Argument and Authority in Early Modern England

Conal Condren offers a radical reappraisal of the nature of moral and political theory in early modern England through an examination of widespread arguments about office. The vocabulary of office-holding and abuse was sufficiently supple and pervasive for us to infer a general presupposition of office cohering the whole spectrum of social discourse, from conceptualising the soul to understanding the responsibilities of the philosopher, poet, parent and priest. The exploration of this vocabulary involves a reconsideration of the nature of early modern social debate, challenging fashionable preoccupations with emerging ideologies and with liberalism, liberty, republicanism, a public sphere, and reason of state theory, through which study of seventeenth-century political theory has been organised. Indeed, the very idea of early modern political theory is called into question. Professor Condren reconsiders the importance of oath-taking, and analyses anew the three great crises of oath-taking that punctuated English history in the seventeenth century. Again, his conclusions challenge widely held beliefs about early modern political argument, the process of secularisation, and the rise of de facto theory. *Argument and Authority* is a major new work from a senior scholar of early modern political thought, of interest to a wide range of historians, philosophers and literary scholars.

CONAL CONDREN is Scientia Professor in Politics and International Relations at the University of New South Wales, Australia.

Argument and Authority in Early Modern England

The Presupposition of Oaths and Offices

Conal Condren
The University of New South Wales

CAMBRIDGE UNIVERSITY PRESS
Cambridge, New York, Melbourne, Madrid, Cape Town, Singapore, São Paulo

Cambridge University Press
The Edinburgh Building, Cambridge CB2 2RU, UK

Published in the United States of America by Cambridge University Press, New York

www.cambridge.org
Information on this title: www.cambridge.org/9780521859080

© Conal Condren 2006

This book is in copyright. Subject to statutory exception
and to the provisions of relevant collective licensing agreements,
no reproduction of any part may take place without
the written permission of Cambridge University Press.

First published 2006

Printed in the United Kingdom at the University Press, Cambridge

A catalogue record for this book is available from the British Library

ISBN-13 978-0-521-85908-0 hardback
ISBN-10 0-521-85908-5 hardback

Cambridge University Press has no responsibility for the persistence or accuracy of URLs for external or third-party internet websites referred to in this book, and does not guarantee that any content on such websites is, or will remain, accurate or appropriate.

To Averil

Contents

Preface	*page* ix
Introduction	1

Part I: The liquid empire of office

1	An overview	15
2	Ceremonies of office: The kiss of the tutti-man	36
3	Institutionalised office: a sense of the scavenger	54
4	The vocabulary of office	80
5	Offices of the intellect: player, poet and philosopher	105
6	Soul and conscience	125

Part II: The authority and insolence of office

7	The cases of patriot and counsellor	149
8	Casuistry as the mediation of office	172
9	The case of resistance to superior power	186
10	Metaphor and political autonomy	209

Part III: 'I, A. B.'

11	An overview of the oath in seventeenth-century argument	233
12	Coronation oaths	254
13	The oath of allegiance of 1606	269

14	Engagement with a free state	290
15	The oath of allegiance and the Revolution of 1688–9	314
	Epilogue	343

Bibliography 353
Index 391

Preface

> *a Man had as good to go to* Court *without his* Cravat *as shew himself in* Print *without a* Preface ... *The Liberty* of Prefacing *against* Prefaces, *may seem a little* Unreasonable; but Common Scribblers *are allow'd the* Priviledges *of* Common Strumpets. *One of the Frankest* Prostitutes *that ever I knew since I was born, had these Words the oftenest in her Mouth*: Lord! *(says she)* to see the Impudence of some Women!
>
> (Roger L'Estrange, *Tully's Offices in Three Books*, corrected edn, 1681, A4)

Preliminary studies have announced many of the themes found in the following pages, and although at times they have made me think I was adequately prepared for the larger work, this has taken an inordinate time to complete. In the process I have felt prematurely blasted by antiquity. But having got this far, there are occasions when I feel as buoyant as Sir Roger L'Estrange after laying down his onerous and odious offices to translate Cicero's. That I can make the comparison is due to many, not least Dr Paul Spira and the Prince of Wales Hospital.

Something long-winded, obscure and purple, had there been light enough to see it by, was passed rapidly to readers Professors Jonathan Scott and John Spurr, who treated it with the astringent professionalism it deserved and the constructive insight that it did not. Great thanks are always due to those who labour to save authors from themselves and to editors like Richard Fisher who handle them with such patience, tact and encouragement.

I am grateful to the Australian Research Council for the generous award that allowed me so much time to write and research; to the Folger Library, and the Huntington Library where I spent time as a Francis Bacon Fellow I owe the gratitude of any scholar privileged to work in these peerless institutions. Thanks are also due to the Master and Fellows of Churchill College, Cambridge for generosity and friendship over many years, and to the Plume Library for such co-operation under pressures of time. More personal debts have been incurred to Pat and John Gibson, Maureen and Charles Fowler, and Professor John and Gail Pryor, Des

Murphy, Mary Lamb and Ben Down, all of whom helped provide the support and conditions in which I could carry out research; to Professor Robert von Friedeburg, my gratitude for ever stimulating company, especially when giving papers in Bielefeld, Amsterdam, London and Rotterdam. I am indebted to all of the following for their learning and generosity in drawing essential materials to my attention: to Professors Tony Cousins, DeAnn De Luna, John Gillies, Jamie Lloyd, David Saunders, John Schuster, Jonathan Scott, Barbara Shapiro and Richard Yeo; to Drs Margaret Kelly, Margaret Rose, J. O. Ward, Eric Nelson, Dirk Moses and John Sutton. Peter Day, the Chatsworth Archivist, and Dr Charlotte Erwin, Caltech Archivist, gave help well beyond the call of duty. I have benefited greatly from the insights, example and companionship of Glenn Burgess, Mark Goldie, Ian Maclean, Noel Malcolm, John Pocock, Richard Serjeantson and Quentin Skinner. Much is owed to ongoing discussions with my research collaborators Professors Ian Hunter and Stephen Gaukroger and Dr Andrew Fitzmaurice; I am even more indebted to Dr Cathy Curtis who generously acted as a third reader with such grace and critical aplomb. One of the great pleasures of academic life is that these professional debts are also ones of friendship, alas making thanks seem doubly perfunctory. My colleagues have cheerfully coped with my erratic presence, or absence, yet have been around when I have needed them; Aoise Stratford Lloyd has reminded me I have other things to write; Allegra Zakis that there are things in the world beyond what I write. My wife Averil has wonderfully born the brunt of the book I have found most difficult to complete in most trying times for us both. She too has critically read it in several drafts, prepared the index, and like all who have seen the bits and bristles of Mr Hume's broom, has swept out rubbish. What is left is mine, I should probably keep it to myself, but while we live we do not learn.

Material towards the end of chapter 3 was first explored in *Contemporary Political Theory*, 1, 1 (2002); a more detailed version of the argument on patriotism appeared in Robert von Friedeburg, ed., *'Patria' und 'Patrioten' vor dem Patriotismus. Pflichten, Rechte, Glauben und die Rekonfigurierung europäischer Gemeinwesen im 17. Jahrhundert* (Wiesbaden: Wolfenbuetteler Forschungen, 2005); some of the argument in chapter 6 was first developed in Philippa Kelly, ed., *The Touch of the Real* (Perth: UWA Press, 2002); much of the material on tyranny in chapter 9 has been adapted from my paper in Robert von Friedeburg, ed., *Murder and Monarchy: Regicide in European History, 1300–1800* (London: Palgrave, 2004). I am grateful for being allowed to re-work these materials.

Introduction

> Indeed it is a strange-disposed time:
> But men may construe things, after their fashion,
> Clean from the purpose of the things themselves.
> (Cicero, in Shakespeare, *Julius Caesar* 1.2)

I

There is now a cohesive literature on political office-holding in early-modern Britain. Following Ernst Kantorowicz's seminal study of kingship has been valuable work on the village constable, on the county Lord Lieutenant, and more broadly on the judiciary and priesthood.[1] The changing scope of socially instituted office has been recognised as crucial to the formation of the modern state, political participation and the outbreak of the Civil Wars.[2] Historiographically, the analysis of office has been held to be central to the reintegration of social and intellectual history.[3] Nevertheless, notions of office have been too narrowly conceived and far less attention has been given to how people argued about offices,

---

[1] Ernst Kantorowicz, *The King's Two Bodies: A Study in Medieval Political Theology* (Princeton, 1958); V. I. Slater, *Noble Government: The Stuart Lord Lieutenancy and the Transformation of English Politics* (Athens, Ga., 1994); J. R. Kent, *The Village Constable, 1580–1642* (Oxford, 1986); Justin Champion, *The Pillars of Priestcraft Shaken: The Church of England and its Enemies, 1660–1730* (Cambridge, 1992); Wilfred Prest, 'Judicial Corruption in Early Modern England', *Past and Present*, 133 (1991), pp. 67–95; Alan Cromartie, *The Constitutionalist Revolution in Early Modern England* (Cambridge, forthcoming).

[2] Michael J. Braddick, *State Formation in Early Modern England, c.1550–1700* (Cambridge, 2000); Mark Goldie, 'The Unacknowledged Republic: Office-Holding in Early Modern England', in Tim Harris, ed., *The Politics of the Excluded, c.1500–1850* (London, 2001), pp. 153–94; Cromartie, *The Constitutionalist Revolution*, chs. 1, 8; Steve Hindle, *The State and Social Change in Early Modern England, c.1550–1640* (New York, 2000); see also Craig Muldrew, *The Economy of Obligation: The Culture of Credit and Social Relations in Early Modern England* (New York, 1998).

[3] Goldie, 'The Unacknowledged Republic', p. 154 and at length; Hindle, *The State*, pp. 1–37.

to what an office was taken to entail, and how and to what ends the vocabulary of its specification was actually deployed.[4]

The argument here is that from the evidence of language, we may properly conjecture what I shall call a presupposition of office broadly characteristic of early modern England. By restricting attention to designated political offices, we decipher, as it were, without a key, and do injustice to debate that went well beyond them. We may even beg questions if, a priori, we marginalise some forms of office talk as only derivative of core political concepts. This study, then, is intended as a change of direction for, and an exploration of the implications of, the literature on early modern office.

It also arises directly from my earlier work and is prefatory to a theoretical account of metaphor, theoretical modelling and concept formation in politics. Thus, it is one of a series and follows principally from *The Language of Politics in Seventeenth-Century England*.[5] That work outlined what I took to be the main patterns of word use in politics from which we hypothesise intentions, theories and dispositions. One initial proposition had been that the putative subject matter of intellectual and cultural history (ideas, concepts, beliefs, ideologies) is largely what is conjectured in order to establish a narrative, or descriptive coherence from surviving evidence. Such processes of hypothetical completion are commonly given a misleading ontological status. That is, hypothetical completions (*X*'s alleged ideas, concepts, intentions and so forth) purporting to explain or make greater sense of what we have, are characteristically projected as an available reality, and this is used to redescribe surviving evidence, so pre-empting understanding. Effectively, the meta-language of explanatory modelling is conflated with the evidence itself, and the past is then easily, even inadvertently, reduced to a series of variations on the present.[6] Consider office-holding and state formation: a modern Weberian model of the state may cast light on the interplay of social office in pre-modern England, but if the terms of the

---

[4] For notable exceptions see Stephen Gaukroger, *Francis Bacon and the Transformation of Early-Modern Philosophy* (Cambridge, 2000); Knud Haakonssen, *Natural Law and Moral Philosophy: From Grotius to the Scottish Enlightenment* (Cambridge, 1996); Ian Hunter, *Rival Enlightenments: Civil and Metaphysical Philosophy in Early Modern Germany* (Cambridge, 2001); Robert von Friedeburg, *Self-Defence and Religious Strife in Early Modern Europe: England and Germany, 1530–1680* (Aldershot, 2002).
[5] Conal Condren, *The Language of Politics in Seventeenth-Century England* (London, 1994).
[6] See also, for example, Philippe Buc, *The Dangers of Ritual: Between Early Medieval Texts and Social Scientific Theory* (Princeton, 2001), pp. 2–3, and pt. 2 at length; Francis West, 'The Colonial History of the Norman Conquest', *History*, 84 (1999), pp. 219–36.

model are read into the evidence, explanatory circularity is almost as inescapable as anachronistic description.[7]

The Language of Politics concentrated on the semantic residue from seventeenth-century England, and how it has been susceptible to rough treatment by modern scholars who, taking their own conceptual vocabulary for granted, have read it into the past. In particular, the terms radical, moderate, conservative, and their near relations left, right, centre, have been used with a redescriptive insouciance that has anachronistically distorted early-modern debate.[8] For all the breadth of brush-stroke, it was argued that my case was incomplete because of inadequate attention to the conjectured principles, ideas and concepts to which I occasionally alluded.[9] The point was well made, and this study is an attempt to rectify the imbalance. The purpose is to hypothesise a presupposition of office as an *explanans* for the sort of word use I have previously described and much more besides. It may or may not play a part in explaining state formation, but a thorough exploration of the linguistic terrain of office would seem to be a precondition for the success of that adjacent enterprise, just as it is for tracing specific theories of office as responses to a changing world. Indeed, if office-talk was as ubiquitous as I claim it was, the whole notion of early-modern political theory needs to be reconsidered.

II

A comment is in order about my vocabulary of intellectual conjecture, lest the body of the argument be mistaken for an attempt to unmask an ideology, or write a conceptual history. A presupposition is something that in a given context is taken for granted; it is apt to be relatively general and constant but may be disclosed in a finite array of differing propositions. Indeed, this adaptive capacity is a salient feature of presuppositional constancy.

Any statement takes something for granted, otherwise nothing can be said. The vision of a philosophy without presupposition has survived from Plato and remains an image of the philosopher's stone,[10] but especially in the cut and thrust of everyday argument much is presupposed. Since any presupposition is a condition for saying certain sorts of things, in a

---

[7] Braddick's reliance on Weberian modelling is taken up in chapter 10; but see also Hindle, *The State*, pp. 20–4. My point, however, is not to dismiss model-building but, in advance of a separate study, to point to the difficulties we share accepting its necessity.
[8] Condren, *The Language of Politics*, ch. 5; Conal Condren 'Radicalism Revised' in G. Burgess and M. Feinstein, eds., *British Radicalism, 1500–1800* (Cambridge, forthcoming).
[9] Glenn Burgess, 'Review', *History of Political Thought*, 16, 4 (1996), pp. 638–9.
[10] E.g. Michael Oakeshott, *Experience and its Modes* (Cambridge, 1933, 1966).

minimal sense it is also a guarantee against saying others. Hypothesising presuppositions, in short, is a matter of the imaginative mapping of a common ground between interlocutors, indicating the limits and conditions that enabled them to debate and differ; it may be to outline a perspective more or less adequately shared, a *habitus*, to borrow Bourdieu's useful term.[11] To hypothesise presuppositions, then, is not to specify anything as cohesive as a doctrine, a theory, a set of ideas, concepts, an ideology or anything that might be mistaken for an independent object or agent. It is simply to suggest what is tacitly accepted at a given point in order that something might be said. Effectively, a presupposition comes to us as the contingent silence that helps structure the diversity of discourse.

If the generality and stability of presuppositions at once frame and facilitate argument, their status is hardly immutable, for a presupposition is a function of language use and may become a focus of debate. Even a clarificatory statement such as 'what I am presupposing is x' places x on the verge of becoming an axiom, an article of faith, or a doctrine. Under pressure, with a breakdown of communication, or with infinite leisure and assiduity, presuppositions can always be converted by explication; but this may amount less to a shared articulation than a crumbling of the commonly held and the alienation from a *habitus*. In the loss of relative constancy, what had been presuppositional may become visible, shaped and constrained in contestation. That survival is the historian's hard evidence of words on paper.

Presuppositions are like the concepts or ideas into which they can be converted in that none of them amount to an available extra-linguistic realm to which the historian has access, a world of ideas to be discovered in any literal sense of that slippery term. Declamations about historical discovery can run the gamut from meaning found, to having made better sense of, to being persuasive. There is, however, much value in R. G. Collingwood's specification of an idea as an answer to a question, with the proviso that frequently the question has also to be conjectured.[12] Often, the absence of a contradictory hypothesis is enough to get the idea established as a conclusive fact. This is not unreasonable, but from there the idea is easily reified as part of a realm of evidence of which histories can be written, and this is less warranted.

So too with the historical notion of a concept: it is largely a metalocution in language signalling a process of classification and alignment of particulars. Seen in this fashion, the word concept is not a reference

---

[11] Pierre Bourdieu, *Esquisse d'une théorie de la pratique* (Geneva, 1972), trans. Richard Nice, *An Outline of a Theory of Practice* (New York, 1977).
[12] R. G. Collingwood, *An Autobiography* (Oxford, 1939), chs. 4, 5.

term for an independent entity that might be discovered or reflected in language. It is a relic of a linguistic practice, and by its use we signal considerable descriptive latitude with respect to the phenomena under discussion, imposing some order on the world, or identifying the attempts of others to do so. Additionally, we may also be making claims for robust continuities within and across natural languages. The importance of this is not to be gainsaid; it is in part what hypothesising presuppositions is about, but tracing broadly stable patterns of usage in language does not seem to me sufficient for positing a distinct ontological realm for basic concepts (*Grundbegriffe*), to be located somewhere between language and social reality, so acting, to employ Reinhart Koselleck's metaphor, as joints linking the linguistic and social worlds.[13] This is an unfortunate image, as the joint suggests less a separate realm than the manner in which two extensions connect and move in concert. It is, nevertheless, exactly this propensity to conceptual hypostatisation that takes *Begriffsgeschichte* back towards its point of critical departure, the Lovejoyan history of 'unit ideas' invented in the service of grand, even whiggish narratives of conceptual consumption.[14] And, to repeat, it is this shared treatment of concept terms that most readily facilitates what *Begriffsgeschichte* wishes to avoid: the projection of 'present day concepts back into the past'.[15]

There is, in fact, a whole family of terms in historiography – presupposition, assumption, concept, idea, belief, intention, motive – that are, as it were, like the spirits of an absent world, largely inferred from marks on paper. We invoke them as a special class of causes for known effects, and such invocations are, as the Galenic theorist of witchcraft John Cotta put it, matters of 'artificial conjecture'. They are voice changes made to maintain or re-establish intelligible order;[16] and they are always vulnerable to alternative conjectures and to accusations of anachronism, over-reading, under-reading and irrelevance. It is the lacunae in evidence that best facilitate accommodation to the present; one way or another we have to supplement what survives for us to ponder or plunder.[17]

---

[13] Reinhart Koselleck, 'Response', in Hartmut Lehmann and Melvin Richter, eds., *The Meaning of Historical Terms and Concepts: New Studies in Begriffsgeschichte* (Washington D.C., 1996), p. 61; this is not dissimilar to words, concepts and things as the parameters of meaning suggested by C. K. Ogden and I. A. Richards in *The Meaning of Meaning*, in 1923.
[14] For astute comment, see Donald R. Kelley, 'On The Margins of Begriffsgeschichte', in Lehmann and Richter, *The Meaning of Historical Terms and Concepts*, pp. 35–40; Hunter, *Rival Enlightenments*, pp. 1–2.
[15] Kosselleck, 'Response', p. 67.
[16] John Cotta, *The Assured Witch* (1624 edn.), pp. 21, 2, 7; cf. W. B. Gallie, *Philosophy and the Historical Understanding* (London, 1964), pp. 105ff.
[17] Conal Condren, *The Status and Appraisal of Classic Texts* (Princeton, 1985), ch. 9.

This study, then, deals principally with the more or less shared vocabulary of seventeenth-century moral discourse and the presuppositions that may plausibly be conjectured from it. By postulating a presupposition of office, I believe it is possible to make good sense of how the vocabulary of social discussion was organised. To put the matter the other way around, from an examination of the vocabulary of argument one can reasonably hazard a fairly simple pattern of presuppositions about human moral, social identity, widely shared over a *longue durée*. This book would not be worth writing if they were our presuppositions, 'our' meaning modern, usually western scholars. But they are not, and by conjecturing or projecting our own understandings of human identity, we, that is modern, usually western scholars, parochialise and impoverish the past. The hypothesised presuppositions central to this study function like Koselleck's 'basic concepts', without the metaphysical baggage that gives us a conceptual realm by separating language from society, and without restricting us to that historical minority who use their vocabulary in an acceptably abstract and philosophical fashion. We can, likewise, recognise John Cotta's sensitivity to the conjectural status of many sorts of inference without believing in a spirit world of angels, witches, demons and familiars.

III

To offer the most general analytic abridgement: the presupposition of office took proper conduct to be by a *persona* as a function of office; conversely, improper conduct was office abuse. In extremis, abuse sloughed off *persona*, and erased, sometimes almost by definition, moral identity and social standing.[18] Superficially, this may seem suggestive of theories of social role-play associated with writers such as Marcel Mauss and, more recently, Erving Goffman.[19] Our now rather diluted understanding of a *persona* would encourage this, especially as the word itself was originally the Latin for a theatrical mask (from Greek, *prosopon*) and later a person. *Persona*, however, conveyed more than the notion of a role-playing individual, which naturally directs attention to the relationship between inner agent and presented identity, to authenticity, dissimulation and appearance. It was, rather, a manifestation, or realisation and

---

[18] If thoroughly schematised, this presupposition might even be reformulated in logical notation as a variation on Leibniz's law of identity; see David Wiggins, *Identity and Spacio-Temporal Continuity* (Oxford, 1988). Or, in Wittgensteinian terms; it is a matter of 'seeing as' a manifestation of one putative office or another.

[19] Erving Goffman, *The Presentation of the Self in Everyday Life* (New York, 1959); Erving Goffman, *Frame Analysis; An Essay on the Organisation of Experience* (New York, 1983); Braddick, *State Formation*, pp. 76–8.

Introduction

representation of a character, or type, such as a young slave, an old man, a free woman.[20] Social role theory can certainly provide insight but it is apt to present a rather fragmented understanding of office that a physical person qua *persona* embodied, and has been developed in the context of rather different perceptions of moral identity. Indeed, so far from merely being roles assumed, *officia* could be formalised as moral beings, making even the notion of an office as a duty itself sometimes misleadingly incomplete.[21] I will touch on the modern fate of office only in the epilogue, but will make clear the differences between office-holding and social role-play where it seems appropriate.

The first part of the book is an attempt to elucidate the nature and pervasiveness of an expectation of office in early-modern, especially seventeenth-century England.[22] My discussion offers a perfunctory sort of descriptive metaphysics. In *Individuals*, P. F. Strawson referred to the relative stability of the presuppositional commonplaces which were at once features of the least refined thinking and the 'indispensable core of the conceptual equipment of the most sophisticated human beings'.[23] I believe something like this applies to evocations of office in the early-modern world. Clarification involves cutting across familiar organisational topics for early-modern intellectual history, such as the concept of citizenship, of liberty, rule and tyranny. The discussion of such words is intended to illuminate differing aspects of the rhetorics of office-holding. This practice might seem initially repetitive and disparate by turns if it is assumed that the concept or idea of citizenship, or say republicanism, and so on, should provide the focus. It will seem less so if it is kept in mind that the office is what matters, other familiar topics being the means to its elucidation. Similarly, there is no systematic single discussion of a figure like Thomas Hobbes, who persists in rounding off a number of my chapters; what is said of his writings is tied to the aspects of office under consideration.

The purpose, however, is not to reduce seventeenth-century argument to some theoretical monochrome. A shared presupposition at a high level of generality hardly prohibits its being worked into many theoretical shapes; and the differences arising from what is shared, of comparable doctrines and of whole types or modes of theorising, may be of more

---

[20] Leonhard Schmitz, 'Persona', in William Smith, ed., *A Dictionary of Greek and Roman Antiquities* (London, 1882), pp. 889–93.
[21] See Haakonssen, *Natural Law*, pp. 40–2; Hunter, *Rival Enlightenments*, pp. 165–6.
[22] The expression 'early modern' must be taken throughout only as a Schopenhaurian nominal classification, a conceptually empty convenience for the period *c.* 1500–1800.
[23] P. F. Strawson, *Individuals: An Essay in Descriptive Metaphysics* (London, 1971 edn), p. 10.

interest than the often unexamined common ground. John Donne's poetic exploration of the imagery of office is a world away from, say, Pufendorf's studied account of society; the solipsistic lovers in 'The Sunne Rising' (see chapter 8) were hardly *entia moralia*. So, too, a posited presuppositional grounding used to collapse one perspective into another risks losing everything that might be interesting about each. Yet Donne's poetic commonplaces, to recall Strawson's point, do touch on Pufendorf's theory; for he played with what Pufendorf would critically examine and affirm – that an office provides an expectation of and the boundaries for proper conduct.[24] For the purposes of this study Pufendorf might be considered an honorary Englishman, not because of his seminal abridgement of a whole philosophy of office, but because he developed it in constructive counterpoint to Hobbes, who in turn had reduced inherited presuppositions of office in a way far more disruptive than Donne's poetic ingenuity. In fact, it may have been Hobbes's draconian subversion of the complex culture of official expectation that provoked Pufendorf to a formal articulation of a theory of the human world as an intersection of offices. He flew, like the proverbial owl of Minerva at dusk, returning to England through translation, redaction and his own astute comments on English affairs.[25] Traversing the common ground between the crepuscular Pufendorf and Donne of the morning sun can be treacherous in the mix of shadows they cast; but the attempt to do so should help explain the specific content of the vocabulary as a whole, and how it was worked into a remarkable diversity of doctrine in England and beyond. Not all of this doctrine was in any helpful sense 'political', either according to seventeenth-century uses of that word, or our own. Indeed, the notion of the political is variable, and an exploration of the pervasive ethos of office will do something to account for its uncertain status and the ease by which those whom we see as political actors could dispense with it.

Presuppositions rarely come to us in splendid isolation; we are not, as it were, dealing with a single refracted broomstick in the water, but with a besom barely bound. And there must remain some distorting partiality about following one presupposition to the neglect of its closest neighbours. Most crucially, a semiotic presupposition about the meaningfulness

---

[24] Samuel Pufendorf, *De jure naturae et gentium libri octo* (1672), trans. C. H. and W. A. Oldfather (Oxford, 1943); Hunter, *Rival Enlightenments*, pp. 164–6.
[25] Andrew Tooke, *The Whole Duty of Man According to the Law of Nature* (1691), translation of Samuel Pufendorf, *De officio hominis* (1673), ed. Ian Hunter and David Saunders (Indianapolis, 2003); Michael J. Seidler, 'Qualification and Standing in Pufendorf's Two English Revolutions', in R. von Friedeburg, ed., *Widerstandsrecht in der frühen Neuzeit, Zeitschrift für Historische Forschung*, Beiheft 26 (Berlin, 2001), pp. 329–52.

of the world, that everything in it is a sign, shadows this study. The very notion of a sign was accommodating, ranging from symptom to synecdoche, effect, residue and prognostic. According to Thomas Browne, all were the marks made by the pencil of God, a God it was also presupposed who had to be feared.[26] The conjunction of the planets might explain or forewarn; the wart might condemn; the very black cat might be the scratch of Satan on the soul of the witch. The flexible faith in the world as one of signs, meaning and interconnections, from medicine and witchcraft to religious ceremony and scientific experiment, helped shape and sustain the ubiquity of office and evidence of its abuse.[27] All things might be 'instruments of fear and warning/Unto some monstrous state', insinuates Cassius, as he spins his conspiracy on a stormy night to cleanse Rome of Caesar.[28] 'The night', wrote Thomas Nashe, 'is the devil's Black Book', and Nashe saw inscribed on its pages forms of illness, human types, the peculiarities of nature, dreams, terrors and spirits, in the realm where Satan could be revealed as a tyrant and a Machiavellian, inverting or challenging all good order glorious in the light of God's sun.[29] For Robert Dingley, when that sun was obscured by thundering clouds we might be hearing His voice, and to stop the ears against the din could be nothing short of rebellion.[30] Although fear of an omniscient deity and a semiotic presupposition are not the focus of this study, so closely are they tied to the vocabulary of office that its exploration is an intimation of them both. This will become most obvious in part III. Oath-taking and administering were not only the quintessence of office in action, but they also generated controversy because of the different ways in which oaths could be signs, and because of their portentous evocation of a most fearsome God. No atheist could hold office, because oaths could signify nothing in the absence of a recognised divinity.

---

[26] For a fine discussion of this presupposition, see David Wootton, 'The Fear of God in Early Modern Political Theory', in *Historical Papers* (Vancouver, 1983), pp. 58–80.

[27] For suggestive explorations of semiotics, John Gillies, *Shakespeare and the Geography of Difference* (Cambridge, 1996); Ian Maclean, *Logic, Signs and Nature in the Renaissance* (Cambridge, 2002).

[28] Shakespeare, *Julius Caesar* 1.3.

[29] Thomas Nashe, *The Terrors of the Night* (1594), in *The Unfortunate Traveller and Other Works*, ed. J. B. Steane (Harmondsworth, 1972 edn), p. 208; also Shakespeare, *King Lear* 3.4, for the tyrannous night.

[30] Robert Dingley, *Vox coeli, or Philosophical, Historicall and Theological Observations of Thunder* (1658), pp. 61, 67; cf. writers like Joseph Glanvill who though seeing 'Real' philosophy as the enemy of such superstition nevertheless saw all the works of nature as provable signs of God's existence: Joseph Glanvill, *Philosophia pia* (1671), pp. 17–23, 48–52; cf. more extensively, Sir Robert Boyle, *The Christian Virtuoso*, part 2, in *Works*, ed. Thomas Birch (London, 1772), vol.VI, pp. 717–96.

In the serious business of studying seventeenth-century political theory it has been fairly routine to brush aside much of this cobweb of presuppositional entanglements, consigning some to a realm called religion, a residue to superstition. Reading, if we bother, the warnings of Mr Dingley, we instinctively side with the voice of Cicero on that stormy night before the assassination of Caesar: 'men construe things after their own fashion, clean away from the purpose of the things themselves'. Indeed: but to abstract a discrete political theory clean away from all such stuff is itself to construe things after our own presuppositional fashions. In fact, much language use such as Dingley's fear of 'rebellion' against God's meteorological messages made it difficult to maintain any clear-cut domain of the political. This was especially where Satan was designated a tyrannical Machiavell and God was ensconced in the office of cosmic rule. Certainly, the political was at times variously identifiable, but it was not the autonomous realm the expression 'political theory' has led us to expect, and which is still sometimes projected as a crucial 'discovery' of the early-modern world (chapter 10). Seeing the world as a text is hardly new.[31] Reading the Bible through notions of allegory, typology and figurative correspondence was often enough a model for imposing order on the rest of creation, and above all for facilitating the celerity of metaphorical movement between established linguistic domains. The vocabulary of office was made to reach from the sun to sunny King James, from the stomach to the philosopher. The darker side of office-abuse was similarly elastic, being stretched from the adulterer or neglectful constable, the stage villain, contumacious counsellor and over-puissant prince, to the inconstant moon and the Prince of Darkness.[32] By the time I reach the epilogue, I will have come as close as I can to suggesting that in the name of historiographical purity we might dispense with the organising notion of early-modern political theory. It is, no doubt, a proof that purity is not everything.

IV

The argument is continuous but is divided into three broad parts. Part I is a preliminary survey of the extent and form of office, but, for orientation, chapter 1 gives an overview, though not a point by point summary, of parts I and II. That chapter ends by drawing out some of the consequences of a presupposition of office for understanding what we see as

---

[31] James Franklin, 'Natural Sciences as Textual Interpretation: The Hermeneutics of the Natural Sign', *Philosophy and Phenomenological Research*, 44, 4 (1984), pp. 509–20.

[32] Robert Anton, 'Satyr of the Moone', in *The Philosophers Satyrs* (1616), pp. 69–75.

seventeenth-century political theory and for a range of fashionable lines of enquiry into it. Enough is said only to show how often unexamined perspectives can impose an anachronistic structure on the past. Chapter 2 outlines sketchily the ceremonies and solemnities expressive of the diversity of office, from folkloric survivals to pageants and masques, while chapter 3 addresses the range of institutionalised social office. Taken together, these chapters provide only a rough backdrop to the more extensive rhetorics of office-talk. Dependent largely on extant literature, they might be tripped over fairly lightly by those expert in social history, but for what is made of the labours of others. The scene set, chapter 4 outlines the terms and expressions broadly constituting the ethics of office and its abuse. It is an overview of the vocabulary of office as a whole, encompassing the ways in which words were used to promote and to criticise office-holders, applied, or withheld to solidify, endow or evaporate official standing. Chapters 5 and 6 explore the extension of this vocabulary away from socially instituted offices in order to map the full range of its deployment with reference to human identity. Within this context of use, chapter 7 deals with the complementary examples of the rather differently contested offices of patriot and councillor. In chapter 8, I examine the function of casuistry in mediating the tensile ethics of office. The principal example, elaborated in chapter 9, is the case of resistance to authority. As the enlistment of the vocabulary of office could often be loose and now appears forced and fancifully metaphorical, part II concludes by explicating some of the problems involved in dealing with metaphors of office. Figurative use was made plausible by assumptions about the world, by meta-assumptions about semiotic interconnection, and in outlining these, the ground is prepared for a reconsideration of the autonomy of politics thesis and reason of state theory.

Like social office-holding, oath-taking is beginning to attract scholarly attention commensurate with its importance in the seventeenth century, but it is yet to be explored within the primary context of the rhetorics of office. Oath-taking was a vital manifestation of asserted and accepted office, and so controversies around the notion of an oath reveal much about the difficulties inherent in an office-driven world. Two short chapters begin part III. Chapters 11 and 12 provide initial orientation by discussing, respectively, oaths in general and coronation oaths in particular. Longer chapters are devoted to the most famous of oath-taking controversies. Chapter 13 is on the oath of allegiance following the Gunpowder Plot in 1605; chapter 14 concerns the Engagement required after the establishment of a republic in 1649; chapter 15 focuses on the oath of allegiance following the Revolution of 1688-9. Were they exhaustive, these discussions would be intolerably repetitive, not least because the vocabulary of office remained remarkably stable, the disputes at the end of the century echoing much earlier stridency of debate. Rather, part III marks the shift from a broadly synchronic mapping of the effects of a presupposition of office to a more diachronic illustration of its workings in argument. This allows for more attention to the development of specific doctrines with the resources of the vocabulary; it allows also for more illustration of the way in which, with the aid of our own presuppositions about the world, we have attributed theories that the evidence inadequately supports. In this way, too, the fairly disparate patterns of illustration necessary for an overview give way to the conventional concentration on relatively cohesive bodies of evidence. The last three chapters explore differing aspects of the intractable difficulties of officeholding and oath-taking in a fissiparous world. Eventually, through deep dispute and presuppositional breakdown, came change; and alterations in the presupposition of office and its vocabulary erratically evidence the erosion of a way of seeing things morally. I do not argue for there being any decisive scene change appropriate to the structure of a pantomime, or a teleological narrative driven by reified concepts emerging clearly and late in full glory. If the ground has been convincingly prepared, the discussion of the cases of oath controversy should not need the Mahleresque crescendo expected of ambitious arguments. An epilogue, however, outlines some of the salient contrasts between what was once taken for granted and more familiar ethical postures; it suggests reasons for a decline in an ethos of office and revisits the consequences of this for understanding early-modern political language and modern political and moral enquiry.

Part I

The liquid empire of office

1 An overview

Yes Socrates.

(Thrasymachus (eventually), Plato, *Republic*)

I

Enter Thrasymachus, blustering and abusive. Socrates had been asking for a general definition of justice and for a good while the sophist had been trying to obtrude himself into the discussion, palpably irritated with the display of Socratic trickery at the expense of the flaccid Polemarchus. Bursting free of his restraining companions, and naming his price, he defined justice as the interest of the stronger.[1] Then, having failed to defend his definition, he appealed to the facts of life. As shepherds exploit their sheep, the strong exploit the weak. The ruler is close to being a wolf in shepherd's clothing and rapacity (*pleonexia*) is justice or superior to it.[2] Thrasymachus' entry anticipated his argument. Socrates inverted the force of the analogy. Shepherds, as shepherds, must attend to the interests of their flocks. The shepherd's art, like any other, is concerned with nothing other than the well-being of its subject. Therefore, the art of ruling considers the interests of the ruled. *Pleonexia* is injustice. In the Homeric and Pindaric senses of the term, the way (*dike*) of the wolf is anything but human excellence.[3]

This may seem an unlikely place to begin a study of the notion of office-holding in seventeenth-century England. Historically speaking, we associate the notion of office with Cicero, whose *De officiis* became a much translated and cited grammar school text-book.[4] And rather than the

---

[1] Plato, *The Republic*, trans. Paul Shorey (Cambridge, Mass., 1969 edn), 366B–338C.
[2] *Ibid.*, 343A–344C.
[3] *Ibid.*, 345D; J. L. Myers, *The Political Ideas of the Greeks* (1927) (New York, 1968), pp. 174–5.
[4] Peter Mack, *Elizabethan Rhetoric in Theory and Practice* (Cambridge, 2002), lists eleven editions between 1573 and 1600, p. 23. Robert Whittinton's translation appeared in 1534, Nicholas Grimalde's in 1556 and 1583 and others would follow in the next century. On Whittinton see Thomas Mayer, *Thomas Starkey and the Commonweal: Humanist Politics in the Reign of Henry VIII* (Cambridge, 1989), pp. 20–5.

relatively stable Ciceronian concept of *officium*, a sphere of duty, Plato's argument gathers round the more nebulous vocabulary of *arche* and *arete*. The former term, notoriously dependent on specific contexts of discourse, could mean anything from rule, initiation, office and causation to the end of a rope.[5] The latter connoted both practical and artistic skills, and so encouraged the characteristic metaphorical interplay between the responsibilities and capacities necessary for rule (*arche*), and the art of the musician or shepherd. The unexamined life of Platonic metaphors of excellence generates sympathy with the irritated outburst of Thrasymachus. In that alone lies an intimation of how the world has changed.

Certainly, something conceptually close to Cicero's *officium* was evident in the philosophical writings of Greek antiquity. Cicero treated Plato and Aristotle as an authoritative lineage and his vocabulary of the dutiful or morally right (*honestas*) is elaborated with reference to the Greek *katorthoma*, the absolutely proper or binding for the wise, and *kathekon*, what is fitting for one's office.[6] For stoicism generally, right action was the conduct appropriate to a *persona*'s realm of duty. This led, at one extreme, to a moral confidence that the diverse demands of office could be reconciled, at least for the wise, so creating a sort of deontological ethics, or a natural law rhetoric of universalism from *katorthoma*. At the other, it terminated in the relentless scepticism of Carneades (214/13–129 BC) who was notorious for claiming that there was always a perspective from which virtue could be seen as vice; the good was contingent on specific interests, aims and identities, and knowledge was only probable. Cicero's assertion, for example, that the fundamental moral claims of sociability, *humanitatis*, varied according to circumstance and duty could be developed in either direction.[7] As I shall argue, ethical expectations in early-modern England continued to move between these polarities, affording a variety of standards by which those in office could be deemed guilty of misconduct.

As we might expect on the precedent of Platonic metaphor, sensitivity to office-abuse extended into the domain of intellectual activity. Plato's hostility to sophists had been to their irresponsible use of reason and language, amounting to the *pleonexia* of rhetoric. The fate of Alcibiades seemed to suggest that the greater the potential for the high office of philosophy, the greater were the consequences flowing from corruption.[8] Festering lilies can smell worse than weeds. When Aristotle, Cicero and

---

[5] Myers, *Political Ideas of the Greeks*, pp. 139–42.
[6] Cicero, *De officiis*, trans. W. Miller (Cambridge, Mass., 1913) 1.3.8.
[7] *Ibid.*, 1.59.
[8] *Ibid.*, 1.8.26; Plato, *Republic*, 491D.

Quintilian reaffirmed the office of the rhetor as central to citizenship, they did so in full awareness of its susceptibility to Platonic critique. Yet, it was necessary to find a significant place for rhetoric in a world of social offices, for the *persona* always needed to be presented in discourse for a suitable audience, thus ensuring attention to the persuasive dimension of language. Eventually, Lucian, in the idiom of Carneades, would turn on philosophy itself by satirising the tendencies of intellectual sects to vanity, dogmatism and the ponderous elaboration of absurdity.[9] Over a millennium later, Erasmus, More and then Hobbes would each selectively endorse the point, becoming Lucianic philosophers of the abuse of the offices of the mind.

The argument is not that Plato might nudge aside Cicero as the true originator of a theory of office, but that both belonged to a world dominated by what may broadly be called an ethics of office, suspending the arts of contemplation and active engagement in much the same web of judgement. Neither, as I have indicated (see introduction), is the point to reduce all doctrines of office to one. Rather, despite strong theoretical differences between Greece and Rome, obscured by the all too easy label of 'classical', and despite the different uses to which Greco-Roman authors might be put, there was a recognisably similar pattern of expectation and concern.[10] Sometimes the early-modern legatees of antiquity exploited differences within the classical inheritance, sometimes they imagined them and sometimes they treated Greece and Rome as one.

It was, moreover because different patterns of moral quality and skill helped distinguish one office from another that the ethics of office was not exhausted by any posited global pattern of virtue. Consequently, notions of decorum were meta-moral categories as well as aesthetic and rhetorical ones. Cicero distinguished a number of distinct *personae*, which, he suggested, were complementary *foci* of duty, to family, friends and country. He also accepted a fourfold delineation of *personae*, defined respectively by spheres of human rationality, capacity, status and chosen life. Because the forms that office might take were not self-evident, for Cicero it was the supervening duty of the philosopher to make other realms of duty clear. This was a self-consciously Platonic understanding of the philosopher's legislative office.[11] Philosophical excellence, however, was taken to be

---

[9] Lucian, *Bion Prasis, Philosophies for Sale*, in *Works*, trans. A. M. Harmon (Cambridge, Mass., 1960), vol. II, pp. 450–511.
[10] Eric Nelson, 'The Greek Tradition in Early-Modern Republican Thought', Ph.D. thesis, (Cambridge University, 2001), pp. 1–17; Martha Nussbaum, *The Therapy of Desire: Theory and Practice in Hellenistic Ethics* (Princeton, 1994) for a detailed account of differences within the Greco-Roman ethical corpus.
[11] Cicero, *De officiis*, 1.1.2; 1.2.4; 3.2.

consistent but not coextensive with the virtues of citizenship or paternity. In this way, Cicero attempted to stabilise and qualify moral modality. Philosophers would continue to find such a general presentation of their significance persuasive.[12]

Many of the threads central of an ethics of office in seventeenth-century England can be teased from Plato's Thrasymachan debate. Here, for example, is an early formulation of a notion of office, an official coalescence of *arche* and *arete*: ruling is defined by discriminate skills, qualities of mind, character and responsibility, the over-extension of which is unjust and tyrannous. Here also is the comforting metaphor of the ruler as shepherd. To be a shepherd is, in Ciceronian terms, to hold an office in the same way that to be a ruler, rhetor or citizen is to hold one.[13] Plato's notion of excellence was not of the human being per se, let alone autonomous agent, the 'Self', but of something more specific. *The Republic* was less about the 'individual's' way of life than the conditions necessary for the philosopher's. To be sure, this was a matter of balance, but we create a modern morality in Plato by replacing the philosopher with the individual, especially the autonomous Kantianised one.[14]

Yet, the anachronism of attributing to Plato a quasi-Kantian individualism nevertheless illustrates the variable scope of office. Cicero's focus was on a civic aristocracy and the active life of citizenship. Plato's was more on the just claims of a tiny aristocracy of the mind, upon the responsibilities of contemplation. Much of the history of office is of the interplay of opposing propensities. There is a continuity of attempts to restrict the burdens of office to a few, leaving a residue of humanity either as voiceless in a wilderness, or Olympian in their distance from practical engagements. Conversely, much of this story also involves stretching the range of office, rendering it remarkably inclusive. As I shall suggest (chapters 4, 14), this extension can be seen as both horizontal, embracing comparable phenomena, and vertical, or rectoral, including the hierarchically ordered.[15] At one extreme, the resources of office were used to insist that everyone remained in his or her appointed station, all callings being given by God. At another, they could be used to affirm that no one was

---

[12] For the notion of philosophical *persona* in antiquity, Pierre Hadot, *Philosophy as a Way of Life*, ed. Arnold Davidson, trans. Michael Chase (Oxford, 1995).

[13] A point strongly associated with Plato by Thomas Palfreyman, (1610) continuation of William Baldwin, *A Treatise of Morall Philosophie* (1557), p. 59v.

[14] Nussbaum, *The Therapy of Desire*, pp. 353-4 on Kantian anticipations in antiquity. The now dated discussions of Plato as a 'totalitarian' and more recent discussions of gender equality and self-fulfilment are largely predicated on the notion that politics should be about individuals and their rights.

[15] Hugo Grotius, *De jure belli ac pacis* (Paris, 1625), 1.i.3, p. 35.

without a voice, or above office and so immune to criticism in its terms.[16] There was little that might not be made into an office, either by extending the range of established terms or by acts of metaphorical dexterity. The shepherd of *The Republic* gave an inkling of what could be done.

Plato's symbolic shepherd had a greatly enhanced resonance by the seventeenth century. Shepherds had attended the birth of Christ, who in turn was called a shepherd; his followers in high office proclaimed authority by carrying crosiers, symbolic of the flocks that had to be fed. Christianity had developed within, and extended an ethos of office, and insofar as this could be cast back onto the pagan philosophers, their voices carried a vicarious weight.[17] By the fifteenth century, Plato's forms could be angels, his Good a glimpse of God, allusions to Hades a conception of Hell. It was, Sir John Harington later reflected, as if he and Virgil 'had red the ghospell'.[18] Cicero was credited with a conception of God's office, and his differentiation of *katorthoma* from *kathekon* was analogous to the New Testament distinction between general and particular callings; the words calling and vocation would become common synonyms for office. If angels were allowed to exist, they did so as office-holders under God. The assimilation of the ancient on Christian terms had, however, also been transformative: before God all souls were equal. Some ancients, such as the Pythagoreans and Plato, had been credited with intimations of the psyche's immortality, but with Christianity this became a postulate of theology, especially significant insofar as the soul's equality before God had reverberations in social life.[19] Indeed, as I shall show (chapter 6), the very relationship of soul to God was characteristically conjectured *officially*.

The shepherd became a potent image of office in the western world. In polemical and occasional literature his evocation was mechanical, even wearisome. It was vital that the shepherd not abuse his office, neglect his sheep, let them wander haplessly – so that sheep might eat men, or mingle with goats; above all, he must not turn wolf, or tyrant, and gobble them up himself. The high charge of office was always shadowed by its tyrannical antithesis, the good shepherd by Gyges, or his ancestor, the villainous shepherd who stole a ring of invisibility to do untold harm

---

[16] John Sharp, '*A Discourse on* the Various Callings in Life', in *Works* (1754), vol. V, pp. 83, 86–7; Richard Brathwaite, *The English Gentleman* (1630), pp. 114–19.
[17] Baldwin, *A Treatise of Morall Philosophie*, prologue, unpaginated, but see also, for example, pp. 56v–58v.
[18] Sir John Harington, 'The Comment, Of Hel', in *The Sixth Book of Virgil's Aeneid* (1604), ed. Simon Cauchi (Oxford, 1991), p. 71.
[19] But see Baldwin and Palfreyman, *Treatise* (1610), arguing that the better part of ancient philosophy was monotheistic and to Plutarch is attributed an awareness of equality of souls before God, pp. 40–1, 52v.

with impunity.[20] The imagery always carried a need for reassurance, as did the claims of office themselves. In 1633 Thomas Heywood's pageant for the Lord Mayor of London included a shepherd and his sheep in St Paul's churchyard, and, to the side, a wolf-in-waiting. At the appointed time, the shepherd handed his authority to the new Lord Mayor, whose office, he proclaimed, was to care for the citizens as his flock.[21] The Thrasymachan wolf was not scripted to muscle in, but his displacement was the point of the occasion.

My argument will thus be that an official perspective on the world was pervasive in early modern Britain in which, despite strains, the ancients might plausibly be presented as one authoritative voice. For Thomas Starkey, a Platonic justice ideally lay in the (Ciceronian) 'offyce & duty' of each part existing in harmonious reciprocity.[22] The dedication to the 1559 edition of *The Mirror for Magistrates* attributes Ciceronian language to Plato. That realm is well governed in which the ambitious do not 'beare office'. From Plato, argued William Baldwin, 'you may perceive . . . what offices are . . . that there is nothing more necessary in a common weale, than that officers be diligent . . . be forced to do their duties'. The ambitious 'seeke not for offices to help others, for which cause offices are ordained, but . . . to pranke vp themselves'. Little wonder, he continued, that the Apostles require us to pray for magistrates. The necessity of office is universal and it is superogatory to go to Greeks, Romans, Jews or any nation to prove the point. A Ciceronian identity was, then, given to God, ruling being 'Gods owne office, yea his chiefe office'.[23] At the beginning of the seventeenth century, Henry Crosse similarly attributed a Ciceronian dictum to Plato. Man was not born for himself but 'as Plato saith, for our friends, parents, country, and such common duties, which are the finall endes of every mans labour'.[24] It proved easy enough to assimilate Cicero, not as an originator, but as witness to the moral universe. In *De officiis*, wrote Nicholas Grimalde, we have 'the whole trade how to live among men'.[25]

---

[20] Plato, *Republic*, 359C–E; François Hotman, *Francogallia* (1573), ed. Ralph E. Giesey and J. H. M. Salmon (Cambridge, 1972), pp. 138–9, naming Gyges as one of the most famous of tyrants.

[21] Thomas Heywood, *Londini euphoria* (London, 1633), sig. B2v.

[22] Thomas Starkey, *Dialogue between Cardinal Pole and Thomas Lupset*, ed. T. F. Mayer (London, 1989), p. 39; Mayer, *Thomas Starkey*, at length.

[23] William Baldwin in *The Mirror for Magistrates* (1559), ed. Lily B. Campbell (Cambridge, 1938), pp. 63–5; see also Baldwin, *Treatise*; Baldwin and Palfreyman, *Treatise*.

[24] Henry Crosse, *Vertues common-wealth* (1603), sig. R3r; see Markku Peltonen, *Classical Humanism and Republicanism in English Political Thought, 1570–1640* (Cambridge, 1995), p. 149.

[25] Nicholas Grimalde, *Marcus Tullius Ciceroes three Bokes of Duties* (1556, 1583), epistle Aiiij.

II

If it was not generated by the material steady rhythms of mundane survival, a sense of life as comprising spheres of responsibility was surely supported by them. Hesiod's *Works and Days* was a celebration of the farmer, whose labour was virtue and whose world was a microcosm of the *arete* and *arche* that would later constitute the Platonic justice of everyman having his own. The farmer's duties to the land, livestock and gods are measured in the decorous response to the seasons. In autumn 'remember to hew your timber: it is the season for such work'.[26] The meta-value of appropriateness found here among the hives and olive groves would sustain a modal morality of office. Early-modern handbooks on husbandry, though less elegiac, nevertheless accept the husbandman as a *persona* in office, for farming was a responsibility. The potential for this specific application of office can be seen in Sir Matthew Hale's *Primitive Origination of Mankind*, where he stretched the responsibilities of stewardship to shape an understanding of the relationship between humanity and creation. Man was but a 'Bayliff or Farmer' of this 'goodly farm', whose care was to maintain order among plants and animals. To emphasise the point, he shifted to another and potent exemplum of office: man is a 'common priest' for the rest of visible creation.[27]

In the ancient world seasonal repetition reinforced the ritual calendars of religion. These infused the diurnal with the divine;[28] and they circumscribed the roles of priest and initiate into patterns of complementary behaviour. The ritual calendar remained important in the early-modern world. The Catholic Church set down and carefully transmitted *The Offices of the Holy Week* itemising individual masses, such as that for the Thursday after Easter, symbolically reminding the faithful of their obligation to thank God for the Apostles. Just so, it was part of the office of the priest to tell them.[29] So we have, as it were, prayer wheels within wheels, an official calendar, describing the offices of belief, and with the

---

[26] Hesiod, *Works and Days* and *Homerica*, trans. H. G. Evelyn-White (Cambridge, Mass., 1936), 422.
[27] Matthew Hale, *The Primitive Origination of Mankind* (1677), pp. 370, 372; for similar imagery of religious husbandry see, for example, John Evelyn, *Sylva, Or a Discourse on Forest-Trees* (1664), 'To the Reader', B1v, John Locke, 'Thus I think', in Peter King, *The Life of John Locke* (1830); vol. II; Richard Baxter, *The Poor Husbandman's Advocate* (1691), on which see W. Lamont, *Richard Baxter and the Millennium* (London, 1979), pp. 306–8.
[28] Hesiod, *Works and Days*, 765–820.
[29] *The Office of the Holy Week According to the Missall and Roman Breviary* (Paris, 1670), p. 550; *The Whole Duty of Man* (1659), pp. 49–55.

Shepherd's Calendar (1493) a latter day Hesiodic co-ordination of duties according to seasons and faith.

By referring to the official as pervasive, I am encompassing more than the philosophically ingrained or theoretically articulated. What seems to have been often, even casually presupposed can be inferred from a surviving vocabulary of office through which the world was organised. That is, we have not strictly speaking a world of offices, but a fairly cohesive vocabulary through which the world was constructed officially. There was little that escaped it, not even Samuel Pepys' foot. Lavatories were 'houses of office', and he notes in his *Diary* discovering an overflow in his cellar from Mr 'Turner's house of office'; John Aubrey records that he was forced to read in the house of office to avoid his father's displeasure, and that the Twisse family's house of office was haunted.[30] To shape the world with the resources of office required of them a robust flexibility. Not only was there an abundance of specific offices, but the vocabulary could also be extended, as Hale exercised that of the husbandman to fashion a metaphysics, reaching to the sun giving forth its rays. The receptive earth could be imagined in the office of a nurse, succouring all who live upon her.[31] The salient terms might variously be understood and related, but from them were formed conflicting doctrines and concepts from the attempts to control the vocabulary and see the world morally. This study is intended to show that disputes over office, who might rightly claim it, or suffer its imposition, and how its vocabularies of justification and accusation might be deployed, constituted the largest part of the development of what we now see as early-modern moral and political theory.

Expressed with sufficient generality, there is an important continuity in the image of the shepherd from Socrates to Heywood, irrespective of whether Heywood read *The Republic*, or any other piece of philosophy. But to understand Heywood's world requires recognition that he did not read Immanuel Kant, Ronald Dworkin or Jürgen Habermas either. We need to read past such eminences more than has been our wont if we are to understand early-modernity as well as we would. We inhabit a different moral universe but one still suggestive of an earlier ethical regime. This is sufficiently the case for there to be no obvious terminus for this study. Although the focus will be on seventeenth-century England, it will be necessary occasionally to move beyond it.

---

[30] Samuel Pepys, *Diary*, ed. Robert Latham and William Matthews (London, 1970, 1977 edn), vol. I, 20 October 1660, p. 269; John Aubrey, quoted in Oliver Lawson Dick, 'The Life and Times of John Aubrey', in *Brief Lives* (Harmondsworth, 1949), pp. 25, 353.

[31] Anon., *The Gentleman's Calling* (1659, 1673 edn), pp. 3–5.

During the sixteenth and seventeenth centuries, the official vision of the social world was subject to controversy and re-specification. Leibniz, for example, mounted a relentless attack on Pufendorf's metaphysical summation, and by the beginning of the eighteenth century reliance on a vocabulary of office was being openly ridiculed. Within about fifty years, Pufendorf's work fell into disuse. Indeed, it may be that as specific official identities, that of the lawyer and physician, achieved institutional, even paradigmatic status, an ethics of office had clear competitors. To an extent, natural law was naturalised, becoming a matrix of drives and material conditions that contextualised conduct. Mandeville had indicated what might be done. And although some formal doctrines of natural law might still be largely doctrines of office, duty gradually ceased to be coextensive with morality. Knud Haakonssen has traced natural law theory from Suarez to Thomas Reid, charting a decreasing reliance on the duties of office and an increasing insistence on rights. And it is rights talk, he concludes, that came to 'flourish, whatever it meant'.[32]

Similarly, Roy Porter has argued that eighteenth-century England saw a decisive shift from duty to individual pleasure, with many ethical problems becoming re-couched in terms of human psychology and happiness. These seem plausible generalisations, but Porter's contrast is crude. The English Enlightenment, he argues, was a discovery of human malleability, a claim that attributes an undifferentiated Augustinian deontology to an earlier world. Yet, curiously, he cites Boswell as 'trying on a whole wardrobe of personae', an observation better suited to showing the survival of older, loosely worn clothes, familiar dress to anyone who still read Pufendorf.[33] It would be truer to say that teleological or developmental malleability, some faith in human perfectibility, gradually complemented, then re-placed, a modal or official one populated by *personae*, a world constructed of Pufendorf's *entia moralia*.[34] If this is closer to the truth, it may further be hypothesised that the change in perspective created the illusion of seeing individuals whole at any one time, and encouraged the eighteenth-century intellectual preoccupation with historical change and with the

---

[32] Knud Haakonssen, *Natural Law*, p. 341. Some natural scientists saw all such traditions of natural law speculation as figurative and to be distinguished from God's natural laws as they applied to materiality; see Peter Anstey, *The Philosophy of Robert Boyle* (London, 2000), pp. 158–9.

[33] Roy Porter, *Enlightenment Britain and the Creation of the Modern World* (Harmondsworth, 2000), pp. 260–3, 288–9; James Boswell, *London Journal, 1762–63*, ed. Frederick A. Pottle (London, 1951), p. 39. Boswell's recorded *personae* are, inter alia, poet, lover, philosopher and client.

[34] Pufendorf, *De jure naturae et gentium, libri octo*, 1.i.23. p. 21; Richard Johnson, 'Early Modern Natural Law and the Problem of the Sacred State', Griffith University (Ph.D. Thesis, 2002), pp. 226–32; Hunter, *Rival Enlightenments*, pp. 263–8.

singularity of the sensitive self.³⁵ Certainly in a world of offices, identity is conspicuously partial and rule-bound; a *persona* is *being as* and *seeing as* and subject to a prior responsibility.

Irrespective of this, my argument ends roughly with the eighteenth century. By the beginning of the nineteenth, Kantians and their antagonists are providing clear ethical alternatives to the world on which I am concentrating, while the romantics are offering a contrast to the understanding of creative achievement. By the beginning of the twenty-first century, these alternatives are so much a part of our tacit knowledge of life that they are easily taken back into an older world – for Porter and others Augustine becomes Kant in a cowl. Wherever the evidence is silent, the past is easily assumed to nod in agreement with our priorities or assumptions. With increasing distance has come, in turn, the baggage of misplaced theoretical enquiries, while manifestations of an ethics of office survive through shrinkage and creative fragmentation; they have become the public adornment of prestigious professions, uneasily worn in a jostling world of journalistic deontology and common-sense utilitarianism. It is perhaps symptomatic of a general change that, in the seventeenth century, the terms 'officious' and 'officiousness' could commend the proper exercise of authority.³⁶ And how far an ethics of office has been buried in the sands of time can be gleaned from standard histories of ethics in which it is barely visible. In its stead are wastelands strewn with broken stones awaiting assemblage into an Osimandean image of someone like Kant.³⁷ 'Look on my works and despair' of recognising anything else. Later writers, who might be placed in a continuous tradition of the ethics of office as it becomes a defensive doctrine, most notably Bradley and Weber, look eccentrically isolated as moral theorists.

This study is first of all, then, an overview of a widespread presupposition of office, an hypothesised ethical *habitus* and the vocabulary from which this can be reconstructed. It is not a specific or thorough account of any particular doctrine of office. It is more concerned with assumptions, expectations, symbolic displays, claims and accusations and, above all, with the resource of a shared vocabulary. As a corollary throughout, it is the adaptive use of a vocabulary that provides the primary context

---

[35] Porter, *Enlightenment Britain*, ch. 12.
[36] William Cavendish, 'Masters and Servants, Horae subsecivae', Chatsworth MS, D3 p. 39; *A Letter from Leghorn from Aboard the Van-Herring* (1679), p. 1; cf. Philip Hunton, *A Treatise of Monarchie* (1643), for the pejorative 'officious propugness', p. 70.
[37] Alistair MacIntyre, *A Short History of Ethics* (London, 1967); J. B. Schneewind, *The Invention of Autonomy: A History of Modern Moral Philosophy* (Cambridge, 1998); John Rawls, *Lectures in the History of Moral Philosophy* (Cambridge, Mass., 2000); Robert L. Arrington, *Western Ethics: An Historical Introduction* (Oxford, 1998).

for discussion, the specific events filtered through it, a secondary one: secondary, because although reference and semantic relationship are biconditional for meaning, the historian can only know to what written evidence refers by understanding the interrelationships of vocabulary on the page. Neither is the first part ordered chronologically, or with respect to discrete areas of reasoning. Important as these are for understanding specific meanings, the emphasis is on what was sufficiently held in common to allow some negotiation and pragmatic transference of language between discursive domains, and on what was sufficiently shared to withstand the buffets of time as specific ideas, concepts and doctrines were not.

III

To reiterate in the most general propositional form: a presupposition of office was the expectation that people must behave according to the requirements of their respective offices. Moral, political and intellectual judgement was a function of office and the agent was a *persona*. This may seem hopelessly abstract and limp; but the ubiquitous presupposition was wrapped, as it were, in a whole semantic economy, capable of infinite pragmatic elaboration and adjustment and which, provisionally and in advance of a fuller discussion in chapter 4, may be outlined as comprising the following rough sectors.

First, there were the most general classifiers of office: the terms calling, vocation, trade, sphere, role, condition, profession, sometimes power, often care, or office. These terms were by no means always synonymous, but their family resemblance is striking, and office shall be taken as the central term. That we have such an overlaid sector of the vocabulary is indicative of the importance of the matter in hand, but the language, as we will see, is as slippery as Mr Pepys' cellar. What is often important about having an office as opposed simply to fulfilling a specific role, as I might if I happen to be giving directions, or having a drink, is a degree of formality in demarcation, an expectation of social continuity and the presentation of a *persona*. In the early-modern world, these aspects were frequently signalled, by ceremonial rites of passage into and out of office, of witnessed oaths cementing office-holder to the burdens of responsibility and frequently requiring semiotic markers to proclaim the *persona*. Claimed offices, such as those of poet, patriot or philosopher, lacking these formalised signs of identity, could be difficult to sustain, but nothing was water-tight. Any office could be controversial, because official status carried with it not only (much emphasised) burdens but serious advantages; its justificatory vocabulary seeped over the whole landscape of social relationships.

If we reduce office and *persona* to modern notions of selves playing roles, we do disservice to the extensive complexities involved.[38] This is not just because a *persona* was an embodiment of a moral economy, but also because we create the impression of some authentic residuum of selves and individuals left over from a limited, usually political world of office. Once hypothesised, these are taken as being available to us as causative agents of social role-play. From there the imposition of a modern distinction between the public (official) and the private (non-official) becomes almost inescapable. My concern, then, is not with a core concept of office (say kingship or priesthood) but with explaining configurations of vocabulary and the character of argument about and beyond institutional formality. To encompass within the ambit of office was to offer a moral, civic and often legal presence. In this light, it may be argued that the enlargement of the political nation, or the democratisation of the polity, is to be discovered less in the expansion of the franchise than in the rectoral extension of office.

Second, we have the vocabulary designating the moral and functional content of offices. Evocation of office entailed statements and presumptions about the status of any office-holder: the (adjectival) qualities relevant to its sphere of operation. These varied in specificity but constituted the touchstones of an ethics of office. The quality of love was central to discussions of parenthood and friendship, not to apprenticeship, and so proper conduct in one office could be improper elsewhere. It was part of the office of the apprentice to sweep out the shop and to avoid language like 'dumb found' and 'oddsbodikins' (as one would).[39] Soldiers might be permitted to curse. It is at this level of specificity that we shift from ethics to what are now styled codes of conduct. Also entailed was an adverbial vocabulary of action. Accommodating notions of *honestas* and *utilitas* provided the most general criteria for proper conduct. Under their auspices may be placed specific affirmations of duty and derivative liberty.

Delineation of any office could only be achieved in relative association with adjacent spheres of social activity. Rationale or *telos* and limit to office were each given prominence depending on circumstances; the question of rationale was likely to be emphasised in defending actions, the notion of limit in trying to control its *personae* (chapter 14). Relational identity between offices was reinforced by widespread understandings of the nature of definition. Whereas *real* definitions purported to label things with words, *nominal* definitions established conceptual and linguistic

---

[38] Braddick, *State Formation*, pp. 76–8, 83.
[39] Anon., *The Whole duty of an Apprentice* (1755), pp. 36.

relationships and protocols for word use. These were particularly important, because the immediate subjects of moral discourse were *personae*, fashioned through words, more than physical beings to which we might simply refer. The distinction between types of definition was most clearly worked out in medieval logic, but something approaching nominal definition also goes back to book 1 of *The Republic*. There it was argued that it ceases to be just to return a knife to its rightful owner if he is transformed into a madman; and Thrasymachus asserted that ineffective rulers are unworthy of the name. In context, this was just fast thinking, but should be seen against a background in which the end, *telos*, defined the *persona*.[40]

By the sixteenth and seventeenth centuries, in a fairly routine if opportunistic fashion, words were often understood nominally; they were taken as having meaning in mutually defining conjunction or opposition. Ruling therefore entailed a delineating notion of people to be ruled.[41] Similarly, a king was a proper ruler who should be obeyed. With slight extension, this gave rise to the common maxim that the king could do no wrong; but this did not necessarily mean that the person (physical being) holding the office was beyond criticism.[42] Those most hostile to a monarch might affirm the maxim. They might employ it, obviously enough, in the process of attacking counsellors as surrogate victims. This was one of the burdens of that ambiguously buffering office (chapter 7). Less obviously, the maxim understood nominally meant only that criticism required a contrasting notion to kingship. The king could do no wrong, but the tyrant could do no right (chapter 9). This sort of meta-belief about word use made central the question of what was to be considered part of the vocabulary of office and it kept vibrant issues of moral re-description. If, in contrast, we assume a more matter of fact or real understanding of definition, or arbitrarily superimpose our own conceptual vocabulary on the evidence when purporting simply to be describing it, we will misconstrue what was said. Such practice has made it easy to construct fixed ideologies from what was more flexible, a point directly relevant to the 'absolutism' of James VI&I (see chapter 13). Nominal definition, then, sustained the understanding of people as pure *personae*; identity in office was predominantly a nominal identity. Pufendorf abridged a wide range

---

[40] R. B. Onians, *The Origins of European Thought* (New York, 1973 edn), pp. 457–9: The *topos* of the return of the knife remained current in later English discussions of the ethics of office; see Cromartie, *The Constitutionalist Revolution*, ch. 2, quoting John Hales.
[41] *The Case of Oaths Stated, in State Tracts* (1705), vol. I, p. 345.
[42] Janelle Greenberg, *The Radical Face of the Ancient Constitution: St Edward's Laws in Early Modern Political Thought* (Cambridge, 2001), p. 192, assumes that the maxim stopped any criticism or rebellion.

of understandings when he wrote that a moral entity should not be confused with a physical one; that the impress of a moral (that is official) status on a physical being does not give an indelible character.[43] His posited *entia moralia* supported also the almost routine belief that offices made sense only in interrelationship. The words in a vocabulary were more than just contingent labels.

Sometimes there were attempts to rank offices in order to avoid contradictory duties, and an awareness that responsibilities might collide was persistent throughout the period under discussion. The fear of incommensurable offices simultaneously held was a spur to Kant's destruction of office by treating ethical activity as only one universal world of duty.[44] Most pertinently for this study, there is occasional appeal to love of country as over-riding or resolving conflicting duties (chapter 7). Yet asserted hierarchies of office were often ad hoc and it was the major function of casuistry to negotiate the tensions, conflicts and uncertainties of the ethics of office (below and chapter 8). Its effective occlusion from histories of ethics is a major aspect of the warping effects of later moral perspectives.[45]

An office, however, was not simply identified in reference to its neighbours; temporal continuity was vital, and imposed on the *persona* a duty to the office itself. So there was a symbolic economy in ceremonies proclaiming entry into office; the repetitions involved might be taken to express the expectation of continuous identity. The advantages of construing office in terms of continuity hardly need stressing when dealing with a monarch, where the fiction of immortality attaching to the *persona* could counteract the disruption of the death of a physical being. Thus notions of office required sophisticated understandings of change, allowing for continuity despite contingent physical mutation. Medieval writers such as Baldus and Accursius, relying on distinctions of form and content had seen office as analogous to ship repair. The ship remains the same though its decking is renewed. The office was thus always a partially reified identity. Such expressions of conceptual stability provided the logical assurance underlying Hooker's theory of a church (chapter 13), Selden's of the common law and even of 'David Hume's Broom'.[46] The principle of continuity is also particularly crucial in comprehending the office of the aristocrat

---

[43] Pufendorf, *De jure*, 1.i.23, p. 21.
[44] Hunter, *Rival Enlightenments*, ch. 6.
[45] Schneewind, *Invention of Autonomy*, mentions casuistry only on p. 395.
[46] Kantorowicz, *The King's Two Bodies*, pp. 293–5; Greenberg, *The Radical Face*, p. 33. According to the anecdote, the step-sweeper at Hume's club argued with the philosopher that he had always used the same broom despite having replaced all its parts.

having a responsibility to a continuing lineage and its reputation (chapter 3). Ironically, such burdens could prove disruptive. The degree to which there might be change in an office without erosion of nominal identity was always potentially problematic. It tied the positive rhetorics of office-holding to those of traditionality, helping to consign notions of innovation to the rhetorics of accusation and suspicion.

So far I have outlined only the sorts of terms and phrases to be appropriated in sustaining or promoting a *persona* in office; but a negative register was just as important as a positive. Again, this was partly a matter of semantics and nominal definition. Without a conception and language of the bad, it was not formally possible to articulate the good. Pragmatics also required a vocabulary of denigration to assist in the protection of one's own. The qualities fitting to status in office were balanced by vices of various kinds, by vocabularies of motive which explained culpable action, and by denigrating descriptors of conduct. The most important members of this group were words such as tyranny, neglect, alienate, engross, oppress, enslave, misrule. As this was a general vocabulary parallel to that of official approbation, it was decidedly redescriptive of any office, and the result was a highly flexible repertoire of accusation. Liberty became licence, prerogative an arbitrary power, subjection slavery. Carneades cast a long shadow, as Montaigne's *Essays* illustrate.[47] The recourse to the negative register of office suggests shared perspectives are breaking down, and that presuppositions are being forced into the open and becoming doctrinally consolidated. The use of a register which others might just as easily employ, however, is not necessarily to forge a doctrine, and take ownership of a set of concepts. In mistaking register for theory, we can fall victim to what C. S. Lewis valuably called the 'dangerous sense' of words, inventing what did not exist.[48]

So, to summarise this provisional account: an office was an identifiable and discriminate constellation of responsibilities and subordinate rights, or liberties asserted to be necessary for their fulfilment, manifested in a *persona* and regarded as in some way socially necessary or acceptable. It was given shape over time, in relation to adjacent offices, and by the patterns of its negation; it affirmed a social being analogous to human corporeal identity of flesh, fluids, bones and humours, seen over time, in space and subject to pathology.

---

[47] See especially Michel de Montaigne, 'Apology for Raymond Sebond' (1575–80), trans. Donald M. Frame, in *The Complete Essays* (Stanford, 1992 edn), pp. 318–457.
[48] C. S. Lewis, *Studies in Words* (Cambridge, 1976 edn), pp. 13–15.

IV

This broad understanding, I believe, provides a common feature of the diversity of early-modern political argument. It may also enhance awareness of the way in which modern disciplinary boundaries can impose misleading perspectives on early-modern exuberance.[49] Tracing expressions of office across the often artificial constraints imposed by notions of literature or philosophy will reinforce the point. Modal distinctions can, as I have noted, be crucial, but frequently our own are not; and, across the board, a recovery of the rhetorics of office compromises them.

I have already touched on the close relationship between presuppositions of office and the recognised ethos of traditionality of the early-modern world. When the common lawyer wrote of rationality and the immemorial, affirmations about tradition and office were entwined. From the mysteries of the law came the shape and authority of the *persona* of the lawyer whose duty was above all to the law. As a corollary, to attack one was to undermine the other.[50] The presumptive sway of tradition, however, could have a more asymmetrical relationship with office. The authority attached to a tradition might be because of faith in some pristine point of origination. And although the cachet of office was enhanced by temporal continuity, its survival a tribute to previous transmitting *personae*, that authority could always be expressed irrespective of tradition. The office could be taken as answering to a timeless theological imperative, a legal Reason, to a social necessity, or to future benefit. As I have noted, an office could always be given an abstract identity independent of contingent temporal mutations.

In contrast to the evocation of tradition, proper behaviour was hardly expressed beyond the confines of office. Acting beyond one's sphere was a form of *pleonexia*; the rim of office was the edge of tyranny. But because the rhetorics of office were adaptable to differing forms of activity, there were prodigious opportunities for conflict in the name of office. There were two principal ways of ameliorating this systemic difficulty. One was to rely on a predominantly modal casuistry, to assert that what was forbidden one *persona* was allowed, or required of, another. The other

---

[49] See, for example, Michael McKeon, 'Politics of Discourses and the Rise of the Aesthetic in Seventeenth-Century England', in Kevin Sharpe and Stephen N. Zwicker, eds., *Politics of Discourse: The Literature and History of Seventeenth-Century England* (Los Angeles, 1987); see also below, chapter 10.

[50] John Warr, *The Corruption and Deficiency of the Laws of England* (1649), in *A Spark in the Ashes: The Pamphlets of John Warr*, ed. Stephen Sedley and Lawrence Kaplan (London, 1992), pp. 89–110.

was to resolve potential conflict a priori by a hierarchical organisation of duties. This more presumptive mode of casuistry had the advantage of reducing mitigation to a relatively simple form. The distinction between presumptive and modal casuistry will be taken up in chapter 8. As one might expect, however, there was no single stable relationship in such patterns of official reciprocity, nor a rigid typology of casuistry. The relational notions of ruler and ruled could be elaborated in terms of complementary offices spun out from the truisms of nominal definition. But the similarly relational terms parent and child (also a relationship of ruling) could be discussed under the auspices of the simple office of parenting.[51] The child's duty to obey was inseparable from having a parent. Regardless of how such terms were related, the very recognition of a delineating office was an acceptance of potential moral difficulties, often incapable of theoretical resolution. The parent had authority until the child was rational and adult, but retained an office thereafter, and it was most likely to be problematic in fulfilling the duty of arranging a marriage. On the one hand, the child was obliged to submit to parental decisions; on the other, it could not marry without love, lest it perjure itself before God in the marriage sacrament.[52]

Acceptance of the obligations of office made arguments decorous or even literal, where now they might seem strained or metaphorical; conversely, the priority given to relationships in office minimised the conceptual significance of distinctions we now see as important. In order to explicate this point, it will be necessary to differentiate autochthonous from analytic patterns of figurative transfer (chapter 10). How the world is intellectually divided has changed and it is no longer obvious, as it seemed to Plato's Socrates and Thrasymachus, that the ruler is a shepherd. Husbands are not kings. But if all such socially contingent classifications are taken to be forms of office, implicit grounds for comparison lubricate the metaphorical imagination, or perhaps render non-figurative what we designate metaphorical. Metaphor is a creature of classificatory specificity and, lacking the requisite categories, we lose the means for identifying figurative transference. In the contentious case of the parent, child and the arranged marriage, it is not difficult to detect a sufficient closeness to rulers and ruled for talk of rebellion and tyranny to rumble around a neighbourhood. Insofar as we recognise familial and political relationships to be different, we might well take the notion of parental tyranny to

---

[51] Anon., *The Office of Christian Parents* (1616), p. 1, B1; p. 229.
[52] Hugh Latimer, *Fruitful Sermons* (1635 edn), fol. 302v; William Gouge, *Domesticall Duties* (1622), pp. 562–5; William Ames, *Cases of Conscience and the Resolution thereof* (1639), ch. 35, pp. 200–1; Anon., *The Office of Christian Parents*, pp. 194, 207.

be metaphorical; but if both the familial and the political are sub-sets of the official to which the tyrannous most properly pertains, then it is not so obvious that we are dealing with a metaphor. The time-honoured homologies between social function and physical attribute have lost much of their power and intimate interconnection. We draw a sufficiently clear distinction between them for a head of state to be understood as merely a figure of speech; but in a world in which corporeal and social identity could be related in a symmetrical and semiotic fashion, the physical could stand for the official. Further, we may talk of affairs of the heart, evoking a moribund yet still recognisable metaphor, but, in the seventeenth century, the heart had an interstitial status between corporeal and non-corporeal identity, a figure for the spiritual or emotional and a literal locus of the passions. The wedding ring, it was noted in *The Gentleman's Magazine*, was traditionally worn on the fourth finger of the left hand because it was believed to carry a nerve directly to the heart.[53] Changes in our knowledge of human physiology, cell and gene structure are far less likely to have an impact on concepts of society than theories of anatomy and corporeal reality had on seventeenth-century political discourse, for each discursive domain now has a degree of conceptual insulation it lacked three hundred years ago.

Analyses of motivation and the psychology of human agency were vital *explananda* for the censure of office. Such failings as pride and greed led to neglecting the proper scope, or transgressing the limits of any office, and they were seen as arising from specific kinds of disposition generated by the physical humours. Thus in a causative as well as an homologous way, the world of offices was related to corporeal identity. The vocabulary of motives sought to explain four sorts of social impropriety: improper occupation, iniquitous exercise, neglect (or alienation) and over-extension of office. This last process of moving beyond one's sphere was a matter of oppressing and reducing others to slavery. Where one form of organised rule might be favoured over another, it was because it was held to satisfy the requirements of the office of rule itself and keep at bay iniquity, turpitude and the ever present threat of tyranny.

V

The explication of all these features of an office-driven world has negative consequences for some fashionable and closely related lines of enquiry into early-modern England. As it is not my purpose to discuss modern

---

[53] *A Selection from the Gentleman's Magazine* (1811, 2nd edn), vol. I (from September 1795), p. 445.

theories extensively, it may be helpful to list something of what is at stake. Over the last generation or so there has been a preoccupation, especially in literary studies, with the emergence of the modern sense of the 'Self', with individualism and with self-fashioning, modern subjectivity, and autobiography. The lineage of this *topos* is an uneven blend of Marxist, Burckhardtian and liberal theory, sometimes processed through Foucauldian notions of power, and sometimes by mistaking Kant's examination of the postulates of the noumenal for features of phenomenal existence. It will, I think, become apparent that a proper attention to the presuppositions of office renders the whole enterprise of self-searching questionable.[54]

Notions of 'self-fashioning' and individualism have a partial genesis in the study of the origins and limitations of liberalism. This is such a firmly entrenched sub-genre of academia at the nexus of political theory, literary analysis and history that it is fairly standard to call Hobbes and Locke liberals, or attach them unreflectively to a liberal lineage when they are not even under discussion. Liberalism seems most plausible in the early-modern world if notions of office lay unnoticed or under-explored. If these are supplemented by the implantation of our own liberal vocabulary, we have not so much evidence of liberalism's continuity as a linguistic fait accompli.[55] I hope that the cumulative effect of the attention to office and the configurations of its language will render liberalism a spurious presence in the seventeenth century. As a corollary, the predominantly liberal notion of human beings as bearers of subjective rights has led to the assiduous search for the origin of a concept of natural law in which such individuals are suspended. If we can find such a theory, and the older the better, of course it commends the writer as modern. We get only fleeting glimpses of such theories in seventeenth-century England, their significance distorted by overlooking that rights were attached not to individuals qua moral agents with needs, but to *personae* tied to duties. Even Grotius, who comes close to being a theorist of subjective rights, uses the notion of a rights-bearing person as a cipher for the diversity of rights and duties that are found in official *personae*.[56] Tracing subjective rights back to the Middle Ages sounds plausible if natural law is isolated from divine and the

---

[54] The formative text is Stephen Greenblatt, *Renaissance Self-Fashioning, From More to Shakespeare* (Chicago, 1980), a work more subtle than much in its idiom.
[55] See, for example, Vickie Sullivan, *Machiavelli, Hobbes and the Formation of a Liberal Republicanism in England* (Cambridge, 2004), and the extensive literature on which she draws, pp. 1–27. Liberalism is seen as a fixture of the political landscape, p. 10; it is its early modern marriage with republicanism that needs explaining.
[56] Grotius, *De jure belli*, 1.i.4–5.

human soul is seen as synonymous with the individual.⁵⁷ But as natural law was subsumed by divine and the soul was largely conceived in terms of relationships of office (chapter 6), the plausibility diminishes; the liberal rights-bearer assumes the shape of a myth.

Related to all of these lines of enquiry is the frequent imposition or casual acceptance of modern distinctions between public and private. Feminist history and political theory have, for example, made much of this and of women being restricted to the private (domestic) sphere. Mapping patterns of disadvantage through the use of dichotomies between public and private is now being recognised as theoretically problematic.⁵⁸ It has also been historically misleading. In the early-modern world, notions of public and private were of diminished and negotiable significance, and they were often used rather differently, sufficiently for the modern binary oppositions to have become distorting global projections. As John Caputo has written in a different context, in making firm distinctions we can invent what we think we are only clarifying.⁵⁹ In the present case, this is not least because, when unpacked, whatever was private could, no less than the public, be discussed in terms of office, or could signal argument about office-abuse (chapter 3). It may be that rather than that handy abstraction liberalism arising from a dichotomy between public and private, it is the other way round. Of recent interest also has been the search for the origins of the Habermasian 'public sphere', itself according to Jürgen Habermas a liberal bourgeois phenomenon which he located in the early eighteenth century as a concomitant, or derivative, of early capitalism.⁶⁰ These origins have gradually been pushed back to the early sixteenth century, but, as I shall conclude in chapter 3, the putative discoveries of this sphere have confused a theoretical model with the evidence, so distorting the past as much as divesting the model of its meaning. The combined effect of putting to one side these customary genealogical categories of analysis that are held to have early-modern origins, is to render problematic what we might take for granted about

---

⁵⁷ Brian Tierney, 'The Origins of Natural Rights Language: Texts and Contexts 1150–1250', *History of Political Thought*, 4 (1983), pp. 429–41; Brian Tierney, *The Idea of Natural Rights* (Atlanta, 1997); Annabelle Brett, *Liberty, Right and Nature* (Cambridge, 1997).

⁵⁸ See, for example, Raia Prokhovnik, *Rational Woman* (London, 1999); Diana Coole, 'Cartographic Convulsions: Public and Private Reconsidered', *Political Theory*, 28, 3 (2000), pp. 337–54; C. Armstrong and J. Squires, 'Beyond the Public/Private Dichotomy: Relational Space and Sexual Inequalities', *Contemporary Political Theory*, 1 (2002), pp. 261–83.

⁵⁹ John Caputo, *On Religion* (London, 2000), p. 46.

⁶⁰ Jürgen Habermas, *The Structural Transformation of the Public Sphere: An Enquiry into a Category of Bourgeois Society*, trans T. Burger and F. Lawrence (Cambridge, 1992).

the political itself, and the apparent discovery of its autonomy in early modernity (chapter 10).

The centrepiece, as it were, of the political turbulence of seventeenth-century England was the execution of a monarch for the most dramatic form of office-abuse and the formal establishment of a republic or commonwealth. This was a revolutionary moment. And fear of the violent precedent it might become informed society deep into the eighteenth century. The monarchy was never quite the same again. The immediate republican past made the restored Charles II a new prince. Because of his Catholicism James II was new, fresher than Mary I. Dutch William was new and so was German George. Even at the end of the eighteenth century, the violent formation of a French Republic did much to bring the fear of English Civil War and king-killing back into the present. So, unlike the preoccupations with the public sphere and the modern, liberal self, an interest in the related questions of the revolutionary character of the Civil Wars and what republicanism might have meant, can all be historically valid. But as the Cromwellian Commonwealth did not last long and people might well suffer if accused of republicanism late in the century, it is all too easy to construct a narrative rather like a Foxean martyrology, pouring the blood of new victims into the old bottles labelled Marxian Revolution, Liberal constitutionalism and Protestant Reformation. Such apologetic trajectories of social time and ideological lineage will be resisted here. Instead, what will, I believe, become clear, is that the nature of English republicanism needs recasting, because much of the evidence for it arises from an unhelpful way of discussing a common feature of all early-modern societies, and much from mistaking register of office-talk for ideology (chapters 3, 7). It is to the disparate evidence of office that I shall now turn.

2 Ceremonies of office: The kiss of the tutti-man

> Ceremony keeps up all things.
> (John Selden, *Table Talk*, 1686)

I

This chapter sketches something of the *habitus* of office beyond institutional form, for the ritualistic or ceremonial was a dimension of activity integral to society.[1] 'Seremoney', insisted William Cavendish, 'though itt is nothing in itt Selfe, yett it doth Every thing.' All artificial relationships of hierarchy were expressed and affirmed through it: '–what is parents & Children, masters & Servants, officers in all kindes, in the Comon wealth, without Seremoney, And order, nothing at all–'.[2] As Selden remarked succinctly, it was 'like a penny glass to a rich spirit . . . without it the spirit [is] lost'.[3] But the glass is an unreliable mirror, or model for any separate social structure.[4] This too contemporaries would have appreciated. As

---

[1] Where possible, I am using the terms ritual and ceremony as interchangeable, though ritual can nowadays be taken to refer to the general character of ceremonial occasions and to specific actions within ceremonies. In the seventeenth century the semantic relationships were rather different. Ceremony was often preferred as a general term to the frequently pejorative ritual. This negativity, however, sometimes rubbed off onto the ceremonial. Much depended on the modes of discourse in which the words were found and specifically on religious affiliations. See Goldie, 'The Unacknowledged Republic', p. 156, on the ceremonial as a principal dimension of political participation; Buc, *The Dangers of Ritual*, at length, on the problem of a 'hazy laundrey list' of practices consolidated by anthropological modelling, p. 5, too broad to be useful, too fashionable to be given up, p. 161. In many cases Buc's 'solemnities', is a better word, p. 9.

[2] William Cavendish, 'Advice' (1660), Clarendon MS 109, Bodleian Library, Oxford, fol. 20.

[3] Albertus Warren, *The Royalist Reform'd* (1650), p. 26; John Selden, *Table Talk* (1686) in James Thornton, ed., *Table Talk from Ben Jonson to Leigh Hunt* (London, 1934), p. 29.

[4] Edwin Muir, *Ritual in Early Modern Europe* (Cambridge, 1997), pp. 5–6 for the qualified distinction between mirroring and modelling. See Tim Harris, *London Crowds in the Reign of Charles II: Propaganda and Politics from the Restoration to the Exclusion Crisis*

Richard Stuart reflected, ceremony was like a 'dumb shew'; it is the moral that commends it, not the act, but 'the *end* of it'.⁵ Therein lay the problem: the semiotic presupposition that so sensitised people to symbolic interconnection made it difficult to limit hermeneutic possibility. Reading the 'end' of it could be re-encoding to a different point, and so the whole field of the ceremonial could be, as Hobbes wrote of metaphor, equivocal and subject to contention.

And so it remains. Much valuable scholarship has been concentrated on the '*end*' or function of the ceremonial within a broader political system. For some the '*end*' was hegemonic containment, for others the opportunity for resistance to that control. Analyses of carnival in early-modern Europe have often moved in this second direction.⁶ Given the variously exploitable character of social rituals, however, global accounts of their social function are likely to be dangerous, and looking for a set of specifically political functions may be a matter of pouring new wine into the old penny glass and investing its 'politics' with anachronistic content.⁷ Even when this is not the case, the identification of the distinctly political can be arbitrary, but political or not, wherever we find surviving evidence of ritual and ceremony, we are likely to find expectations of office, affirmed or disappointed.

II

Throughout early-modern England rituals paced and organised the flow of existence. They often helped palliate wayward contingency even when riding in its most apocalyptic forms. They punctuated and gave structure to the turning points of single lives, to the agricultural year, and constituted the religious calendar.⁸ Prior to the Reformation a complex liturgical calendar was made to coincide with the seasons; thus the productive processes of the year were associated with clerical office. This may or may

---

(Cambridge, 1987), pp. 15–18; at greater length, Tim Harris, 'Problematising Popular Culture', in Tim Harris, ed., *Popular Culture in England, c.1500–1850* (Basingstoke, 1995); Peter Burke, 'Popular Culture in Seventeenth-Century London', in Barry Reay, ed., *Popular Culture in Seventeenth-Century England* (London, 1985), pp. 31–2; Buc, *The Dangers of Ritual*, pp. 7–11.

⁵ Richard Stuart, *Three Sermons Preached by the Reverend and Learned Dr. Richard Stuart* (1656), p. 112.
⁶ Cf. Clifford Geertz, *Negara: The Theatre State in Nineteenth-Century Bali* (Princeton, 1980), with the literature discussed in Muir, *Ritual*, ch. 3.
⁷ Buc, *The Dangers of Ritual*, pp. 8–11.
⁸ Muir, *Ritual*, p. 16; for a detailed study, David Cressy, *Bonfires and Bells: National Memory and the Protestant Calendar in Elizabethan and Stuart England* (London, 1979).

not have functioned to reinforce the authority of the church.[9] It did, however, depict those involved in seasonal activities as souls in a cosmic order that priests themselves might help mediate. After the Reformation, the integration of liturgical and seasonal calendars became controversial, augmenting the vulnerability of the Catholic Church; the signs of popery and the abuse of priestly office could be found almost everywhere. And, because one calendar could symbolise the other, England would prove slow in adopting Gregorian reforms; acceptance could signify compliance to Rome.[10] Nevertheless, throughout England rituals remained, sometimes co-opted and decisively changed.[11] Edwin Muir gives the beautiful anecdote from the history of the vehemently Protestant Emmanuel College. Founded in 1584 upon the ruins of a Dominican priory, the dining hall was on the site of the priory chapel, so the daily breaking of bread ritualistically erased the idolatrous ceremonies of the Eucharist.[12] Later, Marvell would fashion images of perpetual reformation through a house built on a place of papal corruption, so making explicit the meanings of symbolic refounding and reaffirmation in the ceremonies of everyday life.[13]

Numerous rituals were woven like the ribbons worked around the maypole: from sowing seed to cutting the corn, from birth to the dance of death. Ritual performance was a social participation that gave a rationale to the world because it assigned roles; and the acceptance of a role was tacit consent to a world, as one understood it.[14] And, as an office consolidates role-play into an on-going moral entity, we may expect an intimation of office to permeate the ceremonial. As tradition is an idiom of change, the choreography of ritual might be improvised or contested, precisely because people understood its importance as symbolic assertion, a negotiable norm by which to measure any deviating steps.

Older customs, like ancient philosophers, survived by dancing to the tunes of Christianity. 'The Heathens had . . . their *Saturnalia*, and we our *Carnevals* . . . They their Procession of *Priapus*; wee our fetching in, erection, and dancing about *May-poles*; and Dancing is one kind of

---

[9] Muir, *Ritual*, p. 58.
[10] Anon., *The Julian and Gregorian Year* (1700), pp. 15, 17.
[11] Cressy, *Bonfires*, for example, pp. xi–xii, 45–53.
[12] Muir, *Ritual*, p. 176; but see Sarah Bendall, Christopher Brooke and Patrick Collinson, *A History of Emmanuel College Cambridge* (Woodbridge, 1999), pp. 7–10, 43. Muir's conjunction of locations is not specifically supported.
[13] A. D. Cousins, 'Marvell's "Upon Appleton House, to My Lord Fairfax" and the Regaining of Paradise', in Conal Condren and A.D. Cousins, eds., *The Political Identity of Andrew Marvell* (Aldershot, 1990), pp. 53–84.
[14] David Cressy, *Birth, Marriage and Death: Ritual, Religion, and the Life-Cycle in Tudor and Stuart England* (Oxford, 1997), pp. 475–82.

Worship'. Then again, 'Wee never reade of any Christians that went dancing into Heaven; though we read of sundry wicked ones who have gone dancing downe to Hell.'[15] Because so much ritual activity expressed or reaffirmed a particular religious identity, it is little wonder that the rhythms of performance were often disrupted as an expression of social unease and denominational controversy.[16] The very word ritual was a prejudicial Reformation coinage for Catholic rites believed inimical to Christian liberty;[17] but gradually its range was expanded, both to say something serious about social practice and to index spreading controversy. Theologically, ritual was poised on the edge of those things considered necessary for salvation, and so subject to the most sedulous defence, and those belonging to the uncertain realm of *adiaphora*: uncertain, because it could be argued with equal vigour that things indifferent to salvation should be left alone, or controlled in the interests of peace.[18] To move from the ritualised affirmations of salvational necessity to those of *adiaphora* could be to leap from frying pan to fire.

Crucial to understanding ritual as an aspect of expectations of office is the notion of rites of passage, concerning birth, marriage and death. In 1908 Arnold van Gennep identified three stages in them: separation, transition and incorporation. The stages were held to be significant because the specific meanings of actions were dependent upon their immediate ceremonial contexts. David Cressy has suggested that van Gennep's analysis simply closes down historical discussion; but the problem is different.[19] Gennep's structural schema led to a fragmented view of relationships in office. The stage of incorporation was incorporation *as*, and might better be called, an assumption of office. This, in turn, might be less a separation from a group than an enrichment of identity within it. In becoming a priest a man was not separated from his church but assumed an augmented status. This office was of pivotal importance as clerics mediated the transformation of so many *personae* into office, and the Reformation made rites of passage into the priesthood inherently controversial as semiotic encapsulations of theology. For the Lutheran, the

---

[15] Thomas Hobbes, *Leviathan* (1651), ed. Richard Tuck (Cambridge, 1991), ch. 45, p. 457; Morgan Godwyn, *The Negroe's and Indians Advocate* (1680), p. 33; cf. William Prynne, *Histrio-mastix* (1633), pp. 244, 232.
[16] Cressy, *Birth*, pp. 475–82.
[17] George Gillespie, *A Dispute Against the English Popish Ceremonies Obtruded onto the Church of Scotland* (1637), ch. 1; Buc, *The Dangers of Ritual*, pp. 164–72.
[18] For the contrary implications of *adiaphora*, see John Locke, *Two Tracts on Government*, ed. Philip Abrams (Cambridge, 1967).
[19] Arnold van Gennep, *The Rites of Passage*, trans. M. B. Vizidom and G. L. Caffee (Chicago, 1960); cf. Muir, *Ritual*, pp. 19–20; Cressy, *Birth*, pp. 97–8.

change merely proclaimed the duties of an office within an *ecclesia* in which all believers had a priestly aspect. For many others, not necessarily Catholic, the passage into office was through God's grace a radical and mystical transformation.

At this point, a distinction can be drawn between transformative assumption *of* and affirmative performance *in* office. A marriage was a rite of official passage for bride and groom, one in which the bride, to allude to van Gennep, was separated from her parents and assumed a new office after a liminary ceremony of transition. Yet, it was also a performance in office for parents and priest. A recognised assumption *of* was thus dependent upon performance *in* office. The rites surrounding child-birth were always transformative rites of passage for the baby, from unborn soul to child, but with the first child the status of the woman was also altered. Around a single event like birth might be woven subsidiary rituals of child-bed preparation, and there could be an evocation of previous ceremonies. Churching, especially after the birth of the first-born, was a reaffirmation, even in a way a completion, of the marriage sacrament. If one turns attention from transformation to performance, birth rites of passage might generate tension between the official mediators, minister and midwife.[20] Each had an interest of office, a property in the proceedings, but although midwives formally were licensed by the church, expertise and field of operation to the virtual exclusion of men meant that their office was neither clearly subordinate, nor uniformly controlled. That the occasional midwife was a man did not noticeably increase clerical authority. The detailed oath of midwifery, one of the longest recorded in *The Booke of Oathes*, made clear that the midwife's was an office of specific responsibilities and of enabling rights. She was obliged inter alia to help all women in birth regardless of wealth, not to falsify parentage, connive at abortion, or at the death of a child, to forbear the use of charms and witchcraft, to ensure proper burial of the dead and baptism of the quick.[21] She had also to report on any deviant behaviour of any others within the 'roome', or office of the midwife. It was this office that provided also the terms of her protection when conduct was questioned. Elizabeth Gaynsford insisted that it was 'by the authoritie of my office then beying a midwyfe' that she had baptised a child.[22] I shall return to the distinction between the affirmative and the transformative when dealing with the specific issue of oath-taking (chapters 11, 12) for the oath itself was

---

[20] Cressy, *Birth*, pp. 63–70.
[21] *The Booke of Oathes* (1649), p. 288.
[22] 'The Deposition of Elizabeth Gaynsford', October 1543, cited in *A Selection from the Gentleman's Magazine*, December 1795, vol. I, p. 385.

Ceremonies of office 41

characteristically a ritualised act, had a performative dimension and was a sign of what more broadly was taking place.

The mysteries of child-birth were, then, overseen by an officer, at once accountable, yet of independent authority; birth itself was informed by official expectations but not by invariant ritual, or one simple narrative of meaning. Thus the sacrament of baptism became controversial, for it encoded contentious theological claims about the office of the priest, or, in emergency, the midwife, and about the meaning of belonging to a church. Only gradually did the role of the godparents diminish, and probably not much during the period under discussion. Usually in early modern England, their place was central in baptism, for, enlisted in the cosmic fight against evil, their responsibility was to guide a soul, an office that might potentially conflict with parental duty.[23]

Similarly, marriage was preceded to a large extent by differing patterns of courtship to which a considerable literature was devoted dealing with the symbolism and significance of the discrete stages and the strategies for moving through them. These might even be reduced to a set of learnable cribs and aids to seduction.[24] Then, formally status was transformed by sacrament and service; but official expectations could be disrupted by the conflict of action in the name of office. Parents might claim a duty to force or prohibit a union, children might elope, priests might decline to officiate. Some might marry without the exchange of rings. As Cressy points out, during the seventeenth century, the symbolism of the ring also increasingly became a focus for hostility to the vestiges of popery.[25] For George Gillespie, this as well as clerical robes were 'reliques of Romes whoorish bravery' and signs of conformity to Antichrist.[26] William Prynne, in curiously ameliorating vein, considered the ring a matter of theological indifference, to be 'omitted, or left arbitrary to all'.[27] But predominantly it remained a symbol of union before God. To question it was indirectly to subvert the Book of Common Prayer, which after 1662 could itself be defended almost as Holy writ, for the office of the Church of England priest depended much upon it. For the rich, marital disaster might end with another formal rite of official passage, annulment, ejactation or divorce. These terminations could be effected through a diversity of local customs such as the return of the wedding ring. For the poor there was

---

[23] Muir, *Ritual*, p. 21.
[24] Alexander Nicholes, *A Discourse of Marriage and Wiving* (1615); N. H., *The Ladies Dictionary* (1694); Edward Phillips, *The Mysteries of Love and Eloquence* (1658, 1685).
[25] Cressy, *Birth*, pp. 342–7.
[26] Gillespie, *A Dispute*, p.107; pt 2.3, p.15; Cressy, *Birth*, p. 345.
[27] William Prynne, *A Short, Sober pacific examination of some exhorbitancies in Ceremonial Apurtinences to the Common Prayer* (1661), p. 7.

occasionally the option of sale and always the drift into illicit and officially ambiguous relationships.[28]

The termination of life was just as pregnant with symbolic connotations of office, for, as I shall show, the central focus of death was the soul, depicted as being in an official relationship with God (below, Chapter 6). When dissolution was expected, the preparations could be highly ritualised with death-beds as the central props for an *ars moriendi*, the stage for a contest between Heaven and Hell.[29] It was, according to Roy Porter, only during the eighteenth century that death-bed ceremonial gradually dissipated. Wills were more likely to be reduced to their prosaic functions of property transfer, omitting the conventionalised theological prolegomena characteristic of the previous century.[30] Yet, as with baptism, because the service of the dead continued to be informed by official expectations, it was intermittently subject to controversy. First, masses for the dead became tainted within a Protestant environment, then surplices were gathered with the skirts of popery, and even the priest's meeting the funeral procession became contentious.[31] Little of this was, one presumes, the result of an indifference to human feelings, but arose from changing beliefs about what rituals meant and how they squared with the requirements of the priestly office. The more rules and regulations concerning ceremonies in general, reflected Edmund Hickeringill, the more there was likely to be discord.[32] In short, at all recognised stages of life, official expectations proffered hope of order and meaning, often to be dashed in the dissonances of symbolic possibility.

This was true of the solemnities of punishment and execution. So often formally public, executions were performed ceremoniously, often before teeming witnesses, playing their part in creating an almost dramatic ambience. The gruesome relics of this work – London Bridge, for example, with a tiara of boiled heads, the twisting cadavers over the river at Execution Dock – were proclamations of the duties of the sword of justice. They were the droppings of the vigilant. To interfere was itself a serious felony, and could be read as a symbolic rejection of authoritative office. In 1633 the culmination of the notorious Clun murders was not the execution of the young Enock ap Evan for murdering his mother and brother, but the removal of his body from the gibbet to give it some show

---

[28] Muir, *Ritual*, p. 42; the practice lasted – Thomas Hardy's *The Mayor of Casterbridge* begins with such a sale.
[29] Jeremy Taylor, *Rules for Holy Dying* (1651), ch. 4, pp. 178–83; Muir, *Ritual*, pp. 45–6.
[30] Porter *Enlightenment Britain*, p. 211.
[31] Cressy, *Birth*, pp. 396–407; see also Prynne, *A Short . . . Examination*, sect. 4, pp. 30ff; appendix on symbolism of the colours of vestments, pp. 113–36.
[32] Edmund Hickeringill, *The Naked Truth, The First Part* (1680), pp. 8–10.

of decent burial in a saw-pit. The justices were assiduous in winkling out the culprit, even if they decided not to string her up as well. Enock's sister, they concluded, had suffered enough. This acquiescence in a suspension of the law was in turn taken as a sign of a puritan conspiracy involving Enock and the justices who originally had him hanged.[33] Lesser punishments were still weighty with emblematic significance: a necklace of dice for the fraud in the pillory, a whetstone for the liar.[34] Those who walked at large with cropped ears, or spoke with pierced tongue, advertised a whole semiotics of justice.

III

& the next day, being *st. George's*, he went by water to Westminster *Abby.*: when his *Majestie* was entered, the *Dean & Prebends* brought all the *Regalia* ... Then came the *Peres* in their *Robes & Coronets &c* in their hands, til his Majestie was placed in a throne elevated before the Altar ... then rose up the *King* & put off his robes & upper garments ... [that the] Bishop might commodiously anoint him ... Then was a *Coyf* put on & the *Colobium*, Syndon or *Dalmatic*, & over this a *Supertunic* of Cloth of Gold, with *buskins & sandals* of the same, *Spurrs*, The *Sword*... Then the A:B: placed the *Crowne Imperial* on the *Altar*, prayed over it, & set it on his Majesties Head, at which all the *Peres* put on their *Coronets*.[35]

Among the most significant rites of official passage were coronations, municipal elections and ecclesiastical investitures. These were woven around talismanic and sacred robes and baubles, above all the crown and Confessor's throne at coronations. They were performances at once proclaiming the importance of an office and the new office-holder, but it would be unduly reductive to see them only as displays of power. To begin with, they were reassurances of official continuity, drawing on a stock of symbolic associations and of necessity involving a circle of witnesses additional to the central actors. Witness and actor established a relationship of reciprocal responsibility and the prescribed actions furnished a primitive statement of what was entailed. Between being placed on the throne and being anointed, Charles had been presented on every side to the people by the Bishop of London, 'asking if they would have him for their king and do him homage'.[36] Witnesses, in short, were the sanctioning

---

[33] Peter Studely, *The Looking-Glasse of Schism* (1635); Barbara Coulton, 'Rivalry and Religion: The Borough of Shrewsbury in the Early Stuart Period', *Midland History*, 28 (2003), pp. 38–41.
[34] Peter Ackroyd, *London, The Biography* (London, 2000), p. 290.
[35] John Evelyn, *Diary*, ed. E. S. de Beer, 6 vols. (Oxford, 1955), vol. III, 24 April 1661, pp. 282–3.
[36] Ibid.

rim of the action, a sign of limit, framing the performance like the Hungerford tutti-men exchanging oranges for kisses as they marched around the town on its Hocktide or Easter election days, or 'the commons' and 'their clarkes in their surplices' summoned for the Tynwald Day proclamations of law in the Isle of Man.[37] As I will discuss more fully (chapters 11, 12), the solemnities were frequently explicated and cemented with an oath calling on God as the omnipotent witness. If the ceremony publicly affirmed the new status and proclaimed a transfer of rights to the office-holders, it also encapsulated the criteria for judging conduct. The witnesses and the communities they stood for were thus forewarned and forearmed.

Many rites of office made play with circles, for from antiquity the circle had symbolised a form of perfection, something completed, and was a token of a distinct identity. The wedding ring was an unending shape commonly taken as a sign of the undying nature of mutual commitment.[38] The circle, however, not only idealised the virtues of the office-holders, but like the studied repetition of ritual, the continuity of office itself: hence the coronets carried, then worn, in response to the crowning of the king, and the mayoral circlet chain of office. But, as the chain additionally suggests, a circle was associated strongly with constraint and limit, of being tied to a given responsibility and a distinct end; it suggests a *telos*, then, in a double sense of the term, of purpose and completion.[39] There followed the necessity of finding and proclaiming office-holders who were fit because they knew the burdens of their sphere and understood the consequences of neglect or excess.

For centuries in various parts of England there were Ascension Day rituals of beating bounds or circuits of jurisdiction.[40] The common office of schoolmaster was often circumscribed through what Keith Thomas has called 'collusive rituals'. In Tideswell, Derbyshire, for example, the children went around the village and then barred the master from the schoolhouse. He could assume his office only by exercising it to give a holiday.[41] This reciprocity of official bounds and fit conduct seems most explicit in the London Skinners' Company ceremony for a newly elected master. The crown of office, like Cinderella's slipper, was first tried on others before

---

[37] Hugh Pilhens, *The Story of Hungerford* (Newbury, 1983), pp. 19–22; Christina Hole, *English Custom and Usage* (London, 1943–4), p. 121.
[38] Onians, *Origins*, pp. 426–66, esp. 444, 449, 454–9; Cressy, *Birth*, p. 342.
[39] Onians, *Origins*, pp. 457–9, cites Aeschylus as using *telos* to refer to office; Myers, *Political Ideas of the Greeks*, pp. 159–63.
[40] Burke, 'Popular Culture', p. 36.
[41] Keith Thomas, cited in Coulton, 'Rivalry and Religion', p. 30; Hole, *English Custom*, p. 39.

Ceremonies of office

being placed on the master's head, which alone it was proclaimed to fit. Matthew Griffith emphasised this notion of fitness in decoding the symbolism of the wedding ring as an expression of the match between husband and wife.[42] The sense of boundary describing any office could also exhibit a heavy-handed awareness of transgression. At St Mary's parish, Leicester, during bound-beating, newly appointed officials were, apparently, inverted, inserted in a hole and beaten with a shovel.[43]

IV

A little more needs to be said about ceremonial affirmations of office: performances in which office-holders were endorsed in their daily work. Here, however, the movement creating narrative meaning is not of someone assuming a new *persona*, but often literally, a progress, or procession of an office in action. We are still familiar with gaudy crocodiles of judges, or gowned academics processing before their business is properly begun. Nowadays, however, there is often a museum-like quality for the curious onlookers, most of whom are more innocent bystanders than ceremonial witnesses, while the processions themselves may have been streamlined. Judges arriving for the assizes are no longer attended by pikemen and greeted with bells, music and Latin orations, 'awful solemnities', as one seventeenth-century observer put it, designed to impress upon all the majesty of the law.[44] In Elizabethan England, the status of parliament was framed by such events, and the speeches commencing proceedings were ritualistic affirmations of an office and its shared values.[45] Even charitable work could take such a stylised form. John Stow recalls the regular, usually Friday, processions of London citizens and their wives to Houndsditch to place coins at the windows of the needy. In such alms-giving *passeggiate,* they affirmed standing by conduct befitting responsibility and the specific office of alms-giving.[46]

The pageantry of royal progresses associated with Elizabeth I is a similar example: although spectacular progresses were patinated with custom.[47] In announcing her presence and power, they were reassurances

---

[42] Cressy, *Birth*, p. 342.
[43] Hole, *English Custom*, p. 59.
[44] Cited in Braddick, *State Formation*, p. 38.
[45] Mack, *Elizabethan Rhetoric*, pp. 215–52; *Elizabeth I: Collected Works*, ed. Leah S. Marcus, Janel Mueller and Mary Beth Rose (Chicago, 2000), pp. 159, 105, 107, 108, 167, 181, 328–30, 346, 351.
[46] Stow, *A Survay of London* (1603 edn), p. 129; Ackroyd, *London*, p.118; 'Of Alms-Deeds', in *Certain Sermons*, pp. 241–5.
[47] Frances Yates, *Astraea: The Imperial Theme in the Sixteenth Century* (London, 1993 edn), p. 109.

about the protective reach of office. Elizabeth's status was underlined by the pomp with which she and her entourage would pause before the city, town, or palace gates and then formally be received.[48] On such occasions, her studied acts of charity were symbolic of her wider care.[49] At Woodstock in 1575 Sir Henry Lee greeted her with chivalric tilts and a poetic hermit with shepherd's crook who conducted her to an arcadian banquet.[50] In George Peele's Lord Mayoral pageant of 1591, Elizabeth was the shepherdess thwarting the monkish figures of superstition and ignorance. The assurance of the protective nature of true rule is clear: 'Feed on my flock among the gladsome green' (the stress is crucial). Yet more sheep: Elizabeth, 'whose heart is purely fixed on the law,/The holy law . . .' thus stands, or rather sits safe among her flock, swathed in Platonic and New Testament affirmations of office.[51] An account of an extended reception at Cambridge in 1564–5 had also played out the reassuring continuity of responsibility. Elizabeth participated in preliminary processions and receptions with the exchange of gifts, gloves and sugar loaves looming large; and then the event culminated with an oration by the queen decoding the significance by linking herself with her predecessors and expressing her sensitivity to the need to succour learning, but no firm funding promises. All this was to confirm an official space for the university itself.[52]

Expectation of continuity of conduct is most elaborately illustrated by the London pageants.[53] John Stow records commemorations of Edward I's victories over the Scots, with fishmongers moving through the streets with golden sturgeon and silver salmon accompanied by five and forty knights.[54] Often these affairs were sufficiently elaborate and didactic to operate as subsidiary rites of official passage, celebrating the election of a new Lord Mayor. They were frequently scripted by playwrights. Dekker and Heywood drew on eclectic patterns of imagery that presumably sought to reach a diversity of audience.[55] As the participants progressed from one significant point to another, there were tableaux and mottoes, speeches and poetry to decode the action. Such pageants had something of

---

[48] David M. Bergeron, *English Civic Pageantry, 1558–1642* (London, 1971), pp. 3–5; on civic entries, see also Muir, *Ritual*, 239–46.
[49] Christopher Haigh, *Elizabeth* (New York, 1998), pp. 151–2.
[50] Yates, *Astraea*, pp. 94–8.
[51] George Peele, *Descensus Astraeae*, in *Works*, ed. A. H. Bullen (London, 1888), vol. I, pp. 363, 366; Yates, *Astraea*, pp. 60–1.
[52] *A Selection from the Gentleman's Magazine*, vol. I, pp. 75–92; see also Mack, *Elizabethan Rhetoric*, pp. 48–9; Elizabeth I, 'Oration', in *Works* (August 1564), pp. 87–9.
[53] See, at length, Bergeron, *English Civic Pageantry*.
[54] Stow, *Survay*, p. 96.
[55] Burke, 'Popular Culture', pp. 44–5.

the civic mystery play about them. They were, as Bergeron has argued, emblems writ large.[56] The themes all concerned the mayoral office, its responsibilities, the rights and virtues necessary for its exercise and its surrounding dangers. The symbolism of the shepherd was one size that fitted all, mayors no less than monarchs, and citizens were sheep to be protected in the little fold of London from the ever lurking wolves.[57] In 1619 Thomas Middleton made more obvious play with the parallels of office by comparing the mayor with a loving spouse. Dekker and Middleton both used the decorous imagery of maritime adventuring. The mayoralty was like a great voyage of state with all its challenges, dangers and its need for dedication, vigilance, foresight and resilience, imperatives familiar from the world of the Italian republics and which Halifax would later associate with the art of trimming in the tiny boat of state.[58]

Little processions were replicated with local variation throughout the land. At Lichfield the sheriff in the company of mounted witnesses rode annually around the ancient boundary marks of the city, pausing at each to accept the limit and integrity of his sphere.[59] And, aside from all civic pageants, there were, for example, funereal and bridal processions, helping frame transformative rites of passage. More occasionally, processions ending in acts of lavish hospitality might announce the return of a local patron, signalling the resumption of the liberality that was a proclaimed virtue of aristocracy. The end of the journey in one sense expressed the end of the office in another. Gradually such performances were scaled down or abandoned, but they survived into the eighteenth century.[60]

Processions hardly exhausted the symbolic organisation of social space. Within the courtly world, the Tudor progress was superseded by the more intimate Stuart masque: 'come shepherds all let's sing and play'.[61] This was a form of theatre that makes sense best as allegorical comment on the importance of office and its necessary virtues, often with the centrality

---

[56] Bergeron, *English Civic Pageantry*, pp. 274–99.
[57] Heywood, *Londini euphoria* (1633), sig. B2v; Yates, *Astraea*, pp. 60–1.
[58] Thomas Dekker, *Dramatic Works*, ed. F. Bowers (Cambridge, 1953–61), vol. III, pp. 233–4; see also, on Middleton, Bergeron, *English Civic Pageantry*, p. 297; on analogous symbolism in the Italian republics, Quentin Skinner, 'Ambrogio Lorenzetti and the Portrayal of Virtuous Government', in *Visions of Politics, vol.II : Renaissance Virtues* (Cambridge, 2002), pp. 39–92.
[59] Hole, *English Custom*, p. 119.
[60] Cressy, *Birth*, pp. 367–9; David Underdown, *Start of Play: Cricket and Culture in Eighteenth-Century England* (London, 2000), pp. 50–1.
[61] John Blow (?), *An Opera Performed Before The King* (17 April 1664), p. 1; for the shift from pageant to masque, Bergeron, *English Civic Pageantry*, p. 5.

48   Argument and Authority in Early Modern England

of the monarch reinforced by his being both a pivotal participant, even a *deus ex machina*, in the minimal action, and having uniquely privileged perspective from the audience.[62] In the masque, those expectations were Platonically idealised (consider James VI&I as Pan), and so were potential points of vulnerability but for the barrier made of complicit courtly witnesses and performers. This ritual of the static abstraction, incidentally, helps explain some of the uses of the masque motif in revenge tragedy. It could provide the strongest counterpoint for a world just as extremely defined by almost systematic office-abuse. Whether the counterpoint was subversive and ironic, as Darryll Grantly has rather simplistically argued, or reinforcing and condemnatory of the lurid world of corruption and revenge, or not necessarily either, is, however, hardly something that can be neatly read from dramatic structure.[63]

Some distance from court masques were 'rough music', 'skimmingtons' and flitching ceremonies; yet they were all alike in reinforcing expectations of good conduct in office. In some parts of England a flitch of bacon was given to any man, then later any couple, who could plausibly deny ever having repented marriage. By the eighteenth century, the claims were formally investigated and could take the form of mock divorce court proceedings with juries of spinsters and bachelors having fun at the expense of, or perhaps with, the married couple.[64] The flitch ceremonies were the counterpoint to 'skimmington' and rough music, forms of ritualised public abuse of those held to have deviated from moral, especially sexual norms. Being treated to rough music took a number of localised forms. Stow refers to a man carried by four others being led by bagpipe, drum and shawm. In 1748 a man in Billingshurst, Sussex, was treated to rough music by the village women, then put in a blanket and ducked. In Oxfordshire, the threat of rough music survived into the late nineteenth century.[65]

---

[62] See Kevin Sharpe, 'The Court Masque', in *Criticism and Compliment* (Cambridge, 1987); and especially for changes in the masque form, Stephen Orgel, *The Jonsonian Masque* (Cambridge, Mass., 1965), pp. 18–33, 66.

[63] Darryll Grantley, 'Masques and Murderers: Dramatic Method and Ideology in Revenge Tragedy and the Court Masque', in Clive Bloom, ed., *Jacobean Poetry and Prose: Rhetoric, Representation and the Popular Imagination* (London, 1988), pp. 194–212; cf. Inga-Stina Ewbank, '"Those Pretty Devices": A Study of Masques in Plays', in *A Book of Masques* (Cambridge, 1967), pp. 412–33, for the diversity of masque motifs in Elizabethan and Jacobean plays.

[64] Hole, *English Custom*, pp. 64–5.

[65] Stow, *Survay*, cited in Burke, 'Popular Culture', p. 35; Underdown, *Start of Play*, p. 25; Laura Thompson, *Lark Rise to Candleford* (London, 1975 edn), p. 140.

V

Such ceremonies as 'flitching', skimmingtons and rough music provide a context for antitheses of official stability associated with periods of misrule, now so strongly associated with Bakhtin's concept of the carnivalesque. Bakhtin drew on his reading of Rabelais and was correct to claim that prescribed periods of carnival not only inverted order but also became wild and uproarious. But, beyond that, the models of social relationships he attributed to the early modern world are more immediately an abstraction from the experience of Soviet Russia, from which perhaps his historico-literary analyses were something of an allegorical projection.[66] Bakhtin's is a world of simple binary oppositions, of oppressed masses and oppressing élites forming a regime to which resistance can only be made by utopian contradiction and the escapist laughter that reaffirms the authenticity and independence of a prior popular culture that is *sui generis*.

It is probable, however, that medieval and early modern carnival was a vestige of the entanglements of Christian and pagan rites of office, in part an adaptive residue of the Roman Saturnalian festivals in which, after harvest, the whole of Roman society participated. What Hobbes noted as parallels were precedents, partially gathered within the church rather than being completely exorcised by it. It is relevant here also that the earliest examples and accounts of carnivalesque reversals seem to come from what might be taken to be the oppressing élites themselves.[67] Legal fraternities exhibited a very precise understanding of the complexity of exclusive social convention and the protocols of office in the process of parody. And masques too might have their accompanying anti-masques, with 'fools, satyrs, baboons, wildmen, antics, beasts, spirits, witches ... and the like'.[68] At the same time, any straightforward 'trickle-down' effect might be as much a function of inadequate evidence as genuine precedent. In a society that was so ritually ordered, an intricate awareness of social convention was likely to have been pervasive. Irrespective of origins, carnival, like the games and festivities of which Underdown has written, could express belonging as much as alienation. What specific functions were fulfilled is secondary to the fact that carnival required a

---

[66] Aaron Guervich, 'Bahktin and his Theory of Carnival', in Jan Bremmer and Herman Roodenburg, eds., *A Cultural History of Humour from Antiquity to the Present Day* (Cambridge and Oxford, 1997), pp. 54–60.
[67] Noel Malcolm, *The Origins of English Nonsense* (London, 1997), pp. 117–19.
[68] Francis Bacon, 'Of Masques and Triumphs', in *Essays*, in *Works*, ed. Basil Montague (London, 1825), vol. I, p. 130.

clear understanding of order, for it was in all cases a familiar world of offices that was represented through distortion. And the line between inversion of and induction into office could be thin. London journeymen assumed their status through a ceremonial dubbing with a broadsword, and a baptism with ale.[69]

Insofar as one can generalise, it is misleading to see carnival and order as dichotomous expressions of resistance and authority. They were rather aspects of an uneven gradation of social life. In times that some might celebrate as uniquely blessed by 'White peace' there was still black violence;[70] and even in civil war there would be outbreaks of quietude. Formalised rites might variously blend these contrasting threads in counterpoint to some evocation of office. The Kidderminster Kellums, for example, involved a period of mock lawlessness immediately prior to the election of the new bailiff, and as late as 1790 people of every status in the town embarked upon the soft-core anarchism of apple and cabbage stalk throwing.[71]

Carnival and carnival-like events were identified, then, principally with reference to some posited office. As the bounds were beaten on Ascension Day, so London apprentices beat the brothels on Shrove Tuesday.[72] Demonstrations and riots might even have their allotted days. The highly disruptive pope-burnings from 1679 to 1681 were staged on the date of Elizabeth I's succession, 17 November, and had a ritualistic quality. Organised by the Whigs and written by the playwright Elkanah Settle, they were given an unmistakable justificatory narrative telling of the dangers of religion abused and interference with religion reformed. Demonstration walked in the protective dress of pageant.[73] The Tories, no less noisy in their anti-Catholicism, fought back in kind with bonfires, effigies and processions on the verge of loyalist riot. Indeed, Keith Wrightson has remarked generally on how orderly, even ritualised, riots might be.[74] The trick, it seems, was to draw attention to abuse in a way that displayed respect for office.

---

[69] Underdown, *Start of Play*, pp. 22ff; Burke, 'Popular Culture,' p. 35.
[70] Sir Richard Fanshawe, 'Now War is All the World about' (1630), stanza 10, in *Poems and Translations of Sir Richard Fanshawe*, ed. Peter Dudson (Oxford, 1997), vol. I, pp. 55–9.
[71] *Gentleman's Magazine*, vols. LX–LXII (1790), p. 1191; Hole, *English Custom*, p. 133.
[72] Burke, 'Popular Culture', p. 36.
[73] Settle would shortly write enthusiastically for James II: see E. Settle, *A Poem Upon the Coronation of His Most Sacred Majesty King James II* (1685).
[74] Burke, 'Popular Culture', pp. 47–8; Harris, *London Crowds*, pp. 164–72; Paul Kléber Monod, *Jacobitism and the English People, 1688-1788* (Cambridge, 1993), pp. 164–73; Cressy, *Bonfires*, pp. 171–89, especially on the attempts to appropriate festive commemorations, such as 5 November, 30 January, 17 November; Keith Wrightson, *English Society* (London, 1993), pp. 177–9.

Ceremonies of office

But, further, the structure of rule-following that defined a sphere of office always carried its own potential for creative reversal irrespective of the social world of which it was a part. To take the extreme case, the depiction of witches' covens might be generated by nothing more than the inversion of the solemnities of piety; the familiarity with office could be sufficient to stimulate the imaginative nightmare of abuse without any reference point in the reality of witches. It is also in the broad interplay of office and its negative projections that one may place the institution of the court jester. A badge of authority for a prince, the jester was allowed remarkable licence to behave, dress and speak as other subjects could not. Other reversals of official relationships could verge on the mechanical. The Lawless Courts of Rayleigh then Rochford met before a tree not a judge, at night not day, and used coal not ink and quill for signing documents.[75] The belief that certain qualities and achievements are required of a *persona* in office might also be inverted. Fortune could replace capacity at specific points in the ritual calendar: Twelfth Night, Whitsun and May Day.[76] Most familiar is the baking of a Twelfth Night plumcake with a bean or pea in it. Whoever got the appropriate slice became king or queen by virtue of that fortune alone. In the election of the mock mayor of Penryn, journeymen tailors chose the wittiest of their number, in formal contrast (presumably) to the conventional view that *gravitas* and rectitude were the appropriate qualities for the office.[77] The election of May monarchs reversed principles of seniority, capacity and experience; only the young and beautiful were chosen. This principle seems to have been operative in the ecclesiastical business of electing boy bishops on St Nicholas' Day, a pre-Reformation rite involving indecorous and lewd behaviour, the bishop's clothes worn backwards and processing with the Bible upside down.[78]

In all such parodic play there are serious difficulties in reading off social relationships beyond the texts, unless we equate textual parody with social satire, a move made easier if we assume (quite a lot really) a binary oppositional world and notice only the reference functions of language. In a way directly analogous to the relationships between masque and murder in revenge tragedy, the counterpoint of contrasting images is certainly a play with expectations of office, each mirror-like facet explicable in terms of the other. Social meanings, however, are likely to be more specific, contingent and variable, far more to do with the diversely exploitable pragmatics of symbolism than the more structured semantics

---

[75] Hole, *English Custom*, pp. 132–3.
[77] Hole, *English Custom*, pp. 30, 83.
[76] Muir, *Ritual*, pp. 93–4.
[78] Muir, *Ritual*, pp. 95–6.

of textual relationships, or the stylised gestures required by a ritual performance. Parodic language is not necessarily reflective of anything beyond the lineaments of the target text and it allows considerable exploitative possibility.[79] To put the matter a trifle extremely, it was precisely this hermeneutic condition of denotational latitude that enabled Bakhtin to read the USSR into sixteenth-century France.

As a corollary, for contemporaries, symbols like metaphors were not easy to control. Ceremony might rule everything, as Cavendish had it, but what it might be made to convey might not be quite his cup of tea. When Charles II was crowned, was the Bishop of London really asking for consent to his rule? The question was literally rhetorical within the context of the coronation, but at another time, in another place, even at another point in the ceremony, it could feed a theory of authority derived from popular and conditional consent. The coronation could be 'A strange beginning – borrowed majesty'.[80] So from the crux of the coronation oath, suggestive of election and contract, to reading the symbolism of the bean in the pudding. Such events might sometimes have expressed scepticism about the efficacy of virtue in a naughty world, or the capacity of those actually holding office. Yet, authority by lot is unlikely to be romanticised where the acquisition of agricultural skills and herbal knowledge are matters of life and death. It takes a casual attitude to inference to conclude that the institution of the Penryn mock mayor was a sign of a popular ideology in combat with its hegemonic oppressors.[81] It is perhaps, only an intellectual living under someone like Stalin who might understandably mistake such systematic inversions for a desired utopia.

Ritual and ceremony, then, are much like metaphors in that questions of the political function and role are matters of pragmatics and semiotics, of the diversity of narrative potential rather than fixed meaning and function. This potential, political or otherwise, stemmed from a shared grounding in some understanding of office, whether it be affirmed, disputed, disappointed or turned upside-down. Yet, inferential cautions aside, it is plausible to perceive a broadly political dimension to so many of the solemnities of office. It may indeed be misconstrued by the imposition of modern categories that give a fresh content to the 'political', of ideology, power, of resistance and Gramscian hegemony. Nevertheless, it remains striking how much official ceremony concerned rule. This, however, is to be expected by the very notion of an office, entailing relationships of authority, responsibility and duty that could be easily

---

[79] See, at length, Margaret Rose, *Parody: Meta-Fiction* (London, 1979).
[80] Shakespeare, *King John* 1.1.
[81] Contra, Muir, *Ritual*, pp. 230–1.

adapted to cover much beyond any reasonable use of the term political – to the relationships of the poet to nature, or insentient organ to a natural body. More immediately, the involvement of all levels of society in relationships of office was an engagement in ruling as well as being ruled. Collusive ritual gives England just a whiff of the Aristotelian polity. Like the kiss of the Hungerford tutti-man at Hocktide, the institutions of society implicated even those at the margins.

3 Institutionalised office: a sense of the scavenger

> [An officer] is a person of double capacity public and private, and that may be one reason, why he is said to deal doubly with all men that have to do with him. He is but a pimp to his place.
>
> (Samuel Butler, *Characters* 1667–9)

I

As I have noted, a concept of political office is now being used to explain institutional change and state formation in early modern England (above, introduction). The purpose here is not to present an alternative theory. It is, rather, principally to outline the scope of institutionalised office to complement what I have said of the ceremonial.[1] Together, these chapters provide a background to my discussion of the unexplored reach of the vocabulary of office. In outlining this background, however, I shall touch on specific offices such as citizenship and more general notions such as republicanism. This should help avoid the impression that I am positing a social, ceremonial reality on which sits some intellectual superstructure. More significantly, surveying social organisation will also require consideration of the separation, derived from modern theoretical modelling, of a private realm from the 'public sphere' of offices, strongly associated with an emerging state. Neither social organisation nor its language supports such conceptions.

Office was a matter of belonging, of formal relational identity through responsibility; it gave a voice in the commonwealth and it was hardly possible to sustain any other. No man, wrote Edmund de Bohun, is without office, no aspect of life without rule.[2] An awareness of degree was inescapable and easily taken as part of a natural order: 'The heavens

---

[1] Oath-taking and administering were usually good indications of what counted as an instituted office; see chapter 11.
[2] Edmund de Bohun, *The Justice of the Peace, His Calling: A Moral Essay* (1684), A2r–v.

themselves, the planets, and this centre,/ Observe degree, priority, and place,/ Insisture, course, proportion, season, form,/ Office, and custom, in all line of order'.[3] Such an integration of the human into the natural, however, was not necessarily an indication of complaisance. Ulysses's speech on degree was in the context of its absence in the Greek camp before Troy, where 'The speciality of rule hath been neglected'.[4] Throughout the early modern world all the intricacies of status were known to be contingent and fragile. And neither was this hierarchy singular. Any postulation of a solitary chain of being was a triumph of theoretical elegance over experience.

Despite an initially bewildering diversity of hierarchy,[5] early modern England is most easily seen as comprising two overlapping orders of office. 'There bee two mayne partes of Every Body Poleticke Espetially amongeste Christians, *vid*: the state Civill, & The state Ecleseasticall.'[6] The secular dimension of rule was concerned with temporal order, but with strong spiritual associations. The church claimed a spiritual responsibility but with decidedly temporal implications, and its bishops were agents of royal authority. As William Cavendish advised, 'Bishopps they should bee Chosen wise men for Government, rather then Schoole Devines'.[7]

Under the auspices of church and state the country was divided into different units, from parish and village to diocese and county: these were interlaced with legal systems, livery companies and guilds, all overseen by a monarch with a small court, a few paid officials and an irregularly meeting parliament. Despite the willingness of seventeenth-century writers to talk in terms of church and state, the closer one looks, the more tumbled together these abstractions appear.[8] *Aliud distinctio, aliud separatio*, as the haunting aphorism had it, a point to be explored more fully in chapter 13. All units of communal belonging were configurations of office involving some mix of care for bodies, or the husbanding of souls. 'Commonweales, Cities, yae small Townes, do they not assemble together to choose officers, & to establish orders by common consent?'[9] In Maldon, Essex, stands a monument to these conceptually distinguishable spheres of office. The Plume Library is an incongruous amalgam of a rebuilt stone and flint

---

[3] Shakespeare, *Troilus and Cressida* 1.3.
[4] *Ibid.*
[5] Sumner Chilton Powell, *Puritan Village: The Formation of a New England Town* (Middletown, Conn., 1963), p. xviii.
[6] Cavendish, 'Advice', fol. 10.
[7] *Ibid.*, fol. 14.
[8] Braddick, *State Formation*, pt. 4, ch. 7.
[9] George Pettie, *The ciuile conuersation* (1586), trans. of Stefano Guazzo, *De optimo Senatore*, fols. 15 r–v; see Peltonen, *Classical Humanism*, p. 57.

church tower keyed into a two-storey red-brick edifice for books and grammar school teaching. It was designed by Thomas Plume as a standing lesson, a studied iconography of the mutual dependence of the responsibilities of church and state, learning, education and government, framed by that natural symbol of another world, a graveyard.[10]

II

At this point, however, it may be useful to give a more prosaic impression of institutionalised office-holding. There were around 10,000 parishes in seventeenth-century England. A parish was defined by its church and minister, the vestry, its members and the church wardens. The evidence of wardens' and vestry activity is variable.[11] There was the business of applying the Elizabethan Poor Laws, demanding the organisation of work for the indigent, distribution of aid and coping with vagrancy, for 'aliens', 'strangers' and 'foreigners' were always a potential strain on resources. Beyond this, however, the evidence of wardens' work is uneven, from little more than the purchase of candles, at one extreme, to responsibility for an extensive teaching library at another.[12] The situation in late sixteenth-century London was particularly demanding, and, from 1598, an additional overseer's office was created, apparently occupied by higher status parishioners.[13] According to Hindle, the vestry became important as the basic unit of government only during the seventeenth century, and fell more into the hands of yeomen after 1660 when the aristocracy gradually withdrew from such a local level of office-holding.[14]

Some vestries were relatively open, others highly selective; a few had control over the presentation of ecclesiastical livings, the occasional parish was exempt from episcopal control.[15] If all this suggests a sort of political structure within the church, a parish would also have a constable, the common symbol of secular governance and its erratic reach.[16] He was 'a viceroy in the street . . . never so much in his majesty as in his

---

[10] W. J. Petchey, *The Intentions of Thomas Plume* (Maldon, 1985), p. 12.
[11] Hindle, *The State*, pp. 207–15.
[12] Powell, *Puritan Village*, pp. 14–15; Conal Condren, 'More Parish Library, Salop' (Appendix with F. Carleton), *Library History*, 7, 5 (1987), pp. 144, 149.
[13] Ian Archer, *The Pursuit of Stability: Social Relations in Elizabethan London* (Cambridge, 1991), p. 98.
[14] Hindle, *The State*, p. 208.
[15] Archer, *Pursuit of Stability*, pp. 70–1; Coulton, 'Rivalry and Religion', pp. 35, 39.
[16] Michael Dalton, *Country Justice* (1635), ch. 16, and p. 3; Thomas Hobbes, 'Questions relative to Hereditary Right. Mr Hobbes', Hobbes MS D5, Chatsworth; John Locke, *Two Treatises of Government* (1690), ed. Peter Laslett (Cambridge, 1963), 2, para. 202; see also Hindle, *The State*, pp. 167–9, 182–3.

nightwatch'.[17] He regulated inns, checked weights and measures, issued warrants and inflicted minor punishment. No one was more susceptible to accusations of office-abuse because no one was obliged to touch his fellows in so many ways – 'a secular prince of darkness' a small officer, 'most imperious and arrogant'.[18] And, having little reliable support, he was just as easily accused of neglect. The constable might be 'very careful in his office but if he stay up after midnight you shall take him napping'. He was an obvious target for stage amusement: 'I cannot see how sleeping should offend'.[19]

But virtually all touched their fellows in some way. To walk along a street was to sniff the office of the scavenger and his rakers. There was, then, a great immediacy in Locke's remark that to use the highways was to give a tacit consent to a polity, for use was an engagement with the network of offices comprising it.[20] Since David Hume's dismissal of Locke's point, we have lost touch with the world that gave it an emotional plausibility, for we more naturally see the highways and the superadding agency of the regime, the state, as discrete entities; using one does not entail even recognition of the other.[21] Yet, any firm bifurcation between society and a political regime, between *Gemeinschaft* and *Gesellschaft* as Tönnies later formulated it, creates too calibrated an image of Locke's world. Paid officers of court totalled probably only around 1,200 out of a population approaching four million by 1700. Government without bureaucracy or police, and with little or no standing army, must give an alienating inflection to the term 'regime', and we need to be cautious in the way in which we call it a state, especially if the modern state is the outcome of its intricate processes of participation.[22] Ipso facto, the more centralised government turned to legislation, the more the dispersed community was involved.[23] Existing offices had their burdens increased and there was need to have their duties, rights and relationships codified.[24]

---

[17] John Earle, 'A Constable', in *Micro-cosmography, or a Piece of the World Discovered* (1633).
[18] Samuel Butler, *Characters* (c. 1667–9), ed. Charles W. Daves (Cleveland, 1970), p. 261.
[19] Earle, 'A Constable'; Shakespeare, *Much Ado About Nothing* 3.3.
[20] Locke, *Two Treatises*, 2, para. 119; Dalton, *Country Justice*, p. 69.
[21] David Hume, 'Of the Original Contract' (1741–2), in *Political Essays*, ed. Knud Haakonssen (Cambridge, 1994), esp. pp. 192–4.
[22] Cf. Hindle, *The State*, pp. 2–36.
[23] Goldie, 'The Unacknowledged Republic' pp. 154, 176; also Patrick Collinson, 'De republica Anglorum: Or History with the Politics Put Back', in *Elizabethan Essays* (London, 1994), p. 19; Andrew Fitzmaurice, *Humanism and America: An Intellectual History of English Colonisation, 1500–1625* (Cambridge, 2003), pp. 14–15.
[24] A central theme of Braddick, *State Formation*; see also de Bohun, *The Justice of the Peace*, A3r.

Whatever the 'regime' was, then, it had to be highly participatory, a tensile, variable fusion of trust and conflict.[25] Goldie estimates that during the seventeenth century there would have been around 50,000 parish officials at any one time.[26] Additionally there were the office-holders of towns and boroughs. Among London officers, Archer mentions bridgemasters and chamberlains and clerks of the market, not to be confused with clerksitters, pleaders, garbellers, cotton measurers, market overseers and remembrancers, recorders and solicitors, scavengers, town clerks, under-sheriffs, the much put-upon sheriffs, aldermen, their deputies and councillors, all under that particular head of state, the Lord Mayor. Such offices were distinct from those of the livery companies who elected the mayor and whose responsibilities ranged from charity to the control of trade and apprenticeship. Within England, London was unusually Venetian in the intricacy of government. According to Archer, in a rich ward like Cornhill a third of householders might have office in a given year.[27] On Valerie Pearl's estimates, one in ten householders held office across the city annually during the mid-century although Civil War circumstances might have been distorting.[28]

In relative contrast, Hungerford elected around thirty principal officers at its Hocktide ceremonies, and early seventeenth-century Sudbury (population *c.* 3,000) had 110 burgesses and thirty subsidiary office-holders, dividing some forty functions between them.[29] In the Shropshire hamlet of Mainstone, even the poorest cottagers had a voice in the vestry. On the other side of Wenlock Edge at Highley, cottagers were also occasionally church officers.[30] The most significant offices were restricted and correlated carefully to wealth and status. Complaints about this might indicate mobility, or frictions in the business of office-holding.[31] Yet, if an office was necessary someone had to fill it and necessity could be particularly pressing in small communities.[32]

So, too, from the early Reformation to the Civil Wars, clerical shortages could make for ecumenical flexibility. In the 1640s and 50s, a Church of England man might become an Independent and then a Presbyterian; he

---

[25] Hindle, *The State*, pp. 23–4, 66–93; Muldrew, *The Economy of Obligation*, pp. 95–118, 123–47, 199–204.
[26] Goldie, 'The Unacknowledged Republic', p. 161.
[27] Archer, *Pursuit of Stability*, p. 64.
[28] Valerie Pearl, cited in Goldie, 'The Unacknowledged Republic', p. 162.
[29] Pilhens, *The Story of Hungerford*, p. 22; Powell, *Puritan Village*, pp. 42–6.
[30] Mainstone Parish Records, Shropshire County Records Office, 3277/1/2; on Highley, see Goldie, 'The Unacknowledged Republic', p. 163.
[31] Archer, *Pursuit of Stability*, p. 64; Coulton, 'Rivalry and Religion', pp. 28–50.
[32] Powell, *Puritan Village*, pp. 98–100.

might be obliged to lay aside ecclesiological principle in order to fulfil the essentials of office. Some religious deviance was, then, not always an ecclesiological barrier, despite the doctrinaire nature of dispute.[33] Occasional or partial conformity was common after the Restoration among nonconformists; John Humfrey attended his parish church and ran his own.[34] Goldie notes that in Terling, in Essex, eleven convicted nonconformists served in church offices between 1662 and 1688.[35]

At different times and for different sorts of office, principles of election, selection, inheritance, education, wealth or distribution by lot might be used, and although always carrying a social standing, office could be onerous. The constable might be anyone's whipping boy, the sheriff possibly a wiser and poorer man after serving his time. In London, from 1559 to 1600, seventy-one men refused the office of sheriff; the draper, John Bird, complained that his election in 1587 had been driven by malice.[36] There were fines for the avoidance of office and the neglect of duties. Failure could result in dispossession of privilege.[37] Powell remarks of Sudbury, that in becoming a free burgess, a citizen was anything but free. The hyperbole is understandable, but the paradox depends upon anachronistic understandings of freedom.[38] Notions of liberty integral to a world of offices will be explicated in the following chapter. It is enough here to state that burdensome office was the price paid for a social voice and was what freedom amounted to. It was the weight of recognised responsibility. As the Pole Goslicius remarked, voicing a notion of liberty that was also only 'a particular interpretation' by much later standards, a citizen's liberty lay 'chiefly in being capable of offices'.[39]

III

This impressionistic survey naturally begs a number of questions and any attempt to convert the vestiges of social practice into a raw percentage of office-holders would necessarily be inconclusive. Offices were not always occupied, and some people held multiple positions, making social identity

---

[33] Braddick, *State Formation*, pp. 301–3.
[34] Douglas R. Lacey, *Dissent and Parliamentary Politics in England, 1661–1689* (New Brunswick, N. J., 1969), pp. 23–4.
[35] Goldie, 'The Unacknowledged Republic', p. 164.
[36] Archer, *Pursuit of Stability*, p. 21; Braddick, *State Formation*, p. 30.
[37] Powell, *Puritan Village*, p. 46; Archer, *Pursuit of Stability*, p. 35; Goldie, 'The Unacknowledged Republic', p. 168.
[38] Powell, *Puritan Village*, p. 44.
[39] Peltonen, *Classical Humanism*, p. 109, commenting on Goslicius, *The Counsellor: exactly portrayed in two bookes* (1598), pp. 79–80.

concomitantly richer and problematic. Moreover, one needs to distinguish the activities of standing officers from the intermittent responsibilities of jury service and voting, the latter having attracted disproportionate attention. If, as Mark Goldie remarks, democracy is defined in terms of a meaningful franchise, psephology is likely to seem central to charting democratic development.[40] In the mid-seventeenth century, the electorate may have been around 40 per cent of the adult male population and inclusive of some women; by the early eighteenth, it may have shrunk to around 20 per cent of men only. Yet, in an age when most elections were uncontested, and election tended to be a circuit-breaking substitute for selection, little can be made of this.[41]

More important, as Goldie argues, is that voting was played out against a broader background of official participation.[42] Due attention to this led Patrick Collinson to call England a monarchical republic.[43] It is, however, important to distinguish constitutional preference from organisational necessity. Constitutional republicanism is a doctrine about a preferred regime, one without a monarch. This will be discussed in chapter 7. The use of the word republic as a portmanteau for the exigencies of social engagement, however, is another matter. The duty to find someone to scavenge the neighbourhood rubbish does not of itself politically empower whoever we can get to do it, and has no antithetical implications for monarchy. The unacknowledged republic, to allude to Goldie's analysis as an alternative form of democracy, or as the grounding for some ascending theory of legitimation, had been a feature of social structure from time immemorial. What J. E. A. Jolliffe called the 'legal republics' of the shires had existed as a counterpoint and condition for the might of the Angevin kings,[44] a situation that still applied to the uneven authoritarianism of the Tudors and Stuarts.[45] To treat the absence of bureaucracy as a sign of republicanism is to relieve the concept of most of its meaning. Beyond organisational micro-structure, any republican inference from participatory necessity is directly relevant to the response to emergency

---

[40] Goldie, 'The Unacknowledged Republic', pp. 153–4.
[41] *Ibid.*, pp. 157–8; on female franchise see Patricia Crawford, '"The Poorest She": Women and Citizenship in Early Modern England', in Michael Mendle, ed., *The Putney Debates, 1647* (Cambridge, 2001).
[42] Goldie, 'The Unacknowledged Republic', pp. 158–9; Crawford, 'The Poorest She', pp. 197, 203–10.
[43] Collinson, 'The Monarchical Republic of Elizabeth I', in *Elizabethan Essays*, pp. 31–58.
[44] J. E. A. Jolliffe, *Angevin Kingship* (London, 1970 edn), p. 13.
[45] Cf. Hindle, *The State*, p. 26, and the literature there cited; Collinson distinguishes a monarchical republic from constitutional republicanism, but persists with the general term none the less; see, at length, 'The Monarchical Republic'.

in high places. To modern eyes, the formation of 'the Association' in 1584 can easily look republican.[46] This was an agreement of armed fellows to bond in defence of the Queen, a human fasces in the face of the pope. But any 'republicanism' here is created by overlooking the absence of a standing army and presupposing a natural ideological opposition between monarchy and republic. As I shall argue, this can be a misleading projection from the shared rhetorics of office, and it was the need to maintain the office of rule that was the spur to 'the Association', not an embryonic republicanism.

Ultimately, however, the extent of genuine civic participation is hardly more central to my case than the undulations of franchise. It is the extensiveness of the claims themselves that matter, forming a 'liquid empire' of words, flowing, as I have already indicated, across the whole of society.[47] Every city, as William Cavendish warned Charles II in 1659/60, every town and every village could be seen as a little commonwealth, but so too could every vestry, workshop and family.[48] For Winstanley, a man unlikely to agree much with Cavendish, the family was but the smallest link in a chain of magistracy, and so no less subject to the impress of office than the state and church.[49] William Gouge referred to the family as 'a little church, a little commonwealth it is a schoole wherein the first principles and grounds of government and subjection are learned'.[50] Books on marriage and parenting are part of a veritable genre of *De officiis*. The midwife's work, though carried on in a closed domain that we might consider private, was deemed an office. Those who promoted and reflected upon trade did so in terms of the responsibilities of assumed offices, from the Virginia Company, that latter-day byword for economic aggrandisement, to those spokesmen for developing commerce, Scott and Mun.[51] The merchant, insisted Mun, had a vocation and it was above all

---

[46] Stephen Alford, 'The Politics of Emergency in the Reign of Elizabeth I', in G. Burgess and M. Feinstein, eds., *English Radicalism, 1550–1850* (Cambridge, forthcoming); Peltonen, *Classical Humanism*, p. 48.
[47] I am indebted to Dr John Sutton's play 'Kenelm Digby and the Liquid Empire' for this expression.
[48] Goldie, 'The Unacknowledged Republic', at length, esp. pp. 161–7; Powell, *Puritan Village*, p. xviii; Hindle, *The State*, pp. 204–22; above all Braddick, *State Formation*, at length.
[49] Gerrard Winstanley, *The Law of Freedom in a Platform: or True Magistracy Restored* (1652), ed. Robert W. Kenny (New York, 1973), pp. 85, 91–2.
[50] Gouge, *Domesticall Duties*, p. 18; see also Ste B., *Counsel to the Husband* (1608).
[51] Andrew Fitzmaurice, *Humanism and America*, chs. 4, 5; Andrew Fitzmaurice, '"Every Man, that Prints, Adventures": The Rhetoric of the Virginia Company Sermons', in Lori Anne Ferrell and Peter McCullough, eds., *The English Sermon Revised: Religion, Literature and History, 1600–1750* (Manchester, 2000), pp. 24–42.

necessary that he know his duties, for he 'is worthily called *The Steward of the Kingdoms Stock* . . . a work no less of *Reputation* than *Trust*, which ought to be performed with great skill and conscience'.[52] As Craig Muldrew has demonstrated, the material was held generally to be dependent on an ethical economy of responsibility that created a form of social credit; to see isolated economic self-interest as significant in the seventeenth century, to see an economic civil society to which people actually belonged, is to elide post-Smithian categories with the evidence.[53] We may hypothesise an informing motivation of economic aggrandisement, but it has to be read against the grain of the printed word.[54] The liquid empire seeped even into gaols. One inmate of Wood Street wrote of its being a little 'Hole' like 'a citty in a commonwealth, for as in a citty there are all kinds of officers, trades and vocations, so there is in this place as we may make a pretty resemblance between them'.[55]

As office conferred order, and gave a voice, so the range of voices enhanced status. A royal charter of 1319 had laid it down that freedom of the city required first that a man be 'of some mistery'.[56] It was later explained to a stranger in St Saviour's parish, Southwark, that before he could become a vestry man he had 'to make tryall of other offices'.[57] Of the constable, remarked Butler, 'He is never admitted to reign in the street as constable until he has been swabber or scavenger, and made them clean.'[58] Archer concludes on the matter by remarking that '[O]fficeholding . . . served to identify individual citizens with the regime.'[59] It would be truer to say that office-holding was the regime.[60]

---

[52] William Scott, *An Essay on Drapery* (1635); Thomas Mun, *England's Treasure by Forraign Trade* (1664) (reprinted Oxford, 1949), p. 1.
[53] Muldrew, *The Economy of Obligation*, at length, and on Scott, pp. 47, 127; Craig Muldrew, 'Interpreting the Market: The Ethics of Credit and Community Relations in Early Modern England', *Social History*, 18, 2 (1993), pp. 163–5.
[54] Andrew Fitzmaurice, 'Classical Rhetoric and the Literature of Discovery, 1570–1630', Ph.D. thesis (Cambridge University, 1995), ch. 5.
[55] Ackroyd, *London*, pp. 261–2; on such standard homologies between life and prison see, for example, R. Anselment, '*Stone Walls* and *Iron Bars*: Richard Lovelace and the Conventions of Seventeenth-Century Prison Literature', *Renaissance and Reformation* 29 (1993), pp. 17–20; Dosia Reichardt, '"At my grates no Althea": Prison Poetry and the Consolations of Sack in the Interregnum', *Parergon*, new series, 20, 1 (2003), pp. 139–61.
[56] Cited in Margaret R. Somers, 'The "Misteries" of Property. Relationality, Rural-Industrialization and Community in Chartist Narratives of Political Rights', in John Brewer and Susan Staves, eds., *Early Modern Conceptions of Property* (London, 1995), p. 73.
[57] Cited in Archer, *Pursuit of Stability*, p. 64; also Pilhens, *The Story of Hungerford*, p. 22.
[58] Butler, *Characters*, p. 261.
[59] Archer, *Pursuit of Stability*, p. 64.
[60] Braddick, *State Formation*, pp. 19, 21.

IV

Notions of office also provide a context for arguments about citizenship in England. I have previously outlined something of the contentious semantics of this. Thomas Mayer and Markku Peltonen have shown that discussion of political citizenship became integrally related to the assimilation of classical Latin and later Italian writings, and was central to the development of English political vocabulary.[61] These enquiries can be brought together by observing that debates about the word citizen and its relationships to adjacent terms such as subject, trader and merchant, were important because it was assumed to signify a set of official relationships; conceptual space was official space. This is as true of Thomas More's suspicions about the propriety of using the word subject in the context of civic rule as it was to David Owen's contrary insistence, a hundred years later, that the word subject was the only appropriate term for the ruled.[62]

London, however, greatly complicated issues of office and citizenship. It was effectively a primate city and could be called a state. Throughout the whole period under discussion, London was swelled with migration, despite disease, plague and the short life expectancy of its inhabitants. To outsiders it was fearsomely bloated on a constant influx of foreigners. In 1550 the population was roughly 70,000, or 2 per cent of the population, by 1650 it was around 400,000, around 8 per cent. In 1700 its population was approximately 575,000, at which date its nearest rivals, Bristol and Norwich, had populations of 20,000. No other urban area had more than 14,000 people.[63] From the reign of Elizabeth, fruitless attempts were made to curb the unruly spread. Coke expressed concerns, carrying his authority deep into the seventeenth century.[64] It took a developer like Nicholas Barbon to put a case in purely celebratory terms; the bigger London was the better for all: trust me I'm a builder.[65]

London was teeming, rich and jealous of its traditions of self-government. For William of Malmesbury it was a commune and in the fourteenth

---

[61] Condren, *The Language of Politics*, pp. 91–114; Mayer, *Thomas Starkey and the Commonweal*, pp. 43–76, 139–68; Peltonen, *Classical Humanism*, pp. 54–118.

[62] See Damian Grace, 'Subjects or Citizens? Populi and Cives in More's *Epigrammata*', *Moreana*, 97 (1988), pp. 133–6; David Owen, *Herode and Pilate Reconciled* (1610).

[63] Craig Horton, '"...the Country *must diminish*": Jacobean London and the Production of Pastoral Space in *The Winter's Tale*', *Parergon*, new series, 20, 1 (2003), p. 91; Angus McInnes, *English Towns* (London, 1980), pp. 2–4; Braddick, *State Formation*, p. 54.

[64] B&Y, *The Arraignment of Co-ordinate Power* (1683), p. 6; Thomas Violet, 'To the ... Chancellour of England', p. 12, appended to *A Petition Against the Jewes* (1661).

[65] Stow, *Survay*, pp. 557–62; Nicholas Barbon, *A Discourse Shewing the Great Advantages New-Buildings, And the Enlarging of Towns and Cities Do Bring to a Nation* (1678).

century it was called a *res publica*.⁶⁶ In the fifteenth century, Edward IV acted *primus inter pares* among London merchants; in the sixteenth, even Elizabeth was obliged to court as much as she cajoled. Its trained bands could assume the size and status of an army; its play of interests and institutions prohibited any secure court control.⁶⁷ In the seventeenth, Charles I lost London, and in London lost his head. With myths of foundation by refugees from Troy, the city could pretend to the status of a new Rome. Even disaster might play its part in enriching such symbolic associations. Troy, Rome (and Sodom) had all burned. In thieves' cant, London was 'Rome-vill'.⁶⁸ Members of London's ruling élite were sometimes styled *optimates*, lesser citizens *populares*, so linguistically assimilating the understanding of citizenship to ancient models even before the popularisation of Ciceronian and Italianate models of civic autonomy.

The city, then, was a commonwealth, its citizens sometimes having only a selective recognition of any extraneous subjection. London was never so ill as it was now, preached Hugh Latimer in 1548, but the sentiment could probably be repeated in almost any year.⁶⁹ Stow, who presented his *Survay* as an act of citizenly duty, wrote also to reassure the suspicious. 'I confess that London is a mighty arme and instrument to bring any great desine to effect', but it 'is a Citizen, and no Citie, a Subject and no free estate'.⁷⁰ In so far as London was the paradigmatic city, and potentially a microcosm of the wider realm, this had conceptually disruptive potential. It could be 'a mighty beast/ Behemoth or Leviathan at least'.⁷¹ The office of citizen might threaten hypertrophy like the city itself. The Italianate and Latinate theoretical materials of citizenship and love of *patria* assumed a civic politics and fed this expansion. So the proudly proclaimed office of citizen might end up in formal tension with that of subject. London oscillated, as Stow's prose suggests, between being a capital city and a city state; it lurched between Hamburg and Paris, Venice and Madrid. Its corporations were a long-standing model for a body politic.⁷² It is no surprise that the spectre of London overshadows Cavendish's 'Advice' to Charles II. William I had built the tower of alien stone to watch as well as protect the jewel in his crown. Cavendish would go further: London must

---

⁶⁶ Ackroyd, *London*, pp. 48–9–51.
⁶⁷ Archer, *Pursuit of Stability*, at length.
⁶⁸ Ackroyd, *London*, p. 265.
⁶⁹ Latimer, *Sermon* (18 January 1548), in *Fruitful Sermons*, fol. 17r.
⁷⁰ Stow, *Survay*, A3, pp. 557, 558; Anon., *Urbis Londiniensis* (c. 1666).
⁷¹ Anon., *The Character of London Village* (1684).
⁷² W. C., *A Discourse for King and Parliament* (1660), p. 4; *Some Considerations touching Succession and Allegiance*, in *State Tracts*, vol. I, pp. 334–5.

be garrisoned, mewed up, its charters of citizenship scrapped or it would rule.[73] London, as palpitating Richard Baxter put it, was 'the heart of the whole nation'; if infected with false doctrines, the contagion will spread to all.[74] When Hobbes, in *De cive* took the city to mean the state, he insisted that, for the sake of peace, the word citizen meant subject. It was above all London's unpredictable importance that required the domestication of its defining social office.

V

In any realm, however, there were subjects and subjects, just as in any city there were citizens and citizens, and this directs attention to aristocracy standing around the pinnacle of institutionalised office. As Richard Brathwaite remarked, '[none] are less exempted from a Calling than great men' – albeit recognising that many 'offices are deputed to sundrie men'. Those deemed noble, or aristocratic, exhibited the most conspicuous, elaborate and sensitive of social identities; and were likely to attract or engross many social offices. 'The higher the place the heavier the charge.' For Brathwaite, nobility should be the very pattern of office-holding.[75]

The question of what made true nobility had been in the air since the days of Dante and Chaucer; it had been explored in *Utopia*, and became a formal topic for university disputation.[76] It was recognised that the qualities defining the ideal *persona* of the aristocrat – liberality, gentleness, wisdom – might be discrepant with conduct and lineal boasting.[77] Apparel, wrote Sir Thomas Elyot, should be a sign of distinction not pride, for true nobility could be found in any estate. The word noble was the 'surname of virtue' that lay in the metal not the imprint of the gold coins called nobles.[78] Consequently, true nobility in the present required emulation of the past. Such arguments were not merely idealistic, they reiterated the standards by which anyone pretending to nobility should be

---

[73] Cavendish, 'Advice', fols. 1–2.
[74] Cited in Tim Cooper, *Fear and Polemic in Seventeenth-Century England: Richard Baxter and Antinomianism* (Aldershot, 2001), p. 92; see also B&Y, *Arraignment*, p. 6.
[75] Brathwaite, *The English Gentleman*, pp. 115, 119.
[76] See Quentin Skinner, 'Thomas More's *Utopia* and the Virtue of True Nobility', in *Visions of Politics* (Cambridge, 2002), vol. II: *Renaissance Virtues*, pp. 213–44; on university disputation, see Mack, *Elizabethan Rhetoric*, p. 53.
[77] Thomas Rogers, *A Philosophical Discourse Entitled The Anatomy of the Mind* (1576), lib. 2.68; Henry Peacham, *The Compleat Gentleman* (1622), p. 159; Goslicius, *The Counsellor*, pp. 36–7; Warren, *Royalist Reform'd*, p. 1.
[78] Sir Thomas Elyot, *The Book Named the Govenor* (1531), ed. S. E. Lehmberg (London, 1962 edn), 2 iii, pp. 104–5.

judged. George Meriton, drawing more explicitly than Elyot on Plato's myth of metals, blended conceptions of the aristocracy of mind, lineage or wealth to advocate entry into the additional office of the priesthood.[79] In recognising God as our true father, priests may bring together all the virtues associated with nobility. Lineage could thus be a sign, aristocracy a metaphor for a higher office. So to a different end Meriton exploited the commonplaces that nobility did require specific virtues and an august pedigree. Without virtue, Albertus Warren later remarked, the gentleman was 'conspicuously sordid'.[80]

Regardless of 'true' nobility, the maintenance of standing was of intense importance to aristocracy in the setting of a society preoccupied with reputation. The effort involved, however, in sustaining this august form of social office might sully lineage and evaporate honour.[81] Identity was a function of imagined time and the semiotics of social space. A hundred and thirty years after Elyot had argued that inner virtue should shine through dress and display, William Cavendish bemoaned the fact that any woman might have a turkey carpet by her bed. For the survival of the institution of monarchy itself, the symbols of nobility must be maintained: 'to make no Difference between great ladys, & Citizens wifes, in aparrell is abhominable'.[82]

Explorations of the potential tension between virtue and position were framed largely in terms of social office. 'I owe her Maiestie the office: dutie of an Earle Marshall of England; I have bene content to doe her the service of a Clarke', wrote the honour-attentive Earl of Essex, 'but I can never serve her as a villain or a slave.'[83] Her successor saw three sorts of iniquity in the English aristocracy arising directly from the fragility of social position: tendencies to oppress, give indiscriminate support to agents and to fight over any slight of honour. These were all misunderstandings of aristocratic responsibility.[84] In a similar idiom Hobbes, too, emphasised the 'violences, oppressions and injuries' that great persons might do. 'Impunity maketh Insolense; Insolence Hatred; and Hatred an Endeavour to pull down all oppressing . . . greatnesse'.[85]

---

[79] George Meriton, *A Sermon of nobilitie* (1607), B3r–v, D, C2; see Peltonen, *Classical Humanism*, p. 159.
[80] Warren, *Royalist Reform'd*, p. 1.
[81] Muldrew, *The Economy of Obligation*, pp. 149–56; Cavendish, 'Advice', fols. 53–4; Meriton, *Sermon*, C3v.
[82] Cavendish, 'Advice', fol. 53.
[83] Mack, *Elizabethan Rhetoric*, p. 121.
[84] James VI&I, *Basilicon Doron* (Edinburgh, 1599, 1603) in *Workes* (1616), pp. 161–2.
[85] Hobbes, *Leviathan*, ch. 20, p. 238.

Institutionalised office

Most of the literature on aristocracy assumed a mutual interdependency of office arising from the monarch's being the fount of honour, but as Markku Peltonen has argued, things were never so simple.[86] After the execution of Charles I, it became plausible to claim that a democracy gave a greater space for the exercise of aristocratic heroics.[87] William Cavendish's reflections on aristocracy must be seen partially in the light of this alternative. Maintaining the aristocracy (and its carpets), he pleaded, was in the king's interest because it would support him in return, or only replace him with another king – compensation, no doubt, for deposition. But there is a qualification even to Cavendish's Machiavellian stress on self-interest. It was the loyal part of the nobility that, taking the war 'att their owne Charge', kept up Charles I, beyond expectation.[88] This is close to arguing that the aristocracy must be furnished with the means of fulfilling its supporting office to the ruler. It was even closer to asking for cash. The privileges of aristocracy were, however, justified more explicitly through reference to its office when Margaret Cavendish printed the maxims of the 'Advice'.[89] Sustenance of privilege and its display was a duty to lineage and reputation, so profligacy might seem a self-destructive responsibility. Social and financial credit could be semiotically tied to each other as expressions of trust. Butler parodied this attitude in his image of a degenerate noble, debt-ridden and worthless, who exists only in the past of his lineage and to whom present laws do not apply.[90]

Peltonen has applied a valuable analytic distinction between vertical and horizontal dimensions of aristocratic honour. The vertical concerned the aristocrat's place in a social hierarchy; it was something easily augmented and rewarded, or diminished in the business of exercising institutionalised office. Horizontal honour was the relationship of those sharing an official identity and it could be lost, regained, but not augmented.[91] Practices of hospitality and gift-giving were played out on both dimensions, but were vital to vertical honour; its enlargement might depend

---

[86] Markku Peltonen, *The Duel in Early Modern England: Civility, Politeness and Honour* (Cambridge, 2003), pp. 65–79.
[87] Warren, *Royalist Reform'd*, pp. 4–5.
[88] Cavendish, 'Advice', fol. 54.
[89] Margaret Cavendish, *The Life of the Thrice Noble, High and Puissant Prince, William Cavendish, Duke, Marquess and Earl of Newcastle* (1667), ed. C.H. Firth (London, 1896), pt. 4; see Conal Condren, 'Casuistry to Newcastle: *The Prince* in the World of the Book', in Nicholas Phillipson and Quentin Skinner, eds., *Political Discourse in Early Modern Britain* (Cambridge, 1993), esp. pp. 180–3.
[90] Pepys remarks on the notoriously conspicuous Cavendish extravagances, in *Diary*, 26 April 1667; Muldrew, *The Economy of Obligation*, pp. 3–7, 149–72; Muldrew, 'Interpreting the Market', p. 169; Butler, *Characters*, pp. 67–8.
[91] Peltonen, *The Duel*, pp. 35–9, 115–16, drawing on the work of Frank Stuart.

upon material acquisition. The satisfaction of honour, however, took place only among equals, for whom reputation was tantamount to identity. Together these requirements of liberality and honour's jealous defence might generate the 'oppressions and injuries' of which Hobbes warned. They were at the heart of a modal ethics of office that could sit ill with other moral expectations.

There was something of a primitive and Mediterranean ethos to aristocratic patterns of generous display, an inherited understanding that the gift was reciprocal in its bestowal of honour. To trace the gift through the cultural capital of heroic epic poems, from *The Iliad* to *Beowulf*, is to follow the semiotics of identity, achievement and disaster. Sumptuary laws provided some control on extravagance in the early modern world, but aristocrats continued to live in the costly environment of a shame culture. Honour, like the ancient Greek *time*, was itself understood as something largely given.[92] Elizabethan nobles might dread the financial consequences of a visit from Gloriana, but honour demanded appropriate hospitality. As Hobbes put it with imperious sweep:

And riches are honourable; as signs of the power that acquired them. – And gifts, costs, and magnificence of houses, apparel, and the like, are honourable, as signs of riches. – And nobility is honourable by reflection, as signs of the power in the ancestors . . . And the contraries, or defects, of these signs are dishonourable . . . and so we estimate and make the value or WORTH of a man.[93]

During Hobbes's lifetime, the gift relationship and its elaborate rules of decorum continued to proclaim and occasionally disrupt social standing, for the protocols of giving had to be congruent with official relationships. In many cases, such as the convention of thanking judges with gifts of gloves, the offering was subject to some social control in the interests of warding off corruption. And, as Wilf Prest has documented, from the late seventeenth century, the judiciary gradually became sensitised to the difference between gifts and bribes, ever negotiable yet always differentiating exercise of office from abuse. In this process, Sir John Fitz-James and Sir Matthew Hale became bywords for punctiliousness in the niceties of official decorum.[94] Despite the injection of legal families into the

---

[92] Sir Thomas Browne, *Religio Medici* (1643), ed. Henry Gardiner (London, 1845), p. 91.
[93] Thomas Hobbes, *The Elements of Law* (1640), ed. Ferdinand Tönnies (London, 1969 edn), 1.8.5; As he later wrote, 'The honour of great Persons is to be valued for their benificence, and the aydes they give to men of inferiour rank, or not at all.' *Leviathan*, ch. 30, p. 238.
[94] Prest, 'Judicial Corruption', pp. 67–95; James Malcolm, *Anecdotes of the Manners and Customs of London*, 2 vols. (London, 1811, 2nd edn), vol. I, pp. 238–40.

aristocracy during the sixteenth and seventeenth centuries, it is unclear if there was any 'trickle-up' effect to contain display and extravagance.

The right to duel was essential to honour among equals, a recognition of the fragility of an identity contingent upon perceived interrelationships. Its problems were hardly unique to England; casuistic discussions of the violent defence of honour assume a French or Spanish sensitivity to position.[95] It was not entirely the creation of the Renaissance, but duelling was given great impetus from Italian courtesy books of the sixteenth century. This literature blurred the identities of aristocrat, courtier, warrior and counsellor by using much the same vocabulary of office for each, and so the context of discussion for the duel needs to be not one of ideologies and ambivalently emerging self-hood, but, like the other aspects of aristocratic identity, the maintenance of a *persona*, the accretion of social offices and the tensions of ethical modality.[96]

Castiglione's *Il Cortigiano* (1528) attributed an explicitly Ciceronian *officium* to the noble and courtier and made the defence of reputation a perpetual responsibility. Other writers followed in its train.[97] Honour was a gale, as Tuvill put it, driving a man to 'every haughty enterprise';[98] and the little boat of nobility was poled along by the sword, an emblem even more potent than a turkey carpet by the bed.[99] Practice and theory walked in tandem, the increasing practice of duelling being subjected to more critical attention.[100] The Earl of Northampton, hostile only to its extent,

---

[95] Stephen Toulmin and A. R. Jonsen, *The Abuse of Casuistry* (Los Angeles, 1988), pp. 224–5. The proud duelling Spaniard was something of a joke up to the nineteenth century: Jan Potocki, *The Manuscript Found at Saragossa* (1815), trans. Ian Maclean (Harmondsworth, 1995), pp. 35–41.
[96] Cf. Peltonen, *The Duel*, pp. 17–59; on conflicting ideologies and emergent self-hood, p. 306.
[97] Baldesar Castiglione, *Il Cortigiano* (1528), trans. George Bull, in *The Book of the Courtier* (Harmondsworth, 1987 edn), p. 57; see, for example, J. K., *The Courtiers Academie* (1598), trans. of Annibale Romei, *Discors*; Barnaby Rich, *Allarme to England* (1578), discussed in Peltonen, *The Duel*, pp. 42–3.
[98] Daniel Tuvill, 'Of Reputation', in *Essays Politicke and Morall* (1608), fol. 119.
[99] Margaret Cavendish, *Sociable Letters* (1664), cited in Peltonen, *The Duel*, p. 179; cf. Barbara Donagan, 'The Web of Honour: Soldiers, Christians and Gentlemen in the English Civil War', *Historical Journal*, 44, 2 (2001), pp. 365–89, who shows how an office-informed sense of honour could mitigate violence.
[100] In the 1580s, only five aristocratic duels were recorded, in the 1590s, twenty. The number had risen to thirty-three in the second decade of the seventeenth century; see Markku Peltonen, 'Francis Bacon, the Earl of Northampton and the Jacobean Anti-Duelling Campaign', *Historical Journal*, 44, 1 (2001), p. 10. Duelling remained a feature of the army; in 1809 two senior members of Lord Portland's ministry put aside Napoleon as the principal enemy on Putney Heath, and the Duke of Wellington, a notoriously bad shot, also fought a duel with Lord Winchelsea.

suggested that the Marshall's office could channel issues of honour to avoid institutionalising patterns of revenge and feud. In line with this, Jeremy Taylor would permit only judicial duels.[101] The weight of opinion, however, went further. Bacon regarded duelling as expressing an entirely false sense of aristocratic *persona*. For Thomas Comber, the preoccupation with reputation was a delusion and a pretence. The duel was virtually self-murder and its source lay in monkish superstition and pagan impiety. It was an affront to the office of the sovereign and the law.[102] The world of social office could be undone from the top.

To designate the duel a private combat was to see it as unchristian and at odds with true nobility.[103] Yet, despite the strengthening chorus of hostility, it remained a sort of self-defence, where the aristocratic *persona* extended to the perception of family honour. So, the defining right to duel was justified not as private, but as an obligation to the very civility for which the aristocrat stood. For Northampton, despite the abuse of duelling, reputation had to be recovered even if reduced by no more than 'the weight of a graine'. An insult, as Lessius had put it, was a theft beyond money, so defence of honour must be weighed against the consequences of escalating social disruption.[104] The monetary image of theft itself went beyond the material; it tied the duel to the maintenance of proper relationships of office against Gygean acts of rapacity. Being perceived in terms of social office, duelling had an end and a controlling sphere of operation. Hobbes advised the young Charles Cavendish in 1638, 'I beseech you take no occasions of quarrell but such as are necessary & from such men only as are of reputation. For neither words uttered in heate of Anger, nor ye wordes of youthes unknowne in the world, or not knowne for Vertue are of scandall sufficient to ground an honourable duell on.'[105] Concomitantly, it was a highly ritualised practice with intricate conventions protecting its exclusivity. On one occasion, the very short-sighted Sir William Petty was challenged by Sir Hierome Sanchy, and having right of

---

[101] Jeremy Taylor, *Ductor dubitantium* (1660), 3.2, rule 6.
[102] Francis Bacon, 'The Charge of Francis Bacon . . . touching Duels', in *Works*, vol. IV, pp. 110–11; Peltonen, 'Francis Bacon', p. 17; Ames, *Conscience*, ch. 32, p. 182; Thomas Comber, *A Discourse of Duels* (2nd edn 1720), pp. 28, 3–8, 15–18.
[103] Peltonen, *The Duel*, for example, pp. 78–9, 108–10, 212–15; Evelyn, *Diary*, vol. IV, 19 February 1686, p. 501, on this 'unChristian custom'. An exception is Selden, *Table Talk*, 36, pp. 41–2, who allows duelling the authority of the ancient church. When it began depended much on the degree of hostility to it.
[104] Cited in Peltonen, 'Francis Bacon', p. 21; cited in Toulmin and Jonsen, *The Abuse of Casuistry*, pp. 223–7, esp. 224–5.
[105] *The Correspondence of Thomas Hobbes*, ed. Noel Malcolm, 2 vols. (Oxford, 1994), vol. I, 22 August 1638, p. 53.

place and weapon, chose carpenters' axes in a dark cellar. The parodic ridicule was so effective, Aubrey recalls, that the point of honour was dropped.[106]

Aristocracy, in sum, was presented as office-dependent. The difficulty lay in which dimension of office should predominate and how far the social duties undertaken within the polity, such as the Earl of Essex serving as a court clerk, augmented or confused the *persona*, sustained or subverted social order. Formal social office was an emblem of aristocratic standing and expectation, albeit one that could compromise the triumphant *persona* and sap its resources. Yet if these were repaired, standing might be diminished through accusations of corruption and private interest. Throughout the seventeenth century, an uncertain ethical modality sustained an inherent tension of office. Meriton's plea for aristocrats to take on the formal office of the priest demanded a starker choice than his rhetoric indicated; and if the modern state was the unintended consequence of changes in social office, the contraction of the aristocratic *persona* was one part of them.

VI

Offices might be fraught and contentious but acceptance of the social world as necessarily constituted by them was ubiquitous. In the previous chapter, I concluded that the isolation of the purely political can be artificial when read back into the ceremonial dimension of early modern England. With this caveat in mind we need now to reconsider related anachronisms arising from the nature of the distinction between the public and the private. Normally these terms are taken to refer to mutually delineating and equally legitimate domains of experience, with perhaps the public having its rationale in protecting, framing and controlling the private, and not infrequently with the public being a rough synonym for the political or the legitimate reach of the state. Even if a historical awareness leads us to reconfiguring the public sphere as an interaction of offices, this is distorting when imposed on the seventeenth century.[107] A world that could denigrate aristocratic duelling as private, and that saw the most 'private' domains of family and prison life as no less subject to the impress of office than that of the constable or church warden, should alert us to the dangers of taking our own conceptual pairings for granted. Only occasionally do they get superficial support from the way language

---

[106] Aubrey, 'Sir William Petty', in *Brief Lives*, p. 304.
[107] Braddick, *State Formation*, pp. 82–4; less explicitly, Geoff Baldwin, 'Individual and Self in the Late Renaissance', *Historical Journal*, 44, 2 (2001), pp. 346, 363.

was used. Thomas Mun, for example, urged that private gain must run in tandem with public good, but Mun's private gain is still the dividend of the steward's noble vocation. Again, Daniel Tuvill held that private persons can look justice in the eye, whereas public ones must cloak their virtue.[108] But the argument, pivoting on the necessity of secrecy, was about the dangers of court life and the relationships between deliberative and forensic rhetoric.[109] For others, it was the private that was secret.[110] Similarly with Hobbes, the private is sometimes tainted with the illicit and conspiratorial, and what might now be designated the public entails the subject being seen as private, that is without liberties in relationship to the sovereign. This crossover between apparently contrasting concepts should forewarn us of problems to come.[111]

There were several permutations on the meaning of private, each of which expressed a relationship to office. First, the private could designate a worthless residue, life at the bottom of a bottle.[112] Mulcaster's criticism of private education was that as merely individual tutoring it was, socially speaking, worthless; it becomes public, and therefore valuable, simply by involving more students.[113] Second, the word could denote passive duty of obedience of those within a given relationship of office. Tyndale's private world is a shared equality of subjection to Christ.[114] William Willymat's private subjects are those who should all equally obey the magistrate. Yet, when he wrote of these subjects beyond 'publicke charge' and 'office', it was still necessary for the private man to stick to his own 'calling'.[115] In the same vein, Peter Heylyn argued that as all in magisterial office are public persons with respect to those below them, they too were private when considered in relationship to those above them.[116] As Samuel Parker later put it, private men were not properly *sui juris*, being directed by 'the

---

[108] Daniel Tuvill, *The Doue and the Serpent* (1614), pp. 37–9.
[109] *Ibid.*, p. 64.
[110] Rami Targoff, *Common Prayer: The Language of Devotion in Early Modern England* (Chicago, 2001), p. 21; 'Of Swearing', in Anon., *Certain Sermons* (1683), p. 41; Anthony Ascham, *Confusions and Revolutions of Governments* (1649), pp. 113, 143; Anon., *A Letter from Leghorn from Aboard the Van Herring*, p. 2.
[111] Hobbes, *Leviathan*, cf. chs. 21, 22; see also Kevin Sharpe, *Re-Mapping Early Modern England: The Culture of Seventeenth-Century Politics* (Cambridge, 2000), ch. 4.
[112] John Hitchcock, *A Sanctuary for Honest Men: or an Abstract of Humane Wisdom* (1617), pp. 34–5; for discussion, Peltonen, *Classical Humanism*, pp. 158, 149.
[113] Richard Mulcaster, *Positions wherein those primitive circumstances be examined* (1581), ch. 39, pp. 185–6.
[114] Christina Malcolmson, *Heart Work: George Herbert and the Protestant Ethic* (Stanford, 1999), pp. 267–8.
[115] William Willymat, *A Loyal Subjects Looking-glasse* (1604), pp. 47–9, 58–9.
[116] Peter Heylyn, *The Rebells Catechism* (1643), p. 16.

publick Conscience'.[117] Such a meaning survives in the rank of a private soldier.[118]

Consequently, what was private could be no more than an absence of a right in a given situation. In mid-sixteenth century Germany this could make even a prince 'private' (*Privatfurst*).[119] During the same period, Sir Ralph Sadler reported on 'private persons' giving the advice that should be given by counsellors.[120] The use of private in such contexts was occasionally without prejudice. During the Interregnum, Colonel Hutchinson gave counsel as a 'private neighbour' because he refused formal office under Cromwell. Michael Dalton referred to private men as lacking rights with respect to a specific law; hence the private nature of aristocratic duelling.[121] The equation of the private not with a sphere of independence, but with an absence of right, sometimes carried the explicit corollary that the only liberty was liberty of office. As Peter Wentworth protested in 1576, he was no private person, but as a member of the Commons was 'publique and a councellor to the whole'.[122] Private persons submit and obey; lacking the responsibilities of office, they are 'vnweighed by liberty'.[123] So when William Ames argued that in extreme threat to society 'every private man becomes a minister of public justice', he was stating that all those within networks of official relationships took on active responsibilities with the liberties necessary for them.[124] In sum, this common pattern of related uses refers not to anything as absolute as a private sphere of belonging, but simply to the conduct fitting to a given *persona*.

---

[117] Samuel Parker, *A Discourse of Ecclesiastical Polity* (1670, 1671 edn), p. 308; see David Martin Jones, *Conscience and Allegiance in Seventeenth-Century England* (New York, 1999), pp. 178–9; Gordon Schochet, 'Between Lambeth and *Leviathan*: Samuel Parker on the Church of England and Political Order', in Nicholas Phillipson and Quentin Skinner, eds., *Political Discourse in Early Modern Britain* (Cambridge, 1993), pp. 201–8.

[118] 'I cannot put him to a private soldier, that is the leader of so many thousands' (Falstaff), *2Henry IV* 3.2.

[119] See, generally, von Friedeburg, *Self-Defence*, pp. 56–70; cf. Taylor, *Ductor*, 3.2, p. 111: no prince is a private person in following the laws.

[120] Sir Ralph Sadler, 'Embassy to Scotland', letter 10 August 1543, in *State Papers*, 2 vols. (Edinburgh, 1809), vol. I, p. 251.

[121] Lucy Hutchinson, *Memoirs of the Life of Colonel Hutchinson* (London, 1968 edn), p. 293; Dalton, *Country Justice*, ch. 7, p. 33; ch. 117, p. 331; see also John Ponet, *A Shorte Treatise of Politicke Power* (Strasbourg, 1556), pp. 24, 35; Francis Bacon, 'The Charge of Sir Francis Bacon . . . Touching Duels', p. 110.

[122] Cited Peltonen, *Classical Humanism*, p. 45.

[123] Henry Howard, Earl of Northampton, *A publication of his majesties edict, and severe censure against priuate combats and combatants* (1613), quoted in Peltonen, *The Duel*, p. 110.

[124] Ames, *Conscience*, p. 179.

The frequently negative connotations of the private could go further, indicating abuse and corruption, and even marking the nominal transformation of a *persona* beyond office. This usage was well established in Germany by the mid-sixteenth century.[125] Personal or familial resources, such as those of the Renaissance aristocratic diplomat, were proper if put to public, unselfish use, within the bounds of, or serving an office; magnificence was a public virtue, a private vice.[126] People enjoying private wealth, argued Richard Beacon, either neglected their duties or used their resources to pervert public office that ends up 'in open market'.[127] This Machiavellian theme is later evident in Harrington's *Oceana*, and it was in this tradition that Milton and Sidney worked when associating monarchy so closely with a private interest. They helped forge, not a distinction between the public and private, but between a commonwealth and its nemesis, a monarchy. They came to question the validity of the cliché that a king rules for the public good, a tyrant for private profit.[128] Throughout society, private interest threatened a replacement of office-holders with creatures; a bad ruler might become a private person. For de Bohun, it is corruption for a justice of the peace to consider his private interest or think it can be advanced along with his office.[129] The word private, marking the corruption of any official *persona*, is similarly noted with cynical aplomb by Butler. By definition, any officer is 'a person of double capacity, public and private, and that may be one reason, why he is said to deal doubly with all men'.[130]

Beyond such raillery, there is, however, a sense in which it was impossible to sustain any coherent distinction between public and private domains, or, for that matter, public, personal and domestic in a world pervaded by notions of office. When Nicholas Grimalde first translated Cicero's *De officiis*, he promoted it as 'in a manner new again' by urging its equal relevance to 'private life to attaine quietnesse and contemplation: or in office being to winne fame and honour'.[131] The point pivots on the distinction between active and contemplative lives; for Grimalde, both are infused with the values and proprieties of office. Some people, instructed William Gouge in the following century, might think that if they have no

---

[125] Von Friedeburg, *Self-Defence*, pp. 62–3.
[126] Rogers, *A Philosophicall Discourse*, ch. 31, fol. 149v.
[127] Richard Beacon, *Solon His Follie* (Oxford, 1594), pp. 98–9, 50–1; see Peltonen, *Classical Humanism*, pp. 79.
[128] *The Sage Senator* (1660), p. 165; Anon., *An Answer to the Second Letter from Leghorn* (1680), p. 2.
[129] De Bohun, *The Justice of the Peace*, pp. 29, 128–30.
[130] Butler, *Characters*, p. 295.
[131] Grimalde, *Ciceroes Three Bokes of Duties*, epistle Aiij.

public calling they 'have no calling at all': not so. Those wholly employed in private affairs are still part of the microcosm of the domestic commonwealth. Moreover, as the preservation of the family is for the good of the commonwealth, so household duty ' may be accounted publicke worke' undertaken by 'publicke officers'. The 'Horae subsecivae' makes much the same point with respect to masters and servants; they are the representations of a more public government.[132] With such variable delineation between public and private as degrees of office-holding, it is sometimes unclear if reference to the private is synonymous with the domestic, or distinct from it; such matters were of only subsidiary significance in discussions of the importance of office wherever it is found.

If we look at a more studied and sophisticated exploration, it becomes apparent that the vocabulary of office undercuts any coherent delineation of a private world. In the *Advancement of Learning*, Bacon addressed such issues in insisting upon the responsibilities of the philosopher to the active life.[133] He distinguishes 'a private, free, and unapplied course of life' and discusses what he calls 'private and particular good'. He stipulates a double nature of good, personal and public, 'the one a total substantive in itself; the other, as it is a part or member of a greater body'.[134] In the context of such distinctions, he places the difference between the contemplative and active lives. Yet despite the hardly careless language, we are a long way from anything analogous to the private realm and public sphere that we find in the nineteenth century.

For Bacon, a realm of purely self-regarding acts, or purely private contemplation, is for God and angels alone.[135] For mankind, even the contemplative extreme of the monastic life performs the duty of prayers as an office. Bacon expresses this by a formal specification of the private and by an adumbration of its content. First, he divides private good into conservation and advancement, each a form of responsibility, concerning 'the regimen and government of every man over himself' and providing a virtuous disposition to acquit public duties. The world of public office is divided into the civil and politic, as a man is a member of a state, and as he is in a given 'profession, vocation or place', having 'respective duty'.[136] Second, when Bacon outlines the content of these residual offices, he leaves virtually no space for any private or domestic realm beyond them.

---

[132] Gouge, *Domesticall Duties*, pp. 18, 19; William Cavendish, 'Master & servants, Horae subsecivae', p. 32; see also Browne, *Religio Medici*, p. 174.
[133] Gaukroger, *Francis Bacon*, pp. 68–100.
[134] Bacon, *The Advancement of Learning*, in *Works*, vol. II, pp. 223–3, 229–30.
[135] *Ibid.*, p. 225.
[136] *Ibid.*, pp. 233, 234.

76   Argument and Authority in Early Modern England

Respective duty 'doth also appertain the duties between husband and wife, parent and child, master and servant: so likewise the laws of friendship and gratitude, the civil bond of companies, colleges, and politic bodies, of neighbourhood, and all other proportionate duties; not as they are parts of government and society, but as to the framing of the mind of particular persons'.[137] If this fleetingly refers to the civil as well as the politic, in Bacon's vision, the private collapses into preparation for the civic and politic frame. This employment of the nomenclature of office facilitates his realignment of philosophy as a form of public service and a vital office.

Other writers also leave us distant from any private realm of autonomy and non-interference. Goslicius is emphatic: as private life is an ornament to the commonwealth, it is to be controlled. The private, as Robert Sanderson maintained, was not separate from but included in the public.[138] The projectors Robert Chiver and John Cusacke effectively exploited such an incorporation: the monarch's public duty is to impose benefits on the private.[139] Informing this line of argument was a *terra nullius* proposition, itself predicated on an understanding of office, imported, very loosely, from Roman law and reinforced, no doubt, by the parable of the talents (Matthew 25: 14–30). The world was entrusted by God for good use and it was the office of the husbandman to improve his lot; so fens might be drained, land enclosed. Failure to do so was an abuse of stewardship and in neglecting office the husbandman might lose his *persona*.[140] Even for Hobbes, who gives a tantalising glimpse of a private sphere by no more than diminishing reference to any office independent of the sovereign, the contingently residual activities he notes refer to the standard exempla of liberties of office, concerning trade, parental responsibility and the relationship between masters and servants. The true liberty of the subject has no location in any private realm; it is that notoriously minimal right to attempt self-defence when official protection has ceased and when such a person is, strictly speaking, no longer a subject, no longer in a private relationship with the sovereign.[141] As for Hobbes's sometime friend and antagonist, Edward Hyde, he makes a

---

[137] *Ibid.*, pp. 237–8; also Speech to Parliament, 17 February 1607, cited in Peltonen, *Classical Humanism*, p. 144.

[138] Goslicius, *The Counsellor* (1598), pp. 129, 118; Robert Sanderson, *Sermons ad Magistratum*, in *Works*, ed. W. Jacobson (Oxford, 1854), vol. I; also de Bohun, *The Justice of the Peace*, p. 129.

[139] Linda Levy Peck, 'Kingship, Council and Law in Early Stuart Britain', in J. G. A. Pocock et al., *The Varieties of British Political Thought* (Cambridge, 1996 edn), pp. 111–13.

[140] On the guarded use of *res* and *terra nullius* arguments, see Fitzmaurice, *Humanism and America*, pp. 140–4.

[141] Hobbes, *Leviathan*, ch. 21, pp. 148, 150–4; ch. 22, p. 164.

distinction between private and public in the context of exploring private friendship as a Ciceronian *officium*.[142]

In the light of how people actually wrote about public and private as specifications of relationships of office, what can we make of the Habermasian 'public sphere' and the search for its origins in early modern England? The disembodied phrase 'public sphere' currently rattles like a pinball through early modern historiography, an unproblematic concept bouncing into the facts and lighting up the world. It is discovered, to use that treacherous word, by listening to the right voices, be they courtly or marginal.[143] More reflectively, some have identified its presence as something in public but beyond state monopolies of discourse (presupposing a state to monopolise), or alternatively by adumbrating an engagement of the public (members of something later called the public) that prefigured a modern development.[144] At all events, what is needed is more facts to get it right.

It is, however, worth recalling that Habermas was not writing as a historian, but building a theoretical model about the quality rather than the extent of discourse, so historicising the model requires more than added detail, taking its terms for granted and just looking for 'it' somewhat earlier.[145] Like an idealised market, the Habermasian public sphere requires equal participation by similarly informed people, debating issues they have determined for themselves freely and rationally (as philosophers do), and mediating the state and civil society (as intellectuals do). The model was designed to cast critical light on nineteenth- and twentieth-century society, and was predicated on a firm conceptual distinction between public and private domains, of state and civil society, the latter being taken up largely with economic activity. Additionally, Habermas's notion of rationality is very much a post-Enlightenment and secular one. Keeping all this in mind, his own perfunctory attempt to ground the model in history is distracting; and the physical location for the beginnings of the public sphere in the London coffee-house culture of the late seventeenth and early eighteenth centuries has only a knock-about plausibility.

Coffee-houses seem to have been club-like with special shared interests, and while they would have been centres for rumour, news and gossip, it is

---

[142] Edward Hyde, Lord Clarendon, 'Friendship' (1670), in *Essays Moral and Entertaining* (London, 1815), vol. I, pp. 112–14, 116.
[143] For example, Natalie Mears, 'Counsel, Public Debate and Queenship: John Stubbs's The Discoverie of a Gaping Gulf, 1579', *Historical Journal*, 44, 3 (2001), pp. 629–50; Peltonen, *Classical Humanism*, pp. 120, 165, 238.
[144] David Norbrook, *Writing the English Republic: Poetry, Rhetoric and Politics, 1627–1660* (Cambridge, 2000), for example, pp. 13, 74–5, 98–102; Hindle, *The State*, pp. 234–7.
[145] Habermas, *The Structural Transformation of the Public Sphere*.

difficult to imagine any town or village from time immemorial that would not have had some such meeting place. The attention given to, and suspicions of coffee-houses, had a partial context in long-standing concerns about drunkenness and may also have had as much to do with the novelty of the drink, a dangerous competitor to alcohol, and what it might signify, as with the quality or impertinence of discussion around it.[146] Irrespective of the coffee-house, any market or tavern might, given the loose usage current, have been a public sphere: public places for members of the public. Seventeenth-century usage would probably have called it private. It may even have been the case that the dramatic expansion of London and the instability of its population actually disrupted communication on significant issues.[147] Neither did the early eighteenth century convey much confidence that its political debate was better informed and more rational than that to be found in the past. As the word public continued to be so strongly associated with the disinterest and responsibility of office-holding, it would probably be difficult to find anyone engaged in argument not associating themselves and their friends with issues of 'public' concern; and certainly accusations about dishonesty, self-delusion and corruption were largely explained by reference to the 'private'. This suggests something different from the domains of public and private life taken back in the search for the public sphere, and it is hardly surprising that early humanists failed to resolve the tensions in our concepts.[148] And irrespective of any location for debate, clergymen from the authority of the pulpit continued to have remarkable sway in shaping the issues discussed.[149]

These features of discourse around the word public take us a good way from the considerata of Habermasian rationality, and contradict rather than qualify his notion of a public sphere. At the same time, it is probably our own understandings of public, as in space, opinion and members of, together with a greater awareness of the extent of early modern argument

---

[146] Anon., *A Satyr against Coffee* (n.d. c. 1675); Anon., *Rebellious Antidotes: Or a Dialogue Between Tea and Coffee* (1685); see also Anon., *Obsequium et veritas* (1681), p. 2; Anon., *The True Protestant's Appeal* (1680), p. 2; Anon., *Scandalum Magnatum, Or the Great Tryal at Chelmsford Assizes* (1681), p. 3; Anon., *Reflections on a Catholick Ballard* (1675), stanza 2.

[147] On the difficulties of drawing global conclusions from 'print culture' see Harold Love, 'Early Modern Print Culture: Assessing the Models', *Parergon*, new series, 20, 1 (2003) pp. 45–64.

[148] Baldwin, 'Individual and Self', p. 363.

[149] Tony Claydon, 'The Sermon, the "Public Sphere" and the Political Culture of Late Seventeenth-Century England', in L. A. Ferrell and P. McCullough, eds., *The English Sermon Revised: Literature and History, 1600–1750* (Manchester, 2000), pp. 208–34; Conal Condren, 'Between Social Constraint and the Public Sphere: Methodological Problems in Reading Early-Modern Political Satire', *Contemporary Political Theory*, 1, 1 (2001), pp. 92–6.

than Habermas had, that have provided the impulse to seek the origins ever earlier. It would, no doubt, be possible to argue that a public sphere developed as an unintended consequence of discourse at odds with the notions of public and private with which people worked. Such a case, however, cannot be made if the terms of the Habermasian model are simply elided with the evidence of earlier argument. Conversely, if the content of the model is rejected to keep the phrase upon its feet, one wonders what the point is.

4 The vocabulary of office

> And woe unto the people that is brought into such straights and perplexities.
>
> (George Lawson, *Politica sacra et civilis*, 1660, 1689, ch. 15.8)

I

The scene set, I shall now turn to the moral vocabulary of office from which disparate doctrines were developed. A concluding section, however, will comment on the king's two bodies, perhaps the best known of such doctrines, prior to a fuller exploration of the discourse of office in the following chapters. By the end of the sixteenth century, there was a clearly related set of covering terms used to abridge understandings of office: vocation, calling, profession, trade, sphere and end. These were not always synonymous, but their use made claim to similar senses of the ethics of office-holding and to the same complementary registers of justification and critique. To begin with what I am taking to be the central word: office was often used as a general term for a world of duties and purposes, carried out by a *persona* who enjoyed concomitant liberties to those ends. Casually employed, it might indicate only a specific ad hoc favour. Shakespeare, who uses the term office and its cognates some 150 times, employs it thus in *Twelfth Night* when Viola asks Sir Toby Belch to 'do me this courteous office' of saying how she has offended.[1] It sometimes meant a specific field of responsibility and by extension a dedicated function;[2] Walter Charleton surmised that the 'parenchyma' had the 'office of a strainer'.[3] Hence also the lavatory, a house of office, was a room for one purpose. The 'silver sea' served England 'in the office of a wall' and we

---

[1] Shakespeare, *Twelfth Night* 3.4; John Bartlett, *A Complete Concordance to Shakespeare* (London, 1979 edn) listing for office and its cognates.

[2] Henry Sacheverell, *The Perils of False Brethren* (1709), A2v.

[3] Walter Charleton, *Enquiries into Human Nature* (1680), p. 140; Emily Booth, 'A Subtle and Mysterious Machine: Walter Charleton's Medical World' (Ph.D. thesis, La Trobe University, 2002), p. 157.

find commonly, in the mid-seventeenth century, officers as functionaries. The predicate 'officious' could mean dutiful efficiency.[4]

The words vocation and calling were usually interchangeable with each other (from *vocare*, to call) and with office, a point touched on in chapter 3. In the sixteenth century, Hugh Latimer had referred to a general calling or vocation as a position in society, a particular calling as a beckoning from God.[5] William Perkins designated Christianity a general calling that provided the virtues to maintain the integrity of particular callings; the soul's proper demeanour to God had consequences for the way we conduct our lives.[6] Robert Sanderson argued that no man should be without a specific calling, which was not simply a pastime or role, but a form of life. Callings span the whole of society from grand and honourable offices to more mundane employment. When Sanderson alluded to Cicero's *officia* of family, friends and country, he used calling as synonymous with office, and to live in society without office was a sort of theft.[7] John Tillotson illustrates the ease with which people could shift between a wide range of quasi-synonyms for office. He referred to our particular 'work' and 'business' 'Calling and Charge', 'Duty' and 'all Offices', 'Trade and Profession', insisting that 'it is a great mistake to think that any Man is without a Calling'. No one is above obligations and duties.[8] All these terms, employed with such apparent casualness, express an awareness of constrained and relational spheres of responsibility.

The word sphere was often used to complain that someone was improperly going beyond it, or could not see past it.[9] Related to this are the

---

[4] Shakespeare, *Richard II* 2.1; Anon., *The Declaration of the Parliament of England* (1649), in Joyce Lee Malcolm, ed., *The Struggle for Sovereignty: Seventeenth Century English Political Tracts* (Indianapolis, 1999), vol. I, pp. 369–90; Cavendish, 'Horae subsecivae', fol. 39; Anon., *A letter from Leghorn* (1679), p. 1; rulers should be '*officious handmaids to their Trusts*': 'Philodemius', *The Original and End of Civil Power* (1649), p. 22.

[5] Latimer, 'Sermon before Convocation' (1537), in *Fruitful Sermons* (1635), fol. 6v; George Downhame, *Two Sermons* (1609), p. 2.

[6] William Perkins, *A Treatise of the Vocations, or Callings of Men, with the sorts and kinds of them and the right use thereof*, in *Workes* (Cambridge, 1609), vol. I, pp. 727–30; see also James, *Basilicon Doron* (1603), in *Workes*, bk 1.

[7] Robert Sanderson, *Sermons ad Populum*, sermon 4, St Paul's (4 November 1621), in *Works*, vol. III, pp. 118, 95, 99–102.

[8] John Tillotson, 'Of Diligence in our general and particular Calling' (1685), in *Fifteen Sermons* (1702), pp. 226, 228, 230, 237, 241; cf. John Sharp who does not always use the terms synonymously, for he remarked darkly on callings that encourage sin: 'A Discourse on the various Callings in Life', in *Works*, vol. V, pp. 98–9.

[9] For example, Thomas Hodges, *The Growth and Spreading of Haeresie* (1647), p. 25; George Lawson, *Politica sacra et civilis* (1660, 1689), ed. Conal Condren (Cambridge, 1992), 15.5, p. 226; Anon., *The Whole Duty of Nations* (1681), p. 67; Anon., *Vox cleri pro rege* (1688), pp. 53–4; Sacheverell, *Perils of False Brethren*, A2; Anon., *The Ladies Calling* (1673), b; also Gilbert Burnet, *A History of his own Time*, 6 vols. (Oxford, 1823), vol. VI, pp. 154–5.

images of a 'roome', an 'orb', a province, 'place' and a 'size', from the now obsolete meanings of a fixed order and a proper proportion.[10] 'For realmes haue rules, and rulers haue a syse,/ Which if they kepe not, doubtles say I dare/ That eythers gryefes the other shall agrise/ Till the one be lost, the other brought to care.'[11] The word 'care' was sometimes a synecdoche for office and sometimes a specific locus of responsibility within it. Shakespeare illustrates the range of its uses, from not caring, taking care and expressing concern or interest, to meaning office: 'My youngest yet my eldest care'.[12] In *Richard II* care as office is re-enforced when Richard calls his crown his care and Bolingbroke later tells him that 'part of your care you give me with your crown'.[13] Beyond the Bard, Lord Chief Justice Scroggs referred to 'my care at this time' in summing up at a trial.[14] The poem on Richard II, quoted above, also remarks on office-abusers being brought to 'care', carrying the double meaning of being held responsible and being made to suffer. Walter Charleton refers to his care to decide upon authorities used in argument, assuring readers of his responsibilities as a philosopher.[15] The term 'charge' is similar, a shorthand for a responsibility, what one is charged with doing.[16]

Trade could mean more than commerce. Traders as citizens were subject to the demands of office, and from quite early in the sixteenth century a subordinate use of trade conveys the whole decorum of moral intercourse.[17] Work might predominantly mean toil, but if placed in the context of an ethical economy, the presuppositions of office become explicit. Winstanley referred to 'The Work or Office of a Task-Master', of an executioner, judge, the parliament and ministry.[18] Hence 'mystery' which usually concerned the skills of a guild or trade could be extended to mean office; so too 'traffic': 'I give thee kingly thanks Because this is in traffic of a king.'[19] Words like end, purpose or rule could function rather like sphere,

---

[10] *The Booke of Oathes* (1649), p. 288; Burnet, *History*, vol. I, p. 12 (roome); Francis Bacon, 'A Speech to the Speaker's Excuse', in *Works*, vol. VI, pp. 70, 73; Thomas Browne, *True Christian Morals*, ed. Henry Gardiner (London, 1845 edn), p. 265 (orb); Burnet, *History*, vol. I, p. 374 (place).
[11] Baldwin, 'Richard II', in *Mirror for Magistrates*, lines 27–30, p. 113.
[12] Shakespeare, *Two Gentlemen of Verona* 2.1; *The Merry Wives of Windsor* 2.1; *The Winter's Tale* 4.4; *The Comedy of Errors* 1.1.
[13] *Mirror for Magistrates*, line 30, p. 113; cf. Shakespeare, *Richard II* 4.2; see also Andrew Willett, *An Harmonie on the First Booke of Samuel* (1607), p. 154.
[14] *The Trials of Edward Coleman and William Stacey* (1678), p. 89; see also Tillotson, *Fifteen Sermons*, p. 247.
[15] Walter Charleton, *The Darknes of Atheism Dispelled by Light* (1652), 'To the Reader', p. xix.
[16] Burnet, *History*, vol. II, p. 305.
[17] Grimalde, *Three Bokes of Duties*, Aiiij.
[18] Winstanley, *The Law of Freedom*, pp. 100, 101–10.
[19] B&Y, *The Arraignment of Co-ordinate Power* (1683), p. 7; Shakespeare, *1Henry VI* 5.3.

so function as synecdoches. This is particularly true of the abstraction 'power'. As remains the case, it could be something of a 'philosopher's stone', doing and being all things.[20] It could mean force, an army or any resources that might enhance authority.[21] Power was, however, more often seen as a moral quality stemming from omnipotent God, a concentration of the licit exercise of office. John Rocket actually translated *officii* as power;[22] and this was Locke's usage in the *Second Treatise*. Power, then, was often office in action which, when over-extended, either carried a negative predicate variable such as 'arbitrary', or was simply transformed into rhetorical antonyms like force or violence. As the word office could itself act as a synonym for function, we can see how easily Ciceronian terms of office could be mixed with Aristotelian notions of teleology and purpose. 'It is the excellency of our office to be instruments.'[23]

These general descriptors emphasise one of two mutually entailed aspects of office, rationale and limit. Trade, work, end, function, all encapsulated rationality; the spatial images of room, orb, sphere, size and place under-score the necessities of interrelationship and limitation. As the covering terms all expressed subordination to some worthy end, service or duty, they were tied to a compound understanding of representation, a point perceptively accentuated in Samuel Butler's pejorative character of 'An Officer'. He loses his name and nature in his authority, 'has no intrinsic value and nothing to trust to but the stamp that is put upon him'.[24]

The *persona* manifested the office, representing it *pars pro toto*.[25] Yet additionally many *personae* claimed to represent those served or protected by the office, standing for them. This could also be a relationship of the part effectively being the whole, in so far as *personae*, such as shepherds, were not accountable to the sheep under their care.[26] Nevertheless, official *personae* were often held to be accountable in some fashion, because of the limited scope of office. Consequently, representation could either be irrevocable, standing *for*, or it could be accountable *to*. Thus Bacon: the sovereign's officer effectively is the *persona* of the sovereign in executing his duty, but is accountable to the sovereign for his actions.[27] In some

---

[20] John Eachard, *Mr Hobbs State of Nature Considered in a Dialogue Between Timothy and Philautus* (1671), in *Works* (1773), vol. II, p. 22.
[21] Sir Walter Raleigh, *The Cabinet Council* (1658), ch. 16, p. 42.
[22] John Rocket, *The Christian Subject* (1650), p. 119.
[23] Anon., *A Letter from the King of Morocco to Charles I* (1680), p. 3.
[24] Butler, *Characters*, p. 295.
[25] Anon., *The Sage Senator*, p. 1.
[26] Henry Hammond, *A Vindication* (1650), p. 36.
[27] Francis Bacon, 'An Explanation of What Manner of Persons Those Should be, That are to Execute the Power or Ordinance of the King's Prerogative' (n.d.), in *Works*, vol. VI, pp. 102–6.

bodies of literature, the Leveller pamphlets provide a reasonably reliable example; the word representative is usually reserved for someone acting *pars pro toto*, whereas 'officer' implies accountability. Although Hobbes refers to the office of the sovereign, that sovereign is an irrevocable representative, at once the *persona* of the office and, in *Leviathan*, the authorised voice of the protected; officer designates those accountable to the sovereign.[28] Because understandings of representation were shaped by complementary aspects of the notion of office, the vocabulary of representation was flexible, but however deployed, debates about the words representative and officer dissolved into arguments over office: care and accountability, *telos* and limitation.

II

As the office-holder represented the office, the description of office could be approached through the characteristics of the idealised *persona*, the qualities and capacities necessary for true representation. To draw on a distinction I have made before, this was a vocabulary of status and it may be distinguished from a vocabulary of action – the terms specifying the behaviour appropriate to the office-holder's status.[29] Crucially, both patterns of vocabulary come in a positive and a negative register, the latter spelling out, as Hamlet has it, 'the insolence of office'. Together they suggest a rough matrix of adverbial and adjectival language.

Office
(Care, vocation, profession, sphere, etc.)

Status terms +	Status terms −
Action terms +	Action terms −

Status terms referred to all those skills and aptitudes as well as formal virtues that made a person fit for office.[30] According to John Sharp, all callings had their God-given faculties.[31] Some of these were fairly

---

[28] Hobbes, *Leviathan*, ch. 23, also distinguishes public ministers from other officers. All are accountable, but the former are agents of the *persona* of the ruler rather than serving in some other capacity; cf. George Lawson, *An Examination of Mr Hobbs, His Leviathan* (1657), pp. 78–81.

[29] Condren, *The Language of Politics*, ch. 3.

[30] Rogers, *A Philosophicall Discourse*, gives a valuable survey of the semantic content of the attributes and virtues supported by ancient authority.

[31] John Sharp, 'A Discourse on the Various Callings in Life', in *Works*, vol. V, pp. 83–4; Sanderson, *Ad Populum*, pp. 119–43.

specific. Learning and disinterest were required of judges, physical courage and industry of soldiers, love of parents, piety of priests, liberality of nobles. Some qualities were held to be requisite for pretty well all offices. Fulke Greville asserted that 'Mans chiefe vertue, is *Humilitie*,/ True knowledge of his wants, his height of merit'.[32] Browne substituted charity, its having as many forms as there are ways of doing good; to gloss this assertion, as many forms as offices. As a scholar, he wrote, 'I am obliged by the duty of my condition' to foster learning, and not make 'my head a grave but a treasury of knowledge'.[33] Reference to a general calling could express an over-arching presence of office, the virtues of which should infuse particular spheres of activity.[34] Thus, the postulation of, as it were, a quasi-deontological office acted as a counter to the implications of a world defined by the diverging ethical expectations of different offices, implications that if unchecked might terminate in a Carneadean moral scepticism.

The result was a discordance, or a blurring between universal imperatives, such as the New Testament injunctions to love and charity, and the demands of office. Reference has already been made to the tensions between aristocratic honour and more general Christian duty, but recognition of some dissonance between conduct in office and broader expectations was probably common. The 'Swallowfield articles', drawn up in 1596 by the inhabitants of a cluster of Wiltshire villages, stipulated that 'offycers shall not be dislyked of for the doynge of theyr offyce'.[35] A sort of theoretical resolution was possible by maintaining a formal universality which took on meaning only within the context of an office, as we find with Browne's insistence on the primacy of charity. A more pervasive example is provided by prudence which amounted to blending judgement with conduct. As a practical virtue of balanced behaviour it could only be specified modally; its moral content presupposed the ends of an office.[36] Other formally universal virtues were given content as injunctions to stay within the compass of an office. Humility was a form of knowing one's place and duty as an insurance against interference. It was, claimed Selden, a virtue preached by all, practised by none, and if taken to

---

[32] Fulke Greville, 'An Inquisition upon Fame and Honour', in *Certaine Learned and Elegant Workes* (1633), ed. A.D. Cousins (New York, 1990), stanza 33, p. 39.
[33] Browne, *Religio Medici*, p. 158.
[34] Tillotson, 'Of Diligence', pp. 228–36.
[35] 'Swallowfield Articles', 4 December 1596, Huntington Library, cited in Braddick, *State Formation*, p. 74.
[36] Rogers, *Philosophicall Discourse*, chs. 9–10, pp. 83v–90v, ch. 12, p. 92v; Raleigh, *Cabinet Council*, chs. 13, 14; Bohun, *The Justice of the Peace*, pp. 34–5, for whom it is the cardinal moral endowment for the justice of the peace.

extremes, made anyone comprehensively useless.[37] Humility was also the characteristic posture of the soul and perhaps acquired a wider significance because of the importance accorded to the soul's office-like relationship to God. Understanding was also sometimes canvassed as a universally informing value. Mutual trust was in practice so important that honesty was also widely taken to be the sine qua non for virtue in office; although for some writers it was at least qualified by the need for dissimulation in courtly office, and for others was only paradoxically required of the player.[38]

Since antiquity, the cardinal virtue of justice had remained a matter of right conduct within bounds, taking and giving what was due. George Herbert wrote of the country parson, it is his justice not to encroach on the professions of others, but keep to his own.[39] When understood so formally, it is difficult to see justice being much more than a recognition that a world of offices required conduct appropriate to its maintenance. Without going into any awkward detail, Henry Mason asserted that every calling had its own pattern of fitting conduct, and concomitant sins that marred it. All and any might endanger the soul.[40] Beyond such a Platonic guarantee of office, the justice of the judge, soldier, parent, the charity of the scholar and the noble, had, like prudence, varying content. It was thus, as we will see with liberty, a formal quality taking on distinct meaning only as a specification of office. There was little by way of a rigid supervening template of morality, and so the ethics of office exhibited a variable moral modality, sometimes disguised and sometimes modified by reference to universal criteria of judgement.

Some of the characteristics of office-holders were technical skills, others more strictly moral categories. Edmund de Bohun lists prudence, patience, humility, industry, honesty, learning, quick apprehension and chastity as necessary to the justice's *persona*.[41] But as requirements of a sphere of responsibility were coloured by the inherently normative dimension of an office, so an ethics of office blended the technical with the moral such as de Bohun's industry and honesty. Hence Machiavelli's assessment of Agathocles; his wickedness was such that, despite his successes, he was unworthy of celebration. The qualities that make the

---

[37] Selden, *Table Talk*, p. 50.
[38] Elyot, *The Book Named the Governor*, ch. 24, on understanding; on credit, trust and honesty, see Muldrew, *The Economy of Obligation*, pp. 148–95.
[39] George Herbert, *A Priest to the Temple* (1652), ch. 23.
[40] Henry Mason, *The Tribunal of Conscience* (1627), pp. 31, 40–5; see also Sanderson, *Ad Populum*, p. 143.
[41] Bohun, *The Justice of the Peace*, pp. 8–11, 34–9.

good soldier are more than martial skills.[42] Tyrants might be noted for physical courage but this might intensify rather than mitigate tyranny.[43] The ethicising expectation was that skills and capacities always be put to the service of office. It was by conduct in office that we judge and would all ultimately be judged.[44]

'[T]here belongeth further to the handling of this part, touching the duties of professions and vocations, a relative or opposite, touching the frauds, cautels, impostures, and vices of every profession.'[45]

As Bacon's use of 'relative' indicates, office and its abuse were matters of clarifying conceptually interdependent relationships. Good and evil grew together in the world, wrote Milton, and knowledge of one entailed knowledge of the other; ignorance of one is ignorance of both.[46] The necessity for a language of abuse was personified in the image of Lucifer, the rebellious angel driven by pride, the byword for injustice, the father of lies, the rapacious gobbler of souls who would shovel God from his heavenly throne. In the shadow of his engorgement lay the 'frauds, cautels, impostures and vices' of humankind. The vocabulary of vice was also a rhetoric of motives. The mind is a labyrinth of 'crooked windings', Tuvill rumbled, 'beautified by outward imposture'.[47] Motivation, as remains the case, was characteristically hypothesised to explain departure from proper conduct. The voice of Cardinal Wolsey expatiates on his being motivated only by ambition and 'pryde,/ For which offence, fell *Lucifer* from the Skyes'. It is 'A swelling tode, that poysons euery place'. Because of this 'I thought nothing of duty, loue, or feare/ I snatcht vp all, and always sought to clime'.[48]

Humour theory gave a physiological and semiotically rich grounding to motivation, connecting character type, physiology and the structure of the world. Blood, choler (yellow bile), phlegm and black bile corresponded respectively to air, fire, water and earth, and their variable balance created dispositions, the sanguine, choleric, melancholic and phlegmatic, each with its own propensities. A melancholic temperament was so associated with contemplation and philosophy that it was not unusual for authors to allude to this to help establish a *persona*; for Walter Charleton melancholy was a 'tyranny', for Robert Burton, far

---

[42] Niccolò Machiavelli, *Il Principe* (1513), ed. Sergio Bertelli (Milan, 1973 edn), ch. 8, p. 42.
[43] Joan Bennett, *Reviving Liberty: Radical Christian Humanism in Milton's Poems* (Cambridge, Mass., 1989), p. 42.
[44] Sanderson, *Ad Populum*, p. 135; Anon., *The Whole Duty of Nations*, p. 67.
[45] Bacon, *Advancement*, p. 236.
[46] John Milton, *Areopagitica* (1644), in *The Complete Prose Works*, ed. Ernest Sirluck (New Haven, 1959), vol. II, pp. 514, 527.
[47] Tuvill, 'Of Reputation', in *Essayes*, fol. 116.
[48] *Mirror for Magistrates*, lines 358–9, 366, 407–8, pp. 507–8; see also motivations for rebellion 'Homily against Disobedience, fifth part', in *Certain Sermons* (1683), p. 377.

more. The philosopher's ailment was a cause of civil disorder.[49] Conversely, excessive black bile was believed to unsettle judgement and phlegm diluted intellect.[50] The interest in humours was both explanatory and judgemental especially concerning potential imbalance and office-abuse. So the phlegmatic, as Marlowe put it, was slow to anger, quick in lust.[51] Although gradually separated from their physiological grounding, the humours retained their explanatory function, certainly in popular discourse, throughout the early-modern world. Writers such as Hobbes, with his elegant reduction of motivation to aversion (fear), and attraction (broadly ambition), Willis and then Mandeville attempted to reform vocabularies of motive, but the focus remained on socially deviant behaviour and vulnerability of office. It was not until the eighteenth century that Ephraim Chambers could confidently consign humour theory to the archives of the understanding; in doing so he helped perpetuate its popular currency.[52] Again, as with the defence and promotion of office, critique expressed a variable sensitivity to ethical modality, disguised or mediated by reference to general motivation. For Sir Walter Raleigh, the virtues of the general are vices in the common soldier, so to assume them might well be taken to speak of undue ambition or pride; and credulity, hardly a major blemish in most people, becomes 'unfit and perilous' in a ruler.[53]

III

Beyond the nomenclature of character was the vocabulary of action, displaying character, or revealing hypothesised motive. Expressed synoptically, proper action was judged by what was right and useful. The broad Ciceronian strategies of sound rhetorical discourse, the orchestration of *honestas* and *utilitas*, were particularly prominent in discussions of counsel, but effectively functioned as the terms in which criteria specific to any office were organised.[54] The language of proper action comprised a

---

[49] Charleton, *Darknes of Atheism*, p. xxii for discussion; Booth, 'A Subtle and Mysterious Machine', p. 52; Robert Burton, *The Anatomy of Melancholy* (1621), ed. T. C. Faulfer, N. K. Kiessling and R. L. Blair, 3 vols. (Oxford, 1989), 'Satyrical Preface', vol. I.
[50] Marsilio Ficino, *Libra da vita in tres libros divisos* (1489), ed. Carol V. Kaske and John R. Clark (New York, 1989), bk. 1.3.
[51] Christopher Marlowe, *Dr. Faustus, A Text* (c. 1590, 1604), ed. David Ormerod and Christopher Wortham (Perth, Western Australia, 1985), lines 218–20, pp. 20–1.
[52] Ephraim Chambers, *Encyclopaedia* (1728); I am grateful to discussions with Richard Yeo for this point.
[53] Raleigh, *Cabinet Council*, ch. 25, p. 134; ch. 20, p.55; Rogers, *Philosophicall Discourse*, ch. 31, p. 149v; ch. 25, pp. 130–2v, with especial reference to the 'office' of 'strangeness', observing due measure.
[54] Goslicius, *The Counsellor*, pp. 92–3.

consequential vocabulary necessary for the sustenance of the office, and so ideally what was useful tended to the good of the office.

Central to this positive register were words such as duty, care, responsibility, rule, service, right, prerogative and liberty. An appeal to rights did not necessarily involve much reliance on natural law, but reference to natural law could be a rather grand affirmation of the naturalness of office and duty to God; hence Samuel Daniel's claim that 'by the law of nature' he must defend 'the station of his profession',[55] as if literary critics were already a part of a natural order. The projection of self-defence as part of natural law becomes familiar by the seventeenth century as something exercised even by animals, but wherever possible it is assimilated to office defence; self was largely an anaphoric expression for a *persona* (see below, chapters 6, 9).

Because those in office claimed to be serving some end, they asserted rights, prerogatives or duties of ruling and liberties of office. It is important to expand on liberty of office, as it provides a succinct illustration both of the ubiquity of understandings of office and their misconstrual in modern scholarship.[56] Liberty of office was the latitude deemed necessary in order for the *persona* to fulfil its responsibilities. To recall Goslicius' translator, the citizen's liberty lay 'chiefly in being capable of offices'.[57] Concomitantly, when a posited office was thought to be threatened, typically it was defined in terms of its liberty, its area of operation. This will be most familiar from the tenacity with which the Stuart monarchs asserted prerogative right as definitional of sovereignty; and it was a periodic feature of parliamentary debate even on those ceremonial occasions when the office of the parliament was ritually proclaimed.[58] William Noy, speaking in the parliament of 1621, argued that its liberty had to be exercised for its own protection: exercise of liberty maintained the office.[59] Again, Jeremy Collier was similarly insistent upon his liberty; he was a priest and to see him as a servant undermined his office which included the freedom to admonish.[60] Ruling, then, whether we speak of mayors, monarchs, parliaments or parents, was through just command in the interest of the ruled, and so properly was for a public, or greater good. Parents

---

[55] Samuel Daniel(?), *A Defence of Rhyme* (1603), in Edmund D. Jones, ed., *English Critical Essays (Sixteenth and Seventeenth Centuries)* (London, 1956 edn), p. 62.
[56] For a fuller discussion of this point, see Conal Condren, 'Liberty of Office and its Defence in Seventeenth-Century Political Argument', *History of Political Thought*, 18 (1997), pp. 460–82.
[57] Goslicius, *The Counsellor*, pp. 79–80.
[58] Francis Bacon, 'Speech to the Speaker's Excuse', pp. 73–4.
[59] Mack, *Elizabethan Rhetoric*, pp. 239–45; Greenberg, *The Radical Face*, p. 31 quoting Noy, *Commons Journals*, vol. VI, p. 240; see also, for example, Burnet, text of speech 1713, in *History*, vol. VI, p. 155.
[60] Jeremy Collier, *The Office of the Chaplain* (1688), pp. 5, 15, 13.

commanded children because their office gave them this bounden duty and they did so in the interests of the children. Monarchs commanded their people in the public interest because of an analogous responsibility. Because claimed offices were simultaneously centres of responsibility and spheres of liberty for their *personae*, all offices could be discussed purely through questions of liberty and its transgression into wrongdoing.[61]

The confusion of this general feature of all office claims with later more specific and oppositional doctrines has encouraged the projection of liberalism back into the seventeenth century, either to provide a family tree, or as an easy surrogate for attacking genuine liberals who have flourished since.[62] It is true that reference to liberty being so widespread, some of its casual uses sound superficially familiar. Andrew Willett referred to Josephus taking liberties with the Bible and of David's people being tired of kings and seeking liberty.[63] Later in the century, Roger L'Estrange, rather untypically, asserted that if the people cannot rule they want liberty. It is a use suggestive of Sidney's sustained conception of liberty as freedom from the domination of another.[64]

Indeed, when isolated from tacit reference to office, a wide range of statements about liberty can sound like expressions of positive or of negative liberty. Since their clear articulation during the eighteenth century, we have come to take these to be either opposing or complementary concepts of liberty, even if they are not, as Gerald McCallum argued, mutually dependent.[65] To put the matter briefly, negative liberty is taken to be the liberty of non-interference and private endeavour; it is enough

---

[61] Sharp, 'Rules of Conduct for Ourselves', in *Works*, vol. I, pp. 175, 179–97.
[62] See, for example, Sullivan, *Machiavelli, Hobbes, and the Formation of a Liberal Republicanism*, pp. 2–27, citing much in the same vein; William Lund, 'Neither *Behemoth* nor *Leviathan*: Explaining Hobbes's Illiberal Politics', *Filozofski Vestnik*, 24, 2 (2003), pp. 59–83; on Hobbes's rejection of liberalism, p. 61 and failure to be as liberal as he should have been, as we are, p. 83. Instructively, David Armitage refers to liberalism in the seventeenth century as an admitted anachronism and an almost inescapable term of art; see 'John Locke, Carolina and the Two Treatises of Government', *Political Theory*, 32, 5 (2004), p. 1, n.
[63] Willet, *Harmonie on the First Booke of Samuel*, p. 93; *An Harmonie on the Second Booke of Samuel* (1614), p. 117; Hammond, *Vindication* (1650), p. 26 on assuming the liberty to misuse language.
[64] Roger L'Estrange, *A Memento* (1682), p. 72; Algernon Sidney, *Discourses Concerning Government* (1681–3?, 1698), ed. Thomas G. West (Indianapolis, 1996), ch. 3, sect. 33, p. 510; or see Hyde (Lord Clarendon), 'Liberty' (1670), in *Essays*, vol. I, p. 144, where true liberty is being able to do whatever the laws allow, but he had already insisted that no one doubts that liberty involves obligations, p. 143.
[65] Isaiah Berlin, 'Negative and Positive Liberty', in *Four Essays on Liberty* (Oxford, 1969); Charles Taylor, 'What's Wrong with Negative Liberty', in *Philosophy and the Human Sciences* (Cambridge, 1985); Philip Pettit, *Republicanism, A Theory of Freedom and Government* (Oxford, 1997); Gerald C. MacCullum Jr, 'Positive and Negative Freedom', *Philosophical Review*, 76 (1967), pp. 314–19.

that it is possessed formally to enable action and it is commonly held to be the liberty of liberalism. The so-called liberal or 'night-watchman' state, has its rationale in maximising this form of liberty. Positive liberty, associated by Berlin with forms of collectivism, has more recently been attached to republicanism or public involvement, and is the liberty of autonomy, self-fulfilment – in Philip Pettit's salient term, non-domination. It provides a focus on the conditions that enable a meaningful exercise of private, negative liberty.[66]

The plausibility of this oppositional conceptualisation has depended largely upon a fairly robust distinction between a public and private sphere; but just as early-modern uses of public and private are largely at odds with such a distinction, so usage of the word liberty gives flimsy support for any awareness of its positive and negative formulations. There was certainly no scope for liberty to be treated in the libertarian fashion as an end in itself, and a value to trump others. And, despite the shared emphasis on exercise as opposed to mere possession, neither was liberty of office a positive liberty in the modern sense, for it was not about personal autonomy or self-fulfilment. Because it was an assertion of the necessary latitude of action for a *persona* acting in responsibility to something else, it was a right ever teetering on the cusp of duty and subordination. Indeed, it often expressed the meta-duty of the *persona*'s responsibility to the integrity of the office itself. The Stuart insistence on prerogative, Noy's on the liberty of parliament, Collier's on his freedom as a chaplain, are therefore of a piece. The palpable emphasis on vigilance has recently suggested a notion of republican liberty as a conceptual refinement of positive liberty, but this too is historically unhelpful. Republican liberty may better be seen as an emphatic employment of liberty of office and hardly the exclusive privilege of republicans. Recognising this, Quentin Skinner has come to prefer the expression neo-Roman liberty to capture something to one side of positive, negative or republican liberty, namely, the condition of being free.[67] The problem inherent in all these formulations is that they arise from trying to isolate an ideological grouping from the more widespread evidence of a register of office, while the condition of being free does not seem to be a further type of liberty which some might or might not relish, but the security of any office against invasion or curtailment.

As I have illustrated in chapter 3, freedom was very much an accretion of *personae*. If one takes a negative understanding of freedom back to the

---

[66] See also Quentin Skinner, *Liberty Before Liberalism* (Cambridge, 1998); Taylor, 'What's Wrong with Negative Liberty', at length.
[67] Skinner, *Liberty Before Liberalism*, pp. 1–22.

seventeenth century, the liberty of citizenship seems anything but free.[68] Given some anachronistic presuppositions, freedom as being capable of office will certainly sound peculiar; and a life 'unweighed by liberty' oxymoronic or anticipatory of Eric Fromm.[69] As an accoutrement of duty, however, liberty could be the exercise of authority. Such usage can approach, and in discussions of the soul we will see that it can attain, the paradigmatic unity of freedom and authority. It is difficult for us to make literal sense of this sort of configuration of vocabulary, especially since David Hume made such organisational capital out of an opposition between freedom and authority in conceptualising Civil War hostilities. The unending quest for a proper balance between their claims, and the parties attached to each, has been a staple of historiographical analysis, surviving deep into the twentieth century;[70] and it has obscured how people actually used words like freedom and authority, when the freedom was a liberty of office and the authority was derived only from office. The words liberty and freedom can be seen to function, then, rather like justice, or humility, as the formal properties of any office, their content being dependent upon the office itself. It is little wonder that later notions can be read into the vocabulary if first the context of argument about office is ignored.

Once restored, however, what becomes central to liberty is not the adherence to one concept rather than another, let alone in opposition to authority, but a dichotomous relationship with licence and slavery, terms which have their place in the negative register of office talk. Licence was the untrammelled action of the libertine or tyrant. It was immoral or luxurious because it was a movement beyond the sanctioned authority of an office. It was, in a word, the disruptive residuum of action beyond liberty, the formal property of office-abuse.[71] I will say more about this register below, but immediately it can be noted that licence loomed large in attempts to constrain the notion of liberty to an attribute of office, or to challenge liberty claims made from the authority of an office. As Henry IV accuses his son, 'Harry from curb'd licence plucks/ The muzzle of

---

[68] Powell, *Puritan Village*, p. 44; Wilmore Kendall, 'How to Read Milton's *Areopagitica*', *Journal of Politics*, 22 (1966), pp. 439–73.
[69] Howard, *A Publication*, pp. 30–1, quoted in Peltonen, *The Duel*, p. 110.
[70] See, for example, Gerald R. Cragg, *Freedom and Authority: A Study of English Thought in the Early Seventeenth Century* (Philadelphia, 1975), throughout.
[71] Condren, 'Liberty of Office', pp. 467–71; Hammond, *Vindication*, on 'an age of licentiousness', p. 3; a subordinate meaning, now predominant, was 'licence' as a specific permission, e.g. Sir Edward Hoby, *A Curry-Combe for a Cox-Combe* (1615), p. 119; before Hobbes, on whom see below, only occasionally, and casually do we find liberty implicitly at odds with office and elided with licence: for example, Shakespeare, *Measure for Measure*, cf. 1.3 and 2.4. The usage is appropriate to there being a state of licentiousness in the city and a failure of ruling office.

restraint, and the wild dog/ Shall flesh his tooth on every innocent.'[72] In polemic, the distinction is often presented as trouble-free; but sometimes its trickiness is acknowledged. To use the word liberty for sin, wrote John Sharp, conventionally enough, was contradictory; the problem was that there was little latitude between the two.[73] Within a few pages Sharp's liberty has itself become a duty. And it was sometimes noted that the distinction between liberty and licence could involve self-serving justification. The 'ding-dong' about that equivocal term liberty, as *The Parallel* had it, might mean nothing more than licence to rebel.[74] In subverting the disruptive potential of the familiar appeals to endangered liberty, Hobbes had ingeniously undermined any distinction between liberty and licence. The proper, literal signification of liberty was extended so far that licence lost its meaning. It was directly parallel to his insistence that there was no such governmental form as tyranny.

Slavery, in common parlance, was inimical to liberty and was the consequence of tyranny. In a literal sense slavery was familiar enough, but in polemic it is largely an inflated anguish about office-abuse, and the word took on a rather special pattern of meaning in relation to tyranny, the ultimate perversion of office.[75] Milton expressed an almost tautological commonplace of liberty of office when he wrote, in *The Second Defence*, that 'it has been arranged by nature that he who attacks the liberty of others is the first of all to lose his own liberty'; in tyrannically reducing others to slavery, 'he is the first of all to become a slave'.[76] This is much more than a paradoxical consequence. It was entailed by the linguistic relationships Milton was spelling out. The attack on the liberty of others is licence: licence is the action of the tyrant, a slave to unrestrained passion. By our standards this begins to sound a trifle convoluted and removed from the experience of the galley and the cane field; and it suggests that Benjamin Constant was right in intuiting a conceptual sea-change in what he called the 'modern' concept of liberty.[77] His history may have been askew, but he pointed to a contracting sense of office which, like the ebbing tide left exposed an increasing strand of activities,

---

[72] Shakespeare, *2Henry IV* 4.5.
[73] Sharp, 'Rules of Conduct for Ourselves' (1690), in *Works*, vol. I, pp. 175–80.
[74] Anon., *The Parallel* (1682), pp. 21–2; Clarendon, 'Liberty', pp. 142–4, 147.
[75] Hutchinson, *Memoirs*, pp. 293–4: everyone under Cromwell was a slave; on the widespread rhetorics of slavery, see, for example, Quentin Skinner, 'Classical Liberty, Renaissance Translation and the English Civil War', in *Visions of Politics*, vol. II, pp. 308–43.
[76] John Milton, *The Second Defence of the English People* (1654), in *Complete Prose Works* (New Haven, 1954), vol. IV, p. 673.
[77] Benjamin Constant, *Ancient and Modern Liberty* (1838), in *Political Writings*, ed. Biancamaria Fontana (Cambridge, 1988).

flotsam and jetsam, demanding, like Greta Garbo, to be left alone from the responsibilities of office.

It was on this shifting strand of the sea that from the later eighteenth century, a new line was gradually drawn between public and private. These have become complementary domains of legitimate human endeavour; a public sphere and a civil society, with a type of liberty appropriate to each in a way not possible all the time, the discourse of office was a liquid empire colonising the totality of human activity. To designate people of the early-modern world liberals, adhering to something called liberalism, is not just a matter of the technical seeding of isolated alien terms, something to be neutralised by some ad hoc definitional care; we have to implant an awful lot of the modern world into the sixteenth and seventeenth centuries to see liberalism flourishing that long ago. Hardly surprisingly, there was no word for it. We have a compound instance of Caputo's invention by analytic elucidation.[78] In crafting firm distinctions between public, private, negative and positive liberty, liberal and non-liberal, freedom and authority we create the categories by clarification. This may all be conceptually worthwhile for the ahistorical theorist, and my point is not to praise seventeenth-century usage; but when Swift wrote of himself that 'Fair liberty was all his cry', the one thing he was not doing was 'pilfering . . . liberal clothes'.[79] It seems that for Porter Tories could not be enlightened, and as Swift was a Tory he could only be a fake liberal. Curious as such specimens of judgement are, they are also historically irrelevant. Swift was, rather, laying claim to a traditional liberty of office that belonged as much to the ruler shuffling off restrictions as to the citizen resisting slavery. It was loose enough clothing to fit even the unenlightened baby-eating Dean.

IV

Because offices existed in mutually delineating relationships, they could ignite in the frictions that provoked the rhetorics of liberty. Claims on any office could be contentious, hierarchies of office unstable; their dynamics were part of a disputatious world. So the language of office had a negative dimension, and having touched on the terms slavery and licence, it is now necessary to outline it more fully. No more than liberty, or authority, was this accusative aspect of office the property of any one political group. More or less fully available to any putative office-holder, its use was a

---

[78] Caputo, *On Religion*, p. 46; Sullivan, *Machiavelli, Hobbes*, and Lund, 'Neither *Behemoth* nor *Leviathan*', are recent examples.
[79] Porter, *Enlightenment Britain*, p. 33.

response to perceived dangers coming from those resisting the authority of office, be they fellows, superiors or subordinates. It was as necessary to have a battery of accusatory terms as it was to have an armoury of justification. In addition to words like slavery and licence were domination and tyranny, oppression, arbitrary rule, force, neglect, alienation, anarchy, luxury, corruption, revolt, rebellion.

Anyone who comes to political argument is at once constrained and given opportunities by the established resources of language. To use them is almost invariably to counter alternative patterns of judgement and in this process the language is gradually altered, but retaining exploitable traces of earlier states of affairs. In the sixteenth and seventeenth centuries, the complementary registers of office afforded enormous latitude for moral redescription and there were a number of means to this deceptively simple end of presenting one case at the expense of another. Without semantic change, the force of a position might be inverted most obviously by the use of litotes. 'For Brutus is an honourable man; they so are they all, all honourable men'. A position might be subjected to diminishing or derisory comparison, *tapinosis*, such as when Hobbes compared priests with fairies.[80] Although these tropes have redescriptive force, more explicit redescription existed alongside them.[81] Unlike them, however, it was a necessary feature of language, a consequence of the fact that anything that can be classified can be reclassified. Hence anything that can be described can be redescribed. There is, as the ancient sceptics emphasised, no unchallengeable description.

It is possible to make a rough distinction between the following mechanisms of redescription. First, there was the simple act of repredicating a shared common term. The quality of mercy might be deemed a 'lazy passion'.[82] Sometimes repredication took the form of what Chaim Perelman has called the disassociation of ideas. This was a process of co-optive or distributive employment of vocabulary, where a predominant description is at once accepted and subverted in an attempt to replace its associations.[83] Hence expressions such as 'true liberty' or 'so called rebellion', or 'miserably misled Commonwealth's-men (falsely so called)'.[84] Second, an expression, negative or positive, might be 'softened' by a more general

---

[80] Hobbes, *Leviathan*, ch. 46.
[81] Quentin Skinner, *Reason and Rhetoric in the Philosophy of Hobbes* (Cambridge, 1996), at length.
[82] Thomas Walter, *The Excommunicated Prince* (1679), 5.5.3.
[83] Chaim Perelman, *The New Rhetoric and the Humanities: Essays on Rhetoric and its Applications* (Dordrecht, 1979), pp. 23–4; Condren, *The Language of Politics*, pp. 76–9.
[84] Christopher Harvey, *Faction Supplanted* (1663), sects. 2, 7; Anon., *A worthy Panegyrick upon Monarchy* (1658?, 1680); on rebellion see also Sidney, *Discourses*, ch. 3. sect. 36, p. 519.

descriptor that lacked the emotional force of the specific. Parliamentary office could be a 'softer word' for a pension.[85] According to Burnet, persecution was softened by the more encompassing 'prosecution', 'obstinacy' by 'firmness'.[86] Conversely, a general description might be replaced (hardened) by something more pointed; protest could be called riot, remonstrance, rebellion. Third, there was recourse to rhetorical antonymity: the interchange of words in direct opposition to each other. It was a practice that helped sustain the binary nature of much political vocabulary, providing a ready source of redescriptive defence or attack, as the case may be. Power could become force, prerogative deemed arbitrary rule, sloth and cowardice converted into meekness and peaceableness, liberty called licence. As John Hall put it, such words got bounced like so many 'tennis balls' across a court.[87] Hobbes pointed to this feature of discourse by insisting that tyranny was but monarchy misliked; anarchy disliked democracy. He might as easily have said that licence was liberty misliked; anarchy after all was a byword for licentiousness. Clumsy conjurors, he remarked, 'call up spirits, as they cannot at their pleasure allay again . . . Unskillful divines do oftentimes the like; for when they call unreasonably for *zeal*, there appears a spirit of *cruelty* . . . instead of *reformation, tumult*'.[88] Each of these three redescriptive tactics can be seen in the question of what to call what we now neutrally refer to as the Civil Wars, such as revolution, dissolution, rebellion or troubles. Fourth was the use of dramatic metaphorical and allegorical transformations that might accentuate or invert a prior description. David Norbrook's discussion of May's translation and continuation of Lucan's *Pharsalia* offers clear evidence of this, as well as the importance of the terms used to designate the warfare in mid-seventeenth-century Britain. May treated Roman civil war as an allegory, and in doing so transformed what some called a rebellion of subjects into a combat between citizens.[89]

Not all substitutions were redescriptions. Reliance on synecdoche or metonymy could serve to sustain focus. Yet the ways in which perspectives could be altered were easily combined, and thus redescription as a broad process was always a matter of degree, from nuanced qualification and insinuation to allegorical recasting and metaphorical transformation. Because of classificatory contingency, some process of redescription in argument is a condition for us being able to identify anything as political in the

---

[85] Hutchinson, *Memoirs*, p. 63; Anon., *The Certain Way to Serve England* (1681), p. 15.
[86] Burnet, *History*, vol. I, pp. 337, 472.
[87] John Hall, *Of Government and Obedience* (1654), p. 125.
[88] Thomas Hobbes, *The Answer to the Preface Before Gondibert* (1651), in *The English Works of Thomas Hobbes*, ed. Sir William Molesworth (1845), vol. IV, p. 448.
[89] Norbrook, *Writing the English Republic*, chs. 1, 4.

first place, for the predicate political privileges a certain sort of description through an established vocabulary of political terms. But a necessary process could always threaten instability.

With the full array of redescriptive mechanisms in mind, it is possible to identify two principal types of redescription. With one, there is a sufficiently shared tacit understanding of the world for an appeal to the facts, or truth to be used as standards for measuring linguistic ingenuity. Under such circumstances redescription can be controlled, neutralised as poetic amplification, or revealed as a form of misdescription. Hence a principle of decorum could operate as a criterion for language use. It was partially against a background of sensitivity to *paradiastole* and its consequences that one should place the seventeenth-century attempts to establish a universal language, the development of dictionaries to control the meanings of new and difficult words, the heated objections to alien terms, and the attempts associated with the Royal Society to tie words univocally to simple reference functions.[90] The reform of language as a barrier to redescription and the creation of detailed natural histories of the empirical world were related enterprises. The insistence that people should call things by their proper names remains familiar from the seventeenth century to George Orwell. The notions of euphemism and dysphemism are now used to pinpoint dubious deviance from proper use.

There is, however, also a more radical form of redescription where an assumed court of appeal beyond language is unreliable, so rendering contentious any asserted deviation from the acceptable. The possibility had been recognised since antiquity.[91] Aristotle had tried to stabilise moral terms by locating them between extremes – so generosity lay between profligacy and meanness, honesty between exaggeration and understatement. Hobbes regarded this procedure as part of the problem, because it opened a two-dimensional latitude for disputed descriptions, and what had to be effected was a binary, and somewhat Ramist collapse into proper use and misuse – a computer-speak of morality.[92]

I am suggesting here that the problem of moral redescription was recognised as serious because its first form could not be insulated from the second. The opposing registers of office guaranteed the possibility of moral transfiguration, especially in a world in which everything could be taken as a sign for something else. The result was an alarming credence to the claims that the accomplished rhetor could make and re-make the social

---

[90] Barbara Shapiro, *John Wilkins, 1614–1672: An Intellectual Biography* (Los Angeles, 1969), pp. 207–23.
[91] Plato, *Republic*, 561A.
[92] Skinner, *Reason and Rhetoric*, pp. 172–80; 294ff.

world, like a god, or indeed like a devil. This fear helps explain why writers like Hobbes wanted the language purged of words like tyranny. The transformative powers of rhetoric could be like 'the witchcraft of Medea'; the spells cast with them could call up storms of ruin.[93] Roger L'Estrange made the point later in a hyperbolic redescription of the language of nonconformists like Baxter. They *'have a certain* Routin *of* Words and Sayings, *that have the tone of* Magique *in the very sound of them and serve only* (*without any other* Meaning) *like the Drum and the* Trumpet *to rouse up* the Multitude *to* Battle'.[94] These dangers, however, were endemic to the language of office, and all office-holders had an interest in keeping it that way — not least the pot L'Estrange calling the nonconformist kettle black, and the philosopher Hobbes eloquently attacking the philosophies of Mr White: the negative register of office was defence against erosion of the positive. They were bi-conditional and herein lies the full implication of Milton's point about the necessity of sin for a conception of virtue. It was this that Hobbes's draconian solutions to the vocabulary failed to overcome; indeed they seem to illustrate the status quo of contested language use and even to have exacerbated it.

As the occasional recourse to the figures of magic suggests, the extreme of redescriptive hostility relied upon the semiotics of the supernatural. When subjected to Cotta's 'prudent ghesse', all visible signs, acts, performances and coincidental happenings could be transmogrified into an antithetical projection of one's proper relationship with God and one's neighbours, Hell populated 'with Ghosts and spiritual Officers'.[95] As a corollary, the projection of the demonic world easily became entangled with images of religious malefaction, for these too were wayward understandings of the relationship to God. James VI&I argued that the weak in faith were Satan's victims and popish gullibility and useless rites of exorcism the reason for there being so many witches.[96] Over a hundred years later, Defoe was able to evoke a similar ambience of cosmic evil, describing those who 'draw *the Draught* of Arbitrary Power' as 'Infernal States-Men' from 'the Depths of Satan's Kingdom'.[97] Monstrous projections tell us much about the proper order of things, the extremes to which people will go to rid themselves of conjectured evil and shore up conceptions of

---

[93] Hobbes, *Elements*, 2, ch. 9.15, p. 178; *Answer*, p. 448.
[94] Roger L'Estrange, *The Casuist Uncas'd in a Dialogue with Richard Baxter* (1681), Preface, n.p.
[95] Hobbes, *Leviathan*, ch. 12, p. 79; the reference is to pagan religions.
[96] James VI&I, *Daemonologie* (1597), in *Workes*, pp. 119–21.
[97] Daniel Defoe, *Jure Divino* (1706), 6.2, 7.14; see D.N. De Luna, '*Jure Divino*: Defoe's "volume in a Folio by Way of Answer to and Confutation of *Clarendon's* History of the Rebellion"', *Philological Quarterly*, 75 (1996), p. 50.

the good; but they do not necessarily evidence the independent identity of the monsters themselves.[98] Whether they are polemically shaped by hostile redescription, or whether they are actually created by the magic of an inverted world of official probity, can be a moot point. We no longer believe in witches, but some say there be Antinomians and Ranters at the bottom of the seventeenth century.[99]

When Lawson expostulated that Hobbes deserved to be a slave, it was partly in objection to Hobbes's argument that the word tyranny is redundant.[100] For Lawson, conventionally enough, slavery was by definition what tyranny created. Without the language of office-abuse the world was safe for the abusers of office; because their behaviour could not adequately be described, they could not be brought to book. Hobbes, in short, deserved to swim in his own medicine. The issue between them went beyond political forms to the vocabulary of office, to whether words had a reference function sufficient for there to be an appeal in language to realities, so providing a criterion for judging the decorum of redescription; or, whether the sense of reality is created by the language available. The insecurity of any distinction between ontology and epistemology made such matters very difficult to clarify; and Hobbes, formally adhering to the first possibility, seemed to want to purge language on the basis of the second, a remarkable three-card trick.

Just how far the vocabulary of office was subject to destabilising redescription can be seen by William Cornwallis's earlier dangerous experiment in paradox. He took Richard III, the exemplary abuser of kingly office, and then set out less to deny the facts of the case against him than to re-describe his rule through what I am calling the positive register of office. Negative predicates are discounted, 'softer' generalities drained of critical force replace specific accusations, and favourable terms bustle in for hostile antonyms. The tyrant becomes the wise and politic ruler. Cornwallis's paradox was a Gorgian exercise in rhetorical dexterity, a latter-day proof that Helen never went to Troy on the evidence of *The*

---

[98] See, for example, Ian Maclean, 'La doctrine de la preuve dans les procès intentés contre les sorciers en Lorraine et en Franche-Comté autour de 1600', in J.-P. Pittion, ed. *Droit et justice à la Renaissance* (Tours, forthcoming); Peter Burke, *Popular Culture in Early Modern Europe* (London, 1978), pp. 185–91; Peter Lake, 'Deeds Against Nature: Cheap Print, Protestantism and Murder in Early Seventeenth Century England', in Kevin Sharpe and Peter Lake, eds., *Culture and Politics in Early Stuart England* (Basingstoke, 1994), pp. 268–9, 274.

[99] Cooper, *Fear and Polemic*; J. C. Davis, *Fear, Myth and History: The Ranters and the Historians* (Cambridge, 1986). Some awareness of invention by conceptual projection of fear was to be found before modern psychology on which Cooper and Davis draw: see Michael Wilks, *The Problem of Sovereignty in the Later Middle Ages* (Cambridge, 1963), on Augustinus Triumphus' image of a heretical pope, pp. 502–3.

[100] Lawson, *An Examination*, p. 37.

Iliad. It was like trying to prove that syphilis is good for you, which he did.¹⁰¹ Nothing, however, will better illustrate the redescriptive resourcefulness of the vocabulary of contested office than the issue of rebellion (chapter 9).

V

The whole vocabulary of office ensured both that a *persona* in office was contingent and often fragile; and that relationships between offices were crucial to the stability of all of them. These points can be illustrated by concluding with comments on the doctrine of the king's two bodies. It required both an awareness of relational identity, and of its Richardian negation in tyranny; what it was never able to do was to ensure that the *persona* of the monarch was absolute and beyond transforming redescription.

Ernst Kantorowicz produced the major study of the king's two bodies, but his account is misleading if the doctrine is isolated from the world of presuppositions and language use in which it was forged. As Kantorowicz argued, during the late Middle Ages, kingship was seen through a christological metaphor of unchanging divinity expressed in mutable form. Any king was thus conceived as having two natures: the *persona* of office and the body inhabiting it.¹⁰² But if this was so of a king because it was so of Christ, it was so of Christ because the vocabulary of office provided a perspective for understanding divinity (I shall return to such circularity in chapters 6 and 10). This doctrinal specification of kingship was not unique to England, but flourished there because monarchy was perceived to be insecure, its difficulties widely advertised in a discordant chronicle tradition relating with relish kingly failure.¹⁰³

It is, then, not surprising that a doctrine of the king's two bodies expressed the need for continuity of rule, and the potential expendability of the ruler.¹⁰⁴ Neither is it odd that James VI&I's considered theories of kingship were printed when continuity was indeed an issue against a backdrop of instability. In the *Basilikon Doron*, written for his first son, the picture of ruling was a miniature of the imperative of continuity of office organised in terms of three patterns of relational responsibility: the

---

[101] Sir William Cornwallis, Folger MS V.a.132; 'Richard III' in *Essays of Certain Paradoxes* (1616); 'In Praise of the Pocks', in *Essays*.
[102] Kantorowicz, *The King's Two Bodies*, at length.
[103] A point seized upon first, I think, by Ponet, *A Shorte Treatise*, pp. 100ff; see also Greenberg, *The Radical Face*, pp. 206–42; Conrad Russell, *The Causes of the English Civil War* (Oxford, 1990), pp. 134–5, 156–60.
[104] Russell, *The Causes*, pp. 158–60.

Christian calling, the duty to rule and the king's behaviour towards anything not strictly determined by his office.[105] But a pious hope for kingly continuity was only one use to which a doctrine of official identity was put. Parliament's *Apology* of 1604 can be seen in the same context of office redefinition. It, too, re-asserted an abstract identity independent of its changing membership. It was a conceptual and material body, a 'Sovereign Court', whose 'care' is the maintenance of the bonds between king and subjects and making with the king 'one body politic'.[106] The vocabulary allowed an almost infinite multiplicity of duplex bodies. The crucial issue, then, was the relationship between offices under the aegis of which people could give voice. Only God is not dependent upon relationships, as Browne later put it, 'for only he is, all others have an existence with dependency, and are something but by a distinction'.[107]

If official identity was forged in reciprocity, the common understanding was also that occupation of office superadded something special to the office-holder; many held that in becoming a priest a man was mystically transformed. For Catholics, a priest became infallible when made a pope. In this unity with *persona* lay the effectiveness of the office. Identity could thus always be claimed nominally to be specific to office, referring only to bodies considered as *personae*. By the seventeenth century the habits of doing so were ingrained, as was the formulation of Baldus de Ubaldus (1327–1400): an official *persona* was an identity comprehended by the intellect but conceptually separable from its active, physical agent; *dignitas* and substance were different.[108] Notions of relational identity in office created the *personae* that in logic and in apologetics had long provided the currency of ethical discourse.[109] The king, or shepherd, was the image of God in executing his office, stated John of Salisbury, but in abusing it he became the image of the Devil.[110] This principle applied to any office,

---

[105] James VI&I, *Basilicon Doron*, pp. 150, 155, 180ff.
[106] *Form of Apology and Satisfaction* (1604), in J. R. Tanner, *Constitutional Documents of the Reign of James I, 1603–1625* (Cambridge, 1961 edn), pp. 224, 230.
[107] Browne, *Religio Medici*, p. 92; see also, for example, John Pym: only God '*subsists by himselfe*, all other things *subsist* in a *mutual dependence and relation*', *The Speech or Declaration of John Pym* (1641), in Malcolm, ed., *The Struggle for Sovereignty*, vol. I, p. 131; Ste B., *Counsel to the Husband, to the Wife Instruction* (1608), p. 40, on the 'reciprocally related' societies that form a family.
[108] J. P. Canning, 'Law, Sovereignty and Corporation Theory, 1300–1450', in J. H. Burns, ed., *The Cambridge History of Medieval Political Thought, c.350–c.1450* (Cambridge, 1988), pp. 474–5.
[109] They also lie behind Paul Ricoeur's analysis of the philosophical concept of moral identity; see *Oneself as Another*, trans. Kathleen Blamey (Chicago, 1992), pp. 1–26, 169–239.
[110] John of Salisbury, *Policraticus*, ed. and trans. Cary J. Nederman (Cambridge, 1990), 7.17, pp. 163, 202; see also C. H. McIlwain, *The Growth of Political Thought in the West* (New York, 1932), on the *Tractatus Eboracenses*, pp. 211ff.

including the priesthood. The offices of pope and monarch were powerful analogues. The misuse of papal power could be seen as self-deposition. Lewis of Bavaria drew on the same sort of proposition when formally deposing Pope John XXII at Pisa in 1328; the pope had already deposed himself by misconduct.[111] The *Leges Edwardi Confessoris* illustrates what was by the sixteenth century an entirely conventional sort of statement.[112] A king who did not uphold law and religion lost the name of king. It was a name that could easily be held to be meaningless in anything approaching a natural condition. 'When the sea is. Hence! What cares these roarers for the name of king?' Prospero would shortly reflect on precisely this nominal contingency of office. He grew a stranger to his government, lost his office to his brother, who 'new created creatures that were mine . . ./. . . having both the key/ Of officer, and office, set all hearts I' th' state/ To what tune pleased his ear'.[113]

Applied to any office, a doctrine of moral *persona* in office required recognition of no more than a conceptual distinction between the *dignitas* of the official and the fact of the physical body; to collapse them into one created the notion of a quasi-divine figure, a local image of papal *plenitudo potestatis* and divine succession. Although it could never literally be sustained under all circumstances, it was clearly valuable to be able to make this move when conduct in office needed defending; it was a barrier against deployment of its accusative register. Conversely, a separation of *persona* from corporeal person isolated office-holder as mortal and merely human, even 'private', and allowed the person to be attacked or deposed and given a different (im)moral identity while according the office formal respect and allegiance. This was a casuistical move of decided value in a world of potent monarchs. In either case, the defining relationships between the office of kingship and any others were dramatically changed. The problems of separating, or conceptually distinguishing, man from office would be a constant for the troubled Stuart dynasty. We have what might be styled a unity and a separation variant arising from acceptance of nominal identity and expressed in a pattern of shared propositions between which people could shift, depending on circumstances.

During the Civil Wars, the difficulties of sustaining Baldus's precarious formulation between unity and separation became spectacularly apparent. Some distinction between man and office carried superficial advantages

---

[111] Durandus de Sancto Porciano, *De iurisdictione ecclesiastica* (Paris, 1506), fols. 1–8 unpaginated, cited in Wilks, *The Problem of Sovereignty*, p. 224; Augustinus Triumphus, *Summa*, 5.1, p. 50; 67.1. ad 3, p. 353, quoted in Wilks, *The Problem of Sovereignty*, pp. 502, 516.
[112] Greenberg, *The Radical Face*, at length.
[113] Shakespeare, *The Tempest* 1.1; 1.2.

for the motley gathering of royalist supporters. Many were wedded to his cause despite his policies and behaviour, their concern being for his office and the rule of law.[114] Conversely, parliament lacked a focus for personal loyalty and so had perhaps a greater incentive to reify allegiance to offices, initially if awkwardly to the office of kingship itself.[115] Predictably, this backfired when parliament was in turn accused of office-abuse. With splendid polemical sweep, Richard Overton rubbed the parliamentary nose in its own doctrines of office: sovereign authority was separate from the gathering of men who sat in Westminster, for official and personal capacity differ. If war against the king was not war against the office, but a man in relationship with the kingdom, so too this 'very Axeltree' of opposition to Charles is a *'principle'* against the men in parliament now. It allows 'defensive opposition' to their arbitrary and unjust commands.[116] Such interested exploitations of long-shared *topoi* saw a period of particularly intense conceptual confusion, splendidly summed up by Lawson in 1660:

This gave occasion of curious distinctions. For, men did distinguish between Charles Stuart and the King, between his regal and his personal capacity: and on the other side, between Parliament and a party in the Parliament, though the whole Parliament did commission and arm. Thus they found a difference between the King and himself, and the Parliament and itself. These distinctions were not altogether false: yet though Charles Stuart and the King, and so Parliament, and a party in the Parliament, might be distinguished, yet they could not be separated. And woe unto the people that is brought into such straights and perplexities. For if they kill Charles Stuart, they kill the King; and if the King destroy that party in the Parliament, he destroys the Parliament.[117]

Lawson's response was not to reject the curious distinctions, but in taking their formulation to a higher level of abstraction to extend them and offer protocols for the use of the vocabulary of office across society as a whole. All political beings existed in multiple relationships of office and so were to be understood as complementary *personae*. To have a political society is to have an order of subjection required by God. Thus subject and ruler

---

[114] See David L. Smith, *Constitutional Royalism and the Search for a Settlement, c.1640–1649* (Cambridge, 1994), e.g. ch. 7.

[115] See Russell, *The Causes*, ch. 6; Philip Hunton, *A Treatise of Monarchie* (1643); Henry Parker, *Some Few Observations upon his Majesties Late Answer* (1642), on whom see Michael Mendle, *Henry Parker and the English Civil War: The Political Thought of the Public's 'Privado'* (Cambridge, 1995), pp. 84–9, 90–110.

[116] Richard Overton, *An Appeale from the Degenerate Representative Body* (1647), in Don Wolfe, ed., *The Leveller Manifestoes* (London, 1967), pp. 174–5, 177–8.

[117] Lawson, *Politica*, 15.8, pp. 230–1; see also Anon., *A Letter of Spiritual Advice* (1643), on the enormity of separating the king from Charles Stuart; Edward Bagshawe, *The Rights of the Crown* (1660), p. 30, on the imperative of distinguishing without dividing.

were, as Charles I held, plainly different things: mutually defining relative terms, or nominals. But physical beings with a subject *persona* also existed simultaneously in a relationship of fellowship with each other. These beings had the *persona* of citizen with duties to each other and the community as distinct from the hierarchical polity. This communal identity in citizenship was also divinely sanctioned. There were not, then, just two bodies, the physical and the moral *persona* of office, but at least three: the physical and the duplex *personae* of social being. This was to elevate a notion of citizenship not just as conceptually independent of subjection but as partly constitutive of divinely sanctioned human offices. How much followed from this, however, was another matter. Knowing when citizenship or subjection took priority at any time was the way to minimise straights and perplexities by privileging the appropriate sphere of office and its terms of judgement. That was too much for any who saw the polity only as having ruler and ruled and the king's two bodies being inseparable.[118] Beyond that, however, Lawson saw that legislative moral theory had its limits; it was not always possible to say a priori which *persona* should take priority. Complicating the casuistic force of Lawson's case, however, there was a wider problem. The integrity of any office required its delineation from its neighbours, as well as from its underbelly of abuse; but the vocabulary had to be common to all claimed offices including those of citizen and ruler. As I shall now argue, given ingenuity there was little that could not be construed as some sort of office-generating *personae* each with the full *ornatus* of standing, yet subject to an extensive lexicon of reproof and contradiction. Lawson's straights and complexities were endemic to the world of offices, of which the king's two bodies were only an instance.

---

[118] Owen, *Herode and Pilate*; John Maxwell, *Sacro-sancta regnum majestas* (Oxford, 1644); Heylyn, *The Rebells Catechism*; Thomas Hobbes, *De cive* (Amsterdam, 1642, 1646), all illustrate the reduction of citizenship to subjection.

5 Offices of the intellect: player, poet and philosopher

> He is very severe in his supposed Office, and cries, *Woe to ye Scribes* right or wrong . . . He is a *Committee-Man* in the Commonwealth of Letters and as great a Tyrant.
>
> (Samuel Butler, *Characters*, 1667–9)

I

Early modern England exhibited grave suspicion of the protean; but with ethical argument centred on *personae*, the conditions were ideal for constructing the very mutability it feared. The following two chapters will cast light on this tension. The next will show how a presupposition of office was characteristic of accounts of that most immutable and defining inner essence of humanity, the soul. This concerns the rhetorics of office used to sanction socialised, outer identities. Together they should make more historical sense of the post-Renaissance fascination with human identity that has proved to be such a fruitful theme in modern literary studies.[1]

Moral autonomy was neither sought nor celebrated. In Protestant polemic, the denigrated priest is a shape-shifter and dissembler. 'Sometime I can be a monk in a long sad cowl;/Sometime I can be a nun and look like an owl.'[2] The myth of Jesuit transmogrification proved sturdy. Unlike the silly sheep, wrote Daniel Tuvill, near the start of the seventeenth century, man can fashion his voice in as many dialects as ambition demands. Only the honest man, wrote Joshua Barnes a hundred years later, was not a changeling.[3] Any suspicion of plasticity therefore, needed rationalisation.

---

[1] Greenblatt, *Renaissance Self-Fashioning*; Katherine Eisaman Mous, *Inwardness and Theater in the English Renaissance* (Chicago, 1980).

[2] John Bale, *King Johan*, cited in Stephen Greenblatt, *Hamlet in Purgatory* (Princeton, 2002), pp. 30–1; cf. Sir Thomas Overbury (?), 'Jesuit', *Sir Thomas Overbury, his Wife with Additions of More Characters* (1622), n.p.; Evelyn, *Diary*, vol. III, 2 December 1650, p. 23 on a preaching Jesuit as all things to all men.

[3] Daniel Tuvill, 'Of Reputation', fol. 116; Joshua Barnes, *The Good Old Way* (1703), p. 91; Richard Head, *Proteus Redivivus, or the art of Wheedling* (1684), at length.

It was done through the language of office; anything else equalled villainy. It was disputed claims of office that gave a family resemblance to the potentially unreliable identities of courtier, stage player, poet, rhetor and philosopher.

I have already discussed the aristocratic *persona*, noting that as the vocabulary of office could extend to the courtier, these identities might be merged. While both might draw inspiration from courtesy literature, however, the relationship was asymmetrical; courtiers were aristocrats, but aristocrats might shun court. Moreover, a large part of aristocratic identity stemmed from continuity of family name and stability of salient virtues. This was not so obvious for the courtier, and therein lay the opportunity to denude the figure of official standing. For, in contrast to the aristocrat, whose inflexibility, not least on points of honour, was itself a source of difficulty, the courtier was identified with a chameleon-like capacity for adaptation.

Castiglione's *Il Cortigiano* had a number of English printings from 1561, and by appropriating the terminology of office, tried to circumscribe the courtier's need for flexibility. As a modern translator has disapprovingly remarked, much of the work is boldly plagiarised from Cicero, Plato, Plutarch and Livy.[4] At the outset, the allusions to Cicero put the stamp of office upon the ideal: the courtier is not just a shape-shifter, a servant or advisor, but occupies an office to a ruler to entertain, advise and display style and virtue, which in itself enhances the standing of any prince. The courtly office, then, has great tolerance of movement and even dissimulation, but is cohered by a style of performance; hence the centrality of the exclusive virtue of *sprezzatura*, the wit and lightness with which the courtier responds in assuming a diversity of specific roles. Stressing different aspects of a composite identity could stabilise its responsibilities in different ways. Stephen Gosson, relying no less on the authorities of antiquity than Castiglione, isolated counselling as the principal courtly function. On the courtier lay the weight of responsibility for the commonwealth and for its burdens: learning, probity, liberality, justice and courtesy were essential. 'A. D. B.' attends more to the dangers of the courtly environment, justifying flexibility as an insurance against ruin,[5] but here too the line between courtier and counsellor becomes blurred. Markku Peltonen has argued that the adaptation of Castiglione's image to the early

---

[4] Baldesar Castiglione, *The Book of the Courtier* (1528), ed. and trans. George Bull (Harmondsworth, 1987 edn), p. 13.
[5] Stephen Gosson, *The Ephemerides of Philo divided into Three Bookes* (1586), fols. 27r–32v, 33v–36r, 39v; A. D. B., *The court of the . . . most magnificent James* (1619), pp. 60–1, 65–6, 97–9, quoted in Peltonen, *Classical Humanism*, p. 136.

seventeenth century could have been Tacitean.⁶ Court life in an uncertain world required sailing with the wind. But the Tacitean *topoi* of contingency, danger and corruption still operated within the terms of Castiglione's ambit of office and provide thin evidence for any emerging ideology. The Ciceronian and Tacitean alike remain bounded by affirmations of Christian virtue.⁷ Moreover, the formulised requirements of the civil conversation that theoretically lubricated court life had already developed an internal momentum to dissimulation independent of anything exclusively Tacitean. As Peltonen has more recently argued, the civil conversation was, as it were, the life-blood of the courtier, and it led rapidly to what looks like a cult of superficiality. This may do the conversational literature a disservice, for as a grammar of civility, its point was not to exhaust the content of social interaction. And although the result was the formulation of a ritualised shiftiness that made sincerity a solecism, its purpose was still to serve dexterity within office.⁸ Nevertheless, it would make the courtier a hostage to fortune.

For all his play with the vocabulary of Ciceronian office taken from Castiglione, Philibert de Vienne provided a satire of the courtly and its conversation that subverted its official standing, and Shakespeare may have taken a cue from this, for in Polonius we have something close to a personification of a useless mobility. Polonius is at once central and marginal to the action; attached to all in turn, he only gets in the way, and so dies behind the arras, a sort of absent presence. His advice to his son Laertes does little but specify the terms through which social movement was possible, a parody of Aristotelian definition by mean, most tellingly in his advice on the fixation with dress. 'Costly thy habit as thy purse can buy,/ But not expressed in fancy; rich not gaudy;/ For the apparel oft proclaims the man;/ And they in France of the best rank and station/ Are of a most select and generous choice in that.' Curiously, almost the only substantial advice, 'neither a borrower nor a lender be', would have been hopelessly impractical in a cash-strapped society functioning through reciprocal debt.⁹

More directly, in the book of characters attributed to Sir Thomas Overbury, the courtier is depicted as officeless and empty, a display of clothes that belong to another and who follows 'nothing but inconstancy'. For Samuel Butler, the courtier is a cypher, 'a moving Piece of Arras',

---

⁶ Peltonen, *Classical Humanism*, pp. 136–7.
⁷ Tuvill, *The Doue and the serpent*, p. 36.
⁸ Philibert de Vienne, *The Court Philosopher*, trans. G. North (1575), pp. 104–6; see Peltonen, *The Duel*, pp. 19–30, 146–63.
⁹ Shakespeare, *Hamlet* 1.3.

unfortunate in Polonius's case. He is nothing but the cut and flow of his clothing, for which he is probably in debt. The creation of his tailor, he exists only to be seen.[10] Similarly, according to Butler, the court wit is a mere monster of appearance. Here, then, is a parody of *Il Cortigiano*, with possible allusion to *Hamlet*, achieved by draining all vestige of office from the description of social pliancy.

Similar images of instability are found throughout the century, even in court masque: 'Courtiers there's no faith in you/ You change as often as you can'.[11] Predictably, the slight could be directed at any counsellor, or aristocrat in need of attack. 'Dexterity in doing ill' made men think Shaftesbury might do good, wrote one anonymous author. Another called his breath airy compliment. He is the sign of a man made only of clothes and cringes.[12] The courtier, then, could be the counsellor misliked. If for Stephen Gosson the office of counsel had given a justification for courtly plasticity, that office could be contaminated by the courtier's recidivistic shape-shifting. To this end, biblical *topoi* were employed to enhance the image of the mouth without authentic voice. At the beginning of the seventeenth century, Andrew Willett noted Achitophel's relationship with David as typological for Jesus and Judas and for modern times.[13] *Absalom's Conspiracy* (1680) provided a detailed narrative of Achitophel's treachery, easily read as allegory, once David was recognised to be Charles. These may have functioned as pre-texts for Dryden's poem in which the arch-villain, Achitophel/Shaftesbury is an essay in manipulative inconstancy. This simulacrum of satanic evil is also a backdrop to Halifax's *Character of a Trimmer*. Halifax, a prominent and controversial courtier, was accused of persistent vacillation; he too has a place in *Absalom and Achitophel*. His famous defence of trimming will be touched on in chapter 7 to illustrate the construction of country-love as a stabilising responsibility in its own right. It is enough here to anticipate by noting that courtly trimming was defensible only within the constraints of a postulated office.

The homologies between dress and discourse provided opportunities for diminishing the courtier that Butler found irresistible. The courtly concern with dress was, as we would say, fetishistic, a sign of empty words and officeless conduct. The courtier is only his tailor's cut and tailors have no

---

[10] Overbury (?), *Characters*, n.p.; Butler, *Characters*, pp. 69–70. 'I have undone three tailors', boasted Touchstone of his duelling: Shakespeare, *As You Like It* 5.4; Overbury, 'A Taylor', in *Characters*.
[11] Blow (?), *An Opera Performed before the King*, p. 2.
[12] Anon., *The Character of a Disbanded Courtier* (1681), p. 1; Anon., *The True Character of an upstart Courtier* (1682), p. 2.
[13] Willett, *Harmonie on the Second Booke of Samuel*, pp. 104–7.

office either, being unchristian and rejected by Christ.[14] Butler's account of the tailor, who came in with the Fall, sneers at Jews, Turks and Mahometans sitting cross-legged at their dubious work. They are the rhetors of the artisan world, creating an outward appearance to disguise a hidden reality. In this, the age-old associations of dress and words, the common homology between fustian clothes and fustian rhetoric, plain tongue and plain dress from a Quintilianesque metaphor for decorum, are all deftly exploited at the courtier's expense. Sumptuous or simple, dress was a sign pointing in opposite directions; if not a direct expression, it was a disguise, if not of truth, of dishonesty. So, for the hostile, the Quaker's parade of simple dress to symbolise modesty was a proof of hypocrisy.[15]

The insistence on a rationale for alteration is also used to assert the integrity of the actor who, according to Butler, unlike the courtier had a 'calling' and 'profession'.[16] There is good reason to consider the actor as having an *officium* because of the philological origin of *persona* from a theatrical mask; but the *persona* of an *officium* and the player's mask were not self-evidently fused in the early modern world. When the theatre was no longer a sanctioned part of religious performance and yet was increasingly prominent, the perceptible distance between mask-wearer and multiple guises raised questions about the player's status. The legitimacy of the theatre had been a formal topic of disputation in sixteenth-century universities, in which context questions of office, the consequences of poetic imagination and the appeal to the emotions provided a richly entangled opportunity for rhetorical skill.[17] Hamlet's advice to the players draws generally on the questionable place of the actor – a point of direct relevance to the competition between companies in the first years of the seventeenth century, and to controversies surrounding college-sponsored plays in Cambridge where *Hamlet* had early performances. The author of the words to be spoken has authority: 'Speak the speech, I pray you, as I pronounced it to you.' Yet the need for the actor to show flexibility is

---

[14] Butler, *Characters*, p. 174.
[15] Anon., *The Character of a Quaker* (c. 1679), ed. Merritt Y. Hughes, p. 2; cf. John Milton, *Eikonoklastes* (1650), in *Complete Prose Works* (New Haven, 1962), vol. III, pp. 361–2 on signs of piety as proof of hypocrisy in Richard III and Charles I.
[16] Butler, *Characters*, p. 300.
[17] Mack, *Elizabethan Rhetoric*, p. 64; John Rainolds, *Th'Overthrow of Stage-Playes* (1599), gives a sense of university disputation; Stephen Gosson, *Playes Confuted in Five Actions* (1582); Alvin B. Kernan, *The Playwright as Magician: Shakespeare's Image of the Poet in the English Public Theater* (New Haven, 1979), pp. 52–84, for an outline of the uncertain status of the player in the late sixteenth and early seventeenth centuries: the argument draws largely on G. E. Bentley, *The Profession of the Dramatist in Shakespeare's Time* (Princeton, 1971).

evident: 'let your own discretion be your tutor'. If this were all, there might be little difference between player and courtier, but the emphasis is upon eliciting the appropriate response in the audience to the matter at hand. The player, not unlike the priest, has a mediator's responsibility and all interpretative licence serves the theatre's 'end . . . [which] is to hold, as 'twere, the mirror up to nature; to show virtue her own feature'.[18] The play within the play, then, manifests the execution of a moral office to try the conscience of the king.[19] John Earle and Samuel Butler similarly pinpoint the need to craft an identity bounded by office. The result is a deliberately sustained sense of paradox. Like 'our painting gentlewoman', wrote Earle, 'seldom in his own face' or clothes, the more he counterfeits, the better he pleases.[20] For Butler, the player's wit, like his wardrobe, is second-hand. With both he shifts shapes like a witch, assuming 'a body like an apparition', but 'the less he appears himself, the truer he is to his profession – The more he deceives men, the greater right he does them; and the plainer his dealing is, the less credit he deserves': once more the homology of social and material identity. 'His profession is a kind of metamorphosis . . . like a tailors sheet of paper which he folds into figures.'[21] A different image also makes the contrast between the player and the courtier. Butler's 'moving Piece of Arras' is merely part of the 'Furniture of the Rooms, and serves for a walking Picture', whereas the player 'represents many excellent virtues', though knows no more of them 'than a picture does whom it resembles'.[22]

But if the courtier was the creature of his tailor, the actor's integrity lies in being the puppet of the poet, or, as Earle put it, using the language of office-abuse to paradoxical effect, 'the poet is his only tyrant'.[23] The interplay of overlapping patterns of metaphor for social conduct, clothes, bodies, words, furnishing and movement were all ways of expressing office or its absence. If players were to be attacked, office was overlooked; when defended, overworked. Stage plays are the instruments of the Devil, Gosson then Prynne insisted; actors have a vocation, retorted Baker.[24] They are not hypocrites, for there is an end to their activities. They have

---

[18] Shakespeare, *Hamlet* 3.2.
[19] For more extended comment, see Kernan, *The Playwright as Magician*, pp. 94–111.
[20] Earle, *Micro-cosmography, or a Piece of the World Discovered*.
[21] Butler, *Characters*, pp. 300–1.
[22] *Ibid*., pp. 69, 301.
[23] Earle, *Micro-cosmography*, 'A Player'.
[24] Gosson, *Playes Confuted*, B4r–v, C1; Prynne, *Histrio-mastix*, at length, but see Actus secundus, pp. 34–42 (Prynne uses Gosson's conceit of acts for chapters); Sir Richard Baker, *Theatrum Triumphans* (1670), p. 2; it was a long-standing perception that moralists tended to be condemnatory of the stage: Malcolm, *Anecdotes of the Manners and Customs of London*, vol. III, ch. 5, pp. 1–105, but the reasoning changed and was not

a vocation superior to that of the historian or philosopher. Vivid representation in placing moral types before us is 'the proper Office, and work of *Plays*'. It is the 'Office of the Stage to detect *roguery*'.[25] These were Hamlet's sentiments pretty exactly.

Consideration of the player clarifies the importance of keeping distinct the notion of a role-playing agent from a *persona* as a function of office. For the defence of acting was never of role-play as such. It was of an office requiring the *persona* to fulfil responsibilities to roles, to the audience to be delighted and instructed, and to the poet who created the roles to be staged. Conversely, for a critic like Gosson, it was the diversity of mere role-play that actually disrupted vocational order.[26] It is this last responsibility that brings poetry and the stage into such close alignment. Baker's co-option of Sidney's *Defence of Poetry*, and the picture imagery associated with the actor's office, leads from the mundane world of furniture and show to the well-worn commonplace of *ut pictura poesis*, and the poet had claims to serving a very high office indeed; many who wrote on the matter would have known something of Petrarch's being crowned with laurels, so assimilating an intellectual office to one of divinely sanctioned rule.

II

In touching on the literature of poetics, we are confronting a world in which, as Samuel Daniel put it, 'of one science another may be born'.[27] In university study, the organised parts of trivium and quadrivium were neither exhaustive nor incontestably distinct. From the sixteenth to the eighteenth century the shifting domains of intellectual endeavour were variously mapped in order to consolidate human knowledge. There was no certain place, for example, for mathematics touching music, magic, natural science and navigation. Galileo called it the language of God, a claim more conventionally associated with poetry; but the mathematical was itself comprised of competing dialects. Deductive vied with probabilistic, the certainty of geometry with the suggestive mobility of algebra. Richard Mulcaster saw logic as the grammar of mathematics, yet on the eve of Newtonian pre-eminence, John Eachard could see the two as

---

always what it seemed. Before the Restoration enmity was provoked by the religious themes presented on the stage; afterwards overt hostility could be a surrogate for attacking an irreligious and theatre-going court.

[25] Baker, *Theatrum Triumphans*, pp. 110, 178, 133; Anon., *The Immorality of the Pulpit* (1698), p. 7.
[26] Gosson, *Playes Confuted*, penultimate pages, n.p.
[27] Daniel, *Defence of Rhyme*, p. 63.

combining no better than black pudding and anchovy sauce. Logic itself might be included and excluded from philosophy.[28] There was no literature, but in such a fluid environment, there was a crucial but variable understanding of poetics.[29]

In post-Reformation England the poet sometimes needed defending against the ancient accusation of lying, and of being a prop to purgatory, that most self-serving of the delusions of Catholicism.[30] He also needed defending against of taints of Anabaptist prophetic enthusiasm, and the self-indulgence of celebrating carnal trivialities. The poet's faculty has been so discredited, wrote Robert Southwell, 'that a Poet, a Lover and a Liar, are by many reckoned but three wordes of one signification'.[31] Southwell's model of poetic responsibility was the poet-king David. Across denominational divisions the defence of poetry, then, frequently had a theological point or shifted into theology or philosophy on the authority of Aristotle's *Poetics*.[32] Not surprisingly, the poetic also needed to be delineated in tension with competing enclaves of human wisdom, such as history, rhetoric and philosophy. Intellectual identity might simply be assumed in re-characterising poetry;[33] but incantations of office were always available as introductory ploys,[34] and became sharper when asserting intellectual primacy, allaying suspicion, or deflecting accusations of irresponsibility.

Typically, however, the defence of poetry was a defence of its representing *persona*. In the tragedy of the poet Collingbourne (Colyngbourne), gruesomely executed for his lines 'The Cat, the Rat and Lovel our Dog/Do rule al England vnder a Hog', the argument is that under a tyranny the office of the poet is dangerous. If the office of rule sustains other offices, the ultimate form of misrule contaminates them. Collingbourne's voice states that 'The Greekes do paynt a Poetes office whole', and proceeds to outline the necessary qualities through the metaphor of Pegasus. The poet must be chaste and virtuous, 'nymble, free and swyft'; in a tyranny

---

[28] Mulcaster, *Positions*, ch. 41, p. 246; Eachard, *Mr Hobbs State of Nature*, p. 99; Bacon, *Advancement*, pt. 2, pp. 125, 144–5.
[29] McKeon, 'Politics of Discourses', pp. 35–47.
[30] Greenblatt, *Hamlet*, pp. 36–9; Hoby, *A Curry-Combe*; John Donne, *The Pseudo-Martyr* (1610), pp. 115–19, on purgatory and priestly office.
[31] Robert Southwell, 'The Author to his Loving Cosen', in *St. Peter's Complaint, With Other Poems* (1595), in *The Poems of Robert Southwell, S.J.*, ed. James H. McDonald and Nancy Pollard Brown (Oxford, 1967), p. 1.
[32] McKeon, 'Politics of Discourses', pp. 44–5.
[33] For example, Thomas Campion's *Observations in the Art of English Poesy* (1602), or John Dryden's *Essay of Dramatic Poesy* (1668), both in Jones, ed., *English Critical Essays*, pp. 55–60, 104–73, respectively.
[34] Daniel, *Defence of Rhyme*, p. 62.

decidedly swift. Mistakenly, he had thought the poet's ancient liberty to chastise and correct could be pleaded at any bar: 'I had forgot howe newefound tyrannies/ Wyth ryght and freedome were at open warre'.[35] Liberty of office is predictably in tension with tyranny. Yet, however circumspect, indirect or jesting the poet is advised to be, his office remains to trade in moral truths.

For all its abstract economy and emphasis on procedure, Bacon's *Advancement of Learning* illustrates a similar point with respect to rhetoric. The principal distinctions between poetry, history and philosophy are primarily related to a human faculty. Poetry expresses imagination, history is memory and philosophy is reason. Throughout the text, Bacon occasionally shifts from accounts of intellectual procedure to what the practitioner actually does, his virtues and the ends he must serve. If a man as rhetorician speaks to different people, he should do so in different ways, as he should not if the discourse is purely logical. This places rhetoric, as Aristotle argued, between logic and civic knowledge: 'the duty and office of Rhetoric is, to apply reason to the imagination for the better moving of the will'.[36] How a man should speak is a function of *persona*. Further, the complementary scope of each sphere of learning is a way of insisting that conversation between them makes the active life of value to the commonwealth. *The Advancement of Learning* is an elaborate defence of what George Pettie had stated as fact: all learning must be of use, the means to which is conversation. This has its own office in the perfection of learning.[37]

The conventional early modern ideal of the poet remained cloaked in the authority of antiquity. In Greece poets had been associated with divine inspiration. Traditionally draped in purple, the poet was both a maker or creator and a teacher, whose standing Plato, in particular, felt the need to confront in asserting the primacy of philosophy. In lowland Scots as well as English, the term maker could mean poet, and Sidney in his *Apology* and then Jonson in *Timber* drew on the philology of *poietes* to emphasise the poet's divinely creative capacities. Each elaborated on a pattern of responsibility. Jonson explicitly approached the critical ideal of a poem by detailing the qualities necessary for the poet: natural wit, a capacity to imitate nature, industry and

---

[35] Baldwin, *Mirror*, p. 349, lines 69–70; pp. 354–5, lines 183, 198–200. *The Mirror* implicitly condones Colyngbourne's actions by giving him the *persona* of poet for his fragment of verse, but he was executed for something worse, namely treason as an agent of Henry Tudor.
[36] Bacon, *Advancment*, p. 209.
[37] George Pettie, *Ciuile conuersation* (1586), fols. 15–16, esp. 16r.

learning.[38] Rhetoric was commended in much the same terms. As the sophists had donned the purple cloaks of the poets, so there is a sort of clothes-stealing between the theorists of poetry and rhetoric.[39] In this limited context of discussion, then, the promotional literature on rhetoric and poetry can continue to be treated in tandem. Since antiquity each had been associated with magic, boasting the capacity to make and re-make social reality as the magician could re-make nature.[40] The consequences of such transformatory power were disturbing, and so the promoters of the activities pointedly endorsed decorum and service, or subordination to something greater. Even Plato (as Sidney would insist) considered the powers of poetry and rhetoric permissible if subject to the arbitration of philosophy, the love of wisdom. Cicero and Quintilian with respect to rhetoric, Longinus with respect to poetry, trod in his footsteps.

The expectations of poetry and rhetoric from medieval times continued to move within this compass.[41] In part, this was to participate in a tradition of discussion of Man as *imago Dei* that perforce involved the correlates of an omnipotent voluntarist God and a responsible rational creator: Man as the image of God was wonderfully creative but to a point or end. Even in its most hyperbolic celebrations, such as Ficino's, it was an image of office.[42] From the Reformation, however, as I have intimated, the stress on the *persona* of the good rhetorician or poet became burdened with denominational implication and was used to re-specify theology. Thus Richard Pace on the opening of Cicero's *De inventione*: as eloquence founds cities and helps create the arts, so its role in theology is central. The good man, rhetorician and Christian are one in creative responsibility; Christ is the model of great oratory, good rhetoric a form of *imitatio Christi*.[43] The Protestant Thomas Wilson later made similar claims on the authority of the same Ciceronian text. The rhetor approaches God in his capacity to make and civilise, melding limitless power with wise

---

[38] Ben Jonson, 'What is a Poet', in *Timber, or Discoveries made upon Men and Matter* (1641), in *Works*, ed. W. Gifford (London, 1875), vol. IX, pp. 210–12.

[39] Sir Philip Sidney, *An Apology for Poetry* (1595), in Jones, ed., *English Critical Essays*, pp. 50–1; Jonson, *Timber*, p. 218.

[40] Jacqueline de Romilly, *Magic and Rhetoric in Ancient Greece* (Cambridge, Mass., 1975); Kernan, *The Playwright as Magician*, on *The Tempest*, pp. 129–59.

[41] Dr. John O. Ward has informed me of an MS fragment by William of Chartres referring to the *officium* of rhetoric and its end, *finis*, Bruges, Bibliothèque de la Ville, MS 553.s.xiv.

[42] Marsilio Ficino, *Theologica Platonica*: see Charles Trinkhaus, *In our Image and Likeness: Humanity and Divinity in Italian Humanist Thought*, 2 vols. (Chicago, 1970), vol.II, pp. 470–98.

[43] Richard Pace, *De fructu qui ex doctrina percipitur* (Basel, 1517), ed. and trans. Frank Manley and Richard S. Sylvester (New York, 1967); see Catherine Curtis, 'Richard Pace on Pedagogy, Counsel and Satire' (Ph.D. thesis, Cambridge University 1996), pp. 109–14.

ordering. Without him, duty, service, callings cannot be sustained. He is, in short, a microcosm of God's own office of offices.[44] Reclaiming the rhetor's purple to adorn the poet, Puttenham argued that the 'high charge and function' of poetry demanded poets live holy and contemplative lives. Virtue made them fit for prophecy and they were the first lawmakers, politicians and philosophers keeping the commonwealth in order.[45] The poet is the quintessence of decorum, of 'seemliness', a crucially stabilising virtue in the context of court life. Comeliness, discretion, decency, Puttenham's amplifications for seemliness, imply discipline and moderation to bridle the transgressions of figurative creativity. Decorum is the courtly poet's *sprezzatura* that makes him an honest man and not a cunning dissembler.[46] This kind of argument would echo through the pages of *Paradise Lost* in which Christ is the supreme rhetorician and Lucifer the inverted parody, whose eloquence can sustain only a travesty of a properly ordered world.

Sidney's *Apology* is perhaps the most famous instance of these themes. Although an apology for poetry, it is a discourse of the poetic *persona* in the dissonant context of historians and philosophers. The central argument is that, of these, only the poet is a second creator to 'be counted supernatural' and 'ranging freely within the zodiac of his own wit'. The poet is both imitator and maker.[47] This ranging is never a matter of capricious invention or undisciplined imagination, let alone popish fantasy. Even when trading in the comic, the poet is a figure of responsibility.[48] As Rosamund Tuve has persuasively argued, this attitude provides a key to understanding the differences between modern and early modern imagery. The Wordsworthian romantic vision of poetry, as an excess of emotion spontaneously expressed, would have amounted to an impiety. For the poet was neither eccentric nor an individual, revelling in singularity.[49] He was a craftsman, tied to God's creation and in service to an ethical as much as an aesthetic vision. All the intellectual arts and poetry's immediate competitors are, he argued, 'serving sciences'. Their shared end is to draw us as close to perfection as possible. The poet does so by providing perfect pictures that transcend the limited precepts of

---

[44] Thomas Wilson, *The Art of Rhetoric* (1553, 1560), ed. G. H. Mair (Oxford, 1909); see also Angel Day, *The English Secretary* (1586, 1592), ed. Robert O. Evans (Gainesville, Fla., 1967).
[45] George Puttenham, *The Art of English Poesy* (1589), introduction by Baxter Hatherway (Kent, Ohio, 1970), ch. 3.
[46] Puttenham, *English Poesy*, chs. 23, 25.
[47] Sidney, *Apology*, pp. 7, 6.
[48] *Ibid.*, p. 26, on comedy.
[49] Rosemund Tuve, *Elizabethan Metaphysical Imagery* (Chicago, 1972 edn), p. 245.

philosophy and the examples of history.[50] Thus it is the office of the poet to secure reformed religion; poetry can be an idiom of proper devotion.[51] This vision of the poet is further associated with the *personae* of office by reference to Cicero, by comparisons with the standard social offices of lawyer and physician and above all by the Petrarchan metaphor of the poet as monarch, so having the office of creating social office. Poetry, he had remarked at the outset, is 'my own elected vocation'.[52]

In *Timber*, Jonson was reflecting as much on his own chosen vocation of poetic critic as on poetry itself. Poetry is the queen of the arts, supreme in status, above even oratory.[53] This standing had made sound criticism all the more important. It was Aristotle, he remarked, the greatest of philosophers, who taught the offices of proper criticism, judgement and the imitation of virtue. This 'office of a true critic' is no mere tinkering, nor legislating. It is rather a matter of sincere judgement of the poet and subject.[54] Effectively the poetic critic is the mediator, the priest of the poet's divine order.

III

With the authority for such a responsibility drawn from Aristotle's *Poetics*, we have a cue for a further identity hovering behind the arras, though in one sense the philosopher has been on stage all along, for defences of poetry and rhetoric made specific claims to wisdom. As philosophy was love of wisdom, or the possession of all knowledge, this could be to appropriate philosophy to other offices.[55] Sidney, Puttenham and Wilson all exploited the almost indiscriminate range of the word philosophy in this way, revealing how it could refer not to content, method or procedure but to the end of any activity. Philosophical eclecticism encouraged the potential instability. The philosopher could be a hunter and gatherer of others' gems, adhering to no stable propositional doctrine. And, though largely filtered out of professional philosophy's own sense of its past, during the sixteenth and seventeenth centuries, eclecticism was prominent. So, in another sense of the word philosophy, it could be all the more important to establish the philosopher as having a distinct *persona*.

Plato had made the most ambitious claims for the intellectual authority of the philosopher. Aristotle had muted them and Aquinas had argued

---

[50] Sidney, *Apology*, pp. 11–14, 19–24. [51] Targoff, *Common Prayer*, pp. 73–4.
[52] Sidney, *Apology*, pp. 15, 21, 2. [53] Jonson, *Timber*, p. 218.
[54] *Ibid.*, p. 220.
[55] Goslicius, *De optimo senatore* (1593), p. 107 for philosophy as any knowledge under Heaven.

explicitly that metaphysics in particular had an office, conceived of in virtually platonic terms as a duty of the highest wisdom to rule other disciplines and lesser claims to knowledge.[56] Sidney's poetic office had a long-standing and formidable opponent. For others, philosophy, more or less precisely understood, offered a guide for the active or the contemplative life. This was the case for Bacon: as the office of the stomach was to nourish the whole body, so philosophy made sense of all other professions.[57] His was a restatement of long-standing arguments; it is the duty of philosophy to make other realms of duty clear. Additionally, this provided a rationale for the most eclectic of philosophers; and, as it were, modelled the office of the philosopher (like that of the rhetor or the poet) on the metaphorical projection of the office of God, to create and order all subordinate offices in the natural and human world. By the same token it was to make philosophers kings.

Philosophical identity was thus protean in a double sense. It had an unstable relationship with rhetoric and poetry, and for some writers it offered a vision of human potential, not unlike the picture of invention painted by the apologists of rhetoric.[58] The shared vocabulary of office used to define differences and priorities did much to confuse them. The philosopher as living the highest form of contemplation or as the instrument of the life of social engagement persistently treads on the toes of the poet and rhetor.[59] Directly or indirectly, he serves the commonwealth, although always the immediate end of his office is the quest for truth and wisdom. For Bacon it was the specific means to this end that principally gave the philosopher distinction. He was obliged to pursue free and thorough enquiry, and this had the attendant duty of taking nothing on authority and having a preparedness to dismiss even the most elevated quacks of antiquity.[60] Informing this decisive liberty of office was a sceptical demeanour, and for philosophers in Bacon's increasingly fashionable idiom, dogmatism was inimical to the office. Boyle's *Skeptical Chymist* would have Carneades as its spokesman.[61] Just as with rhetoric,

---

[56] Aquinas, *Commentary on Aristotle's Metaphysics*, pp. xxix–xxxi, as discussed in Johnson, 'Early Modern Natural Law', p. 41.
[57] Bacon, *Advancement*, pt. 2, p. 93; for a succinct discussion of Bacon's counter-claims to Sidney's poet, see Gaukroger, *Francis Bacon*, pp. 48–57.
[58] W. G. Craven, *Giovanni Pico della Mirandola, Symbol of his Age* (Geneva, 1981), for a valuable discussion.
[59] Bacon, *Advancement*, pp. 229ff; Goslicius, *De optimo*, pp. 57–9.
[60] Gaukroger, *Francis Bacon*, pp. 105–110; Julian Martin, *Francis Bacon, the State and the Reform of Natural Philosophy* (Cambridge, 1992), pp. 147–50.
[61] Robert Boyle, *The Skeptical Chymist* (1661).

however, intellectual status was tied to the reassuring display of a socialised and decorous *persona*, the peripatetic image of the office.

The early modern world inherited the view that the office of the philosopher involved a way of life.[62] If, as Harvey famously put it, Bacon wrote philosophy like a Lord Chancellor, it was in no small part because the lawyer and the philosopher were alike forms of intellectual office in service to mankind.[63] Even for Hobbes, a most procedurally minded defender of a discipline of philosophy, there should be a style of life fit to the calling: 'My Life and Writings speak one Congruous Sense', a rough translation of the more litotic '*Nam mea vita meis non est incongrua scriptis.*' In his aphorism that he and fear were born twins, a central explanatory concept of Hobbesian philosophy was given a poetically autobiographical origin.[64] Hobbes's critics saw this unity in a different light. He was accused of arrogance, singularity and libertine atheism, allowing his philosophy to be attacked through the *persona*. Although Hobbes appeared to lack the decorous modesty usually signifying the true philosopher, he was at least suitably melancholic. In this light, it seems likely that Aubrey's elaborate 'Life' took a cue from the asserted unity of life and doctrine; it was itself 'the last Office' to his dear friend. Fittingly, it was a defence of philosophy through exemplification of virtuous conduct, an indirect rebuttal of Hobbes's critics. Hobbes, the philosopher of motion, had a mind, remarked Aubrey, that was never still, but always controlled by the perpetual quest for aetiological understanding. The personal qualities Aubrey attributed to his friend – his curiosity, openness, generosity and charity, his energy, enjoyment of good company, discipline, consideration and abstemiousness – were all qualities echoing those attributed to Socrates, and they were appropriate to the Epicurean *persona* Aubrey defends. He noted in his 'Life' that Hobbes would not wear a beard, wanting his reputation to depend upon his wit not the self-advertising symbol of the sage.[65] This probably alluded to the beard-wearers derided by Lucian, and Hobbes certainly made a Lucianic commitment explicit in *De corpore*, although, as Butler maintained, whether with Hobbes in mind or not, nowadays philosophers have to shave to maintain their reputations.[66] The fusion of proposition and

---

[62] Gaukroger, *Francis Bacon*, pp. 50–1, 44–56; Hadot, *Philosophy as a Way of Life*; Hunter, *Rival Enlightenments*, ch .1, are all studies recapturing this point.
[63] Martin, *Francis Bacon*, at length, for a detailed study of this relationship.
[64] Hobbes, *Life of Mr. Thomas Hobbes of Malmesbury* (1680), p. 18, *Thomae Hobbesii Malmesburiensis Vita* (1679), pp. 14, 2.
[65] Aubrey, *Brief Lives*, pp. 83, 233.
[66] Hobbes, *De corpore* (1655), in *English Works*, ed. Sir William Molesworth (1839–45), vol. I, p. ix; Butler, *Characters*, p. 95.

persona helps explain the ease with which philosophers like Hobbes shifted into satire and *ad hominem* argument and could be treated in the same fashion. Attacking a *persona* was hardly the irrelevance it might now seem when occupation of the office not just the proposition was at issue.

Hobbes was also capable of running poetry and philosophy together in a way that Sidney had made thoroughly familiar.[67] In praising Davenant's *Gondibert*, he discussed the poet's office by elaborating on a counterpoint between the responsibilities of the ancient and the Christian poet, and by stressing the dangers in the abuse of the powers of eloquence and figurative creativity. Initially distinguishing poetry from philosophy, he then went on to suggest that, where philosophy has failed in its responsibilities, poetic fancy must take its place.[68] The reference to office here is so reified that it overrides the procedures that Hobbes normally took to define philosophy to the exclusion of poetry's reliance on metaphor. At the same time that Hobbes was writing *Leviathan*, and still pondering the strict *regulae* of the philosopher's office that would appear in *De corpore*, he was extolling the almost primeval mystery of the poet's calling, a voice in unison with Sidney, Puttenham and Jonson and conjured from antiquity.

During the seventeenth century, the philosopher and the natural philosopher became more distinct. Daniel superficially sounds like a prophet: 'of one science' another was indeed 'born'.[69] There was no single or simple reason for this. Charles Schmitt, for example, has suggested that it had much to do with the logistics of text-book production.[70] But Bacon's re-orientation of the office of the philosopher and then the momentous work in natural philosophy by figures such as Boyle and Newton are also crucial. Their work, together with the energies and controlled image of the Royal Society (and others established in its train), could, retrospectively, be seen as vindications of Baconian procedure.[71] Irrespective of achievements, Bacon's insistence on natural philosophy as an inductive communal endeavour of public importance seemed to be borne out in the development of networks of scholars communicating problems, experiments and discoveries in a way that distinguished them from the more isolated and text-based work of deductive metaphysics, theology and

---

[67] On Sidney and Hobbes, see Raia Prokhovnik, *Rhetoric and Philosophy in Hobbes's Leviathan* (New York, 1991), ch. 3.
[68] Hobbes, *Answer*, p. 450.
[69] Daniel, *Defence*, p. 63.
[70] Charles B. Schmitt, 'The Rise of the Philosophical Textbook', in Charles B. Schmitt and Quentin Skinner, eds., *The Cambridge History of Renaissance Philosophy* (Cambridge, 1988), pp. 792–804.
[71] L. Boschiero, 'Natural Philosophizing inside the Late Seventeenth-Century Tuscan Court', *British Journal for the History of Science*, 35, 4 (2002), pp. 383–410.

logic, and from the restrictive conventions of court culture. In the courtly environment, the scientist was accepted on the precedent of the artist or even courtier, to bestow honour on his patron by doing as required; the ethos was hierarchical and often combative.[72] The Royal Society presented a contrasting Baconian group *persona* at odds with the evidence of activity.[73] Moreover, by establishing an organisation under the patronage of that highest social office-holder, the king, having rules of conduct, a selective membership, oaths of initiation and an advertised ethos of shared endeavour, the Society assimilated itself to established, institutionalised patterns of official expectation in a way that was denied the poet, or the philosopher outside the university or monastery.

By the end of the century there has been a partial change of focus, from the relationships between the offices of poet, rhetor and philosopher to those between philosopher, natural philosopher and mathematician, but these remained relationships of office specified through its resilient vocabulary. Stephen Shapin has inferred an intimate relationship between the emerging image of natural science and the development of modern 'selfhood'. Because the new science was a communal enterprise among gentlemen, it required modesty and respect for the arguments and experiments of fellows, the openness to attend to all relevant evidence and for hypotheses to be tested in a public forum, sustained by the technologies of print. He is right to stress the relationship between proposition and *persona*, and that the shift away from this conjunction constitutes a change of ethical perspective.[74] It is clear, however, that the presentation of a *persona* was hardly a singular achievement. In taking over the philosophical dialogue, for example, scientists like Boyle worked with canons of civility that had been characteristic of its functioning from antiquity to the Renaissance. In *The Republic*, even Thrasymachus is tamed. Neither was a gentlemanly preoccupation with civil conversation in any way new when Boyle emphasised its importance. It had been an aspect of aristocratic and courtly offices for sufficiently long for the duelling provoked by its breakdown to be seen as native.[75] Boyle further adapted the aristocratic virtue of liberality to the ends of enquiry – it was an undogmatic generosity towards the work of others in the scientific community. His chastity was a

---

[72] Peter Burke, *The Italian Renaissance: Culture and Society in Italy* (Princeton, 1986), ch. 3.
[73] John A. Schuster and Alan H. B. Taylor, 'Organising the "Experimental Life" at the Early Royal Society: The Production and Communication of Experimentally Based Knowledge', Princeton University, History and Philosophy of Science Seminar, 2003. I am grateful to Professor Schuster for access to this.
[74] Stephen Shapin, *A Social History of Truth: Civility and Science in Seventeenth-Century England* (Chicago, 1994), e.g. pp. 409–10.
[75] Peltonen, *The Duel*, pp. 178–9.

virtue appropriate to the true Epicurean's love of knowledge. There was also an insistently Christian dimension to this.[76] The Pauline injunction (2 Timothy 2: 24, 25) was a familiar text concerning heresy. Those in error should be treated with gentleness, patience and meekness, as the similarly chaste Hobbes reminded his critics in an attack on dogmatism.[77] Here are dicta of the utmost civility that are anything but the preserve of the new men of science, issuing from one of the old, too easily accused of incivility and not neatly to be tied to the honour-driven competitiveness of court science.[78] The continuing vitality of a register is uncertain evidence of a new ideology. So it seems misleading to see a *persona* like Boyle's as fashioning a modern self.[79] Natural science and philosophy might well be diverging activities, but no more than with poetry, or rhetoric at the end of the sixteenth century, was one *persona* denied the authenticating clothing of the other.

Robert Boyle lived the scientific *persona* with conspicuous success, to be sure, and his critiques of Hobbes were an effective way of presenting the openness of eclecticism, labouring in the interests of wisdom as an alternative to the prioristic over-reaching of untrammelled speculation. Locke went further in calling philosophy a matter of under-labouring for natural philosophy.[80] In some ways, we have come a long way from the world of Sidney and 'the poet Collingbourne', but Locke's image of philosophy still draws on the promotional rhetorics of office. The philosopher's modesty is the humility of knowing an office and its limits; his argument is cast in the language of duty and responsibility, of ends and what has impeded their fulfilment. The answer is cut and stitched with much the same materials of intellectual office and its abuse as Bacon and Hobbes had used: the over-reaching obfuscation of past philosophy and the delusions of rhetoric which are attacked *tout court* by *ad hominem* accounts of motivation, so stigmatising the *persona* of the rhetorician as the enemy of the under-labourer.

---

[76] See above all Boyle, *The Christian Virtuoso*, in *Works*, vol. V, pp. 508–40; vol. VI, pp. 673–716, 717–96.
[77] Thomas Hobbes, *An Historical Narration concerning Heresy and the Punishment thereof* (c. 1668), in *English Works*, vol. IV, pp. 407–8.
[78] Hobbes did operate largely within the courtly Cavendish circle and for most of his life was a servant of the Cavendish family. He enjoyed the eristics of courtly debate; but his employers were in many ways his fellows and friends. He drove his own agenda of enquiry which William Cavendish facilitated rather than directed.
[79] See Shapin, *Social History*, pp. 160–8; for systematic discussions, see John H. Schuster and Alan H. B. Taylor, 'Blind Trust: The Gentlemanly Origins of Experimental Science', *Social Studies of Science*, 27 (1997), pp. 503–36; Michael Hunter, *Robert Boyle (1627–91): Scrupulosity and Science* (Woodbridge, 2000), at length.
[80] John Locke, *An Essay Concerning Human Understanding* (1690), Epistle.

As Locke's under-labouring efforts amounted to an argument about what and how anything in the world can be studied and knowledge communicated, his philosophical vision can be encompassed by Bacon's analogy of the stomach and by Ciceronian priorities. And for Locke also, this was not just a matter of digesting dry doctrine but of knowing enough to live as we should.[81] In this respect Locke's revised image of philosophical responsibility is at one with Shaftesbury's reassuring echo of Platonic *eudemonia*: the purpose of philosophy is to make us happy; it is tied to and is an expression of character.[82]

Office, then, provided a currency of advertisement, defence and critique for intellectual activity, a vocabulary to be co-opted to the extent that it kept fluid, or could blur substantively different intellectual endeavours. Fuller disciplinary demarcation perhaps required a diminution of the status of the language of office; or perhaps an increasing differentiation in the minutiae of practice gradually over-stretched the common resources of advocacy and demonisation. Either way, we now live in a world in which the promotional rhetoric of office has a less certain place and a lower threshold of plausibility when applied to intellectual life.

IV

One consequence of this change is that it has become easy to overlook the *persona* of the philosopher and put in its stead the somewhat evasive 'selfhood' of the modern individual. Discriminate claims have been universalised, philosophy is over-simplified and a premature modernity is invented. To an extent all this is understandable. As I have laboured sufficiently, philosophy was a particularly unstable term, and the ubiquity of the vocabulary of office hardly assisted in fixing a discursively insulated discipline. Nevertheless, the philosopher, even as the more general scholar or man of letters, was well short of the modern individual. Since Burckhardt's search for nascent individualism in the Renaissance, Pico della Mirandola's seminal *Oration on the Dignity of Man* has largely been read as an unrestricted argument about human individuality, a joyous indulgence in Man's protean capacity. Yet, as Bill Craven has shown, Pico uses the notion of Man as a metaphor for philosophic creativity.[83] In

---

[81] John Locke, 'Thus I think', in King, *The Life of John Locke*, vol. II, pp. 126–7.
[82] Anthony Ashley Cooper, Lord Shaftesbury, *The Characteristics of Men, Manners, Opinions and Times* (1711), ed. Philip J. Ayres (Oxford, 1999), vol. II, p. 207.
[83] Craven, *Giovanni Pico della Mirandola*, esp. ch. 5; cf. Trinkhaus, *In our Image and Likeness*, vol. II, pp. 753–60.

overlooking this, connotation is mistaken for denotation and so the frame of reference greatly expanded past the rhetorical exercise of praising philosophy. Pico claimed for the philosopher what Wilson, Puttenham and Sidney would use to vindicate poets and orators; the protean nature of philosophy is to be celebrated, because the philosopher's is an office of such weighty responsibility. Discussion of Pico, then, should be placed in the context of the shared resources of contested intellectual modality, not in that of a projected definition of modern individualism. The clothing of office was torn in the mutual attempts to rip it from the backs of intellectual competitors; the tatters get stitched by the latter-day tailor into something else.

Similarly, it is unduly modernising to read More's 'Dialogue of Council' as a debate about a private individual and public life, an inner self confronting the dangers of a public role, freedom versus obligation or constraint. It is, rather, a debate about the tensions between the responsibilities involved respectively in the active and contemplative lives as patterns of conduct that might best fulfil the office of the philosopher. To this end, as Catherine Curtis has argued, More drew on complementary figures from Menippean and Lucianic philosophical satire: Hythlodaeus the traveller, 'the latter-day Menippus, caped and bearded', free of social burdens that he may serve knowledge, considering only issues of *honestas*; and Morus, the man tied to the practicalities of the offices of lawyer and counsellor, who must be circumspect and always consider the consequences, *utilitas*. Eric Nelson has related this distinction specifically to More's use of a Greek conception of the superiority of contemplative philosophy to counter-point a Roman requirement that philosophy engage with the commonwealth.[84] The questions explicitly raised by More are whether the contemplative philosopher, Hythlodaeus, whose Greek is better than his Latin, can become a councillor to any good effect; and whether the man of practical engagements is morally and philosophically compromised in trying to be helpful. To fulfil one sort of office seems to involve failure by the standards of another, for the ethics and liberties of each are discordant. Contested philosophy is, as it were, stretched across a moral modality. Certainly, there is a dialogue between these personified positions, but the dramatic delineation is well served by More's resisting a resolution, and thus leaving in the air the question, to be answered so emphatically by Bacon, of what really is true wisdom.[85] That indeterminacy inviting the reader's active participation, however, is more congruent

---

[84] Curtis, 'Richard Pace', p. 277; Nelson, 'The Greek Tradition', ch. 1.
[85] Thomas More, *Utopia*, ed. George Logan, Robert Adams and Clarence Miller (Cambridge, 1995), bk. 1.

with the office of the rhetor whose dress the author More was wearing, than with the philosopher about whom he was writing. For the rhetor had perforce, as Bacon would also insist, always to adapt a case according to audience and circumstances and it was, according to the ancient Quintilian and the modern Machiavelli, not always possible to argue from *honestas* or to reconcile it with *utilitas*.[86] To lose sight of this interplay between and with intellectual office is to drain the *personae* from the text and leave us only with the misplaced voices of individuality. More significant than the twisting of the protean philosopher into the Self, however, has been the secularisation of the soul, and it is to this illusive essence, sometimes the inner philosopher, that I shall now turn.

---

[86] Quintilian, *Institutio oratoria*, trans. H. E. Butler (Cambridge, Mass., 1920–2), vol. III, 8. 30–7; Niccolò Machiavelli, *The Prince* (1513), trans. Russell Price, introduction by Quentin Skinner (Cambridge, 1988), pp. xvii–xx; see also Fitzmaurice, *Humanism and America*, pp. 118–19.

6 Soul and conscience

> For my Soul, I confess I have heard very much of Souls, but what they are, or whom they are for, God knows.
> (Nathaniel Brent, *The Last Will and Testament of the Earl of Pembroke*, 1681)

I

One sympathises: it was hard not to hear much of souls in seventeenth-century England, but what they were was indeed debatable. Since antiquity, the soul (*psyche*) could refer both to the moving principle inherent in all living things and to the conjunction of will and intellect in humans, usually considered immortal. This chapter is mainly concerned with the second, intellective understanding of the soul, but initially it is important to disengage what were often confusing patterns of meaning.

Plato had used *psyche* in both senses in the *Timaeus*, a somewhat Pythagorean dialogue that became a touchstone in Renaissance discussions.[1] To these he added the notion of a world soul to explain the apparent coherence of creation itself. Aristotle's *De anima* provided seminal material for scholasticism and Reformation theology, but it seemed to have no use for a world soul, while from Epicurus and Lucretius came a notion of a material soul, the intellective soul conceived as mortal and composed of atoms. Varieties of Stoicism qualified and continued to mix theories of the *psyche* as principle of life, divine spark of humanity, with the *psyche tou pantos,* or world soul.[2] A full account of the understandings of the *psyche* found in the seventeenth century would also need to include postulated animal spirits that could affect it; to say nothing of folkloric survivals from Greek and Germanic mythology, of transmogrifying and separable souls, hidden talismans of power, like the purple hair on the

---

[1] Plato, *Timaeus*, 34a–37c; 41a–44, trans. H. D. P. Lee (Harmondsworth, 1965), pp. 44–9, 56–60.
[2] F. E. Peters, *Greek Philosophical Terms: A Historical Lexicon* (New York, 1967), pp. 166–76.

head of King Nisus of Megara, a soul plucked out by his daughter Scylla to his and his city's destruction.³

When *psychologia* was coined around 1575, to refer to the study of the soul, it had, predictably, no exclusive disciplinary location, being used from theology, metaphysics and morality to natural philosophy, medicine and what is now called psychology.⁴ Elaborate taxonomies of study stemming from the soul as vegetative and/or sensitive, or as intellective gave an indication of the ground *psychologia* had to cover.⁵ Superficially, it might seem that these understandings could be kept separate, given that only the human intellective soul was taken as a defining principle of immortality.⁶ Indeed, during the pontificate of Leo X it was deemed heretical to deny human immortality.⁷ This unique soul continued to be affirmed in Protestant speculation. Melanchthon's much printed *Liber de anima* was largely at one with Thomistic belief; Aristotelian authority was a common grounding. To paraphrase Melanchthon's definition, the rational soul was the immortal part of man.⁸ Such an apparently clear point of demarcation, however, could nevertheless be compromised, and by the seventeenth century some diminished form of immortality could be accorded souls in animals.⁹

Irrespective of degrees of immortality, there was a more fundamental reason for the continuing slippage between the varieties of soul-talk. In all uses the soul was intangible, an inaccessible essence that had to be expressed in a publicly shared language. This was a business that doomed discussion to metaphorical inadequacy, exemplifying the limitations characteristic of reference to divinity itself. The concept of God as beyond human comprehension was a consequence of the postulate of divine

---

[3] For a detailed account of the interactions of ancient uses of *psyche*, *anima* and their survivals, see Onians, *Origins*, pp. 93–122, 169–73.

[4] Katharine Park and Eckhard Kessler, 'The Concept of Psychology', in Schmitt and Skinner, *The Cambridge History of Renaissance Philosophy*, pp. 355–7.

[5] Katharine Park, 'The Organic Soul', in *ibid.*, pp. 465–6; Elyot, *The Book Named the Governor*, 3.24, pp. 224–5.

[6] See, for example, Hale, *Primitive Origination*, pp. 27–8.

[7] Donne, *The Pseudo-Martyr*, ch. 12, p. 375; Pietro Pomponazzi (1452–1525) provoked extensive controversy over his *De immortalitate animae* (1516), defended in his *Apologia* (1518), arguing, to put it bluntly, that philosophically speaking the soul was mortal, theologically, immortal. This had severe ramifications for the relationships of the office of theologian and philosopher; see Charles H. Lohr, 'Metaphysics', in Schmitt and Skinner, *The Cambridge History of Renaissance Philosophy*, pp. 602–7; Eckhard Kessler, 'The Intellective Soul', in *ibid.*, pp. 500–7.

[8] Kessler, 'The Intellective Soul', pp. 517–18, and n. 233, quoting Philipp Melanchthon, *Liber de Anima*.

[9] See Samuel Haworth, *Anthropologia: or a Philosophic Discourse Concerning Man* (1680), discussing Henry More and Ralph Cudworth, pp. 40–1.

omnipotence, and it was a commonplace by the seventeenth century.[10] Omnipotence could not be contained in any single definition, and so comprehension might only be grasped at by complementary predications. This led at once to a sort of theological scepticism which could be as pious as polemical, and to a metaphorical fecundity that could be as disturbing as it was devout.[11] Such a God was a model for understanding the putative spirit realm and the unknown within the physical; so 'the forms of things unknown' are named, and 'airy nothing' given 'A local habitation'.[12] The spiritual, argued Cotta, is only conjectured in mundane terms, its likely marks and manifestations matters of 'prudent ghesse'.[13] But sensibility to human inadequacy also allowed scope for paradoxical play with words, tumbling different conceptions of the soul into one. The soul, claimed Samuel Haworth, is so far above sense that only the soul can explicate its nature – an assertion that approaches intelligibility only because he proceeded to reduce the soul to an incorporeal cogitant, to wit, an immortal rational faculty with a ruling function.[14]

As one common way of glimpsing God's nature was to see Him as having the office of ruling, expectations of office gave a predictable form to any postulated angelic host. Devoid of their reciprocal offices, wrote Christoph Scheibler, the angels of the republic of Heaven would be but a common herd.[15] If office secured angels from plummeting into the bestial, we can expect the relationship of soul to God to be conjectured in similar fashion. To allude to Marsilius of Padua's prescient distinction, we are habitually confronted with a world of intransient (*non transeunt*) acts between God and soul, grasped only through the transient language of human social interaction.[16] Hobbes commented of Walter Warner, 'I wish he could giue good reasons for ye facultyes & passions of ye soule, such as may be expressed in playne English. If he can, he is the first (that I ever heard) speake sense in that subiect.'[17] Again one sympathises, but plain

---

[10] Browne, *Religio Medici*, pp. 74, 94; Hobbes, *Leviathan*, ch. 3, p. 21; ch. 34, p. 271.
[11] Browne, *Religio Medici*, pp. 23–5, K n. 25.
[12] Shakespeare, *A Midsummer Night's Dream* 5.1.
[13] Cotta, *The Assured Witch*, pp. 21, 2, 7; John Cotta, *A Short Discovery of the unobserved Dangers of . . . Physicke in England* (1612), p. 7. Such awareness of the limitations of human knowledge naturally fuelled the sort of rigorous scepticism of Hobbes, who could take a Cotta-like understanding of the spiritual to the totality of the external material world.
[14] Haworth, *Anthropologia*, pp. 14, 21.
[15] Christoph Scheibler, *Metaphysica duobus libris, universum hujus scientiae systema* (Giessen, 1617, Oxford, 1665), lib. 2, punctum II, p. 638. I am most grateful to Ian Hunter for bringing this to my attention, if not with quite the *gravitas* it deserves.
[16] Marsilius of Padua, *Defensor pacis* (1324), ed. H. Kusch (Berlin, 1958), 1.5.4.
[17] *Correspondence of Thomas Hobbes*, ed. Noel Malcolm, 2 vols. (Oxford, 1994), vol. I, 15/25 August 1635, p. 29.

English, being approximate English, was part of the problem, and plain English was infused with the vocabulary of office. So, if it could be used of God, it could become an almost irresistible resource for prudent guesses about the soul. Metaphors of office, then, persistently offered hope of a higher understanding. On close inspection, however, these frequently collapse into circular affirmations of office-talk itself, at once a language of morality and explanation. They could even coalesce the ostensible polarities of divine inner essence and the outer protean *persona* of the philosopher. For the remainder of this chapter I propose only to illustrate permutations on this common theme of soul and soul–God relations given 'local habitation' through office.

In antiquity Cicero and Epictetus had defined human beings in terms of four *personae* or realms of duty, one of which is the essential shared rationality of all humanity, that is, in some sense a soul.[18] The vocabulary of office continued to be available in this way from the Church Fathers to beyond the medieval scholastics. Thomas More's *Dialogue of Comfort* illustrates some of the intricacies that could result. A. D. Cousins has shown that More presented a series of *personae*, to construct a lasting composite image of himself that was then propagated by family and disciples. The first is that of the father, whose duty is to leave an ideal of morality to guide his family; the last is the *persona* of the Boethian and Silenic philosopher who has discovered that true knowledge is found in subordination to Christ. True philosophy is, then, an expression of the soul's proper demeanour to the supreme office-holder; the true philosopher is thus an exemplum for any soul.[19]

When, towards the end of the sixteenth century, writers such as Montaigne and Charron redefined the intellective soul in exploring notions of inner identity, the language and exempla of office were to hand. For the figuratively inventive Montaigne, the soul, the inner self, the conscience, was, most simply, a judge, a court assessing the vanities of the world; for Charron it could even be a republic.[20] As for More, the object of the enquiry was to define the duties of the true philosopher, so the language of office is used to reconcile notions of inner being and philosophical judgement; the result gained familiarity and authority through the force of the

---

[18] Epictetus, *Discourses*, trans. W. A. Oldfather (Cambridge, Mass., 1925), 2.10.
[19] A. D. Cousins, 'Role-Play and Self-Portrayal in More's *A Dialogue of Comfort Against Tribulation*', *Christianity and Literature*, 52, 4 (2003), pp. 457–70.
[20] Carol Clark, 'Talking about Souls: Montaigne and Human Psychology', in I. D. MacFarlane and Ian Maclean, eds., *Montaigne, Essays in Memory of Richard Sayce* (Oxford, 1982), pp. 67–9.

descriptive terms themselves.[21] There is, then, nothing strained in William Perkins writing of Christianity as a general calling, and seeing the Christian soul as in an official relationship with God. This image, passing into common usage, was studiously developed by George Herbert as a doctrine about the relationships between the calling of a Christian and, within this, the vocation of the priest, whose office was devoted to assisting the soul in its relationship to God.[22]

Donne played paradoxically with the need to rely upon the familiar image for the inscrutable in a sermon in which he suggested that as prophets penned scripture through metaphors drawn from their prior professions, so, as the sinful soul turns fully to God, its prior passion shapes its new relationship. His argument is thus a variation on Cotta's problem of inference from the indescribable. The covetous, urges Donne, will be spiritually covetous, for as a servant of God, he will have his wages.[23] Although the term soul functioned as an abstract noun, above all it expressed a relational identity of total subjection to God, an office of constant exercise. Ideally, wrote Donne, the soul is so thoroughly turned towards God, that it prays even in ignorance of its activity.[24] Yet precisely because no single description touching divinity was adequate, total, private subjection did not exclude liberty – quite the contrary; as the Church of England liturgy insisted, God is he whose service is perfect freedom. At one point, using the model of the equally mysterious Trinity, Sir Thomas Browne elaborated a triple vision of the soul comprising affection, faith and reason, all related through the vocabulary of office and rule.[25] For Matthew Hale, it was altogether more simple: the soul was a microcosm of God's rule over the universe.[26] Hale's conventional formulation embraces the soul as divine human essence and principle of life. It resides in the noble faculties of head and heart, where it governs, but 'pervades' the 'Body and exerciseth vital Offices'.[27] So, too, the pathology of the physical world, the failure of the soul as life principle, could be styled a failure

---

[21] Pierre Charron, *De la Sargesse* (1601), trans. S. Lennard, *Of Wisdome Three Bookes*, n.d.; cf. also David Hume, *A Treatise of Human Nature* (1745), ed. L. A. Selby-Bigge; second edn P. H. Niddich (Oxford, 1978), p. 261.
[22] Malcolmson, *Heart Work*, at length.
[23] Donne, Sermon 18, in *Sermons* (1660).
[24] Donne, Sermon 9, in *Sermons* (1640); Robert Boyle, 'Of Piety' (1645–7), in John T. Harwood ed., *The Early Essays and Ethics of Robert Boyle* (Carbondale and Edwardsville, 1991), p. 173; cf. Nussbaum, *The Therapy of Desire*, p. 363, citing Diogenes Laertius, claiming that the good person is always using his soul.
[25] Browne, *Religio Medici*, pp. 51–2; not to be confused with Reisch's tripartite soul.
[26] Hale, *Primitive Origination*, p. 33.
[27] *Ibid.*, p. 23; see also Haworth, *Anthropologia*, p. 61, on the analogy of the vacuum to prove extension of the immaterial.

of office.[28] This also had been intimated in antiquity where the soul's function was sometimes depicted as vitalising and governing.[29]

Covenant theology figuratively imagined a solemnity of passage by which the Christian soul came into a new relationship of office with God, accepting a moral responsibility of total subjection. And even those who rejected the imagery of covenant might turn to that of office to express the relationship between Christ and the souls he saved. Hobbes, for example, insistent enough on God's incomprehensibility, deemed Christ to have an office.[30] Sir Harry Vane the younger (no conspicuous Hobbesian) was fully cognisant of the metaphorical and paradoxical nature of soul descriptions, and relied on the vocabulary of office to affirm a spiritual tutelage, a freedom in captivity, and a harmony of liberty and necessity.[31] Referring to the inner obligations of the soul to God, George Lawson remarked on how hard it was not to speak in tropes; the very notion of an obligation was a metaphorical approximation.[32] The expression of inner being needed the resources of official relationships.

II

Understanding the obligations, of course, was a further issue and knowing one's duty to God was a matter of conscience. Theories of conscience, intricate and highly speculative as they could become, were grounded in the Latin *conscientia* combining the meanings of inner awareness and consciousness.[33] A standard starting place was Aquinas's *De obligatione conscientiae*, treating conscience as a mental operation, both a form of knowing and an application of principles to conduct – a specification already trailing intimations of intellectual office.[34] Compressing this understanding, conscience was also the principle of movement, or judgement in the soul: a natural power of the soul, as Christopher St German

---

[28] See also Charleton, *Enquiries into Human Nature*, p. 394; Booth, 'A Subtle and Mysterious Machine', p. 155.

[29] Peters, *Greek Philosophical Terms*, p. 175, citing Plotinus; more generally, Onians, *Origins*, pp. 93–123.

[30] Hobbes, *Leviathan*, ch. 41, p. 332; cf. Ames, *Conscience*, p. 73.

[31] Sir Harry Vane the Younger, *Two Treatises* (1662), quoted in David Parnham, *Sir Henry Vane, Theologian: A Study in Seventeenth-Century Religious and Political Discourse* (London, 1997), p. 145.

[32] George Lawson, 'Amica dissertatio', Baxter Treatises, Dr Williams's Library, London, 1, fols. 99–130b, item 9.

[33] Lewis, *Studies in Words*, pp. 181–3.

[34] Ames, *Conscience*, pp. 2–4; Robert Boyle, 'The Aretology' (1645), in Harwood, *Early Essays*, pp. 46–7.

put it.³⁵ Thus the conscience could become a synecdoche for the soul, for each was a matter of intellect and will subordinated to God. Similarly, the mind from the same root in *conscientia* could be the seat of consciousness. The *OED* cites usage of this sort from the fourteenth century, so the word mind could function as a synonym for the intellective human soul. A preamble to an act of 1512 refers to the will and mind (*OED*), suggesting the very distinction made with respect to the conscience, knowledge and the will to apply it. By the sixteenth century *mind* could refer to the whole social being – 'To humble broken minds, this Lord is ever, ever neare'³⁶ – and could become synonymous with soul and conscience. The verb to mind was to care, or take responsibility for, and the *OED* cites the imperative to be mindful as being strongly associated with that most prominent of offices, counsel. Much of the diverse usage of the terms conscience, mind and soul is strung on a thread of associations with office.

The metaphors of conscience and those of the soul could be much the same, but the conscience was taken to be a source of knowledge of what was right with respect to external offices as well: of what people needed to be mindful of. For Jeremy Taylor, it was a kind of Platonic or Ciceronian philosopher, or priest, its offices being to dictate, testify, bear witness, excuse, accuse, loose and bind.³⁷ On scriptural authority, Taylor equated conscience and heart, then with spirit ministered by the offices of the body. The conscience is the mind of God, ruling in men.³⁸ The description of conscience, like that of God and soul, was driven by metaphor frequently derived from but also feeding back into understandings of office. Henry Mason, for example, used the terms soul and conscience as synonyms in his exploration of the importance of self-examination. Conscience is an inner tribunal, judging and passing sentence. It is analogous to that similarly clear case of relationships of social office, that of the physician and patient. Both general and particular callings, he argued, have their characteristic failings and need regular scrutiny.³⁹ The result of this constant subjection of offices to office, the self-examination before one's own inner court, is greater awareness of duty and enhanced preparedness of the soul for God. '[E]very man', wrote the Quaker Samuel Fisher, 'is a little world within himself, and in this little world there is a court of

---

³⁵ Christopher St German, *A Dyaloge in Englysshe bytwyxt a Doctoure of Dyvynyte and a Student in the Lawes of England: of the groundes of the sayd lawes and of Conscyence* (1530); see Jones, *Conscience and Allegiance*, pp. 38–9.
³⁶ Sidney-Pembroke, *Psalter*, 34.9 quoted in *OED*; see Targoff, *Common Prayer*, pp. 77–81.
³⁷ Taylor, *Ductor dubitantium*, p. 11; see also Anstey, *The Philosophy of Robert Boyle*, pp. 74, 188–90, on Robert Boyle's elision of rational soul and mind.
³⁸ Taylor, *Ductor*, pp. 4–5.
³⁹ Mason, *Tribunal of Conscience*, pp. 2, 12, 36ff, 31, 40, 53.

judicature erected, wherein next under God the Conscience sits as the supream judge . . . that passeth sentence upon all our actions.'[40] Ecumenical as such formulations were, adequate preparation for judgement was known to be no easy matter: as Browne put it, the 'inward opticks and crystalline of [the] soul' was the hardest sort of vision. 'Conscience only, that can see without light, sits in the Areopagy and dark tribunal of our hearts surveying our thoughts and condemning their obliquities.'[41]

The conscience rarely escaped images of perception, seeing and knowing. The analogies between sense and intellection to be found, for example, in Plato's *Republic*, where sight is used synaesthetically, and Aristotle's *De Anima*, III, had become so established that sense, especially vision, provided both the standardised metaphorical vocabulary for understanding, and a model of expectation in the early modern world.[42] As ideally the conscience directed us to duty, and the soul towards God, so too there was a responsibility to follow its beckoning. Applying the knowledge of the conscience was, then, effectively an office of the soul, the duty of following what was seen in the dark.

I have already discussed the relationships between public and private being at odds with modern concepts, and in the light of metaphors of office used for the conscience of the soul we can also appreciate contradictory understandings of the private: as inaccessible and in a relationship of total subordination to God, the soul was private; but it was also possible to reduce the inner conscience to nothing more than doing the duties required of public office. James VI&I insisted on this conjunction of conscience and duty over and above any private conscience.[43] As Kevin Sharpe has shown, a similar collapse of a knowing conscience into the exercise of office helps explain why Charles I's conscience had to override the consciences of those he governed. As God ruled the soul, so Charles ruled in God's place. God was the king of men's consciences and Charles was his vicegerent. The conscience was also God's vicegerent. It was around this contentious office-shaped rock of conscience that the controversies surrounding the *Eikon Basilike* would flow.[44] Samuel Rutherford

---

[40] Samuel Fisher, *The Bishop Busied beside the Businesses*, Epistle, quoted in Jones, *Conscience and Allegiance*, p. 188; Clarendon, 'Of Conscience' (1670) in *Essays*, vol. I, p. 196.
[41] Browne, *Christian Morals*, pp. 331–2; see also Bohun, *The Justice of the Peace*, p. 124, tying this visual imagery to Matthew 6: 23.
[42] Richard Rorty, *Philosophy and the Mirror of Nature* (Princeton, 1979), introduction, ch. 1; Richard Tuck, 'Optics and Sceptics', in Edmund Lietes, ed., *Conscience and Casuistry in Early Modern Europe* (Cambridge, 1998), at length.
[43] Sharpe, *Re-mapping*, pp. 158–60.
[44] *Ibid.*, pp. 183, 194, 178; Charles I (?), *Eikon Basilike*, p. 78.

had already disputed Charles's conception of his authoritative conscience with metaphors of his own: 'the people Have a natural throne of policy in their conscience to give warning ... against the king as a tyrant'.[45] Yet the two men drew alike on the standard vocabulary of rationality, knowledge and office.

Such fluid language makes the notion of a public conscience, whether the king's or the people's, quite plausible. It could be a shorthand way of affirming knowledge of one's duty to maintain the integrity of one's office. Thus Heneage Finch, in 1674: 'there is a twofold conscience, viz *conscientia politica et civilis et conscientia naturalis et interna*. Many things are against natural and inward conscience which cannot be reformed by the regular and political administration of equity.'[46] In a closely related way, James Harrington, then John Toland, used the analogical patterns of soul-talk and government, both equally informed by an overtly Ciceronian awareness of office, to speak of government as the soul of the nation, and to use this, as Finch would have approved, to restrict the office of the priest from government and law.[47]

The practical consequence of this sort of metaphorical circularity was that, however insubordinate it might seem, following one's conscience could be presented as a paramount duty sprung fully armed from knowledge of one's office.[48] Indeed, it may have been that only when cloaked in relationships of office could conscience carry authority. This can be seen slightly differently from a suggestive argument put forward by Bishop John Sharp. Rather than objectifying soul and conscience as definable and almost perceptible objects and independent authorities, Sharp dismisses the importance of definitions to ask the Wittgensteinian question of how we use the word conscience, for what purposes and in what forms of discourse. It is employed, he answers, to insist upon rule-following in contexts of moral discourse.[49] Conscience is a recognition of duty, a function of understanding offices.

Regardless, then, of whether conscience is typically defined through the nomenclature of office, or is seen as a usage about office, it is to be expected that the question of whether any other person could direct it,

---

[45] Samuel Rutherford, *Lex, Rex* (Edinburgh, 1644), Q.24.
[46] Heneage Finch, 'Treatise of Chancery Learning', in D. E. C. Yale, ed., *Lord Nottingham's 'Manual of Chancery Practice' and 'Prolegomena of Chancery and Equity'* (Cambridge, 1965), p. 194. I am grateful to Professor David Saunders for bringing this to my attention and for a copy of his unpublished paper 'Our Artificial Conscience: Lord Nottingham, Judicial Impartiality, and the "conscientia politica et civilis"'.
[47] Champion, *Pillars of Priestcraft*, pp. 198–210.
[48] Ames, *Conscience*, ch. 3, p. 7; Taylor, *Ductor dubitantium*, pp. 111–13.
[49] John Sharp, 'A Discourse of Conscience', in *Works*, vol. II, pp. 172–3, 181.

of whether the voice, the judge, the eye, could be represented and controlled, became a highly controverted issue. The arguments surrounding the consequences of the postulate of a conscience became, not arguments about selves, but about *personae*, not least that of the priest as putative mediator, and souls as office-holders. A shared faith in the imperative of subordination of the soul to God was highly divisive. At one extreme, a humanly directed conscience lost the Christian liberty of direct subordination, which was why papal or priestly authority could be seen as inimical to the health of the soul. At the other, the Christian liberty of the soul without informed mediation could be a sort of anarchy, every man becoming his own pope.[50] So, typically, Hobbes had cut to the quick challenging the long-standing ecumenical appeals to conscience: it could not be a matter of knowing. Either (in the Marsilian idiom) it is a matter of purely intransient belief, thus definitionally lacking social consequence, or it was only a matter of privileged opinion.[51] Hobbes diminished conscience by erasing associations with office. By the end of the century, although the older uses retain a vibrancy in pulpit literature, the Hobbesian view is endorsed and made palatable by Locke's *Essay*, and almost made orthodox by the latitudinarian Sharp. Conscience is an opinion about the moral propriety of our own behaviour. If every man is his own pope, the papacy is no more; even heresy can be of positive value in the quest after truth.[52]

The multivalence of the word soul casts light on the relationships between those projections from the vocabulary of office, natural and divine law. Broadly, one can say that divine law had provided a context of posited relationships for the immortal soul, natural for the animate soul. So, too, one may say that until the seventeenth century God was a necessary postulate of natural law subordinated to divine. In one way or another, the soul could be seen as suspended in the context of either. Gradually, during the seventeenth century, there were attempts to desacralise natural law. In this context Grotius and Hobbes have attracted considerable attention. As Haakonssen synoptically expresses it, both assumed a theistic world, but wanted an understanding of morality that was independent of a concept of divinity and so less reliant upon priestly mediation. God is an occasional and ghostly intruder into Hobbes's discussions of natural law, yet as he insisted in *De cive*, natural law is subsumed by divine, and he concludes *Leviathan* leaving much the same

---

[50] Charles I, *Eikon Basilike*, p. 114.
[51] Hobbes, *Elements*, 2.6.3; 2.6.12.
[52] Locke, *Human Understanding*, 1.2.8; Sharp, 'On Heresy', in *Works*, vol. VI, pp. 11–15.

impression.[53] For Grotius the moral being became a person as a constellation of apparently subjective rights in a natural order. But the natural rights bearer could easily dissolve into a soul with divinely ordained duties.[54] Richard Johnson has pointed out that when Grotius cashes in his purely abstract or provisional notion of subjective rights, he does so entirely in terms of offices.[55] Gradually, from the late seventeenth to the eighteenth century, the loosening of the ties to divine law effectively allowed natural law to function as an explanatory and metaphysical context for understanding the human; a hierarchical relationship between divine and natural law was gradually reconfigured into a parallel one.[56] Yet throughout this time, the residual shadow of the divine remained significant, and this was partly because human individuation continued to be predicated in terms of the soul.[57] A full secularisation of natural law probably had to await the replacement of the soul by the individual or the self, or for the reduction of the soul to its naturalistic dimension, allowing natural law to be re-conceived as an abstracted context of universal drives and needs that gradually decontaminated self-interest.[58]

III

It was, wrote Lord Ellesmere in Calvin's Case (1608), always dangerous to separate man from office, king from crown.[59] In such contexts of argument the notion of someone, a 'man' distinct from an 'office', should not be taken as a stable moral category but as an underspecified residuum, which when given attention resolves into further patterns of office. This is when man is not a synonym for a *persona*. When Thomas Fuller etched in his elegiac image of the yeoman, he remarked that 'as he is called *Goodman*, he desires to answer to the name, and to be so indeed'. The man is the yeoman and the yeoman is a description of the responsibilities, attitudes and demeanour of 'a gentleman in ore'.[60] Moral identity, then, was multiform just as it was being discovered, corporeal identity was a layering

---

[53] Hobbes, *Philosophicall Rudiments Concerning Government and Society* (1651), ch. 4, p. 58; *Leviathan*, p. 491; Selden, *Table Talk*, finds it incomprehensible that natural law is not subsumed by divine; paras. 70, 78, which would seem to suggest that relationship could not be taken for granted, pp. 55, 60.
[54] Haakonssen, *Natural Law*, pp. 31, 28.
[55] Grotius, *De jure*, I.i.4–5; Johnson, 'Early Modern Natural Law', pp. 102–5.
[56] See, for example, Tooke, *The Whole Duty of Man*.
[57] This is especially so of Richard Cumberland's riposte to Hobbes, *De legibus naturae* (1672).
[58] Muldrew, *The Economy of Obligation*, pp. 328–31.
[59] Cited in Russell, *Causes of the English Civil War*, pp. 157–8.
[60] Thomas Fuller, 'The Good Yeoman,' in *The Holy State and the Profane State* (1642).

of complementary systems, skeletal and muscular, nervous and circulatory, themselves hardly immune from the vocabulary of office. Similarly, the naked corporeal identity would have social presence through layers of clothes. Indeed, as I have illustrated, corporeal and sartorial metaphors were pervasive in dealing with the elusive complexity of social identity.

This helps reinforce a point made in chapter 3 that the higher the social status the more complex the official identity was likely to be; and the more privileged, the more vulnerable to critical examination. I want to reiterate that there is no need to assume some inner moral, psychological agent to adopt self-consciously the social roles it played, other than the soul impressed with its own official identity.[61] Both these matters may be illustrated by reference to Shakespeare's emblem of social being, Prince Hal, then king Henry. When, at the outset of *Henry V* we are introduced to 'one man imagined into a thousand parts', we must, I think, take Lord Ellesmere's understanding of king and crown to the assertion. It is a physical man imagined into his constituent social offices and the ethics of each.[62] Henry is in turn son, friend, brother, king, judge, soldier, soul before God and lover. The notion of some autonomous moral agent playing, then shifting between these roles either heroically or hypocritically is purely the creature of modern expectations of psychological unity.[63] And these, I think, simply miss the point that the Henriad as a whole is an exercise in the interplay and problematics of office-holding. Henry V *is* his offices, not some prior flawed person taking them up. He is defined in the drama in relationship to other emblematic figures: his father the troubled usurping king, Hotspur the honour-driven aristocrat, Falstaff his riotous inversion whose only merit lies in the joy of irresponsible friendship.[64]

All the scenes concerning Hal, then Henry, are explorations of official decorum, and the apparent inconsistencies – what Stephen Greenblatt refers to as the juggling – are the consequences of the differing requirements of office. There is, in short, no sign that the 'me' on whom 'This new and gorgeous garment Majesty sits' is anything other than the layered offices on the corporeal body.[65] Indeed, in the same scene he affirms his

---

[61] Cf. Goffman, *The Presentation of the Self*.
[62] Philip Edwards, 'Person and Office in Shakespeare's Plays', *Proceedings of the British Academy*, 56 (1970), pp. 93–109.
[63] Phyllis Racken, *Stages of History: Shakespeare's English Chronicles* (New York, 1990), e.g. p. 235; Stephen Greenblatt, *Shakespearean Negotiations: The Circulation of Social Energy* (Berkeley, 1988); cf. Edwards, 'Person and Office', pp. 94ff. The main target is the tragic division between inner self and social role imagined by Terry Eagleton, in *Shakespeare and Society* (1967).
[64] John Dover Wilson, *The Fortunes of Falstaff* (Cambridge, 1970), at length.
[65] Shakespeare, *2Henry IV* 3.2; Edwards, 'Person and Office', pp. 103–7.

identity as more than a ruler, in terms of standard official *personae*: 'Not Amurath an Amurath succeeds, but Harry, Harry . . . I'll be your father and your brother too'. The peremptory rejection of Falstaff, 'I know you not, old man', often eliciting such sympathy for the victim, was something of which Hal had forewarned his friend, knowing full well that the boyish identity of tavern carouser in Falstaff's court manqué would be superseded by the behaviour fitting the ruling prince. The rejection when it comes is an immediate response to Falstaff's consistent lack of decorum; he is a fraud who aims to use friendship to exploit the new monarch.[66] The injunction that immediately follows the dismissal, 'fall to your prayers', brutally reminds Falstaff that he is an old man, shortly to be a naked soul before God. As King Henry, he then proves his worth by taking to his counsel the man who had exercised his own office fearlessly by imprisoning the young wayward Hal. For the young king to have complied with Falstaff's imprecations would have been a form of corruption, of rule by cronies and flatterers which had been precisely the failing of the king Harry's father replaced. And Richard II is also little more than an emblem of office, explored through the confusions of affection and conduct unbecoming to his royal identity, all of which contradicted his high sense of the ceremonies of office. But crucially, in *Richard II*, ceremony is not the substance of office; and when Richard sits in his cell deprived of his 'care' and the respect that shored up his being, he is almost literally deprived of a social identity. He tries vainly to people his world with images and they dissolve before him.[67] To lift Goffman's expression, there is always, explicit or implicit, some frame of office in which to analyse identity.[68] The irony, presumably intended, is that Richard is nothing if not a king but, like some gorgeous courtier, he was really only a ceremonial husk of the office that requires a Henry to wear majesty to full effect. Henry V is a triumphant resolution of the inadequate aspects of office personified in his father and the man whose throne he took.[69]

These brief comments on Shakespeare have been made in part because he has proved such a happy hunting ground for those in search of modern individuality, and what Harold Bloom has flatulently dubbed the invention of the human.[70] Shakespeare, however, no less than his contemporaries, inhabited a world permeated by assumptions of office. This, of course,

---

[66] Dover Wilson, *The Fortunes of Falstaff*, pp. 61–81, 120–1.
[67] Shakespeare, *Richard II* 5.5.
[68] Goffman, *Frame Analysis*, ch. 1.
[69] Edward Hall, *Chronicles* (1809), pp. 46–7; cited in Mack, *Elizabethan Rhetoric*, pp. 170–1, 308.
[70] Harold Bloom, *Shakespeare: The Invention of the Human* (London, 1999).

is not to criticise modern requirements for performance, and it is probable that a greater attention to historicity makes Shakespeare decidedly more difficult to stage. Post-Stanislavski theatrical expectations of intimacy and psychological realism would have been impossible given the physical context and limitations of the early modern theatre, but have been crucial in cutting it into a dramatic shape.[71] Theatrical practices, however, are part of a broader pattern of assumptions about human identity, and, to list the slippery semi-synonyms, modern individuality, self-hood, subjectivity, moral autonomy have to be read into the early modern world in order to assimilate it to our own: perfectly proper for the boards, not so for books purporting to be about the past.

IV

The mechanisms by which modernity is prematurely applauded indicate that a rather high price of historical understanding is being paid, and because so much study is presented with the garnish of historicity this requires brief comment. If, despite all the references to primary sources, we can triumphantly proclaim that Falstaff's character is one of demystification threatening freedom, something does need explaining.[72] In the previous chapter, I noted the modernising replacement of Man for philosopher and I want now to turn to the replacement of *persona* with person, or rather the autonomous, free individual, or Self. As Katherine Eisaman Mous has indicated, selves are most readily discovered simply by secularising the notion of the soul.[73] Paradoxically, some early modern uses of soul, or *anima*, for corporeal beings has encouraged much the same translation into modern creative individuality as did Pico's celebration of the philosopher.[74] The use of the soul as a shorthand for office-holders and abusers alike also makes the conversion superficially plausible. The king might be called a soul, those plotting against him guilty souls.[75] What

---

[71] Geoffrey Borny, 'Direct Address and the Fourth Wall: The Then and Now of Shakespearean Performance', in Philippa Kelly, ed., *The Touch of the Real: Essays in Early Modern Culture* (Perth, 2002), pp. 221–38.
[72] Racken, *Stages of History*, pp. 235, 238; Brian Vickers provides a bracing polemic on such forced readings in *Appropriating Shakespeare: Contemporary Critical Quarrels* (New Haven, 1993).
[73] Mous, *Inwardness and Theater*, pp. 27–8.
[74] Lohr, 'Metaphysics', p. 573, specifically on Ficino, *De vita, libri tres* (1576), bk. 3, for whom the human soul has the duty or office of mediating between the divine and material. This remains much closer to the protean rhetor, poet or philosopher than the individualistic genius Lohr sees it as anticipating, p. 574.
[75] Ponet, *Shorte Treatise*, pp. 40–1, 50; Anon., *A Poem to His Sacred Majesty on the Plot, by a Gentleman* (November 1678); Hunton, *Treatise*, p. 2.

does it matter if we think of them all as individuals? They can all be counted individually. This sort of abridgement makes it easier to slip modernity into the evidence, and half-noticed offices get reduced to roles that selves assume. Because such roles compromise the projected moral autonomy of the self, they become, to use Phyllis Racken's tiresome term, mystifications of the reality, that is of our own projected theoretical vision.[76] Stephen Greenblatt's elegant and influential study *Renaissance Self-Fashioning* established a clear agenda of enquiry in these terms under the auspices of 'new historicism'. Although strongly indebted to Foucault for the belief that power curtails the proper development of individualism, Greenblatt concluded his study with an almost Burckhardtian peroration about the Renaissance self doing its own fashioning, making its autonomy, craving its own freedom.[77] Studies in his idiom have been legion, from Stanley Fish reading Herbert as an autonomous agent who retreated from the implications of his own autonomy, or Deborah Shuger seeing in Herbert a strict dichotomy between social office and the 'autonomous, ethical' self, to Annabel Patterson who, by dint of describing people in Rawlsian terms, is quite sanguine about finding modern liberal selves in the sixteenth century – as one would.[78]

As I suggested at the outset of this chapter, such studies have hit on something important, but, as attention to the range of the vocabulary of office shows, have done so in historically inappropriate terms. Keeping in mind what has already been said about the distinction between public and private, the following might be added. The need for an inner psychological and moral agent, a self to fashion, fail to fashion or otherwise don the raiment of office, sounds like a Rylean category mistake. In analogy with the concept of mind, Ryle gave the example of the visitor to Oxford who asks to be shown the university, not realising that the university is the organisation of colleges.[79] So too with moral agency and office. We might now need to postulate some inner self as a moving *explanans* for the diversity of social identity, but there is little to suggest people in the early modern world actually did so. Rather, what was taken to be a moral person was the constitution of offices. This may seem to us now suggestive of a moral schizophrenia, but to think of it in such terms is itself a case of

---

[76] Racken, *Stages of History*. The term is sprinkled throughout.
[77] Wesley Morris, *Towards a New Historicism* (Chicago, 1972); Greenblatt, *Renaissance Self-Fashioning*, pp. 256–7.
[78] Stanley Fish, *Self-Consuming Artifacts* (Berkeley: 1972), pp. 156–8; Deborah Shuger, *Habits of Thought in the English Renaissance: Religion, Politics, and the Dominant Culture* (Berkeley, 1990), pp. 93, 95; Annabel Patterson, *Reading Hollingshed's Chronicles* (Chicago, 1994), pp. x–xii.
[79] Gilbert Ryle, *The Concept of Mind* (London, 1949), p. 16.

petitio principe: it presupposes the very unity we now routinely expect; even if it is a moral schizophrenia, that, historically, is what we need to understand.[80]

Moreover, from what I have outlined of the way in which people wrote of the soul, they left little or no space for selves, or individuals to provide sites for this unity, or to occupy zones of moral autonomy.[81] What was regarded as licit action within the bounds of an office was no more autonomy in a modern sense than it was private, and to see moving constellations of *personae* as subjective rights-holders and standard-bearers for Grotius, and Grotius for a world after Kant, requires detaching natural from divine law and again replacing soul with person.[82] A plausible emblem of nascent individuality like Girolamo Cardano in the sixteenth century, writing extensively in a personal and autobiographical fashion, remarks that when we look in a mirror, or read our own books, we are confronting the exteriority of the soul. As even that emblem of modern individualism Bernard de Mandeville put it in the early eighteenth century, 'when we speak of our own selves, and mean our own persons, Socrates tells us in Plato nothing is understood but the soul'.[83]

Such notions of malleable identity variably relating official *personae* to a soul became highly problematic when entangled with the soul as a general principle of life, sometimes material and mortal. Matters were complicated by the neo-Platonic tendency to posit the soul as somehow located between the material and spiritual, investing animals and the world at large with some sort of soul, in the resilient idiom of the *Timaeus* and the Stoic *psyche tou pantos*.[84] Conversely, discussions of the soul could take place in a context of reductive materialism. Hobbes, the most famous voice in this respect, came from a sufficiently substantial and Christian tradition for it to be necessary throughout the seventeenth century to reaffirm the soul as life principle and as spark of immortality.[85] Thomas Willis was probably typical of most natural scientists in sticking with a form of dualism. He situated the organic soul in the brain and insisted on

---

[80] Ricoeur, *Oneself as Another*, for a subtle if convoluted exploration of the dimensions of malleable personal identity consistent with an identity in office.
[81] Tierney, *The Idea of Natural Rights: Studies on Natural Rights*, pp. 66–9, 327–9.
[82] See Johnson, 'Early Modern Natural Law', ch. 3.
[83] Girolamo Cardano, *De libris propriis* (1562), ed. Ian Maclean (Milan, 2004), p. 329, Maclean, 'Introduction', pp. 34–5; Bernard de Mandeville, *A Treatise of the Hypochondriack and Hysterick Passions* (1711, 1730), pp. 50–1.
[84] Ficino, *De vita libri tres*; Pietro Pomonazzi, *De immortalitate animae* (1516), discussed in Kessler, 'The Intellective Soul', pp. 500–4; Lohr, 'Metaphysics', pp. 570–4.
[85] R. O., *Man's Mortalitie* (1643), who regarded the immortal and immaterial soul as a heathen and 'ridiculous invention', pp. 10–11.

its being responsive to external stimuli. To a soul still comprehensible in terms of office to God, he added something very suggestive of the Lockean personality.[86] Locke studied under Willis and the potential ambiguities created by the dual soul provide some context for Locke's understanding of a *person* and his use of the term 'self', a significant point in a shift away from identity in office towards identities taking office.

In tackling the issue of human non-corporeal identity, Locke took a person to be the whole ensemble of perceptible characteristics, which he explicitly referred to as a Self.[87] This sounds like Willis's material or organic soul, but it was an answer to a number of entangled problems. It was partly an attempt to deal with what has since been called Leibniz's law of identity: the assurance with which we can say x has a given identity is a function of the covering terms, in Locke's expression, 'sortal concepts' through which it is discussed.[88] So we can be the same, or a different person (or especially *persona*) depending on the aspects of existence considered. Less directly, his theory was also a response to one of the perceived consequences of a thorough-going materialism. If the soul is an inner core of identity, how can it be hypothesised and where can it be found? Cartesian dualism, with the soul in the pineal gland linking material and spiritual reality, was hardly satisfactory; the Hobbesian, Miltonic and Muggletonian material soul was theologically disturbing.[89] Willis's conventional embrace of a range of possibilities under the auspices of the term soul remained in need of more adequate discrimination. Locke's respecification of the person, or Self, plausibly but only partially bypassed such issues by treating it not as a fixed inner identity, or an inner moral agent, but as a whole 'personality' shaped through time and in space, sustained and circumscribed by the stability and limits of consciousness. This consciousness, however, remained inhabited by a soul and it is this

---

[86] Thomas Willis, *Two Discourses Concerning the Soul of Brutes,* trans. S. Pordage (1683); see Philip Hilton, 'Bitter Honey: The Disillusioned Philosophy of Mandeville's Treatise' (Ph. D. thesis, University of New South Wales, 1999), pt. 2, ch. 1; see also Seth Ward, *A Philosophical Essay* (1652), pp. 35–42, where the understanding of the soul as an incorporeal substance covers the indiscriminate range of the terms from spiritual essence to self-consciousness and physical perception shared with animals; also M. S., *A Philosophical Discourse on the Nature of Immaterial Souls* (1695), defending Willis and Bacon, attacking Ralph Cudworth. The understanding of the immaterial soul is accepted as being dependent upon Scripture, and thus remains within the ambit of duties to God.

[87] Hobbes, *Leviathan*, ch. 16, pp. 111–12; Locke, *Essay*, bk. 2, chs. 27–9.

[88] Wiggins, *Identity and Spatio-Temporal Continuity*, pp. 1–5; Udo Thiel, 'Individuation', in Daniel Garber and Michael Ayers, eds., *The Cambridge History of Seventeenth-Century Philosophy* (Cambridge, 1998), pp. 212–52, esp. 245–9, for a valuable survey.

[89] Haworth, *Anthropologia*, pp. 31–40; Glanvill, *Philosophia pia* on the Sadducism of modern atheists, pp. 23–8, and numerous others on Hobbesian materialism.

soul, on most aspects of which Locke could afford some scepticism, that is still an inner essence confronted by God at the resurrection.[90]

The whole argument was to set a troubling agenda of debate in morality, theology, natural science and psychology. It was satirised by the Scriblerians and Laurence Sterne and taken to sceptical extremes by Anthony Collins, David Hume and Dugald Stewart who would see the soul as only an inference from consciousness.[91] Roy Porter has argued that in this way soul became a concept of psychology as well as a postulate of theology, but the soul had always had this among its functions.[92] If anything, Locke's partial accommodation of the soul to the personality, as inhabiting it for the purposes of having something to be resurrected, suggests that the soul's usefulness was being constrained to theology. With Locke we are a long way from a prototype of Kantian moral agency, requiring a concept of the noumenal, but we do have the abstract language of the Self as personality weakening a reliance on *persona* and so of office. The difficulty, however, of reading the modern self back into Locke underlines the implausibility of more distant projections into the deep Renaissance.[93]

This brings me directly to the central question of how the word self was used before Locke converted it to the abstract precondition for such modern locutions as 'Selfhood'. It existed as a term of emphasis, as in 'one self-same commonweale', 'self same instrument';[94] occasionally it could mean something close to same or specific: 'Hell hath no limits, nor is circumscribed/ In one self place, for where we are is hell'.[95] Usually, however, it is found as a pronoun and so anaphorically tied to a given identity.[96] When, in that most famous of lines, Polonius instructs Laertes 'to thine own self be true', we should not look forward to modern

---

[90] Locke, *Essay*, bk. 2, ch. 27, esp. paras. 15–23, and 15 for the soul inhabiting consciousness; Thiel, 'Personal Identity', in *The Cambridge History of Seventeenth-Century Philosophy*, pp. 888–93.
[91] Christopher Fox, *Locke and the Scriblerians* (Los Angeles, 1988); Anthony Collins, *An Answer to Mr Clarke's Third Defence* (1708); Hume, *A Treatise of Human Nature*, pp. 246–53; Thiel, 'Personal Identity', pp. 897–904; Porter, *Enlightenment Britain*, pp. 256–7.
[92] Porter *Enlightenment Britain*, p. 170.
[93] Baldwin, 'Individual and Self', is a partial corrective, p. 364, but nevertheless identifies proto-modern concepts of the self by restricting office to a 'public sphere', and by taking evidence explicitly about souls to mean selves, and some of that evidence is about the *persona* of the true philosopher.
[94] Beacon, *Solon his Follie*, p. 64; Browne, *Religio Medici*, p. 41.
[95] Marlowe, *Doctor Faustus*, lines 568–9.
[96] A rare partial exception is to be found in Shakespeare's *The Phoenix and the Turtle* (1601), stanza 10: 'Property was thus appalled/ That the self was not the same'. Although this is anaphoric, the definite article gives an intimation of the later abstraction; see also *Richard III* 4.4.

'selfhood' but back to what he has just specified as the ambit of action proper for an aspiring young courtier. In fact, it is usually a denial of what we might see as 'autonomy' that is found in a positive register. 'Self-denial', 'self-control' (the soul's), 'self-humiliation' to God, 'self-command' and 'self-government' as designating of inner discipline are all expressions of subordination to something else. Self-government was an internalisation of the expectations of office in the hallowed idiom of Plato's metaphors of the *psyche*, the inner or microcosmic regimen of the *polis*. To speak of government of the soul was, whatever its precise rules, to evoke a relationship in office.[97] For Kant, self-government would cohere with his Lutheran understanding of office as obedience to a moral law. Reflexive uses such as 'self-conscious' and 'self-knowing', 'self-distrust',[98] 'self conversation',[99] are apt to be strongly associated with knowing limits and duties, echoes perhaps of the scholastic notion that in reflexivity lay a vital part of human identity.[100] Marlowe's apparently odd usage about hell not being in 'one self place' is related exactly to a limit.

Conversely, negative compounds connote indifference to the responsibilities of office, as with the widely used 'self love', 'self-conceite',[101] 'self-credulity', 'self idolatry',[102] 'self-ended',[103] 'self-made authority,'[104] 'self-centred', 'self-glorious', 'self-tempted', 'self-deprav'd'.[105] Self-will is nothing but a will that 'usurps the place and office of reason'.[106] Similar patterns of association are found in the generally less accommodating pronouns of French and Italian. The importance of reference to self-willed behaviour explaining office-abuse is long-standing, as the seminal texts of Machiavelli and Guicciardini attest, but it is probably not until the eighteenth century that, on the initially disturbing basis of Hobbesian and Mandevillian psychology, we find the calm acceptance, or celebration of selfishness.

Similarly in aesthetics, a vogue for singularity, individuality, originality and enthusiasm is not firmly established before the late eighteenth century.

---

[97] See, for example, Baldwin, *Treatise* (unpaginated but p. 77v).
[98] Daniel, *Defence of Rhyme*, p. 62.
[99] Browne, *Christian Morals*, p. 230.
[100] Annabel Brett, *Liberty, Right and Nature: Individual Rights in Later Scholastic Thought* (Cambridge, 1997), p. 16.
[101] Tuvill, *The Doue*, proem; John Wing, *The Crown Conjugal* (1620), p. 57.
[102] Browne, *Christian Morals*, p. 264.
[103] Winstanley, *Law of Freedom*, p. 85.
[104] T. B., *Logoi apologetikoi* (1649), sub-title.
[105] John Milton, *Paradise Lost* (1667), in *The Poems of John Milton*, ed. Helen Darbishire (London, 1960 edn), bk. 3, line 130, p. 56.
[106] Cavendish, 'Of Self Will, Horae subsecivae', p. 27.

Some form of originality was given a legitimate place in the world depending on the nature of the intellectual office under consideration. The impropriety of argument from authority in philosophy and natural science made it difficult to condemn intellectual novelty out of hand. Browne distinguished novelty in science from novelty in theology; and at the end of the century, a hagiographic biography of Descartes lists his questing after the new as among his greatest virtues.[107] In religion and morality, however, newness retained its opprobrium. But gradually originality as a virtue of a specific office becomes a more general expectation for the poet, a sign of a modal ethics changing. The craftsman in office became the authentic individual creator whose sensitivity, according to Porter, eventually 'validated the inner self'.[108] Before then, selves approaching autonomy are likely not to be expressions of self-fashioning at all, but moral accusations levelled by others. Autonomy is probably about the worst term we can find to describe this most particular projection of office-abuse.

The most autonomous and protean identities in Shakespeare's or Jonson's plays (they are in this respect typical) are the quintessentially villainous. Free of all sense of being bound to an office, they fulfil the stage office of villain. When that self-obsessed chameleon Richard III remarked that 'I am myself alone', he had just abandoned the office of brother that Henry V affirmed on becoming king. He was free of all constraints on his tyrannous quest for rule, just as a thorough-going tyrant should be. The pointed repetitions of the word 'self' in the latter stages of *Richard III* emphasise the tyrant's moral isolation in another way: he has wronged so much he can only swear on himself; there is nothing but evil to which the pronoun can relate.[109] Similarly Iago is a moving tableau of evil. *Othello* involves taking the different dimensions of the office of the soldier and imagining them into separate parts.[110] Each is subject to fortune, the great counterweight to martial integrity, but of these Iago is so difficult to play because there seems such flimsy psychological grounding for his systematic abuse of the aspects of office through which others see him. Cassio expects the soldierly loyalty of a fellow in arms and is undone: Othello requires the obedience of a subordinate and the plain speaking of a trusted advisor and receives only their beguiling simulacra. In Iago we have a clear

---

[107] S. R., trans., *The Life of M. Descartes* (1693), pp. 251–2.
[108] Edward Young, *Conjectures on Original Composition* (1759), in Jones, *English Critical Essays*, pp. 270–311; quotation, Porter *Enlightenment Britain*, p. 281.
[109] Shakespeare, *3Henry VI* 5.6; *Richard III* 4.4.
[110] For a contemporary discussion of these aspects of the *persona*, see Raleigh, *Cabinet Council*, chs. 22–3, 25, pp. 68–7, 132–4.

case of the early modern fear of the protean power of the rhetor freed of the restraints of office; Iago fashions his own image and the social world according to self-interest, even to the extent of re-describing the human world as the bestial, inverting what was seen as a natural order, so displacing his own monstrousness.

As true villainy was the absence of office, it extended from kings and generals to the offices of the mind. Marlowe's Dr Faustus is the intellect's Iago. He is 'swollen with cunning of a self-conceit,/ His waxen wings did mount above his reach.'[111] It is the limitation of every art he masters that makes it inadequate for one fretting to eat of the tree of a knowledge that promises unbridled power. He dismisses, in turn, the philosophy and logic of Aristotle, its 'chiefest end' being in effective dispute, Galenic medicine, law and divinity. Magic alone gives 'omnipotence'. 'A sound magician is a mighty god', whereas 'Emperors and kings/ Are but obeyed in their several provinces'. Marlowe makes complementary play with understanding the interrelationships between the spheres of the firmament, but Faustus's burning desire is to have the power to disrupt them, have 'the moon drop from her sphere' and be unhindered by any sphere himself.[112] Such ambition was more than optimistic; it was tyrannous and sacrilegious. And a legacy of this feared restive excess, against which, as I have suggested, we find defences of rhetoric and poetry both fighting, is still evident in accusations of philosophical over-reaching well into the seventeenth century. Hobbes argued against Thomas White that he went beyond the sphere of philosophy by entangling it with matters of theology; Bramhall accused Hobbes of subjecting everything to causative analysis, so leaving no sphere for God's works beyond philosophy.[113] This critique was not unrelated to the belief that Hobbes was an atheist, erasing divine mystery and impervious to the mind's, or soul's, dependence on God. To be sure, there is nothing as luridly dramatic as Marlowe's *Faustus* as an imaginative personification of intellectual *pleonexia*, but there is a shared presumption about the tyranny of intellectual over-extension. These were failings at the heart of Faustian ambition and what was at stake in Faustus's case was nothing less than the fate of his soul, a prize distinct from the good doctor's individualistic disdain for the constraints of office.

---

[111] Marlowe, *Doctor Faustus*, Chorus, lines 20–1.
[112] *Ibid.*, lines 35–9, 83, 91, 86–7, 665ff, 278.
[113] Hobbes, *Critique du De mundo de Thomas White* (1643?), ed. J. Jacquot and H. W. Jones (Paris, 1973), pp. 367–72; John Bramhall, *A Defence of True Liberty* (1655); see Vere Chappell, ed., *Hobbes and Bramhall on Liberty and Necessity* (Cambridge, 1999), pp. 43–68, 1–14.

V

The obvious exception to the arguments presented here would seem to be found in Hobbes's descriptions of a natural condition comprised of unsocialised individuals. These clashing Calibans hardly appear as souls before God and their state is plausibly taken as presenting a post-Grotian vision of a world of persons armed with rights. Here at least, adaptive translations do not seem necessary to discover a thorough-going autonomy, the rampant individualism Burckhardt feared as bursting from the Renaissance. Coming from an office-driven environment, Hobbes's natural condition is indeed a remarkably imaginative conceptual achievement, an example of what he would call an act of privation, imagining the empirical world away in order to fashion a cogent explanation for it.[114]

There are, however, two crucial qualifications to this appearance of modern individuality. First, all variations of a natural condition were intended to explain the necessity of offices: the horrors of that condition are threatened by our not accepting the reciprocities entailed by there being a ruling office. Second, there still remains a trace of office in the ghost of a soul-like relationship to God. Natural law is subsumed by divine and the capacity of humans to reason is God-given and is sufficient to recognise His requirement to seek peace.[115] Depending on how seriously commentators take the divine injunction, the laws of nature remain echoes of an empty sense of office, or a set of commands from a lawgiver. The rights and wrongs of such debates are not the issue here. Rather, the point is to suggest that this most rebarbative image of modern individuality was not formulated by Hobbes without a touch of circularity in the residue of office it was put forward to help rescue. For Hobbes, everything hung on understanding aright office and the language appropriate to it. This was what moral and political theory amounted to, a point to be illustrated over the next four chapters.

---

[114] Hobbes, *De corpore* (1655), in *Opera latine*, ed. Sir William Molesworth (1845), vol. I, 2.7.1.
[115] Hobbes, *De cive*, ch. 4.

Part II

The authority and insolence of office

7 The cases of patriot and counsellor

> Who is here so vile, that will not love his country?
> But when I tell him he hates flatterers,
> He says he does, being then most flattered.
> (Shakespeare, *Julius Caesar* 3.2; 2.1)

I

The interplay between the positive and negative registers of the vocabulary of office was persistent in the disputes concerning the offices of counsellor and patriot. Although plausibly combined, one office was universally accepted and largely institutionalised, the other was not. Discussion of each can help explore the range of contention over the duties of political *personae* and the dynamics of the resources employed. Brief comment on republican theory in the context of patriotism, and sovereignty theory in that of counsel, will illustrate the importance of not confusing the vocabulary of office with specific theoretical development.

The direction of argument can be indicated by preliminary reference to the words patriot and patriotism. Conventionally they have been studied as markers for a doctrine in relative counterpoint to the ideology of nationalism.[1] In exploring their use as responses to offices asserted or denied, however, it will become apparent that there may be no single doctrinal history to be written. The English 'patriot' dates from the early sixteenth century and is closely related to 'nation', a term sometimes referring to the people of a given country. Thus the patriot could serve

---

[1] Cf. Mary Dietz, 'Patriotism', in Terence Ball, James Farr and Russell Hanson, eds., *Political Innovation and Conceptual Change* (Cambridge, 1989), pp. 189–90; Johann Huizinga, 'Patriotism and Nationalism in European History', in *Men and Ideas*, trans. James S. Holmes and Hans van Marle (New York, 1965 edn); for timely scepticism, see Alisdair MacLachlan, 'Patriotic Scripture: The Making and Unmaking of English National Identity', *Parergon*, new series, 14, 1 (1996), pp. 1–5.

nation, or country.² It is difficult to find a necessary opposition between nationalism and patriotism, especially as the abstract neologisms had yet to be invented and so have histories partially distinct from their linguistic roots. Throughout the early modern world the location of the patriot was debatable; his, and occasionally her, allegiances were all variable. England was a powerful locus of patriotic commitment, subsuming or obliterating Wales and war-like Scotland, swelling to the sceptred Isle girt by a silver sea.³ Yet England's counties could also be objects of patriotic loyalty, a point most evident during the civil wars when bands of 'Clubmen' tried to keep the contesting armies out of their respective counties.⁴ John Stow proclaimed himself a patriot of London with a duty to defend and celebrate it.⁵ Also variable were the evils exciting patriotic commitment, corruption, tyranny, foreign incursion, factional, private and party interest, and Rome. It is relevant that the first recorded use of the neologism 'patriotism' referred not to any doctrine, but to the disputed registers of office-talk. According to Pope and Arbuthnot, by the golden law of rhetorical transformation vices could be changed into virtues, corruption metamorphosised into 'patriotism'.⁶

What appears common to patriot and its cognates is an attempt to craft a distinctive *persona* through them because other more institutionalised offices needed augmenting, or were insufficiently tractable. Without their protective mantle comment could look impertinent or rebellious, so it was helpful to be able to shape criticism as a form of loyalty, an alternative subordination to some worthy end.⁷ There is, then, a frequent air of defensiveness about the patriot's proclaimed official duties. My impression is that by the mid-eighteenth century claims and counter-claims about the patriot had this almost habitual function, the principal disputes about the patriot being matters of tactical redescription and disassociational predication. What was at issue was the difference between true and

---

² Ponet, *Shorte Treatise*, pp. 54–5, 60, 61, 147ff (for country); 7, 175, 176, for 'nacion'.
³ Shakespeare, *Richard II* 2.1; also *Richard III* 3.1; Anon., *Sir Thomas Overbury's Vision* (1616), p. 55; Anon., *A Pindarick Poem to His Grace Christopher Duke of Albermarle* (1682), p. 2.
⁴ John B. Morrill, *The Revolt of the Provinces: Conservatives and Radicals in the English Civil War, 1630–1650* (London, 1976), on the 'Clubmen' in general and occasional synonymity of country and county, p. 14.
⁵ Stow, *Survay*, A3; Anon., *Urbis Londiniensis* (c. 1666).
⁶ Alexander Pope, *Peri Bathous, or The Art of Sinking in Poetry* (1727), ed. E. L. Steeves (New York, 1952), ch. 14, pp. 79–80. The argument for co-authorship is in Conal Condren, *Satire, Lies and Politics: The Case of Dr Arbuthnot* (London, 1996), Appendix B.
⁷ It would not be until the nineteenth century that opposition in parliament was claimed to be an office in its own right, a ritualised service to the monarch. His Majesty's Loyal Opposition was a long way from Overton's 'just and necessary *defensive Opposition*'. Overton, *An Appeale* (1647), in *The Leveller Manifestoes*, p. 177.

false patriotism, between a spurious and an authentic public voice. The word patriot proved to be a wild card of office.

But, from early evidence, the insistence on patriotic responsibility was greatly elevated if combined with piety. Cicero had presented love of country as an expression of citizenly *pietas*. Augustine had dramatically re-worked Ciceronian objects of love into a theological vision of society, and on the basis of such groundwork, the crusades were promoted by Louis VI of France as marrying love of country to love of God. On the eve of the Reformation, Machiavelli remarked forcefully to Vettori that he loved his *patria* (Florence) more than his soul; such intensity of expression could itself be worn as a badge of pious commitment.[8]

There was, therefore, precedent for what became a potent Reformation *topos*, the combined duty to God and country, useful in emergency, because arguably overriding other obligations. The rhetorics of the *patria* can appear first, not as an emotion or a rarified concept, but as an idiom of largely modal casuistry. The Marian exile John Ponet relied heavily on this double appeal to responsibility in his attacks on Queen Mary, a betrayer of England and true religion by her adherence to Rome. The patriot's duty was to stand against Antichrist.[9] A beleaguered Elizabeth proved noticeably effective in collocating the rhetorics of piety and patriotic loyalty and they were common in parliaments of the period.[10] In undated notes for a speech, Sir Ralph Sadler claimed to be speaking at once for his country and for the queen, the 'patronesse and protectrix' of Protestants. He concluded a later speech in 1563 as 'a naturall and good Englishman' giving no less 'honour and suretie to my prynce, then aperteyneth to thoffice [sic] and duetie of a trew subject'.[11] The most obvious expression of this unity was that Bond of Association of 1584, through which Elizabeth's most vocally loyal subjects affirmed armed defence of her person, religion and country. Love of country and Protestantism would continue to be precariously linked to more formal expressions of office. James VI&I was fond of the homology between father and king, and so attached the Ciceronian tag *pater patriae* to himself.[12] In defending as patriotic his proposed reforms to the office of the philosopher, Francis Bacon ironically listed selfless love of country among the faults of the ancient sages Plato, Cato, Cicero and Demosthenes.[13]

---

[8] Dietz, 'Patriotism', p. 181. [9] Ponet, *Shorte Treatise*, pp. 98–126, 147–83.
[10] Mack, *Elizabethan Rhetoric*, pp. 236–7.
[11] Sadler, 'Notes of Speeches', in *State Papers*, vol. I, pp. 549, 561.
[12] James VI&I, *The Trew Law of Free Monarchies* (1598), in *Workes*, p. 204.
[13] Bacon, *Advancement*, pp. 27–8.

Despite the roster of authorities, such rhetoric was not securely possessed by the monarch or those who would buttress his office with new learning. James's desire to unify Scotland and England as Great Britain foundered on semi-submerged rocks of patriotic opposition. He may have styled himself emperor of Britain on his coinage, but local identities were not eclipsed given the love of mutual suspicion shared by Englishmen and Scots.[14]

During the Civil War and Commonwealth period, the country, or nation, could easily house office-based opposition to any in authority. The Leveller tracts overflow with references to the nation, or people of England, sometimes using it to isolate a patriotic identity tangential to expected obligations: thus the imperative 'make this Nation a *State*, free from the Oppression of *Kings*'.[15] At the Savoy Conference debate in 1660, Richard Baxter was directly accused by the Bishop of Carlisle of using the word nation in order to avoid recognition that he was once again subject to a king.[16]

In 1681, the Elizabethan Bond of Association became a template for urging the exclusion of the Duke of York from the succession in the names of patriotic duty and the defence of the Elizabethan Settlement. Such display of the accoutrements of tradition hardly escaped the Earl of Shaftesbury's enemies, who, holding him responsible for the new Association, considered his paraded piety and love of country a hypocritical mask for rebellion. He calls himself a patriot who has lost all respectability; the word is an empty vainglorious name.[17] He had 'Usurp'd a Patriot's All-atoning Name./ So easie still it proves in Factious Times,/ With publick Zeal to cancel private Crimes.'[18] The true patriot, according to *The Parallel*, is a man of peace and quietness, steering a course between Catholicism and fanaticism. He was not a 'Factious Associator' but a loyal member of the Church of England.[19] Sir Roger L'Estrange alias 'The Observator' was equally determined to co-opt the term and did so

---

[14] See Sybil M. Jack, 'National Identities within Britain and the Proposed Union in 1603–1607', *Parergon*, new series, 18, 2 (2001), pp. 75–102; Judith Richards, 'English Allegiance in a British Context: Political Problems and Legal Resolutions', *Parergon*, new series, 18, 2 (2001), pp. 103–121; Christopher J. Wortham, 'Shakespeare, James I and the Matter of Britain', *English*, 97, 45 (1996), pp. 97–122.

[15] John Lilbourne, *A Remonstrance of Many Thousand Cittizens and other Free-born People of England* (1646), in *Leveller Manifestoes*, p. 125.

[16] Burnet, *History*, vol. I, p. 312.

[17] Anon., *The Two Associations* (1681); Anon., *The Parallel*, pp. 4, 30; Anon., *The Character of a Disbanded Courtier*, p. 3.

[18] John Dryden, *Absalom and Achitophel* (1681), Pt. 1.

[19] Anon., *The Parallel*, p. 4.

in the hallowed ovine imagery of office. 'Observator' was a patriot, the stout mastiff keeping whiggish wolves from worrying the flock.[20]

Unlike Shaftesbury, Halifax proved a survivor, but not without suffering similarly serious accusations of being an unprincipled courtly creature, 'a state Hermaphrodite', 'a church *Spread-Eagle*'. Another anti-Shaftesbury tirade referred to 'The Trimmers office, as some term it well,/ Because it squints both toward Heav'n and Hell.'[21] In his own *Character of a Trimmer* (c. 1684), Halifax deftly inverted the accusation by drawing on the latent potential of the metaphor. Only by trimming sails can a good sailor keep the little boat afloat, but always within the principled bounds of love of religion and country; because of them, the trimmer is no cypher-like and protean courtier. Halifax declaimed that he would not tolerate the damage done to one 'spire' of English grass by an invading boot.[22] In the spire he brought together the four patterns of association: religion, fixed points of navigation, the down-to-earth specifics of patriotic love, and the grass on which a flock might safely graze.

Pasi Ihalainen has shown how the word patriot could displace and re-describe accusations of party interest, and in this rhetorical context, perhaps increasingly, it attracted qualifying predicates such as 'worthy' and 'true'. The 'abandoned faction' of Whigs and Dissenters, according to the clarion voice of Dr Sacheverell, had no right to the term patriot.[23] During the early eighteenth century there seems to have been an intensification of attempts to co-opt the word patriot to a range of causes. 'Patriot' becomes a pseudonym in print. Richard Steele produced a thrice-weekly paper as the Englishman, but gave it up in 1714, tired of the alternative 'mushroom' patriots around him.[24] Standing firm in a world of party affiliations, the patriot assumed an aura of the alienated prophet which itself was an implicit accusation of corruption and carried a concomitant expectation of martyrdom. The Catholic Roger Palmer, Lord Castlemaine, called himself a known patriot walking incognito.[25] The patriot's 'soul by Nature is design'd/ to rescue Nations, and to save mankind'. His lot is to warn 'the state of coming Storm', and is called to

---

[20] Sir Roger L'Estrange, *A Vindication of the Observator* (1685), at length.
[21] Anon., *The Character of a Trimmer* (1683), p. 2; Charles Argall (?), *The King of Poland's Ghost* (1683), p. 2.
[22] George Savile, Marquis of Halifax, *The Character of a Trimmer* (c. 1684), in *Complete Works*, ed. Walter Raleigh (Oxford, 1912), p. 97.
[23] Pasi Ihalainen, *The Discourse on Political Pluralism in Early Eighteenth-Century England* (Helsinki, 1999) p. 226.
[24] Richard Steele, *The Englishman, Being the Close of the Paper So-Called* (1714), pp. 3, 10.
[25] Roger Palmer, Lord Castlemain, whose name only appears on a MS version of *The Englishman's Allegiance* (c. 1690), bound in with Samuel Butler *Hudibras* (1674), pp. 203–19, 413–21. The MS is held by the Caltech Archives, California.

bear 'The weight of Nations and the Public Care'.[26] Bolingbroke's *Patriot King* and *The Craftsman* took this attempted co-option to an extreme. His averred belief in the wholesale corruption of tradition since the civil wars that spawned party, left him with little in the way of offices in which he could place faith. His response was an appeal to the ruler, supported by a truly patriotic party, which consequently was no party. Elizabeth, not surprisingly, was the English ideal.[27] Effectively, patriotism was opposition to that man of party Walpole.

Given the ethos of defensiveness in the name of duties to God and Country, there was an industry in redescription into the odious. The patriot could be 'rough and boistrous',[28] 'so called', pretended, hypocritical, a rebel, a knave, a factious disputant, a man of private or party interest. There was little that could not, as Ihalainen has shown, be negatively transformed by connecting 'party' to something else with a hyphen.[29] But because it was self-assumed, lacking institutional protection and the formalities of initiation, the posited office of the patriot was particularly vulnerable. Any few can pretend to being the sounder part of the polity, wrote George Hickes, by claiming an interest for their country.[30] As Bishop Berkeley put it, only by consulting his heart can a man tell if he is really a patriot; bystanders find it harder. The true patriot nevertheless is a sort of guardian, a man of religion aiming at the public good, treating his countrymen as God's creatures.[31] Because any man might consult his heart to his own satisfaction, patriotism became, in Dr Johnson's expression, the last refuge of the scoundrel. This pseudo-definition did not stop Johnson seeking sanctuary in the rhetorics of last resort. In attacking the 'American usurpation', he accepted that patriotism often originates in opposition to those in office.[32] Yet its quality is 'to be jealous and watchful . . . to see public dangers at a

---

[26] George Sewell, *The Patriot, A Poem* (1712), pp. 1, 5, 6.
[27] Henry St John, Lord Bolingbroke, *The Idea of a Patriot King* (1749), ed. Stanley W. Jackman (New York, 1965 edn), p. 80; many of the same points could be made with reference to J. Trenchard and T. Gordon, *Cato's Letters: or Essays on Liberty, Civil and Religious, and Other Important Subjects (1720–3)*, ed. Ronald Hamowy, 2 vols. (Indianapolis, 1995).
[28] Edward Hyde, *The Lord Chancellor's Speech to the Two Houses at their Prorogation*, 9 May 1662, p. 16.
[29] Ihalainen, *Discourse on Political Pluralism*, pp. 363–7. Not all usage was prejudicial, however; see Hutchinson, *Memoirs*, pp. 65–6, 313.
[30] George Hickes, *An Apology for the New Separation* (1691), p. 3; also Burnet, *History*, vol. V, p. 196.
[31] George Berkeley, *Maxims Concerning Patriotism* (Dublin, 1750), in *The Works of George Berkeley*, ed. A. A. Luce and T. E. Jessop (London, 1953), vol. VI, pp. 253–4.
[32] Samuel Johnson, *The Patriot* (1774), in *The Political Works of Samuel Johnson*, ed. J. P. Hardy (London, 1968), p. 96.

distance'. The patriot does not peddle false opinions, or adhere to parties, he acts in the public interest as a lover of his people and of justice. He is, in short, a counsellor for the public good. Much the same pious platitudes issued from Johnson's usurpers across the Atlantic, where, as Mary Dietz notes, selected seventeenth-century patriots were being elevated to the status of martyrs.[33]

II

The lack of a specific institutional focus and limit for the assumed responsibilities of the patriot made the surrounding polemics inconclusive; but, as a corollary, patriotic rhetoric was invaluable in extending the range of people given official identity within the commonwealth. This did not mean that patriotism was simply an adjunct to arguments about citizenship, or an idiom of republican or democratic commitment. In offering an ad hoc casuistry of inclusion, it was a lubricant for official flexibility, a common denominator for monarch and aristocracy, above mere citizenship and for the disfranchised below it.

During the continental Reformation, it may have been that the impetus to such a rectoral expansion of office was more closely tied to citizenship, as the early Protestant reformers tried to gather forces to defend their princes and their independent cities. Gradually the imperatives of patriotic defence were extended to citizens and to the household.[34] Similar moves were made in England, but with the appeal to country-love being spread as a cloak of office to cover the excluded and to smother other forms of duty.[35] The notion of a general calling to Christianity potentially added a theological reason for inclusion and it provides a further impetus behind the redescriptive energies devoted to words in the ambit of *patria*. In the mid-sixteenth century the Marian exiles embraced all English Protestant souls in their anti-Catholic polemics. Cardinal Allen returned the compliment: true religion and love of country sanctioned decisive action against Elizabeth even by the most humble. The spread of literacy, relatively cheap print and the circulation of stories of England, above all Foxe's *Acts and Monuments* (1563), probably did much to inculcate a popular sense of Englishness to which patriotic appeal could be made. To advance the honour of 'our Countrie', wrote Richard Hakluyt, ought

---

[33] *Ibid.*, pp. 93–4; Dietz, 'Patriotism', pp. 186–7.
[34] Von Friedeburg, *Self-Defence*, ch. 2.
[35] Before Agincourt, Henry V's soldiers were his band of brothers, even the meanest gentled by loyalty to king and country; Shakespeare, *Henry V* 4.3.

to be the aim of 'every good man'.[36] After the shock of the gunpowder discovery, James VI&I responded with a similarly open-ended appeal. When king, country and religion are at 'hazard no good countryman ought to withhold his tongue or his hand according to his calling and facultie'.[37]

In the following reign, Sir John Eliot, whose opposition to the king had by 1630 deposited him in prison, sat translating Arnisaeus, *De Iure majestatis* (1610), but in doing so, the patriotic and protective duty of the prince was extended to the Englishman cherishing his country. It was a sign of things to come.[38] *The Protestation* was drawn up in more elaborate but familiar terms, to the same inclusive ends. When religion, law, the liberties of subjects, the power and privilege of parliament and the monarch's person and estate are at risk, piety and country-love impose duties of defence. In 1641 it was presented to those in institutional office for subscription, but then promoted across the country. All who embraced its terms, citizens or not, men or women, were effectively made officers for the defence of all that was good and holy about England.[39] Doctrinal content was another matter.[40] Some would subscribe only if they could determine meaning, others refused because of its equivocal language. *The Protestation* was, indeed, variously understood: bishops subscribed, altar rails were broken.[41] What it shows is how the appeals to piety and country had become part of the positive register of office and could be used to galvanise a participatory sense of responsibility.

Later, Burnet recalled that after the disaster of the Battle of Dunbar, in 1650, the Scots debated whether those who had not served the Kirk should 'be received into public trust, and admitted to serve in the defence of their country'. One argument was that it was a law of nature and nations that whosoever a government defends has a duty to come to its aid. Here country is collapsed into meaning state, with the duties of office extending far beyond citizenly privilege. To allude again to William Ames'

---

[36] William Allen, *An Admonition to the Nobility and People of England and Ireland* (1588); Greenberg, *The Radical Face*, pp. 81, 94–8; Richard Hakluyt, *Divers Voyages*, cited in Fitzmaurice, *Humanism and America*, p. 47.

[37] James VI&I, *A Discourse of the Manner of the Discovery of the Powder Treason*, in *Workes*, p. 223.

[38] Von Friedeburg, *Self-Defence*, pp. 194–5.

[39] David Cressy, 'The Protestation Protested, 1641 and 1642', *Historical Journal*, 52, 2 (2002), esp. pp. 254, 259, 252; Crawford, 'The Poorest She'.

[40] *The Protestation*, 3 May 1641, in Samuel Rawson Gardiner, ed., *The Constitutional Documents of the Puritan Revolution, 1625–1660* (Oxford, 1979 edn), p. 155; on the importance of recognising inclusive generality in seventeenth-century argument, Glenn Burgess, *The Politics of the Ancient Constitution* (London, 1992), chs. 5–6.

[41] Cressy, 'The Protestation', pp. 256–79.

casuistry, emergency makes a public officer of any private man.[42] Deeming him a patriot could be sufficient. The imperative could as easily be directed to protect the country's church. If godly, every man and woman might be called upon to carry out this duty.[43] Ponet, James VI&I, Ames and the debaters after Dunbar were all making much the same sort of casuistic moves, extending the responsibility of office by reference to country, its people, the government, or the nation. As I shall eventually suggest, it is in this idiom that we may best see Locke's inclusive appeal to the people to respond to tyranny (below, chapter 15). The difficulty, especially given a veritable tradition of such patriotic casuistries of inclusion, lay in controlling the spirits so conjured from the vasty depths.

By the mid-seventeenth century, the word patriot was sufficiently well established for it also to be used beyond polemic and special pleading, in the processes of conceptual refinement. Lawson associates patriotic commitment with communal loyalty, and so it helps shape his concept of *real* majesty, the universal dimension of sovereignty founding and authenticating political order. A patriotic Englishman is more than just a subject.[44] Adam Smith would develop a similar point more fully. In the furore over the French Revolution, Dr Richard Price had argued that although patriotism was usually just self-serving parochialism, true patriotism was support for the new France.[45] For Smith, however, the vexed issue of patriotism was never reducible to a simple commitment, it resided in the question of when the duties of citizenship took precedence over the law to which there was also an obligation.[46] Patriotism is used to abridge a pervasive feature of moral responsibility in any polity, but appeal to it is not necessarily decisive; as for Lawson, the patriot is precisely one who recognises the imperatives of considered judgement.[47]

This comment on the pragmatics of patriotism may help us move on from the rather sterile ontology of patriotism and nationalism, preoccupied with when it, or they (as doctrines, theories, ideologies or forces, 'isms'), really began, of whether one was the unhealthy off-shoot of the

---

[42] Burnet, *History*, vol. I, p. 95; Ames, *Conscience*, p. 179.
[43] Stephen Marshall, *Meroz Curs'd* (1641), p. 2; a transgression of the duty of the priest to be a minister of peace, according to Anon., *A Letter of Spiritual Advice* (1643), p. 4.
[44] Lawson, *Politica*, e.g. pp. 111–12.
[45] Dr Richard Price, *A Discourse on the Love of our Country* (1790) in Ellis Sandoz, ed., *Political Sermons of the American Founding Era, 1730–1805* (Indianapolis, 1991), pp. 1010–25; Adam Smith, *A Theory of Moral Sentiments* (1759, 1790), ed. D. D. Raphael and A. L. Macfie (Indianapolis, 1984), editorial note, p. 231.
[46] Smith, *Moral Sentiments*, VI.ii.2, pp. 10–18.
[47] *Ibid.*, VI.ii.2.11, pp. 231–2.

other. Overall, the broad awareness of office enabled an appeal to the *patria* to be used to mobilise and justify extraordinary or questionable actions, and such rhetorical practices played a role in changing and inventing parental lands and nations. That the *patria* rather than the nation was the prime focus may also be explained without recourse to some prior logic of doctrinal development, or by taking the reality of the 'ism' for granted. Because 'nation' referred to nativities, and not necessarily to units of affiliation, it was altogether less flexible. So although there was no contradiction in a patriot's being committed to the English nation, as there might well be if we are dealing with differing ideologies, the words nationalistic and nationalist were not developed as were the terms patriotic and patriot, and there is no 'nationalism' until the nineteenth century. The considerably earlier 'patriotism' was to a large extent the consequence of the interested arguments over office.

III

In chapter 3, I suggested that the organisational character of early modern society has created the impression of a ubiquitous republican practice and that a participatory ethos needs distinguishing from a doctrinal commitment to constitutional republicanism. It is on this that the rhetorics of love of country cast light. Discussion of the best form of government became familiar in early modern England and in often being about England, it helped create a site of patriotic commitment. Non-monarchical societies were known from antiquity and contemporary Europe, and so intellectually there was no reason why rule without a monarch could not be considered the best form of English government. Charles Merbury offered a patriotic vision of the Elizabethan monarchy that came close to seeing its main virtue as proximity to somewhere like Venice. At the death of Elizabeth, Walter Raleigh thought that England might dispense with kingship, to avoid subjection to the 'beggarly nation' of Scotland. During the Civil Wars Nathaniel Bacon attributed a republican form of rule to Anglo-Saxon England before its clergy-driven degeneration.[48] The Levellers occasionally gave voice to the sentiment that kings were inimical to good government in England. Despite such patriotic salvoes, it is difficult to find unambiguous adherents to any constitutional republican cause much before the execution of Charles I.[49] This is perhaps most

---

[48] Charles Merbury, *A briefe discourse of royall monarchie* (1581); Aubrey, 'Sir Walter Raleigh', in *Brief Lives*, p. 319; Nathaniel Bacon, cited in Richard Tuck, *Philosophy and Government, 1572–1651* (Cambridge, 1993), pp. 238–40.

[49] Raia Prokhovnik, *Spinoza and Republicanism* (London, 2004), pp. 117–53, for a helpful survey.

obviously because the difference between a monarchical and non-monarchical form of government was rarely clear-cut.[50] Monarchs might be elected or hereditary, and be variably bounded by law. But once armed with the potent if rather indiscriminate abstraction republicanism, it is easy now to misrepresent the character of argument and the nature of political commitments.

Three points of reference in recent historiography will help re-orientate the issue. John Pocock, recognising how minimal constitutional republicanism actually was in England, famously referred to it as a language not a programme, his paradigmatic republican being James Harrington, the authentic legatee of Machiavellian republicanism.[51] Partially with Pocock's image of Harrington in mind, Jonathan Scott has argued that the model republicans are rather Sidney and Milton (Harrington was really a Hobbesian and no friend of liberty), and that republicanism was above all a set of moral principles.[52] Both recognise an aura of indeterminacy around the phenomenon and are helpful in pointing towards the vocabulary of office. The crucial question, however, is how some employment of it gets isolated as being properly republican. Justin Champion has identified one simple mechanism: men like Milton, Sidney and Harrington all had idealised visions of society as a church under one king in Heaven, and nothing more easily fabricates a modern republicanism than discounting the religious dimensions of their selected texts.[53]

The imagination of an ideal heavenly commonwealth under the most absolute of monarchs was commonplace and it rather muddies the waters of English constitutional republicanism.[54] It nevertheless alerts us to the fact that through appeals to office such figures needed to be self-proclaiming pious patriots to justify arguments that looked disruptive of order.[55] Indeed, much of what has been accepted as republicanism was a particular

---

[50] For discussion see Robert von Friedeburg, 'Introduction', in Robert von Friedeburg, ed., *Murder and Monarchy: Regicide in European History, 1300–1800* (Basingstoke, 2004), pp. 5–28; for exceptions see, Bacon, *Advancement*, pp. 64 and 83; Raleigh, *Cabinet Council*, ch. 26, pp. 162–3, 172; *The King's Answer to the Nineteen Propositions* (1643), in Malcom, *The Struggle for Sovereignty*, vol. I, pp. 154–78, and *The Solemn League and Covenant* (September 1643), in Gardiner, *Constitutional Documents*.
[51] *The Political Works of James Harrington*, ed. J. G. A. Pocock (Cambridge, 1977), at length, 'Introduction'; J. G. A. Pocock, *The Machiavellian Moment* (Princeton, 1975), pp. 384–6.
[52] Jonthan Scott, *England's Troubles: Seventeenth-Century English Political Instability in European Context* (Cambridge, 2000), pp. 317–18.
[53] Champion, *Pillars of Priestcraft*, pp. 170–8, 264; a point endorsed by Scott, in *England's Troubles*.
[54] See, for example, Scheibler, *Metaphysica*, bk. 2, punctum 2; George Lawson, *Magna charta ecclesiae universalis* (1665), p. 144; for the ultimately Augustinian imagery.
[55] Pocock, *The Machiavellian Moment*, pp. 371–2.

exploitation of the positive register of office, a point obscured by setting up any figure as paradigmatic.[56] Playing favourites in this way is apt to confuse use of language with rightful ownership embedded in exclusive doctrine, creating a general phenomenon in the image and likeness of the favoured text. To repeat, the notions of ruling for the good of the commonwealth, in the public interest of England, of proper, or just participation in rule, of liberty and the protection of rights were terms used by all when they argued over offices of ruling. It would be hard to find anyone not embracing the virtues of justice, courage and constancy, the republican principles Scott associates so strongly with Milton and Sidney; such language could be used by any self-respecting nun. Conversely, protested commitments to good rule were sharpened in opposition to the salient terms of office-abuse. Republicans were implacably against tyranny, oppression, ruling in a private, party, foreign or factional interest (Catholic priests were particularly practised in this). Slavery or arbitrary rule and backsliding towards Rome were all feared as threats to England.[57]

This commitment made it imperative that Charles I, or his ghost writer in *Eikon Basilike*, co-opt the appropriate registers. The reader is assured that Charles acted in the people's interest, and for the good of the commonweal. He, being a man of reason, law, and loving the proper participation of his parliament and the 'true liberty' of the people, had found himself confounded by faction which, dominating parliament, tried to dictate and command his duty.[58] And so sensitive is he to tyranny that he warns his son to use his prerogative to soften the rigours of the law rather than relentlessly following the letter, which is but a legal tyranny. There is more of the same, but one gets the drift; the issue is between good government and its subversion. The explosive *Eikonoklastes*, heavily freighted with the rhetorics of commonwealth and nation, country-love and Reformation, retorted (I abbreviate) that the tyrant had no right to use such language.[59]

But, like it or not, he had done so and in taking sides as to who is the true republican, we obscure the processes by which a constitutional republicanism did develop. After 1649, people violently opposed over the abolition of the monarchy were in agreement that good government and

---

[56] Tuck, *Philosophy and Government*, pp. 221–59; Scott, *England's Troubles*, pp. 317ff.
[57] It is apparently common dislike of tyranny that helped synthesise liberalism and republicanism by the early eighteenth century; such a salve would glue everyone together; see Sullivan, *Machiavelli, Hobbes*, pp. 15, 237, 267.
[58] Charles I, *Eikon Basilike*, pp. 2, 79–80, 239, 284, 286, 79.
[59] *Ibid.*, pp. 239; Milton, *Eikonoklastes*, pp. 344, 348, 456–69, 580–1.

religion were the main issues, and that the words commonwealthsman and republican should designate the same constitutional situation – the absence of a king – but the agreement on a label was for diametrically opposed reasons. For some there was a contradiction between good English government and monarchy; for others good rule demanded a monarch, and commonwealthsman could be consigned to a lexicon of abuse, becoming roughly synonymous with rebel, traitor, regicide, etc. Ironically, then, there was something of a semantic marriage of convenience between those at loggerheads over the execution of Charles. Brought together by grasping for the vocabulary of good rule and country-love, they gradually entrenched an opposition between monarchy and republic.[60] Certainly by the end of the century predominant usage has changed. In the 1630s William Cavendish had styled himself a good commonwealthsman, one who served the commonwealth (*res publica*). In the 1680s, Richard More needed vehemently to deny that he had been a republican in order to stand for office.[61]

The issue of good rule, however, could still complicate the question of republican identity. Republicanism versus monarchy becomes, quite literally, a cosmic false dichotomy when taken to *Paradise Lost*, that most self-consciously patriotic and ambitious of epics. The question of where the poet really stands has generated a substantially misconceived literature, divided over whether Milton was true to his republicanism, or abandoned the Cause.[62] Satan stands for abuse of office (fair enough), so naturally he is manifested as a bad king; not surprisingly a composite of Cromwellian apostacy and bad thing Charles of *Eikonoklastes*, with Hell sounding like a parody of a parliament, or a participatory assembly in its chaos, self-interest and corruption of rhetoric. In contrast, God is office in its just execution, so although a heavenly king, his relationship with the angelic hosts can seem 'republican', hardly a novel or eccentric use of the vocabulary of office; and Lucifer needs to misuse 'republican' arguments in attempting to corrupt the heavenly throng. Of course: good angels actually like good government, so how is poor Lucifer going to corrupt them,

---

[60] See, for example, Peltonen, *Classical Humanism*, for true republicanism, quasi-republicanism, aristocratic republicanism, etc., all inferred from the positive register of office; Prokhovnik, *Spinoza and Republicanism*, p. 149.
[61] William Cavendish, later Duke of Newcastle, Harleian MS 6988, art. 62 in Margaret Cavendish, *The Life of the Thrice Noble, High and Puissant Prince, William Cavendish*, appendix, pp. 326–30; Richard More, 'The Defence of Richard More against the Rev. Mr. Billingsley's Charges' (*c.* 1681), MS in private hands.
[62] For discussion, see William Walker, '*Paradise Lost* and the Forms of Government', *History of Political Thought*, 22, 2 (2001), pp. 270–300.

other than by misappropriating its vocabulary?[63] What is unhelpfully styled 'republicanism' of Heaven under a king is the perfection of ruling activity, described as such through the conventional positive register of office. Having God as a king was hardly Milton's problem; it neither needs explaining nor explaining away.[64] We do not ask why he makes Satan so bad, though some have worried about why he is so interesting.

Decoding a poem that pivots upon office and its abuse as if it were, or should be, about a specific ideology is part of heavier baggage commonly carried back to the early modern world. As I have argued before, we can hardly expect to be well attuned to distant disputes if we read modern uses and dichotomies back into them. The point here is that, generally, more attention is needed to the capital of seventeenth-century debate before we can understand the development of distinct doctrines within it; and, specifically, that a good deal is bound to be mythologised if we take the mutually delineating registers of office necessarily as markers for opposing theories – consider the careless and word-blind assertions that people defended rights to rebellion and revolt, developed ideologies of the same, or conversely justified arbitrary rule. During the final troubled stages of Charles II's reign good and bad rule continued to be heatedly contested, but as the registers of each were common currency, they were not exclusive to doctrinal difference. Those like Sidney, Marvell and Locke were sure that the monarchy was leading to slavery and tyranny, while others fearing the boisterousness of un-English republicans were as insistent that alteration in the succession would mean slavery. It had been the Commonwealth that had been arbitrary, a proof that all rebels were tyrants in the making. The true patriots were on all sides.

IV

I want now to turn to the office of counsel. Throughout medieval and early modern Christendom counsel was a multidimensional phenomenon, disputed in its workings yet accepted as central to the fabric of government. The institutionalisation of counsel, through committees, parliaments, chapters, consistories and assemblies, provided the principles around which constitutions and arguments were organised. The questions of who could call a council, what authority it might have and why,

---

[63] Norbrook, *Writing the English Republic*, pp. 445–6; 'Devils soonest tempt, resembling spirits of light': Shakespeare, *Love's Labour's Lost* 4.3.

[64] As Paul Rahe points out, a monarchy might be acceptable to Milton if the ruler properly fitted the office: see 'The Classical Republicanism of John Milton', *History of Political Thought*, 25, 2 (2004), pp. 256–8.

generated a mighty literature in ecclesiology alone of which the conciliar movement provided an impressive monument. It is, however, symptomatic of wider issues that there was no agreement as to what, for example, the Council of Constance (1414–18) actually proved. It could be argued that by deposing alternative popes it exemplified the authority of rational advice formulated in concert, or that the Council affirmed the proper authority of a genuine pope whose position was hardly weakened by its advisory deliberations.

At one extreme, a council could be, as with the Italian Republics, the ruling *persona* of the polity.[65] At the other, it might be little more than a courtly accessory, an assurance of the integrity of rule.[66] The medieval English barony may be seen as moving between these extremes. Sometimes docile, cowed or on display, just occasionally toppling monarchs, it was armed as a self-styled council. The rhetorics of the office might be enriched by the literature from wider Christendom, but their force would have been familiar enough.[67]

Just as councils were central to the governance of Christendom, so was the office of counsel, ambiguously tied as it was to social institutions.[68] For Sir Thomas Smith, all those with an interest in the health of the commonwealth may speak to counsel those who rule it.[69] Society itself was thus implicitly conciliar, and like some appeals to the dutiful love of country, Smith's argument gave a touch of office to all. Commonly, however, counsel carried an aura of exclusivity and in the advice to princes literature counsel had almost a genre to itself. The ruling God was also counsellor (Isaiah 9: 6; Psalms, 73: 24) and so good counsel stood in the divine shadow.[70] It was, however, as dangerous as it was important. Lucifer, Achitophel and Judas were the archetypal figures of evil counsel and Dante had consigned all such to the ninth circle in Hell.

But counsel, even without being evil, was a responsibility that might be at odds with others, a central theme of *Utopia*. The counsellor might do good in the world but was always potentially morally vulnerable or

---

[65] David Wilcox, *The Development of Florentine Humanist Historiography in the Fifteenth Century* (Cambridge, Mass., 1969), Appendix C, pp. 211–12.
[66] Gosson, *The Ephemerides of Philo Divided into Three Bookes*, bk. 2.
[67] John Guy, 'The Rhetoric of Counsel in Early Modern England', in Dale Hoak, ed., *Tudor Political Culture* (Cambridge, 1995), pp. 293–302.
[68] *Ibid.*, p. 293.
[69] Sir Thomas Smith, *De republica Anglorum* (1583), ed. L. Alston (Cambridge, 1906), pp. 11–13.
[70] Wing, *The Crown Conjugal*, p. 79; Francis Bacon, 'Of Counsel', in *Essays* (1625), in *Works*, vol. I, p. 68; Guazzo, trans. Pettie, *Ciuile conuersation*, fol. 15v; Willett, *Harmonie on the Second Booke of Samuel*, p. 1; Baldwin, *Treatise*, unpaginated, but p. 85 (1610 edn), p. 62v (attributed to Aristotle).

useless. Whether the greater danger lay in being listened to or ignored was an unsettled issue. In either case, the office was distinct enough to stand in tension with other offices of human identity, above all that of the dispassionate scholar. Counsel was a principal humanist *topos* in the early years of the sixteenth century, and More's discussion was itself part of a dialogue among friends.[71] In a time of new rulers Henry VIII's early reign promised much. Inexperienced and talented, Henry must have seemed to be one of those rulers precious to Machiavelli, who needed and would respond to good counsel; and when More wrote *Utopia*, he had already decided to enter the king's service. But many besides More might be confronted by the problems he had considered. Counsel could be presented as the cure for the sickness in any office, and so wife, child, servant, priest, lawyer, jester might all assume the potentially disruptive liberties of a counsellor.[72]

Overall the liberty of giving honest advice was a necessity of the office. Surviving notes for speeches before the Privy Council might allude to such responsibilities in prolegomena, or by way of conclusion; thus the patriotic Sir Ralph Sadler, c. 1561, who craved to speak directly 'without fayning or dissimulation' and though only speaking like a fool, meaning 'well to your majestie and my countrey'.[73] The uncertainties of the office are well illustrated by the unusually detailed oath for privy counsellors. The specifications alone suggest the need to tie down every possibility, and enfolded in the verbal straightening of an inherently ductile position is the crux upon which so much swings. The counsellor, as Bacon summarised, is a servant acting always and exclusively in the interests of the counselled, but with this unwavering loyalty and subordination must come the duty of fearless advice.[74] The freedom of tongue was an expression of duty, the troublesome nub of liberty of office. Omit no opportunity to forewarn, instructed Goslicius. Yet both the end and the means must be good, wrote Willett with the wicked Ionadab in mind.[75] This sentiment was to the fore when John Pym later attacked the counsels of the Earl of Strafford: 'There is a *liberty* belongs to *Counsellors*, and nothing corrupts Counsels more than *fear*.' The liberty may be central to the office but is a hardly controllable means to an end. It can justify the otherwise inexcusable, hence the formal imperative also emphasised by Pym, that

---

[71] Curtis, 'Richard Pace', ch. 1.
[72] William Cavendish, 'On Self Will, Horae subsecivae', pp. 27–30.
[73] Sadler, 'Notes', in *State Papers*, vol. I, pp. 562, 563.
[74] Anon., *Booke of Oathes* (1649); Bacon, 'Of Counsel', p. 71.
[75] Goslicius, *The Counsellor*, pp. 93, 88; Willett, *Harmonie on the Second Booke of Samuel*, p. 80.

counsel keep within 'just bounds', furthering a good beyond itself, specifically what is beneficial to 'King or common-wealth'.[76] Exercising the *persona* easily excluded others and might press uncomfortably upon the ear of the counselled. There could be but a hair-line between fearless counsel and attempted control, between liberty of office and the licentious abuse of attempted tyranny.

So, to claim a right or duty to counsel was to lay hold on a potent but dangerously interstitial office, for ignoring good counsel was itself an abuse of the office of rule. Just how invasive of ruling counsel could seem can be gleaned from Goslicius' definition. Counsel's office is to punish wicked citizens and defend the good for the love of justice alone.[77] Similarly, Sir Walter Raleigh maintained that counsel has no authority and should be given exclusively on request, only to reflect that it is where counsel rules that commonwealths prosper.[78] Goslicius' adaptive translator resorted to a curiously destabilising metaphor to capture counsel's ambivalent position: it is the fingers that allow the hand to grasp.[79] As such, the office was vulnerable to complementary accusations and a choice of redescriptive options. If the advice became too vehement the office might readily be perceived as a tyrannous encroachment on rule. The whole force of Hobbes's chapter on the office of counsel was to separate it absolutely from that of the sovereign.[80] The existence of counsellors was a mark of ruling, and what Henry Parker had called the 'vast businesse of Government' required good counsel,[81] but the office of ruling was distilled precisely by its capacity to set counsel aside. How a fingerless hand could do this was another matter.

But from those insufficiently noticed in the process of counselling, the problem might be less the overreaching than the negligent *persona*: the disliked counsellor became a mere flatterer, or the negatively portrayed courtier. It is not incidental that in counselling the young Lorenzo de'

---

[76] Pym, *The Speech or Declaration* (1641) in Malcolm, *The Struggle for Sovereignty*, vol. I, p. 140.
[77] Goslicius, *De optimo senatore*, p. 93; see also Willett, *Harmonie on the Second Booke of Samuel*, p. 10.
[78] Raleigh, *Cabinet Council*, cf. ch. 7, pp. 14–17; ch. 14, p. 35; see also Elizabeth I, 'The Queen's Last Speech', 19 December 1601, where she commends her reign as always council bound and driven, in *Collected Works*, p. 347; Stephen Alford offers an excellent case study of this understanding of counsel as integral to rule: see *The Early Elizabethan Polity: William Cecil and the British Succession Crisis, 1558–1569* (Cambridge, 1998), esp. pp. 32–3, 98–105.
[79] Anon., *Sage Counsellor*, 1660, pp. 11, 162.
[80] Hobbes, *Leviathan*, ch. 25.
[81] Henry Parker, *The Oath of Pacification* (1643), sig. B4, see Mendle, *Henry Parker*, p. 122; Bacon, 'Of Counsel', pp. 68–9; Goslicius, *The Counsellor*, pp. 30–1; Willett, *Harmonie on the Second Booke of Samuel*, p. 104.

Medici, Machiavelli had included a protective chapter on the recognition of flattery. It was a common enough theme in England, and Andrew Willett would distinguish two types of flatterer, the 'palpable and gross', who 'say and unsay' to please, and those (by implication far worse) who pretend to a 'kinde of liberty', simulating the counsellor's liberty of office.[82]

Unwelcome advice was correspondingly disassociated from the office of counsel by being called new, ill, evil or 'preposterous'. The malignancy of evil counsel, as it was called in the 1640s, often provoked a rhetoric of motives which, as it condemned evil counsellors, affirmed the office of counsel itself. Evil counsel typically arose from motivations such as greed, pride and ambition, and was above all advice given to serve a private not a public interest. It might also arise from ineptitude. According to Parker, Charles I was surrounded by a council of 'green headed Statists'.[83] Naturally a ruler's position was enhanced if such counsels and counsellors were rejected. Similarly, although good counsel added lustre to rule, the office was as valuable as a pen for scapegoats as it was for surrogate attacks on a ruler. Insofar as rulers could do no wrong, the rhetoric of counsel was a corrective necessity.[84] There were, then, multiple patterns of usage sustaining the uncertainties of relationships defining the office; redescription was never hard.

V

Above all, the institutional centrality of that uncertain office meant that any sustained attempt to negotiate its scope could be seen to threaten revolution, a problem central to the Civil Wars. What have been isolated as issues of sovereignty were explicitly posed as problems of counsel, but at the same time the imposition of counsel could seem like a claim to the sovereign office under another name. Agonies of counsel became acute in Charles's reign from 1629. The parliament was characterised by increasing distrust of royal policy, balanced by royal resentment of advice deemed impertinent. Charles held that factions in parliament were attempting to interfere with his office and to dictate in his council's stead. For their part, the concerned parliamentary voices expressed alarm at the misdirected counsel that was leading policy astray. Taken to the very brink,

---

[82] Elyot, *The Governor*, 2, 14, pp. 154–5; Gosson, *Ephemerides*, bk. 2, 40r–43v.Willet, *Harmonie on the First Booke of Samuel*, p. 332.
[83] Parker, *Oath*, sig. B3, 4; Mendle, *Henry Parker*, p. 122.
[84] Smith, *Constitutional Royalism and the Search for a Settlement*, p. 189.

neither offices of counselling nor of ruling, nor of parliament understood as a counselling body were challenged.[85]

The eleven years of personal rule that followed would provide a sharpened focus on counsel, on the Privy Council in particular, and when in 1640 Charles was obliged to call first one parliament then another, the vocabulary of counsel would convey the predominant mode of hostility.[86] All the ambiguities of the necessity of counsel for sovereign office were exploited, jurisdiction and counselling persistently blurred. Those hostile to the king's policies presented themselves as counsellors by virtue of being in the realm's great council.[87] In due order they would displace evil and new counsel, of which the king was an innocent victim;[88] they would veto his choice of counsellors; they would subordinate the Privy Council; their advice would be close to obligatory.[89] Penultimately, they would save him from himself. Ultimately both his bodies would be lost and they would replace his sovereign power. When William Prynne referred to parliament as housing the king's 'companions' with a duty to restrain and bridle him, one can see how easily the office of counsel could slide into a doctrine of co-ordinate sovereignty.[90] But there was nothing new in the language of this companionable pressure; Prynne used the terms traditionally associated with the burdens of counsel not sovereignty. His readers would have picked up the allusion to the authoritative Bracton.

For his part, the king saw his choice of counsellor as a necessary condition for the maintenance of his own office: a factional noise, under the guise of counsel, was rebellious.[91] The asserted liberty of office was thus converted into licence and tyrannous intent. With such clear deployment of the registers of office, the mutually accepted responsibilities of counsel provided the means of a surrogate attack on Charles, whose

---

[85] L. J. Reeve, *Charles I and the Road to Personal Rule* (Cambridge, 1989), ch. 3.
[86] See, for example, Henry Parker, *Some Few Observations Upon His Majesties Late Answer* (1642); Parker, *Oath*.
[87] Mendle, *Henry Parker*, p. 76; Smith, *Constitutional Royalism*, pp. 189–93; this itself had been contentious, as Guy shows in noting Elizabeth's objection to free speech as necessary for parliament's office, in 'The Rhetoric of Counsel', p. 302. The confusions and ambiguities concerning parliament's status are noted by Cromartie, *The Constitutionalist Revolution*, ch. 8.
[88] Pym, *The Speech or Declaration*, pp. 140–4; *The Grand Remonstrance* (1641), in Gardiner, *Constitutional Documents*, pp. 203–6.
[89] *The Nineteen Propositions made by both Houses of Parliament* (1642), in Malcolm, *The Struggle for Sovereignty*, vol. I, pp. 148–54.
[90] William Prynne, *The Treachery and Disloyalty of Papists to their Soveraignes: The Soveraigne power of Parliaments and Kingdoms* (1643), p. 3; see Greenberg, *The Radical Face*, p. 77.
[91] Smith, *Constitutional Royalism*, e.g. pp. 189–98.

understanding had been overtaken by bad counsel, and in turn allowed him the privilege of finding scapegoats, albeit with unusual reluctance. Strafford was sacrificed by sophistical reliance on the two bodies doctrine of Charles's own office; but sacrificed he was.[92] Nevertheless, counsel allowed a certain diplomatic latitude. It delayed outright attack on the king and the reliance on egregious and isolating theories of sovereignty. It offered an orchestrated idiom of litotes, a hope of peace and settlement; up until the Newport negotiations, it was less of a sticking point than the specifics of militia control, reformation and the extirpation of malignants.[93] As so often with the shared language of office, the devil was in the details because these afforded less room to move, whereas the problem of counsel was by its nature negotiable at the edges: the importance of the office to the polity was common ground. To generalise from this with a synoptic extremity, the identification of doctrinal difference depends far less on the most abstract theoretical propositions in which it is usually sought, than on differing patterns of application. Regardless of this, if any issue ceased to allow a latitude of judgement, it became unrecognisable as an issue of counsel. On the basis of Smith's astute analysis, it becomes one of the ironies of Charles's rule that, although he and his supporters were aware of what was at stake in matters of advice, trust in him broke down because he was unable to negotiate the imponderables of judgement at the heart of the office itself and its relationship with ruling. He died of a surfeit of counsel.

VI

Analysis of two proof texts of an ideology of sovereignty can flesh out these points. They do appear in a context of argument that was partially about the location and limits of sovereignty, but neither the *Nineteen Propositions* of June 1642, nor *The King's Answer*, formulate matters as we might, or as Milton would, only to project a simple (loaded) issue back into that debate.[94] Modern analyses have replicated this pattern of oversimplification, prematurely consolidating the centrality of sovereignty by ignoring the ambiloquies of counsel.[95]

---

[92] Sharpe, *Re-Mapping Early-Modern England*, pp. 188–9.
[93] Smith, *Constitutional Royalism*, pp. 189–218.
[94] Milton, *Eikonoklastes*, pp. 456–9.
[95] See, for example, C. C. Weston and Janelle Greenberg, *Subjects and Sovereigns: The Grand Controversy over Legal Sovereignty in Stuart England* (Cambridge, 1981), ch. 3. Counsel is not indexed: Malcolm, *The Struggle for Sovereignty*, vol. I, pp. 146–7 notes that the tone of the *Answer* is misread, but the issue is still sovereignty. The best full study is Mendle, *Dangerous Positions*. He is most severe on Professor Weston,

The Nineteen Propositions was confrontational and there was little precedent for the concessions demanded.[96] Comparison with the *Apology* of 1604 is instructive. The *Apology* is more fulsome on the matter of due obedience to the monarch. Neither document blames the monarch directly for the problems addressed, but only at the end of the *Apology* does 'misinformation' to the new monarch about parliament become 'sinister informations or counsel'. The *Apology*'s insistence on conscientious free speech is to remind James of parliament's office as a court and subordinate conciliar helpmate. There is nothing that approaches a claim on sovereignty.[97] *The Nineteen Propositions*, however, may more plausibly be taken in just this way, but this still involves discounting what the document insists upon: that the king's dutiful subjects wish to reform his council.[98] Evil counsels have damaged 'your Majesties Honour and Safetie ... Publicke Peace and Prosperitie'. It is proposed therefore that the king's counsellors be approved by parliament, swearing an oath devised by both houses; that only such sworn counsellors give advice; that (as listed) the principal officers of state be chosen 'with the approbation of both houses'.[99] The voice of the dutiful subjects sounds disingenuous. The propositions following these ground rules deal with the specifics of policy, concerning the education of royal children, marriages, reform of the liturgy, role of clergy, control of the militia, the treatment of Catholics, and foreign policy towards co-religionists.[100]

To the accusation that the king had been subject to new counsels, *The Answer* retorted that *The Propositions* fabricated a 'new Doctrine', a 'new Utopia of Religion and Government'. The main objection is to the king's actually choosing his own counsellors.[101] To accept the *Propositions*

---

remarking (p. 191, note to p. 17) that concerns over counsel have been much under-estimated; the corrective move was made by Guy, 'The Rhetoric of Counsel', pp. 308–10.

[96] Smith, *Constitutional Royalism*, pp. 190–3; Edward Hyde, Lord Clarendon, *The History of the Great Rebellion*, ed. W. Dunn Macray, 6 vols. (Oxford, 1958), bk. 5, vol. II, pp. 171–2, states that initially the king considered that the people could judge the enormity of the *Propositions* without his needing to reply; but cf. Cromartie, *The Constitutionalist Revolution*, for whom it is far less extreme.

[97] Tanner, *Constitutional Documents of the Reign of James I*, p. 230; cf. Goslicius, *The Counsellor*, pp. 30–1, 88, 92, 93, 121.

[98] *A propos* of this, we may have some explanation for why *The Protestation* did not formally require an oath; such a demand might have looked like an alienating claim on sovereign power. See below, chapter 10.

[99] *Nineteen Propositions*, in Malcolm, *The Struggle for Sovereignty*, vol. I, pp. 148, 149.

[100] The asserted role in the education of children unduly distracts Mendle as the most outrageous of demands, *Dangerous Positions*, but royal education was no private matter and was also vital to religious continuity.

[101] *Answer*, in Malcolm, *The Struggle for Sovereignty*, vol. I, pp. 155, 160.

would be to undermine the 'care of Our Service', would be to 'depose both Ourself and Our Posteritie', reduce us to only 'the signe of a King'. Sovereignty, therefore, becomes an explicit issue, not as a claim, but an accusation that parliament misunderstands the limits of its office. The choice of counsel is vital to kingship and this entails that advice cannot be given as 'Commands or Impositions'. Yet, it is lavishly conceded, the king will reject bad counsels and counsellors as the Houses of Parliament also desire. On this understanding of counsel, nothing is conceded by referring to parliament as 'Our Great Counsel'.[102] It does, however, sound accommodating and prepares the verbal common ground for describing the whole polity as composed of complementary estates. Thus it capitalises upon the accepted reciprocity of offices, locking monarch and parliament in a relationship of rule; how much it accepted, how much it sought to stymie parliamentary independence is unclear.[103] This is reminiscent of the earlier *Apology* in positing king and a counselling court of parliament as comprising the polity.[104] Moreover, the *Answer* assigns to the estate of aristocracy the specific role of counselling. 'The good of Aristocracie is the conjunction of Counsell in the ablest Persons of a State for the Publike benefit.'[105] Uncertainty of official relationships was crucial, but whether disputed sovereignty was an underlying cause, or a consequence of arguments over counsel, is not evident. The emphasis on counsel helps explain what Mendle has called the equivocal nature of the *Answer*.[106] Much depends on whether we accept the redescriptive accusation levelled at *The Nineteen Propositions* – what had been presented as counsel was really grasping at sovereignty. On either side, supporting pamphlets sustained this tussle over issue saliency; for those supporting Charles the issue was sovereignty, for those defending parliament it was counsel.[107] But naturally, if first we inadvertently take sides, by assuming sovereignty to be

---

[102] *Ibid.*, pp. 162, 164; cf. Charles I, *Eikon Basilike*, pp. 79, 130 (misnumbered p. 230).
[103] Mendle, *Dangerous Positions*, pp. 10–12; Cromartie, *The Constitutionalist Revolution*, ch. 8.
[104] *Apology*, in Gardiner, *Constitutional Documents*, p. 224.
[105] *Answer*, pp. 167–8; cf. Goslicius, *De optimo*, an assumption more than an argument.
[106] Mendle, *Dangerous Positions*, pp. 9–10.
[107] For Anon, *The Contra-Replicant, His Complaint to his Majestie* (1642), the issue is really about counsel and a proper reason of state, pp. 18–22. Conversely, for Anon., *A Discourse upon the Questions in Debate between the King and Parliament* (1642), p. 9, it is about sovereignty, but in the peroration (p. 19) it is about replacing private counsel with good counsel. For Henry Parker, *Observations upon Some of his Majesties Late Answers and Expresses* (1642), pp. 7–13 the issues are counsel (p. 13) and legislation. In the slightly earlier and previously cited *Some Few Observations*, the argument shifts from around halfway through from counsel and the King's council to sovereign power: see for example, p. 35; cf. William Ball, *A Caveat to Subjects* (1642), in which the issue is sovereignty because the king is a free monarch, p. 6.

fundamental to politics, the matter is settled; whatever is said, somewhere there has to be the ideological commitment to sovereignty; selection and appropriate redescription will make it clear.

Yet even where sovereignty was an agreed issue, there was no wholesale move from the rhetorics of counsel. Accusations of evil counsel would shortly be thrown back in the face of the parliament as the effective ruler of the nation.[108] Parliament continued to be a counsel, still on the frontiers of advising and sharing in rule. In 1682, *A Plea for the Succession* remarks darkly that the late rebellion began with the attempts to get rid of evil counsellors, but the unease is more immediate.[109] Veiled threats about evil counsel marked the increasing suspicion of Charles II's religious policies. Marvell's explosive *Growth of Popery* is ostensibly an appeal to Charles to save the kingdom from evil counsel and in this he explicitly recalled Charles's determination, in a speech to his parliament, not to become the mere sign of a king, an almost precise quotation from the *Answer*. On the eve of his trial for treason, the Earl of Shaftesbury maintained what was surely a justificatory myth of a fallen counsellor, to be construed as martyr or fallen angel, depending. His has been the voice of honest counsel, of one standing between and desiring to reconcile king to people, and in doing his duty has risked being too plain.[110] He was, of course, also a patriot. A hand-written note on one copy simply remarks 'Burnt by the Hangman'.

---

[108] Overton, *Appeale*, p. 176.
[109] Anon., *A Plea for the Succession* (1682), p. 5.
[110] Cooper, Anthony Ashley, Lord Shaftesbury, *A Speech made lately by A Noble Peer of the Realm* (1680), p. 7. The handwritten note is on the copy in the Verney Tracts, Cambridge University Library.

8 Casuistry as the mediation of office

> And not *rather*, (as we have been slanderously reported, and as some affirm that we say,) Let us do evil that good may come? Whose damnation is just.
>
> (*Romans* 3: 8)

I

Like the proverbial Jesuit in a black cloak, casuistry has for long enough been hovering at the edge of this study. It now warrants elaboration. And, a little like the shape-shifting Jesuit of myth, casuistry was, and remains, too complex a phenomenon to be seen as any single school, or doctrine of moral reasoning. It was, rather, a constellation of propensities sharing the recognition that principles under-determine conduct.[1] Even if the conscience was furnished with perfect knowledge of the principles of proper conduct, they still needed applying in situations that might qualify their authority.[2] Of dress codes and sumptuary laws, wrote Donne, what may approach sin under some circumstances, is 'not alwais, nor everywhere'.[3] He was bolder about the prohibition on suicide. 'No law is so primary and simple, but it fore-imagines a Reason upon which it was founded: And scarce any Reason is so constant, but that Circumstances alter it.'[4] Such a casuistic insistence on the ethical necessity of a principle of specific judgement had long been prop to the priestly office regardless of Reformation divisions, but was vital as a moral move well beyond pastoral care and the confessional.

In law the recognition of the limitations of rules had institutional expression in the court of equity which was seen as a court of casuistry; and from the Aristotelian concept of the equitable (*to epieikes*), seventeenth-century

---

[1] Toulmin and Jonsen, *The Abuse of Casuistry*, pp. 6–11; Ames, *Conscience*, p. 2.
[2] Jones, *Conscience and Allegiance*, p. 77; Ames, *Conscience*, p. 4.
[3] Quoted in Meg Lota Brown, *Donne and the Politics of Conscience in Early Modern England* (Leiden, 1995), p. 23; cf. for example, 'Of Excess in Aparel', in *Certain Sermons*, p. 193.
[4] John Donne, *Biathanatos* (1624, 1700), p. 22.

lawyers explored both the limits of rules and the protocols of deciding who could ignore them and when.⁵ On Aristotle's authority, it was commonly held that the equitable was a just correction to a legal rule.⁶ In government an acceptance of rule inadequacy was entailed in the authority, beyond custom, claimed by medieval kings.⁷ This became the prerogative powers that strained mercy to the condemned. Pufendorf and his translator, Andrew Tooke, drew a distinction between the necessary prerogatives of dispensing with a law, and equity as a recognition that no law in nature is adequate to all cases.⁸ Michael Hunter has shown that a preoccupation with the cases of casuistry informed Robert Boyle's scientific research as it did his spiritual reflection.⁹

As I shall illustrate in the next chapter, much of what we inadvertently reclassify as political theory was pervasively casuistical. Sometimes the casuistic turn is signalled by reference to what lay beyond normal cases, where the extraordinary is allowed, or is necessary. In Henry Parker's not untypical case it is signalled by reference to the ends or scope of law rather than the law itself, to the supreme law of the people's safety and to developing what Michael Mendle has a little misleadingly called a political theory of permanent emergency.¹⁰ Sometimes it is signalled by reference to the virtue of prudence and discretion, 'the Gouernesse of vertue, the rule of our behauiour'. Rules are important but as assessment is required, experience becomes the soul of wisdom.¹¹ In short, casuistry shadowed the whole of social behaviour, and philosophically it remains a necessary dimension of ethical reasoning. There was, however, a fragile line between extenuation and a kind of antinomianism, between arguing that a dubious act is not really sinful and a seeming denial of sin. 'Evil is not in the nature of a thing', wrote Donne, 'nor in the Nature of the whole Harmony of the World'. Everything depends on what is commanded.¹² In so saying, he placed a foot, as it were, on a road that led to Hume, Nietzsche and Foucault.

---

⁵ Brown, *Donne*, p. 22; Cromartie, *The Constitutionalist Revolution*, chs. 2 and 7.
⁶ The crucial locus is Aristotle, *Ethica Nicomachea*, 1137a–b, trans. Sir David Ross (Oxford, 1915, 1966), bk. 5, 9–10.
⁷ Jolliffe, *Angevin Kingship*, p. 18.
⁸ Pufendorf, *De officio*, trans. Tooke, *The Whole Duty of Man*, ch. 2, sects. 9–10, pp. 47–8; see also the formulation in Rogers, *Philosophicall Discourse*, ch. 8, 106v: equity is judgement as to the good and honest.
⁹ Hunter, *Robert Boyle*, pp. 68–71.
¹⁰ Mendle, *Henry Parker*, p. 93; Mendle, *Dangerous Positions*, p. 179.
¹¹ Robert Johnson, 'Of Discretion', in *Essaies, or Rather Imperfect Offers* (1601), fols. 37, 55, 16; Taylor, *Ductor dubitantium*, pp. 10–11.
¹² Donne, *Biathanatos*, p. 12.

In its Catholic manifestation, casuistry led to the reliance on church authority; in its Protestant form, to the abstracted, if similarly accommodating, seal of conscience, with biblical citation replacing canon law.[13] Despite interested polemics which typically saw casuistry deplored in name and deployed in spirit, the denominational divide was deceptively negotiable.[14] A Jesuit authority might be an isolated church voice, authorities in concert might only be probably correct. A volume of Protestant cases could carry the weight of gathered precedents, none of which could be presumed automatically as adequate to the matter at hand. The education of conscience was a continuing battle. For Catholic and Protestant, the rules and criteria, the meta-language used to appraise ordinary and extraordinary cases, were likely to lead only to probably right or wrong courses of action, hence to the notorious Jesuit doctrine of moral 'probabilism'. This was first enunciated in 1577 by Bartolomeo Medina, arguing that a probable opinion might be followed even if less probable than another. It was then developed by Suarez who became its byword. Protestant case theologians similarly recognised that moral reasoning afforded only what Aristotle had regarded as probable certainty.[15] 'Probable arguments', wrote Jeremy Taylor, 'are like little starres', which when seen together 'make a constellation . . . to guide . . . our way . . . This heap of probable inducements, is not . . . Mathematical and physical demonstration which is in discourse as is the Sun in heaven, but it makes a Milky and a white path visible enough to walk securely.'[16] He barely stops short of the Jesuit argument that a less probable argument may be preferred to a more probable one.[17] The little stars of casuistry lit the way down to the waters of scepticism which seemed to threaten so many certainties in the early modern world.

If casuistry was a reaction to the delusions of rationalistic reductionism, it easily led to a world of perplexing uncertainty: seeing trees without clear vision of the wood. When a high churchman like Donne could seem so decidedly relaxed about suicide, it is little wonder that casuistry was taken to erode principle.[18] Moreover, both Catholic and Protestant forms of casuistry were open to the same forms of condemnation. Jansenists traduced the Jesuits for evaporating sin; High Churchmen tarred case

---

[13] Ames, *Conscience*, p. 11; Toulmin and Jonsen, *The Abuse of Casuistry*, p. 161.
[14] Toulmin and Jonsen, *The Abuse of Casuistry*, p. 161.
[15] *Ibid.*, pp. 160–5.
[16] *Ibid.*, p. 162; Taylor, *Ductor dubitantium*, p. 122.
[17] Taylor, *Ductor dubitantium*, pp. 121–3.
[18] Donne, *Biathanatos*, pp. 1–8.

divines with the Jesuitical brush.[19] The vital anti-casuistical injunction came from Romans 3: 8: do not evil that good may come of it. It is remarkable just how many cite this in the process of developing casuistic argument.[20] Hostile eyes could see the inherent danger in all casuistry as a form of sophistry developed to relieve people of their obligations.[21] Yet, as Bishop Burnet reflected, those most suspicious of arguments from necessity (like Burnet) would plead it in their own extremity (like Burnet).[22] So a necessary impulse in ethical reasoning became contaminated with immorality. It is easy to see the unfairness in this but it did arise, as it were, from the underside of casuistic intellectual virtue.

The difficulties were not lost on those drawn to casuistic reasoning. The emphasis on cases, persons, circumstances, to test a rule, the authority of a commanding office and the general ends that rules and offices served, all required some awareness of the criteria that might be used in judgement. 'Let the end try the man', remarks Hal in full awareness of being seen as hypocritical and unfeeling.[23] In this context can be placed many appeals, to the virtue of prudence and to natural, or fundamental law. These presented deviance in the guise of another set of laws, so countering the accusation of arguing merely casuistically. Samuel Rutherford identified a court of necessity as of no less importance than a court of justice, and in it 'the fundamental laws must then speak, and it is with the people in this extremity as if they had no ruler'.[24] Paradoxically, a further casuistic response to the contingent authority of global principles was the generation of meta-rules and procedures to maintain intellectual order. Casuistry might be restricted to physical locations. Initially the Jesuits gave it sanctuary in the confessional, but as Sir Simon Harcourt would argue in defence of Sacheverell in 1710, if there are extraordinary cases, they should not be aired in the pulpit; it should dwell only on

---

[19] John Killcullen, *Sincerity and Truth* (Oxford, 1998), pp. 10ff; David Clarkson, *The Practical Divinity of the Papists Discovered to be Destructive of Christianity and Men's Souls* (1675), chs. 7, 8; William Reeves, *The Nature of Truth and Falsity* (1712); also L'Estrange, *The Casuist Uncas'd*, p. 51.
[20] Peter Martyr Vermigli, 'De tyrannide', Commentary on Genesis 34, in *The Political Thought of Peter Martyr Vermigli*, ed. Robert Kingdon (Geneva, 1980), p. 109; Willett, *Harmonie on the First Booke of Samuel*, p. 346; Leonard Wright, *A Display of Duty* (1616), fol. 20r; Boyle, 'Aretology', in *Early Essays*, p. 38; Reeves, *Truth and Falsity*, and Clarkson, *Practical Divinity*, both make much of this tag. It is cited widely in the literature discussed in chapters 10, 14 and 15, below.
[21] John Wilson, *The Cheats* (1662, 1671), 5.4.
[22] Burnet, *History*, vol. V, pp. 434–5.
[23] Shakespeare, *2Henry IV* 2.2.
[24] Rutherford, *Lex Rex*, Q.24.

normal morality.[25] Casuistry controlled in the confessional might become acceptable if thrown out of church.

In an earlier discussion I outlined what I took to be two types of casuistry, exceptional and extensive.[26] By exceptional I referred to the sort of unadorned appeal to emergency or necessity that might excuse wrongdoing. In Machiavelli's *Prince* it is insisted that necessity sometimes requires that princes behave badly. Unadorned, this provides a morally thin defence, and as Thomas Fitzherbert argued forcibly, as a generalised rule it was hopelessly incoherent.[27]

My suggested typology, however, now seems to me to be unhelpful. It may generally be truer to say that exceptional casuistry is less a clear type of moral argument than an overly elliptical justification tacitly assuming some good end to mitigate desperate means. And the appeal to a general end, or rationale for a rule in order to override qualms about the conduct of those in office, was a tactic found across the moral landscape: 'governors in cases of great extremities', wrote Richard Beacon of Irish unrest, 'may proceede against offendors, without observing the usual ceremonies of lawes. After this manner did *Cicero* proceede against *Lentulus*, and *Cethegus*'.[28] Such actions, he assures the reader, are not tyrannous: for Reformation's sake, hammer the Irish. Necessity, claimed Robert Darlington, gave a latitude in the management of great affairs.[29] Daniel Tuvill wrote that in matters undertaken for the 'well-ordering of a State or commonweale, [there] may seeme sometimes, seeme (I say) to have in them . . . some ruder lineaments and traces of unjustice' but a public person must so 'conforme his carriage that the benefit of the publicke weale maybe the only . . . scope of his endeavours'.[30] When William Ames referred to the court of equity as having more law than the law itself because it did not consider the law so much as the ends of the law, he was making exactly this sort of move.[31] He was committing neither himself nor the court to a type of argument. The great maxim, 'the good of the people is the supreme law' (*salus populi suprema lex est*), which reverberated throughout the seventeenth century, proves a reliable guide

---

[25] See Burnet, *History*, vol. V, pp. 427–8; John Sharp, 'The Duty of Subjection to Higher Powers' (1700), in *Works*, vol. II, pp. 34–5.
[26] Condren, *Satire, Lies and Politics*, ch. 6.
[27] Niccolò Machiavelli, *Il Principe* (1513), in *Il Principe e Discorsi*, ed. Sergio Bertelli (Milan, 1973 edn), ch. 15, pp. 65–6; ch. 18, pp. 73–4; cf. Thomas Fitzherbert, *An sic utilitas in scelere* (Rome, 1616), at length.
[28] Beacon, *Solon his Follie*, p. 16.
[29] Peltonen, *Classical Humanism*, p. 157.
[30] Tuvill, *The Doue*, pp. 36–40; see also Peltonen, *Classical Humanism*, p. 158.
[31] Brown, *Donne*, p. 21.

to the casuistic insistence on the scope, or end of law to override the normally binding force of its specifics. So Strafford apparently urged Charles I that having tried all normal means, in dire necessity, 'and for the Safety of Your Kingdom and People, You are loose and absolved from all Rules of Government'.[32] Bring in the Irish. When Bishop Burnet remarked that Oliver Cromwell was all too willing to excuse his actions in terms of necessity, and indeed when Burnet himself made much the same move in justifying the ousting of James II, neither was really relying on a distinctive type of casuistry, but presupposing the moral imperatives and awareness of office that necessity served – the duty of Englishmen and Christians to preserve the Reformation and the whole frame of good government.[33] In a different context, Burnet, like Beacon, makes use of the authority of Cicero to justify dispensing with the niceties of law; and elsewhere summarises debates in parliament as arguing that 'real necessity . . . extraordinary occasions, must supersede the forms of law . . . Forms were only rules for peaceable times'.[34] This was what could be meant by reference to the supreme law. Even with Machiavelli's *Prince*, my principal example of exceptional casuistry, we find some residual trace of the office of the good soldier, even if there is little inkling of service to the state or the public good (see below, chapter 10).

The medieval doctrine of extreme necessity had allowed the appropriation of the means to live because, being God's property, we could not wilfully die.[35] In early modern England, assertions about natural law became a way of limiting such casuistry, insofar as natural law theory was a projection and rationalisation of a world of moral offices. By natural law, then, we are given rights of self-defence and appropriation, but for a reason. That is, exceptional casuistry was apt to assume a context of moral imperatives, and the need to defend action characteristically led to the justificatory explication that I had called extensive casuistry. In effect, the appeal to necessity stood between specific infringements and the scope of an office. We are dealing not with types, but with the difference between the presupposed and the explicit.

With extensive casuistry, I argued, the casuist redescribes the questionable course of action in a way that shows it not to be a breach of a moral

---

[32] Tuck, *Philosophy and Government*, p. 223, quoting Rushworth, *Memorials*, vol. VIII, p. 545.
[33] Burnet, *History*, cf. vol. I, pp. 78, 136 with vol. III, pp. 227–8.
[34] *Ibid.*, vol. IV, p. 334, and pp. 72–3.
[35] S. G. Swanson, 'The Medieval Foundations of Locke's Theory of Natural Rights: The Rights of Subsistence and the Principle of Extreme Necessity', *History of Political Thought*, 18, 3 (1997), pp. 403–6; see also below on Anthony Ascham, chapter 14; see also James Tully, *A Discourse on Property: John Locke and his Adversaries* (Cambridge, 1982).

requirement at all, but really an adherence to a further, unrecognised moral value, even the defence of an office. So, for example, Aquinas had argued that a just cause was needed if rulers were to go beyond the law.[36] It may be that this is the point of reiterating the biblical mantra to do no evil that good may come of it; the reader might be reassured that what was being recommended was not really evil; hence Tuvill's crucial (Thomistic) qualification, already cited, that apparently dubious actions may seem, 'seeme (I say)', to be unjust. Judged by a relevant standard, or when the activity's scope is explicated, actions are shown to conform to the ethics of an office. As John Pym justified his opposition to Charles I in 1643, like Cicero defending Rome against Catalinus, law was broken only for a greater good. But his enemies, Pym protested, had made his actions vicious when they were in fact 'my principal Virtue, my Care to the publicke Utility'.[37]

II

A better, though still slippery distinction now seems to me to be between what I shall call presumptive casuistry, where an office and its most salient obligations can be taken for granted, and modal casuistry where the relevant office is itself the issue. Much of what we recognise to be casuistry operated under the auspices of a unitary perception of office or moral *persona* and so concerned a single line of ethical imperatives. Depending on circumstances, these might be largely implicit and presupposed, understood precisely, or stretched to accommodate differing patterns of action. Thus Aristotle's discussion of *to epieiketes* had addressed the question of whether equity is opposed to justice. Because Aristotle concluded that it is a form of justice opposed only to the application of a given rule, it was easy to assimilate Aristotle's text to predominantly presumptive casuistry. This was ideal for lawyers who could use the discussion to reinforce the belief that exceptions to the law had to be within the scope of the law and determined by lawyers.[38] Again, a stable and shared set of values, say those of the Catholic priest, might be assumed, and the question becomes how to fit the specific case to it. And if the values pertaining to the office could be ordered hierarchically, so much the better. If a range of similar values is accepted (say charity, humility, piety) there may be nothing in such reasoning to disturb a universalist ethical deontology.

---

[36] Thomas Aquinas, *Summa theologiae*, II.i.96.5; II.i.97.4 cited in Wilks, *The Problem of Sovereignty*, p. 223.
[37] Tuck, *Philosophy and Government*, p. 226.
[38] Cromartie, *Constitutionalist Revolution*, ch. 2.

For simplicity's sake, or perhaps for the purposes of reassurance, this is the focus of Gabriel Daniel's defence of casuistry. As he pointed out, the bulk of Catholic casuistic reasoning is advice to priests about their confessional duties and not for everyone to use as he or she will. Moreover, he argues, what might be condemned if considered only in terms of justice might well be praised if considered under the neighbouring, possibly greater virtue of charity.[39] In this context, prudence becomes the clerical virtue of discerning when normal rules are inadequate, or when the implications of governing virtues are not adequately understood.

Frequently, however, casuistic argument was more than a matter of trading in virtues under the aegis of a single office and its end. When multiple offices were involved, it could be altogether more difficult to presume an established hierarchy of virtues as unambiguous criteria for judgement; a highly generalised virtue term (humility, prudence, love), if shared, could be given different content in reference to diverging realms of responsibility. If casuistry is most important where morality is most difficult, it was most needed where people were caught between conflicting patterns of duty. There might not be just single values at play, but alternative *personae*. Thus to return to the seventeenth-century lawyer and the authority of Aristotle: if it could be argued that the lawyer's office was restricted to the application of legal rules, equity in the form, say, of clemency could be the virtue appropriate to the sovereign who stood outside the legal framework; so equity belonged to the prerogatives of the sovereign's office. This was the line taken by writers deemed 'absolutist', and it was the fear of such a virtue to override the application of law that provided a driving force behind common lawyers' attempts to encompass equity within legal purview. The clash between common law and sovereignty was thus partially channelled by the presumptive or more modal dimensions of casuistry. This modal style of casuistic move was a natural, if intermittent consequence of positions such as Donne's, that wrong-doing was a function of disobedience to proper command. When authorities commanded differently, the demands had to be weighted in any definition of sin. So even parricide might be allowable.[40] One way to resolve the possibility of incommensurable moral imperatives was to posit hierarchies of office beyond hierarchies of virtue within the scope of a given office. There was, however, something rather ad hoc in such reasoning, and it could itself be subject to casuistic exception. The force of the scepticism of Carneades, towards what he had taken to be the

---

[39] Gabriel Daniel, *The Discourses of Cleander and Eudoxus on the Provincial Letters* (1694, 1704), p. 444.
[40] Donne, *Biathanatos*, pp. 10–11.

naiveties and evasions of stoicism, lay in the persistent tensions between the ethical demands of adjacent offices. The upshot was his principle that virtue in any absolute sense is unattainable and paradoxically tainted with vice. The point had been confronted pretty directly by Cicero, who devoted Book III of *De officiis* to a range of cases in which duties appeared to be in conflict. Toulmin and Jonsen call it the first 'case book' of casuistry, but correctly point out that Socrates' dilemma when awaiting execution was a matter of resolving a conflict between duties in tension.[41] Overall, moral theory in the ancient world was noticeably concerned with the case law needed to supplement and modify the modal morality of office.

In medieval legal casuistry it was precisely the special status, or office, of a ruler that permitted actions denied to others. In Book 1 of *Utopia*, as I have already discussed, More intimated similar tensions between what is proper for the scholar and what is needed of the counsellor. Hitchcock and Raleigh read Machiavelli in such a casuistical tradition. For Hitchcock, a prince had to assume 'the skinne of the Foxe and the Lion'. He could rightly do for his own protection and the public good (Hitchcock's ethicising adjustment) what in 'private persons' would be 'vicious and unlawfull'.[42] For Raleigh, also, because a ruler had his chief care in the good of the people, it was sometimes necessary to do what in a private person would be reprehensible. But if necessary for some good end, dissimulation must remain within the bounds of virtue and piety. In a world of craft it was necessary to presuppose evil intent in others, and a prince must be prepared to play both fox and lion, up to a point. Any man might be caught between the requirements of private friendship and public duty: he might have to 'omit the Offices due to . . . Country or draw . . . dearest friends into danger'. In the last analysis (at least on this occasion) the offices to country must take priority.[43] Goslicius made a parallel point about the citizen: he may in other ways be unjust, intemperate and cowardly, but as a citizen he is good if diligent in 'the service of the state'.[44] As I will conclude in chapter 10, the so-called autonomy-of-politics thesis is largely a distorted recognition of such modal casuistry. It is, however, all more than a matter of politics. The principal mechanism by which *Othello* moves to its grisly culmination is Emilia's entrapment between her duties as Iago's wife and as servant to Desdemona. She is, in fact, quite sanguine about casuistical reasoning: 'who would not make her husband a

---

[41] Toulmin and Jonsen, *The Abuse of Casuistry*, p. 75.
[42] Hitchcock, *A Sanctuary*, pp. 85–6; discussed in Peltonen, *Classical Humanism*, p. 158.
[43] Raleigh, *Cabinet Council*, ch. 20, p. 55, ch. 25, pp. 120, 145–6.
[44] Goslicius, *The Counsellor*, p. 37; see Peltonen, *Classical Humanism*, p. 109.

cuckold to make him a monarch? I should venture purgatory for 't'. Too late she realises the enormity of Iago's conduct in which she has connived out of obedience: "Tis proper I obey him – but not now.'[45] Robert Browne, in writing of the different 'orbs' of men and women, attributed to each appropriate virtues and vices. The ground for such suggestions of moral modality was prepared by his general fideism, the belief that what might hold for divinity, might not be acceptable in philosophy.[46] This indirect descendant of the medieval Averroistic two truths doctrine, and the more recent and much publicised views of Pietro Pomponazzi, rationalises a binary modal morality.[47]

Lying provides a specific focus, especially as before the sixteenth century St Augustine's absolute prohibitions against it were taken by most writers as universally binding.[48] Honesty, then, might seem to have been a value shared by all offices, and, unlike charity, one that maintained singular form. Nevertheless, distinctions between types of lie softened Augustinian demands to differing senses of office. Leonard Wright distinguished lying for delight from lying out of spite, lying perniciously and lying politically.[49] Such qualification allowed variable degrees of condemnation. The politic lie, which Wright designated as any lie for advantage, was justified casuistically if the scope of the office were considered. Redescribed as subtlety or prudence, it was accommodated to the ethics of the office of rule.[50] As we have already seen, however, the actor provided a thorough exception. The player had to lie to be true to his office. Conversely, if lying was universally to be condemned, acting was denied official standing; it could only be immoral role-play. At the beginning of the eighteenth century, Dr William Reeves, an obdurate defender of honesty under all circumstances, allows only Christ the latitude of allegorical lying; parables were necessary for his office.[51]

What gave so much casuistry a quasi-utilitarian ethos was not the proposition that the end justifies the means, but that a questionable act in one capacity might become allowable if subordinated to the moral requirements of an office; the means must serve a moral scope. To claim

---

[45] Shakespeare, *Othello* 4.3; 5.2.
[46] Browne, *Christian Morals*, pp. 265, 275; Browne, *Religio Medici*, p. 122.
[47] See Lohr, 'Metaphysics', in *Cambridge History of Renaissance Philosophy*, pp. 602–7; Antonino Poppi, 'Fate, Fortune, Providence and Human Freedom', in *ibid.*, pp. 653–60.
[48] Peter Abelard seems to be a recently discovered exception, see Peter von Moos, 'Literary Aesthetics in the Latin Middle Ages: The Rhetorical Theology of Peter Abelard', in Constant J. Mews, Cary J. Nederman and Rodney M. Thompson, eds., *Rhetoric and Renewal in the Latin West, 1100–1540* (Turnhout, 2003), pp. 81–97.
[49] Wright, *Display of Duty*, fol. 20r.
[50] Rogers, *Philosophicall Discourse*, p. 107.
[51] Reeves, *Truth and Falsity*, pp. 8–9.

office was to lay hold of the defence that, in a given case, one sort of duty took precedence over another. What the servant could not say, the counsellor must; what the woman could not steal, the mother might. What the subject must accept, the citizen, or the patriot, might stand against. The moral discourse of early modern Europe is littered with cases of this sort, the surviving shards of the constant attempts to control the potent and contestable rhetorics of office. Richard Baxter in his almost unending correspondence is persistently taken up with the pastoral work of settling doubts as to the moral framework in which a man or woman was acting, as well as the more straightforward cases restricted to what a parent or a neighbour might do. Voices at law were relentlessly casuistic in both the presumptive and modal senses.[52] By the same token, the moral ties of honesty might be loosened if unjust demands were imposed by someone abusing office.[53]

For Donne casuistry provided a poetic as well as a moral motif. *Biathanatos* is perhaps the most extensive and brilliant example of his grappling with presumptive casuistry, for suicide is largely pertinent to the office of the soul; but, as Meg Lota Brown has elegantly argued, the case the poet puts in 'The Sunne Rising' is a casuistic one. Under normal circumstances one should be up and about one's work, the conduct of one's office, even as the country ants should obey the sun's beckoning them to their offices.[54] The sun was a constant image of the office of rule that ordered subordinate spheres of activity.[55] Its 'duties bee/ To warme the world'. The refusal to let the sun through the curtains and to obey its brazen call is initially couched in terms of the lovers knowing no limit and being deaf to moral imperative. 'Love, all alike, no season knowes, nor clyme', it recognises only its own demands; the voice of the lover is an appeal to necessity. The ground for this hostility is prepared from the opening lines; the sun is personified as an invader ('Busie olde foole, unruly Sunne'), abusing its office ('sawcy pedantique wretch'), and by entering the lovers' room provokes a casuistically justified resistance. The poem's final stanza,

---

[52] Richard Baxter, *The Christian Directory* (1673); Ames, *Conscience*; William Perkins, *A Whole Treatise of the Cases of Conscience* (1608); Boyle, 'The Aretology', in *Early Essays*, pp. 3–143; Lamont, *Richard Baxter and the Millennium*, esp. pp. 33–40 on Baxter's advisory energies.

[53] Toulmin and Jonsen, *The Abuse of Casuistry*, p. 201, citing Azor, *Institutionum*, I.x.iv; III.xiii.iii.

[54] Brown, *Donne*, pp. 112–13.

[55] Bennett, *Reviving Liberty*, pp. 36–8; the opening lines of Shakespeare's *Richard III* provide an intricate pun on this association; Gosson, *The Ephemerides*, bk. 2: 'the Sunne reciuethe the day to his charge', 25r; also Bacon, 'Speech to the Speaker's Excuse', in *Works*, vol. VI, pp. 70–1; Andrew Marvell, 'The Last Instructions to a Painter' (1667), in *Complete Poems*, ed. Elizabeth Donno (Harmondsworth, 1978 edn), lines 957–9.

however, resolves the tensions between a range of dichotomous pairings, human, natural, young, old, inner and outer. It seems to claim an office higher than princely rule for the lovers themselves ('Princes doe but play us'); this at once converts the bedchamber into a microcosm of the world, and subordinates the sun's office to their own. The invading sun is invited in to do its duty and warm them. The invitation is a gracious condescension to one whose 'age askes ease'; and so with a play on two metaphors for office, the walls of a room become the sun's 'spheare'.[56]

I have noted that the stage image of Henry V was of a multiple *persona*, an exhibition of seamless movement between offices (chapter 6). Nevertheless a disquieting spectre of casuistry overshadows the centrepiece of his reign. It is, after all, two plotting clerics who at the outset let loose the war-like Harry on hapless France. Threatened by a bill that might impoverish the church, the bishops of Canterbury and Ely decide to distract the young king by reactivating the questionable claim to his cousin's throne. They are themselves compound *personae*, churchmen and counsellors, and they justify their proposed manipulation of the monarch to each other as protection of the church. Henry, however, reminds them of their solemn obligations as counsellors. Well he might, knowing that the proposed enterprise would cause 'much fall of blood whose guiltless drops/ Are every one a woe'. 'We charge you in the name of God take heed . . . that what you speak is in your conscience wash'd/ As pure as sin with baptism.'[57] In this he already exhibits his understanding of the relationships between rule and counsel. Frank, honest counsel must be taken seriously; the better the king at listening, the more burdensome the office of counselling, for the more it is joined in rule.

Had the play started with Henry's portentous warnings, there would be no evidence to suggest a casuistic disingenuousness in the advice he gets and in the detailed genealogical adumbration of the right to the French crown. But we have already been privy to the whisperings of Canterbury and Ely whose words have all the moral ambiguity of modal casuistry. In response to Henry, the cleric/counsellors put their case, sliding between responsibilities in potential conflict and persuading him his cause is just. It is not clear that the invasion is ever really just or justified; but having delegated his responsibility to his counsellors, Henry can proceed with some moral assurance carrying his potential scapegoats with him.[58] His

---

[56] Shakespeare, *Love's Labour's Lost* for a further variation; according to the elegiac Berowne, who has also appealed to necessity (1.1), love blesses inferior offices with its power, 'gives every power a double power,/ Above their functions and their offices', 4.3.
[57] Shakespeare, *Henry V* 1.1.
[58] See Hall, *Chronicles*, p. 46; cited in Mack, *Elizabethan Rhetoric*, pp. 171, 308.

victory is their vindication, but this is not a sense of ethical assurance we now share. A morally autonomous individual cannot delegate such responsibility, a *persona* can. As Raleigh put it, in a good state counsel rules. Shakespeare returned to the difficulties of *persona* and responsibility in the debates before Agincourt. It was no business of the ordinary soldier to understand the justness of the cause. Only his soul was his own, which is to say directly God's; for the rest he was but the obedient soldier. Following orders was a virtue of his office; it was Henry who must carry any weight of guilt, if it had not already been deflected onto his clerical counsel.

Casuistry was not simply displaced or superseded by alternative theories of ethics. There has been no simple dialectic or progressive change in the history of ethical reasoning. This is partly because casuistry has survived as it has contracted with the restricted scope of office; academically it is now almost co-extensive with practical ethics. It is partly because the now commonplace opposition between universalist deontology and consequentialism separates into distinct doctrines, the principles of the right (*honestas*) and the useful (*utilitas*), when traditionally these had been combined whenever possible. It is also because these more abstract alternatives arose from casuistry's perceived shortcomings; indeed they formalise the negative dimensions of casuistry itself. That is, if casuistry was an idiom of ethical reasoning essential to the mediation of office, it was as much a part of the armoury of accusation where, in a given case, that mediation was rejected in the name of office. Hence it is from a world of offices that we find a clear insistence that casuistry can be the art of justifying the wrong, of rule-mongering to find exceptions to binding precepts.[59] The Kantian attack on the partiality of casuistry, its inherent drift towards the evaporation of general moral principles, was at one with accusations against the art by those fearful for the integrity of official relationships; casuistry seemed to allow the collar of office to be slipped and replaced by a cloak of spurious responsibility.[60] The elevation of the consideration of consequence, *utilitas*, to pre-eminence in moral judgements, associated most emphatically with Bentham, is the isolation of a procedural principle in much casuistic reasoning. The consequences for the *telos* of an office had always to be considered. Somehow, in ethical reasoning *utilitas* became opposed to *honestas*, around which have hardened oppositional theories of ethical conduct and reasoning, and I

---

[59] Killcullen, *Sincerity and Truth*, Essay 1.
[60] On Kant's critique of casuistry, as well as his failure to escape it, see H. D. Kittsteiner, 'Kant and Casuistry', in Edmund Leites, ed., *Conscience and Casuistry in Early Modern Europe* (Cambridge, 1998), pp. 185–213.

suspect that it was disputes on the misuse of casuistry that did most to bring this about.

In a more positive sense, if office can be assumed, what I have called presumptive casuistry can seem close to universalist deontology rendering irrelevant problems of ethical modality. If a single sense of office cannot be assumed, modal casuistry, in stressing ends and differing functions, is suggestive of utilitarianism. Casuistry, then, was janus-like playing a part in both the positive and negative registers of the ethics of office. As an instrument of office it excited as much assiduous attention to perceived misuse as it was needed wherever moral discourse had practical relevance – where, in short, there were real problems about what values should guide one's action, or in what capacity one should act. The habitual omission of casuistry from standard histories of ethics is not only distortion, it is the sacrifice of an opportunity to explain the existence of more familiar moral positions, the responses to its inescapable but disturbing importance. Casuistry, then, marked the line between normality, the ordered conduct under the regimen of an office, and the abnormality, necessity or emergency where rules and principles suddenly seemed problematic. Gross social abnormality made casuists of everyone. What divided people, and so their necessarily shifting attitudes to casuistry, was disagreement on the grossness of the abnormality. This is easily overlooked if political discourse is reduced to a clash of principles and ideologies, or as the dramatic transformation of embedded political dispositions. The question, for example, of just when the conservative puritans became radical revolutionaries, in advocating resistance to the monarch, is a weirdly anachronistic case in point.[61] It leads directly to the general issue of resistance: less as theory, doctrine or ideology than as an illustration of the necessary evil of casuistry.

---

[61] William Lamont, 'Richard Baxter, Popery and the Origins of the English Civil War', *History*, 87 (2002), pp. 336–52.

9 The case of resistance to superior power

> What is the cause that Europe groans at present under the heavy load of a cruel and expensive war, but the tyrannical custom of a certain nation, and the scrupulous nicety of a silly Queen.
>
> (John Arbuthnot, *The History of John Bull*)

I

If hostility is any guide, resistance theory was pervasive in the early modern world, but the tacit academic assumption has been that theory means justification, or advocacy – what else are theories about? In this ideological guise, resistance has assumed singular significance in narratives about sovereignty, democracy, liberty, liberalism and individualism. Yet, if scholars have been enthusiastic in its pursuit through the tomes of early modernity, they have often been left with the task of constructing theories from fragments and asides in order to do what previous writers should really have done for themselves.[1] Duncan Forbes's remark, however, that expecting political philosophy to be preoccupied with resistance is like expecting treatises on marriage to be about divorce, has more than witticism to commend it.[2] The analogy points to the casuistic nature of the problem.[3] This was not lost on that spouse of Britain James VI&I. The notion that the people may act to preserve the commonwealth against

---

[1] Frank Grunnart, 'Sovereignty and Resistance: The Development of a Right of Resistance in German Natural Law', in Ian Hunter and David Saunders, eds., *Natural Law and Civil Sovereignty: Moral Right and State Authority in Early Modern Political Thought* (London, 2002), pp. 123–38.

[2] Duncan Forbes, *Hume's Philosophical Politics* (Cambridge, 1975), p. 323.

[3] Margaret Sampson, ' "Will you Hear what a Casuist he is?" Thomas Hobbes as Director of Conscience', *History of Political Thought*, 11, 4 (1990), pp. 721–36; Margaret Sampson, 'Liberty and Laxity in Seventeenth-Century English Political Thought', in Lietes, ed., *Conscience and Casuistry*, pp. 72–119; Glenn Burgess, 'Religious War and Constitutional Defence: Justifications for Resistance in English Puritan Thought, 1590–1643', in R. von Friedeburg, ed., *Widerstandsrecht in der frühen Neuzeit* (Berlin, 2001), pp. 185–206, for valuable treatments of political theory as casuistry.

the Free Monarch is to be condemned, he asserted, for the Bible tells us that no evil can be done that good may come of it.[4] The purpose of this chapter is to return 'resistance theory' to the casuistry of office from whence it came.

During the early modern era, the term resistance was predominantly a negotiable, near-empty classifier, argument being largely divided between competing patterns of redescription: at one extreme, resistance was really rebellion, at another just defence. Between these lay a good deal of rhetorical ingenuity, but we need to start with rebellion, for alternative descriptions were responses to its power. As rebellion, resistance was emphatically accommodated to the negative register of the vocabulary of office and the vast majority of statements can probably be placed under this rubric. With rebellion came accusations of conspiracy, tumult, treason, sedition, insurrection, violence and murder. The motivations explaining this not nice behaviour were equally lurid: ambition, pride, rapacity and envy. The authority of the Bible was persistently pressed to the excoriation of rebellion. With rare exception, such as Israel's rising against Rehoboam and the house of David (1 Kings 13: 19), rebellion lurked in the shadow of the 'son of the morning' (Isaiah 14: 12), the angel of the bottomless pit (Revelation 9: 11). Lucifer was the first rebel.[5] Under such circumstances even those openly in arms against authority might need circumlocutions for apparently overt acts of resistance. Those involved in 'Kett's Rebellion' were but violent petitioners.[6] They lost and were rebels. Predictably, Civil War disruption deepened the almost indelible opprobrium of the words rebellion and rebel, with rare exception.[7] The odium of rebellion was such that equation with resistance was itself condemnation; thus Henry Ferne at the outbreak of the Civil Wars: parliamentary resistance to the king is rebellion, therefore the deaths it will cause will be murder.[8] Looking back on the wars, Lawson argued that justifying rebellion was hardly possible. The issue had to be rephrased.[9] The question was whether the alleged 'Devil of Rebellion' might be

---

[4] James VI&I, *The Trew Law of free Monarchies*, in *Workes*, p. 206.
[5] Anon, *Against Wilful Rebellion*, in *Certain Sermons*, p. 352; Heylyn, *The Rebels Catechism*, p. 2; see, additionally, Condren, 'Liberty of Office', p. 462; J. C. Davis, 'Religion and the Struggle for Freedom in the English Revolution', *Historical Journal*, 35 (1992), pp. 507ff.
[6] Rev. F. W. Russell, *Kett's Rebellion in Norfolk* (London, 1859), the documentation in which shows rebels presenting themselves as petitioners, at one with the king, and only hostile accounts calling them rebels and traitors, e.g. pp. 48–56.
[7] Sidney, *Discourses*, ch. 3, sect. 36, p. 519; rebellion is only to re-open a war.
[8] Henry Ferne, *The Resolving of Conscience* (1642).
[9] Lawson, *Politica*, ch. 15.8, pp. 230–2.

described as something like 'an Angel of Reformation'.[10] This issue of redescription reverberated throughout the early modern world. Addressing it had been Philip Hunton's brief in defending the actions of parliament against Charles I. He was unusual, however, in making the word resistance the focus of attention.

Hunton distinguished negative from positive resistance arguing that each must be considered differently in the contexts of absolute and limited monarchies. Negative resistance covered flight, the appeal to law and concealment,[11] and it stemmed from the recognised virtue of suffering.[12] Additionally, the articulate might petition, and the holy might admonish the mighty.[13] Limited, or mixed monarchies gave more scope for such negative resistance without its being rebellion than did monarchies tending to absoluteness. Positive resistance was the use of defensive force and here Hunton imposed major restrictions: it could not be undertaken in contravention to oaths of obedience; it must stop short of violence to the person of the ruler.[14] Resistance, whatever it amounted to, arose in the context of these slippery qualifications to obedience. In the same year, Peter Heylyn's brief had been to refute every reformulation and casuistic exception to obedience as really cases of rebellion. Assertions about evil counsel, defence of property, religion and law against alleged tyranny were all rebellions of heart, hand and mind. And whether hand be armed with pen, or sword under the pretext of defensive arms, was all one.[15] Later, stepping back from Heylyn's capacious notion of rebellion, Christopher Harvey accepted that a few acts were only so-called rebellion, but those properly designated remained satanically wicked; while Jeremy Taylor, who had ways of qualifying most absolute injunctions, insisted that the rule prohibiting subjects taking up arms against a sovereign was among the most binding.[16] What is called resistance theory, then, was the casuistry involved in finding descriptive latitude for presumptively rebellious acts against office, the attempts to maintain a verbal and moral space quarantined from Luciferian pollution. The 'word "rebellion" – it

---

[10] Charles I, *Eikon Basilike*, p. 235; A. Sellar, *The History of Passive Obedience* (1689), p. 132.
[11] Hunton, *Treatise*, pp. 4–9, 25 and pt. 2; pp. 8, 14.
[12] Rogers, *Philosophical Discourse*, p. 156; Willett, *Harmonie on the Second Booke of Samuel*, p. 12; Sellar, *History of Passive Obedience*, p. 132.
[13] Hugh Latimer, sermon (8 March 1549) before King Edward, in *Fruitful Sermons*, fol. 25v; Thomas Bell, *The Regiment of the Church* (1606), pp. 4–5.
[14] Hunton, *Treatise*, pp. 66, 15, 28, 55–61, 64, 65.
[15] Heylyn, *Rebels Catechism*, pp. 3–9, 10; see also Anon., *A Looking Glass for Rebels* (1643); Seth Ward, *Against Resistance to Lawful Powers* (1661, 1710), pp. 8–9.
[16] Harvey, *Faction Supplanted*, sect. 7 and pp. 28–9; Taylor, *Ductor dubitantium*, pp. 149–50.

had froze them up,/ As fish are in a pond. But now the Bishop/ Turns insurrection to religion.'[17]

II

Nothing illustrates better the ecumenical nature of casuistry than arguments about the limitations of obedience. To be sure, what is called Catholic resistance theory required the sanction of papal authority, and within Catholicism there were disputes about whether papal power was direct or indirect, spiritual or partially temporal. Such questions left English Jesuits horribly exposed from the last years of Elizabeth's reign. But despite the absence of pontifical authority for Protestants, casuistic justifications were interdenominational. William Barclay's coinage *monarchomachi*, king killers, applied to the implications of the arguments of Huguenots and Catholic Leaguers alike.[18] David Owen referred to an evil concord of 'puritan-Jesuitisme'; James VI&I called Jesuits 'puritan papists'.[19] Gradually from an intellectual consanguinity grew a mythic rebellious and regicidal alliance. Owen's puritan lineage includes Goodman, Knox and Buchanan, Marsilius of Padua and the 'lewd learning' of pagan antiquity.[20] So in writing for a Protestant audience Hunton had the challenging task of distancing himself from Jesuit contamination.[21] It was no easy matter when the Civil Wars were already pulling on their marching boots. After the dust had mostly settled during the Restoration, the accusations about a puritan–Jesuit conspiracy gained polemical momentum, especially for a very royalist Church of England, a proclaimed *via media* between these hated extremes. For a while, the church even created the illusion that principled obedience could be immune from casuistic exception (see below, chapter 15).

The strength of Owen's case had lain in his recognising the largely common casuistry derived from shared presuppositions of office rather than upon nosing out any genuine plot. The unwillingness to explore what casuistry might sanction in emergency, arose from an equally ecumenical awareness of how difficult it would be to control the consequences. Accepting extraordinary remedies risked normalising them and

---

[17] Shakespeare, *2Henry IV* 1. 1.
[18] J. H. M. Salmon, 'Catholic Resistance Theory, Ultramontanism and the Royalist Response, 1580–1620', in J. H. Burns, ed. (assisted by Mark Goldie), *The Cambridge History of Political Thought, 1450–1700* (Cambridge, 1991), pp. 219–53, esp. 235.
[19] Owen, *Herode*, pp. 36–43, 47ff; James VI&I, *Premonition*, in *Workes*, p. 305.
[20] Owen, *Herode*, pp. 47, 45, 44.   [21] Hunton, *Treatise*, pp. 54–5.

encouraged accusations of wanting to do so. Argument from implication was one of the first resorts of polemic.[22]

III

In an unstable world, however, total acceptance of a principle of subordination was difficult to sustain. Unqualified obedience was, theologically, owed only to God; therefore all human obligations had some limit.[23] This rabbit was always in the hat as it passed around divided Christendom. The solution to its lurking presence lay in equating some privileged patterns of human subordination effectively with obedience to God. Nevertheless, there remained circumstances when even the most acquiescent might need occasional recourse to a casuistry of non-compliance.

In its presumptive form, this casuistry pleaded that the virtue of submission to immediate authority had been misunderstood. This form of argument is common to political documents that are denominationally poles apart. For the Marian exile Christopher Goodman, as tyrants are an affront to God, accepting them is complicity with Antichrist. It is therefore not rebellion but a doctrine of Godly peace that demands of everyman the eradication of tyranny, a topic to which I will return below.[24] Goodman's casuistry was taken over in William Allen's incitement to rise up against Elizabeth I. It is she, Allen declaims, who has rebelled against God's laws, and a proper understanding of submission requires her removal. Catholic resistance is obedience to true religion, quite unlike heretical rebellion.[25] Thomas Bilson and Andrew Willett would shortly concur. True religion was indeed obeyed by disobeying the false; they simply tipped the pope from the content of the truth and poured him into the bucket of iniquity.[26] Leonard Wright was adamant that even the tyrannical must be obeyed: except (he notes parenthetically) in matters contrary to faith and salvation.[27] True obedience can

---

[22] Cooper, *Fear and Polemic*, pp. 5–7.
[23] Theodore Beza (?), *Du droit des magistrats* (1573), ed. R. M. Kingdon (Geneva, 1971); Hunton, *Treatise*, pp. 8–9. The importance of this limit was underlined by the Israelites' flirtation with theocratic monarchy, with the kings after David obscuring the place of God in the minds of his people. It would be a powerful theme in post-Civil War England.
[24] Ponet, *Shorte Treatise*, pp. 33, 50, 98ff; Christopher Goodman, *How Superiours oght to be Obeyd of their Subjects* (1558), pp. 9, 62, 191.
[25] Salmon, 'Catholic Resistance Theory', p. 242; Allen, *An Admonition*; the title seems to allude to Ponet's peroration, 'An exortacion or rather warning to the Lordes and Commones of Englande', in *Shorte Treatise*, p. 147.
[26] Thomas Bilson, *The True Difference between Christian Subjection and Unchristian Rebellion* (Oxford, 1585); Willett, *Harmonie on the First Booke of Samuel*, pp. 293–5.
[27] Wright, *Display of Duty*, fols. 6v–7r.

be disobedience, tyranny can really be rebellion. In the wake of the Gunpowder Plot, Owen found all such arguments anathema. Endorsing the sort of high monarchical claims that had James VI&I whistling in the Scottish winds, Owen insisted that God made the monarch and the rest as subjects owed obedience, full stop. Any qualification invited anarchy. Such views were current throughout the seventeenth century. With faith in an office of rule, they offered nothing more complex than a subject *persona* whose duty is to obey the office itself. The general language being shared, what divides writers is who is classified as what, creating oppositional doctrines from the same resources and patterns of presupposition. As I shall show, they had unexpected doctrinal reformulation in the Engagement and oath of allegiance controversies of 1649–50 and 1689–90 respectively (chapters 14, 15). What can be called the Marian question – who is really guilty of rebellion – retains its contested vibrancy into the eighteenth century. The true rebels, insisted Defoe, were those who introduced the novel doctrines of *jure divino* rule before the Civil Wars, and those who in reactivating them caused the Revolution of 1688–9.[28]

In casuistry's more modal manifestations, there is not just a higher but a somewhat different duty that could be invoked to deflect accusations of rebellion. As I have argued, the claimed offices of patriot and counsellor could have this protective function. Such forms of redescription had been a feature of argument during the turbulent years of Angevin kingship and became a striking aspect of apologetics during the French Wars of Religion.[29] They later cohered the debates between Charles I and his parliaments in 1629 and from 1640 to 1642. Through counsel it was possible to draw on the Bractonian and Seysselian metaphors of the counselling *persona* as 'bridling' the ruler through advice. There emerged, however, other variations on this theme.

IV

From the sixteenth century, insistence on the corrective duties of lesser magistrates provided defence against accusations of rebellion. It was, initially, a less ambiguous claim on the office of rule than counsel allowed. Calvin saw the Spartan Ephors as a lesser magistracy constraining the Spartan kings, and exemplifying the necessity that all office under God be

---

[28] Defoe, *Jure Divino*, see De Luna, '*Jure Divino*', pp. 43–66.
[29] Jolliffe, *Angevin Kingship*, ch. 1; Salmon, 'Catholic Resistance Theory', at length.

limited.³⁰ Beza and Althusius presented more sustained arguments. Although private men might be at most passively disobedient, the lesser magistracy had a duty of resistance when the office of rule was abused. Lesser magistrates were plausibly identified in France, and especially in an imperial context where such figures were armed independent princes with diplomatic and legal standing.³¹ Adjustments, however, were needed for lesser magistracy to be seen as directly relevant to England; once made, an initially precise and exclusive office became highly accommodating.

Protestant civic hostility to imperial Catholicism, most notably in the Magdeburg Confession of 1550, extended lesser magistracy to include elected city officials, which thus became particularly helpful in a polity with London at its centre. The Marian exiles stretched lesser magistracy by urging the duty to protect true religion. Peter Martyr feared that this would allow the wicked to 'doe violence unto godly Princes: and so should nothing be left holy and unviolated'. Notwithstanding, he insisted that inferior magistrates should act whenever princes 'transgresse the endes and limites' of their power.³² As precedents, he cited both the German imperial Electors and the senate and people of Rome. The associations between Rome and London need not be laboured further, but the allusion to Rome left the door ajar for a very humble lesser magistrate. Within a generation, Anthony Gilby warned that if magistrates neglected their duties, men like the one-legged Miles Monopodios, soldier, that is an officer of Christ, would act in their stead.³³

By the Civil War period, references to lesser magistracy were common in England. Predictably for Peter Heylyn, they amounted to rebellion, anything but for John Goodwin. He was succinct and inclusive: 'the procurement of the publique good, doth not lie by way of Office, or duty, upon the chiefe Magistrate only, but upon all subordinate Magistrates also, and Officers whatsoever'.³⁴ In 1649 'Philodemius' endorsed this in a way that points again to the most extensive scope of office. The efficient

---

[30] Jean Calvin, *Institutes*, discussed with an acidic accuracy in Harro Höpfl, *The Christian Polity of John Calvin* (Cambridge, 1982), pp. 171–2.
[31] Robert von Friedeburg, 'Self Defence and Sovereignty. The Reception and Application of German Political Thought in England and Scotland, 1628–1669', *History of Political Thought*, 23 (2002), pp. 238–65; Kathleen Parrow, *From Defense To Resistance: Justification of Violence during the French Wars of Religion*, Transactions of the American Philosophical Society, vol. LXXXIII, pt. 6 (Philadelphia, 1993), pp. 38–42.
[32] Goodman, *Superiours*, pp. 43–4; Peter Martyr Vermigli, *Political Thought*, p. 11.
[33] Anthony Gilby, *A Pleasaunt Dialogue Between A Soldier of Berwicke and an English Chaplaine* (1581), pp. A2–B4.
[34] Heylyn, *Rebel's Catechism*, p. 15; John Goodwin, *Right and Might well Mett* (1648) in Malcolm, *The Struggle for Sovereignty*, vol. I, pp. 317, 316.

cause, or womb of all political power is the people, that is, any 'person whatsoever', whether their professions and callings be honourable or 'base and extreme'.[35] A people as such, however, needs lesser magistrates to act for it. That every person had some kind of office made it easy for the corrective powers of the lesser magistrate to include the army. In the 1640s Miles Monopodios was on the march, or rather hop, and the execution of Charles was an exercise of magesterial office.

Here it must be reiterated that, as with the related motif of patriotism, there was no straightforward democratic trajectory, with the doctrine of the lesser magistrate in the Reformation leading to Locke's, or more individualistic insistence on the people's right to resist. The Marian exiles, confronting the most exceptional of circumstances had been willing to give everyman an ad hoc official status in the accommodating names of religion, love of country and hatred of Queen Mary. There was, however, little more than a sporadic casuistic application of the randomly applicable theological axiom that every man has an office:[36] sporadic because so potentially disruptive. Moreover, the point of this theological axiom was often more directed at the powerful who might place themselves above office than at the lowly who had been denied it. Designation in terms of office acknowledged accountability for the onerous exercise of liberty.

During the Civil Wars the Earl of Essex, who by accepting parliamentarian command was particularly exposed to accusations of rebellion, acted under a local and very exclusive adaptation of lesser magistracy: to wit, the medieval office (vacant since 1521) of High Constable, whose responsibility was to keep the monarch to the terms of the coronation oath.[37] His sheltering under this illustrates the easy flow between distinguishable rhetorics of conciliar control, baronial bridling and lesser magistracy and, more generally, that wherever there was an office there was a rhetoric of its defence. As the soul itself could be depicted as in a relationship of office to God, defence of this could be the rock upon which any might stand. We come, then, to the polar opposite of resistance as rebellion, to resistance as really self-defence.[38]

---

[35] 'Philodemius', *Original and End of Civil Power*, 'To the Reader'; see also John Milton, *The Tenure of Kings and Magistrates* (1649), in *Complete Prose Works*, vol. III, pp. 190–258.
[36] Anon., in *Excess of Aparel*, in *Certain Sermons*, p. 194.
[37] Smith, *Constitutional Royalism*, p. 191; see below, chapter 12.
[38] Hunton, *Treatise*, pp. 8–9; von Friedeburg, 'Self Defence and Sovereignty', pp. 238–65; Condren, 'Liberty of Office', at length.

V

For some, self-defence was a universal right of nature, stemming less from the gnash of fleshly and fishy teeth, than the axiom that God's creatures had no right of self-destruction.[39] In practice, defence sanctioned by the laws of nature and under a Christian dispensation were apt to blur, for it was the latter that really mattered.[40]

The result was something much more than a purely individualistic right of self-defence. Because the self was largely anaphoric for a *persona*, defence could also be an expression of the meta-duty to the relevant office, and this in turn involved the protection of those seen under its aegis.[41] The self could be the group in office defending law or religion, the shepherd guarding sheep, the mother killing for her child. Even as a naked soul, the self was a locus of responsibility. If such extensive notions of defence provided a powerful counter to the accusation of rebellion, they were difficult to disentangle from revenge and feuding. At law, the scope of defensive homicide was reasonably clear where it was limited to previous action. In broader contexts, however, analogies from legally justifiable defence, against highwaymen, footpads and ravishers in dark alleys, were more tricky.[42]

In sixteenth-century France, for example, the notion of the self had been limited by the extent of the *persona* of the office deemed threatened. Self-defence required the perception of a genuine and immediate threat, whereas feud and revenge could be dishes eaten cold. Because the distinctions could be difficult to apply, the royal *persona* was extended through the fiction of *cas royaux*: whatsoever touched the crown must be defended by the crown, and theoretically this took revenge away from injured parties. In Germany Philipp Melanchthon also saw revenge as a function of magistracy, separating it from the self-defence allowed by the law of nature.[43] In England, this was affirmed by Peter Martyr. 'We ought to knowe, that God will revenge our injuries, and that we must not take upon us his office. But God will declare his wrath, either by himselfe, or by the Magistrate.'[44] Given Peter Martyr's extensive notion of

---

[39] William Ames, *Conscience*, pp. 186–7; Browne, *Religio Medici*, pp. 73–5.
[40] Rutherford, *Lex, Rex*, Q.31; Tully, *A Discourse on Property*, e.g. pp. 22–4, 36–40; Milton, *Tenure*, argues from principles of nature and birthright distinct from theological duty, see Rahe, 'The Classical Republicanism of John Milton', pp. 250–1.
[41] Von Friedeburg, *Self-Defence*, at length.
[42] Ascham, *Confusions*, p. 49.
[43] Parrow, *From Defense to Resistance*, pp. 16–21; Philipp Melanchthon, *Loci theologici* (1535, 1543); see von Friedeburg, *Self-Defence*, pp. 58–61.
[44] Peter Martyr Vermigli, 'De Bello', in *Political Thought*, p. 77; Wolfgang Musculus, *Loci communes*, trans. John Man as *The Commonplaces of Christian Religion* (1578), pp. 1332–3.

the lesser magistrate's duties to control the ruler's wrath, his scattered remarks might seem contradictory, but revenge is not defence. Nevertheless, in practice, the problems separating revenge from defence persisted. The aristocrat's *persona* stretched to name and lineage, and defence of this could easily look like revenge and feud; and so in the mid-seventeenth century Anthony Ascham found it necessary to condemn what he prejudicially defined as 'an insolent *delight* in the sufferings or paines of another, whom we judge to have injured us'.[45] If defence was necessary for order, revenge was inimical to it; the basic point was as old as Aeschylus.

Defensive acts also, like revenge, were definitionally reactive; it was thus alleged or implied interference that activated the casuistry. But if fear of wrong was intense, defence could be anticipatory. As Grotius was abridged, 'he which prepares to do me injury gives me a right against himself ad infinitum'.[46] The care of office was never a momentary thing. The response to rumours of Irish invasion around the outbreak of the British Civil Wars was to make defence talk both inclusive and anticipatory. It was a heady combination. When the Civil Wars broke out in England, parliament claimed to be involved in a form of self-defence which was readily decoded, or expanded, to mean a defence of the office of parliament, the laws of the realm, the Reformation and even the office of the king against the man – that man of blood and private person, Charles. Henry Parker's writings are pretty systematic evidence for this response to alleged abuses of office. That parliament might be acting illegally weighed little in Parker's scales of justice.[47] His consistent response was a hallmark of casuistic argument: it is the scope of the law that must be considered more than the minutiae of action. The question was what maintains the safety of the people, because it is for this that government exists.

The fear of future threat also allowed a supplementary casuistry; for true religion's sake, a neighbouring prince might intervene, as Philip II attempted in 1588, as William of Orange would one hundred years later. The casuistic line between rebellion, defence, open war, invasion and intervention was uncertain. When the Bracton text had referred to an appeal to Heaven if a people should be desperately oppressed, it was clear that they should pray for intervention from

---

[45] Ascham, *Confusions*, p. 190.
[46] Mack, *Elizabethan Rhetoric*, pp. 190–1, on Cecil's defensive aggression to Scotland in 1559; Sampson, 'Liberty and Laxity', p. 95.
[47] Mendle, *Henry Parker*, p. 93.

somewhere distant.[48] Similarly, Peter Martyr wrote that '[Because] powers be of God, tyrannie must be abbiden.' For the righteous, appeal is 'onelie unto the tribunall seate of GOD'.[49] But an appeal to Heaven in the seventeenth century could well mean a recourse to arms: let God judge on the battlefield as he would – 'Providence' as the New Model Army proclaimed in defensive battle array.

'Rebellion!' was the conventional reply. As Henry Sacheverell insisted in the notorious sermon that would lead to his trial in 1710, self-defence was used to avoid calling *'Rebellion by its Proper Name'*.[50] And the easy accusation of rebellion explains the unwillingness of people to admit that resistance had taken place; it was asking for trouble.[51] Henry Sacheverell's relentless equation of resistance with rebellion, and therefore his denial that the Revolution of 1688–9 had been an act of resistance, is a tribute to the power of this rhetorical synonymity. When Benjamin Hoadly responded by defending the Revolution in Hunton's terms as justifiable defence, there was, remarked an incredulous Burnet, 'a great outcry ... as if he had preached up rebellion'.[52] But, on all sides, the response to the question rebellion or defence, was the creak of jerking knees. This made it difficult to sustain understandings of social disruption independent of conversion into either extreme. The proposition that government had dissolved is the prime example.

The dissolution of government for whatever reason was recognised as a fact of life. For Hunton, Hobbes and Lawson dissolution was definitionally the absence of sovereignty.[53] Therefore, according to Lawson, if a government dissolves, all predicates of sovereignty, such as resistance and rebellion, dissolve with it; Hobbes would have concurred.[54] Yet, by the end of the century, this alternative description also becomes dragged into the orbit of rebellion (below, chapter 15). Similarly, if rebellion was taken to encompass all resistance, Hunton's negative as well as positive, crafting an alternative description to either for action in the

---

[48] Henry de Bracton, *De legibus et consuetudinibus Angliae*, ed. G. E. Woodbine and S. E. Thorne (Cambridge, Mass., 1968–77), vol. II, pp. 109–10; more generally on the Bractonian text, see Cary J. Nederman, 'The Royal Will and the Baronial Bridle: The Place of the *addicio de cartis* in Bractonian Political Thought', *History of Political Thought*, 9 (1988), pp. 419–29.
[49] Peter Martyr Vermigli, *Political Thought*, p. 108.
[50] Sacheverell, *Perils of False Brethren*, p. 22; see also Heylyn, *Rebels Catechism*; William Sherlock, *The Case of Resistance to Supreme Powers* (1684), pp. 186–96, 203–6.
[51] Russell, *The Causes*, pp. 22–4, 132–4; Mark Goldie, 'The Revolution of 1689 and the Structure of Political Argument', *Bulletin of Research in the Humanities*, 83 (1980), p. 489.
[52] Burnet, *History*, vol. V, p. 424.
[53] Hunton, *Treatise*, p. 67; for Lawson's dissolution theory see Conal Condren, *George Lawson's 'Politica' and the English Revolution* (Cambridge, 1989), pp. 128–9, 153–68.
[54] Lawson, *Politica*, pp. 229–33.

name of true religion was no easy task. William Sherlock put forward 'non-assistance', with assurances that 'this is no rebellion, no resistance'.[55] It was probably difficult for most to grasp how non-assistance was not a species of disobedience, or another 'softer' name for negative resistance. Through a domino effect, by which one description after another is stained by the associations each was initially developed to avoid, expressions like dissolution and non-assistance were taken to be semantic ruses for avoiding the word that, according to Sacheverell, the guilty would not own.

Ownership appears acknowledged only during the eighteenth century; as the taint of rebellion faded, the need for alternatives abated. There is a hint of this in Hume's essay 'Of Passive Obedience' where he refers to the just provocation of rebellion, but the change is sustained in a Stephen Case (?) sermon. The author confirms that 'rebellion is a damnable sin except where the word is taken in a lax sense'; this he proceeds to do. There can be 'a good rebellion and a clear duty', as with the American rising: a firm example of an armed defence. The criterion for distinguishing good from bad lies in whether the rising is against 'lawful authority' or against tyrants, making it a lawful rebellion.[56] The sanctity of office and the horrors of its abuse continue to provide the crucial dividing line; but, in placing the word rebellion on either side of it, the semantic order of the language begins to change, and the conditions are established for the modern roughly neutral synonymity of resistance and rebellion.

In sum, the ingenuity of arguments gathering around counsel, lesser magistracy or defence were not put forward to justify rebellion; to think in these terms endorses a denunciation, or mistakes an anodyne idiom of modernity for something very different. Either way, we hardly grasp what was going on. Such arguments were casuistic responses to the power of an accusation, and I want now to turn to the prior, or anticipated deviance from office that prompted them.

VI

Rebellion generated four basic counter-accusations: illicit acquisition, neglect or alienation, over-assiduous exercise of office, and outright tyranny. First was the claim that *ab initio* irregularity in the assumption of office

---

[55] Sherlock, *Case of Allegiance due to Sovereign Powers*, p. 50; see Mark Goldie, 'The Political Thought of the Anglican Revolution', in Robert Beddard, ed., *The Revolutions of 1688* (Oxford, 1991), pp. 116–17.

[56] David Hume, 'Of Passive Obedience' (1748), in *Political Essays* (1777), ed. Knud Haakonssen (Cambridge, 1994), p. 204; Stephen Case (?), *Defensive Arms Vindicated* (1783), in Sandoz, *Political Sermons*, p. 722.

resulted in an incapacity to exercise authority. From the fourteenth century distinctions had been drawn between tyranny of acquisition and conduct.[57] It was accepted from St Augustine and from Roman mythology that most polities were likely to have originated in wolfish violence. Time might render bloody foundation irrelevant, but this was no help in the immediate aftermath when it could be argued that there was sufficient office-abuse to warrant disobedience to rulers without title. As Peter Martyr remarked, though 'it be lawfull to resist Tirantes which assaile a Kingdome, yet when they have obtained the same and doe beare rule, it seemeth not to belong unto private men to put them downe'. As he elsewhere insisted, using the case of Jehoiada, the issue was whether the action came from office. Jehoiada confronted tyranny not as a private man but as a high priest.[58] The argument from incapacity could also apply to irregularities of election and natural frailty. John Knox and Christopher Goodman argued that because women were unfit for rule Queen Mary could not have authority. With a woman of the right religion the argument required adjustment.

Second, an office might be neglected or alienated: these were technically different but can be outlined together. John Ponet ominously warned that neglect of office had brought about God's intervention in Sodom and Gomorrah. In running from his calling, as Willett had it, King David was tarred with the brush of neglect. Charles II defeated after Worcester, Richard Cromwell abandoning the protectorate, might similarly have been condemned, much as Mr Hobbes senior was in running from his cure and dying excommunicate beyond London.[59] *In extremis* neglect or alienation could lead to the argument that action was not against authority; for by neglecting office or alienating it to another, a ruler ceased in its *persona*, becoming a 'private' person, or a pillar of salt, an entirely conventional process of ethical redescription.[60] Such was the strength of nominal definitions of rule that even those, like Thomas Bilson most stalwart in defending absolute authority, might add a qualification in the case of alienation. Subjects are not rebels if a monarch has ceased to be by alienating the kingdom. Because of his impeccable

---

[57] Bartolus of Sassoferrato, *Tractatus de tyrannia* (c. 1356), in E. Emerton, ed., *Humanism and Tyranny* (Gloucester, Mass., 1964), ch. 5, p. 132; Coluccio Salutati, *De tyranno* (1400), *Humanism and Tyranny*, ch. 1, p. 78.

[58] Peter Martyr Vermigli, *Political Thought*, pp. 100–2, reiterated by Michael Hawke, *Killing is Murder* (1658), p. 40.

[59] Ponet, *Shorte Treatise*, p. 51; Willett, *Harmonie on the First Booke of Samuel*, p. 303; Aubrey, 'Thomas Hobbes', in *Brief Lives*, p. 227.

[60] See, for example, the *Tractates Eboracenses*, and the discussion by McIlwain, in *The Growth of Political Thought*, pp. 211ff; John of Salisbury, *Policraticus*, ch. 17, pp. 190–2.

orthodoxy, Bilson's name would almost amount to a proof text during the Civil Wars.[61] This line of argument, used against the papacy in the fourteenth century, and against James VI&I in the seventeenth, remained highly serviceable in 1689–90 (see below, chapter 15). For vociferous nonconformists like Richard Baxter and John Humfrey, owing obedience to a monarch who could be succeeded by a Catholic made alienation a crucial concept, and Bilson's authority was valuable protection. Humfrey worried that King John had already set the precedent for alienation, and Baxter drew the line of true Christian subjection before being eaten by the 'Romish Wolf'.[62] Obedience is due to office only insofar as it operates within its sphere. Neglect or alienation were potent accusations, because they paraded respect for the office itself. In the late eighteenth century, the same moves are still being made. William Barclay's *De regno* (1600) is quoted with some glee by Stephen Case (?): 'if a king will alienate, and subject his kingdom', it 'is actually lost, and the people may not only lawfully resist, but also depose him'.[63]

Third, there was over-assiduous exercise of the office. In law most felonies were potentially capital offences, but a judge who routinely hanged the guilty would have a severely damaged reputation. This was the form of tyranny that Antonio's rule took in *Measure for Measure*; it was the legal tyranny Charles I explicitly warned his son against, by way of affirming his own innocence of the crime.[64] In this accusation of office-abuse, there was a casuistic understanding of the under-determination of principles, an affirmation of the importance of judgement and discretion as virtues necessary to the exercise of responsibility. It worried the very people most likely to rely on casuistries of defence against what they were apt to call arbitrary power and tyranny.

Fourth, there was rebellion's doppelgänger tyranny. This was the over-extension of office: simultaneously it damaged the office from which the tyrant acted, adjacent offices and their *personae*. The tyrant existed in the shadow of the Thracian shepherd Gyges. This accusation echoed with the authority of antiquity and activated the rhetorics of bridling and counsel as preventatives and self-defence as office defence in its most obvious forms, deposition and tyrannicide.[65] John of Salisbury's

---

[61] Bilson, *Christian Subjection*; See William Lamont, 'The Rise and Fall of Bishop Bilson', *Journal of British Studies*, 5, 2 (1966), pp. 22–32.
[62] Lamont, *Richard Baxter*, pp. 98–9.
[63] Case, *Defensive Arms*, p. 731, citing Grotius, *De jure*, 1.4; cf. Cumberland, *De legibus naturae*, 9.6; trans. John Maxwell as *A Treatise of the Laws of Nature* (1727), p. 351, where sovereigns 'destroy themselves' by opposing what is necessary for the common good.
[64] Charles I, *Eikon Basilike*, p. 239.
[65] Plato, *Republic*, 359D–360B; Hotman, *Francogallia*, pp. 138–9.

Policraticus certainly canvasses the possibility of tyrannicide in a way that makes it clear how tyrants were the real rebels. If the ruler is a shepherd and the image of God, the tyrant is the image of the first rebel, Satan. There is no automatic injunction to act, as the imagery might imply, and John qualifies his position in ways that Salutati would certainly find unsatisfactory.[66] In the face of powerful monarchs like the Angevins, there was a two-stage defence against high-handed conduct rather than an immediate escalation to cosmic warfare. The monarch might be accused of erratic wilfulness (*actus per voluntatem*) and therefore be in need of an encouraging bridle, or if he persisted, be held to account for systematic tyranny and threatened with deposition, or tyrannicide.[67] Deposition did not necessarily mean tyrannicide. Rehoboam (1 Kings) stood as the image of a tyrant who could be deposed without being killed, and throughout the early modern period there were those who, although accepting tyranny as a horrid reality, nevertheless refused to countenance violent action. Wolfgang Musculus, echoing John of Salisbury's analogies between God and rule, Satan and tyranny, and his reluctance to develop an unequivocal commitment to tyrannicide washed his hands of moral judgement. In circumstances so beyond normality, there could be no moral legislation.[68] Others balked at tyrannicide by combining arguments from consequence and principle: the possibilities of immediate confusion and destabilising precedent were unacceptable; subject status itself was a moral prohibition reinforced by oaths of allegiance. It was usually possible to say with Leonard Wright, cited above, that even tyrants should be obeyed when commanding what lay within the law, which was at once to express obedience to the law and bracket the problem of action against tyranny. Overall, the fears for the consequences of instability made calls for tyrannicide less common than accusations that disobedience would lead to such violence.

There were nevertheless considered arguments that offered destruction of country and true religion as prospective criteria for tyrannicide. Such abuse of office made the tyrant an enemy against whom defence is a right of nature.[69] Here we confront the full force of the well-worn formulas

---

[66] John of Salisbury, *Policraticus*, bk. 8, cf. chs. 17, 18; Salutati, *De tyranno*, p. 90.
[67] Jolliffe, *Angevin Kingship*, pp. 4–5.
[68] Musculus, *Commonplaces*, cf. pp. 1283–5, 1265 with 1340.
[69] Ponet, *Shorte Treatise*, pp. 98ff; see also pp. 11, 34, 161; George Buchanan, *De jure regni apud Scotos* (Edinburgh, 1579); Johann Gerhard, *Loci theologici*, 560–1, quoted in von Friedeburg, *Self-Defence*, p. 130; John Cook, *King Charls His Case* (1649), pp. 21–3, on whom see Glenn Burgess, 'The Execution of Charles I and English Political Thought', in von Friedeburg, *Murder and Monarchy*, pp. 223–9; the right could be a duty: see, for

of nominal identity.[70] To become a tyrant, summarised Rutherford, is to cease to be a king. 'If the office of the tyrant (so to speak) be contrary to the king's offices, it is not from God, and so neither is the power from God.'[71]

As with incapacity and alienation, the obloquy of tyranny separated office from office-holder by redescribing a moral entity. This transmogrification into the private was the shared ground on which the *topoi* of defence and restitution of office could be run together. For writers like Buchanan and Rutherford, the polemical edge is sharp enough, but we find the same structure of argument with Philip Hunton and the compliant Jeremy Taylor. If a prince abides by the law, wrote Taylor, he can never be a private person, for private men have no power of punishment.[72] The notions of ruler and ruled are 'relatives', Hunton argued, so that if a ruler goes beyond his authority he becomes a private person, his act one of private violence. 'No power can challenge obedience beyond its own measure; for if it might, we should destroy all Rules and differences of Government, and make all absolute and at pleasure.'[73] The ring of office becomes the ring of Gyges.

This will now sound familiar enough but it was, nevertheless, always a delicate issue, for identities contingent upon office were rhetorically unstable. Andrew Willett, like Peter Martyr, insisted that only a public office gave warrant for dealing with a tyrant. Yet, Willett continues, if a private man is stirred by an extraordinary spirit, he thereby assumes an 'extraordinary vocation'; dealing with the tyrant makes him a public governor.[74] The fluidity of such nominal identities could result in a conditional obedience even to the most absolute of monarchs. Equally, they made a stable criterion for tyrannicide difficult to sustain, offering mainly a bridge of polemical flexibility across confessional divides. Suarez would urge the same point about the transformation of a private *persona* into a public agent when killing a tyrant. The king Willett treated with kid gloves was the tyrant Suarez had in mind.[75]

---

example, *Cato's Letters*, vol. II, letter 68, p. 414, summarising widespread sentiments; see Sullivan, *Machiavelli, Hobbes*, pp. 236–7.

[70] *Tractates Eboracenses* (c. 1170), discussed in McIlwain, *The Growth of Political Thought*, p. 213; Bartolus, *Tractatus de tyrannia*, ch. 2, p. 127; on the *Leges*, see Greenberg, *The Radical Face*, pp. 62 ff.

[71] Cf. Rutherford, *Lex Rex*, Q.24; John of Salisbury, *Policraticus*, bk. 8, chs. 17, 18.

[72] Taylor, *Ductor dubitantium*, pp. 111, 107; Hawke, *Killing is Murder*, p. 40.

[73] Hunton, *Treatise*, pp. 1, 15, 54–5, 27.

[74] Willett, *Harmonie on the First Booke of Samuel*, p. 294; cf. Peter Martyr Vermigli, in *Political Writings*, pp. 100, 101–2; the argument would be repeated in Anon., *Conscience Puzzl'd* (1650), in Malcolm, *The Struggle for Sovereignty*, vol. I, p. 440.

[75] Francisco de Suarez, *Defensio fidei Catholicae et apostolicae* (Coimbra, 1613), 4.4.14 (see below, chapter 13).

During the Civil Wars, arguments from tyranny surfaced only sporadically and late in the proceedings and, according to John Morrill, it was Charles who first made capital out of the accusation.[76] If so, it was a superficially safe escalation of verbal hostilities, for the tyranny of parliament did not carry an obvious injunction to tyrannicide. But the issue is not that clear-cut. Charles may have been responding to an insinuated accusation. To 'marry the power or Office of a Prince to his will' wrote Henry Parker (?), is unacceptable because the will indiscriminately includes the good and the bad. What is good about the prince's will 'makes him a king', what is bad 'makes him a bloody tyrant'.[77] This is pretty close to name-calling. Again, Charles's own accusations may have been reacting to parliament's early indirect warnings about tyrannous conduct. It sponsored a translation of Buchanan's *Baptistes* (1579), a play about Herod's descent into tyranny on the evil counsel of women. A copy of this allegorical accusation against Charles and his queen was presented to him, a gift that would have been difficult to reject, awkward to refute and impossible to stomach.[78] When the deposition and then execution of Charles became clear possibilities, the question of the monarch as *persona* was central to the separation of Charles I from Charles Stuart. Charles Herle, like Hunton, specifically replying to Ferne's equation of defensive resistance with rebellion and murder, had argued earlier that parliament may defend '*King, Lawes, and Government*' even against 'the King's *personall* Command'. Six years later, others justified Charles's execution as tyrannicide; abuse of office had brought about the necessity. Charles is designated an officer with dogged repetition and the very notion of an unaccountable officer is dismissed as 'a strange monster'.[79]

Beyond the protection of office lay the perversions and shadows of Satan, his witches and Antichrist. At the least tyranny was 'monstrous and unnatural'.[80] In Milton's attacks on Charles, then on Satan in *Paradise Lost*, depictions of tyranny are taken to the most dramatic

---

[76] J. S. Morrill, 'Charles I and Tyranny', in *The Nature of the English Revolution* (London, 1996), pp. 293–6.
[77] Anon. (Henry Parker?), *The Observator Defended* (1642), p. 9.
[78] George Buchanan, *Tyrannical Government Anatomized* (1642); see Conal Condren, 'The Office of Rule and the Rhetorics of Tyrannicide', in von Friedeburg, *Murder and Monarchy*, pp. 63–5.
[79] Charles Herle, *A Fuller Answer to a Treatise* (1642), in Malcolm, *The Struggle for Sovereignty*, vol. I, pp. 226–7; *The Declaration of the Parliament of England* (1648), in ibid., vol. I, pp. 372, 379; see also Cook, *King Charls His Case*, pp. 20–3, and *Monarchy No Creature of Gods Making* (Waterford, 1651) discussed in Burgess, 'The Execution of Charles I', pp. 223–9.
[80] Hunton, *Treatise*, p. 9.

extreme.[81] Both Charles and Satan are fiends in beguiling shape, each claims divine right, each is a rebel, enslaved as he destroys. This is all ultimately in the Platonic idiom: the overreaching inversion of the just man, the victim of his own lust, and the invisible ring-wearer, transformed and implicated in any manifestation of evil. This is not paranoia, it is metaphysics. Milton's tautology, discussed in chapter 4, that the tyrant is enslaved by abusing the liberty of others, is central also to Edward Sexby's promise to treat Cromwell to tyrannicide, so making him genuinely significant.[82] Only with the Protector's death will liberty be restored, the Reformation furthered and justice cease to be the Thrasymachian sort. The verbal shape-shifting of the tyrant through radical *paradiastole* is complete in Sexby's work. Tyrants are like beasts of prey that may be destroyed on sight.[83] Thereafter, however, the simile contracts into metaphor: the tyrant is made of the skin of the lion, the tail of the fox; he is an ulcer, a disease, a wild beast, a viper and a devil to be exorcised.[84]

Lurid, yes, but Sexby's justification for tyrannicide pivots on the same kind of nominal transformation outlined by Goodman and Willett – a private man becomes public by acting against tyranny. The tyrant converts the commonwealth into a condition of slavery; it loses its name because the tyrant destroys the end for which men enter society.[85] Everyman thus assumes the office of a soldier. The high priest Jehoida, whose tyrannicidal actions Peter Martyr had justified, becomes a model for all. Tyranny makes everyman his own magistrate.[86] Michael Hawke's riposte to the 'Jesuit' Sexby is just as revealing. All government originates from God through force; it is only tyranny of exercise that matters. Unlike Sexby, Hawke had a precise and more literal understanding of the marks of tyranny, a dozen or so kinds of action forming a fine mesh of criteria through which the Protector could not fall into a pit of privacy. Concomitantly, he refuses to countenance the transformation of the private man into the officer, the soldier, armed priest or magistrate. It is nothing more than the creation of that unthinkable natural condition against which Hobbes and Cicero warn.[87]

---

[81] Joan Bennett, *Reviving Liberty*, ch. 2.
[82] John Milton, *A Defence*, in *Complete Prose Works*, vol. IV, p. 310; *The Second Defence*, in *Complete Prose Works*, vol. IV, p. 373; see Bennett, *Reviving Liberty*, p. 50; Edward Sexby, *Killing No Murder* (1657, 1689 edn).
[83] Sexby, *Killing No Murder*, Dedicatory Letter, p. 3.
[84] Ibid., pp. 5, 10, 24; see also Abraham Nelson, *A Perfect Description of Antichrist* (1644? 1660), dedicated to Charles as a precise description of Cromwell.
[85] Goodman, *Superiours*, pp. 76–7; Willett, *Harmonie on the First Booke of Samuel*, pp. 294; Sexby, *Killing No Murder*, pp. 10, 9.
[86] Sexby, *Killing No Murder*, pp. 13, 11.
[87] Hawke, *Killing is Murder*, pp. 18, 26, 40, 7. Hawke may have believed Sexby was a Jesuit, but the naming might have been discreditation.

The four distinct denunciations of office-abuse could be run into an integrated indictment designed to erase or re-direct the notion of rebellion. Thus John Goodwin: when a ship's pilot is rendered useless and is 'uncapable of acting the exigencies of his place' any one or more of the 'inferiour Mariners, having skill, may in order to the saving of the Ship, and of the lives of all that are in it' take over.[88] By their actions rulers might cease to be, becoming frenzied or drunken tyrants, private men, beasts, vipers and ulcers and thus exposed to actions exempt from the accusation of rebellion. Against a private man rebellion was impossible and one who so abused office could himself be a rebel against true order. Equally, in doing right in extremity, even private men might become public officers, their actions being killings, not murders. In this destabilisation of the rhetorics of rebellion, we have the authentic echoes of the Jesuits Suarez and Mariana as well as Buchanan. As the Earl of Devonshire would put it in 1688: 'we call it rebellion to resist a King that governs by law, but to resist a tyrant we justly esteem no rebellion but a necessary defence'.[89] In terms of immediate force this is a long way from James VI&I who insisted that kings could do no wrong; in terms of presupposition, we are no distance at all – a point indirectly supported by the willingness of those of much the same mind as the earl to cite James as an authority on kingship when his grandson had, as a king, ceased to be.

Perhaps the best illustration of identity in office as an inconclusive necessity for mediating casuistries of resistance is to be found in George Berkeley's *Passive Obedience*. It is a considered piece, implacably hostile to all doctrines of resistance, and at one with the most extreme arguments for passive obedience that swirled around the Sacheverell controversies from 1710.[90] Obedience is an absolute moral rule. Any qualification is rebellion, and all rebellion is criminal. He dismisses all arguments derived from defence and tyranny as nothing more than casuistical errors arising from the mistaken belief that evil may be done that good may come of it. Yet there remains one limitation to obedience.[91] It is due only to a proper authority, qua authority. That is, the injunctions of the law of nature apply only to the thing, the office of rule, and not to madmen or invasive interlopers. 'Which I shall not go about to prove, because nobody has denied it.'[92] Formally, we are taken back to Socrates' debate with Polemarchus – is it just to return the knife to the madman? But

---

[88] Goodwin, *Right and Might Well Mett*, p. 319.
[89] See Condren, 'Liberty of Office', p. 480.
[90] George Berkeley, *Passive Obedience* (1712, 1713) in *Works*, vol. VI, pp. 22–4, 28.
[91] *Ibid.*, pp. 26, 18, 35–44.
[92] *Ibid.*, p. 45; cf. Cumberland, *De legibus*, 9.6, Maxwell, trans., *Laws of Nature*, pp. 350–1.

implicitly the argument unravels; for all the huffing and puffing, begged questions are not blown away, for 'Resistance' was never said to be to just authority, it was defence against madmen, usurpers and tyrants. The identity and actions of *personae* in office was everything.

VII

Around 1678, the Earl of Devonshire had sought advice from Hobbes on whether *Leviathan* could furnish arguments to control the monarchy by changing the succession. Within ten years he had come to a more Lockean conclusion. This invites consideration of Hobbes's and Locke's statements on and around the question of resistance. Each man's political theory is to be sure very different. The point here is to use the casuistry of defence to illustrate only how they shared presuppositions of office and nominal identity and employed the common vocabulary derived from them.

Neither writer justifies rebellion, though Hobbes was accused of doing so, and Locke has often enough been carelessly commended for the same achievement. Each accepts that resistance as defence is a right of nature to be exercised when relationships of government have dissolved. Each, then, is dealing with exceptional circumstances of casuistic mitigation. Without denying the right of defence *in extremis*, all Hobbes's theories minimised its disruptive significance. *De cive* sabotaged the argument from tyranny. In a state of war, civic relationships are dissolved; thus the vocabulary appropriate to them becomes irrelevant. Whereas Buchanan had treated the equation tyrant and enemy as an imperative, that is, a tyrant should be dealt with as an enemy, Hobbes formulated it as definitional redundancy; in a state of war, enemy is sufficient.[93] If there is a sovereign, then by definition there are subjects whose duty it is to obey. Nevertheless, unlike Berkeley, Hobbes did allow self-defence within the ambit of the peaceful polity. It was, however, restricted to the isolated physical being whose (private) subject status in a relationship of office has been destroyed. The defending self could not be a *persona* acting with or for others. Self-defence cannot enlist, or put at risk those still subject to the sovereign. We are asked to believe that such scrupulosity could be a consideration for one returned to the natural condition. It is here that Locke uses notions of nominal identity so differently.

---

[93] Hobbes, *Philosophical Rudiments*, p. 177; Hawke, *Killing is Murder*, p. 28, who had read Hobbes, attributes this definitional evaporation of tyranny to Wolfgang Musculus. No text is cited but possibly he had in mind *In Epistolam D. Apostoli Pauli ad Romanos commentarii* (Basel, 1600), or earlier editions.

Protective relationships can be dissolved by those who in exceeding their power are transformed into tyrants and rebels. Against these, the people may defend themselves. When this is discussed more fully (chapter 15) it will become apparent that the Marian question of who was really guilty of rebellion was as pressing in 1690 as it had been in 1550. From another route we are confronted again with the problem of what may be called Ellesmere's axiom, the danger of distinguishing man from office; and the 'straights and complexities' that arise whether we do or don't.

VIII

And woman too: after John Bull had heaved the fateful bottle at his first wife's head and killed her (obviously self-defence), he found among her papers a 'Vindication of the Rights of Cuckoldom'. It was enough to have rotated John Knox in his grave. 'Mrs Bull's Vindication' is a parody of the speeches delivered at the trial of Dr Sacheverell but it has a much wider significance.[94] Asking at what point can there be a limit to passive obedience and whether the Church of England really subscribed to such a principle without exception, were questions recognisably central to any 'resistance theory'; and Mrs Bull's 'Vindication' amounts to an allegorical abridgement of the casuistry prompted by accusations of rebellion.

'It is evident', she begins with glib Jeffersonian assurance, 'that matrimony is founded upon an original contract' in which the wife gives over her rights to her husband who thus acquires 'the property of all her posterity'. The obligation, however, is mutual and if broken on either side ceases to bind.[95] 'Where there is a right, there must be a power to maintain it . . . This power I affirm to be that original right, or rather that indispensible duty of cuckoldom, lodged in all wives.' No wife, she continues, is bound without consent. Originally all 'economical government' is lodged in husband and wife, the husband being the executive part. But the wife's share and original right of cuckoldom remain. Can anyone affirm that she has no remedy other than prayers and tears, or an appeal to a supreme court? There is no universally fixed relationship between the terms husband and wife. 'In some eastern nations [husband] signifies a tyrant with an absolute power of life and death . . . in Italy

---

[94] John Arbuthnot, *The History of John Bull* (1712), in George Aitken, ed., *The Life and Works of John Arbuthnot* (Oxford, 1892), ch. 8, p. 208, ch. 13, pp. 214–17; Patricia Koster, 'Arbuthnot's Use of Quotation and Parody', *Philological Quarterly*, 48 (1969), pp. 201ff.

[95] Arbuthnot, *The History of John Bull*, ch. 13, p. 215; cf. Robert Sanderson, 'The Case of the Validity of a Matrimonial Contract', in *Works*, vol. V, p. 123.

it gives . . . the power of poison and padlocks'. Yet in England, France and Holland, the word husband implies 'free and equal government', securing in 'certain cases' the 'liberty of cuckoldom'. There is, then, no 'absolute unlimited chastity' (obedience). The exhortations to chastity are meant only for 'ordinary cases'; without qualification it is an unreasonable reflection on the church, taking it to condone oppression. In contrast, the 'doctrine of the original right to cuckoldom' is from the law of nature, superior to all human laws, and has never been relinquished by English wives. To deny it is to damage marriage and the necessary means of perpetuating families. The recent European conflagration brought about by the failure of a dynasty because of the 'scrupulous nicety of a silly Queen' is one of 'the effects of the narrow maxims of your clergy, that one must not do evil that good will come of it'. If the true basis of marriage be sapped and 'tyrannical maxims introduced, what must follow but elopements instead of peaceable cuckoldom?'[96]

In this fashion Arbuthnot exhibits an easy familiarity with the casuistic nature of arguments from defence against unqualified obedience. There is the characteristic slippage from right to duty integral to conceptions of liberty of office; and the emphasis on considering the scope of an office. In exceptional cases, obedience cannot hold, and doctrines demanding it indiscriminately are at once at odds with natural law and English custom and encourage oppression and tyranny. The 'narrow maxim' that one must not do evil in hope of some good following, is itself only for ordinary cases. To put the matter another way, if this whole 'Vindication' is an exercise in gentle *tapinosis* at the expense of the verbal posturing surrounding the Sacheverell trial, it is an echoing concatenation, of 'state casuistry' what we have since deemed resistance theory, a playful pastiche of the themes of defence and extremity that go back in English to Peter Martyr Vermigli. Duncan Forbes was clearly wrong after all about marriage and divorce.

Arbuthnot was a High Church Tory, of sorts, sympathetic to Dr Sacheverell and so distinctly ambivalent about the Revolution of 1688, if it was considered as an act of resistance. But in the chapter immediately following 'Mrs Bull's Vindication', he describes how parties formed around her doctrine. Husbands tried to force their wives into signing papers detesting it. The wives divided into opposing camps, the Devotos who complied, the Hitts who refused. The distinction, he remarks, was often 'more nominal than real', some Devotos exercising

---

[96] Arbuthnot, *The History of John Bull*, ch. 13, pp. 215–16.

their original rights regardless of what they signed, some Hitts being 'very honest'.[97] The moral was not to rely upon agreements made under duress, and for husbands to behave decently rather than believe their wives. One man, he remarks, having had complete faith in the principle of absolute fidelity, discovered one day that his wife had eloped. James II took too literally the principle of absolute obedience. Yet the pulpiteers of the High Church who promoted it avoided the issue of its casuistic limit. As Arbuthnot teasingly insinuated, the difficulty for them lay in accepting that the alternative to absolute obedience, namely defence in the teeth of innovation, tyranny and the usual cast of ethical suspects, was indeed a form of the very casuistry they normally abhorred.

Arbuthnot's shift from doctrinal parody to the extreme situations that generated casuistic mitigation illustrates what Hobbes called the equivocal nature of metaphor. It is no more likely that Arbuthnot set out to defend a theory of resistance than he seriously proposed a practice of infidelity; yet it takes some determination to keep this in mind. It was, after all, what he styled the 'scrupulous nicety of a silly Queen' that, on his understanding, brought about thousands of deaths through war once the Spanish succession had ended. In 1712 Arbuthnot was very much one of the peace party. Might he have had some sympathy for a variation of Emilia's choice – to cuckold a husband for the sake of preserving a kingdom? Moreover, the allegory works with long-standing homologies between marriage and governance, the family and the polity. The plausibility, thoroughness and uncontrollable nature of these stem from the vocabularies of office that could be moved indifferently between them. Some attention to this will serve as a conclusion to the first two parts of this study.

---

[97] *Ibid.*, ch. 14, p. 217.

10 Metaphor and political autonomy

> He shews that People have a Right to private Truth from their Neighbours, and oeconomical Truth from their own Family; that they should not be abused by their Wives, Children and Servants; but, that they have no right at all to *Political Truth*.
>
> (John Arbuthnot, *The Art of Political Lying*, 1712)

I

From God and the sun to the mice in the fields; between them kings, constables, prison life and the protean philosopher. All were informed by the vocabulary of office, and so it is now necessary to confront the distinction between central and peripheral use, literal and figurative. There is, after all, a difference between the House of Lords and the house of office, between the sun calling the mice to their offices and anyone calling Charles I an 'officer'. Yet such differences need handling with care; the grounds for making them are not unproblematic. The terrain covered here is at times difficult but the journey across it is important for understanding the argument and its implications for the study of history and politics.

A metaphorical use involves carrying a locution from one established field of discourse to another, hence the original Greek, *metaphora*, a carrying across, from *meta* + *phorein* (to convey messages), and hence the Latin *translatio*. Consequently, any understanding of the metaphorical is dependent upon awareness of a prior conceptual demarcation of experience. Metaphor is thus a creature of the specificity and adequacy of classification. For if lines of demarcation are uncertain, the difference between the metaphorical and what linguists call extensional use within a domain can be hard to pin down. It is difficult to see, for example, at what point if any the noun settle (Old English, a seat or chair) becomes metaphorical with such a noun as settlement, meaning dwelling place, diplomatic conclusion, legal termination, or constitutional arrangement. Inigo Jones's notebooks provide a more pointed case. Jones wrote of the design of a building through the nomenclature of rhetoric, of ornament, arrangement and disposition. This seems metaphorical, yet he was drawing on Alberti's architectural theory, employing the Italian *disegno*, a much broader notion that encompassed rhetorical organisation. Thus, insofar as *disegno* was carried into English, Jones's conceptual language is ambivalently on the edge of the metaphorical and extensive.[1] Or, consider the following, from a book addressed directly to the literal and not the 'equivocal' (metaphorical) conception of parental office, often enough extended to refer to the magistrate:

> Some mens office is about stones, timber, metall, and such like: some handle plants, herbs and flowers: some cattell, foules of the ayre, or fish of the sea: the Physitian looketh to the health of the body, the Lawyer to the state of the lands or goods; but the Parent is put in trust with a more honourable charge, to govern the chiefest creature under heaven.[2]

It is not self-evident where office is being used metaphorically when ranging over the whole terrain of social relationships. It is, moreover, difficult to distinguish cause from effect: does the diversity of overlapping meanings of office prepare the ground for metaphorical transfer, or evidence its power? In any given case it could be either.

The dependence of metaphorical movement upon classificatory adequacy raises a further issue insofar as even general classifications change over time. The domains of the natural and supernatural, animate and human, organic and mechanical, all have histories. This suggests the usefulness of making a meta-distinction between autochthonous and analytic metaphors. A locution may be an analytical metaphor, and may seem metaphorical now because we draw a firm line between domains of word use where none was made in the past. It may be, as has been argued since Vico, that we perceive more patterns of demarcation than people did in ancient and medieval times; universities certainly have more disciplines that purport to evidence and explore a greater complexity in the world than was once apparent. We are apt to draw firm lines between philosophy and science as people in the sixteenth century did not, and so treat locutions moving from one to the other as figurative as contemporaries would not. Conversely, autochthonous metaphors are those that have sprung directly from past patterns of conceptualisation; their erosion may inhibit our recognition of figurative usage. Vico's belief that in antiquity everyone spoke in metaphors may have been a function of

---

[1] I am grateful to Dr Liam Semler's paper, 'Designs on the Self: Inigo Jones, Marginal Writing and Renaissance Self-Assembly', delivered at the 'Theory and Practice of Early Modern Autobiography' seminar, Humanities Research Centre, Australian National University, December 2002.
[2] Anon., *The Office of Christian Parents* (1616), B1, p. 9.

not understanding how the Homeric world was conceptually organised. Analogously, the belief that the Greeks were colour-blind arose from not understanding the organisation of the semantic field of colour terms in Greek.

Leaving aside the question of what might be read metaphorically now, there are three broad ways in which the metaphorical was contentious in the seventeenth century. Metaphor as such might be considered inappropriate to a form of discourse; individual metaphors might be rejected or their implications challenged. It is in this third form of controversy that meanings are most obviously changed. But new meanings are created simply by the analytic invention of the figurative, or by not seeing its autochthonous creation. Either process gives a different semantic status to words we nevertheless share with our forebears. Pico's metaphor of 'Man' for philosopher becomes the concept of the modern individual if its figurative status passes by unnoticed. This is akin to Henry Smith's explanation for the doctrine of transubstantiation: it was a metaphor that had been mistaken for a literal transformation.[3] So, too, the soul is secularised whenever we take within its metaphorical range the modern 'Self', or morally autonomous agent as a rights-bearing person. Thus, in large measure, the reconstruction of the past into manageable semi-modern shapes is the progeny of the often inadvertent treatment of metaphor. A theory of the humours, once believed literally, retains plausibility in a metaphorical half-life; conversely, a metaphor is revivified by being made to be literally about something else.

Shifting patterns of presupposition add further complications. For many in early modern society, the world was cohered by reading analogically, typologically, allegorically or microcosmically. This, for example, allowed a word like *oeconomia* to refer both to the ordering of a household and the structure of creation, resulting in the seventeenth-century body of writings on *oeconomia animalis*. Assumptions of microcosmic relationships helped standardise a metaphor as a technical term in materialist natural philosophy.[4] Because there were no digressions in God's universe, everything could be seen as a sign of something.[5] The semiotics of God's love was a pervasive example.[6] Charles II's failure to produce a legitimate heir was a problem for the succession; it was also a symbol of moral corruption, for although 'Man' and office might be separated physically,

---

[3] Mack, *Elizabethan Rhetoric*, p. 262.
[4] Walter Charleton, *The Natural History of Nutrition* (1659); discussed in Booth, 'A Subtle and Mysterious Machine', ch. 4.
[5] See, in particular, Maclean, *Logic, Signs and Nature*, ch. 8.
[6] Sharpe, *Re-Mapping*, p. 109.

one could always be used symbolically for the other.[7] Encouraged by a semiotic optimism, metaphor at once instantiated such reading and helped confirm the rationality of the cosmos.

A presupposition of meaningful interconnection required, then, figurative ingenuity. Hardly surprisingly, adjacent presuppositions of office assisted the mobile armies of terms to forage from the magistrate to the minister and the mouse. As I stated at the outset, presuppositions do not come down to us in splendid isolation. Thomas Hobbes polemically exploited the highly conventionalised pastoral metaphors of office in the process of diminishing that of priests to little more than a walking sign of virtue; the long-asserted responsibilities of correcting, judging, admonishing were appropriated to ruling office. 'The Civill Soveraign is the Supreme Pastor, to whose charge the whole flock of his Subjects is committed, and consequently that it is by his authority, that all other Pastors are made.'[8] In this way, presuppositions can be seen as figurative lubricants, making plausible what I have elsewhere called prodigal's return. An expression from one domain is taken into another and such a metaphor might 'stick',[9] become acclimatised and assume some conceptual space of its own. One reason for such transference lies in the domain into which the metaphor is taken (the area of metaphorical attraction) already being prepared. Far from being a merely colourful incursion, the metaphor blends with established nomenclature. There is nothing like shared presuppositions for easing the process. Such a grounding creates an aura of appropriateness; metaphors, as Aristotle remarked, should not be too far-fetched.[10] When they seem suitably decorous, the new terms might only be returning home like prodigal children.

Thus, in anatomy, the vocabulary of office helped explain the opaque complexity of the body, once it was assumed that all parts were purposive, had some *telos*, for God whose office was to order all things would leave no redundancies. Functionality thus inserted the thin end of a wedge of intentionality and responsibility that could be attributed to the material and inert; organs and bodily functions were relationally defined in terms

---

[7] Steven Zwicker, 'Virgins and Whores: The Politics of Sexual Misconduct in the 1660s', in C. Condren and A. D. Cousins, eds., *The Political Identity of Andrew Marvell* (Aldershot, 1990), pp. 89–91.
[8] Hobbes, *Leviathan*, ch. 42, p. 373.
[9] Cavendish, 'Of Affectation, Horae subsecivae', p. 20.
[10] Aristotle, *Rhetoric*, trans. W. Rhys Roberts (New York, 1954), 1404, 17–22. Prodigal's return is also characteristic of larger transdisciplinary theories; one doctrine might seem to provide independent confirmation of another because its origins from a shared source have been forgotten; see, for example, Buc, *The Dangers of Ritual*, pp. 229–30, 237–8.

of their offices.[11] Charleton's later lectures reveal another typical manifestation of terminological circulation lubricated by metaphors of office.

As the design or end of the [Segovian Mint] was to Coin money, which is the bloud of all States... for the support of Government: so the office and work of [the heart] is to stamp the character and Vitality upon the mass of bloud, for the maintanance of life in all parts of the body, and regulation of the whole Animal oeconomy.[12]

The incipient circularity in such processes of reasoning need not be laboured: recall the terms used of soul and conscience often derived from the language of office, then taken back to explicate the duties of office (above, chapter 6). By the same token, a jarring diversity of figuration in a relatively cohesive body of literature might itself signal discordancy in conceptualising office. Counsel might be the 'staff and guide'; the fingers on the hand; ripened fruit; or the sun set by the dial.[13] The patterns of association that individual images form are clear enough, but they create differing expectations of the relationships between counsel and rule.

II

The point here is that we need to pay attention to such presuppositions lest we inadvertently replace them with our own, so misconstruing the surviving evidence, even when being attentive to the words concerned. Insofar as there was a general presupposition of office it was likely to subordinate distinctions that we habitually and unselfconsciously privilege. When we do so, conceptual schemata and priorities are plausibly projected onto the past because language is superficially shared; models of change can then get embedded in the evidence for which they end up being mistaken. Because the distortions are often subtle, the point may best be made through illustration. Michael Braddick's splendid account of English state formation is marred in this way. In salutary fashion he explores the manner in which changes to established social offices had the unintended consequence of making England much more like Weber's conception of a state by 1700 than it had been in 1550. But in organising

---

[11] Charleton, *Enquiries into Human Nature*, p. 140; see Booth, 'A Subtle and Mysterious Machine', p. 153; Haworth, *Anthropologia*, p. 177 on the 'office' of respiration.
[12] Walter Charleton, *Three anatomical lectures* (1683); Booth, 'A Subtle and Mysterious Machine', p. 201 who notes that Charleton was relying on Kenelm Digby, *Two Treatises* (Paris, 1644), p. 208. Images of circulation and coinage became common after William Harvey's work.
[13] Cavendish, 'Self Will, Horae subsecivae', p. 28; Goslicius, *The Counsellor*, p. 162; Anon., *A Worthy Panegyrick* (1658?, 1680), stanza 8; *The Letter of Sir John Suckling* (1640, 1679), p. 2.

his material through Weberian conceptual vocabulary and using a Weberian ideal type as a measure of change, occasionally he elides the evidence with his model; office is reduced to social or political office, and all offices are accepted as derivative expressions of a Weberian conception of legitimate power defining the state. This must obviously accommodate the conclusion but sits oddly with much of the talk of office that has come down to us; it reverses the priorities of the evidence in which what we designate legitimate political power was often closer to being understood as a species of something more general.[14] Similarly, Michael McKeon has valuably explored the contingent nature of intellectual demarcation in the seventeenth century, especially with reference to the crucial absence of a field of 'literature'; yet he takes for granted the primacy of the political in the context of which we have developed and imposed later disciplinary boundaries. Thus he refers to the book-list of the printer and possibly agent for the Earl of Shaftesbury, John Starkey, and notes that Starkey used no classification for 'literature', consigning Suetonius and Rabelais to 'history'. Starkey used no category of 'politics' either, but on this more striking discrepancy McKeon is silent, perhaps because he presupposes the importance of seeing things politically.[15] It is additionally relevant that Starkey's probable collaborator in re-printing Lawson's *Politica* in 1689, the parliamentarian Richard More, used much the same classifications and omitted the political in cataloguing his library, which included works by Plato, Aristotle, Cicero, Machiavelli, More and Hunton.[16] At least in these cases there is some organisation to act as a barrier to the inadvertent salting of the evidence with our own conceptual priorities, but not so with Samuel Jeakes of Rye. His modern editors commend political radicalism as an 'exciting feature' of Jeakes' collection, despite neither the political nor the radical featuring at all as principles of classification; feature *of* is simply conflated with imposed *upon*.[17]

This may seem a churlish criticism of fine scholarship, but prepares the ground for showing how putting one foot, as it were, beyond the chalk circle of our own tacitly accepted conceptual schemes can lead to

---

[14] Braddick, *State Formation*, pp. 82–4.
[15] Anon., *A Letter from a Person of Quality to his Friend in the Country* (1675), p. 2 names Starkey as an agent; McKeon, 'Politics of Discourses', p. 46; see also Michael McKeon, *Politics and Poetry in Restoration England: The Case of Dryden's Annus Mirabilis* (Cambridge, Mass., 1975), Introduction.
[16] Condren, 'More Parish Library, Salop', pp. 145–6.
[17] M. Hunter, G. Mandelbrote, R. Ovenden and N. Smith, eds., *A Radical's Books: The Library Catalogue of Samuel Jeakes of Rye, 1623–90* (Woodbridge, 1999); cf. the greater conceptual care shown by Petchey, *The Intentions of Thomas Plume*, p. 18, who does not elide how we might classify the books with Plume's own Jeakes-like organisation in terms of date and size.

difficulties. Kevin Sharpe, acutely aware of how an untenable distinction between public and private has helped make part of the oeuvre of James VI&I 'political', nevertheless refers to *Counsell to the Husband* as systematically politicising the relationships between husband and wife.[18] The book does describe marriage through the vocabulary of rule, but it is we who are apt to equate this with politics. Marriage is taken as a matter of reciprocal duty, with both partners subject to the office of the teacher in order to establish a foundation for the family in Christ. A structure of official relationships articulated through such words as government, tyranny and rebellion was just as easily called a church as a commonwealth; a bullied husband could be a crucified St Peter as easily as a deposed monarch.[19] The work in fact seems to show a presuppositional acceptance of office informing the civic and domestic, and it was this that eased the circulating movement of vocabulary between these permeable (and variously named) spheres of experience. Nicholas Grimalde, who was apt to equate reason with an understanding of human offices, had almost made the point explicit. A man of reason must transfer it to 'the governance both of his household privately', and to 'the whole commons openly'.[20] Indeed, even to imply a two-way movement is simplification. In much marriage literature marital relationships are theologised analogously to the way in which the office of the humble shepherd was sanctified as an expression of the grandeur of rule. Marriage was a potential microcosm of the universal battle between God, the exemplum of office and good rule, and the ever disruptive 'ghostly enemy' Satan; no wonder it could be a church as much as a polity.[21]

To refer to *Counsell to the Husband*, then, as politicising the family gives a modernising primacy to the specifically political that is clear only because it is abstracted, assumed and projected onto the evidence. It conflates what is analytically necessary, or taken for granted now, with what the agent seemed to be doing in using his words. From the same anachronistic perspective we might conclude that John Evelyn politicised husbandry at every turn. After all, he called deforestation usurpation and tyranny and commended planting as the work of 'Patriots and good commonwealthsmen' caring for England's 'wooden walls'.[22] But Evelyn took husbandry to be an office, and this enabled him to graft a Themistoclean civic virtue to

---

[18] Sharpe, *Re-Mapping*, pp. 164–5, 108–9.
[19] Ste B., *Counsel to the Husband*, pp. 2, 41–2, 22–3, 7–8, 71.
[20] Grimalde, *Ciceroes Three Bokes of Duties*, pp. Ciiij–v.
[21] 'The State of Matrimony', in *Certain Sermons*, p. 320; Ste B., *Counsel to the Husband*, p. 8; 'The State of Matrimony', pp. 322, 321; Gouge, *Domesticall Duties*, p. 698 on the office of the master.
[22] Evelyn, *Sylva*, B1v, pp. 1–2.

the practicalities of arboreal management in a way that was less metaphorically fanciful than it might seem now when we treat the political as a sort of natural kind. To read that priority into *Sylva* is to stand the tree upon its branches.

A work such as Wing's *The Crown Conjugal* would initially support this sort of inversion. Wing distinguishes the political from the domestic and personal, and at times suggests no more than an analogical relationship between them.[23] 'As reason and policie is the crowne *monarchicall*, so wilbe [sic] our guide in the crowne matrimoniall.' But again, the shared grounding for the analogy lies in patterns of duty and office. This allows the relentless exploration of the imagery of a crown that to modern eyes politicises marriage. As the wife is the husband's crown, so he is a king, and a disobedient wife a 'house rebell a house traytor';[24] but for writers like Wing, a king was a father and the previous monarch had been married to her people. After her death, James in a speech to parliament made laborious play with these linked metaphorical patterns for office. 'What God has joined', he said, 'let no man rend asunder. I am the husband the whole Isle is my lawful wife; I am the Head and it is my body; I am the shepherd, and it is my flocke.' And, he added, he sought unity between his kingdoms, for he would not be a polygamous husband.[25] To read such arguments as politicising is to miss the ebb and flow of the prodigal's return made plausible by a presupposition that was a good deal more than political. In partial contrast to Wing, the author of *The Office of Christian Parents* insisted that designating a magistrate as a parent was figurative, but seemed to take quite literally a notion of parental tyranny.[26] As Samuel Rutherford later insisted, in writing of the most 'political' of issues: there is no moral difference between a monarch's betrayal of trust and any other who holds an office; physicians, parents, masters, patrons, husbands and the pilots of ships all might be resisted. 'Every tyrant is a furious man.'[27] What is at issue is a specific case of the ethics of office not an insulated political doctrine. It follows from explicating such a widespread presupposition of office that what we have come to regard as early modern political theory is an artificial and potentially misleading construction.

The argument, then, is not that distinctions concerning the civic, the domestic, the legal and the political passed unnoticed in the

---

[23] Wing, *The Crown Conjugal*, p. 6. [24] *Ibid.*, pp. 69, 80ff, 140.
[25] James VI&I, Speech (19 March 1603), in *Workes*, p. 488.
[26] Anon., *The Office of Christian Parents*, pp. B1, 194.
[27] Rutherford, *Lex, Rex*, Q.28.

seventeenth-century night. On the contrary, Aristotelian traditions had long insisted on family and polity having different *tele*. Before Thomas Aquinas adapted Aristotle, Hugh of St Victor in his *Didascalicon* defined the political as synonymous with the civic and public and distinct from the domestic and economic.[28] John Ponet could later write confidently of 'politicke power' without needing to define his terms; it was but one manifestation of God's power to be found in the vocational relationships between masters and servants, husbands and wives. Sovereignty theory in seventeenth-century Germany certainly built on an inherited literature to create a perceptible form of political theory; and Edward Gee could use the expressions civil magistracy and political power interchangeably.[29] The argument is, rather, that shared presuppositions in office made these distinctions far more negotiable metaphorically than they have become, and made them, above all, derivative of what was presupposed about the world as a whole: they were framed, as it were, by God and Satan, one the epitome of office, the other of its abuse. There was nothing novel about this in the post-Reformation world. The literature that Maurizio Viroli discusses as defining a language of politics for modernity to inherit, did nothing of the sort. It was shot through with the interplay of conceptual vocabulary and imagery that compromised any such isolated identity; activity beyond the political was still properly a matter of offices, and political relationships could be described as marriages.[30] Thus, in a post-Reformation world, the Lord Mayor of London could be presented in pageant as a spouse (chapter 2). Defoe could write of the 1688 Revolution as divorce; Arbuthnot could concoct 'Mrs Bull's Vindication' as a cautionary tale about the casuistry of passive obedience.

I have argued before that the conceptual domain of the political was far less secure than we have taken it as being, and, when we find it, had a significantly different semantic content, and that 'politics' and its cognates had variable and somewhat different meanings from those they have since acquired. A politician might be an idealised counsellor, or an atheist.[31] Writing in the *politica* genre was jurisprudential and it was still common during the seventeenth century to keep politics and its cognates distinct

---

[28] Hugh of St Victor, *Didascalicon*, discussed in Maurizio Viroli, *From Politics to Reason of State: The Acquisition and Transformation of the Language of Politics 1250-1600* (Cambridge, 1992), pp. 31-2.

[29] Ponet, *Shorte Treatise*, pp. 51, 47; Edward Gee, *The Divine Right and Original of Civill Magistracy* (1658), p. 26.

[30] Viroli, *From Politics to Reason of State*, on Henry of Rimini, pp. 40-1; on Lucas de Penna, pp. 62-3.

[31] Condren, *The Language of Politics*, chs. 1, 2; Cf. Anon., *The Sage Senator*, sub-title; Anon., *The Catholike's Supplication for Toleration* (1604), p. 10.

from the vocabulary used for what we call political communities. In this uncertain linguistic environment, our politically central concept of the state still had an ambivalent place. Machiavelli, who had used the word state in *The Prince* to designate effective possession, had referred to the republics and states of Christendom in a way suggesting a novel dubiety in the latter.[32] As late as 1660 the word state could still carry this connotation.[33]

I am suggesting now, as an explanation of this fragility, that the reliance on a moveable vocabulary of office may have diminished the need, or inhibited the capacity, for maintaining any clear-cut demarcation between political and non-political as later it has become customary to draw it; so habitual that it passes unnoticed when etched back into the evidence. Further, that it is the under-determination of the figurative use of the vocabulary of office that has facilitated this anachronistic slippage. That is, lacunae in the evidence together with patterns of figuration ease the restrictive conventions of discourse, erode safeguards of meaning and encourage supplementation with later understandings. This point applies not only to the domestic and the political but, as I have evidenced (chapter 3), to the parallel distinction between the public and the private. It reinforces the claim that much of what we designate political theory might have been seen differently, and through a different discursive prism, consigned to a well-established discipline such as theology, law or rhetoric, or regarded, for better or for worse, as casuistry. Thus the absence of official and political as organising categories in book-lists can be seen to be for diametrically opposed reasons. 'Political' animals like More and Starkey did not necessarily need *libri politici* (law, theology, history, even miscellaneous, might do), but the official was so pervasively informing it was not helpful in classifying anything beyond, perhaps, editions and translations of *De officiis*.

This raises the question of whether the erosion of a presuppositional grounding in office is a principal condition for the development of political theory as we understand it. If, as Braddick concludes, the formation of the modern state was largely the unintended consequence of the tensions between older social offices, the question has extensive resonance and it will be touched on again briefly in the epilogue.[34] And, certainly, what we have gathered together as early modern political theory is easily rendered accessibly modern by erasing its groundings in perceptions of office. The issue is, no doubt, too simply put, but it requires that we

---

[32] Machiavelli, *Il Principe e Discorsi*, Disc. 1, ch. 12.
[33] Anon., *The Sage Senator*, p. 170.   [34] Braddick, *State Formation*, at length.

look afresh at that allegedly defining mark of modern political understanding, the autonomy of politics thesis. This is, above all, because it has been widely held that Machiavelli discovered political autonomy and early modern argument refined and propagated awareness of it – not least in England where Starkey printed Neville's translations of the famous Niccolò.[35] Reconsideration of the autonomy thesis and its main variant, reason of state theory, is a condition for us to be able to write a history of political theory in this period that is not significantly artifical.

III

To put the thesis in the most general terms, political activity is held to be autonomous from morality. It operates either by no morality, or by moral rules of its own. On either variant, external standards are irrelevant, or only of conditional importance. This may be deplored, celebrated or stated as a fact about the world but, regardless, the autonomy thesis is predicated on there being a cohesive awareness of the political in the first place, to be contrasted with a monolithic (implicitly deontological) moral perspective. Benedetto Croce appears to have been the first to claim that Machiavelli discovered '*la necessità e l'autonomia della politica*' and it is still common enough to hold him responsible.[36]

Machiavelli's *Prince* was published posthumously and had probably not been intended for print. One clue lies in the off-hand way in which Machiavelli introduced the central metaphor of the state, *lo stato*, the first and quite unexplained noun in the body of the work and one used some 114 times in the text that followed.[37] Yet although *lo stato* does not seem to be an established term of print discourse, Viroli has evidenced its prior existence in the manuscript world of Florentine politics; Machiavelli's taking it for granted suggests less his metaphorical imagination, as I have mistakenly argued, than the use of an idiom appropriate to an audience whose actions were part of the *arcana imperii* of his city.[38] This would also explain the use of *lo stato*, albeit less frequently, in *The Discourses*. The work is also strikingly more meagre than *The*

---

[35] Henry Neville, trans., *The Works of the Famous Niccolo Machiavell* (1675), printed by John Starkey, who was also implicated in the bogus letter by Machiavelli prefacing *The Prince*, for which he provided a provenance.
[36] See Benedetto Croce, 'Elimenti di politica' (1929), in *Etica e politica* (Rome, 1973 edn), pp. 204–5; cf. Sharpe, *Re-Mapping*, pp. 67–70, 160, 178; the most important study in this tradition is still probably Gennaro Sasso, *Niccolò Machiavelli. Storia del suo pensiero politico* (Naples, 1958).
[37] J. H. Hexter, 'Il Principe and lo Stato', in *The Vision of Politics on the Eve of the Reformation* (London, 1973), pp. 150–78.
[38] Viroli, *From Politics to Reason of State*, pp. 134ff.

Discourses in its use of the rhetorics of moral justification to be found in printed books. It is not, then, a work that assumes any obvious sense of office. Moreover, the central figure of the prince is, despite appearances, ideally one of protean adaptability. Indeed, with a touch of parodic critique, he is not unlike the pilloried courtier of character literature and a plausible inspiration for the 'Machiavels' of the stage. In a different moral environment Burckhardt seized on the apparent autonomy to make Machiavelli's *Prince* central to his own argument about the emergence of modern individualism. In his steps trod Croce.

What is significant about *The Prince* is not its acceptance of immoral behaviour. It had long been held in medieval legal casuistry that the special status of the ruler in having official responsibility for the condition of the *regnum* allowed conduct that was otherwise reprehensible.[39] It remained the case that an appeal to office mitigated villainy, and placed a control on activities such as studied hypocrisy and fraud. From this notion of *status regni* comes one aspect of the rich metaphor of *lo stato*. One can find Machiavelli arguing in such terms in *The Discourses* (1.9); but what is striking in *The Prince* is that all the emphasis on the importance of being able to dissemble in necessity is almost without justification. Survival in a dangerous world seems virtually an end in itself. The need to control the environment of activity, almost as a personal property, provides a second metaphorical dimension to Machiavelli's *lo stato*.[40]

A qualification, however, is needed. To begin with, there is the casuistic emphasis on necessity, presupposing that the breach of normal ethical expectations should not be gratuitous, something upon which Machiavelli insists. In any case, as Renaissance ethical judgement was predominantly tied to the specific offices in which people found themselves, it is important to note the residue of office in *The Prince*. This ethical trace is military rather than political and it is easy for us to overlook it, because, after all, we see Machiavelli as a political theorist. This despite his work not being organised around the vocabulary of *politica*, and being sparing even in the use of words with the *polit* root.[41] In this context, seeing him as a civic writer would be an improvement, potentially covering a variety of offices beyond the political and including that of the soldier. In a number of ways Machiavelli moves to collapse the civic into the military, insisting on the martial as the sine qua non for civic life. Neal Wood has argued that military life, down to and including the ranking structure of an army,

---

[39] Gaines Post, *Studies in Medieval Legal Thought. Public Law and the State, 1100–1322* (Princeton, 1964), p. 308, n. 141.
[40] Hexter, *Vision of Politics*, pp. 150–78.
[41] J. H. Whitfield, *Discourses on Machiavelli* (Cambridge, 1969), ch. 9, esp. pp. 169ff.

was a clarifying model for the political. He has pointed out that in *The Art of War* (1521) Machiavelli used the term *principe* to mean ruler and general, and in *The Prince* itself an image of the prince as soldier is persistent.[42] He is advised to make the practice and study of war his central concerns – even hunting should be an exercise in the military exploration of topography – and the work culminates by urging the military adventure of liberating Italy from the barbarians. The structure hinges on several chapters devoted to the type of army he should have and the exemplars of princely conduct are largely soldiers.[43] Fortune, such a central preoccupation in warfare, thus becomes vital to civic life.

One aspect of this is that the moral qualities of the soldier, especially as inherited from Roman theory, fortitude, courage, discipline, hard work, foresight and initiative, are tacitly accepted as the moral qualities of the prince.[44] Not all these would necessarily be ethical in any post-Kantian way and, as Franciscans and Cistercians could attest, they were not the exclusive preserves of pagan Roman and stoic theorising. The point is simply that these qualities were accepted as aspects of the military *persona*, and of the general especially. In the uncertainties of war, fortune required the virtues of flexibility and foresight, the dangers demanded discipline, industry and courage. These qualities by no means exhaust the richness of *virtù* in Machiavelli's work; but they cover much of it and they are enough to constitute the ethics of a particular office, their exercise amounting to a form of prudence.[45] And rather than separating morality from politics, or discovering an autonomous political morality, Machiavelli never questions these martial attributes. When he wrote, notoriously, that it is necessary for a prince to know how to be bad – '*sapere intrare nel male, neccessitato*' – there was no implication that badness meant rejecting soldierly virtue.[46] The specific virtues he rejected, namely piety, liberality, honesty, are questioned, because if practised automatically they would be at odds with what must always be fostered: vigilance, foresight, flexibility and courage. Here, then, are affirmed the qualities Othello is supposed to exhibit and which, we are told, have made him a potent servant of Venice. Moreover, it is a part of Machiavelli's understanding of the office of the

---

[42] Neal Wood, 'Introduction' to *Niccolò Machiavelli, The Art of War*, trans. Ellis Farnworth (Cambridge, Mass., 2001), pp. iii–lxxxvii.
[43] Neal Wood, 'Machiavelli's Concept of Virtue Reconsidered', *Political Studies*, 15 (1969), pp. 159–72.
[44] *Ibid.*, for a discussion of the implications of this.
[45] On the full diversity of meaning attached to *virtù*, see J. H. Whitfield, 'The Anatomy of Virtue', in *Machiavelli* (Oxford, 1947), pp. 95–105; Russell Price, 'The Senses of *Virtù* in Machiavelli', *European Studies Review*, 3 (1973), pp. 315–45.
[46] Machiavelli, *Il Principe*, ch. 18, pp. 73–4.

general that he behaves in ways that can be celebrated; thus the moral imperative of ridding Italy of the barbarians and thus, too, the explicit denial of Agathocles' *virtù*.[47] It is this residue of office that has to be overlooked, as it was by Innocent Gentillet, to convert the prince into an emblem of evil, to transform the figure into an unrestrained self-fashioning and autonomous individual, or to see Machiavelli's use of the term *virtù* as systematically amoral, or immoral. Over the full range of its employment, it is neither. Insofar as the military ethos is important, we are a very long way from the autonomy of politics.

As an addendum, it is noteworthy that when Machiavelli was appropriated to nineteenth-century nationalism, then to fascism, it was done in part by reading into his loose and metaphorical usage of the term *lo stato* the later deified concept of the nation state which his prince could then be seen as serving. In that service heroism was regained through ideologies stressing the ennobling subordination to the greater good. A remnant of office was transformed and re-created, a form of *status regni* was donned in a black shirt.

The early modern world remains a plausible locus for the origins of political autonomy as it does exhibit an insecure and variable perception of moral modality detectable in Machiavelli's *Prince*. From the sixteenth century there are certainly hints of something occasionally approaching a moral autonomy for the polity in affirmations of reason of state. It has been quite conventional to posit reason of state as a pretty coherent doctrine, codified during the mid-sixteenth century and used to justify political policy in contradistinction to morality or religious orthodoxy. In this way, reason of state theory has been presented as some version of the autonomy thesis and, like that, has even been taken to have enjoyed some sort of ideological triumph.[48] A simplistic view of Machiavelli has, then, had wider ramifications. As Harro Höpfl has pointed out, however, the use of the expression, seemingly coined and used once by Guicciardini circa 1520 (*la ragione e uso degli state*),[49] does not point in any singular doctrinal direction. Sometimes used in the processes of demonising Machiavelli, it could also signal nothing more than acceptable casuistical adjustment, neither opposed to morality nor to religious orthodoxy. Unless the expression was part of the lurid armoury of polemical accusation, in which context it is a reliable guide only to hostility,

---

[47] *Ibid.*, ch. 8, p. 44.
[48] See Viroli, *From Politics to Reason of State*, pp. 238ff.
[49] Quoted in Harro Höpfl, 'Orthodoxy and Reason of State', *History of Political Thought*, 23 (2002), p. 214, n. 10.

it makes best sense in a context of casuistic prudence.[50] It illustrates the ease with which later doctrines can be projected into the invitingly casual, fugitive and fragmented.

What some usage amounted to was a recognition that there could be discourse about the civic or political, and touching the *arcana imperii* to one side of extraneous moral considerations, but not necessarily beyond office. This is about as much, I have suggested, as we get from Machiavelli, who had a sort of autonomy thesis thrust upon him by way of condemnation. Some evidence to support such a hypothesis can be found in Viroli's research into the raw conceptual materials for reason of state arguments found in the papers of fifteenth-century Florentine committees. More can be gathered from Scipione Ammirato and Arnoldus Clapmarius writing directly on the issue and for whom Tacitus was the authoritative touchstone. Their arguments pivoted on a distinction between a good and bad reason of state: the good, certainly involving dissimulation, was predictably a function of service and office, with ends and limits to its use; the bad was an abuse of office.[51] A little more can be gleaned by comparing William Cavendish's direct manuscript advice to Charles II with the modifications made by Margaret for publication. In what she presented as a series of moral *sententiae* we can detect an ethicising redescription of some fairly brutal practical maxims to the end of maintaining Charles on his throne. To the question of whether princes should rule by love or fear, William concludes, use both 'as occasion serves' and force only on necessity; to the same question Margaret summarises, on William's behalf, always rule justly.[52] In fact, her paraphrases of his maxims often insert references to words like justice and mercy where they were quite absent from the advice actually given to Charles.

Of the two variants of the autonomy of politics thesis the first, that the political domain is immoral, would seem to be little more than a conventional expostulation about the abuse of office. The second, that the political has moral requirements of its own, is, I think, closer to what people did argue when accepting the value of some reason of state. What

---

[50] *Ibid.*, pp. 217–18, 223ff; see also Donne, *Pseudo-Martyr*, pp. 47–8; see also Peter S. Donaldson, *Machiavelli and the Mystery of State* (Cambridge, 1988), pp. 112–19; tracts printed around the outbreak of the Civil Wars make this casuistic status abundantly clear, see for example, Anon., *The Contra-Replicant* (1642): reason of state must not be renounced in circumstances of extremity, p. 19; also in Anon., *The Moderator Expecting Sudden Peace or Certaine Ruine* (1642), reason of state is used in necessarily dispensing with rules of law, and every prince should do so if he is as wise as he is pious, p. 21.
[51] Scipione Ammirato, *Discorsi sopra Cornelio Tacito* (1594); Arnoldus Clapmarius, *De arcanis rerumpublicarum* (1605), on whom see Donaldson, *Machiavelli*, pp. 113–40.
[52] Cavendish, 'Advice', fol. 79; Margaret Cavendish, *Life of . . . Newcastle*, p. 4, p. li; see Condren, 'Casuistry to Newcastle', pp. 180–1, and at length for other examples.

is misleading is to see this as some exclusive and coherent theory of politics per se.[53] It would be truer to say that the beginnings of something like an autonomy of politics, and an acceptance of reason of state, are to be found in patterns of modal casuistry. They are reinforced wherever that casuistry could be assumed to be acceptable for a given audience. This, I hazard, was the case for both Machiavelli and William Cavendish. Each wrote manuscript advice directly for, or directed at, a prince who must first be a general and who will survive only by exercise of the skills and policies that maintain effective control. It was a form of argument arising from an understanding of office in which the specific virtue of prudence, as appropriate and balanced conduct according to the end or *telos* of an activity, was an indispensable criterion for good conduct. Just as one would expect, given the porosity of the notion of the political, prudence was not a defining feature of politics as such. The 'domestic' saying 'spare the rod and spoil the child', which Cavendish uses, was an adage of prudent discipline, implying a casuistic autonomy of parenthood. Indeed, the specificity of ethics of office could offer all sorts of moral autonomies for particular callings.[54] In maintaining that 'extraordinary cases' allow a departure from the authoritative ancient principles of church government, Lawson suggests a distinct reason of church. In asserting that the separate 'orbs' of men and women have their characteristic virtues and vices, Browne may be taken as intimating a reason of gender. Francis North insisted that what in a private man was a culpable failing, namely proud ostentation, was in a judge a necessary virtue of office. This sounds like a clear autonomy of law.[55] If these be written off as cases of ad hoc apologetics of scant theoretical consequence, presumably the same attitude should be adopted to those who wrote passingly of reason of state. Ammirato's and Clapmarius's exposition of reason of state, however, cannot be treated in this way, and what is crucial is that their arguments alike stem from modal casuistry. No single body of law, they argue, offers adequate imperatives and sanctions for all human situations; thus we have different bodies of law to complement each other. Reason of state is the corrective mechanism that mediates the

---

[53] In *Behemoth*, for example, Hobbes shows a clear-eyed awareness of both, but this does not mean that he is part of a Tacitist or reason of state ideology; his own science of politics was presented as a coherent alternative to such practices and ad hoc explanations of the social world. See Noel Malcolm, '*Behemoth Latinus*: Adam Ebert, Tacitism and Hobbes', *Filozofski vestnik*, 24, 2 (2003), pp. 118–20.

[54] Mason, *Tribunal of Conscience*, pp. 40–2.

[55] Lawson, *Politica*, p. 185; Browne, *Christian Morals*, p. 337; Chief Justice Francis North, *The Lord Keeper's Speech* (1682); see also de Bohun, *The Justice of the Peace*, Preface, p. A (mispaginated).

laws impinging on the state and, for Clapmarius, sovereignty.[56] Andrew Tooke's adaptive translation of Pufendorf's *De officio* similarly universalises the issue in terms of offices rather than politics: equity might even be styled a reason of natural law. It is impossible, to recall Tooke's (and Pufendorf's) point, that all cases can be 'compriz'd in the *Universal Law*' and equity demands its suspension given a peculiar case.[57] In short, wherever there is a rule of conduct established by and for an office, there is a potential autonomy from extrinsic moral expectations, or normal conduct within its ambit.

To assume the historical validity between morality and politics, between private morality and public political life, is simplistic and distorting; and it is in mislocating such presupposed dichotomies that the autonomy thesis looks to be established by the seventeenth century. Overwhelmingly, we need to recast putative assertions of autonomy, political or otherwise, in the light of the casuistry of office-holding. The end of any office could be taken to override normally expected behaviour seen under its auspices and, I think, what might be isolated as expressions of a theory of reason of state, or a recognition of the autonomy of politics, must very often be taken as examples of modal casuistry reliant on the accepted *tele* of valued offices. Reference has already been made to the Earl of Strafford and William Pym (chapter 8), and to Richard Beacon and Gilbert Burnet, both of whom cited the authority of Cicero for the justification of peremptory and arbitrary conduct in order to save Rome.[58] Richard Beacon, again, in *Solon His Follie* asserted more generally that what for a public magistrate is policy, in a private man is deceit.[59] It is an exonerating redescription of lying, but it has its place in the Reformation imperative of dealing with Ireland; it is a piece of modal casuistry. Just as easily, Lord Burghley had concluded the opposite: considering the *telos* of counsel, deceit was allowable only in private men.[60]

Daniel Tuvill provides a more sustained case, exhibiting a sceptical awareness of the corruptions and dangers of public as opposed to (his distinction) private life. The direct honesty and justice of the private man is in contrast to the suspicious conduct appropriate to the public. The somewhat alien scope he gives to public and private has already been noted (chapter 3), but Tuvill's main point was that, in a corrupt age, the

---

[56] Donaldson, *Machiavelli*, pp. 119, 124–7.
[57] Tooke, *Whole Duty of Man*, ch. 2, sect. 10, pp. 47–8.
[58] Beacon, *Solon his Follie*, p. 16; see Peltonen, *Classical Humanism*, p. 157; Burnet, *History*, vol. IV, p. 334.
[59] Beacon, *Solon his Follie*, p. 12; cf. Ponet, *Shorte Treatise*, pp. 128–9.
[60] William Cecil, Lord Burghley, letter to Sir Robert Cecil, 21 May 1593, cited in Mack, *Elizabethan Rhetoric*, p. 182.

courtly world is that in which it is safest to assume office-abuse, the private that in which the requirements of office are fulfilled. Thus it is not so much that in court life, if you will, political morality is absent, but that it must be guarded.[61] The dove of simple virtue must ally herself with the cunning serpent. This may plausibly be written off as obfuscation, but it is the sort of obfuscation that stops well short of attributing autonomy to the courtly world. The valorous lion must don 'the outer hide' of the fox.[62] To enter the world of court life requires adjustments, but always within the ambit of Christian integrity; it is a sphere of prudence subservient to Christianity. In a world of office-abuse there must be the constant exercise of supreme intelligence; only Christ could unmask Judas who had fastidiously 'performed all the ceremonious offices' that love required.[63] Despite isolated expressions, this amounts to much less than a theory of political autonomy, and despite well-digested Machiavellian imagery it takes us no further from casuistry than did *The Prince*. Those like Hitchcock and Raleigh who embraced a sort of Machiavellianism qualified it, as I have noted above (chapter 8): dubious means must serve a moral end.

Nevertheless, to repeat, from exercises in the casuistry of office, specifically state casuistry, or reason of state, to be found in the writings of Tuvill, Beacon and many others back to the legal doctrine of *status regni* that preceded Machiavelli, it is easy to construct a coherent doctrine of the autonomy of politics. This seems to have been done first (dangerous word) not by writers adapting Machiavelli's work but by those hostile to and caricaturing modal casuistry. In the mid- to late seventeenth century, arguments for the acceptance of new rulers were distorted by their opponents in ways that insinuated some domain impervious to the righteous moral judgements of the clergy, the religious who Machiavelli would not have imposing their ethical priorities on the civic world. To some extent a kind of political autonomy was a *reductio* of a feared erosion of the authority of clerical office. As we will see, this was a feature of George Hickes's response to the new monarchy of William and Mary.[64] On the basis of such polemic and by a considerable leap of poetic imagination, John Arbuthnot developed a modern and clearly recognisable doctrine as a satiric exploration of the implications of the 'state casuistry' men like Hickes found so abhorrent. Arbuthnot's *Art of Political Lying* (1712) is an ironic descant on at least one hundred years of casuistic

[61] Tuvill, *The Doue*, pp. 37–9; Tuvill, 'Of Accusation', in *Essays*, fols. 124–7.
[62] Tuvill, 'Of Accusation', in *Essays*, fol. 125.
[63] *Ibid.*, fol. 82; Tuvill, *The Doue*, p. 36.
[64] Hickes, *Apology*, pp. 7–8.

analyses of office, and it does offer a firm distinction between public and private much as we would now take it. The private and the economical, that is the domestic, are informed by shared values quite properly absent from the political.[65] Only in the private realm, pontificates Arbuthnot's spurious 'Author', are we entitled to expect honest dealings. He offers a general description of political discourse, action and the institutions that serve and channel them, that is systemically discrepant with everyday moral life. The political is not simply evil or anarchic, but it is autonomous in the modern sense of following its own rules; it has a weird coherence, vocabulary and decorum of its own and is therefore amenable to a thorough scientific analysis of its laws. The 'Author' has discovered, distilled into print and will sell what Machiavelli was thought to have known. Doctrines are not always developed by people who believe in them, or expect them to be taken literally.[66]

IV

If, to sum up, we survey the political structures and modes of discourse in early modern England, it can appear that we are dealing with social roles that individuals might take up, or from which they might be excluded, within a regime on which they may have reflected in some way. This all sounds innocent enough but it is not. First, it virtually reads into the past a firm, almost universal distinction between public and private, of institutionalised political role and private individuality, or public and private spheres. Second, to this binary pattern can be attached fitting notions of negative (private) freedom and positive, political, participatory liberty. Third, this in turn leads to presupposing an interplay of socially constructed identity and inner autonomy. I have suggested along the way that the impositions of all of these pairings are, regardless of permutations, inadequate to the patterns of presupposition about human moral identity in an office-driven world. One result has been to imagine commitments to only later concepts of liberty (chapter 4); another has been to mythologise a doctrinal republicanism from a positive register of office entailment (chapters 3, 7) and so exaggerate the cohesiveness and exclusivity of an ideology. Another, noted immediately above, has been

---

[65] John Arbuthnot, *Pseudologia Politike, Or The Art of Political Lying* (1712); for discussion, Condren, *Satire, Lies and Politics*, esp. chs. 6 and 7; see also Head, *Proteus Redivivus* for the closest antecedent.

[66] I know only of one apparently gullible buyer, who thought the author was genuine and the opus in preparation c. 1710 regrettably lost. There may be one born every 250 years: see Robert M. Adams, 'The New Art of Political Lying', in *Bad Mouth: Fugitive Papers on the Dark Side* (Berkeley, 1977), pp. 43–4.

to firm up an awareness of the autonomy of politics from altogether less conclusive intimations gathering around understandings of the contested integrity of office and the equity that was taken to complement any practice of official rule-following. In some form, however, a good range of questionable oppositional pairings are needed if we are to see even embryonic liberalism in the early modern world. Using liberalism to effect an historiographical redescription is to insinuate a whole perspective (above, chapter 4).

Partially at issue in all this are the anachronisms caused by mislocating our own later vocabularies. It has been a long-standing custom to embed them in the past, as if they were shared despite differences of language. In Russellian terms, it is a confusion between object and meta-language. We may, for example, want to call the *Basilikon Doron* a piece of ideology, and in doing so we may realise that we are re-classifying to render more accessible a world which did not have the concept term ideology. We may proceed in this way, either because a limited historical imagination confines us to the play of the conceptually familiar, and so, at least without uneconomic effort, we have little option but to read a document as if it were ideology. The use of scare quotes around the salient terms signals an unwillingness to go too far in understanding a suspiciously alien world and a willingness to try and have our cake and eat it. Or, we designate something an ideology because, despite the absence of that concept term, we hold ideology to be a necessary category of the political; therefore, if there is politics, there must be ideology. If the language of the past does not adequately express the concept, it is our job to rectify the failure and properly disclose the political. If such linguistic correction becomes sufficiently self-conscious, it may be philosophically defensible. It is, however, clearly to hypostatise our own concept of the political and so shift from historiography to the metaphysics of politics. Yet, for whatever reason, when we say that James VI&I's opponents *intended*, or tried to repudiate his ideology, that he was worried about their radicalism, or hostile to their liberalism, or conservatism, we have confused object and meta-language, what is inherent in the evidence with the explanatory and elucidatory tools we take to it: 'Dryden spoke both commonplace and ideology, and he was understood accordingly by his contemporaries.'[67]

Ultimately, the metaphor of the tool for language has its limitations; words are more than a set of optional instruments aiding or confounding historiographical understanding. Eventually we all reach some conceptual threshold, some Kantian antinomy, a limit to imagination beyond which

---

[67] McKeon, *Poetry and Politics*, p. 42.

we cannot move without treating object and meta-language as one, a point at which our language constitutes an inescapable perspective for viewing the evidence. This may be posited as a limitation or a condition of human understanding, but historians are rarely dealing with problems at such an ultimate terminus. The pretence that they are is euphemistic for a refusal to set aside present priorities. If we can recognise a difference between myth-making and historiography, it pivots on our tolerance of concept implantation by redescription by (let us call a spade a spade) how relaxed we are about altering the evidence. And if we describe the intentional activity of figures like James VI&I or Dryden in terms of their understandings of ideologies, we are augmenting it. To generalise the matter, it is little better than giving up the ghost if we admit the anachronisms involved in our descriptive vocabulary and then proceed as if they do not matter.[68]

This, however, is only part of the problem. More insidious is the misreading of conceptual relationships where individual items in the vocabulary remain invariant and even enjoy a continuity of emotional force, as is the case with the terms liberty and corruption. For this there is no simple clue to help identify what is going on; and for this sort of structural anachronism a simple Russellian distinction between object and meta-language is hardly adequate. But the occlusion of the full ramifications of early modern presuppositions and language of office has played no small part in ensuring its continuing practice.

---

[68] Greenberg, *The Radical Face*, p. 3; Racken, *Stages of History*, pp. 94–5.

Part III

'I, A. B.'

11 An overview of the oath in seventeenth-century argument

> Now Oaths are so frequent, they should be taken like Pills, swallowed whole; if you chew them you will find them bitter; if you think what you swear,'twill hardly go down.
>
> (Selden, *Table Talk*, 1686, para. 94)

I

The ancient and sacrosanct practice of oath-taking epitomised office in action, and like the term office, the English 'oath' was one of a whole family of quasi-synonyms and potentially casuistic qualifiers, such as protest, vow, promise, confess, affirm, declare, believe and know, incitements all to controversy. A vow, for example, could be a promise to God, an oath called upon Him as a witness, but sometimes the words could be interchangeable. In *Twelfth Night*, Sir Toby Belch tells Viola that Sir Andrew Aguecheek will fight only 'for's oath sake', referring to this as 'his vow'.[1] The vow of a nun taking holy orders is included in *The Booke of Oathes*.[2] At the end of the century, while Roger Palmer called oaths and vows synonyms, White Kennett insisted they were different.[3]

Other terms in the ambit of swearing, such as protest, or declare, could seem less onerous than the specific oath. Their presence in oath-like documents is partially explained by a common distinction made between assertory and promissory oaths.[4] The assertory oath was in Austinian terms a constative: it attested to a state of affairs, such as one's identity in a court of law. The promissory, however, was an Austinian performative; like a wager, it was a creative act, having 'constructive power'.[5] The

---

[1] Shakespeare, *Twelfth Night* 3.4; also Browne, *Christian Morals*, p. 337; Earl of Orrery, *The Black Prince* (1672), 5.4, p. 60.
[2] *Booke of Oathes* (1649), p. 194.
[3] Kennett, *Dialogue*, p. 15; Palmer, *The Englishman's Allegiance*, p. 207.
[4] Robert Sanderson, *De juramento* (1655), 1.8, pp. 17–18; also *Works*, vol. IV, pp. 243–306; see also Tooke, *The Whole Duty of Man*, ch. 11, 10, p. 127.
[5] Sanderson, *De juramento*, 1.13, pp. 31–2; 'The Case of the Rash Vow', in *Works*, vol. V, p. 64; cf. John Austin, *How to Do Things with Words*, ed. J. O. Urmson (London, 1955);

233

assertory, then, could easily be synonymous with declaring and it might only require subscription to its terms.[6] The promissory oath was more problematic and accepted as binding only on tacit conditions. These Sanderson summarised as being sworn with God's permission, consistent with a superior power, existing oaths, and assuming circumstances were not radically transformed.[7] Keeping these in mind was enough to ensure that oaths were never impervious to casuistic exception.[8] Additionally, there was always the meta-duty incumbent upon any office-holder to consider the end of the office, and therefore give priority to the point of any oath in question. The difference between assertory and promissory oaths, however, was not absolute, for the importance of asserting often lay in the performative dimension of oath-taking. So, during the Restoration, any potential officer had to 'declare and believe [constative] that it is not lawful upon any pretence whatsoever to take up arms against the King'.[9] If this were not taken as implicitly promissory, it would have been pointless.

There is a less than clear distinction between performatives and constatives as such, and the uncertain barriers between assertory and promissory oaths allowed a vocabulary of knowing, asserting and subscribing to be swept into the vortex of swearing, abjuring and vowing. A number of terms, then, might simply have been used to make promissory oaths, or fashion something less rigorous than swearing. This negotiable indeterminacy meant that words in the immediate context of the oath could look suspiciously 'soft', and appear as euphemistic displacements for it. The 'domino effect' of language might make agreements and affirmations oaths in all but name.[10] In early modern England there was widespread

---

on the more general relevance of Austinian terminology to Renaissance law, see Ian Maclean, *Interpretation and Meaning in the Renaissance: The Case of Law* (Cambridge, 1992), pp. 168–70, 209.

[6] As God was all-knowing, the assertory vow was redundant and this might suggest a clear difference between oaths and vows, as Sanderson argued, 'The Case of the Rash Vow', pp. 63–4, but in practice this was not so.

[7] Sanderson, *De juramento*, 2.10, pp. 32–3; Joseph Hall, *The Lawfulness and Unlawfulness of an Oath or Covenant* (Oxford, 1643), pp. 1–3; Anon., *A Mirrour of Allegiance* (1647), p. 17; Anon., *New Quaeres of Conscience Touching the Late Oath: Desiring Resolution* (Oxford, 1643), fols. Ar-v; see also Selden, *Table Talk*, pp. 70–1; Tooke, *The Whole Duty of Man*, ch. 11, 6, p. 126.

[8] Sanderson, *De juramento*, pp. 54–5; Shakespeare, *Love's Labour's Lost* 1.1.

[9] The Corporation Act (1661); the Act of Uniformity (1662) and the Act for Restraining Nonconformists from Inhabiting in Corporations (1665), quoted in Jones, *Conscience and Allegiance*, pp. 279–80.

[10] Thus to subscribe could be a specifically written act appropriate to assertion or declaration, and so not be taken to signify a promissory oath, but it could be the written form of a promissory oath. Compare Shakespeare, *Love's Labour's Lost* 1.1, in which the young King of Navarre insists that he and his fellows subscribe to a promissory oath

recognition of the latitude that language allowed in clarifying or obscuring meaning.[11] So, one function of ritual was to isolate acts of swearing, guaranteeing that an oath and its end was unambiguous.[12] This reinforced the *gravitas* of the oath but was not always effective in eradicating interpretative latitude. The Solemn League and Covenant was ceremonially buttressed by sermons and distributed throughout the country with instructions for swearing to it as an oath. It was even prefaced with the biblical text 'And all Judah rejoiced at the oath' (2 Chronicles 15: 15). Although for some its oath-like status only inflated its impropriety, others insinuated that its implications had been deviously disguised. Why, asked one critic, is it presented as a vow and covenant; is it thought that avoiding the term 'oath' will make it easier to take?[13] Sometimes there were indeed advantages for an authority in avoiding the term. In issuing *The Protestation*, parliament had enhanced its own office by encouraging people to do something very close to swearing, yet as Robert Sanderson surmised may have avoided the ominously exacting 'oath' with its requirement to swear.[14] Given a culture so attentive to such discriminations, it is unlikely that Sir Robert Boyle operated on a double standard in refusing to swear oaths himself while requiring that his servants 'promise & ingage' to him.[15] Boyle's insistence was consistent with his distaste for swearing.[16]

Oaths entailed a triadic relationship between people in official capacities and divine power as an absent presence.[17] They were expressions of

---

(or vow) to study without interruption, frivolity or women for three years, with Anon., *A Letter from a Person of Quality* (1675) in which subscription is contrasted with swearing, see below, n. 94.

[11] Robert Parsons, *A Treatise Tending to Mitigation* (1607), chs. 7, 8, pp. 275–81, 296–306, 313–18, 328–30; Henry Mason, *The New Art of Lying Covered by Jesuits under a Vaile of Equivocation* (1624), ch. 1; Sanderson, 'The Case of the Engagement' (1650), in *Works*, vol. V, p. 23.

[12] Henry Parker (?), *The Oath of Pacification* (1643), p. 6; Thomas Comber, *The Nature and Usefulness of Judicial Swearing* (1681/2), pp. 17–20; Hobbes, *Elements*, 1.15.16–18; Rogers, *Philosophicall Discourse*, digests a range of ancient symbolic acts accompanying swearing, ch. 47, pp. 200v–1r.

[13] Anon., *The Anti-Covenant; or A Sad Complaint* (Oxford, 1643), pp. 24–5.

[14] Sanderson, 'The Case of the Engagement', pp. 18–34, see below, chapter 14; Sanderson, *The Reasons of the Present Judgment of the University of Oxford* (Oxford, 1647), in *Works*, vol. V, pp. 387–8, seems also to distinguish oath from protestation in referring to *The Oath of Supremacy* and the *Protestation*; see, additionally, Cressy, 'The Protestation Protested, 1641 and 1642', p. 255.

[15] Boyle papers, Commonplace book 189, fol. 13r, quoted Shapin, *A Social History of Truth*, p. 403; cf. Sir Robert Boyle, *Free Discourse Against Customary Swearing* (c. 1647, 1695), in *Works*, ed. Thomas Birch, London (1772), vol. VI, pp. 1–32.

[16] Boyle, *Free Discourse*, p. 11; see also Boyle, 'The Dayly Reflection', pp. 220–1.

[17] A rare exception is found in Samuel Harsnett's reading of Ezekiel, 31: 11 where God's 'As I live' is taken literally to have been an oath sworn to the Jews, but as Harsnett also

religion as *religio*, bonds forming the 'safest knot', for the performance of duty.[18] This mainstream belief did, however, need reiterating. If the religion of an oath fails to bind, insisted Archbishop Tillotson in 1681, nothing will.[19] One might, depending on context, 'know', or 'affirm', or 'protest' without explicit invocation of religious faith; but calling on, or vowing to God, was to wager the soul; swearing, therefore, had to be by a god in which one believed – it could be taken as a form of worship.[20] Swearing, as Dante had it, relinquished God's gift of free will, and as others explicated, had to be in good conscience with conscience being followed even when erroneous. Mind and words must always be as one.[21] If an oath is lawful, wrote Hunton, citing Ezekiel, it is obligatory and the king of Judah should not have broken his oath even though to keep it was to harm his people.[22] A diversity of biblical texts could have been cited to reinforce the responsibility, not least the Third Commandment, 'Thou shalt not take the name of the Lord thy God in Vain' (Exodus 20: 7). A public fundamental oath, Hunton insisted, is the equivalent of divine law and William Prynne would relentlessly contrast Old Testament allegiance to divine law with the alacrity with which he believed new oaths were sworn in contradiction to old.[23] Because swearing was conventionally assumed, or asserted to be a God-given institution, it dangerously entangled religion with potentially more tractable issues and through judicial oaths bonded law to religion.[24] One might, and some

---

insists that oaths have to be sworn by something higher, the argument might better be considered a mess rather than an exception. See Richard Stuart, *Three Sermons by the Reverend and Learned Dr. Richard Stuart, to which is added a Fourth Sermon by Samuel Harsnett* (1656), pp. 122–3, 126.

[18] Thomas Alcock, cited in J. C. D. Clark, 'Religion and Political Identity: Samuel Johnson as Nonjuror', in J. C. D. Clark and Howard Erskine Hill, eds., *Samuel Johnson in Historical Contexts* (Aldershot, 2002), p. 81; also John Spurr, 'Perjury, Profanity and Politics', *Seventeenth Century*, 8, 1 (1993), p. 29; see also Christopher White, *Of Oathes* (1627), pp. 1–3, and numerous others. The oath as religious bond was almost a phatic utterance.

[19] Sanderson, *De juramento*, 1.2, pp. 5–6; Comber, *Judicial Swearing*, p. 3; Tillotson cited in Clark, 'Religion and Political Identity', p. 82.

[20] Hobbes, *Elements*, 1.15.16–18; Tooke, *The Whole Duty of Man*, ch. 11, 6, p. 126; on the oath as worship, Boyle, *Free Discourse*, p. 11.

[21] Dante, *The Divine Comedy*, ed. and trans. Charles S. Singleton (Princeton, 1970–5), Paradise, 5.19–30; see Joan Ferrante, *The Political Vision of the Divine Comedy* (Princeton, 1984), pp. 260, 360–1. Sanderson, *De juramento*, 1.11, pp. 23–4; Mason, *Tribunal of Conscience*, pp. 2–10; Tooke, *The Whole Duty of Man*, ch. 11, 6, p. 126; Taylor, *Ductor dubitantium*, pp. 111–13; Miles Coverdale, *A Christe exhortacion* (1574), fol. 13.

[22] Hunton, *Treatise*, pp. 6–7; Sanderson, *De juramento*, p. 2.

[23] Hunton, *Treatise*, p. 4; William Prynne, *Concordia discors* (1659), pp. 17–29; de Bohun, *The Justice*, p. 157.

[24] Coverdale, *A Christe exhortacion*, fol. 3; John Sharp, Sermon 16, c. 1680, in *Works*, vol. IV, p. 284; Comber, *Judicial Swearing*, pp. 27–8, 17; de Bohun, *The Justice*, p. 160.

did, swear on a surrogate for God, a sign, according to Stillingfleet, of dangerous atheistic drollery.[25] To swear on one's honour, the stars in the firmament, on one's lady's foot, by 'thine own fair eyes', on a 'parcel-gilt goblet',[26] or by Grimalkin the Rebel Cat, threatened to destabilise and weaken the potency of the institution without which offices could not be sustained.[27]

There are additional ways in which the oath concentrated the imponderables of office-holding. First, because those involved were *personae*, the question of to whom and in what capacity one swore could provide leeway. As John Humfrey asked of the Abjuration Oath, if we swear to do nothing to alter the government, are we swearing to the king, his office or his will?[28] Bishop Burnet warned that whereas Catholic princes were bound to their oaths as men, 'their oaths, being acts of religion, were subject to the direction of their confessors'. So, when Louis of France swore in the coronation oath to observe the Edict of Nantes, Protestants were probably made less not more secure.[29] The scope given by awareness of identity in office would be central during the Engagement controversy (below, chapter 14). Second, just as the language of office could be used, albeit with stresses and strains, to defend or attack almost any conduct, so too any strict typology of oath-taking over-simplifies the slipperiness of the activity. *The Mirror of Justices*, for example, had stated baldly that recognition of fealty provided the principal form of oath-taking. William Prynne recorded that when old enough to take any office, every man had to swear such an oath at an annual court leet. In this way oaths of fealty were much like, and retrospectively could be called 'state oaths', those oaths designed to ensure allegiance to established rule.[30] Some preliminaries aside, I want instead to suggest no more than a heuristic continuum of oath-taking, the thread of continuity being provided by a common process of performative utterance, or promissory force in assertive swearing before divine power and evoking relationships of office. 'State oaths', among others, do not fit neatly on any one point of such a

---

[25] Cited in John Spurr, 'Perjury, Profanity and Politics', pp. 39–40; Comber, *Judicial Swearing*; and Sharp, 'Against Common Swearing', in *Works*, vol. IV, p. 297.
[26] Shakespeare, *Henry V* 3.7; *The Merchant of Venice* 5.1; *2Henry IV* 2.1.
[27] Coverdale, *A Christe exhortacion*, fols. 11–12, 23; Sermon, 'Of Swearing' (1562?) in *Certain Sermons*, pp. 41–3; Butler, 'A Swearer', in *Characters*, pp. 202–3.
[28] John Humfrey, *The Free State of the People Maintained* (1702), p. 3.
[29] Burnet, text of speech (1713), in *History*, vol. VI, pp. 157–8.
[30] Andrew Horn (?), *Speculum justiciorum* (c. 1300), trans. 1642 (New York, 1968 edn), ch. 3, sect. 37; Prynne, *Concordia discors*, p. 1; Lawson, *Politica* (1689), p. 360, marginal gloss University of New South Wales copy, by Thomas Winter c. 1810, tags them as state oaths; Jones, *Conscience and Allegiance*, ch. 2, p. 15.

vector. The purpose is less to fashion a set of definitional boxes than to outline just how complex and controversial an oath could be.

II

At one extreme, one may place what I shall call oaths of passage. Recall a distinction with respect to the solemnities of assuming office, between transformative assumption *through* and affirmative performance *in* ceremonial activity (above, chapter 2). Oaths of passage encapsulated this: one party exercised office in requiring of another an oath to behave appropriately to a newly assumed social *persona*.[31] Under this rubric may be placed those rare oaths that stripped the oath-taker of an identity, as when a subject swore to accept banishment.[32] More normally, the oaths of 'private persons' at marriage,[33] the midwife before the bishop, the scavenger before aldermen, were oaths of passage proclaiming an altered identity, attempts to induct, announce and contain. In laying out the content of the office, the oath denuded the initiate of excuses for non-performance. A number of the oaths collected in *The Booke of Oathes* (1649 and 1689), such as those required of doctors of divinity, are oaths of this sort.[34] So too, obviously enough, is the oath of a Lord Mayor to treat fairly all within his authority, and not to be bribed or swayed by gifts.[35] Yet there is sufficient emphasis on the importance of the mayor's allegiance to the monarch to give this oath some of the expected features of a state oath. And if it therefore disrupts neat classification, this too is not surprising given the state-like significance London at times achieved.

Oaths of passage, however, fall into two broad groupings, or rather could be seen in two ways. There were what might be called directly performative or transformative oaths, where swearing in the ceremony itself was taken as the act that formed the new *persona*. *Ipso facto*, to assume an official *persona* prior to taking an oath of passage could be to behave without right.[36] According to the Churches of Rome and England,

---

[31] Coverdale, *A Christe exhortacion*, fol. 8.
[32] *Booke of Oathes* (1649), pp. 208–9, 296; Shakespeare, *King Lear* 1.1, where Cordelia is 'stranger'd with our oath'.
[33] Sermon, 'Of Swearing', in *Certain Sermons*, p. 41.
[34] There are well over 200 oaths in each volume; the additions to the second edition include not only oaths pertinent to the reigns of James and William and Mary, but also, for example, the oaths of ale-tasters and leather-searchers. It is all better set out but the pagination is worse.
[35] *Booke of Oathes* (1649), p. 374.
[36] Donne, *Pseudo-Martyr*, ch. 12, p. 348.

the spinster and bachelor became a married couple through the ceremony in which the oath was taken. But other oaths could be held to be more constative and might better be called proclamatory oaths of passage, for they concluded, or simply announced an already changed *persona*. It was the person who had been chosen as a mayor who ceremoniously concluded his transition through an oath. The analytic distinction between the transformative and proclamatory can help focus important lines of dispute. The more transformative the oath of passage, the greater the narrative significance of the ceremonial context. The more proclamatory, the more issues of its meaning were diffused. These diverging possibilities are particularly important with respect to coronation oaths to be discussed in the following chapter.

If seen as proclamatory, oaths of passage shade into what, for want of a better term, may be called oaths of explication. With these, it was not that a new *persona* had been assumed, but that new or specific tasks were required of the office-holder, effectively enhancing the extant *persona*. The oath of a Knight of the Bath on his induction is one thing, the oath of such a knight taken at a coronation was another; an oath taken by a soldier and an oath by a captain of Berwick were distinct, the latter adumbrating specific expectations for one who held a martial office. A full exploration of these oaths would provide important evidence to test the argument that the modern state was formed through the augmentation of office.[37]

Oaths of explication merge into a second main class: what might be called diurnal oaths. These were taken by people in acknowledged capacities in order to re-establish or maintain predictable expectations of conduct. From Anglo-Saxon times, there were highly specific oaths of this sort, and, perhaps to be included with them, the oath of an oath-helper.[38] As Miles Coverdale put it, these oaths were mechanisms for ending controversies among neighbours. The oaths of the Duke of Gloucester and Bishop of Winchester to end disputes between them, ratified by the arbitration oath of the Duke of Bedford in 1419 acting as an oath-helper, are an example of what Coverdale would have had in mind;[39] but they also look a little like state oaths, testing allegiance of those in high office who carried with them armed retinues. Diurnal oaths were often taken to give voice at law in order to facilitate a formal judgement. Many

---

[37] Braddick, *State Formation*, at length.
[38] Carl Stephenson and Frederick Marcham, *Sources of English Constitutional History* (New York, 1937), p. 25.
[39] Coverdale, *A Christe exhortacion*, fols. 7–8; *Booke of Oathes*, p. 249; Anon., *The Book of Oaths* (1689), pp. 143–4.

were what James Morice called judicial oaths.⁴⁰ Among such may be classed oaths to be taken between party and party, oaths of jurymen, or women investigating pregnancies.⁴¹ As in all the previous cases they were administered by someone in authority, but unlike oaths of passage they involved only a continuity of *persona* and they were largely assertory in form.

With all of these oaths there were considerable burdens placed on those requiring them. Oaths might not be regarded as mutually binding contracts, but because all parties had some office, they entailed a heavy ethical reciprocity.⁴² To demand oaths trivially or improperly, to impose oaths requiring the impossible or self-condemnation, were all regarded as serious abuses of office, a direct affront to God and an injury to souls. 'Love no false Oath: for this is a thing that I hate, saith the Lord' (Zechariah 8: 17).⁴³ There was 'an office of dewtye belonging unto them under payne of goddes hei displeasure' to use the oath with probity.⁴⁴ This was liberty of office in miniature: the right of office to impose oaths was itself a duty to do so appropriately, and in unambiguous terms so that controversies might indeed be ended and the heinous sin of perjury avoided.⁴⁵ It was 'impious' and 'execrable' to impose oaths inconsistent with extant obligations. A principle of non-contradiction was thus a vital criterion in deciding whether an oath was licit.⁴⁶ It is in the context of such responsibilities that strong objections were made to the *ex officio* oath of ecclesiastical courts, demanding a commitment to answer 'all such Interrogatories as shall be offered unto you and declare your knowledge therein'.⁴⁷ For Sir Edward Coke it was a Satanic device for condemning souls to hell, for others, a necessity for ascertaining loyalty. Nothing good, Coverdale had remarked, might not be turned to evil ends;⁴⁸ and if there were dangers of misuse in all the above kinds of oath, they were most important in a final broad set.

---

⁴⁰ James Morice (?), *A Brief Treatise of Oathes* (1590), pp. 4–5.
⁴¹ *Booke of Oathes*, p. 206; *Book of Oaths*, p. 250.
⁴² Sanderson, *Reasons of the Present Judgment* (1647), pp. 379–80; Anon., *Magna veritas, or John Gadbury not a papist* (1680), p. 5.
⁴³ Coverdale, *A Christe exhortacion*, fols. 9–10; Sanderson, *De juramento*, 7.13, p. 267; Morice, *Brief Treatise*, p. 6; Charles I, *Eikon Basilike*, p. 111.
⁴⁴ Coverdale, *A Christe exhortacion*, fol. 8.
⁴⁵ Sanderson, *Reasons of the Present Judgment*, pp. 419–20; Tooke, *The Whole Duty of Man*, ch. 11, 9, p. 127; Bohun, *The Justice*, pp. 167–70.
⁴⁶ Prynne, *Concordia discors*, p. 17; Kennett, *Dialogue*, p. 38; Palmer, *Englishman's Allegiance*, p. 207b and numerous other writings on oaths.
⁴⁷ Cited in Jones, *Conscience and Allegiance*, p. 57; see also Morice, *Brief Treatise*, pp. 5, 7–8.
⁴⁸ Jones, *Conscience and Allegiance*, p. 57; Coverdale, *A Christe exhortacion*, fols. 7–8.

These might be called oaths of circumstance, and with them there is neither an obvious change of *persona*, nor a simple adumbration of established responsibilities. The oath is called upon precisely because waters were sufficiently rough and uncharted to require a public reaffirmation, or confession of current obligations.[49] The previous authority may have changed, and so the extraction of an oath was a proclamation of the continuity of office. It is at this point that we can more confidently begin to locate most of what have been isolated as state oaths, for these are clearly tests of continuing loyalty for crucial office-holders.

Clear examples are *The Oath to the Succession* (1534); *The Bishop's Oath* required by Henry VIII when he assumed the effective office of pope in England and, more broadly, *The Oath of Supremacy* (1536). Occasionally there is no change of authoritative office, but circumstances have made it sufficiently insecure to require holy reiterations of allegiance. James VI&I's *Oath of Allegiance* (1606) is the clearest example (below, chapter 13). There was, however, precedent for this during the Wars of the Roses in the oath required of Richard Duke of York and his followers by Henry VI. Given Charles II's status in 1660 as both a hereditary monarch and a new prince, and the fact that the Church of England was newly re-established after 1662, the Restoration oaths demanding loyalty to church and king, are partially in this broad tradition of circumstantial oaths.

Some of these oaths designed to sort sheep from goats (not to be confused with the oath for sheep numbering)[50] were phrased with a fine mesh of words, to sieve and exclude the dangerous or unwanted. The oaths required by the Act of Uniformity to re-establish a Church of England were, according to Burnet, aimed at pushing out 'the old men who had taken the covenant'.[51] But some did more than this. For irrespective of the Covenant, the status of oaths of passage into the priesthood lay at the heart of the re-ordination controversies of 1662. At one Lutheran and proclamatory extreme, the oaths could not significantly transform a priest, for the church as a whole was a priesthood of believers. At another, the oaths and ceremonies of ordination were mystic transfigurations. John Humfrey, ordained by a presbyter during the Commonwealth for want of any bishop, was confronted with a demand to go through the process again at the restoration of episcopacy. Initially he was prepared to do so as a matter of theological indifference (*adiaphora*), but was persuaded that this would entail swallowing more than he

---

[49] John Donne, *Pseudo-Martyr*, ch. 12, p. 349.
[50] *Booke of Oathes*, pp. 344-5.
[51] Burnet, *History*, vol. I, p. 313.

could chew, for the oath implied a whole theory of episcopacy as *jure divino* and a fundamental inequality among priests.[52] The result of the re-Establishment with its oaths like the eyes of needles, was a high degree of ecclesiological purity and a running sore for the whole Restoration. Many clerics found the new oaths for old unacceptable and lost their livings after what Presbyterians saw as a new St Bartholemew's Day Massacre.[53]

Other oaths of circumstance, however, most clearly the new oath of allegiance sworn to William and Mary after 1689, were altogether more latitudinarian, being phrased, as we will see, to minimise sticking points. The problem with accommodating formulations, however, was that they entered the penumbra of uncertainty clouding the promissory. Just what was being sworn to and how it might be manipulated could thus be an inhibition to swearing, as was the case for the proposed Test in Scotland of 1682. The qualification that obedience to authority was absolute all the time it remained within the bounds of office, could be insufficiently reassuring, and the Earl of Argyll ended up in prison because the promissory dimension concerning obedience to the status quo seemed to undo the authority of the legislature.[54]

An important sub-group of circumstantial oaths deserves a label of its own; these are what might be called Horatian or associative oaths, taken in emergency in order to protect, or establish proper authority, despite the formal lack of imprimatur on the occasion of swearing. These, which may also be seen as state oaths, have some of the formal features of a Hobbesian contract or agreement among equals to create a sovereign. With associative oaths, there is no literal state of nature, but there is the Hobbesian spur of dramatic insecurity, and it is uncertain whether, in swearing, the oath-takers assume new *personae*, so making associative oaths a sub-set of oaths of passage, or whether they are simply oaths of explication, most commonly adumbration of the soul's piety and the patriot's loyalty. Their status is ambivalent, and they were recognised potentially to be as subversive as they might be supportive.

The Elizabethan Association (1584) set a wayward precedent for the following century. It was a 'vow and promise' before God to form 'one firm and loyal society', a signal mark of allegiance and devotion to a beleaguered queen who, flattered, honoured and, nay, overwhelmed

---

[52] R. A., *A Letter to a Friend* (1661); John Humfrey, *A Second Discourse* (1662).
[53] Burnet, *History*, vol. I, pp. 313, 318; see also Spurr, 'Perjury', pp. 35–6; Anon., *A Letter from a Person of Quality*, p. 2.
[54] Burnet, *History*, vol. II, pp. 300–8, 309–10.

by the love and courage of her subjects, claimed to have known nothing of it.[55]

True or not, this joyous surprise furnished added force for Catholic and exterior consumption. A free expression of loyalty and an oath of determination to revenge Elizabeth's murder was an unlikely response to tyranny and would be a decided barrier in trying to overthrow her. At the same time, Elizabeth's formal innocence of the Association left no room to suggest that she was any more bound by it than, say, would be an Hobbesian sovereign to an original contract. Not far removed from the Association was the oath of association, which *The Booke of Oathes* claims was taken by the Gunpowder conspirators: to bond together in the face of tyranny, heresy and intolerable persecution and act in the name of the true religion, to re-establish it and to remain bound to each other until released from the terms of the oath.[56] During the Civil Wars, there were probably many oaths of association taken, especially by county 'Clubmen' banding together against the forces of either official army. Some saw the *Solemn League and Covenant* as a league, or conspiratorial association. And, from the Civil Wars, associations are increasingly subject to suspicion.[57] In 1662 the Catholic Earl of Bristol gathered allies at his home to organise another such oath, possibly emboldened by his knowledge that Charles II was already a co-religionist; but this time, it was an oath taken to galvanise concerted Catholic support for a general toleration to which the monarch was sympathetic but his parliament hostile.[58]

The close structural symmetry between conspiratorial and acceptable acts of bonding can be seen by the proposed Association of 1681. Touched on in a different context (above, chapter 7), this was to be sworn to stymie the Catholic Duke of York succeeding to the throne, so overthrowing the English Reformation Elizabeth had properly established. Despite being punctiliously modelled on the Association of 1584, its force was very different from the original. An associative vow, promise or protestation '(or whatever else you please)' had become perceived as conspiratorial.

---

[55] Elizabeth I, *Collected Works*, text of the Bond of Association, pp. 183–5; see Alford, *The Early Elizabethan Polity*, pp. 196–8; 'The Queen's Speech to the Committee of Both Houses', 12 November 1586, in Elizabeth I, *Collected Works*, pp. 184; 189–90.

[56] *Book of Oaths*, p. 206; see also J. Williams, *The History of the Gunpowder Treason* (1678), p. 5.

[57] Anon., *Plain English, Or a Discourse Concerning the Accommodation, the Armie, The Association* (1643), proposing an association for peace, pp. 27–8; and the anonymous reply, *An Answer to a Seditious Pamphlett intituled Plain English* (1643); see also Anon., *Certain Observations upon the New League or Covenant* (Bristol, 1643), p. 10; Anon., *Certaine Observations upon the two Contrary Covenants* (Oxford, 1643), pp. 5–6. The word 'league' had prejudicial connotations from the Catholic League of sixteenth-century France.

[58] Burnet, *History*, vol. I, p. 333.

Those hostile to the Association had aggravated its enormity by calling it an oath, and to swear to it, as the author of the *Remarques* had it, was 'downright Rebellion'.[59] In this we have a microcosm of the disputed rhetorics of the office of the patriot and rebel.

The associative oath comes full circle in 1696, rehabilitated by the attempted assassination of William III. Members of both Houses of Parliament formed a protective association for the king much in the idiom of that originally sworn to Elizabeth.[60] In its reach far greater than the Association of 1584, it also attested to the erratic vertical extension of office. The danger inherent in associative oaths was that, in the absence of an uncontentious authority, being initiated by one whose official status was debatable, or only casuistically justified, they could either support or challenge established powers. That they all involved affirming allegiance to some higher authority was neither here nor there; that was merely to project the demeanour appropriate to any *persona* in office.

III

Additional to the potential disruption of associative oaths was the feared trivialisation of all oath-taking once it escaped the control of responsible authority. This amounted to a veritable tradition of lamentation. 'We have nothing in our pastime but Gods blood', hectored Hugh Latimer before young King Edward VI. Around one hundred and fifty years later John Sharp concurred. Swearing is 'the crying sin of the nation'.[61] Situated between the two, Samuel Butler wrote that the swearer 'stakes his Soul to nothing' and becomes 'the Devil's Votary'. Some saw what Sanderson called 'comminatory oaths' as an affectation of the nobility, or of the wayward soldier 'Full of strange oaths and bearded like the pard'.[62] Others saw it as ubiquitous, with the lower sort addicted to swearing in the

---

[59] Anon., *Remarques Upon the New Project of Association* (1682), p. 5; see also Anon., *The Two Associations*; Anon., *The Parallel*; cf. *The Addresses Imputing an Abhorrence of an Association Pretended to have been seized in the Earl of Shaftsbury's Closet* (1682), insisting that associations of loyalty were no less important than they had been in Elizabeth's day, pp. 3–4.

[60] Burnet, *History*, vol. III, p. 319; vol. IV, pp. 298–9, 432–3; William Atwood, *Reflections Upon a Treasonable Opinion . . . Against Signing the National Association* (1696), regarded it as implicit in the oath of allegiance, p. 6; M. Percivall (?), *The Tragedy Called the Popish Plot Reviv'd* (1696).

[61] Latimer, *Fruitful Sermons*, fol. 97v; Sharp, 'All Oaths not Unlawful and Against Perjury', in *Works*, vol. IV, p. 285; de Bohun, *The Justice*, feared a 'National Judgement' for the widespread sin of perjury, p. 162; John Taylor, *Christian Admonitions* (1630), col. 2.

[62] Samuel Butler, 'Swearer', in *Characters*, pp. 202–3; Boyle, *Free Discourse*; Sanderson, *De juramento*, 1.9, p. 19; Coverdale, *An Christe exhortacion*, fol. 23; Cavendish, 'Of Affectation, Horae subsecivae', p. 21; Shakespeare, *As You Like It* 2.7.

processes of trade.⁶³ Fears for the trivialisation of swearing had, predictably, an uncertain range. Because all vows and oaths created an obligation, they were particularly dangerous when rash, driving the swearer to irresponsible action. 'No, not an oath', cried the anguished Brutus to his fellow conspirators.⁶⁴ The rash vow is a manifest theme of both *Love's Labour's Lost* and *The Merchant of Venice*, in both of which the burdens of the oath are in tension with the ease with which people swear. It is the crux of *Hamlet*, who is forced to swear revenge by the ghost. Much depends on whether it is indeed the ghost of Hamlet's kingly father, or of some demon, which would indeed make Hamlet 'the Devil's votary'.⁶⁵ King Herod was condemned as a tyrant not just because he had the head of John the Baptist on a plate, but because he did so to keep an irresponsible oath to a young woman.⁶⁶ But trivialisation could move a long way from the wildness of the comminatory. It also embraced the more formal affront to the Third Commandment – 'emphatic oaths', as Aubrey describes Hobbes's predilection; these were expletives for emphasis, or punctuation that wasted into the phatic dimension of language. Here too there could be discriminations. An expletive reference to God was blasphemy and there could be a greater tolerance of some *personae* blaspheming than others.⁶⁷ Obscenity, however, while improper, was generally less disturbing. Both the comminatory and the expletive were strongly associated with that other national sin of drunkenness which acts of parliament in the reigns of James and Charles I sought to control, extending the constable's tricky office, apparently to little effect.⁶⁸ We can hardly ask a question, said John Sharp, without swearing or cursing. As 'Daredevil' explains in *The Atheist*, 'Rot me, Sir, Confound me, Sir means no more than So, Sir; And, Sir, or Then Sir, at the worst'.⁶⁹ Plausible and bland as

---

⁶³ Sermon, 'Of Swearing', in *Certain Sermons*, p. 43; Sharp, 'Arguments against Common Swearing', in *Works*, vol. IV, p. 288; Walter Powell, *A Summons for Swearers, and a Law for the Lips* (1645), pp. 28, 46–7, on whom see Muldrew, *The Economy of Obligation*, pp. 310–11.
⁶⁴ Sanderson, 'The Case of the Rash Vow', in *Works*, vol. V, pp. 60–4; Shakespeare, *Julius Caesar* 2. 1.
⁶⁵ For discussion of the central mechanism of the oath in Shakespeare's plays see, especially on the tragedies, Frances Shirley, *Swearing and Perjury in Shakespeare's Plays* (London, 1979); Elena Glazov-Corrigan, 'The New Function of Language in Shakespeare's *Pericles*: Oath Versus "Holy Word"', in Stanley Wells, ed., *Shakespeare Survey*, vol. XLIII (Cambridge, 1991), pp. 131–40, on the declining effectiveness of the oath within the plot structure of later plays.
⁶⁶ Buchanan, *Baptistes, Tyrannical Government*.
⁶⁷ Shakespeare, *Measure for Measure* 2.2. 'That in the captain's but a choleric word/ Which in the soldier is flat blasphemy.'
⁶⁸ Malcolm, *Anecdotes*, vol. I, pp. 232–7.
⁶⁹ Sharp, 'Arguments against Common Swearing', p. 288; Thomas Otway, *Works*, ed. J. C. Ghosh (Oxford, 1932), vol. II, p. 327, cited in Spurr, 'Perjury', p. 46.

this now seems, it was more likely to be taken, as Otway's play indicated, to be a sign of atheism. It was a trivialisation that eroded the status of the oath in language, at once sinful and foolish.[70]

Here the significance of the slippery distinctions between public and private again come into play. A private oath could be illicit, secret or conspiratorial, but it might also be a licit diurnal oath. A public oath was one taken for the public good.[71] So, as I have cited above, this understanding of public allows a marriage vow to be referred to in a sermon as between 'private persons', that is those not holding a commonwealth office, or perhaps irrespective of office.[72] It may be that the importance of private, that is, diurnal oaths diminished gradually during the seventeenth century, particularly as formal contracts became more common. Yet one mark of the continuing importance of diurnal oath-taking is to be found in the statistics of Bible production. There were more than enough Bibles for every household in England by mid-century, and as literacy remained patchy, it is a reasonable hypothesis that their pervasive use was as objects on which to swear oaths. Bibles were artefacts of social cohesion.

Overall, one may say that oaths were expressions and instruments of uncertain trust, designed to maintain the fragile world of offices, modulating the movements of its changing *personae*. Concomitantly, the tensions between offices were articulated through extensive discussion of oaths. Edmund Hickeringill was taken to court in 1681 for abuse of his clerical office because he had argued that the oaths required of the clergy contradicted those of secular allegiance, and that the oath required of churchwardens put them in an impossible position between clergy and laity. He admitted to adjusting the oath to make the office easier. This led to the question of whether the specific office of the priest was itself valid.[73] A more famous case is found in the Anonymous *Letter from a Person of Quality*, usually attributed to the Earl of Shaftesbury, possibly in association with John Locke, an inflammatory account of debates in the House of Lords. It has attracted attention largely as a

---

[70] Comber, *Judicial Swearing*, pp. 27–8; Sharp, 'Arguments Against Common Swearing', pp. 297, 517.
[71] Coverdale, *An Christe exhortacion*, fol. 11; Morice, *Brief Treatise*, pp. 4, 5, 7.
[72] 'Of Swearing', in *Certain Sermons*, p. 41.
[73] Edmund Hickeringill, *The Naked Truth, The Second Part* (1681), pp. 5–10, 45–6; also Edmund Hickeringill, *The Horrid Sin of Man-Catching Explained in a Sermon* (1682), pp. 2–9, 11; Philip Hickeringill, *A Vindication of the Naked Truth, The Second Part* (1681), pp. 12–17; Anon., *The Late Famous Tryal of Mr Hickeringill* (1681); Anon., *Scandalum magnatum: or, The Great Tryal of Chelmsford Assizes* (1681).

precursor of the Exclusion crisis and because of its 'country' Whig and quasi-Harringtonian hostility to the tyranny that might arise from standing armies.[74] In fact, a largely overlooked and yet far more prominent theme is the discussion of oath-taking. Different parts of the attack on the court and episcopal moves to impose oaths are attributed to different noble lords fighting a courageous rearguard action. To use oaths out of fears for security was argued to be foolish and counter-productive; the promissory requiring swearing and assertory only requiring subscription should not be confused; promissory oaths should not, according to the Bible, be taken; an oath against any change to government was technically impossible (what of legislation?). These abuses of the oath, the noble lords agreed, threatened to change the monarchy from a bounded to an absolute one. Despite earlier misuse by evil men, it was essential to distinguish swearing allegiance to office and occupant.[75] They found similar difficulties in swearing never to change the church. It suggested a degree of perfection and infallibility to present arrangements; it confused the necessary with the indifferent and could place the mitre above the crown.[76] Additionally, qualifying or counter-oaths were proposed to thwart the court: an oath enshrining freedom of parliamentary speech and one requiring that voting be according to conscience after free debate.[77] With this document we are on the edge of a precipitous slide into distrust that barely stopped short of civil war; it is a narrative of a clash of offices and conceptions of office fought by debating oaths. But the issues of office in conflict and uncertain trust were hardly unique to this particular concentration of suspicion.

IV

From the Reformation, trust was severely compromised by the perceived need to impose uniformities of religious practice in the face of feared insincerity of those forced to comply. Along with the conventional Aristotelian belief that habit helps create virtue, lay the recognition that people might conform disingenuously before the right habits were in place. Nicodemism, as such insincerity was called, encouraged authorities

---

[74] See, for example, Pocock, *The Machiavellian Moment*, pp. 405, 415; Scott, *England's Troubles*, pp. 356–7, 374–5.
[75] Anon., *A Letter from a Person of Quality*, pp. 10, 14–15, 26, 16, 17–18; but, as I have evidenced above, n. 10, subscription was not so tightly tied to the assertory.
[76] *Ibid.*, pp. 20–1; the implicitly papal and innovatory implication of this is stressed by Scott, *England's Troubles*, pp. 374–5.
[77] Anon., *A Letter from a Person of Quality*, pp. 26–9.

to tread carefully.[78] To impose oaths too readily might generate dishonesty and contribute to the subversion of the holy institution itself;[79] not to impose them at all was to neglect a necessary instrument of rule.

Until the end of the sixteenth century, two forms of insincere swearing were feared; outright perjury and swearing in ways that loosened the oath by exploiting ambiguities in language. These arose in oath texts largely through generality and imprecise formulation. Perjury was not a statute offence until 1563, but its meaning was often wider than it is now. According to John Selden, it ought to apply only to assertory oaths.[80] Nevertheless, after an oath of passage any failure in office could be construed as perjury. It was a further variation on argument from implication and created pressure on those who swore to find ways of accommodating compliance to their situations. During the Restoration Slingsby Bethel was given extensive advice on how to take the oaths necessary for public office, and the result was an interpretation that was apt to negate the ends of the oaths themselves.[81] White Kennett in brilliantly casuistic form would argue that even the most exacting Carolinian oath of allegiance could embrace disobedience if the ends of oaths and offices were considered. 'Oaths are straws and men's faiths are wafer-cakes.'[82]

From the end of the sixteenth century, however, equivocation was added to fears of perjury and hermeneutic dexterity. This was the practice of reserving a qualification or contradiction to an explicit statement (see below, chapter 13). 'Call not Jove to witness', later wrote the finger-wagging Browne, 'with a stone in one hand, and a straw in another; and so make chaff and stubble of thy vows.'[83] For the English Jesuits who developed it, the theory of equivocation provided an alternative to lying; for most others, it was lying. Notwithstanding the seriousness of the accusation, equivocation was no more straightforward than lying. Blurred by ambiguity, it was an anathema publicly abused and piously practised.[84]

---

[78] Perez Zagorin, *Ways of Lying: Dissimulation, Persecution and Conformity in Early Modern Europe* (Cambridge, Mass., 1990), pp. 10ff; Malcolm, *Anecdotes*, vol. I, pp. 171–2 according to whom the Reformation created an age of such perjury.

[79] Boyle, *Free Discourse*, pp. 1–32; Hutchinson, *Memoirs*, p. 313 on Sir Arthur Hasilrigg and the impositions of oaths in Interregnum parliaments.

[80] Spurr, 'Perjury', pp. 30–1; John Selden, *Table Talk*, para. 94, p. 71.

[81] Spurr, 'Perjury', p. 38; see also Sharp, 'All Oaths not Unlawful', p. 285; Clarendon, 'Promises' (1670), in *Essays*, vol. I, pp. 137–8.

[82] Kennett, *Dialogue*, pp. 30–5; Shakespeare, *Henry V* 3.2.

[83] Browne, *Christian Morals*, p. 337; White, *Of Oathes*, p. 3

[84] Edward Vallance, 'Oaths, Casuistry and Equivocation; Anglican Responses to the Engagement Controversy', *Historical Journal*, 44, 1 (2001), pp. 70–7; Spurr, 'Perjury', p. 31.

Richard Baxter and Jeremy Taylor were among the few brave non-Jesuits to speak in its favour.[85] To complicate matters, oath-imposers might be suspected of it no less than oath-takers. Intentions were not always transparent; the ends of an oath might be opaque, giving licence for them to be variously understood, a point crucial to such documents as the Engagement and the oath of allegiance to William and Mary (see chapters 13, 14).[86]

The imagined erosion of the sanctity of oaths resulted in greatly adumbrated detail in the content of the oath and the use of an elaborate vocabulary to the oath-taking act itself. This may evidence a declining faith in the efficacy of oath-taking, but given the diversity of oath-taking, generalisations are dangerous.[87] Nevertheless, oath texts do confront the possibility of evasive reaction. Many were not content with one descriptor for what was demanded. *The Sacred Vow and Covenant* 1643, formulated in response to a plot to undermine London's defences, required a vow and covenant before God, which was also called an oath. The members returned for the parliament of 1654 had to 'freely promise and engage', and after the Restoration 'declare' could substitute for, or be added to 'swear'.[88] The new oath of allegiance to William and Mary insisted on 'promise and swear'. The Abjuration Oath (1702) can almost be watched in the act of trying to cover every imaginable base, yet despite being 'penned as fully as words can go', it failed to allay all fears of mendacity.[89]

I, A. B. do truly and sincerely acknowledge, profess, testify, and declare in my conscience, before God . . . And all these things I do plainly and sincerely acknowledge, and according to the plain and common sense . . . understanding of these same Words, without any Equivocation, mental Evasion, or secret Reservation whatsoever; and I do make this Recognition, Acknowledgement, Abjuration . . . willingly, and truly, upon the true Faith of a Christian.[90]

Fear of equivocation was caught on the horns of a linguistic dilemma. The opportunities for it might seem curtailed if the language of an oath were kept plain and simple.[91] But as plain English lawyers have later found out, plain English is often imprecise English, through which horses

---

[85] Baxter, *Christian Directory*, ch. 9; Taylor, *Ductor dubitantium*, pp. 98, 99, 100.
[86] Charles I, *Eikon Basilike*, p. 114.
[87] Conrad Russell has rather boldly referred to a total faith in oath-taking during the sixteenth century, in *The Crisis of Parliaments* (Oxford, 1988 edn), p. 52; cf. Ponet, *Shorte Treatise*, who mentions oaths, pp. 138, 139, 143 only to doubt them.
[88] See Jones, *Conscience and Allegiance*, pp. 279, 280.
[89] Burnet, *History*, vol. VI, p. 210.
[90] Jones, *Conscience and Allegiance*, p. 281.
[91] Sanderson, *Reasons of the University of Oxford*, pp. 419–22.

and laden carts of meaning can be driven. So anticipated equivocation was also apt to generate the wordiness found in the Abjuration Oath, though it must be stressed that where a relevant office afforded much latitude of action, an initial oath of passage was also likely to be detailed.[92] Qualification aside, the many oaths cast across the social landscape of seventeenth-century England were signs of the insecurity that lengthy formulations might assuage. *The Lawes and Ordinances of Warre* (1639) contains the following sacred prolixity, as fearful as it is anticipatory of the impending terms of dispute between king and parliament.

I, A. B. do sweare before the Almighty and everlasting God, that I will beare all faithful Allegeance to my true and undoubted Sovereigne Lord King Charles, who is lawfull King of this land, and all other his Kingdomes and Dominions, both by Land and Sea, by the Lawes of God and Man, and by lawfull sucession: and that I will most constantly and cheerfully, even to the utmost of my power, and hazard of my life; constantly oppose all Seditions, Rebellions, Conspiracies, Covenants, Conjurations, and Treasons whatsoever, raised up or set up against his Royal Dignity, Crowne, or Person, under what pretence or colour whatsoever: and if it shall come veiled under pretence of Religion, I hold it more abominable before God and Man. And this Oath I take voluntarily in the true faith of a good Christian and loyall Subject; without any equivocation or mentall reservation whatsoever; for which I hold no power upon earth can absolve me, in my part.[93]

By the early eighteenth century, the habit of lengthy oath-making was used commonly to convey not just the ethics of the relevant office but also something approaching codes of conduct. The Goldsmith's oath of passage made initiates into the liberty of the guild swear to be true to the monarch, work metals honestly without use of glasses and counterfeit stones, keep all good ordinances, pay all fees, and inform the wardens of any deceit. In this is an admixture of general virtues and the specific requirements for conduct within a trade.

The acute awareness of the functions, dangers and limitations of swearing meant that there were always likely to be two dimensions to controversies over office-holding. There were those dealing with the rights and wrongs of the offices brought together by the institution of the oath; there were also disputes about the status of the oath itself, behind which lurked varying understandings of language and the semiotics of social performance.[94] For the majority, oaths should be sworn, or imposed at peril

---

[92] The oaths for a counsellor and a midwife are the longest in *The Book of Oaths*.
[93] Anon., *Lawes & Ordinances* (1639), pp. 25–6.
[94] These were hardly issues unique to the seventeenth century, however; Lorenzo Valla traverses them arguing that oaths, vows and promises are largely redundant in order to deny the standing of the contemplative life; the vow adds nothing to accepting God's

because they were taken as so decisive in structuring legal conduct and religious faith.[95] For a few, such as the anonymous Leveller writer in *No Papist nor Presbyterian*, 'compulsory Oaths' should be dispensed with. According to Sanderson, both Anabaptists and Socinians refused oaths.[96] Sir Robert Boyle was particularly reluctant to swear. For reasons that remain obscure, in 1680 he refused the promissory oath required of the president of the Royal Society although he had taken a similar one that inducted him onto the Society's council in 1673. It is possible that the arduous nature of the position, or the heightened controversies concerning oaths from 1675, deterred him. Either way, he never assumed the presidency.[97]

It was the Quakers, however, who would attract most sustained attention. Standing defiantly on the Sermon on the Mount against the Old Testament, these 'obstinate adversaries' rejected all oaths:[98] 'Again, ye have heard that it hath been said by them of old time, Thou shalt not foreswear thyself, but shalt perform unto the Lord thine oaths. But I say unto you, Swear not at all: neither by heaven: for it is God's throne; Nor by the earth; for it is his footstool' (Matthew 5:33–4). 'But let your communication be, Yea, yea: Nay, nay' (Matthew 5:37). There had been no need of oaths among the early Christians, and so it should be now, wrote Samuel Fisher. Drawing a firm distinction between an oath and a promise, he claimed that which the Quakers promised was proved in performance, while others swore '*themselves* To *and* Fro *into the* Favour *of every* Form *of* Government *as it* Stands *its time upon the* Stage'.[99] The Quakers were effectively gathered up with the Jesuits, to form a new proof of a puritan-Jesuit conspiracy and there was some plausibility as well as polemical convenience in this. Thomas Comber, for example, associated

---

authority; the word religion was abused in being co-opted by fear-driven disputatious philosophical sects. Despite its similarities to a number of Hobbesian positions, it was not, however, an argument known in post-Reformation England. See Lorenzo Valla, *De professione religiosorum* (*c.* 1442), in *Opera omnia*, 2 vols. (Turin, 1962), vol. II, pp. 135–41.

[95] Sanderson, *De juramento*; Jeremy Lawson, *Lawson of Oaths and Witnesses* (1681); Comber, *Judicial Swearing*; Tooke, *The Whole Duty of Man*; White, *Of Oathes*, pp. 1–3.

[96] Anon., *No Papist nor Presbyterian* (1649), in *The Leveller Manifestoes*, p. 308; Sanderson, *De juramento*, 7.10, pp. 251–2.

[97] Boyle, *A Free Discourse*, pp. 1–32; 'The Dayly Reflection', *c.* 1646, p. 220; Hunter, *Robert Boyle*, pp. 64–8. As the presidential oath specified employment, he may have baulked at swearing on grounds similar to those that may have informed his requirement that his servants only promised and engaged to him, namely that to insist on an oath was trivialising and dangerous. But, then again, it was an oath that stipulated promising, not swearing.

[98] Comber, *Judicial Swearing*, p. 8.

[99] Samuel Fisher, *Rusticus ad Academicus or . . . or The Rustick's Alarm to the Rabbies* (1660), fol. b2v.

Quaker austerity with popish enthusiasm and indeed Robert Parsons, like Fisher, had argued that a simple yea or nay had been good enough for the early Christians. It was only the corruption of the age that required oaths before anything could be believed.[100] The world, Justice Twisden remarked to a jury, seemed divided between those who would swear to nothing and those who would swear to anything.[101]

Once sworn, any oath's sacred nature could be used as a barrier against demands from authority. Conversely, the asserted power to impose or to release from an oath could be a litmus test for the scope of office. In 1686, James II attempted to get the University of Cambridge to offer honorary degrees to Catholics on the precedent of one having been conferred on the King of Morocco's ambassador. But the Fellows refused, arguing that such an honour was a violation of their oaths. James countered that as king he could release them from such oaths.[102] Clearly recognising that the oath could irritate the rubbing sores of office, some attempted to dissipate its importance. Oaths were useful, it was held, but only as ceremonial signs of agreement and markers for anticipated conduct.[103] In this way, oaths of passage were reduced to a proclamatory dimension. There were those who could take oaths in good conscience as long as they could arbitrate the sense of the words for themselves. To ask in whose sense an oath should be taken, Selden remarked, is like asking on whose legs one can walk.[104] Conversely, there were those adamantine in their insistence upon the authority of authorial intention in crafting the words.[105] There were others who stressed the overall point of the oath, even despite the specificities of wording, hypothesised intentions and motives of the imposers.[106] And there remained that feared and indeterminate number thought to be unbound to any oath or agreement,

---

[100] Comber, *Judicial Swearing*, p. 13; Parsons, *Treatise*, ch. 7, p. 275; see also Boyle, *A Free Discourse*; William Prynne, *Quakers Unmasked* (1664), calls them the spawn of Jesuitical frogs, sub-title; *Certain Observations upon the New League or Covenant*, refers to dispensing with oaths as Jesuitical, p. 29.
[101] Cited in Spurr, 'Perjury', p. 33.
[102] Burnet, *History*, vol. III, pp. 139–43.
[103] Bell, *Regiment of the Church*, p. 4; Robert Filmer, *Patriarcha* (1680), ed. Peter Laslett (Cambridge, 1949), pp. 21–2; Anon., *A Letter of Spiritual Advice* (1642), on breach of promise and prior power, p. 7; Hobbes, *Leviathan*, ch. 14, p. 100; Tooke, *The Whole Duty of Man*, ch. 11, 10, p. 127.
[104] Selden, *Table Talk*, para. 94, p. 71; Sanderson, *Reasons*, pp. 419–20; Anon., *Conscience Puzzel'd* (1650), in Malcolm, ed., *The Struggle for Sovereignty*, vol. I, pp. 438–43.
[105] Taylor, *Ductor dubitantium*, p. 358; Sidney, *Discourses*, 3.17, pp. 408–17; Anon., *The Sheriffs Case* (1680), p. 1.
[106] Sanderson, *De juramento*, pp. 54–5; Tooke, *The Whole Duty of Man*, p. 127; Kennett, *Dialogue*, at length.

who by destabilising known meanings through the doctrine of equivocation, would make chaff of all social bonds.

Just as oath-taking was central to contested office, so it is tantalisingly suggestive of contemporary controversies over the interpretation of texts and the social functions of language. Adherence to a sort of reader response, or textual autonomy theory of the oath, was offset not only by a clear insistence on the authority of authorial intention, but also by the attribution of a sort of post-modernist deconstructive mischief in the Jesuitical doctrine of equivocation. Concern over equivocation was like a fear of *différance*, at once an alarming feature of language, an opportunity for a policy of deception and deferral of responsibility for what is said and what the oath text demanded. Something of this indeterminacy is expressed metaphorically by the Porter in Macbeth, 'much drink may be said to be an equivocator with lechery: it makes him, and it mars him; it sets him on, and it takes him off; it persuades him and it disheartens him; makes him stand to, and not stand to; in conclusion, equivocates him in a sleep, and giving him the lie, leaves him.'[107] This was the sleep that Macbeth had murdered in his quest to be crowned a king.

---

[107] Shakespeare, *Macbeth* 2.3.

12 Coronation oaths

> O, let thy vow
> First made to heaven, first to heaven be performed. . .
> (Shakespeare, *King John* 3.1)

I

The five coronation oaths sworn during the seventeenth century were part of a remarkable semantic and ceremonial continuity dating from Anglo-Saxon times, when the hegemonic kings (*bretwaldas*) swore to uphold religion, peace and the *folcricht*, of those who gave fealty. For these duties the kings asserted their necessary prerogatives, *cynerytha*. William I's oath reassuringly echoed earlier ones, replacing *folcricht* with the custom of the English, *consuetudo Angliae*, but maintaining an expectation of reciprocal responsibilities.[1] How far this formal translation of office qualified the disruption of conquest would become contentious; yet coronation oaths seem to have departed little from each other in the principles they enunciated; in some fashion all new monarchs swore to act justly, and maintain law, custom, religion and the office itself.

This continuity was made possible only because of the skiagraphic, or amphibolous open-endedness of the language used. It is symptomatic of the slipperiness of oath-taking that, despite appearances, the meaning of coronation oaths was debatable whenever a monarch was in trouble. The contrast with France is striking. There too, the king swore an oath at his coronation but the hereditary principle was dramatically more secure and the meaning of the oath symptomatically more straightforward. Between the accession of Hugh Capet (987) and 1789, no king was deposed and none assumed the throne devoid of accepted right.[2] For the first 200 years of the Capetian dynasty, each was able to crown his successor in

---

[1] M. R. L. L. Kelly, 'King and Crown', Ph.D. thesis Macquarie University (1996), vol. I, pp. 55–61.
[2] J. H. Shennon, *Government and Society in France, 1461–1661* (London, 1969), p. 15.

a pre-coronation ceremony.³ In England only the sequence from Henry VIII to Charles I came close to emulating such seamless transitions. The meanings of the oaths so ritually taken were concomitantly less easy to contain.

II

Coronation oaths took place in the context of wider symbolic action, most crucially the anointing. The oath of passage that usually followed this completed and proclaimed the sacred transformation of a new *persona*. So much was generally accepted, but because the ceremonies themselves were ritualised annunciations, they were as multivalent as metaphors and could be fashioned into widely diverging patterns of meaning and imperative. The ceremony in which the oath was embedded was encrusted with religious import, held within a church and presided over by the clergy. Robert Parsons, deliberately undermining any hereditary principle, read the oath as an 'agreement a bargayne and contract' to uphold true religion which thus stood as a criterion for continued obedience. The chief end of government was upholding *cultus Dei*.⁴ He stood firmly on the laws of Edward the Confessor and the notion that he was no king who did not maintain religion. It was an exposed line of argument in a post-Reformation world. Again, formally there seemed to be an act of consent involved, a residue from Germanic understandings of kingship as elective.⁵ But whether this was just an alien trace, an instance of *différance*, or a narrative principle was another matter.

The oath and anointing ceremony as a whole could be taken as directly transformative: the process by which the new *persona* was mystically created. The Earl of Argyll went to his execution for treason in 1685 maintaining that he owed no allegiance to James II until the coronation oath had been sworn.⁶ Conversely, it could be considered as assertory, proclaiming what had come to pass. This had been Archbishop Cranmer's position at the coronation of Edward VI, and as anointing could be taken to signify the authority of the officiating priest, this specific implication of the whole event could be countered by adding that 'the oil, if added, is but a ceremony'.⁷ In this diminishing idiom the coronation would later be

---

³ Muir, *Ritual*, p. 249.
⁴ Robert Parsons, *A Conference About the Next Succession* (Antwerp, 1594/5), pp. 119, 207.
⁵ Bertie Wilkinson, *The Coronation in History* (London, 1951), p. 8; Kelly, 'King and Crown', vol. I, pp. 27–52.
⁶ Burnet, *History*, vol. III, p. 28.
⁷ Thomas Cranmer, cited in Richards, 'English Allegiance in a British Context', p. 108; see also James VI&I, *God and King* (1615), pp. 42–3; cf. Shakespeare's Richard II, whose own tears alone could remove the sacred oil.

called a solemn declaration of the monarch's 'antecedent vocation'.[8] If the oath were merely assertory, consent dwindled into acknowledgement, but if it was taken to be directly transformative, the people's proclaimed assent could become a ritualised re-enactment amounting to a culmination of considered choice. Thus what it meant to acclaim a monarch was itself subject to redescription depending on what the monarch was doing in swearing. Each description of so symbolic an event effectively redefined the nature of the polity.

An appeal to precedent did not necessarily clarify matters. Henry II and John, for example, had been abroad when their respective predecessors died, and in their absence rule was maintained by the Chief Justiciar.[9] Royal arrival and coronation in spritely order could give crowning the appearance of a rite of passage like that of the marriage ceremony, or of the priest who was transfigured through ordination. From the succession of Edward I (1272), however, the new reign was usually dated from the day following the death of the previous monarch and so the coronation and its oath could be taken as ratification and proclamation. There was, therefore, a case for seeing the oath either as expressive of a hereditary principle, or of contract, consent and election. As an oath of passage, it could be an annunciation or transfiguration.

In practice, the result was an aggregated appeal to potentially conflicting principles that might have differing prominence on different occasions. Richard II was deposed and Henry Bolingbroke assumed the throne claiming right of hereditary succession. This he buttressed with a ceremonial device by which, after due prayer, the parliament petitioned Henry to settle the succession; it was a performance suggestive of communal participation in the creation of a new line.[10] The coronial recognition of Richard III, whatever its role in 1483, referred to him as 'rightful and undoughted enheritor . . . to the corone . . . [and] elected chosen and required of all of the iij estates of this same lande to take upon him the saide crowne'.[11]

Because it was sworn within a frame of ritualised obeisance, the oath was also a little like a state oath, acting out the truisms of nominal definition – there can be no king without subjects. This could be applied in two ways. It could be held that the *persona* of the monarch was created

---

[8] Edward Gee, *A Plea for Non-Subscribers to the Engagement* (1650), p. 48.
[9] William Stubbs, ed., *Select Charters and Other Illustrations of English Constitutional History* (Oxford, 1957 edn), pp. 438–9.
[10] Kelly, 'King and Crown', vol. I, pp. 93–4.
[11] *Ibid.*, pp. 74, 104; Anne F. Sutton and P. W. Hammond, eds., *The Coronation of Richard III* (Gloucester, 1983), p. 213.

only with reciprocal affirmations of fealty or subjection; or, that the reciprocities were simply a symbolic acceptance of a fact of language. Moreover, as the language of the coronation oath was itself so formulaic, it could be sworn without entailing impossible restraints. This was a necessary feature of the oaths because the monarch had to judge what was appropriate and possible within the bounds of the office. The terms of each oath thus provided a rhetoric of justification for the exercise of office as much as a set of substantive obligations. This could be understood to mean that the oath itself added nothing to the requirements of an already familiar office. Promulgated by an Accession Council, it was sworn after the monarch had begun to rule. As a peacetime event, any coronation oath presupposed a social stability that might be invoked to qualify allegiance to the monarch.[12]

Nevertheless, however formulaic, coronation oaths were adjusted by the monarchs who were to swear them and at the Accession Council seemed to have accepted the responsibilities of rule. This at once indicated the exceptional status of the office and that the words were important in binding the office-holder.[13] If the oath added nothing substantial to the office, its content did not much matter. Given the divergence of symbolic possibilities, rather than debating now whether coronation oaths were binding contracts, whether they ceased to be so under the Tudors, or Stuarts, we might get further by seeing them as encapsulating the language of office, thereby necessarily offering opportunity for unleashing its vocabulary in both its defensive and accusatory registers. Endeavouring to keep the peace and exercising judgement were essential to the crown's endurance but provided avenues for dispute. The scope each oath offered the monarch through prerogative and judgement to maintain the protective office allowed critics to counter that enough had not been done, that judgement was wrong, that the prerogative had become arbitrary rule; they might conclude that, because of the oath, the office needed protecting from the office-holder. The prerogative was a Greek gift to all monarchs who embraced its necessity for the exercise of office.

Thus, for example, Edward III was asked to swear to keep and confirm laws and customs of the people, those granted to the clergy by Edward the Confessor, to keep peace and justice according to his power, and again according to his power have law, justice and discretion in mercy and truth in all judgements, to keep the rightful laws and customs of the

---

[12] See, for example, Hunton, *Treatise*, pp. 23–4; this theme will re-surface in the discussion of Ascham and Locke, chapters 14 and 15, respectively.
[13] Kelly, 'King and Crown', vol. I, pp. 227–81; Hunton, *Treatise*, pp. 24–5, 37.

kingdom as much as 'in you lieth'.[14] Henry VIII amended the coronation oath. He had sworn to do nothing prejudicial to the crown according to conscience and judgement, which was to swear to be judge in his own cause.[15] He swore to keep the laws that the nobles and people had chosen with *his* consent, to keep his power in those things required by honour and equity.[16] According to *The Booke of Oathes*, the promise to keep the laws that the people have chosen was changed for James VI&I to a promise to protect what they had. It was some reassurance that there would be no invasion of Scottish civil law. The situation with respect to Charles I is predictably rather confused and it will be discussed at greater length below. What is clear is that he swore to keep law and custom, to rule according to the laws of God and the Gospel and in agreement with previous prerogative and custom.

In 1655 a draft oath as part of a new constitution was prepared for Oliver Cromwell who, as an elected officer, was to swear in the presence of God to do the uttermost in his power to maintain the purity of the Protestant reformed religion, according to Holy Scripture and encourage its profession; to call parliaments, not to infringe on parliamentary privilege, and to the best of his understanding govern according to law, custom and the liberties of the people. He had also to seek their peace and welfare according to those laws and customs and to uphold and administer justice. The *Humble Petition and Advice* (1657), reasserting a potentially hereditary principle, offered a similar but simplified variation in its addendum.[17] Parliament ceased to be present in the oath the Protector swore. Verbally, the Commonwealth formulations provide the greatest departure from the norm with their religious specificity. In the first of these, reference to Cromwell as an elected officer would imply that the oath was not being seen as transformative, but the lineaments remain at one with what had been sworn before. Like all the rest, Cromwell would be asked to swear to do his best according to his understanding of his office; the word was not there, but the latitude of action remained a prerogative power.

Charles II reverted to his father's oath, itself a symbol of restoration. His brother James confirmed the laws and customs granted by his lawful

---

[14] Kelly, 'King and Crown', vol. II, p. 588, document quoted in full.

[15] *English Coronation Records*, ed. L. G. W. Legg (London, 1901), p. 249; a variation is printed in *The Booke of Oathes* (1649); the word 'conscience' is missing from this clause in the Legg version.

[16] *Booke of Oathes*, p. 3; Kelly, 'King and Crown', vol. II, p. 619; Kelly's invaluable sources are compiled and adapted from L. G. W Legg, *A History of the English Coronation*, trans. P. Schramm (Oxford, 1937).

[17] Gardiner, *Constitutional Documents*, pp. 428–9, 448–9, 42.

predecessors, a phrase that could be taken as erasing any residual relevance of the Commonwealth. He swore to uphold the clergy according to the laws granted by St Edward, the Gospel and true profession as agreeable to the prerogative; to keep peace according to his power; to keep law, justice and discretion in mercy, to maintain the laws and rightful customs of the commonalty, and to defend and uphold the laws of God.[18] It was all unarguably sedimented in tradition and leaving room for a less than Protestant reading of the laws of God. When erected on the precedent of the oaths of previous godly princes, and upon the reliquial incantation of St Edward the Confessor, this was an ominous sign of innovation for his Protestant subjects.

So William and Mary swore differently. Edward the Confessor's regalia retained a ceremonial presence, but his disputed laws disappeared.[19] The oath itself was the first coronation oath to be finalised by parliament, providing an echo of the Commonwealth and carrying a contractarian undercurrent.[20] It required the monarchs to rule according to the statutes, laws and customs, maintaining the spiritual and civil rights and properties of the people, to execute justice in mercy, to do their utmost to maintain the laws of God, the true profession of the Gospel and the Protestant reformed church established by laws and all such rights and privileges of the bishops and clergy. Despite reference to statutes, and to civil and spiritual rights and properties, no changes removed what had always been significant room for monarchical manoeuvre. Everyone, above all William, accepted that the *arcana imperii* could not be reduced to a set of specific instructions. Monarchs were crowned as rulers and discretion was a defining feature of rule.

The enduring language of the coronation oath joined people in affirmative generalities about office; they were rent asunder when meanings were cashed into the specific and when patterns of perceived implication diverged. One hallowed implication was that as the monarch swore to fulfil the office, the obedience of the people was to this rather than the person.[21] Another was that the monarch was bound to the limits of office, a restriction, as Fortescue put it, that helped make England a *dominium regale et politicum*.[22] Such common views of the significance of the oath, together with the insecurity of royal tenure, probably had much to do

---

[18] *The Book of Oaths*, pp. 260–1.
[19] Greenberg, *The Radical Face*, pp. 51, 279.
[20] Kelly, 'King and Crown,' vol. I, pp. 375–6.
[21] 'The Declaration of the Magnates' (1307), see Jones, *Conscience and Allegiance*, p. 20.
[22] Sir John Fortescue, *De laudibus legum Angliae*, ed. S. B. Chrimes (Cambridge, 1949), p. 79; for later endorsement, see, for example, Hunton, *Treatise*, p. 37.

with the alterations that, until the oath taken by William and Mary, apparently augmented royal power, at least by diminishing, as Jones suggests, reference to the people's consent. At the end of the seventeenth century also, swearing to keep the laws of God and true religion become exclusively Protestant. James II could not in good faith have sworn to the coronation oath of William and Mary, in which the reformed religion, its bishops and clergy loom large. Just as, indeed, he did not take the Scottish oath which required extirpation of all enemies of the Kirk. In William and Mary's oath no doubt was the hand of those who had helped bring William to England. It was a small unsung victory for the Commonwealth; after a fashion William and Mary were being inducted into the Protector's office.

III

There was a more specific problem with the coronation oath apparent from 1642 when the relationship between the king and parliament became so fraught. It was perhaps a red herring, as the crux of dispute seems to have arisen not from Charles's own oath but a medieval antecedent of the oaths associated with Edwards II and III.[23] This carried ominous precedent, as Edward II was deposed for breaking it. Parliament had it printed as Charles's oath and William Prynne made it central to debate about the king's conduct. The Edward oath-text was claimed to be the model for, or assimilated to what Charles should have sworn at his coronation (Prynne is evasive on the matter), and a crucial part of the oath was the monarch swearing *corroborare justas leges et consuetudines quas vulgus eligerit*.[24] Assuming, as people did, that what survives is the oath actually sworn by either Edward (although *The Booke of Oathes* only gives a French version), this was probably a clause insisted upon by his suspicious barony in 1307.[25] There was no problem with the monarch's assent to the just laws and customs. The difficulty in the 1640s lay with *vulgus* (people), stretched to mean parliament, and with whether the verb *eligere* (to choose) was in a past or future tense. If in a past tense, the oath sanctioned a status quo. If, as Prynne argued, *eligerit* should be translated as *shall be chosen*, the oath became a promise to

---

[23] See Weston and Greenberg, *Subjects and Sovereigns*, pp. 78ff, who seem not to have noticed that the oath discussed was never sworn by Charles.
[24] William Prynne, *The Soveraign Power of Parliaments* (1643), pp. 25–30; cf. Edward Hyde, Lord Clarendon, *History of the Great Rebellion*, ed. W. D. Macray, 6 vols. (Oxford, 1958 edn), vol. II, p. 123, bk. 5, paras. 225–6.
[25] Jones, *Conscience and Allegiance*, p. 19; *The Booke of Oathes*, p. 291.

comply with the legislative activity of parliament.[26] This was decidedly confrontational. Despite the glib enthusiasm for Lawson's extreme radicality on such matters, he developed a more accommodating argument possibly from Prynne's case.[27] Like Prynne he took *vulgus* to refer to parliament as a representative of the people, but he argued that *corroborare* meant to guard the just laws, for when there was no sitting parliament, there was still the executive monarch with the sword of justice. *Elegerit* is not picked out as troublesome, but on Lawson's reading of *corroborare* there is clearly no need to decide between past and future tenses, and monarchical power is not necessarily diminished as it had been for Prynne. Legislative power, Lawson insisted, is with the unity of king, lords and commons.[28]

As Matthew Hale later admitted, surveying the controversies and comparing French and Latin versions of the Edward oath-text, the perfect tense was grammatically correct.[29] It was also historically plausible, as coronation oaths had never been made in the context of parliamentary insistence on legislative power, either as a matter of shared sovereignty or conciliar responsibility. Notwithstanding, Archbishop Laud was accused by Prynne of changing the oath for Charles to subvert the role of parliament. He was said to have inserted the qualification to *corroborare*, and he later believed it would help cost him his life.[30] As Kelly patiently points out, and both versions of *The Book of Oaths* in fact recorded, Charles I swore in English to assent, or corroborate, insofar as was consistent with the prerogatives of the kings who preceded him. This was a qualification that may have had precedent beyond the Edward oath-text, and was a formally innocent abridgement of the requirements to protect the office itself.[31] Yet, in a context of debate in which sovereignty was becoming an issue, it could only generate suspicion. Was

---

[26] Prynne, *The Soveraigne Power*, p. 29; see also, more straightforwardly, Henry Ireton, 'Putney Debates', 1 November 1647, in A. S. P. Woodhouse, *Puritanism and Liberty* (London, 1938), p. 111.
[27] See, most recently, Greenberg, *The Radical Face*. Lawson was one of a 'radical quartet if ever there was one', p. 231, on the curious grounds that he cites John Sadler to confirm the validity of a combined hereditary and elective principle in monarchy: being elective 'in a certain line' was desirable, especially where the heirs are truly virtuous, *Politica*, ch. 8.11, pp. 100-1. You cannot get more radical than that.
[28] Lawson, *Politica*, pp. 109-10.
[29] Weston and Greenberg, *Subjects and Sovereigns*, p. 215; Kelly, 'King and Crown', vol. I, p. 362, who does make clear the dubious status of the Edward oath-text; Sir Matthew Hale, *The Prerogatives of the King* (c. 1645, London, 1976), p. 85.
[30] Jones, *Conscience and Allegiance*, p. 26.
[31] Kelly, 'King and Crown', vol. I, pp. 284-5; *Booke of Oathes*, p. 272; *Book of Oaths*, p. 154; Legg, *English Coronation Records*, pp. xxix, 251.

the alleged emphasis on prerogatives code for unlimited sway, the exercise of arbitrary power and the means of introducing a foreign absolutism?

Historically and grammatically strained it might be, but there was some plausibility to Prynne's putting *elegerit* in the future tense. It drew attention to the scope of the whole text, which was concerned less with the assertory than the promissory force of the oath and in a way that recognised the possibility of change. Henry Parker had already hit the nail on the head with the customary waft of his casuistic hammer: the tenses of *elegerit* did not matter; what counted was the end of the king's office to protect, and therein lay his dignity and the force of his oath.[32] Kelly maintains that the oath taken by Edward VI was the first we have that makes an explicit distinction between established and future law. As she interestingly argues, it also had a little-noticed precedent in a manuscript of the 'Device' for the coronation of Richard III. This was an aid for the service and may not have been sworn, but it did require the king to grant and promise to defend those laws that 'as to the worship of God shalbe chosyn by your people (in parlement)'. She also suggests that this was consistent with Richard's intention to involve parliament in policies of reform.[33]

By the seventeenth century, however, Richard III's name was not one to venerate, and Prynne's point, when he had side-lined the notorious tyrant, was to find a long-standing precedent for a greatly enhanced and creative role for the *vulgus*, alias parliament, whose own responsibility would be to choose just laws, to which the monarch assented.[34] 'I really do believe this was the agreement that the people of England made with their Kings', urged Ireton; it was 'most apparent by the oath itself, and by all the practice since'.[35] Parliamentary, or popular consent, then, was a matter of choosing; anything else was contrary to the letter and spirit of the oath. At once this argument made legislation decidedly important, and a sharing in rule a sacred obligation of monarchy. This could be seen as worryingly innovative. Making legislation central to rule raised the spectre of European civil law. Making it central to parliamentary activity threatened also to turn parliament into the sovereign, the king into the shadow of the Doge. As we have seen with respect to the office of counsel, Prynne had referred to parliament as the companion to the monarch, so moving between tactical evocations of counsel and sovereign

---

[32] Parker, *Observations* (1642), p. 3.
[33] Kelly, 'King and Crown', vol. I, pp. 275–6; 232–5; see also Sutton and Hammond, *The Coronation of Richard III*, p. 220.
[34] Prynne, *Soveraigne Power*, p. 29.
[35] Henry Ireton, 'Putney Debates', in Woodhouse, *Puritanism*, p. 111.

co-ordination. Either way, Charles I certainly regarded such arguments as an over-extension of the parliament's proper care at the expense of his own.[36] Of course, to accept any principle of co-ordination in rule was not much of a clarifying ideology; it left most touchy issues about sovereignty still open to debate, and merged with the traditionally unstable relationship between rule and counsel. In all this, the conflation of the Edward oath-text, however its clauses might be read, with what Charles I actually swore was the secondary issue; in the archaic grammar of a medieval oath lay a clash of more immediate offices.[37] But in this we are taken little further in determining whether an aggressive conciliar bridling was code for a new theory of sovereignty or whether that was an outcome.

In sum, however ritualised, coronation oaths outlined a series of responsibilities of office and it was consequent upon these that subjects cheered their acceptance of the monarch; the form they took, empty or otherwise, was of a reciprocal, almost contractual agreement with those swearing allegiance. It was typical of the accession to any office that in emphasising responsibilities that sanctioned status, it armed others with criteria to judge performance. The difficulty was just how far such conventional phrases of swearing carried a residually dangerous content for the office-holder. Grappling with this problem led, on the one hand, to the unbending insistence on oaths being taken as their words must have been intended; upon describing the oath as an expression of a contingent contractual agreement and so down-playing the solemnities of the occasion. Instead it was seen as what I have called a transformative oath of passage by men as otherwise doctrinally different as Robert Parsons and Algernon Sidney.[38] As Janelle Greenberg has argued, reference to the pre-conquest laws of Edward the Confessor was sometimes a means to this end.[39] On the other, the oath within the rituals of crowning supported the argument that it was only a ceremonial proclamation of an already established relationship in rule.[40] One extrapolation would mew up the office-holder, much like a constable, the other promised elevation to the status of an earthly God, sweeping aside the use of any aspect of the oath as a means of criticising the office-holder. There is a certain irony of positioning here: those who would make the monarch in office almost impregnably divine, were apt to see as superficial a deeply

---

[36] Clarendon, *History*, vol. II, p. 155, bk. 5, paras. 292–307.
[37] Legg, *History of the English Coronation*, pp. 251–2; Kelly, 'King and Crown', vol. II, pp. 630, 634–5, 362–3.
[38] Parsons, *A Conference*, ch. 1.5; Sidney, *Discourses*, 3.17.
[39] Greenberg, *The Radical Face*, at length.
[40] Samuel Eaton, 'An Answer to a Paper', in *The Oath of Allegiance and the National Covenant Proved to be Non-Obligatory* (1650), pp. 9–10.

religious ceremony; those Protestants who, like Algernon Sidney, would use the oath as ammunition to be fired at ill-performing royal targets were most insistent upon the oath's character as a sort of transubstantiation. There is little doubt that each general position on the nature of oaths per se was driven by the argumentative fecundity of the coronation oath in particular. It always teetered on the edge of office and its abuse and it symbolised the inherent tensions of the world as an interaction of offices. Its necessarily formulaic nature threatened to undermine its credibility but at the same time was the condition of its hallowed continuity.

IV

The tendentious nature of coronation oaths casts some light on seventeenth-century social contract theory. A contract, or sometimes a compact, was a specific and bounded agreement between *personae* for mutually agreed reciprocal ends, and it was typically cemented with an oath. Depending on circumstances, the oath might be one of passage, as in a marriage contract, or of a diurnal nature, as in a contract between merchants. Within England, there was an increasing reliance on formal contracts during the seventeenth century;[41] and travel to the Americas, after a symbolically cleansing sea passage, had given a certain literality to the notion of a contract between peoples to form a new society. Contractual verisimilitude was also enhanced by a civil war followed by a formal restoration of the monarchy in 1660 and the abnormalities around the convention parliament of 1689. Something like a contract could be seen in all such show-pieces of political re-settlement.

For all this, the so-called great age of social contract theory is an exaggeration of later theoretical enthusiasms. An integrity and independent theoretical identity has been given to something that was certainly common but often little more than a casual way of expressing the moral importance of consent in governmental relations and of approaching the question of what could be done in the face of office-abuse.[42] No explicit theory of contract was needed to explore such issues. Lawson accepted a contract theory of society in his *Examination of Mr Hobbs*, but three years

---

[41] Muldrew, *The Economy of Obligation*, pp. 123–5, 315–28.
[42] See, for example, Anon., *A Discourse upon the Questions in Debate Between the King and Parliament*, p. 5, where it is but a garnish to the distinction between tyranny of origin and exercise; for a valuable survey, Harro Höpfl and Martyn P. Thompson, 'The History of Contract as a Motif in Political Thought', *American Historical Review*, 4, 84 (1979), pp. 919–44; see also below, chapter 15.

later in *Politica* he retained a vocabulary redolent of contract without developing any specific theory.[43] Variable notions of trust and its breach could subsume, replace or refine reference to contract. Writers generally given scant attention in the contract tradition, most notably Milton, Rutherford and Sidney and, uncomfortably for them, the Jesuit Robert Parsons, and uncomfortably for him Presbyterian George Buchanan, are more typical of the contract motif than those bywords of contractarianism, Hobbes and Locke. Certainly the doctrinal diversity of the smaller fish of contract makes it difficult to assimilate them to liberal ideology latterly housed in the abstraction 'contract theory'.

Broadly one can say that from the late sixteenth century the coronation oath became an obvious proof-text to justify talk of governmental contract.[44] This in turn meant that what might be argued through a contract motif could just as well and was probably more commonly formulated as oath-breaking.[45] If this effective synonymity is ignored, as it routinely is, in discussions of 'contract theory', what is presented as coming from the seventeenth century will remain an implausible distance from it. Rhetorics of contract and oath-breaking could be bound so tightly because each could be expressed through the clichés of nominal identity: governor and governed are 'relatives', wrote Anthony Ascham (?) and if one ceased, the obligation of the other is automatically destroyed.[46] For writers like Buchanan and Parsons, in breaching a coronial contract (or oath) a monarch conceptually ceased to be; therefore, by definition, no monarch had an absolute power – all standard fare in dealing with the *personae* of office. Parsons, citing the authority of Plato and Aristotle, insisted that the monarch's end was in making the commonwealth happy, the tyrant's was the reverse. As the end of government lies in religion, manifest injustice requires acts of defence.[47] The unequivocal point of such propositions was to pinpoint the heretical nature of Protestant rulers who broke their oaths by abandoning true religion.

These patterns of proposition carried a very different force when redeployed by parliamentarians during the Civil War period. Rutherford reiterates a Parsonian insistence on the reciprocity involved in the oath,

---

[43] Conal Condren, 'Confronting the Monster: George Lawson's Reactions to Hobbes's *Leviathan*', *Political Science*, 40 (1988), pp. 67–83.
[44] Parsons, *A Conference*, pp. 73–4, citing the authority of Cicero, *De officiis*; Rutherford, *Lex, Rex*, Q.14.
[45] See, for example, Eaton, *The Oath of Allegiance*, p. 1; 'An Answer to a Paper', in *The Oath*, p. 7.
[46] Anthony Ascham (?), 'E. P.', *An Answer to the Vindication of Doctor Hammond* (1650), p. 5.
[47] Parsons, *A Conference*, pp. 78, 207–8, 20.

citing the crowning of David as exemplary.[48] A pre-social state of systemic insecurity (hardly a monopoly of Hobbesian theory) was also easily used to underline the desperate need for government. The coronation oath was thus taken as a ritual re-enactment of the contractual nature of government: the office of rule was for a purpose, the oath made this clear, and by it rulers could be judged. The office-bounded reading of the oath functioned, then, as a way of associating the sanctity of oath-taking with arguments from self-defence and for deposition and tyrannicide. Although anti-royalist, in the hands of writers like Rutherford, Prynne and Parker it could be turned against any claimant to rule. In contrast, it was asserted that, as the oath was sacred, there could be no release from it simply because one party was thought to have behaved badly; consider marriage, or the office of parent. Two wrongs do not make a right.[49] It was argued that contracts presupposed consent, and no governments were in fact founded on free consent, a reasonable case if consent meant choice.[50] Oaths, being specific, were acts of choice.

The lines of Hobbes's counter-argument to the predominant Buchananesque–Parsonian tradition are sufficiently well known not to need rehearsing except to note the following points. First, he may have been elaborating on James VI&I's denial that the Scottish coronation oath was contractual.[51] In doing so, he was also shoring up royalist arguments that if a power is given, it cannot be taken back.[52] Secondly, as the outcome of contract, a ruler was not a party to its terms, but was definitionally bound to the ruling office, the arbiter of its meaning accountable only to God. This was, indeed, James VI&I's view of the Scottish monarchy. Concomitantly, Hobbes insisted that oaths were very different from transformative contracts, being proclamations of prior agreement. This was like Thomas Bell's rebuff to Parsonian contractual readings of coronation oaths.[53] At once, then, Hobbes inverted the logic of any posited social contract somehow manifested in a reading of coronial oaths and drove a wedge between the conjoined rhetorics of contract and oath-taking by discounting the importance of oaths as such. These

---

[48] Rutherford, *Lex, Rex*, Q.14; 'Philodemius', *The Original and End*, pp. 31–2.
[49] George Hickes, *A Word to the Wavering* (1689), p. 5; George Berkeley, *Passive Obedience* (1712, 1713), in *Works*, vol. VI, pp. 28–9.
[50] Filmer, *Patriarcha*, the effective thrust of an otherwise convoluted critique.
[51] James VI&I, *The Trew Law, of Free Monarchies* in *Workes*, pp. 206–7; cf. Hobbes, *De cive*, chs. 7.2–3; 12.1–2.
[52] For example, Maxwell, *Sacro-sancta*; Dudley Digges, *An Answer to a Printed Book* (1642).
[53] Bell, *Regiment of the Church*, p. 4; tangentially see also Lorenzo Valla, *De professione*, in which the vow only proclaims a proper obedience, while specific vows as to poverty were at best tokens of an inner humility, *Opera omnia*, pp. 113–15; 124–7.

were powerful moves in the process of advancing sovereignty theory but Hobbes's attitude to swearing had complicating consequences in the context of the Engagement controversy (below, chapter 14, VII).

At the same time, it should be noted that both Hobbes's understanding of a social contract and the arguments of those positing a contract in the oath were extrapolated from complementary aspects of oath-taking. The coronation oath specified the protective ends of the ruling office and its maintenance, so accepting the exercise of sovereign judgement. Hobbes was happy to transpose this to formulate a contract between those seeking protection.[54] But the oath also offered justice, religion and the prior customary properties of the ruled as givens, not as terms to be interpreted howsoever the sovereign thought best, although the oaths taken by Henry VIII and Charles I approach a Hobbesian ideal. Such words as justice, religion and custom could be used to invoke standards independent of royal will, limiting the sovereign and justifying bridling, correction or deposition. The paradox of Hobbes's position was that unless the oath were diminished to a ceremonial husk and its affirmations abstracted into a contract that hardly touched the sovereign, the ruling office would be undone.

Just as the presuppositions and language of office are found throughout the seventeenth century, so it is a shade artificial to isolate the separate controversies over oath-taking around the Gunpowder Plot (1605–6), the Engagement (1649–52) and the Allegiance controversy (1689–90). So far, I have largely bypassed evidence from these crises to minimise pleonasm. Nevertheless, they provide concentrated eruptions of problems that rumbled throughout the century.

To give a general overview of each oath and the arguments about it would lead to intolerable repetition. The resonance of 1606 was evident in 1689 when that unlikely rabbit James VI&I emerged from the hat as a hero of true rather than free monarchy, and the shadows of the Engagement were still thick enough to cast Thomas Hobbes somewhere rather dark. My purpose is to use each controversy to disengage complementary aspects of the problems of oath-taking and office-holding. The focus in the following chapter will be on the question of demarcation of office, as this was both a local and a Christendom-wide dispute. The controversy of that first oath of allegiance thus enfolds the whole political culture of Christendom. King James himself will be the principal guide, as he was both instigator and defender of the oath, a philosopher and a king. The Engagement controversy will be used to plot a localised

---

[54] Hobbes, *Elements*, 1.15.16.

but more extreme examination of the offices of priest and ruler, more importantly to explore the reification of the office of rule and the way in which defining aspects of office became competing doctrines. Anthony Ascham's *Confusions and Revolutions of Governments* will be the main text discussed. The final chapter will be broader in that it will draw on the themes of the previous two to help bring the study together. Although there is an emphasis on continuity, certain points of change will also be clear by examining the arguments eddying around the Glorious Revolution: the extension of anti-papal rhetoric to all priests, the reliance on tyranny for all abuse of office and the surfacing of established presuppositions about consent as fundamental to rule. The main guide here will be the anonymous *A Friendly Debate* of 1689. Throughout the full repertoire of oath-construction and oath-taking strategies will be apparent; and in this context, the promulgation of oaths of allegiance at the end of the century can be seen as a response to the failures of those formulated at the beginning. The consequence of a fresh focus will be to question several established images of these crises; that the Engagement controversy was over might versus right, or pragmatism versus principle is simply not supported by the evidence. Indeed, despite the weight of modern scholarship devoted to refining its precise shape, scope and adherence, there was no de facto theory. As a corollary, the Revolution of 1689 was not a victory for the exponents of that theory or ideology, any more than it marked a decisive stage in the march of democratic rights to resist. It is to the first oath of allegiance controversy that I shall now turn.

13 The oath of allegiance of 1606

> O, come in, equivocator. Knock, knock, knock.
> (Shakespeare, *Macbeth* 2.3)

I

With its blood-red suns suspended low in the sky, chill November was Blotmonath in Anglo-Saxon, the month of blood; and so it was in 1605, with plans to blow the royal blood sky-high; but in searching the cellars under the House of Lords, Sir Thomas Knevet found powder kegs and a tall lurking fellow, with 'three matches, and all other instruments fit for blowing vp the powder'.[1] The discovery of the Gunpowder Plot was the new king's Armada. Its providential failure would enter the ritual calendar of English Protestantism, its celebration marking the light, the way and the *ignis fatui* of confusion and sedition. One match to the powder was the legacy of Elizabeth's harsh religious policies. A second was the reciprocated hostility of Rome and Spain to the heretic queen. Both were severe tests for indigenous Catholic loyalism.[2] A third was the discrepancy between the hotter sorts of Protestants prominent in the Church of England and the diversity of lay belief, approaching independency at one extreme, remaining close to a native Catholicism at another. The *via media* of the Church of England was a hope for a road of uncertain width and smoothness and was little more settled than its new monarchical head. James's accession, however, was initially a cause of some Catholic optimism, 'we have a Kinge [who] will restore us to our rightes', wrote Katharine Gawen, and Henry Garnet anticipated 'a golden time of unexpected freedom'.[3] The glister did not last and by 1605 persecution had been renewed. Thoughts of relaxation and reform can be dangerous for an oppressive rule and so it proved for James. As

---

[1] James VI&I, *A Discourse*, p. 230.
[2] Patrick McGrath, *Papists and Puritans under Elizabeth I* (London, 1967), pp. 253–98, for a survey of divisions among Catholics under Elizabeth.
[3] *Ibid.*, pp. 339, 364; see also John Lacey/Lay, *A Petition Apologeticall* (1604).

there was talk of toleration and peace with Spain, the plot was hatched.[4] A time of crisis was one of opportunity, but the oath that bound the conspirators to decisive action was followed by the oath that made the plight of English Catholics desperate.

II

The oath of allegiance of 1606 was one of circumstance, the centrepiece of two acts punishing the bulk of obedient Catholics for the blown conspiracy of the few. Its messages were mixed. It evidenced a collapse of trust and offered hope of its restitution should the oath be sworn. It also exhibited remarkable faith in the power of an oath, partially justified by the agonies of conscience excited in the English Catholic community.[5] Jesuit theory, however, as understood beyond the order, gave reason to believe oaths might be meaningless, so the symbolic act of swearing gave questionable assurance to Protestants in and beyond England, all of whom were an audience for the royal response to the plot. The form of the oath was largely assertory but promissory in force. 'A. B.' (any suspected recusant) had to acknowledge James's rightful sovereignty; that the pope could not depose or release subjects from their obligations, and could give no licence for subjects to bear arms against the king or his government. In more explicitly promissory mode 'A. B.' had to swear to be true to the king and his heirs and successors, defending them 'to the uttermost of my power against all conspiracies and attempts whatsoever'; to endeavour to disclose 'all treason and traitorous conspiracies [of] which I shall know or hear'. Doctrines of king killing were to be abhorred, the pope's capacity to release the swearer from the oath was rejected. All was to be sworn to sincerely without equivocation, evasions and with the words being taken in their normal senses, after all of which he or she subscribed by name, or mark.[6]

In his remarkable study of James, W. Brown Patterson has argued that the oath was careful in demanding only a temporal allegiance, being based on those required of Catholic clergy to give civil allegiance in return for a degree of toleration.[7] Thus it seemed to conform to the

---

[4] Theophilus Higgons, *A Sermon Preached at St Paul's* Cross (3 March 1610) (1611), on the temperature of many English Catholics, p. 53; James VI&I, *Discourse*, p. 231.

[5] Arnold Pritchard, *Catholic Loyalism in Elizabethan England* (London, 1979), at length.

[6] Jones, *Conscience and Allegiance*, p. 272, gives the text in full from *An Act for Discovering and Representing Popish Recusants* (January 1606).

[7] W. Brown Patterson, *James VI&I and the Reunion of Christendom* (Cambridge, 2000 edn), p. 79.

conventional ethics of oath administration. If the insistence upon an oath was a right of rule, an impossible one was abuse of power and likely to be counter-productive. To force Catholics to abandon spiritual allegiance to Rome would have been an incitement to swearing in bad faith, a fear that pervades the oath itself. Indeed, James repeatedly insisted that the oath was an act of favour and clemency towards those who 'though blinded with the superstition of Poperie, yet carried a dutifull heart towards our Obedience'.[8] A touch of salt is needed for the clemency and favour, but James did tacitly accept a spiritual authority for the pope.[9] Does the oath, he asked rhetorically, say anything about religion?[10]

It must have been known, however, that James and his Council were testing the very rim of rule. We are returned to that most difficult of themes in early modern England *aliud est distinctio, aliud separatio*. To distinguish spiritual from temporal was an act of understanding, to separate them was a matter of policy, and churches were enmeshed in temporal as well as spiritual activity.[11] The oath might only demand the civil allegiance of the 'popishly affected', but swearing was an act of the soul before God.[12] If only temporal obedience were being sought, the problem was to contain the consequences of allowing even a residual spiritual obligation to Rome.

Troubled Catholics responded differently. Archpriest George Blackwell, to be found somewhere between a rock and a hard place, chose to swear on James's terms. He was joined by the Appelants and those hostile to the Jesuits in England.[13] Antonio De Dominis would temporarily defect to the Protestant cause. Given the timing of a papal interdict on Venice in 1606 for its civil subjection of priests, there might almost be said to have been a London–Venice axis of anti-papal argument.[14] At one point, James even suggested that the papacy address the criticisms of

---

[8] *Ibid.*, p. 78; also James VI&I, *An Apologie for the Oath of Allegiance*, in *Workes*, p. 248; *His Maiesties Speech in This Last Session of Parliament* (1605), in *Workes*, pp. 503–4.
[9] James VI&I, *Apologie*, pp. 248, 256.
[10] *Ibid.*, p. 269; *A Catalogue of the Lyes of Tortus, Together with a Briefe Confutation of them*, in *Workes*, p. 341; *A Praemonition to the Monarchs*, in *Workes*, pp. 292, 297; for defensive explication, see, for example, Donne, *Pseudo-Martyr*, pp. 347ff.
[11] Bell, *Regiment*, ch. 6.
[12] James VI&I, *Apologie*, p. 248.
[13] George Blackwell, *A Large Examination Taken at Lambeth . . . together with the Cardinal's Letter and M. Blakwell's said Answer to it. Also M. Blakwell's Letter to the Romish Catholickes in England* (1607); Richard Sheldon, *Certain General Reasons Proving the Lawfulnesse of the Oath of Allegiance* (1611), pp. 2–10; William Barclay, *Of the Authoritie of the Pope* (1611), esp. chs. 2, 33.
[14] Patterson, *James VI&I*, pp. 220–59; Salmon, 'Catholic Resistance Theory', pp. 250–1.

the Venetians before bothering him further.[15] This strong coincidence of interests was given additional support by the Gallicans of the Sorbonne. Much of the Catholic hostility to the Pope stemmed from a belief that the church was too apt to interfere with temporal power in the name of spiritual authority. The over-extension of priestly office, argued the Catholic Richard Sheldon prophetically, would lead to its discreditation.[16] The oath, however, did come perilously close to requiring a rejection of Rome's spiritual authority, and for some Catholics it was theologically offensive because it made a heretic the arbiter of heresy.[17] James's denial that it said nothing about religion seemed disingenuous and Pope Paul V lost no time in twice forbidding Catholics to take it.[18] Cardinal Bellarmine insisted that the force of the oath was to abrogate the papal office.[19] These arguments were to be extended, largely through repetition and personal imputation, by Robert Parsons in dispute with Thomas Morton; by Bellarmine again, in his *Apologia*, and by Martin Becan and Francisco de Suarez.[20]

If the oath had to stop short of erasing all papal authority for Catholics in England, it also had the task of reassuring suspicious Protestants that even minimal tolerance was safe policy.[21] A demarcation dispute exacerbated by an oath was a problem that persisted and made imperative a reaffirmation and clarification of monarchical office, a context that invites reconsideration of James's claims to being an absolute ruler and a god on earth (see below, section IV). First, however, it is necessary to go back in order to outline the terms in which the domains of temporal and spiritual office were debated, because these remained of direct relevance to the escalating oath controversy, defining for the rest of the century what was to be a fundamental problem for the office of the priest as much as for secular rule.

---

[15] James VI&I, *A Catalogue*, p. 346.
[16] Sheldon, *Certain General Reasons*, pp. 14–20, 29, 74.
[17] Pritchard, *Catholic Loyalism*, p. 193, n. 213.
[18] Patterson, *James VI&I*, p. 83; James VI&I, *Apologie*, pp. 250, 258.
[19] Robert Bellarmine, *Admonitum . . . Georgio Blacuello* (1607), in Blackwell, *A large Examination*, fols. B–b3, English C–c3; see also in James VI&I, *Workes*, pp. 260–2; *A Catalogue*, pp. 339–40.
[20] Parsons, *A Treatise Tending to Mitigation* (1607); Robert Parsons, *The Judgement of a Catholicke English-man* (1608); Thomas Morton, *A Full Satisfaction* (1606), *A Preamble unto an Incounter* (1608); Robert Bellarmine, *Matthaei Torti . . . responsio* (St Omer, 1608); Robert Bellarmine, *Apologia* (Rome, 1609); Martin Becanus, *Controversia anglicana de potestate regis et pontificis* (Mainz, 1612); Martin Becanus, *Dissidium anglicanum de primatu Regis* (Mainz, 1612); Suarez, *Defensio fidei Catholicae*.
[21] Gabriel Powell (?), *The Catholicke's Supplication* (1604, 1606).

III

As offices were defined in mutual relation, and as the pope's spiritual authority for his followers was crucial, the oath effectively re-affirmed the traditional terms of debate for the Christendom-wide controversy it provoked. These had been set down by the Galatian 'two swords' doctrine of the fifth century. In this image, taken from Luke 22: 38, Pope Gelatius (492–6) had formally acknowledged the claims of the Emperor without compromising his own authority. Christ had given two swords, one of temporal and one of spiritual authority. Each sword was an office and together they came to circumscribe the dimensions of Christendom. The most uncompromising reading of the doctrine was in Boniface VIII's *Unam sanctam* (1302), for it placed both swords in the hands of St Peter, so denying divine origin for temporal authority. Even where the independence of the temporal sword was accepted, the terms of the metaphor made rejection of papal authority difficult. Dante systematically disputed the metaphors commonly used to bolster papal superiority; yet he accepted that the imagery of the swords expressed the pope's spiritual office for the soul and this required that the Emperor must show the reverence (*pietas*) due from a son to his father.[22] Understandably the two swords argument remained a crucial and flexible weapon in the armoury of papal polemic: what it did not claim directly through a swinging ambidexterity, it could assert indirectly with one hand behind its back. By accepting the authenticity of temporal office, the sword could always be presented as needing to be drawn only in cases of extremity when the temporal authority's soul might itself be endangered. Sheathed with the sword, then, was a well-honed modal casuistry. When admonition failed there was recourse to the spiritual thrust of excommunication, meaningless without temporal consequences such as deposition.

In the pre-Reformation world, it had principally been Marsilius who had refused to accept the implications of the *topos*: give the pope a spiritual sword, as Dante had, and the grounds were already in place for the abuse of office that had been the story of Christendom's degeneration. Marsilius dismissively listed the swords as among a number of images used to accumulate priestly power, and argued instead that Christ had excluded himself, his apostles, and hence all priests from every *officium*

---

[22] Dante Alighieri, *De Monarchia*, ed. E. Rostagno (Florence, 1921), 3.1, 4–6; 3.16; Wilks, *The Problem of Sovereignty*, pp. 144–6, who points out that in the *Convivio* Dante sometimes uses reverence and obedience synonymously, p. 145.

concerning jurisdiction in this world.[23] The result was a severely restricted, egalitarian conception of pastoral office, and an independence of all temporal authority derived directly from God.[24]

At the Reformation Luther was accused of being a Marsilian, and for the Protestant laity the Marsilian solution would have considerable appeal. William Marshall's translation of *Defensor pacis* had been provided for Henry VIII's bishops immediately after the break with Rome. The text was used in Venice under the most severe threat from Pope Paul V.[25] But it had corrosive consequences for the office of any priest, and so, across the Reformation divide, there remained a clerical investment in some distinction between the swords and a sphere of authority for the priest touching temporal affairs. The priest, insisted Hugh Latimer in 1550, had a sword of spiritual reproof for the correction of rulers. Make not a 'mingle mangle' over what is due to God and to Caesar.[26] For Protestants, the problem would remain with which sword the line was drawn in the sand. It would make a formal distinction, though metaphorically plausible, arbitrary and difficult to apply. Spiritual exercise could always be construed as priestly interference, and thus popery.[27]

For Catholics the Reformation made some reliance on the swords almost inescapable. Francisco Vitoria, in defending the Castilian monarchy, at one point reduced the two swords argument to an impotent literality, yet insisted on the papacy's duty to exercise authority in matters of spiritual emergency. The pope was a casuistic necessity.[28] Cardinal Reginald Pole argued in similar terms. The temporal office of the king was for the body, the church was for the higher service of souls; the natural law mediated by the priesthood overrode the positive law and if the monarch endangered souls, the church should act. There was, he made clear, precedent enough for this in England.[29] Cardinal Bellarmine fighting on both the Venetian and the English fronts had, then, a hallowed tradition on which to draw and reiterate. He repaired to the Bonifacian position; both swords were rightfully in the hands of the

---

[23] Marsilius of Padua, *Defensor pacis*, D.2.3.6; D.2.4.4.
[24] *Ibid.*, D.2.29.5; D.2.4.12; cf. also Lorenzo Valla, *De professione*; between them Marsilius and Valla put in place most materials needed for the Lutheran Reformation.
[25] See Gregorio Piaia, *Marsilio da Padova nella Riforma e nella Controriforma* (Padua, 1977), for a survey of usage.
[26] Latimer, *Fruitful Sermons*, fols. 6v, 25v, 94v.
[27] Bilson, *Christian Subjection*, pp. 126–8, 146; 164–5; 251–2; 247.
[28] Francisco de Vitoria, *On Civil Power* (1528) and *On the Power of the Church* (1532), in *Political Writings*, ed. Anthony Pagden and Jeremy Lawrence (Cambridge, 1991), 5.9, p. 99; 5.6–7, pp. 90–1.
[29] Reginald Pole, *Pro ecclesiasticae unitatis defensione* (Rome 1536, 1539); see Mayer, *Thomas Starkey*, ch. 7.

church, excommunication allowed the deposition of heretic rulers and Christendom's unity depended upon re-asserting papal sovereignty. In contrast Giovanni Marsilio defending the Venetian Republic read the gladiatorial imagery like Dante, as an acceptance of the distinct spheres of temporal and spiritual, a complementary relationship of office, not a hierarchical one, awkwardly supporting his reading with additional images of arms and metals.[30] Back in England, Richard Sheldon remarked more bluntly that priests who took up the temporal sword were likely to perish by it.[31]

Thus the oath of allegiance, in not explicitly denying the pope all spiritual authority, offered an uncertain hostage to fortune and helped ensure the spread of the accusation of popery to almost any cleric laying a hand on the hilt of spiritual reproof. The heavily patinated imagery of the swords continued to offer hope of some modus vivendi between complementary offices, but in practice collapsed either into theocracy or erastianism. Immediately, this was not a conspicuous aid for James's loyal Catholics. They had no doctrine as Catholics that could really reassure the suspicious Protestant; time, obedience, an understanding pontiff and suffering, as George Blackwell enjoined his flock, were all they could rely upon. This, however, was not much in a society capable of systemic hostility to Rome. It was certainly symbolically appropriate to their situation that it was from the office of London's Clink Prison that Blackwell defended the oath as expressive of the independence of the temporal sword.[32] He was sacked by Pope Paul. Later in the century, as a testimony to the continuing difficulties they faced, a few Catholics, such as Sir Kenelm Digby and Thomas White, were to toy with the idea of English Catholicism without a pope; as Sheldon had remarked, in supporting James, it is lawful to resist even the pope when he invades our souls.[33]

In defending kingly office after 1606, James and his supporters needed to sharpen parallel claims about state and church. First there was the need to reassert sovereignty against what Donne would call the 'new Alchimy' of priestly immunity, interference and usurpation of Christ's

---

[30] See William Bowsma, *Venice and the Defence of Republican Liberty* (Los Angeles, 1984 edn), pp. 428–9, 434, 430.
[31] Sheldon, *Certain General Reasons*, pp. 14, 49.
[32] Blackwell, *M. Blakwell's Letter to the Romish Catholickes*, pp. 169–70; Peter Lake, 'Anti-Popery: The Structure of a Prejudice', in R. Cust and A. Hughes, eds., *Conflict in Early Stuart England* (London, 1981), pp. 72–106; and at length Anthony Milton, *Catholic and Reformed: The Roman and Protestant Churches in English Protestant Thought, 1600–1640* (Cambridge, 1995). Sheldon also wrote from prison, *Certain General Reasons*, p. Av.
[33] Sheldon, *Certain General Reasons*, p. 55.

office.³⁴ Second, the specifically episcopal Church of England needed to replace the exorcised ghost of Rome: one sword in the hands of the king, the other transferred to his bishops, a strategy that would merely localise the clash of steel. On the first score, it was reasserted that the monarchy, being directly instituted by God, was not answerable to any other office. As an attribute of his supreme authority, the king's absolute right to impose oaths was a crucial test: absolute allegiance was required by all subjects.³⁵

There was an urgency and shrillness to this independent of the oath of allegiance, but James, no less than Bellarmine, came to the crisis theoretically armed. He had been educated by George Buchanan, who had argued that tyrannicide was justified for abuse of office, that allegiance was conditional and that sovereignty lay with the whole community of the people.³⁶ Buchanan, instrumental in having James's Catholic mother removed from the Scottish throne, had dedicated his theory to the young king. Catholic Scholastic writers had taken a similar line about the duty to remove erring monarchs, and Cardinal Allen, from a safe distance, had urged the purgative of tyrannicide for Elizabeth.³⁷ Although the papacy stopped short of the decisive rebuke of assassination, James was understandably insistent that Catholic interference in temporal affairs left him in much the same position as Elizabeth. Excommunication had given her over 'as a prey', 'setting her subjects at liberty to rebell'.³⁸ The spiritual weapon of excommunication was really temporal, and to use it was, indeed, to make a 'mingle-mangle' of what was due to God and Caesar. As James reminded the Catholic princes of the empire, 'yee are in the Popes folde' and whenever he pleases may be led by 'that great Pastor as sheepe to the slaughter'.³⁹ The king needed as thick a hedge of divinity as he could manage.

IV

The result was an absolutist theory of kingship, elaborated before James became king of England. *The Trew Law of Free Monarchies* drew on

---

³⁴ Donne, *Pseudo-Martyr*, pp. 93–4, 98.
³⁵ *Ibid.*, p. A2v chs. 3, 4, 12, pp. 248ff; James VI&I, *Apologie*; *God and King* (1615), pp. 28–36; Bell, *Regiment*, pp. 4–5; Owen, *Herod and Pilate*, at length.
³⁶ Buchanan, *De jure regni apud Scotos* (1579). For a recent assessment, see Roger Mason, 'George Buchanan on Resistance and the Common Man', in Robert von Friedeburg, ed., *Widerstandsrecht in der frühen Neuzeit* (Berlin, 2001), pp. 163–81.
³⁷ Allen, *An Admonition*; also William Allen, *A True Sincere and Modest Defence of English Catholics* (1584).
³⁸ James VI&I, *Apologie*, p. 252; *God and King*, p. 7; Patterson, *James VI&I*, p. 80.
³⁹ James VI&I, *A Praemonition*, p. 296.

medieval dicta about the divine origination of rule, and on hierocratic and post-Bodinian sovereignty theory.[40] It was directed at the rumbustiousness of James's subjects, especially his aristocracy, against spiritual interference from Rome, the Kirk and against his old tutor's theories of limited monarchy and tyrannicide. It was not an absolutist theory of sovereignty per se, but it was uncompromising. In any free monarchy, there must be an unchallenged source of effective law; an analogous claim was also being developed in republican Venice.[41] The free monarch is accountable exclusively to God, and only his will ties him to the law.[42] However labelled, this text manifestly provided an implacable defence of the oath of allegiance against any attacks from Rome and propositions from it, or akin to it, did much to sow absolutist dicta across the English political landscape.

Absolutism as a general classifier, however, is unstable, being used to cover a doctrine of principle, a moveable rhetoric of office defence, an accusation of abuse and the institutionalised practice that the early Stuart monarchy never managed. Only occasionally in a work like *Trew Law* does it approach the reductive clarity it enjoyed in France and the theoretical coherence appropriate to twentieth-century categories of ideological analysis.[43] Yet the exception has been taken as the rule, and the study of Stuart thought has been organised through related polarities: democratic or popular (sometimes revealingly elided with constitutional) versus divine right absolutism, or, more generally, through Walter Ullmann's now exploded model of necessarily competing ascending or descending ideologies of legitimation.[44] This has been convenient but distorting. All power might formally descend from God, but the efficient cause of its manifestation could be the people (as in Venice) from whom it also ascended.[45]

---

[40] Vitoria, *Civil Power*, 1.3, p. 10; Jean Bodin, *Six livres de la République* (1576), translated into Latin, then English. Richard Knolles' English translation, *The Six Books of a Commonweale*, ed. K. D. McRae (Cambridge, Mass., 1962); see also Bilson, *Christian Subjection*, pt. 2.

[41] Bowsma, *Venice*, e.g. pp. 430–3.

[42] James VI&I, *Trew Law*, pp. 200, 206, 203; *God and King*, pp. 18–21; 30–6.

[43] See Johann Sommerville, 'Absolutism and Revolution in the Seventeenth Century', in *The Cambridge History of Political Thought*, pp. 249–50, for measured qualification. For Scotland's ally France, see Mark Greengrass, 'Regicide, Martyrs and Monarchical Authority in France in the Wars of Religion', in von Friedeburg, *Murder and Monarchy*, pp. 176–92.

[44] See, for example, Walter Ullmann, *Law and Politics in the Middle Ages* (Cambridge, 1975); for a devastating critique, Francis Oakley, 'Celestial Hierarchies Revisited: Walter Ullmann's Vision of Medieval Politics', *Past and Present*, 60 (1973), pp. 1–48; see also Hindle, *The State and Social Change*, pp. 25–6; this model was applied by Johann Sommerville in his standard *Politics and Ideology in England, 1603–1640* (London, 1986).

[45] Cf. Marsilius, *Defensor pacis*, D.1.12; D.2.4.12; Vitoria, *Civil Power*, Prologue, 1.1; cf. Bowsma, *Venice*, p. 430; and later Rutherford, *Lex, Rex*, Q.4; Hunton, *Treatise*,

Such compound causative propositions and theological axioms might tell us little about principles of rule and accountability.[46]

The potential tensions, however, between absolute and bounded rule brought into relief the distinction between the normal and the reserve, or prerogative power. With this we are returned to the casuistic nexus, the junction of ordinary and abnormal cases. Much debate about absolute rule concerned an idiom of casuistic adjustment, analogous, as it were, to God's occasionally working miracles, to the pope's occasionally acting in the temporal realm, or to the more mundane court of equity. Anyone who made a casuistic appeal to a principle of prerogative for exceptional cases might be accused of absolutism and it is probably more helpful to say that absolutists were those who could see no way in which any such line could, or should, be drawn.[47] As Carl Schmitt would much later summarise, the sovereign is whoever decides in emergency. Meanwhile, there were few writers in Jacobean England systematically willing to embrace such a doctrine, though there would be many who would spy absolutists everywhere because of the difficulty of limiting the recourse to prerogative powers. It was a troublesome case of the control over casuistry itself.

With the emergency of the Gunpowder Plot close behind them there were certainly many who had absolutist moments, employing maxims casuistically that have since been widely regarded as expressing commitment to an absolutist ideology.[48] Glenn Burgess has doubted this, arguing convincingly that absolutism as found in the secondary literature is largely an anachronistic invention, and that many contemporary statements now deemed absolutist accepted some limitation and could be accommodated to law.[49] His case raises the further issue of whether identifying an ideology is anything more than a matter of abstracting from certain sorts of language use, and at what point in surveying the evidence it is plausible to conclude that we are confronted with an ideology. This, if it has been considered, affords no simple answer. For although many absolutist propositions immediately after 1605 may themselves fall short of ideological affirmation, they can be read in the context of Bodin's work, available in three languages and, most immediately, James's own theory.

pp. 3–4. Absolutism could also be fashioned to what would later be seen as liberal and tolerant ends.
[46] Burgess, *Politics of the Ancient Constitution*, ch. 5.
[47] Glenn Burgess, *Absolute Monarchy and the Stuart Constitution* (New Haven, 1996), pt. 1, for the best discussion of these issues.
[48] Sommerville, 'Absolutism and Revolution', pp. 348–9; cf. Burgess, *Absolute Monarchy*, ch. 2, and the literature there cited and ch. 4.
[49] Burgess, *Politics of the Ancient Constitution*, ch. 4; Burgess, *Absolute Monarchy*, chs. 1–2.

If we are to rely on the concept of absolutist ideology, this surely fits the bill. As some would universalise the matter, any state was an order of command and obedience, and wherever the sovereign is located its office is to make and execute the laws.[50]

At this point it may be helpful to turn to a commentator unaware of the conceptual modelling on which modern scholars have relied. At the outbreak of the Civil Wars Philip Hunton would abstract from Jacobean materials three degrees of absoluteness in rule. One tied the ruler to the law only by will, the degree expressed by Scottish James in *Trew Law*; a second was that found in a prerogative power above the law for abnormal cases, the degree to which English James seemed to adhere; a third was that in which the ruler formally promised to be limited by the law, the degree to which he also later attached himself.[51] Crucially in Hunton's analysis, these degrees of absoluteness all concerned the nature and scope of an office, a moral power, not elaboration of an unlimited capacity to act which absolutism as a practice might approach, and which the 'blandishments' of later parliamentarian propaganda feared.[52] Thus, for Hunton, transgression was not a form of government but a move beyond it.[53] The ruler in office no matter how absolute was like a shepherd. The absolutism lay in an awareness of office whose limits are internally and divinely guaranteed. Little wonder that the king's conscience, as James said, lay in executing his office.[54] The important corollary of this, as I have argued, is that identity was a function of office. As a *persona* the king could do no wrong, but in doing wrong he might cease in that *persona*. This crucial qualification could accommodate apparently absolutist maxims to critical purposes: subjects must obey kings but tyrants are not kings.[55]

Again, however, *Trew Law* is distinctive in prohibiting such linguistic moves. Only God can give judgement. Yet, in arguing this, James reasserts the importance of seeing the relationship between rulers and ruled in terms of office. The sub-title highlights the main theme: *the reciprock and mutual dutie betwixt a Free King and his natural subjects*. His freedom is a freedom of office, to see justice done, to be a good pastor. The reality of tyranny as abuse of office is never denied, but subjects have no avenue of office through which to act but for recourse to prayers, tears and flight. By

---

[50] Henning Arnisaeus, *De iure maiestatis libri tres* (Frankfurt, 1610); *De auctoritate principum in populum semper inviolabili* (Frankfurt, 1612).
[51] Hunton, *Treatise*, p. 7.   [52] Burgess, *Absolute Monarchy*, p. 123.
[53] Hunton, *Treatise*, p. 1.   [54] Sharpe, *Re-mapping*, p. 159.
[55] Willett, *Harmonie on the First Booke of Samuel*, pp. 52, 294.

precisely this token, James's supporters after the Gunpowder Plot could train the argument where it was most needed, against the claimed immunities and bogus authority of priests whose office lies only in admonition and reproof.[56] If it reproved with the word tyranny, James's reply was to ask, Who is to judge? In such cases, for king or people to judge each other would be to usurp the office of God. Similarly, if the people, including the priests, cannot judge the king, the king cannot treat a rebel as an 'vtter enemy'.[57] Reciprocal office entails limitation. However unsatisfactory we might find such limitation, it is a defining feature of the argument;[58] his absolutism is an idealised ethics of office, the manifestation, in Hunton's terms, of a moral power.

To indicate the doctrinal fragility of early Stuart absolutism, it is worth returning to James's unqualified assertion that the king is above human law and obeys the laws only out of his will. This, it seems to me, is clear enough and is directly analogous to, or derived from, the theological proposition that a voluntarist, omnipotent God chooses to work through the laws of nature; but it takes only a slight change of inflection for it to crumble into something little more than a tautology. And so it would prove. In a speech before parliament in 1609, James argued that although all kings were originally absolute, this is qualified in practice; a king binds himself by a double oath to the fundamental laws of his kingdom. He 'leaves off to be a king and degenerates into a tyrant' as soon as he ceases to rule through the law.[59] It would be fitting, then, that Hunton would refer not to types of absolutism but only to degrees of absoluteness of which this is the third, though James stopped short of denying the prerogative power it might seem to imply. It was a degree that still allowed accusations of tyranny to be made by lawyers, or priests who saw the old religion as part of the legal fabric of the nation. Despite royal reassurance, the pervasive casuistic worry remained: the prerogative to move beyond all law might only be for exceptional cases, but who is to judge? What is to stop the exceptional becoming the norm? So argument from consequence compressed absolutism into tyranny. But this was a polemical projection, not a commitment to be found around James – except as an accusation levelled against the pope. There is a certain irony in Locke

---

[56] James VI&I, *Trew Law*, pp. 208, 194; *God and King*, p. 51.
[57] James VI&I, *Trew Law*, p. 208. The practical implications of 'vtter' may be obscure given the treatment of convicted rebels.
[58] Burgess, *Absolute Monarchy*, pp. 18–20, on the confusions between limitation and mechanisms of control.
[59] James VI&I, *The Kings Majesties Speach to the Lords and Commons*, 21 March, 1609, n.p.; but see *The Political Works of James I*, ed. C. H. McIlwain (Cambridge, Mass., 1918), pp. 301–10; cf. the very different Ponet, *Shorte Treatise*, pp. 108, 98–9.

extolling James as a king while he was collapsing prerogative power into tyranny.

The frequently nominal understanding of the rights of *personae* coextensive with action in office underscores the importance of trying to keep object language conceptually distinct from the meta-language of theoretical modelling, hence the flagged scepticism in the preceding comments about the category of ideology through which the nature of Jacobean absolutist writing has been filtered.[60] It may be safer to think in terms of moveable vocabularies of office defence and critique, tantalisingly suggestive of what we call ideology. There may be so few systematic absolutists despite the wide scattering of absolutist propositions because the functions of proclaiming absoluteness in rule were largely restricted to the crises of office surrounding the Scottish monarchy and oath of allegiance. The more extreme the theory, the more discrepant it could be with the situation to which it responded. Bellarmine's and later Suarez's image of absolute papal right provided a strong contrast to the world in which they lived, and James fell well short of being the free monarch of all he surveyed in Scotland.

V

Here endeth the excursus on absolutism; ideology or not, its *sententiae* were of inestimable value in defending the king's oath, and we can now briefly pick up the second imperative arising from the controversy: to fill the spiritual void of Rome. Catholic and anti-Catholic polemic in England provides hermeneutic problems not dissimilar to those clouding absolutism. The on-going debates exhibited shifting views and intensity of expression on all sides, perhaps as much concerned with positioning within denominations as with facing down an extrinsic foe.[61] The Gunpowder Plot and the subsequent oath provided a sharpened focus for a diversity of factions, and by 1616 the Venetian Ambassador Foscarini reported on twelve broad groupings: three Catholic, two puritan, three others and four in different ways supporting James.[62] It is with caution, then, that I rather drastically streamline the problem of spiritual office in England.

---

[60] See also Jones, *Conscience and Allegiance*, pp. 230–1.
[61] Jeanne Shami, 'Anti Catholicism in the Sermons of John Donne', in Ferrell and McCullough, eds., *The English Sermon Revised*, pp. 136–66, drawing much on Milton, *Catholic and Reformed*.
[62] Milton, *Catholic and Reformed*, pp. 7–9; Shami, 'Anti Catholicism in the Sermons of John Donne', p. 137.

Cardinal Bellarmine's attack on the English church was at one with a number of English Jesuit tracts, holding that although arbitrarily deviant and born of expediency, it remained sufficiently close to Rome to be rejoined and, for the sake of Christendom, must return to the fold; there was hope in that it was not unredeemably heretical Geneva. The Jesuits had enemies within their church who were likely to disagree with the substance and tone of what they argued. Conversely, the more reformed Protestants in England agreed effectively with the Jesuitical analysis. Some left the English church because they saw it as crypto-Catholic, and some urged more reform to stop the slide back to Rome. Hooker, though formally rejecting Rome, had directed his attentions to those who wanted such further reform, and not surprisingly he was commended by the Jesuits for being close to Rome and condemned by more thorough reformers for the same reason.[63]

Arguments in Hooker's idiom put forward after 1605 had perforce to be re-directed towards Rome in order to maintain the tenuous claims to a *via media*, and there were three complementary dimensions to this, each alienating Catholicism from England. The first was to rehearse the abuses of office by the Roman Church in England. A robust native martyrology, established earlier by Foxe, was appended to the lurid accounts of early Christian suffering under pagan Rome. To this was added the biblically based argument that bishops were sanctioned by the Bible and that episcopacy could stop short of papacy and its temporal aggrandisement. In developing these arguments in direct reply to Bellarmine, Lancelot Andrewes elaborated on James's own defence of the oath against the cardinal.[64] With the defence of the Church of England went, in fact, the increasing insistence on episcopacy as *iure divino*.[65] In any event, the force of such arguments is clear: if episcopacy is *iure divino*, then in having bishops the English church has no need of a pope, a claim directly analogous in structure and function to James's *iure divino* claims for monarchy. It was not without insight that James insisted that no bishop meant no king. The third dimension which had been magisterially adumbrated by Hooker was the argument that any church must evolve in keeping with the community it served; its office was specific to the character of the flock. His defence of the English church provided a variation upon arguments that had long been used to distinguish the nature

---

[63] Diarmaid McCulloch, 'Richard Hooker's Reputation', *English Historical Review*, 117 (2002), pp. 773–88.
[64] Lancelot Andrewes, *Tortura Torti* (1609); Donne, *Pseudo-Martyr*, ch. 3.
[65] George Downhame, *Two Sermons* (1607, 1609), although in George Downhame, *A Defence of the Sermon* (1611), the position is qualified, p. 2.

of an office from contingent physicality.[66] To this was added a third localising force making it possible to accept Rome as a church for offshore people, while denying it any authority over a national church founded in the consent of the English. This was Richard Field's contribution. The visible church of Christendom was comprised of self-governing separate churches. Synods provided the means of dealing with any ecclesiological disputes, so conciliarism became again an alternative to the bogus supremacy of Rome. Such arguments helped fuse the rhetorics of reformation and patriotism for a further generation.[67]

Antonio De Dominis' *De respublica ecclesiastica* presented a broader position, for he had perforce to counter the supreme Jesuit Francisco de Suarez, who taking up the cudgels from Bellarmine insisted that the oath was an heretical abuse of office, a tyrannous over-extension of James's title. By virtue of his care for souls and true religion, the pope, as pastor, had a right of excommunication and deposition, and was absolute. Entailed in this aggressive reiteration of the duty to force-feed his sheep was the papal right to release men from improper oaths.[68] De Dominis, rehearsing the abuse of papal power in a way that was encouraging both in England and Venice, reasserted a conciliarist ideal and elaborated on Paolo Sarpi's fundamentally Marsilian analysis of the causes of Christendom's troubles. The abuses of the church were systemic and based on wilful misreading of the Bible. By interfering with temporal matters, its own office was corrupted and Christendom destabilised. The absolute papal monarch had become a tyrant. James's position on the oath of allegiance was re-affirmed and re-stated in the face of excommunication with temporal teeth. De Dominis's Jacobean counterblast assumed a sense of almost cosmic threat.[69]

Either, then, Rome was alien to England, its imperialism transforming it into a Gygean shepherd; or, to those more unbending than Field, Hooker, and even De Dominis, Rome was Antichrist, the inverted projection of religious office. This proposition had been put forward by John Ponet in the most incendiary fashion, and it remained current in the rabid, or strategic anti-Catholicism of late Elizabethan and early Jacobean England. By turns both these positions were adopted after

---

[66] See Kantorowicz, *The King's Two Bodies*, pp. 294ff.
[67] Richard Field, *Of the Church* (1606).
[68] Suarez, *Defensio fidei Catholicae*, 3.23.17, 10–11; this is a brutal and, in other contexts of argument, probably a useless summary of a sophisticated reformulation of medieval hierocratic theory.
[69] For accounts of De Dominis, see Patterson, *James VI&I*, ch. 7; and Noel Malcolm, *De Dominis (1560–1624): Venetian, Anglican, Ecumenicist, and Relapsed Heretic* (London, 1984).

1605, not least by James himself, whose audience was sufficiently diverse to need a range of arguments. In the *Apologie* he had only raised the spectre of Rome as Antichrist. In the *Praemonition*, however, he took the matter further in a way that sits ill with Patterson's image of James as the moderate remediator. In a substantial digression, James heightened accusations he had only insinuated before his succession to the English throne, and concluded directly that the pope indeed rode the pale horse and his time was due.[70] This might have encouraged other Protestant princes and reassured some of his co-religionists in Scotland.[71] He might even have expected a distant cheer from beleaguered Venice, but, in fact, a frustrated Paolo Sarpi rounded on James's efforts: the king's office was in government and action (arms and money for the Republic, please), not in theological discourse.[72] Under circumstances that engendered a reflexive sensitivity to the assumed office of participants in debate, James may have anticipated such a reaction.[73] Scholastic disputation, he had accepted, was not proper for a king whose calling was 'to set forth decrees in the Imperative mood'.[74] Yet unashamed of the deed of writing to warn his fellow princes of Antichrist, he reminded them that the office of a king lies both in leaving the liberties of others and in maintaining his own. James's arguments must have intimated rather worrying imperatives for his loyal Catholics, followers of Antichrist for whom the oath was apparently such an 'Acte of great favour and clemancie'.[75]

Despite, then, the adjustable nature of James's arguments, the variety and intensity of dispute, the Gunpowder Plot controversy was bound by an unbroken thread – how and at what points could the spiritual and temporal offices be distinguished and related? These were old issues, and so the whole culture of Christendom was evoked, or its unwanted implications lurked like a fellow with matches in the interstices of argument. Curiously, the problems of distinction and separation were only aggravated when explored with reference to that instantiation of offices in collision, an oath – a spiritual act concerning temporal conduct. To be sure, the controversies did much to refine and make notions of sovereignty immediate. Yet because James and most of his supporters seemed to begin any defence of the oath from a presumption that there was some

---

[70] James VI&I, *Apologie*, p. 272; *Praemonition*, pp. 308–28; cf. *A Fruitful Meditation* (Edinburgh, 1588), in *Workes*.
[71] James VI&I, *Praemonition*, p. 72; Patterson, *James VI&I*, pp. 95–6.
[72] Paolo Sarpi, letter to S. Contarini, 13 December 1615, in Bowsma, *Venice*, p. 526.
[73] For example, Donne, *Pseudo-Martyr*, Preface, p. B3r.
[74] James VI&I, *Praemonition*, p. 290.
[75] *Ibid.*, pp. 291, 338; cf. Patterson, *James VI&I*, p. 78.

demarcation between spiritual and sovereign power, Jacobean absoluteness in rule was asserted always on the cusp of compromise.

VI

The oath of allegiance insisted with laborious repetition that it must be sworn sincerely, without equivocation or mental reservation, as the words were normally understood. These formulas echoed down the rest of the century but were never empty. They attested to the fear not just of insincerity, but the English Jesuit doctrine of equivocation. At risk were the integrity of all oath-taking, human trust and the destruction of social office, because ultimately the very function of language was perverted by it.

The doctrines were developed by Henry Garnet and especially by Robert Parsons, during the oath of allegiance controversy. The fundamental argument had been an immediate response to the pressures of Elizabethan policy, and the trial of the poet Robert Southwell in 1595. Like James's articulation of the absoluteness of the Scottish monarchy, its importance was increased in the aftermath of the Gunpowder Plot. The claim was that under exceptional circumstances of persecution, the true believer was justified in avoiding questions and concealing the truth, for this was not to lie. If, to cite the salient case, a priest was hiding in your house, it was right to conceal him. When asked by his hunters if you knew where he was, it was right to say 'no', reserving to God the full statement, 'at least not for you to find'. In this way, the priest might be saved and God honoured with the truth.[76] Equivocation, then, was a circumnavigation of dishonesty through a mental reservation serving the overall scope of the statement, the act it was trying to bring about, or thwart.

The spurious ingenuity of the doctrine had a partially linguistic source. The trick lay in converting a necessary feature of language into a redescriptive strategy. From medieval times it had been recognised that many if not all statements were incomplete because dependent upon networks of implicit understanding and presupposition. This came to be seen as a vital feature of promissory oaths. Insofar as meaning depended not just on internal structure but also upon the tacit and contextual, a statement was held to be of a mixed mode. John Austin would develop a philosophy

---

[76] See, especially, Henry Garnet, *A Treatise of Equivocation* (1595); Parsons, *A Treatise Tending Towards Mitigation*; for a lucid discussion, Toulmin and Jonsen, *The Abuse of Casuistry*, pp. 195–215; at greater length see the excellent survey by Johann Sommerville, 'The New Art of Lying', in Lietes, ed., *Conscience and Casuistry*, at length.

of language analysis on a similar basis; and in a related fashion it lies behind the Derridean theory of *différance*. Martin Azpilcueta (Navarrus, b. 1492) developed the theory of mixed modes in the Jesuitical direction through a concept of *amphibologia*. The word was chosen carefully, for behind it lay in the traditional Greek rhetorical notion of *amphiboly*, the process of casting general terms wide, like a fisherman's net, to catch a diversity of auditor.[77] *Amphiboly* exploited ambiguities and differences of meaning in language and was a form of *skiagraphia*, the verbal painting with a broad brush necessary when dealing with a large, unknown audience.[78] *Amphibologia*, however, involved a process of distancing oneself from the words spoken, and this resulted in a mixed mental operation, extending away from irony and litotes, the tropes that were most akin to it. According to Perez Zagorin, *Enchiridion* was much used in Jesuit education, and as Garnet pressed the matter, *amphibologia* went well beyond irony or litotes, for the recognition that either trope was governing a statement would undo any mental reservation. Equivocation became as dramatic a form of redescription as definitionally equivocal metaphor; both could be lumped together as lies.[79]

There was also a clear moral imperative behind equivocation; it was because lying was such a sin that the persecuted felt a need to generate an alternative to it. But, more immediately, the logic of the ethics of office came into play. Rights adhered to *personae* in office, not to office-abuse. Further, insofar as the soul and its duty of subordination to God took precedence over any other relationship, then honesty before God was what really mattered. Likewise, the Jesuits effected a more general evaporation of sin. A distinction would be drawn between philosophical and theological sin, only the latter, comprising acts consciously and purposely directed by the soul against God, were unforgivable. All others might be mitigated, or dissolved by the priest in the confessional, when considering the scope, or point of the action concerned and the knowledge of the sinner. This was an extension of priestly authority that would prove no more palatable to Jansenists in France than equivocation had to so many in England.[80] Casuistry that directed attention to the end or scope of any practice might encourage people to break oaths in the name of the scope of an oath, and so, irrespective of bad faith, oaths

---

[77] Navarrus, *Enchiridion* (1549), see Zagorin, *Ways of Lying*, pp. 165–70.
[78] Aristotle, *Rhetoric*, trans. W. Rhys Roberts (New York, 1954), 1414a, 5–10, p. 186.
[79] See, most succinctly, Reeves, *Truth and Falsity*.
[80] See the excellent discussion in Kilcullen, *Sincerity and Truth*, pp. 16–53. See also Anon., *The Jesuit's Gospel* (1679), pp. 23–33.

might be sworn too lightly.[81] And the more general the language in which the scope of the oath was formulated, the less restrictive its actual terms became.

For many, equivocation was tantamount to lying, for like hidden irony, it involved intention to deceive. The Jesuits were aware of this and its destructive consequences if used beyond clerical office. This, however, was to rest on an authority not granted in Protestant England, and equivocation was unacceptable to many Catholics who also condemned it and helped isolate the Jesuits from Christian respectability.[82] It was widely agreed that this was a new and unheard-of doctrine, which was not quite true, as Parsons emphatically argued.[83] But in such debates newness was as much an accusation as an empirical assertion, the force of which was to undermine any grounding that the Jesuits might offer from classical rhetoric and the New Testament.

There were two main lines of argument taken up more or less in tandem. First, at a meta-level, as a theory, the doctrine was misdescription at its most dangerous. The very term equivocation was a redescription of a lie.[84] Second, as a practice, it destroyed reliability and trust in language itself. Because, as everyone accepted, language was imperfect, communication depended upon competence, good will and trust. With these, definition, example, clarification could minimise the ambiguities of equivocal terms. The oath, in fact, was a prime case of the attempt to shore up trust in society and overcome the limitations of ordinary language use. Equivocation as a tactic of language, however, was another matter. It rendered every word uncertain, because a reserved completion might contradict whatever was said.[85] Every word, as it were, suffers a *différance* in Derridean terms and we cannot know where we

---

[81] Shakespeare, *King Lear* 3.4: '[I] swore as many oaths as I spake words, and broke them in the sweet face of Heaven', Edgar, feigning madness to Lear; also see Charles I, *Eikon Basilike*, p. 114; Kennett, *Dialogue*, pp. 30–2.
[82] Mason, *The New Art*, pp. B2, 25, 29, 37; Anthony Coply, *An Answer to a Letter of a Jesuitical Gentleman* (1601), pp. 198–200; see Zagorin, *Ways of Lying*, pp. 196–9.
[83] Coply, *An Answer*; and, most extensively, John Barnes, *Dissertatio contra aequivocationes* (Paris, 1625); see also the writings cited in Higgons, *A Sermon Preached at St Paul's*, pp. 54–5; Thomas Morton, *A Full Satisfaction concerning a double Romish Iniquitie* (1606); Mason, *The New Art*; contra Parsons, *A Treatise*, ch. 7, pp. 275–81, 296–306; ch. 8, pp. 313–18.
[84] Coply, *An Answer*, p. 199; for variation on this see, for example, John King, *A Sermon Preached at Whitehall* (Oxford, 1608); Robert Tynely, *Two Learned Sermons* (1609); Mason, *The New Art*, pp. 2, 12.
[85] Morton, *A Full Satisfaction*, pt. 3, pp. 47, 85; Mason, *The New Art*, ch. 1; Sommerville, 'New Art', p. 179.

stand. The upshot, as Thomas Morton revealingly put it, was to fashion a Gygean language, making plots invisible to Protestants.[86]

In sum, equivocation threatened what Hobbes would regard as a natural condition of language use, unsocial and solipsistic. As Quentin Skinner has observed, Hobbes's state of nature is a condition of the most radical *paradiastole*; only by escaping it can we establish a society.[87] The disputes between temporal and spiritual can thus be seen to be secondary to these issues, for if we have Jesuit theory and practice neither sphere of office can stand. Of course, such operatic extremes were generated by the standard tactic of argument from implication. What was crucial, however, as Mason stressed, was the uncertainty engendered by the very possibility of reservational ploys; it could even infect the oaths that had hitherto bound society together. The Jesuits were insistent that England was no longer a defensible polity, and its rulers no longer operated within their proper sphere, so if oaths and weaker social bonds are still respected, how can we know?

The ingenious convolutions attempted by Robert Parsons proved largely unconvincing in the atmosphere following the Gunpowder Plot. He assured readers that Catholics and Protestants could still live peaceably together; that equivocation was only used in extremity and when blessed by the priestly office; and that no one abhorred lying more than he. Oaths remained sacrosanct (if imposed by a proper authority within its sphere) and yet he downplayed their significance. In an uncorrupt world they would be unnecessary.[88] The Jesuits would, in fact, back away from the doctrine of equivocation, dealing with truth less in terms of a duty to tell than a right to hear, this being directly contingent on the conventional question of *personae* in office.[89]

It is not unreasonable to see the arguments over equivocation as a context for a man writing a generation later. Hobbes grew up with such controversies and they rolled on beyond his death. For the whole seventeenth century, the possibility of equivocation provided some of the tacit conditions that necessarily informed oath-taking and certainly oath formulation. Moreover, the doctrine was defended in France when Hobbes

---

[86] Morton, *A Full Satisfaction*, fol. A4, pt. 3.15; Mason, *The New Art*, pp. 21, 32–3; Donne, *Pseudo-Martyr*, p. 48: equivocation is a tower of Babel in placing its practitioners above earthly majesty and in destroying communication.

[87] Quentin Skinner, 'Hobbes on Rhetoric and the Construction of Morality', in *Visions of Politics*, vol. III, *Hobbes and Civil Science* (Cambridge, 2002), pp. 116–20.

[88] Parsons, *A Treatise*, Epistle; ch. 7 (the specific defence against Morton); ch. 8 on the antiquity and biblical basis of the doctrine. Despite the weight of Augustinian prohibitions, there was also some support from writers (uncited by Parsons) like Peter Abelard.

[89] Grotius, *De jure*, 3.1; Toulmin and Jonsen, *The Abuse of Casuistry*, pp. 211–13.

was moving in high clerical and scientific circles. Cardinal Richelieu hired Charles de Condren, a respected non-Jesuit and an influential court confessor, to write a defence of equivocation. In measured, simple but distancing prose, itself suggesting the touch of *amphibologia*, de Condren put the case that the truth might be concealed under figures, or be partially presented if circumstances were trying and the cause good. Naked truth, except to God, was not the only virtue, and it might damage the exercise of others. This modal casuistry would come back to England later in the century with the reiterations that equivocation was a theory for the confessional, and that oaths were exempt.[90] But the Jesuit head and bloody bones were too valuable as relics of the oath of allegiance controversy, and so a lurid redaction of the doctrine was but more fuel to anti-Catholic and by extension anti-clerical fires, heaped around the celebrated pre-yule log of the Gunpowder Plot itself and its ritualised recollection on the fifth of November.

---

[90] Charles de Condren, *Traité des équivoques* (Paris, 1643) in *Oeuvres complètes*, ed. Abbé Pin (Paris, 1847–8); Gabriel Daniel, *Discourses of Cleander and Eudoxus on the Provincial Letters* (1694, 1704).

14   Engagement with a free state

> [B]ut what state the body can be in, if the head, for any infermitie that can fall to it, be cut off, I leave to the readers judgement.
> (James VI&I, *The Trew Law of Free Monarchies*, in *Workes*, p. 205)

I

In the winter of 1650, the Reverend Thomas Washbourne sent his servant from his parish at Dombleton in Gloucestershire to the deeper chill of Boothby Paynell, Lincoln, with a letter for the logician and theologian Dr Robert Sanderson. It sought advice on The Engagement.[1] After the brisk execution of Charles I and the abolition of the House of Lords, England had been declared a Commonwealth and its Council of State promulgated something like an oath of allegiance to it. This Engagement required of ministers of state was extended by January 1650 to include all adult males.[2] Subscription gave a voice at law, refusal risked loss of property without redress.[3] So confronting Mr Washbourne had been an apparently simple document with apparently straightforward consequences upon his decision.

'I, A. B. declare and promise, that I will be true and faithful to the Commonwealth of England, as it is now established, without a King or House of Lords.'[4] That was all. Except, of course, it was not. As Washbourne wrote to Sanderson, oaths were sacred, so in taking this, previous oaths were undone; but perhaps circumstances had undone them already, perhaps it was not an oath, and perhaps it was something to be

---

[1] Sanderson, 'The Case of the Engagement', pp. 19–21.
[2] Gardiner, *Constitutional Documents*, pp. 380, 384; John M. Wallace, 'The Engagement Controversy, 1649–52: An Annotated Checklist of Pamphlets', *Bulletin of the New York Public Library*, 68, 6 (1964), pp. 385–6.
[3] Marchamont Nedham, *The Case of the Commonwealth Truly Stated* (1650), ed. Philip Knachel (Virginia, 1969), pp. 28–33.
[4] Gardiner, *Constitutional Documents*, p. 391.

taken in one's own sense. Just what had the imposers intended and did they have authority?[5]

The decision to impose an engagement had only been taken after considerable discussion. A confrontational version was abandoned and the one promulgated had been extended against a background of unrest.[6] It was at once a symbolic proclamation of new authority and a 'careful indulgence' for continuity of law.[7] Whether, as some hoped, it would help flush out malignancy was another matter.[8] The loyal hardly needed it, while 'malignants' and 'apostates' would not blench at equivocation and perjury.[9] The apparent displacement of a demand to 'swear', a loophole noted by Mr Washbourne, would not have escaped wider notice. As Blair Worden cites a contemporary newswriter, known royalists, swallowing the Engagement with alacrity, would vomit it up with ease.[10] This had some encouragement from the exiled Charles II and such disingenuousness was justifiable on established theories about the tacit conditions necessary for licit oaths.[11] There was, it was said, always a 'fast and loose' to promissory oaths.[12] So only tender consciences would be likely to agonise; if left to sleep they would lie, if woken by a call to engage, they would make a fuss about needing to.

None of these possibilities should have seemed strange to the imposers, for the main issues of taking oaths to conquering powers were hardly

---

[5] Sanderson, 'The Case of the Engagement', p. 19.
[6] Vallance, 'Oaths, Casuistry and Equivocation', p. 61; Wallace, 'Engagement Controversy', p. 386; Blair Worden, *The Rump Parliament* (Cambridge, 1974), pp. 213–15, 226–31; Sarah Barber, *Regicide and Republicanism: Politics and Ethics in the English Revolution, 1646–59* (Edinburgh, 1998), pp. 174–201.
[7] Warren, *The Royalist Reform'd*, p. 41.
[8] John Moyle, cited in Worden, *Rump Parliament*, p. 227; cf. Margaret Sampson, '"Giving Obedience for Peace and Quietnesse": The Political Thought of Anthony Ascham and the Engagement Controversy, 1648–50', B.A. Hons. thesis, Australian National University, undated, pp. 18–19; Jonathan Scott, *Algernon Sidney and the English Republic 1623–1677* (Cambridge, 1988), p. 93; Anthony Ascham, *A Discourse Wherein it is Examined, What is Particularly Lawful during the Confusions and Revolutions of Government* (1648), p. 84; Anon., *Arguments & Reasons to prove the inconvenience . . . of taking the New Engagement* (?1650), p. 7.
[9] Anon., *Some considerations about the nature of an oath* (1649), ms note on Folger copy. See also Wallace, 'The Engagement', p. 392; John Dury, *Objections against the taking of the Engagement answered* (1650), pp. 20–4.
[10] Worden, *The Rump Parliament*, pp. 228, 231; but according to Clarendon, *History*, bk. 9, vol. IV, pp. 499–500, it was taken as an oath and many lost office because they could not swear to it.
[11] Sanderson, 'The Case of Engagement', p. 23; Vallance, 'Oaths, Casuistry and Equivocation', pp. 64, 68.
[12] Ascham (?), *The Bounds and Bonds of Publique Obedience* (1649), p. 48; at greater length, Nedham, *Case of the Commonwealth*, pp. 41–50.

new.[13] But the Engagement controversy was played out in immediate counterpoint to *The Solemn League and Covenant* of 25 September 1643. Between it and the extended Engagement England had made a conquest of itself. Although the king's execution had harnessed well-worn arguments about tyranny releasing its victims from obligation, such casuistry could not avoid the awkward piety of *The Solemn League*.[14] It had been drawn up by a parliament at war with the king, yet swearing to defend his 'person and authority'.[15] It exemplified the 'straights and complexities' of identity in office but never encompassed casting 'the Kingdome old/ Into another Mold'.[16] It had left no room for equivocation, insisting twice that the oath was taken 'sincerely, really and constantly'. All who swore, with 'hands lifted up to the most high God' did so, as the formula had it, according to his vocation, or calling.[17] Then, in 1648, Anthony Ascham printed an argument for settlement regardless of established rights, for the government of England was already so dramatically altered that the question of obedience to an illegal regime was apparent.[18] The very totality of victory had 'destroyed the great work of time', and thus any purchase on traditional authority.[19] So now for something completely different, only six years after those pious covenanting arms had been so solemnly lifted to Heaven. It is not surprising that Mr Washbourne's servant had to saddle up and brave the long north-easterly trudge to Dr Sanderson. The advice, when it came, was instructive for its subtlety and for its insistence that the sanctity of oaths is dependent upon relationships of office.

Allegiance, Sanderson wrote, does not arise from any oath as such, but is entailed in the notion of a subject and the idea of rule. Under duress it can be suspended, but in principle, obedience to the ruler remains virtually

---

[13] J. G. A. Pocock, *Obligation and Authority in Two English Revolutions* (Wellington, 1973), pp. 6–7; Hunton, *Treatise*, pp. 4, 22–3.

[14] See, especially, *Parliament's Declaration*; Milton, *Tenure*; Cook, *King Charls His Case*; Quentin Skinner, 'Conquest and Consent: Thomas Hobbes and the Engagement Controversy', in G. E. Aylmer, ed., *The Interregnum: The Quest for Settlement* (London, 1972), pp. 79–81; Barber, *Regicide*, pp. 175–82; Gee, *A Plea*, pp. 42, 5, 49, 52.

[15] Gardiner, *Constitutional Documents*, p. 269; Clarendon, *History*, bk. 7, vol. III, pp. 206–12.

[16] Andrew Marvell, 'An Horatian Ode of Cromwell's Return from Ireland', in Elizabeth Donno, ed., *The Complete Poems* (Harmondsworth, 1978 edn), lines 35–6. Heylyn insisted, however, that overthrow was the whole point of parliament's actions, *Rebells Catechism*, pp. 5–8; Anon., *The Iniquity of the Late Solemn League or Covenant Discovered* (1643), pp. 2–4, 5–7; Anon., *Certaine Observations upon the Two Contrary Covenants* (Oxford, 1643), pp. 3–4.

[17] Gardiner, *Constitutional Documents*, pp. 268, 269.

[18] Ascham, *Discourse*; Wallace, 'The Engagement', p. 389.

[19] Sampson, 'Giving Obedience', p. 9; Marvell, 'Ode', line 34.

in the subject. Therefore, where possible, attempts should be made to restore the king. Thus also, *The Solemn League* could only have been taken in ways consistent with allegiance. As for affirming the Engagement in one's own sense, that was to be abhorred as equivocation. Yet, the new king seems to permit subscription in some fashion and there is hardly any part of the text that cannot be construed differently. Loyalty to the Commonwealth, for example, might refer to those in power, or to the nation or country, to which all patriots had a duty.[20] Through a detailed analysis, Sanderson offered two extreme readings: a 'high' one making the Engagement a sacrilegious oath to usurpers, and a 'low' one which did not preclude re-establishing allegiance to the rightful ruler. But if the document is so demonstrably ambiguous, Sanderson suggests that the real equivocation is to be found among the imposers; the Engagement was much as he had understood *The Protestation,* deliberately evasive and encompassing. But it is not, he assures Washbourne, the swearer's business to fathom motives. Invited latitude is enough to justify subscription in a 'low' sense, if it cannot be avoided altogether.[21] Equivocation might be a heinous sin but nothing illustrates its accommodating elasticity better than Sanderson's letter.

The 'protean ambiguity' of the Engagement was noted by others;[22] and it may well have encouraged acceptance. John Lilbourne illustrated just how its brevity could be exploited. Always his own man, his vindication of the Engagement was an audible slap in the face to the government.[23] Mostly, however, the print controversy was more earnest and anguished. It concentrated on adjacent issues of oath-taking in the context of office, and these presumed the document to be read in Sanderson's 'high' sense.

II

With qualification, John Wallace dates the beginning of the controversy from the publication of Francis Rous's *The Lawfulness of Obeying the Present Government,* in April 1649. Wallace's checklist of the main

---

[20] Sanderson, 'The Engagement', pp. 21–2, 24, 29; cf. Anon., *Arguments & Reasons,* pp. 3–4; cf. also Anon., *Memorandums of the Conferences held between The Brethren scrupled at the Engagement and others who were satisfied with it* (1650), pp. 12, 15–16; John Lilbourne, *The Engagement Vindicated and Explained* (1650), pp. 2–4.
[21] Sanderson, 'The Engagement', pp. 26–8, 30–4.
[22] Gee, *A Plea,* p. 10.
[23] Lilbourne, *Engagement Vindicated,* at length; Commonwealth meant the people, or the Leveller ideal; it could not mean government as trustees, any of whom could be tyrannous.

contributions is probably a statistically reliable guide to the undulations of argument. In 1649 some twenty items appeared, equally divided between those supporting the Engagement and their critics. In 1650, a further thirty-five tracts were printed (I am excluding pirated versions of Hobbes's works), twenty-three favouring subscription. In 1651, of thirteen titles, only one was hostile. In 1652 only two pro-Engagement tracts came out.[24] Additionally, Edward Gee's *Divine Right and Original of the Civill Magistrate* (1658) provides a summation of his earlier anti-Engagement arguments and there was substantial comment in newspapers, poems, broadsides and satires. Most notable was the manuscript of Marvell's 'Horatian Ode' in mid-1650, printed in 1681.[25] Finally, there is the cuckoo in the nest, *Leviathan*, the conclusion to which, with its allusions to the controversy, has had the effect of inserting the whole of Hobbes's civil philosophy into the debate. This is not without reason, as part of *The Elements of Law* and Cotton's translation of *De cive* gave the exiled Hobbes a mighty presence.[26] Because the discussion was assimilated to long-standing arguments about usurpation, conquest and tyranny, the controversy as a whole was a fly in the amber of office. The subsequent reliance on similar tests of loyalty during the Restoration, and an Engagement-like new oath of allegiance to William and Mary in 1689, made sure that the initial discussions lost none of their point. Oaths treated as necessary instruments of security, bred a nagging incubus of doubt and a good deal of hermeneutic dexterity with which the ingenuity of oath texts did battle.

The main debate probably fizzled out because after a period of uneven subscription the Engagement was repealed partially in 1653 and completely in the following year.[27] The marked preponderance of pro-Engagement tracts prior to this may evidence concerns over subscription rates, yet the new regime was surviving. In this respect, those urging

---

[24] Perhaps this should be twenty-two. Eaton's *The Oath of Allegiance* is largely taken up with 'An Answer to a Paper' attacking Eaton's original position; Wallace, 'The Engagement', p. 400.

[25] See Worden, *Rump Parliament*, p. 231, citing *A Perfect Diurnal . . . Armies* (1650); Charles Steynings, cited in David Underdown, *Somerset and the Civil War and Interregnum* (Newton Abbot, 1973), p. 158; Annabelle Patterson, *Marvell and the Civic Crown* (Princeton, 1976), p. 26. Other valuable studies are J. A. Mazzeo, 'Cromwell as Davidic King', in *Reason and the Imagination* (New York, 1962); Norbrook, *Writing the English Republic*, pp. 254–72; Christopher Wortham, 'Marvell's Cromwell Poems: An Accidental Triptych', in C. Condren and A.D. Cousins, eds., *The Political Identity of Andrew Marvell* (Aldershot, 1990), esp. pp. 16–29.

[26] Noel Malcolm, 'Charles Cotton, Translator of Hobbes's *De cive*', *Huntington Library Quarterly*, 61, 2 (2000), pp. 259–87.

[27] Glenn Burgess, 'Usurpation, Obligation and Obedience in the Thought of the Engagement Controversy', *Historical Journal*, 29 (1986), pp. 515–36.

subscription were correct: people did prefer peace to another war.[28] Broadly this would remain the case even though the government was unpopular, the Rump ridiculed and the settlement sought by the 'restless Cromwel' remained unsecured at his death.

The controversy of 1649–52 covered much the same ground as that following the oath of allegiance in 1606, but there were clear differences of emphasis. First, against a backdrop of such stark governmental change, the nature of rule itself loomed as a central issue. Second, the relationships between the temporal and spiritual guidance took on a new significance. These points need explication, for the first has been misread, the second largely overlooked.

Zagorin set the reductive terms of debate on the nature of rule: it was all a matter of right versus might.[29] While those urging refusal of the Engagement denied the Commonwealth any right to rule, those justifying subscription pointed to its might; there was no practical option but to engage with it, hence the tag 'de facto' theorists. Irrespective of Zagorin's impatient caricature, the existence of a group of de facto theorists in opposition to those adhering to the principle of de jure rule has been unchallenged.[30] A corollary to this ideological delineation has been a strong association of the de facto writers with a secular political pragmatism.[31]

The following features of argument, however, confound the accepted polarities: that the Commonwealth originated in de facto violence and that it had to be accepted out of prudence, *utilitas* or *necessitas* was largely common ground.[32] So too was the axiom that God instituted human governance. This allowed both sides to make strong moral claims about obedience to the office of rule, each relying on pragmatism and self-interest to support argument from principle. Both sides recognised that the Engagement demanded a moral commitment, so those defending it would have missed its point had they mainly urged the de facto acceptance

---

[28] Ascham, *Bounds and Bonds*, p. 11.
[29] Perez Zagorin, *A History of Political Thought in the English Revolution* (1954; New York, 1977), pp. 62–7, esp. 63, 70.
[30] For recent examples, see Conal Condren, *Thomas Hobbes* (New York, 2000), pp. 116–17; Barber, *Regicide*, pp. 188–90, on the 'defactoists'; and even Burgess, 'Usurpation, Obligation and Obedience'.
[31] Skinner, 'Conquest'; the view is more nuanced in the revised version in *Visions of Politics*, vol. III, pp. 290–3.
[32] Anon. (Nathaniel Ward?), *A Discolliminium, Or Reply to a Late Book called Bounds and Bonds* (1650), p. 1; Nedham, *Case of the Commonwealth*, title page; W. S., *The Constant Man's Character* (1650), pp. 69–70; Anon., *The exercitation answered* (1650), esp. ch. 4; the Augustinian colouring to this is clear in R. F., *Mercurius heliconicus. Or the result of a safe conscience* (1651): all crowns began as robberies.

of conquering force. It was, rather, those refusing the Engagement who took this stand and did so by insisting on a strong prejudicial dichotomy between might and right; rightful rule was not 'ambulatory' but usurpers might have to be accepted de facto.[33] In contrast, subscribers could retort that such de facto compliance actually undermined the office of rule by a 'lingering consumption';[34] and some argued that the distinction between de facto and de jure exercise of rule was spurious.[35] There was always a moral obligation to God's offices.[36] We might even conclude that modern scholars, in swallowing the refusers' formulation of the issues, have simply attached the right label, 'de facto', to the wrong people, but the problem goes deeper.

The principal point of dispute between the subscribers and refusers may be clarified with help of an analytic distinction between the vertical and horizontal extension of office. The vertical (that process by which every man might be accorded an office) has already been discussed. What is important about the subscribers, however, was the attempt to achieve, as it were, a horizontal extension from established rule, giving moral sanction to any rule that could be placed under the auspices of office. As John Rocket put it, we must obey for our soul's sake, for we are confronted with 'Error personae, non Officii, The Person not the Power'.[37] Only tyrants press a mere title, when the office is otherwise occupied.[38] It was on this basis that the subscriber Joseph Caryl was adamant. The very idea of de facto government was logically invalid: as God's office requires obedience, it can only be to those fulfilling it, and should they be killed, like officers in an army, others must replace them.[39]

---

[33] Edward Gee, *An exercitation* (1650), pp. 1–10; Gee, *Divine Right and Original*, pp. 15–18; see also *A Plea*; Anon., *The Westminsterian Iunto's Self-Condemnation* (1649), p. 7; J. Reynalds (?), *The Humble Proposals of Several Learned Divines within the Kingdom Concerning the Engagement* (1650), pp. 2–3.

[34] Anon., *Memorandums*, p. 8; see also Anon., *A word of councel to the disaffected* (1651), 'who swares to future powers, doth strife increase;/ who swares to present is a friend of peace', p. 2.

[35] For example, Nedham, *Case of the Commonwealth*, ch. 4, p. 40; N. W., *A Discourse Concerning the Engagement, or The Northern Subscribers Plea* (1650), refers to de jure and de facto only with respect to keeping oaths and indicates that one amounts to the other, p. 16.

[36] Anon., *Conscience Puzzel'd* (1651), in Malcolm, *Struggle for Sovereignty*, vol. I, p. 448; Malcolm, presumably following Julian Franklin, *John Locke and the Theory of Sovereignty* (Cambridge, 1975), attributes this to George Lawson. This may by chance be right, but no evidence has been offered and Franklin's reasoning is erroneous.

[37] Rocket, *Christian Subject*, p. 119.

[38] John Dury, *Disengaged Survey* (1650), p. 8.

[39] Joseph Caryl, *A Logical Demonstration of the Lawfulness of Subscribing to the New Engagement* (1650), p. 3; Anon., *Memorandums*, p. 7.

This horizontal extension made the range of office central and reinforced the objectification of a concept of magistracy. It was analogous to resorting to the court of equity. When the specific obligations of any office were contentious, its defining purpose came to the fore.[40] Here the protective function of rule was isolated, as modern scholars have recognised, but less as an end in itself than as the necessary condition for godly living. So protection and obedience were held to be morally, even theologically complementary. God requires us to live in peace, therefore protective office has to be continuous despite contingent occupation. Such an insistence, sometimes isolated from its ultimately theological rationale, was hardly unprecedented. Edward II had been warned of the higher obligations to office per se in the Barons' Declaration of 1307; it had been enunciated as a principle in 'Calvin's Case'; it is characteristic of Jacobean writers deemed absolutist; and at the time of the controversy, the royalist Dr Henry Hammond insisted on a firm distinction between power and those who exercised it. Some of us, remarked the subscriber N. W., have taken in this doctrine from the Schools. Others might have taken it from *King Lear*: 'A dog's obey'd in office'.[41]

On no side was a moral obligation to office as such ever denied, but whereas the subscribers traced an ultimately theological purpose for it, the refusers could qualify, or nominally transform the moral imperatives of obedience. They preferred locutions like submission, passive obedience, or suffering to obedience as expressive of a full moral reciprocity. Instead, the refusers' alternative emphasis was on the limits of magistracy; without understanding these, conscientious commitment was meaningless. Magistracy straying beyond its bounds was morally self-destructive. They would not accept a Rocket-like separation of *personae* from *officii*. But it was also the subscribers' emphasis on the divine function of rule that armed the refusers with their most effective consequentialist riposte: allegiance to 'de facto' occupation of office is destabilising.[42]

Further differences were gathered around the fault-lines of end or rationale versus limitation. For subscribers, the importance of *telos* diminished the relevance of violent origins; protective exercise of office was what mattered – something very different from tyranny, widely agreed to be protective of nothing.[43] For the refusers, tyrannous origin was

---

[40] J. G. A. Pocock, 'Political Thought in the Cromwellian Interregnum', in P. S. O'Connor and G. A. Woods, eds., *W.P. Morrell, A Tribute: Essays in Early Modern History* (Dunedin, 1973), pp. 22–3.

[41] Hammond, *A Vindication*, p. 30, an argument not addressed to the issues of engagement; N. W., *A Discourse*, p. 8; Anon., *Memorandums*, p. 8; Shakespeare, *King Lear* 4.6.

[42] Gee, *Exercitation*, pp. 12–13, 81.

[43] Nedham, *Case of the Commonwealth*; the very term usurpation is slanderous, ch. 5, p. 41.

crucial: foundational de facto force contaminated subsequent exercise of office, so the republic was condemned.[44] With the relationship between tyranny of origin and exercise being glossed so differently, opposing conclusions were drawn from the brassy mouth of providence. As Caryl argued, because both sides in the Civil Wars had appealed to God, the result was reasonably read as providential, underscoring His moral requirement to obey; the Israelites had obeyed David after the death of Saul.[45] For the refusers, William Prynne retorted that English history was full of providential punishment for rebels, and a number of those who had taken the Engagement had suddenly died and one had committed suicide: Caryl, take note.[46] The arguments were never clinching on either side. The shared assumption that the ruling office was God-given for protection insufficiently overcame what was at times *un dialogue de sourds* – allegiance to office opposed to allegiance to the right *personae* only within their sphere. The normally complementary aspects of office, function and limit became for a while competing doctrines, nudging each other as they passed in the night, and having contact more with respect to the imponderables of consequence than principle. The problem of *aliud distinctio, aliud separatio* when dealing with *persona* and office remained irresolvable. Once the contest over the moral category of office is revealed as common ground, the division between pragmatism versus principle, de facto versus de jure can be seen to have distorted genuine differences almost as much as the trivialising banality of might versus right. In a word, there was no de facto camp of theorists but there was, as will become evident in the following chapter, an increasingly shared de facto idiom of accusation; de facto acquisition of office and merely de facto submission to it countered each other across an ethical chasm. Selective reliance on these confused echoes has helped create the myth of an emerging ideology.

IV

A second less sustained aspect of the argument was a further variation on the clash of spiritual and temporal offices after 1606. Many of those who agonised over the Engagement were ministers, displaying a clerical

---

[44] Anon., *An enquiry* (1649); Anon., *The Westminsterian Iunto's Self-Condemnation*, p. 6, insisted on a people cozened not conquered.
[45] Caryl, *Logical Demonstration*, pp. 5–6; also N. W., *Discourse*, p. 7. Anon., *Conscience Puzzel'd*, p. 438. The centrality of providence was first emphasised by Wallace, 'The Engagement', pp. 384–5, but most significantly explored by Burgess, 'Usurpation, Obligation and Obedience'.
[46] William Prynne, *A Brief Apologie for all Non-Subscribers* (1650), pp. 2–6, 12–13.

persona and exercising spiritual office in giving guidance. At what point, however, did this become meddling in matters of state? The admonitory Hugh Latimer might well have insisted that there should be no 'mingle mangle' between the dues of God and Caesar; but who was to distinguish mingle from mangle?[47] In the Engagement controversy we find warnings by divines, especially by the prolific John Dury, about self-discrediting clerical interference. The civil magistrate had authority for this world; the priest's was just a watchman's office over the soul, and in exceeding their calling priests worked against Christ's model, and caused disruption; and please, gentlemen, some public decorum, or no one will take us seriously.[48] It was much in the idiom of Richard Sheldon's earlier warnings to Rome. There were laymen who re-enforced the point, not without unseemly glee. There was a 'pack of old puritans' on both sides argued one; Dury himself was an example of exploded credibility, concluded another.[49] 'Clergy men', wrote Albertus Warren (gent) always 'neigh after new quarrels', seeing themselves as 'Gods little special ones', standing in their pulpits, doing evil that good may come of it; but discretion is superior to their authority, for the 'Parsons anger is not as the breath of Gods nostrils'.[50] When Nedham also applied the conventional honorific '(gent)' to his authorship of *The Case for the Commonwealth*, it carried this implicitly anti-clerical force. Battle-lines may even have been drawn between the counselling offices of priest and lawyer. As one tract surmised, ministers might not take the Engagement because lawyers would.[51] Conversely, the author of *The Plea* was adamant: we have no wish to move beyond our sphere but within it we will move freely.[52] Ministers will be discredited as 'men of ductile spirits and prostituted consciences', condemned as equivocators should they be forced to subscribe to an ensnaring oath.[53] It is not difficult to understand the variable mix of defensiveness and hostility. Presbyterian clerics had been foremost among those lifting their hands to Heaven in the days of *The Solemn League* (a point relished by their enemies);[54] and there is more than a whiff of disingenuousness in

---

[47] Latimer, *Fruitful Sermons*, fol. 94v.
[48] John Dury, *A Case of Conscience Resolved* (1649), pp. 1–2, 5–6, 10–12; J. D. (John Dury), *Just Re-Proposals to Humble Proposals* (1650), pp. 18–19, 21; Anon., *Considerations*, pp. 11–13, 25.
[49] Anon., *A Pack of Old Puritans* (1650), p. 1–2; Anon., *The Time Serving Proteus . . . Uncas'd to the World* (1650).
[50] Warren, *Royalist Reform'd*, pp. 16–22, 26, 29–30.
[51] Anon., *A Discolliminium*, p. 40; see also Warren, *Royalist Reform'd*, chs. 2–3.
[52] Gee, *A Plea*, p. 5; see also Anon., *A Brief Answer to the Late Resolves of the Commons* (1649); the Commons as constituted has no authority, p. 3, and must stop interfering with priestly office, pp. 4–6.
[53] Reynalds (?), *Humble Proposals*, pp. 4, 5, 6.
[54] Anon., *The Westminsterian Iunto's Self-Condemnation*, p. 3.

so many clerics wearing their pondering consciences on the preambles of their pamphlets. When we get to the meat of Gee's *Exercitation*, we hear not the voice of considered moral judgement, but implacable hostility to Cromwell, thinly disguising the desire for continued hostilities. It was a case of what Dury considered priestly obtrusion. Conversely, the unctuous Rocket, displaying pious humility through a prayerful prolegomenon, unfrocks himself as an egregious Cromwellian.[55]

One feature of debate is that it brought abstruse nostrums down to earth. For it was conducted not by people calmly reflecting on bloody origins in antiquity: 'So when they did design/ The Capitol's first Line/ A bleeding Head where they begun,/ Did fright the Archetects to run'.[56] Rather, it was between those who had seen the heads bobbing under the bridge. The advice was for ordinary people suddenly living under new princes; it approached the obverse of Machiavellian casuistical coinage.[57] But what sort of *persona* had authority to advise? Issues of office have moved from Christendom and the swords of kings and popes to people in the parlour and parish church. Between them, Francis Rous's *Lawfulness*, and the anonymous *Grand Case for Conscience* did most to establish the terms of debate and can now be used to flesh out the argument.

V

Rous's contribution followed hot on parliament's *Declaration* and was re-printed the following year, no doubt to encourage taking the extended Engagement. The *Declaration* had attempted to justify the tyrannicide of Charles, and implicitly accepted that re-shaping the office of rule to avoid tyranny was itself beyond the normal compass of law. Rous's complementary argument was an elegantly structured casuistic exercise, moving from theological axioms to the present situation, concluding with a resolution to the problem of reneging on *The Solemn League*. He argued that although the change in government might be believed unlawful, 'yet it may be lawfully obeyed'.[58] Lawful obedience might mean mere

---

[55] Gee, *Exercitation*, p. 66; Rocket, *Christian Subject*, at length.
[56] Marvell, 'Ode', lines 67–70.
[57] Irene Coltman, *Private Men and Public Causes* (London, 1962), p. 199, makes this point about Ascham; Nedham, *Case of the Commonwealth*, refers obliquely to the newness of many princes with reference to Machiavelli, ch. 4, p. 35; Mazzeo, 'Cromwell as Davidic King', pp. 29, 42–5; but the qualification is crucial given the moral tone of debate.
[58] The significance of Rous is made particularly clear by Skinner, 'Conquest', in *Visions of Politics*, pp. 291–6; Francis Rous, *The Lawfulnes of Obeying the Present Government* (1649), re-printed in Malcolm, *Struggle for Sovereignty*, vol. I, p. 396.

compliance to a 'de facto' power, or justly required.⁵⁹ It was the moral claim that Rous set out to establish.⁶⁰

All power was of God, and at Romans 13 there was an injunction to obey the higher powers. The reliance on this had an irresistible attraction, for it had been prominent in royalist Civil War polemic. Now it expressed the fundamental principle of official reciprocity and intimated continuity despite the execution of Charles. Power as office clothed persons in authority.⁶¹ Rous relied on the familiar distinction between the acquisition and exercise of this authority, arguing that the rule of the Emperor Claudius, beginning in violence, was nevertheless legitimate for its exercise.⁶² In England, until the sixteenth century, barely three monarchs in a row came to power 'by true lineal succession', yet they were obeyed.⁶³ Understandably so, for, Rous insists in a shift to consequentialism, confusion is even worse than tyranny. We need always to consider, then, 'the maine end of Magistracie, to live a peaceable life in godlinesse and honesty'.⁶⁴ As he cites James VI&I, the king exists for the commonwealth not the commonwealth for the king, so we must not destroy the end for the means. An appeal to *utilitas* and the point of any form of rule thus supports the initial theological axiom.⁶⁵

Rous then turns directly to the sticking point of oaths. They are normally sacrosanct, but 'to impossible things there is no obligation'.⁶⁶ We

---

[59] See also Anthony Ascham (?), *A Combate between Two Seconds* (1649); Anon., *A briefe resolution of that grand case of conscience* (1650), pp. 5–6; Caryl, *Logical Demonstration*, p. 5; the somewhat chaotic *Conscience Puzzel'd* shifts between these senses of lawful within a few paragraphs, pp. 438 and 440–1.

[60] Nedham, *Case of the Commonwealth*, chs. 2–5; and especially Caryl, *Logical Demonstration*, pp. 1–3.

[61] The argument had been attacked by John Canne, *The Golden Rule* (1649), in ways that might have forewarned Rous of what was to come. Rous, *Lawfulnes*, pp. 396, 399; see also Rocket, *Christian Subject*, pp. 115–20; Anon., *Exercitation Answered*, chs. 3–4; Anon., *A word of councel*: God demands obedience to the higher powers and rewards commitment with peace, p. 2.

[62] Rous, *Lawfulnes*, p. 396; see also Nedham, *Case of the Commonwealth*, chs. 1–2 for biblical and Roman examples of dubious acquisition.

[63] Rous, *Lawfulnes*, pp. 398, 399; see also Ascham, *Combate*; Lewis de Moulin, *The Power of the Magistrate* (1650); Nedham, *Case of the Commonwealth*, chs. 1–2, ch. 4, pp. 37–8.

[64] Rous, *Lawfulnes*, pp. 400–1; see also Rocket, *Christian Subject*, p. 116; Dury, *Disengaged Survey*, on the text of Romans 12: 18; Nedham, *Case of the Commonwealth*, ch. 3, pp. 30–1, ch. 5, pp. 41–2.

[65] See also, for example, Ascham, *Bounds and Bonds* (1649); Anthony Ascham, *Reply to a Paper* (1650), p. 50; N. W., *Discourse*; Dury, *Considerations* (1649); Nedham, *Case of the Commonwealth*, Appendix, pp. 135–9; de Moulin, *Power of the Magistrate*, accepts this would include the rule of the Turk, pp. 29–31.

[66] Rous, *Lawfulnes*, p. 401; Dury, *Disengaged Survey*, p. 10; Richard Saunders, *Plenary possession* (1651); John Dury, *Conscience eased* (1651); Ascham, *Bounds and Bonds*, pp. 38–66; Nedham, *Case of the Commonwealth*, ch. 5.

cannot keep that part of *The Solemn League* touching the king, but we should keep that concerning the purity of religion and requiring obedience to Charles's heirs and successors. Obedience to Henry VII as the successor to Richard III was a clear precedent.[67] Thus, the contradictions between *The Solemn League* and the Engagement are exaggerated. As a piece of presumptive casuistry, Rous's argument may be summarised as an enthymeme: rule is ordained by God; whoever rules fulfils the main end of the office, therefore we should obey; so too with oaths in microcosm. We can swear only to what is possible; therefore, having sworn, we should keep what we can. In sum, acquisition of power may be de facto, exercise is not, so allegiance to office in exercise is a moral, not a de facto requirement.

It was this erasure of a concept of de facto exercise that provoked the author of *The Grand Case*. Obedience to the unlawful is unethical. Rous has loosened our sense of obligation by ignoring the crucial question – by what right can our inheritance be changed?[68] Any justification in terms of convenience is unacceptable.[69] Convenience gives a thin guarantee that soldiers will be paid.[70] Having set the scene pragmatically, the author follows the development of Rous's case. Romans 13 has been misunderstood.[71] Obedience to higher powers means only properly constituted power. Of course, the law of nature allows compliance as self-defence.[72] He himself would submit to the conquerors.[73] A wife, however, is obliged to obey her lawful husband; she has no duty to a murdering impostor, although she may be forced to submit de facto.[74] Moral obligation, therefore, assumes a limit to action within an office. It follows that the extension of the range of office leaves us with 'the greatest inlet to tyranny ... and the speediest means of destroying states that could be invented: for none should govern ... any ... longer than their swords ... could bear

---

[67] Rous, *Lawfulnes*, pp. 401–3.
[68] Anon., *The Grand Case for Conscience Stated* (1649), re-printed in Malcolm, *Struggle for Sovereignty*, vol. I, pp. 408–33; see also Gee, *A Plea*, pp. 21–39.
[69] This would not bother Samuel Eaton, *A Resolution of Conscience* (1650), pp. 7, 8–48, Samuel Eaton, *The Oath of Allegiance and the National Covenant Proved to be non-Obligatory* (1650), p. 2; cf. Anon., 'An Answer to a Paper', in Eaton, *The Oath*, pp. 10–18; Edward Gee, *A vindication* (1650).
[70] Anon., *Grand Case*, p. 408.
[71] See also Nathaniel Ward (?), *A Religious Demurrer* (1649), postscript; Gee, *Exercitation*; and, at greater length, *Divine Right*, b3, pp. 5ff.
[72] Anon., *Grand Case*, pp. 414, 409–11, 419; Anon, 'An Answer to a Paper', in Eaton, *The Oath*, p. 17; Anon., *Second part of the Religious Demurrer*, pp. 2–3.
[73] Anon., *Grand Case*, p. 417; see also Anon. (Robert Sanderson), *A Resolution of Conscience in Answer to a Letter Sent with Mr. Ascham's Book*, in *Works*, p. 3; Anon., *Second part*; Gee, *A Plea*, pp. 27–9; Anon., 'An Answer to a Paper', p. 7.
[74] Anon., *Grand Case*, p. 410; Anon., 'An Answer to a Paper', p. 7.

them up.'⁷⁵ But right, the author insists, is not so easily extinguished. The imprisoned husband, unable to fulfil connubial duty, remains a husband.⁷⁶

Rous's historical analogues are dismissed: that the Romans submitted to emperors tells us nothing about right. Rome was never sworn 'to a particular government as we have been. Things in themselves indifferent are made necessary, when by an oath engaged to.' The legendary instability of English monarchy existed within a sort of constitutional structure that accommodated deviation from strict primogeniture.⁷⁷ But now we see only 'a minor part relict' of previous legality and the country governed by 'bustling Colonels', confronting 'committees with their arguments by their sides'.⁷⁸

As for oaths, circumstances can make keeping them impossible, a case hardly to be pleaded by those who first destroyed their monarch. A woman is not released from her marriage bonds by murdering her husband. We were obliged to obey the entire *Covenant*; if we swore to all when only part could be kept, that itself is a sin.⁷⁹ And, manifestly, the obedience to the king's heirs and successors did not encompass anyone who should succeed.⁸⁰ The implicit injunction throughout is to avoid moral obfuscation through the misuse of the Bible to support a usurping regime. Such confusion creates the illusion of a clear conscience, which can only have the practical consequence of perpetuating instability. Rous had urged that the scope of government must always be considered, being a means to the ends of peace and godliness. The author responds that 'he that destroys the means in its tendency to the end, will scarcely preserve that end'. Rous's overall emphasis on the conditions needed for a godly life is countered by a similar insistence on the conditions necessary for a moral commitment to those in office. He finishes his refutation with the motto of anti-casuistic rectitude: let us not do evil that good may come of it.⁸¹ When de facto possession displaces office held de jure, de facto compliance is all that can be expected.

---

[75] Anon., *Grand Case*, pp. 412, 420; Anon., *Second part*, p. 6; Gee, *Exercitation*, pp. 12–14; see also, at length, Anon., *Trayters deciphered* (1650).
[76] Anon., *Grand Case*, p. 420; also Anon., *A Copie of a Letter* (1650), p. 5.
[77] Anon., *Grand Case*, p. 414; see also Anon., *Second part*.
[78] Anon., *Grand Case*, pp. 416, 422–3; also Gee, *Exercitation*, p. 6; Anon., *The Westminsterian Iunto's Self-Condemnation*, pp. 2–3.
[79] Anon., *Grand Case*, pp. 425, 424, 427; see also Anon., *Second part*; Sanderson, *Resolution*; Gee, *Vindication*; and Anon., *A Plea for Non-Subscribers to the Engagement* (1650), pp. 39–66.
[80] Anon., *Grand Case*, p. 429; much the same position was adopted by Richard Vines and Richard Baxter, see Lamont, *Richard Baxter*, p. 173, and n.
[81] Anon., *Grand Case*, pp. 420, 433 (Romans 3: 8); cf. Anon., *Conscience Puzzel'd*, p. 440; Anon., *Copie of a Letter*, p. 6.

VI

There is an unusual piquancy to Anthony Ascham's *Confusions*. It repaired the sort of case put forward by Rous, and the Commonwealth rewarded its author with a diplomatic mission beyond its protective reach to Spain. Ascham had presciently remarked on the 'ticklish and deplorable' conditions 'of those who live upon frontiers'.[82] Almost on arrival, he was murdered by exiled royalists who had entered his lodgings as merchants.[83] *The Confusions* is given a double relevancy to this work by being re-printed, as a 'seasonal' commentary on the Revolution of 1688–9.[84] Its first and second editions place it alongside *Leviathan* and the *Two Treatises*, respectively, with each of which it has decided affinities.

Ascham's argument provides an emphatic horizontal extension of the office of rule. Any government is a contingent superstructure upon the community. As he quotes Augustine, 'what matters it under whose government we, who are hourly expiring, Live, if they, (who ere they be that rule over us) command us not in Impious things?'[85] Consider rather the protective purpose of rule allowing a peaceful and godly life.[86] The safety of the people being the supreme law, they have a reciprocal duty to obey.[87]

Rule, then, the condition for all social goods and godly living, is a locus of authority, and by virtue of that is to be obeyed.[88] As expedience agrees with this moral requirement, the perplexities concerning obedience are assuaged.[89] Ascham accepts that the violences in the acquisition of office do not transmute into virtue, a point conceded to the refusers; but a firm distinction between might and right is irrelevant in need to escape a state of war. We do so by accepting a 'narrower swing of Liberty' under some form of rule than might otherwise be enjoyed.[90] Society, as it were,

---

[82] Ascham, *Confusions*, p. 44.
[83] Edmund Ludlow, *Memoirs*, 3 vols. (Vivay, 1698–9), vol. I, p. 291.
[84] Ascham, *Confusions* (1649, 1689), Advertisement.
[85] *Ibid.*, pp. 163, 158, 134, cf. Augustine, *De civitate Dei*, bk. 5, ch. 17.
[86] Ascham, *Confusions*, p. 125; see also pp. 21, 24–5, 107–8; Ascham, *Combate*, p. 13. This hardly suggests the meaningless universe or anti-social attitudes Coltman oddly attributes to him in *Private Men*, p. 208.
[87] Ascham, *Confusions*, pp. 115, 107, 125–6, 112; see also Ascham, *Combate*, p. 15; Ascham, *Bounds and Bonds*, p. 24. It is misleading to say, as Coltman has, that rulers and ruled have no shared interests and inhabit different moral universes, *Private Men*, p. 201, if they are joined in reciprocal obligations.
[88] Ascham, *Confusions*, pp. 10, 32, 131, 136, 151–2; it makes no sense to call Ascham 'anti-authoritarian', Coltman, *Private Men*, pp. 203, 234.
[89] Ascham, *Confusions*, p. 154; see also Rocket, *Christian Subject*, p. 115; Nedham, *Case of the Commonwealth*, ch. 3.
[90] Ascham, *Confusions*, pp. 33, 24–5, 108, 109.

converts a destructive natural liberty into the liberty of office entailed in relationships of government. We are driven to this by the need for self-preservation: everything inside the skin does its best to save it.[91] So, too, accepting a new rule is not an open door to instability; the people for and on behalf of whom Ascham writes want only peace and quiet.

Unlike Rous, Ascham does not burn his fingers on the text of Romans 13. Neither does he avoid the problem of tyranny, setting down criteria to delineate effective rule from tyrannous excess. One criterion lies in the theological imperative to lead a godly life, interference with which is contrary to the end of government. This informs the whole discussion. As Ascham insists, quoting James VI&I and the oath of allegiance, obedience was never against 'faith and salvation to soules'.[92] Additionally, there is an excursus into the notions of money and property. It contradicts the view that the new regime was a tyranny of exercise and the sequestration of malignants' property was theft of the pudding. Refusers played upon the relationship between theft and tyranny; but the attention Ascham gives to property may also have been occasioned by the demonisation of the Levellers as wanting to destroy all property relationships.[93]

The natural condition makes *meum* and *tuum* meaningless, so society introduces variable rules of ownership and the attendant institution of money. Subsistence property is the equivalent to life, and the function of rule is to protect life and property in this minimal sense. Invasion of property thus suffices as a criterion for distinguishing protective office from tyranny.[94] Surplus property is different. Only God owns all; we are as stewards in the world and balancing our right to subsistence is our duty to give charitably – points usually insisted upon by divines. In extremity, the necessitous poor are effectively in a state of war and may take what they need.[95] Government, then, having duties to everyone under its protection, may alter contingent property relationships to that end. The difference between rule and tyranny is as precarious as the line between tax and theft. Allegiance is destroyed when the ruler attacks people and property, inhibits a godly life, or when protection ceases. These cases

---

[91] *Ibid.*, p. 4; but see Anon. (Sanderson), *A Resolution of Conscience*, p. 5.
[92] Ascham, *Confusions*, pp. 125–6.
[93] Nedham, *Case of the Commonwealth*, pt. 2, ch. 4; on the anxiety over property and theft, see J. M. Beattie, *Policing and Punishment in London, 1660–1750* (Oxford, 2002 edn), ch. 1 and pp. 277ff; Ascham, *Confusions*, p. 18; the anti-Engagement *Copie of a Letter* accepts that if appropriation of property had been the primary intention, a more demanding oath would have been insisted upon, p. 10.
[94] Ascham, *Confusions*, pp. 79, 4, 15, 22; Ascham cites Machiavelli approvingly: 'a man will not lament so much the losse of his publique Parent, as of his private Patrimony', p. 74.
[95] *Ibid.*, pp. 47, 13–14.

make the ruler a private person. Nero virtually declared he would not govern when he set Rome alight; a father attempting to destroy his child is no father.[96] Right, therefore, attaches only but always to the office in exercise: the people can do an ex-ruler no wrong. Again we see an explication of the presupposition that offices are populated by *personae*; the problem of obedience lies in whether we can separate or only distinguish one from the other.

At the junction of temporal things and 'salvation to soules' grew the thorny issue of oaths. For Ascham they were fundamental social ties; the problem here was to stop them rubbing against the protective scope of rule. He defined an oath as 'a Religious attestation of God where we assert or Promise that which is lawfull and in our Power, and is then at its height when we put ourselves under Gods severe wrath if we deal fraudulently'.[97] There are, he argued, always tacit conditions, especially to promissory oaths, the uncertainties of which have led some to believe they should be unlawful.[98] Promissory oaths cease to bind by dispensation, absolution, extinction and violation, only the last of which is a sin.[99] A 'true harmony of oaths' requires only the utmost striving to keep them. Should we then fail, we are freed without guilt. If one considers the oaths among princes, they bind only insofar as they remain in power. Oaths sworn to them are compelling insofar as they are rulers, yet even oaths to tyrants must be kept if they obliged within the ambit of the law. This is to say that the obligation is to the law irrespective of the tyrant. Under all circumstances, swearing is dependent on shared language and must be in good faith, without equivocation.[100] Disapproving of casuistry in this context, and predictably citing the tag that no evil should be done, etc., etc., he nevertheless comes close to suggesting that in extremity something like dissimulation is allowable. Above all, oath-keeping is contingent upon the stability of offices and the continuity of the *personae* of those involved.

It will be evident that we need to be cautious in identifying Ascham's argument as secular. It was not in his emphasis on self-interest, for the selves, although occasionally physical beings, are more characteristically souls needing protection for God's work on earth.[101] There is a suitable irony in Irene Coltman's error in stating that *Confusions* ends

---

[96] *Ibid.*, pp. 47, 68, 79; see also, Anon., *Conscience Puzzel'd*, pp. 440-3.
[97] Ascham, *Confusions*, pp. 51, 38, 52.
[98] *Ibid.*, pp. 37, 54-7; also N. W., *Discourse*, p. 16.
[99] Ascham, *Confusions*, pp. 86-92; cf. also Nedham, *Case of the Commonwealth*, ch. 5.
[100] Ascham, *Confusions*, pp. 81-2, 86, 68-70, 61, 64-6.
[101] *Ibid.*, cf. pp. 4, 16 with pp. 316, 45, 50, 51; Burgess, 'Usurpation, Obligation and Obedience', on the unsecular nature of the debates in general.

with reference to *De civitate Dei*.[102] For the extensive quotation, some forty pages earlier, is a culmination of a powerful Augustinian theme. Additionally, *Confusions* makes persistent reference to the Bible (it ends citing Genesis 28: 20) and accepts a providential world. Oaths are so dangerous because they may excite God's wrath.

There is, however, one sense in which *Confusions* is decidedly secular. On the Jacobean assumption that a firm line can be drawn between temporal and spiritual matters, Ascham undermines the authority of the cloth to give guidance on either. His advice is a reason of state to troubled souls and he restricts the front on which advice can be given. We are born to two distinct worlds and our actions in this should never endanger our place in the next. Beyond this, however, institutionalised religion is largely a function of circumstance and internal faith removed from the mysterious workings of worldly justice.[103] We are, for example, largely ignorant of the original rights of rule. We cannot read minds, only conjecture from external signs. Conscience is but ingrained opinion. It is all unnecessary perplexity to fret about such matters, and to lay hold of what certainty there is we need no cord of clerical contrivance. Only God obliges conscience and His injunctions to live godly lives in neighbourly peace are plain enough.[104] This effective removal of the middle-man from all earthly transactions touching on salvation is to make priestly authority redundant, or spurious.

More slyly, he adapts two clerical arguments about the integrity of a church to urge acceptance of the new Commonwealth; the pervasive grounding in understandings of office facilitates the analogies. As the continuity of a church is found not in persons, but purity of doctrine, so too, with temporal rule, it is continuity of office not office-holders that matters.[105] As it takes more than occasional sin to destroy a church, so it takes more than ad hoc transgression to convert protective rule into tyranny. Ascham's challenge to priestly authority casts light on his references to natural law. Priests were conventionally the mediators of divine and, by extension, natural law, but for Ascham the natural is uncertainly connected to the divine. It is natural law that informs us of the transcendent right of self-preservation.[106] Yet the human creatures under its auspices, being souls, are locked in a relationship of official subordination to God. His argument illustrates how the divine and the natural could not

---

[102] Coltman, *Private Men*, p. 237; a possible confusion with *A Discourse*.
[103] *Ibid.*, pp. 7, 161, 196, 154.
[104] *Ibid.*, pp. 32, 44, 63–4, 78, 45.
[105] *Ibid.*, p. 137; cf. Bilson, *Christian Subjection*, pt. 2, p. 302.
[106] Ascham, *Confusions*, pp. 148, 44, 48–50, 107.

separately exist until the soul became the individual (above, chapter 6). Anti-clericalism was an impetus towards this transformation, but for Ascham it is enough that he offers consolation independently of the pulpit. If he gives advice to Everyman about how to react to new princes, he also recommends to all the *ataraxia*, the state of repose that Richard Tuck has seen as central to the Grotian response to Charron and Montaigne. Ascham's use of Grotius and his studied if conventional scepticism would support this association.[107]

VII

There is, no doubt, an irksome tidiness in concluding another chapter with a comment on Hobbes. Yet, as the Engagement controversy has been so important as a context for his theory of obligation, this is unavoidable.[108] His work was seized upon by Nedham, who having cited one royalist to show that obedience to the new government was morally required, used *De corpore politico* for a greater stress on the *self-interest* of submission.[109]

Ascham's arguments, however, suggest a more thorough and less opportunistic familiarity with Hobbes. His discussion of the natural condition as a state of war in which property rights are meaningless is at one with *The Elements*. He gives the nominalist priority to particulars over generals, and treats contract as the paradigm of law.[110] Shared also is a scepticism about heresy, conscience and direct knowledge of the mind. For each writer, in entering society there is a justifiable trade-off between natural liberty and its more restricted 'swing' under rule.[111] Although, given all this, Hobbes is properly aligned with the subscribers' cause, Ascham, like the refuser Edward Gee, thought otherwise. In his longest comment on Hobbes, he took *De cive* to insist upon an irrevocable, idolatrous allegiance to an established monarchy.[112]

This was to overlook Hobbes's insistence that no agreement can bind to impossibles;[113] and so Hobbes's explicit contribution to the Engagement debates is principally an explication. In the 'Review and Conclusion' to *Leviathan*, Hobbes sided precisely with Ascham's case. He

---

[107] Tuck, *Philosophy and Government*, pp. 172–3.
[108] See, for example, Quentin Skinner, 'The Context of Hobbes's Theory of Political Obligation', in *Visions of Politics*, vol. III: *Hobbes and Civil Science*, pp. 264ff.
[109] Nedham, *Case of the Commonwealth*, pp. 135–9.
[110] *Ibid.*, pp. 22, 24, 62.
[111] *Ibid.*, pp. 196, 128, 163–4, 109.
[112] *Ibid.*, pp. 122–3, 107; see Coltman, *Private Men*, p. 224. Gee, *Divine Origin*, p. 141.
[113] Hobbes, *Elements*, 1.15.18.

would add as a law of nature that a man is bound *'to protect in Warre, the Authority, by which he is himself protected in time of Peace'*. In the early Civil War context, this had been a sentiment much approved by royalists. Concomitantly, if a ruler can no longer function, it becomes lawful to seek a new allegiance and this is formed at the point at which an express or tacit consent can be given to a conqueror, or adverse party. It is held to be but an inference from the natural laws commanding peace adumbrated in the body of the work.[114]

I have already touched on Hobbes's deflationary treatment of oaths in the context of arguments from contract (chapter 12). It is additionally important in aligning him with the subscribers. Oaths should not be taken trivially.[115] Yet for all its associated ceremonies, any oath is purely proclamatory, '*a forme of Speech, added to a Promise*'. It 'addes nothing to the Obligation'. For if lawful, a covenant binds in God's sight regardless of any oath; if not lawful, 'it bindeth not at all'.[116] In *The Elements* he had added further qualifications, that any oath increases the risk of divine punishment should it be violated and that neither oath nor covenant binds beyond 'our best endeavour'. In this respect we are the interpreters of our obligations.[117] On this earlier doctrine, the value of any imposed oath becomes close to negligible. As I have noted, no coronation oath could be seen as a transformative contract and potentially a block for a ruler's head.

In the Engagement controversy this doctrine had direct relevance for both the coronation oath and *The Solemn League*. Mentioning neither, Hobbes marginalised both. In the immediate context of argument, then, neither oath was a barrier against the honourable acceptance of new protectors who henceforth had to be supported according to natural law. But, a fortiori, neither was the Engagement a barrier against returning to the Stuart fold should a future king be able to shepherd his flock. In diminishing the significance of oaths, Hobbes reinforced a Sandersonian 'low' reading of the Engagement.[118] And Sanderson sounds just like Hobbes in insisting that obligation arises from the nature of the relationship of sovereign and subject, not from any subsequent oath. The disadvantage for Hobbes, however, was that paving the way to an honourable peace could loosen allegiance. If oaths added nothing, support for

---

[114] Hobbes, *Leviathan*, 'Review & Conclusion', pp. 484–5.
[115] *Ibid.*, ch. 14, p. 100; also *Elements*, 1.15.16.
[116] *Leviathan*, ch. 14, pp. 99–100; *Elements*, 1.15.17.
[117] Hobbes, *Elements*, 1.15.17, 18.
[118] See also Hobbes, *Considerations upon the Reputation, Loyalty, Manners and Religion of Thomas Hobbes* (1679), in *English Works*, ed. Sir William Molesworth (London, 1840), vol. IV, pp. 422–4.

rulers could evaporate precisely when they relied upon such forms of speech. So, those antagonistic to Hobbes could easily traduce him as a self-interested de facto Cromwellian, a mere casuist. Nedham's use of Hobbes to give authority to the self-interested dimension of his own pro-Commonwealth argument would not have been helpful. There was, Hobbes remarked, no good constellation for truths such as his 'to be born under'.[119] Nevertheless, his later denials of any sympathy for the Commonwealth under which he thrived still need treating with caution, for they were made in a context of Restoration antipathy to anything smacking of qualification to monarchy.[120]

What *Leviathan* offered was the most systematic horizontal extension of the office of rule with a concomitant diffusion of most of the issues surrounding the sanctity of oaths. In the short term, this eased Hobbes's return to England; in the median, it became embarrassing when the difference between a Sandersonian 'high' and 'low' reading of the Engagement was conveniently forgotten. In the longer term, the awkward generality of his work had its implicit ties to impassioned causes erased to leave a purer text of philosophy than he wrote. Equally, however, as the issues of engagement were themselves but a concentration of long-standing problems of office, the controversy does not provide a self-contained context. Its importance for Hobbes's doctrines of obligation has certainly been established by Skinner and its need for supplementation has been shown by Burgess.[121] The argument here is that, abstracted from the established preoccupations with oaths and office, its relevance has been misread or overlooked.

When finishing *Leviathan*, Hobbes wrote to a friend referring to it as 'Politique in English'.[122] Two connotations of 'politique' lead beyond the Engagement to a European context: to the '*politiques*', who had resisted Rome's authority in France, although he was opposed to their maintaining a two swords position protective of priestly authority;[123] and to *politica* writing. Works in this genre following Bodin's *République* (1576) were attempts to define the sovereign's office, mapping social order to help maintain peace, and every German university produced at least one during the early seventeenth century.[124] In many respects *Leviathan* is an

---

[119] Hobbes, *Leviathan*, p. 491.
[120] Hobbes, *Considerations*, p. 413, quoting Wallis.
[121] Skinner's position is adjusted, or clarified, in 'Conquest' in partial response to Glenn Burgess, 'Contexts for the Writing and Publication of Hobbes's *Leviathan*', *History of Political Thought*, 11 (1988), pp. 675–702.
[122] Cited by Richard Tuck, in Hobbes, *Leviathan*, 'Introduction', pp. ix–x.
[123] Hobbes, *Leviathan*, ch. 47.
[124] Von Friedeburg, *Self-Defence*, pp. 101–5.

eccentric example of this literature, given its elaborate metaphorical structure, rhetorical force and satiric style. It is distinctive, too, in its relative lack of scholarly apparatus and its scant respect for the talismanic figures of office theory, Cicero and Aristotle (though Plato is not bad for a Greek). There may have been an irony in Hobbes's use of the word *'politique'* to describe his efforts, but in particular *Leviathan* has marked affinities with Henning Arnisaeus' *De jure majestatis* (1610) and with James VI&I's *Trew Law*. It was assimilated to the European heartland of *politica* writing. If Anthony Ascham became seasonal in 1689, a laundered Hobbes came back in Pufendorfian clothing through Tooke's translation of *De officio hominis* (1673). In this guise, most of Hobbesian sovereignty theory proved more comely than *Leviathan*.

Above all, then, *Leviathan* is a discourse on sovereignty, defined in terms of reciprocal offices. The fragile achievement of social order is the result of a transformative contract among denizens of the natural condition by which simultaneously they re-create themselves as subjects in authorising their sovereign. As Arnisaeus had it, any sovereign state is an order of subjection. In this way, Hobbes provided a rationalisation for William Willymat's and Peter Heylyn's polemical understandings of a purely 'private' person as the passive member of a relationship in office (above, chapter 3). In doing so, Hobbes tried to curtail the capacity of the vocabulary of office to generate the clamours of competing social demands. The only limitations to obedience are consistent with the point of assuming the *persona* of a subject in the first place.

The Hobbesian sovereign is not similarly obliged, but the issue of obligation is reductive, hardly trapping the reverberations of official reciprocity. The sovereign as a representative is, as I have noted above, a responsible *persona*, having an end or purpose to maximise an ambience of peace and well-being.[125] And only through sovereign office can God's requirement to live in peace be satisfied. Hobbes's position is that recognising the true nature and necessity of sovereignty will itself contribute to peace, a practical conclusion at one with the thrust of *politica* literature, with Ascham and the other subscribers. In short, with respect to the extent of sovereignty and the available options around the time of its dissolution and acquisition, the Engagement controversy provided Hobbes with an adventitious opportunity for clarification. It is additionally valuable in helping us to distinguish the problem of the reach and rupture of sovereign power from the grounds of obligation to it. Again, Hobbes is in general agreement with the subscribers in relying on a

---

[125] Hobbes, *Leviathan*, ch. 30.

variable blend of argument from *honestas* – what is morally required and so should bind in conscience, according to natural and/or divine law; and from *utilitas* – what self-interest and an eye to consequences demand.

Insofar as the context is right, however, the conclusions drawn from it have been wrong. Just as the subscribers were not de facto theorists, neither was Hobbes. He concludes that 'an inviolable observation' of the 'mutuall Relation between Protection and Obedience' is required both by divine law and the interests of human nature.[126] To choose one as being the authentic voice is to ignore the scope of the argument. Hobbes's contemporary critics, however, had an interest in doing just that. He was held to have no awareness of the limits that gave office definition and meaning. This was exactly what worried refusers about what I have called the horizontal extension of office, for to them it encompassed tyranny. Ascham faced the issue squarely, but Hobbes's earlier denials that there was any tyrannous form of government must have sounded like a musket ball in the foot. To abstract a pure secular self-interest and a de facto allegiance was to conjure up an atheist susceptible to the most convenient routines of condemnation, a strawman easily burnt. And, it is worth repeating, some subscribers were willing enough to accuse their critics of being the real de facto theorists because they could give only de facto compliance when a moral commitment to sovereign office was required. The Engagement controversy unleashed an indiscriminate idiom of accusation, and Hobbes would become a principal victim of its success; but it offers highly selective evidence for the secular ideological identity, for which he might now be praised.

Finally, however, there is in *Leviathan* a dramatically enhanced anti-clericalism from Hobbes's earlier works, which, though concentrating on Catholicism's 'Kingdom of Darkness', embraces all priests as potential threats to peace and religion. The Protestant shamanistic divines shadowing the edges of Cromwell's army, the Presbyterian pastors arbitrating conscience, had all left an intense distaste in his mouth – and he would later have to swallow re-established bishops, men particularly prone to slip off the yoke of subjection.[127] Hostility to the cloth would not win Hobbes a conspicuous number of friends, but it tied him roundly to subscribers like Dury, Warren and Ascham determined to contain troublesome priests.[128] Here, I suspect, this largely overlooked aspect of the controversy is vital in understanding a trajectory of development; after

---

[126] *Ibid.*, p. 491.   [127] *Ibid.*, p. 374.
[128] Champion, *Pillars of Priestcraft*. For some of the friends it did win him when they put his sovereignty theory aside, pp. 134–6.

1651 Hobbes never retreated from his reductive Marsilian vision of the cleric as lacking authority in this world.

The necessary inadequacy of a context for understanding the politics of Hobbes's philosophy can be illustrated most succinctly from *Leviathan* chapter 42. There we find the central Engagement *topos*, Romans 13, Hobbes insisting like Rous that obedience is owed to the higher powers not only out of self-interest, '*but also for conscience sake*'. This does not chime too well with Hobbes's more characteristic scepticism about arguments from conscience, but it posits obligation as morally required. Yet the chapter is not about obedience to a usurping civil ruler, but the relationship between priestly and magisterial office and the effective collapse of one into the other. It is not Cromwell who stands empower'd upon the grave of Charles I, 'to fright/ The spirits of the shady Night' but the ghost of Cardinal Bellarmine, still to be exorcised.[129]

In this we see a sort of historiographical *différance*. Because intellectual contexts are constructed and shaped by the questions historians ask, the language and materials they use, we must expect them to be unstable at the margins. I have argued earlier that the Jesuit doctrine of equivocation enriches our understanding of the insecurities of the Hobbesian natural condition. James VI&I might well have recognised Hobbes's blow to Bellarmine as a belated prop to his own throne. As the frontispiece of *Leviathan* makes manifest, sovereign power depends upon a substitution for the Jesuit's double-handed gladiatorial grasp. Yet, if supportive of 'free' sovereigns, *Leviathan* was a critical comment on James's futile attempt to separate spiritual from temporal authority in the oath of allegiance. A Hobbesian response would be endorsed in the oath of supremacy formulated for William and Mary, a context not for his problems, but for the economy of his answers; there can be but one sword to protect and cut the Gordian knot of office claims; the other hand wields the crosier.

---

[129] Marvell, 'Ode'; Hobbes, *Leviathan*, ch. 42, pp. 343, 341.

15 The oath of allegiance and the Revolution of 1688–9

> ... and from the mouth of England
> Add thus much more, that no Italian priest
> Shall tithe or toll in our dominions ...
> So tell the Pope, all reverence set apart
> To him and his usurp'd authority.
> (Shakespeare, *King John* 3.1)

I

Throughout the seventeenth century, ritualised winter bonfires kept the Gunpowder Plot bright in the minds of English Protestants, and in 1688 they were barely cooling to grey embers when James II's reign itself crumbled into ashes. The son of Orange, with guns and printing press, had arrived on a Protestant wind, landing at Torbay on the anniversary of 'gunpowder treason day'. As the semiotically attuned Gilbert Burnet remarked, this was of 'good effect on the minds of the English nation'. William moved cautiously towards London. An Association was formed to make his gradually swelling support more than 'a rope of sand'.[1] By December, he was encamped at the tutti-man town of Hungerford. There were riots in London. James's daughter Anne fled to her co-religionists, his wife to France. The king followed in disguise, consigning the great seals of government to the Thames. But he was taken, returned to London and given a perplexingly popular welcome. This confusion of movement complicated any uncontentious account of his fall.[2]

His initial flight was an 'earthquake' for his allies;[3] his capture made it difficult to determine how he should be treated. Had he deserted the throne, or had his rights been usurped? These questions created immediate

---

[1] Burnet, *History*, vol. III, pp. 310, 319.
[2] Monod, *Jacobitism*, pp. 166–7.
[3] Lord Clarendon, cited in Robert Beddard, *A Kingdom without a King: The Journal of the Provisional Government in the Revolution of 1688* (Oxford, 1988), 'Introduction', p. 64.

diplomatic embarrassment and a longer-term Jacobite party.[4] Ejected from London by William's soldiers on 18 December, James left England, against advice, five days later. However it would be read, the reign collapsed, wrote Burnet, like a spider's web, at a finger's touch.[5] The oath of allegiance arguments following the crowning of his replacements would stretch back to entangle the whole Stuart monarchy and its mid-century rupture. The controversy rounds off the century with more than superficial symmetry; it was a fearful, if sometimes triumphalist commentary on the crises to which ruling office was prone. Discussion of this wider context before dealing directly with the oath will help to pull the strands of this study together.

II

Towards the end of Charles II's reign, attempts to deal with the impending James left England on the brink of re-opening the Civil Wars.[6] Suspicions remained deep at the accession in 1685, for if James was a Godly Prince in the English tradition, he was not in the English religion. The coronation was on St George's Day, a reassuringly symbolic affirmation of continuity with the Restoration. James swore a conventionally general coronation oath but took neither Communion, nor the Scottish coronation oath with its specifically Presbyterian insistence on the 'trew Religioun of Jesus Christ', 'preicheing of his haly word', and extirpating 'all fals Religioun contrare to the samin'.[7]

The coronation itself was an ill-omened occasion. The crown slipped, then 'totter'd extreamly'; the throne's canopy broke; the top of the 'Scepter did then fall'. The celebratory fireworks exploded all at once, which at least could be redescribed as an excess of nature's enthusiasm for the monarch.[8] His illegitimate son died on the same day, which could not.[9] London skinners would have needed no help to decode the meaning of an over-sized crown sliding down the royal face (above, chapter 2). The pious hope was, no doubt, that a Catholic king would not rule for long, meanwhile, keeping duty to his people distinct from allegiance

---

[4] Burnet, *History*, vol. III, pp. 329, 333–4.
[5] Beddard, *Kingdom*, pp. 58–65; Burnet, *History*, vol. III, p. 1.
[6] Burnet, *History*, vol. II, pp. 202–6, 269.
[7] Scots coronation oath (1567), in *Statutes in Force* (London, 1978), cited in Kelly, 'King and Crown', vol. II.
[8] Aubrey, *Brief Lives*, pp. 57, 58; R. Lowman, *An Exact Narrative and Description of the Wonderful and Stupendous Fire-Works in Honour of Their Majesties Coronations* (1685), pp. 1–2.
[9] Burnet, *History*, vol. III, p. 20.

to the pope. Significant trust was thus placed in the very separation of offices and *personae* on which James VI&I had been unconvincingly insistent. Sceptics were doubtful; separating distinguishable offices was a persistently uphill battle, and it was questionable whether any Catholic could be trusted further than the pope might be thrown. The oaths of office could hardly be sacrosanct if His Holiness could release princes from their burdens.[10]

An innovator by faith alone, and perilously close to being a Machiavellian new prince, James sent disturbingly mixed messages. Reform of a slothful court and reassurance for the safety of his subjects' property and established church were balanced by a perceived disregard for law and open practice of his religion.[11] The non-Catholic loyalist aristocracy and the bishops of the Church of England had, then, a particularly fraught office of counsel. The attempt to keep James adjacent to the straight and Reformation narrow of the Elizabethan Settlement was, for the clerics, a necessity of their office, and any neat delineation between temporal and spiritual spheres, counsel and subject status was compromised further. After crushing Monmouth's Rebellion, James increasingly placed Catholics in key positions. Even a small standing army began to look perilous. He appeared as close as his brother had been to Louis of France and to be emulating his cousin's style.[12]

Surveying Christendom, Burnet deemed 1685 one of the great crisis years of Protestantism (among many others).[13] James's determination to be a Catholic king involved flexing the muscles of prerogative and gradually shunning the Church of England, on the grounds that it could be relied upon to practise the passive obedience it preached. So with promises of toleration and advancement for Presbyterians, Independents, Anabaptists and Quakers, James tried to tie obvious enemies to his cause. By Church of England stigma these were the detritus of the Reformation. A monarch was finally forming the alliance of king-killers that Owen and Barclay had feared at the beginning of the century. When James's cunning was blessed with an heir in 1688, the prospect of a Catholic dynasty stretched into the unforeseeable future: the Elizabethan Settlement could well be flushed away with the Reformation bath-water. The Church of England bishops considered it imperative

---

[10] *Ibid.*, vol. II, pp. 202–7; vol. VI, p.157; cf. the more optimistic John Evelyn, *Diary*, 2–8 October 1685, vol. IV, pp. 478–9.
[11] Burnet, *History*, vol. III, pp. 5–13.
[12] See, for example, James II, *His Majesties Most Gracious Speech to both Houses of Parliament* (9 November 1685), pp. 3–4; Burnet, *History*, vol. III, p. 11.
[13] Burnet, *History*, vol. III, p. 69.

to stand firm on the cusp of matters civil and spiritual and came close to controlling James, thus subverting the justification for William's arrival.[14]

From the outset, there were grounds for the accusation that James's religion would dictate an alienation of the crown, or an exercise of rule that was, by Rome's overreaching, tyrannical.[15] By the trial of the seven bishops in 1688, many in the Church of England saw the king as misusing civil power to invade spiritual authority. As parliament would resolve the matter once he had fled, a popish prince was inconsistent with the 'safety and welfare of this Protestant Kingdom'.[16] From the *topoi* of tyranny of origin and exercise, he was vulnerable to being called a wolf in shepherd's clothing.

Reluctantly, the Church of England clergy magnified the casuistic small print in their manifestos of loyalty. Passive obedience presupposed the ruler's protection of true religion. *In extremis*, there might be defence of religion, and at least, 'the bare refusing to aid and assist'. With impeccable hindsight, Burnet claimed to have warned James not to rely on the doctrine of passive obedience, a 'disputable opinion' carrying 'distinctions and reserve'.[17] Burnet records approvingly (for once) a speech by the Earl of Shaftesbury in 1675, emphasising the necessity of obedience, while underscoring its cessation with the alienation of the kingdom. So too William Sherlock: the Church of England was profoundly loyal, but loyalty to prince means loyalty to religion, and it is no true loyalty to suffer the erosion of 'our religion and its legal securities'.[18] As one tract would put it, there was a 'common abuse of the term loyalty'.[19] Expressed less prejudicially, the word became highly susceptible to co-optive predication (above, chapter 4). As Goldie has aptly remarked, James relied

---

[14] Mark Goldie, 'James II and the Dissenters' Revenge: the Commission of Enquiry of 1688', *Historical Research*, 66, 159 (1993), p. 53; Burnet, *History*, vol. III, pp. 151–2, 97–8; Mark Goldie, 'The Political Thought of the Anglican Revolution', in Robert Beddard, ed., *The Revolutions of 1688* (Oxford, 1991), pp. 107–9.

[15] Burnet, *History*, vol. II, pp. 27–8; 202–6; vol. III, p. 43; Lamont, 'Richard Baxter, Popery', pp. 336–52.

[16] 'Grey's Debates' (1688), p. 29, text in David Lewis Jones, ed., *A Parliamentary History of the Glorious Revolution* (London, 1988), p. 125.

[17] Edmund de Bohun, cited in Goldie, 'The Political Thought of the Anglican Revolution', p. 117; Burnet, *History*, vol. II, p. 27; see also Thomas Long (?), *A Resolution of Certain queries concerning submission to the present Government* (1689), pp. 6–8; and Thomas Long (?), *Reflections upon a Late Book* (1689), pp. 9, 15–16.

[18] William Sherlock, *A Sermon Preached at Westminster* (1685), pp. 31–2; Goldie, 'The Political Thought of the Anglican Revolution', p. 113; see also Burnet, *History*, vol. III, p. 7.

[19] Anon., *Important Questions of State, Law, Justice and Prudence both Civil and Religious*, in *State Tracts* (1705), vol. I, p. 171.

on the support of an Anglican political theology carrying the intellectual materials to justify his overthrow.[20]

This political theology, however, involved an inter-denominational understanding of priestly office with shared casuistic resources for its protection and an immediate implication for oaths of allegiance. An oath was invalid if it undermined true faith, or over-taxed conscience. Only tyrants, not rulers, as Parsons and Goodman had been ecumenically insistent, would impose such oaths. Conversely, stated Philip Hickeringill, Henry VIII might have broken with Rome, but the very notion of the clergy sustained a form of popery into the present.[21] Arguments about religious office loomed as large as they had in 1606; and casuistry remained the necessary and sublimated means of dealing with them.

To be sure, Burnet's spider's web consisted of more than the sticky threads of priesthood and domestic unease; also relevant were problems in Ireland, frictions in Dutch politics, and the hostilities between France and William, who had abandoned a futile alliance with the Stuarts for a working one with the disaffected Protestant aristocracy.[22] There would be no uncontested description of what it was all about. The Dutch Republic had invested heavily in William's enterprise and with its army on English soil, William's arrival could be called an invasion. Yet, made easy by collusion, it could be presented as a neighbourly intervention, so circumventing awkward notions of conquest and helping explain the absence of the Dutch presence in many accounts.[23] Rather than a reprise of 1066 or 1649, William's armed arrival could be celebrated as an answer to a Bractonian prayer – when unduly oppressed, the people may get down upon their knees and appeal to Heaven for relief by a distant power. He came, they saw that God conquered.

Ostensibly, William's purpose was only to help. Coy about dynastic ambitions, he might have been more pushed than driven to the throne.[24] But, equally, in seeming to be pushed, William did not need to drive. Kingly ambition would itself have aroused suspicions of tyranny, success would look like conquest, oaths sworn to him would be questionable.

---

[20] Goldie, 'The Political Thought of the Anglican Revolution', p. 111.
[21] Philip Hickeringill, *A Vindication of the Naked Truth, The Second Part* (1681), p. 17.
[22] Scott, *England's Troubles*, pp. 458–9.
[23] Jonathan Israel, 'The Dutch Role in the Glorious Revolution', in J. Israel, ed., *The Anglo-Dutch Moment* (Cambridge, 1991), pp. 105–10, 122, 128–9; cf. Evelyn, *Diary*, 27 October 1688, vol. IV, p. 601 and 8 November 1688, p. 609, on the impending invasion, with 1 November 1688, pp. 604–5, on the invitation; Thomas Comber, *A Letter to a Bishop Concerning the Present Settlement and the New Oaths* (1689), pp. 18–21.
[24] Beddard, *Kingdom*, 'Introduction', pp. 27–8.

So William's declarations were fittingly reassuring; he sought only the restoration of good government and the Protestant way.[25] James countered that he had intended to call a parliament. The manner of his departure, however, abandoning seals and destroying parliamentary writs, created the impression that he intended to create chaos.[26] It made plans for a negotiated settlement irrelevant. Seen thus, his departure was a terminal abuse of office, not unlike the one Anthony Ascham had attributed to Nero. A ruler who refuses to rule ceases to be a ruler. Among all the maxims and clichés of debate, this affirmation of the nominal identity of a *persona* would be pressed relentlessly.

If William initially lacked kingly ambitions, Whig pressures and James's scorched earth retreat enlivened his mind, by creating a vacuum that could be advertised as a vacancy, or, to use a slippery term, an abdication.[27] In place of a king an ad hoc provisional government of peers ruled from 11 to 16 December. Once William had established an effective presence, he gathered a sympathetic élite to decide how to proceed. On Christmas Eve it was broadly agreed that, to use the most accommodating term, a 'demise' of the previous government had occurred, and after long debate William was asked to call a convention and assume government until it met.[28]

Albeit with no unambiguous office to settle the kingdom, Peers and Commons met in a volatile and violently anti-Catholic city, effectively controlled by the Dutch and heavily preached upon and encouraged by the Church of England.[29] The Convention's work was to achieve a settlement balancing the prerogatives of rule with the protection of the laws and religion of the ruled. The choice was between a regency, narrowly defeated in the Lords,[30] a new king, or a permanent interregnum, a commonwealth. The last option was not much canvassed beyond the occasional pamphlet during the early, most open-ended stage of proceedings.[31] A king bound by office was a virtually unchallenged proposition, but a Catholic one, insufferable. This left a single person, with an

---

[25] See, for example, Burnet, *History*, vol. III, pp. 286–8.
[26] Beddard, *Kingdom*, 'Introduction', p. 32 states this as a fact; cf. Burnet, vol. III, pp. 326–7.
[27] John Miller, 'The Glorious Revolution: Contract and Abdication Reconsidered', *Historical Journal*, 25, 3 (1982), pp. 541–4; in reply to Thomas P. Slaughter, '"Abdicate" and "Contact" in the Glorious Revolution', *Historical Journal*, 24, 2 (1981), pp. 323–37.
[28] Beddard, *Kingdom*, 'Introduction', p. 65.
[29] Israel, 'The Dutch Role', pp. 128–30; Harris, *London Crowds*, pp. 226–7.
[30] 'Notes of a Noble Lord', in Jones, *Parliamentary History*, p. 81.
[31] Anon. (John Humfrey?), *Good Advice Before it is Too Late* (1688); Anon. (John Wildman?), *Some Remarks*, in *State Tracts* (1705), vol. I, p. 162; discussed in Mark Goldie, 'The Roots of True Whiggism', *History of Political Thought*, 1 (1980), pp. 212–14.

army, and mob-handed, uninterested in regency, who had already been asked to rule pro tem. Deciding on him seemed to some to offer the choice of an elective monarchy (almost unthinkable) or chaos (marginally worse).[32]

William's assumption of the throne, then, amounted to a final stage in a crisis of allegiance that had been brewing for several years. Yet oaths had been sworn; a properly crowned king was absent and another was effectively in command. Was this a re-enactment of the conquest or usurpation of Cromwell and the army a mere generation ago? Did this simply explicate the limitations in swearing? Had the throne been alienated or vacated? Had James neglected his duties? Could he be said to have ceased to be a king by virtue of his flight, or by his action in office? Had he ceased to be king by breaking the contract entailed in his oath, or simply by breaking his oath? Had there been resistance to office, a defence against tyranny, or a plain rebellion? Bypassing these loaded possibilities it could be urged that the government had simply dissolved. But if so, in what capacities could people act to re-establish it? The redescriptions of who had done what to whom were the means by which the central issues of identity in office and its implications were addressed. Thus the presupposition of office that set the terms of debate itself became a problem when the actors argued reflexively. Each of the above rudimentary accounts of James and his departure was canvassed in parliament. Each would be disputed, distinguished and run together in what was to prove one of the most hectic periods of print since the invention of the press. Over 2,000 titles were published in 1689, two-thirds being related to the Revolution. For the printers, it was one of the four golden years of the century.[33]

III

It is tempting to see the controversies following the Revolution as a synthesis: issues of spiritual and temporal office from 1606 combined with those of ruling function from the Engagement debates. The result, a revolutionary consummation greatly to be wished – to wit, the beginnings of effective and secular rule and the long triumphantly stable eighteenth century. Certainly, if we isolate the issue of oath-taking and office, the Allegiance controversy offered little that was not at one with these previous concentrations of dispute and the white noise of oath argument that

---

[32] 'Notes of a Noble Lord', in Jones, *Parliamentary History*, p. 86; Burnet, *History*, vol. III, pp. 355–6, 373.
[33] Goldie, 'The Revolution of 1689', p. 478.

can be heard throughout the century. Yet, if anything, it was the long seventeenth century that would march boisterously past 1715.[34] One can almost hear men breathing 'providence' over recent events with an audible sigh of relief in much the same way as that sanctifying breath of God had dissipated the Armada and blown out the Gunpowder Plot. Assimilation to a providential past was the surest way of making moral sense of the present.

Some awareness of the tenacity of old arguments can be gleaned from the number of re-printed volumes and by the familiarity of those arguing from 1690 onwards with the texts of earlier years.[35] After a fashion, the Revolution of 1688 walked backwards into a newer world, redeploying the inherited and almost unchallenged vocabulary of restoration, reform and conservation.[36] Numerous works such as Ascham's *Confusions* and an adjusted Lawson's *Politica* offered templates for analysis. Of these, Hunton's *Treatise of Monarchie* and Buchanan's *De jure* had only recently been burnt. Their phoenix-like rebirth indexes a striking change of atmosphere. Locke's *Two Treatises* finally saw the light of day. If the oath of allegiance controversy of 1689 replayed the major issues of 1606 and 1649, there were nevertheless subtle departures. Gradually the received vocabulary of office was reconfigured, and problems perhaps previously relatively distinct were more easily run together. Four predictable topics illustrate the process: clerical office, consent, tyranny, and de facto rule. They are worth highlighting before focusing on specific arguments.

IV

With respect to 1606, James VI&I's attempt to keep civil and spiritual allegiance separate was abandoned, bringing into ever stronger relief the limits of clerical office. This problem, a veritable sub-text of debate on almost all social issues from the Reformation onwards, was apparent during the Engagement controversy and augmented during the Restoration, when oaths were such prominent instruments of conformity.[37] Debates in the House of Lords over the rights of bishops to vote in

---

[34] Jonathan Scott, *Algernon Sidney and the Restoration Crisis, 1677–83* (Cambridge, 1988), pp. 4–17; Monod, *Jacobitism*, Introduction and ch. 1.
[35] For example, Anon., *Animadversions on a Discourse* (1691); Peter Allix (?), *An Examination of the Scruples* (1689); William Atwood, *The Fundamental Constitution* (1690); Anon. (Charles Blount?), *The Proceedings of the Present Parliament Justified* (1689).
[36] Scott, *England's Troubles*, pp. 455ff.
[37] Jones, *Conscience and Allegiance*, ch. 4; Champion, *Pillars of Priestcraft*, pp. 53–82.

Danby's treason trial (1679) spilt over into heated anti-clerical protests.[38] Ten years later anti-clericalism is a persistent theme in the advice from the self-conscious laity.[39] The spiritual office must needs be kept out of civil matters. Knowing one's office was knowing one's place; not knowing it easily became tyranny – as John of Salisbury had insisted long before. It was a position endorsed by some clerics, such as John Sharp, who like John Dury sought to retain authority by withdrawing his office to safer ground. But whereas Dury had been a marginal ecclesiastical figure, Sharp was central and senior.[40]

In the accusation of interference one can see the rationale for the erratic pejorative expansion of the term popery to elide ecclesiological difference. In 1606 the accusation of popery was usually denominationally specific, but became increasingly stretched in response to Archbishop Laud's promotion of the cloth and the intrusions of Scottish Presbyterianism. By the 1640s it could cover what formally might still be civil and secular policy. In 1651 *Leviathan* had warned that any priest might meddle with sovereign right, and in this lay the seeds for the development of new cults, a proposition central to Hobbes's Restoration works on the intellectual history of heresy and Christianity.[41] My kingdom is not of this world, a theological axiom for most, was an ecclesiological imperative for some. By the 1690s priestly abuse of office was more easily and probably more often called popery than ever before. The word 'priestcraft', remarked Burnet, was in fashion and all religious controversies were seen as plots to advance clerical interest.[42] In opposing the incursions of James II upon their understanding of office, the Church of England clerics had effectively recaptured the medieval 'two swords' doctrines concerning the relationships between *regnum* and *sacerdotium*.[43] These were popish enough for a suspicious laity, and accusations of priestcraft

---

[38] Burnet, *History*, vol. II, pp. 208–10; see, for example, Anon., *That Bishops in England May and Ought to Vote in Cases of Blood* (1680); Anon., *A Discourse on the Peerage and Jurisdiction of the Lords Spiritual* (1679); E. W., *The Bishops Courts Dissolved* (1681).

[39] For example, Anon., *Animadversions on a Discourse* (1691); Anon., *The Doctrine of Passive Obedience and Jure Divino Disproved by a Layman of the Church of England* (1689).

[40] John Sharp, 'General Directions for a Holy Life', in *Works*, vol. I, pp. 226–49; Sharp, 'The Duty of Subjection to Higher Powers', in *ibid.*, vol. II, pp. 34–51. But, to qualify, Bishop Bilson had also been central and senior, and in defending Elizabeth against the Jesuits had done his best to withdraw the clergy to safer ground with as blunt an argument from the swords as could be managed. See *Christian Subjection*, pt. 2; it did much to explain his continued popularity.

[41] For printed works in this idiom, especially Burnet's *History of the Reformation* (1679–1714), see Champion, *Pillars of Priestcraft*, pp. 77–98.

[42] Burnet, *History*, vol. IV, p. 378.

[43] Goldie, 'The Political Thought of the Anglican Revolution', pp. 25–6.

served less to denigrate religious discussion, as Burnet feared, than to stop up priestly mouths, often with the authority of Cicero's *De officiis*.[44] Whilst some wished only to constrain priests in the idiom of Dury and Sharp, an occasional voice regarded any clerical office as an invention of the pope and the devil. This draconian reduction of office could itself be collapsed into Hobbism.[45]

The position of the non-jurors, Jacobeans, or *'florid Gentlemen* of the long robe' was straightforward.[46] Easily accused of popery, they sought to occupy the high moral ground by dismissing alternative positions as casuistic expediency. As they largely applied the arguments of the Engagement refusers, positioning themselves close to the martyred Charles I, the gist will be apparent: oaths and the hereditary principle were sacrosanct. Swearing obedience entailed accepting royal prerogative.[47] James had not deserted, but had been deposed. Swearing new oaths violated old, a fast road to perdition. Knowing this, usurpers were rarely so foolish as to insist on oaths; even 'honest Cromwell' avoided them.[48] The new regime, cobbled up upon the sins of the forsworn, might have to be accepted de facto, but never de jure.[49] Even praying for William and Mary could be tantamount to swearing allegiance to usurpers. If not binding when inconvenient, oaths meant nothing. Thus allegiance did not end with the ruler's incapacity to protect – the question should be why was he not protected when in need.[50] A large part of their case depended upon the danger of distinguishing man from office; it verged on separation and that, as the high theory of Restoration kingship had insisted, was a sign of treasonous intent.[51] For W. Anderton (soon to be executed for treason) the political declension was simple: there had been a king, there has been a rebellion, there remains a king. People

---

[44] Champion, *Pillars of Priestcraft*, pp. 175–8, 194–5.
[45] E. W., *The Bishops Courts Dissolved*; Hickeringill, *A Vindication*, pp. 12, 17, 35; the view had authority from Luther's understanding of a church as a priesthood of all believers.
[46] William Atwood, *Reflections upon a Treasonable Opinion . . . Against Signing the National Association* (1696), p. 1; Roger Palmer, Lord Castlemain, identifies himself as of the long robe in *The Englishman's Allegiance*.
[47] Anon., *Reflections on our Late & Present Proceedings in England* (1689), in *Somers Tracts*, vol. X, p. 7; Palmer, *The Englishman's Allegiance*, pp. 203, 207b; Anon (Jeremy Collier?), *Vindiciae juris regii* (1689), p. 32; Dr. G. B., *A Word to the Wavering* (1689), pp. 4–5.
[48] Palmer, *The Englishman's Allegiance*, p. 217, presumably taking the Engagement to have been less than an oath.
[49] Theophilus Downes, *A Discourse* (1690), pp. 16–18; 13; Jones, *Conscience and Allegiance*, pp. 218–19.
[50] Palmer, *The Englishman's Allegiance*, pp. 203, 212–14, 217; Anon., *A Caution against Inconsistency, Or The Connexion between Praying and Swearing in Relation to Civil Powers* (1689?), A2v.
[51] Sherlock, *The Case of Resistance to Supreme Powers* (1684), p. 198.

are being taught to name things with the wrong words.[52] In Jacobean eyes, Hobbes assumed the shape of the arch-casuist of rebellion.[53] George Hickes was explicit in tying the 'uncouth' and 'unheard of' principles of Hobbism to the Engagement and was scathing on the 'unlimited sense' given to obedience to higher powers. It makes any man who can mount Bucephalus an Alexander.[54] Because such latitude would let in Turkish rule, it was a threat to the church and Christianity, the obedience of 'protean subjects' being the least regarded by any ruler.[55] He rounded waspishly on Sharp's attempt to maintain the integrity of clerical office by drawing a line between 'state points' and matters of religion: as if morality and priestly duty could be so easily constrained.[56] In attributing an acceptance of irresistible power to the subscribers of the Engagement and many of his contemporaries, he condemned them as companions in Cromwellian evil, and projected as a clerical nightmare something Arbuthnot would urbanely turn into a theory of political autonomy (above, chapter 10). The spectre of 'state points' would shortly become a smoothly inverted vision of routine amorality.

V

The proposition that government depended on consent was neither new nor revolutionary. It permeated the workings of society, was formally evoked in the symbolism of crowning and in elections and was not necessarily inconsistent with the virtually axiomatic notion that the office of rule was established by God. The notion of consent, however, was capacious, covering inferred acceptance, tacit consent, considered choice

---

[52] W. Anderton, *Remarks on the Present Confederacy* (1693); Anon., *A Caution against Inconsistency*, Av.

[53] See, generally, Collier, *Dr. Sherlock's Case* (1691); Anon., *A Confutation of Sundry Errors* (1691); George Hickes, *A Vindication of Some Among Ourselves* (1692); Theophilus Downes, *An Examination of the Arguments* (1691); but especially Hickes, *An Apology for the New Separation* (1691), p. 6.

[54] Hickes, *Apology*, pp. 3–4, 6; 'The Duchess of York's Ghost', Huntington MS EL 8770 (35/B/43): 'Nor is confirm'd to any certain line,/ Possession makes all Government Divine.'; see also Palmer, *The Englishman's Allegiance*, p. 213 on the invitation to William 'of our great men'.

[55] Hickes, *Apology*, p. 6; Collier, *Dr Sherlock's Case*, pp. 5–9; the allusion to the 'Turk' may seem hyperbolic, but Socinians and others were deeply admiring of Islam as superior to established Christianity, and were Hobbesian fellow-travellers: Champion, *Pillars of Priestcraft*, ch. 4. Others also feared 'Turcism' as an implication of Erastianism; its head had been raised in the Engagement controversy, de Moulin, *The Power of the Magistrate*, pp. 29, 31.

[56] Hickes, *Apology*, pp. 5–8; cf. Sharp, 'General Directions' at length; Burnet, however, would show how aggressively such a restricted view of his proper 'sphere' could be used. See his speech of 1713, in *History*, vol. VI, pp. 154–61.

or contractual agreement. To point to the discrepancy between the rhetorics of consent and the lack of choice and narrowness of franchise may be to lose much of the point. Whatever its content, the *topos* of consent affirmed a sanctioning origin for office; the absence of consent was the sign of office-abuse. Moreover, as oath-taking always entailed consent, and oaths were central to debate, so too was consent.

Additionally, consent provided verisimilitude to the proceedings through which William became king more plausibly than those through which Cromwell became Protector: as noted, the monarchy was now arguably elective.[57] If so, reference to consent might undermine the view that the new rulers were usurpers. Yet the elasticity of consent complicated any simple contrast. As writers in a Hobbesian idiom could argue, even in conquest, consent preceded settled rule.[58] Consent was central because although its formal meaning might be clear, its application remained contested and could be tantalisingly unspecific. Concomitantly, reliance on the rhetorics of consent enabled the accusation of tyranny to flourish. This had become central to the later stages of the reign of Charles I when a controversial emphasis on tyranny gradually emerged, justifying his execution as tyrannicide.

After 1688 talk of tyranny seems infinitely more widespread, casual and generalised than it had been earlier. I have touched on a partial explanation. James's rule could be construed almost a priori as tyrannical; he was a shepherd turned wolf.[59] This, of course, was no novel casuistical ground for disobedience. The Elizabethan Bishop Bilson continued to be cited for having argued that alienation of office was grounds for action.[60] James VI&I battled the very tyranny his grandson invited into the kingdom and so assumed the virtuously emblematic status that Elizabeth had held for those critical of him.[61] James II helped restore James I. To a sort of tyrannous incapacity, could be added 'the late daring *Pranks of Tyranny*', suspension of laws relevant to the established church and challenging its spiritual authority.[62] A number of writers rehearsed the

---

[57] See also Burnet, *History*, vol. III, pp. 355–6; but cf. Israel, 'The Dutch Role', pp. 128–30, on the constraints imposed by the Dutch presence.

[58] See Anon., *Some Short Considerations relating to the settling of the government humbly Offer'd*... (1689), in *State Tracts* (1705), vol. I, p. 175.

[59] Edward Stephens, *Four Questions Debated*, in *State Tracts* (1705), vol. I, p. 164; Richard Baxter, *Against the Revolt to a Foreign Jurisdiction* (1691), at length; Francis Fullwood, *The Agreement Betwixt the Present and the Former Government* (1689), pp. 32–5.

[60] See, for example, Allix, *An Examination* (1689); Anon., *Anatomy of a Jacobite Tory* (1689); Long (?), *A Resolution of Certain Queries*, p. 23; Atwood, *The Fundamental Constitution* (1690, 1705), pp. 447–50; Lamont, 'Richard Baxter', pp. 342–5.

[61] Fullwood, *The Agreement*, p. 34.

[62] Ibid., p. 36; Atwood, *Reflections*, p. 59.

Parsonian reading of the coronation oath, although the Jesuit's name was conspicuously absent. It was a contract, and having sworn to uphold religion James had broken his trust, automatically releasing his subjects from obligation. Such arguments allowed accusations of breach of contract or violation of oaths to be blurred and become largely interchangeable.[63] Burnet draws attention to the new-found popularity of a contractual reading of the coronation oath and a denial of its being merely proclamatory. It was an easy means of reiterating a purely nominal identity in office.[64] Finally, once James had gone, tyranny was simultaneously a lurid and safe abridgement of office-abuse because more easily severed from the horrific injunction to commit tyrannicide, with its feared consequence of confusion and the conjuring of the ghosts of Charles I and Cromwell. Defoe, for example, would be able to celebrate liberation without contemplation of chaos:

> But if the Mutual Contract was dissolv'd,
> The Doubt's explain'd, the Difficulty solv'd
> That Kings, when they descend to Tyranny,
> *Dissolve the Bond, and leave their Subjects free.*[65]

With this general indictment of tyranny now synonymous with office-abuse, it became easier to run together quite distinct accusations about departure from office that might justify a new allegiance. According to the non-jurors, this was 'loose and impertinent'.[66] Yet they could be equally loose in associating William with the tyrant Tarquin, whose wife Tullia was like Mary, the daughter to the king he replaced.[67] Generally, the word tyranny was a staple of argument and one not much subject to discrimination.[68]

---

[63] Thomas Erle, 'Paper of Instructions', in Erle papers, Churchill College, Cambridge, Archives, 4/4, fol. 3v: 'All oaths of compacts and agreements (being the strongest ligaments [of] sosieties) carries always about them tassit salves and savings, of Generall and implied conditions. The King first breaking his oath with his subjects, they are no longer bound by their oath of allegiance to him'; Kennett, *Dialogue*, pp. 31–5, for whom William I's coronation oath was 'a Bargain and Compact', p. 14; Anon., *Counsel to the True English: Or a Word of Advice to the Jacobites* (1691), p. 9.

[64] Burnet, *History*, vol. III, pp. 357–8; Richard Claridge, *A Second Defence of the Present Government* (1689), p. 28; Anon., *An Examination of the Scruples of those who refuse to take oaths of allegiance*, in *State Tracts* (1705), vol. I, p. 302.

[65] Daniel Defoe, *The True-Born Englishman*, in *Selected Writings*, ed. John Boulton (Cambridge, 1975), p. 72.

[66] Hickes, *Vindication* (1692), pp. 41–2.

[67] 'The Duchess of York's Ghost'; 'Tarquin and Tullia' (1689), Huntington MS EL 8770 (35/B/43), pp. 78–93, 52–60.

[68] Anon., *A Justification of the Whole Proceedings* (1689); K. William, *Wherein it is Set Forth* (1689); Richard Claridge, *A Defence of the Present Government* (1689); Claridge,

VI

William and Mary could be seen as rulers by de facto acquisition, although the rupture was less decisive than in 1649; a repeat performance had, by definition, precedent.[69] It was also rather different from the brutal sequence of king, axe, Cromwell. There was still a king and the ruling queen was a Stuart. James's Protestant daughter was now in waiting; the family could be re-affirmed as the unit of hereditary continuity.[70] Irrespective of the gradations of de facto practice, to see the Revolution as marking a triumph of de facto theory is decidedly wide of the mark.[71]

I have argued that might versus right, de facto versus de jure, was only a prejudicial formulation of the issues of the Engagement. It was now sustained by the non-jurors, who collapsed different propositions into one accusatory phrase that could be given additional currency by being turned back on them. As they admitted, they could give only non-moral, de facto compliance, pro tem.[72] The issue of who was really a de facto supporter was a formulation of the Marian question of who was really rebellious, arising more clearly than it had in the wake of the Engagement. It was a matter of asking not just who might have acquired office de facto, but also of who really ruled de facto, by force.[73] Here we see the fuller point of the redescriptive energies surrounding William's arrival; invasion by an ambitious foreign prince or a selfless response to a plea were opposed preconditions for locating the true origin of de facto rule, not government but tyranny.[74] As with the Engagement, some did not accept the validity of the loaded distinction between de facto and de jure.[75] Given the persistent blending of arguments from right, usefulness and necessity, this was not unreasonable. Emphasis on the tyranny of

---

A Second Defence (1689); Anon, *A Defence of Their Majesties* (1689); B. R., *Satisfaction Tendered* (1689); Anon., *The Anatomy of an Arbitrary Prince* (1689); Daniel Defoe (?), *The Advantages of the Present Settlement* (1689).

[69] Defoe, *Jure Divino*, bk. 10.
[70] Thomas Comber, *The Protestant Mask* (1692/3); Fullwood, *Agreement*, pp. 25–9; see also Lawson, *Politica*, p. 101.
[71] J. P. Kenyon, *Revolution Principles: The Politics of Party 1689–1720* (Cambridge, 1977), ch. 3; Goldie, 'The Revolution of 1689', p. 487.
[72] Claridge, *A Second Defence*, pp. 23ff.
[73] Anon., *A Remonstrance and Protestation of all Good Protestants of This Kingdom . . . together with Reflections Upon it* (1689). This is, incidentally, the first text of which I am aware to make use of Marvell's recently published 'Ode of Cromwell's Return from Ireland', pp. 13, 16.
[74] Anon., *A Remonstrance*, succinctly puts both sides, pp. 5, 7, 11, 13.
[75] Comber, *A Discourse* (1689); Atwood, *Reflections*, p. 62, it was groundless and wicked. Even 1066 is massaged into the shape of 1689, pp. 20–1, as it was by Kennett, *Dialogue*, pp. 12–14. Defoe, *Jure Divino*, p. viii, dismisses de facto and de jure as a new distinction.

James's rule was a denial of purely de facto triumph by William. Righteous restoration of good rule was always going to be more than mere possession; only tyranny occupied office de facto.[76]

To misread the arguments of the Allegiance controversy as a triumph of de facto 'theory' really needs explaining and may be a result of giving disproportionate weight to the writings of William Sherlock and his opponents.[77] From being an outspoken advocate of passive obedience, he justified allegiance to William and Mary on grounds that strongly echoed the arguments of the subscribers of 1649–52; consequently, the guns primed by the original refusers could easily be trained on him. Condemned as a man of expedience, an oath-breaking Hobbist turncoat, he excited anger by denying any prudential plasticity. But, whatever his motivations, his argued position, like that of the original Engagers, was never one of preferring might over right, or pragmatism over principle. His faith in the moral reciprocity of protection and obedience remained commonplace, retaining its strong connotations of God's required obedience to office.[78] Additionally, he drew on a number of justifications for his outspoken allegiance to the new rulers, rejecting the analogy with Cromwell, who having failed to settle the country, was never properly its protector. As with so many, providence played an arbitrary role in his case and there were always the moral obligations of his sacred clerical office to put true religion even before obedience to rulers. On this he had been insistent when preaching before James in 1685. To see 1689, then, as a victory for de facto theory may be to side inadvertently with the nonjurors' outrage. It is certainly to mistake a widespread accusation from the negative register of office for a theory that could triumph; it is a little like discovering the ascendancy of Communism in McCarthyist America. At least that was a dominant ideology somewhere.

Ascham may have been seasonal again in 1689, because his arguments for a moral reciprocity between ruling and obeying did not rely on Romans 13, the perceived weakness of Rous and of Sherlock. In 1689, the lines of this kind of moral claim, again, like so much else, are more tumbled with others than in 1649–52. The Convention parliament of 1660 provided a sanctioning model for the Convention of 1689–90, so from this authoritative historical resource was drawn a constitutional

---

[76] Fullwood, *The Agreement*, pp. 68, 33–9; Anon., *A Remonstrance*, pp. 11–15.

[77] Anon., 'The Female Casuist' and 'An Epitaph for Passive Obedience' (1688), Huntington MS EL 8770 (35/B/43), pp. 164–6, p. 23, both suggest that self-interest was typical in changing sides.

[78] Fullwood, *The Agreement*, p. 68, citing Calvin's Case; see also Long, *Reflections*, at length.

precedent justifying the new rule irrespective of dynastic rupture, or issues of might versus right.[79] This also gave allegorical plausibility to arguments from trust and contract, increasingly important, if unstable, variations on a general theme of consent.[80] Further, any move beyond the boundaries of consent allowed a right of resistance which if exercised (an option most seemed reluctant to extertain) facilitated redescription of the whole sequence of events in an adaptable amalgam of damning indictments. Superficially there was an element of ad hoc-ery in this, but a presupposition of office facilitated the kaleidoscopic combination.

VII

Parliamentary debates provide ample illustration. According to John Howe, the king's tyranny had ended his government.[81] Sir Robert Sawyer thought the words to describe James's departure 'all one'; the issue was whether government had dissolved. Turning the state 'Topsy Turvy' had been a refusal to govern, and abdication was the most plausible descriptor if it referred to the exercise of office.[82] The king's office, according to Sir William Poltny, is from the people, and is not for their destruction. James II's conduct has been 'a Cessure of the Trust', an abdication; it was necessary and not treasonable to distinguish the person from the power. If a constable acts within the king's authority he must be obeyed, if drunk and abusive self-defence is allowed. The king, stated Sir John Mainard, 'has deposed himself'.[83] Monday, 28 January: 'Resolved, That King James the Second, having endeavoured to subvert the Constitution . . . by breaking the original Contract between King and People, and, by the advice of Jesuits, and other wicked Persons, having violated the fundamental Laws, and having withdrawn himself out of this

---

[79] 'Grey's Debates', Serjeant Maynard (20 February 1688), p. 93, in Jones, *Parliamentary History*, p. 189.

[80] Burnet, *History*, vol. III, p. 357, misleadingly writes of contractarian and anti-contractarian parties. For the diversity of contract uses, see Miller, 'The Glorious Revolution', pp. 545–54.

[81] 'A Journal of the Convention', in Jones, *Parliamentary History*, p. 234.

[82] *Ibid.*, pp. 236, 238.

[83] *Ibid.*, p. 239; cf. Hobbes, 'Questions'; 'Journal', in Jones, *Parliamentary History*, p. 242; possibly an allusion to Lewis of Bavaria, but more likely to the *Leges Edwardii confessoris*: see Greenberg, *The Radical Face*, p. 278. This style of argument was partially identified by Thomas Slaughter in his claim that to abdicate actually meant to have been deposed, from which he reaffirmed the dominance of resistance theory, but the opposite conclusion is more warranted: abdication of responsibility was self-deposition, so a means of avoiding 'resistance theory'. See Slaughter, '"Abdicate" and "Contract"', pp. 323–8.

Kingdom, has abdicated the Government.'[84] Nominal identity and the elision of the terms of office-abuse gave enormous descriptive latitude.

It also lubricated discussions concerning the office held by those deciding what James had done and how to re-settle the nation. 'There is only one Question ... whether we are a Parliament, and what we shall do when we are a Parliament.'[85] The alternative, that the sitting was a convention, had the considerable appeal of evasive reach, suggesting little more than a special status of parliament's business, or designating some foundational act, or contractual moment from which constitutions and normal parliaments might arise.[86] Contractual or not, a myth of popular foundation through a convention was also more plausible in 1690 than it had been in 1649, and it facilitated an understanding of the Revolution as a thorough restoration and a bulwark for the work of reformation. These were considerable advantages in undercutting any idea that here stood a brave new world, ramshackle on pure de facto power. And the general designation of a convention stuck in imperfect and impatient times.[87] In January, Sir Thomas Clarges remarked to his fellows that 'you are here as a Convention, which is a resemblance of a Parliament'. On 19 February, Sir Robert Sawyer pointed out that the earlier Convention had started as a parliament, yet Charles and it had been in their positions de facto. Hugh Boscowen remarked that the present Convention was more of a parliament than the one of 1660, and should proceed in its business.[88]

But, like the situation as a whole, no self-description was unproblematic and the two issues ran in tandem. If the Convention arose from a dissolution, this could well call up the spectre of levelling and of a Hobbesian natural condition deemed a 'bold and dangerous assertion' and a 'ridiculous notion'.[89] Thus Sir Robert Sawyer: if there has been a dissolution, the proceedings have no authority; but if James is taken to have abdicated, those involved can still be representatives. To this the palpably irritated Boscowen retorted that if it was necessary to wait for a better 'way to sit

---

[84] 'Grey's Debates', in Jones, *Parliamentary History*, p. 121.
[85] Anon., *Proposals to the Present Convention*, in *Somers Tracts* (1689), vol. VIII, p. 34; Maynard, 'Grey's Debates', in Jones, *Parliamentary History*, p. 197.
[86] Humfrey (?), *Good Advice* (1688); Fullwood, *Agreement*, pp. 44–6; Anon., *A Discourse Concerning the Nature, Power and Proper Effects of the Present Convention* (1689), in *State Tracts* (1705), vol. I, pp. 218, 220, 221–4.
[87] Burnet, *History*, vol. IV, pp. 41–2, 72–3.
[88] 'Grey's Debates', in Jones, *Parliamentary History*, pp. 101, 181–2.
[89] Burnet, *History*, vol. III, p. 362; *A Letter to a Member of the Convention*, in *Somers Tracts* (1689), vol. VII, p. 25; see also William, *Wherein it is Set Forth*; see also Tim Harris, 'The Leveller Legacy: From Restoration to Exclusion Crisis', in Michael Mendle, ed., *The Putney Debates* (Cambridge, 2001), pp. 219–40.

than as you are, you may sit till doomsday'.[90] Abdication solves nothing, for there is still 'a little one beyond the sea too, that will pretend ... Therefore declare "that the throne is void," and fill it'.[91] This resolution was sent up to the Lords, where it too was found difficult; a vacant throne implied an elective responsibility.[92] In one form or another, some understanding of consent becomes inescapable as a criterion for settlement. Ultimately, as Francis Fullwood reflected, the Convention opted for the words abdication and vacancy as the least contentious to describe the situation.[93] There had been neither forfeiture nor resistance.

In the Declaration of Lords Spiritual and Temporal, and Commons, Assembled at Westminster (13 February), those involved would style themselves as 'a full and free Representative of this Nation'. In this grand if under-determined capacity they resolved to offer the throne to William and Mary. In accepting, William stated that he regarded the Declaration as a great proof of trust. He reiterated that he had come to England only to preserve 'your Religion, Laws and Liberties' and assured them that he would act only for the good of the Kingdom, 'to advance the welfare and glory of the nation'.[94] Those who flourished new oaths of allegiance were formally consenting to the joint rule. This studiedly ceremonial occasion thus concluded with the flavour of a coronation oath.

VIII

Behind the oaths that would be sworn to king and queen lay an attempt to avoid another Engagement controversy. A carefully balanced committee of the loyalists lords Nottingham, Rochester and the Bishop of Peterborough, together with the emphatically Williamite lords Wharton and Delamere, had been given the task of formulating new oaths. Previous ones that might cause agonies of conscience and conflicting obligations were repealed. Replacement oaths of allegiance and supremacy proposed by the committee formed the peroration of the Declaration before William and Mary. The oath of allegiance read: 'I, A. B. do sincerely promise and swear that I will be faithful and bear true Allegiance to their Majesties King William and Queen Mary.'[95]

---

[90] 'Grey's Debates', in Jones, *Parliamentary History*, pp. 118–19; see also Sir Thomas Lee, Col. Birch, 20 February 1688, in *ibid.*, pp. 199, 198.
[91] *Ibid.*, p. 119.
[92] 'Notes of a Noble Lord', in *ibid.*, p. 80.
[93] Fullwood, *Agreement*, pp. 33, 56.
[94] Jones, *Parliamentary History*, p. 45.
[95] Jones, *Conscience and Allegiance*, p. 280.

What Burnet called the oath's 'ancient simplicity' strongly suggests that it was set on encompassing rather than sorting sheep from goats.[96] The range of people being required to swear, of 'all office or employment ecclesiastical or civil', supports this.[97] Yet again it illustrates the wide scope of office in the polity to which James VI&I had appealed in the wake of the Gunpowder Plot and the appropriateness of a short skiagraphic oath, in the idiom of the Engagement, to an adequately encompassing end. It was all the more easy to take if it was read as a proclamation of the reach of subjection.[98] The new oath of supremacy, however, sought to exclude all Romish interference, so going beyond James VI&I's demands for only civil allegiance. The distinction between temporal and spiritual offices had proved too porous. Thus, 'A. B.' had to swear abhorrence from the heart of 'that damnable doctrine . . . that princes may be excommunicated or deprived by the Pope or any authority of the See of Rome, may be deposed or murdered by their subjects or any other whatsoever'. And A. B. had further to declare, in a manifest tightening of the oath of 1606, that 'no foreign Prince, person, prelate, state or potentate, hath or ought to have any jurisdiction, power, superiority, pre-eminence or authority ecclesiastical or spiritual within this realm'. As Beddard tellingly remarks, in this the Augsburg principle was inverted. The religion of a people would determine that of the monarch; the Reformation in England, brought in by a king, had undone primogeniture.[99]

Out of 10,000 clergy only 400 could not take the oath of allegiance. Among them, however, were eight bishops who, forced to alienate official administrative tasks to laymen, created in their dioceses a temporary but symbolic erosion of priestly office.[100] From the evidence of print, the issue for them remained the sanctity of spiritual office epitomised in the oaths already sworn.[101] Passive obedience was a theological doctrine and clerics claimed to be arbiters of what this meant. If this situation contrasted starkly with the numbers who lost their livings after 1662, it also probably inflamed fears of equivocation. The simpler an oath, the more it might accommodate Sandersonian 'high' or 'low' readings and the more the imposers might themselves be suspected of equivocation. Conversely, the more it closed loopholes, so challenging conscience, the more it might be rejected or be taken with indifferent sincerity. The new

---

[96] Burnet, *History*, vol. III, p. 380.
[97] Jones, *Conscience and Allegiance*, p. 280; Goldie, 'The Revolution of 1689', pp. 482–3.
[98] Kennett, *Dialogue*, p. 30.
[99] Jones, *Conscience and Allegiance*, pp. 280–1; Beddard, *Kingdom*, p. 65.
[100] Goldie, 'The Revolution of 1689', p. 479; Burnet, *History*, vol. IV, p. 12.
[101] Evelyn, *Diary*, 15 January, 1689, vol. IV, p. 614; 26 April, 1689, p. 637.

oath of allegiance was subject to the first danger, that of Supremacy subject to the second. The oath of allegiance was probably meant to be decidedly latitudinarian, its force depending upon understandings of 'faithful' and 'true allegiance' where there was no mention of right. All these points were rehearsed in both Houses.[102] As one tract put it, the 'highest' reading was that faithful and true meant defending the new monarchs against all comers; the 'lowest' meant little more than de facto acceptance of them until James II had an opportunity to recover his throne.[103] This protean potential, so strongly echoing the Engagement, may itself explain the small numbers of non-juring clergy. An abjuration oath was much debated in parliament in 1690, and when James died the 1701 Oath of Abjuration unceremoniously insisted on allegiance to William as right and lawful king.[104] For a minority, the agonies of conscience rippled well into the eighteenth century. Dr Henry Sacheverell remains in the wings.

Drawing on Hickes's *Apology*, Mark Goldie has suggested that there were six or seven hypotheses as to what had happened when James ran and William came: resistance, from historical precedent, or natural right; breach of contract, justifying deposition, or as action taken *in extremis*; possession, as effective protection; abdication, a conquest, or providential deliverance.[105] These hypotheses fall into two rough sub-groups: those concentrating on what James had done, and those using his actions to assess what was done by others.

A number of things are crucial about this. First, because Hickes was a less than disinterested guide, his account needs treating with caution. Contract and resistance are disproportionately significant, perhaps, as Paul Monod has noted, because non-jurors regarded contract as particularly vulnerable to refutation. Goldie, in fact, has observed a reluctance by those supporting the Revolution to accept that it had been an act of resistance. This is because resistance remained easily reconfigured as a euphemism for rebellion, setting a dangerous precedent in an uncertain future; it could even be an expression of popery.[106] No wonder Hickes subsumed so much under its auspices, and that arguments from defence and dissolution are absent from his listed hypotheses. Defence was the

---

[102] Burnet, *History*, vol. IV, pp. 76–7.
[103] Anon., *A Discourse Concerning the Signification of Allegiance* (1689), pp. 1–2; Clark, 'Johnson', pp. 84–5.
[104] Burnet, *History*, vol. IV, pp. 76–7; The Abjuration Oath reprinted in Jones, *Conscience and Allegiance*.
[105] Goldie, 'The Revolution of 1689', pp. 486, 529.
[106] See Monod, *English Jacobitism*, p. 21; Goldie, 'The Revolution of 1689', p. 489; Long (?), *Reflections*, pp. 2, 10.

most noticeable counter to the accusation of rebellion; dissolution could be used, albeit with diminishing success, to avoid resistance and rebellion altogether.[107] For Hickes it was all euphemistic of rebellion. If all the eggs could be dropped into one rebellious basket, they might be easier to break at a blow. Secondly, in a vibrant print environment, with unknown and even unimagined audiences, diversity of argument had appeal on the basis of quite conventional rhetorical injunction. The arguments in print, therefore, like those in the Convention, ran together and slipped between *topoi* such as conquest, possession, natural right, abdication and defence. What, to repeat, generated this flexibility of argument was an extensive grounding in a belief that James's rule had been tyrannical. On all sides, then, the issue actually in dispute was the limits and functions of the office of rule and what it entailed for the ruled as concentrated in the act of swearing an oath; all of this functioned theoretically as preconditions to justify taking new oaths for old. Questions of consent become difficult to avoid because an awareness of rupture was inescapable; and re-affirming rule through an oath meant nothing if it did not presuppose some consent of the soul.

IX

The anonymous *Friendly Debate* was one of the lengthier pamphlets, presented as the private papers of a modest minister, so displaying and exploiting the clerical tensions in the crisis of allegiance. A dialogue between a non-juror, Dr Kingsman, and his Williamite neighbour Gratianus Trimmer, it is set before a thanksgiving sermon for the new monarchs.[108]

It opens in Platonic style, with a journey. Kingsman is visiting his friend, and after initial skirmishes they adjourn to Trimmer's chilly study, allowing both access to the authorities they need. Kingsman's role is to raise objections to abandoning oaths, exhibiting disloyalty, rebelling and rejoicing at the triumph of de facto rulers. His is the pious non-juring voice of passive obedience, drawing on the anti-Engagement arguments of Robert Sanderson.[109] Trimmer dextrously handles one distinct account of affairs after another, but always to the same end: allegiance to

---

[107] Lawson, *Politica*, pp. 226–34; Comber, *A Letter to a Bishop*, pp. 5, 14; for the use of Lawson, see Condren, *George Lawson's Politica*, chs. 13, 14.
[108] Anon., *A Friendly Debate between Dr. Kingsman, a Dissatisfied Clergy-Man and Gratianus Trimmer, a Neighbour Minister* (1689); see also Kennett, *Dialogue*, which has a less elaborate structure to similar ends.
[109] Anon., *Friendly Debate*, p. 14; see also Downes, *Discourse*; Dr G. B., *A Word to the Wavering*, p. 2.

the new regime is morally required, abuse of office has destroyed the old, and only in that context must the sanctity of oaths be considered. The subject's obligation entails judgement that makes passive obedience a dereliction of duty.[110] Only the trimmer understands true loyalty and, as Halifax had it, keeps the little boat of state on a true bottom. Because James did not keep 'his Religion to Himself', he threatened the kingdom. Therefore, loyalty to him is disloyalty to Christ.[111] Here, in short order, is an initial co-optive predication of the crucial terms loyalty and duty as attributes of the subject's responsibility, followed by an awareness of the difficulties of keeping the spiritual and temporal realms distinct, an insistence on allegiance being to office rather than person and a faith in the sanctioning power of providence. These are all shaped into a piece of extensive casuistical argument. The litany of James's misgovernment, undefended by Kingsman, allows Trimmer to extend loyalty to office to the point at which identity in office dissolves the issue. 'I am subject to the King, and not to him who . . . hath made Himself none.' He continued, '[As] Sir Thomas More said, the Lord Chancellor is gone, when his Person was there present, but out of Office.'[112] Lawson's authority reinforces the argument: obligation to the king ceases with the monarch's death, with tyrannous conduct, or with actions that dissolve the constitution. 'If one term of the relation be changed or ceased, the obligation of the other relate and Correlate ceaseth.'[113] On this basis it will be urged that James was not deposed and there was no rebellion.

Kingsman meanwhile has repaired to the law of nature. Obedience is from nature, to which Trimmer replies that obedience to the pope is not, and by it James relinquishes any natural right to rule. How is it, then, asks Kingsman, that men swore obedience at his coronation? They swore, states Trimmer, and suffered in good faith, but James broke his trust and threatened tyranny. Thus there was no rebellion or breach of oath only defence; the invasion was a deliverance providentially arranged.[114] Kingsman's reiteration that there had been a rebellion because of 'our

---

[110] Anon., *Friendly Debate*, p. 3; Kennett, *Dialogue*, pp. 31–2.

[111] Anon., *Friendly Debate*, pp. 2, 60, 3, 49; see also Long (?), *A Resolution*, fol. Ar.

[112] Anon., *Friendly Debate*, pp. 6–7; 25–6, 71, misprinted as 17, 72–3; see also Fullwood, *Agreement*, pp. 32–4; Anon., *The Doctrine of Passive Obedience* (1689), pp. 1–2; Anon., *An Enquiry into the Present State of Affairs* (1689), pp. 10–11; Comber, *Letter to a Bishop*, p. 4.

[113] Anon., *Friendly Debate*, pp. 6–7, 21. The references are to the first edition; recall also Ascham (?), *An Answer to the Vindication of Dr. Hammond* (1650), p. 5, on the terms governor and governed as 'relatives'.

[114] Anon., *Friendly Debate*, pp. 6, 7–8, 39, 12–13; Kennett, *Dialogue*, an 'unfathomably stupendous deliverance', pp. 1, 11–12. See also Anon., *The Doctrine of Passive Obedience*, p. 2; Anon., *An Enquiry*, p. 10.

Oaths' opens discussion of the limitations of all promissory oaths. Ordinarily these should be kept, states Trimmer, but because of their reciprocal nature, when rule becomes tyranny, they must cease. Tyranny now stretches beyond papal *pleonexia* to the systematic misuse of necessary prerogative, a criterion for marking abuse of office and the transformation of its inhabiting *persona*.[115] Kingsman insists that prerogative cannot be so restricted; the liberties of the subject are concessions and therefore resistance is rebellion. This synoptic view of absolutism is supported by Filmerian arguments from Adam as the universal father, introduced by Trimmer for the purpose of ridicule, and by the serious proposition that rights and ownership are the contingent gifts of the sovereign. Rejecting this, Trimmer enlists Queen Elizabeth as a ruler who recognised that sworn allegiance was limited by what was due. The crown was absolute only in being imperial: she owed no fealty to a foreign prince;[116] so oaths are conditional upon offices being maintained, and upon a veritable hierarchy of loyalty to those in office, to country and to God. How, asks Trimmer rhetorically, 'can I swear to . . . the Imperial Crown, when [James] hath parted with . . . Authority . . . to the Pope? This would be to swear against Him and not for Him.' James was not an absolute monarch where his office required it. Swearing under Charles II to be loyal to his successors meant Protestant successors.[117] Oaths cannot be taken *in vacuo*; they assume stable constitutional relationships.

Loyalty, then, necessitates consideration of the English monarchy which is neither absolute nor entirely hereditary. Trimmer now argues more generally, introducing a notion of contract, to which he returns in an addendum. Government, having begun in families, gradually grew into kingdoms and the 'derided Contract and Consent of the People' has provided a sound principle for distinguishing rule from tyranny.[118] His authority is Hooker. As the coronation oath shows and the Convention plausibly illustrates, consent does not require a gathered multitude to be meaningful.[119] Indeed, an original contract is more than 'a *Popular Flourish*', it is close enough to the work of the Convention to sit with the traditions of a polity that has always negotiated the office of rule.[120] This allows yet another justification for taking new oaths for old.

---

[115] Anon., *Friendly Debate*, pp. 13–14; Fullwood, *Agreement*, p. 38; cf. Hickes, *Apology*, pp. 2–6.
[116] Anon., *Friendly Debate*, pp. 15–17, 18–19; cf. Burnet, *History*, vol. III, p. 92.
[117] Anon., *Friendly Debate*, pp. 25–6; cf. Bilson, *Christian Subjection*, pt. 2, pp. 145–6; also Anon., *An Enquiry*, p. 10.
[118] Anon., *Friendly Debate*, pp. 28, 61–78, 29; Kennett, *Dialogue*, p. 14.
[119] Anon., *Friendly Debate*, p. 30; Kennett, *Dialogue*, pp. 14–15.
[120] Anon., *Friendly Debate*, pp. 62–5; contrast Anon., *Vindiciae juris regii*, p. 21.

Breach of contract can mean forfeiture of office as well as dissolution of government.[121]

In this expository layering of arguments around a simple principle, Kingsman's responses gradually compress to a splutter 'Conscience and Allegiance'.[122] In contrast, Trimmer expatiates and dialogue becomes declamation. There is something authentically Socratic in this encroachment of tedium and something structurally Platonic in the argument coming full circle, back to the meaning of duty and what is due to office. In this there is also a typically Platonic inversion. Kingsman eventually signals agreement, but his last two short sentences suggest latent disloyalty to the new regime. He will keep his oath to James and do nothing to harm his cause should he return: real rebellion and disloyalty under pretext of sacred oaths is to be looked for in the non-juror.[123] A distributive predication balances the opening co-option of true loyalty. A compound rhetorical question hangs in the air: who really knows his duty, who is really rebellious, who really should be tarred with the de facto brush?[124]

X

In the following year John Locke's *Two Treatises* was also printed anonymously. It was well tuned to the surrounding debates, and can be used to illustrate the widespread tendencies to elide discrete conceptual vocabularies. The work's overall similarity to *A Friendly Debate* is evident. Both reject Filmer's arguments as biblically implausible and theologically obnoxious. Both rely on consent to sanction rule and qualify the hereditary principle.[125] Each subverts what is taken to be the fundamental feature of absolutism: untrammelled prerogative. In terms almost identical to the language of Trimmer and the earlier 'Philodemius' (Anthony Ascham?), Locke summarises prerogative as *'nothing but the Power of doing publick good without a Rule'*.[126] But later he reverts to the conventionally hostile understanding, like Trimmer, collapsing

---

[121] Cf. Defoe, *Jure Divino*, bk. 6, p.15: 'And they who what they should defend invade,/ Forfeit their Office, have their Trust betray'd.'
[122] Anon., *Friendly Debate*, p. 60.
[123] Ibid., p. 62; cf. Anon., *The Case of Allegiance to a King in Possession* (1690), p. 3; William Sherlock, *The Case of Allegiance due to Sovereign Powers* (1691), pp. 46–7.
[124] Cf. Defoe, *Jure Divino*, p. i; Fullwood, *Agreement*, pp. 60–1.
[125] Locke, *Two Treatises*, 1, paras. 9–11.
[126] Locke, *Two Treatises*, 2, para. 166; see also 'Philodemius', *The Original and End*, p. 23; for a recent discussion of this topic see C. Fatovic, 'Constitutionalism and Contingency: Locke's Theory of Prerogative', *History of Political Thought*, 25, 2 (2004), pp. 276–97. Despite seeing Locke as an advocate of rebellion, p. 285, Fatovic rightly sees prerogative as central to casuistic theory, see p. 295.

prerogative into arbitrary power and both into tyranny.[127] This creates slavery because the tyrant is unbounded and acts in self-interest. Rights, argues Locke, are only for the fulfilment of duties; freedom is not allowing '*every Man to do what he lists*', it is bounded by law.[128] Against tyranny stands liberty of office.

Like the author of the *Friendly Debate*, Locke relies upon the contingency of official identity to invert the language of political condemnation. Father, magistrate or master (the conventional examples of social office) exist in the same man, but their continuity depends upon rule-bound conduct. A *persona* may cease through ill actions, and in this respect there is no difference between great and petty officers.[129] To avoid slavery, a people might defend itself against those *who had once been* their magistrates.[130] Thus what is called rebellion can really be self-defence against tyranny, dissolution of government and violation of contract. Those who have been entrusted with office and tyrannously bring about such a situation 'are truly and properly *Rebels*'.[131]

The same well-worn *sententiae* of nominal identity are found in Locke's comments on oaths: they presuppose social, rule-bound activity.[132] Like 'Trimmer', he insists that allegiance is but 'an *Obedience according to Law*'; and is contingent on the prince remaining the representative of the public will. Once a prince quits this *persona* and behaves as 'a single private Person', he loses right, for obedience is owed to the public will of the society, that is, to its offices. When the *Two Treatises* was written, Charles II was widely feared to be in contravention of his oaths, and the disquiet had remained relevant to James.[133] Locke's and Trimmer's entirely conventional position springs from the same source as the doctrine of equivocation: recognition that meaning partially depends upon the tacitly accepted, especially concerning the point and limit of office. Locke's was clearly not a doctrine of equivocation, but that a statement might be under-determined by its own content could have similarly qualifying effects when applied to swearing. It is also the burden of Locke's song to collapse both arbitrary and absolute rule into the state of war in which reciprocal responsibilities are impossible.[134] The sort of

---

[127] Locke, *Two Treatises*, 2, paras. 210, 224, 137, 164, 166; Kennett, *Dialogue*, p. 24.
[128] Locke, *Two Treatises*, 2, paras. 199, 57.
[129] *Ibid.*, 2, para. 202.
[130] *Ibid.*, 2, paras. 227, 239, 220; cf. also Wildman (?), *Some Remarks Upon Government* (1688/9), in *State Tracts* (1705), vol. I, p. 152.
[131] Locke, *Two Treatises*, 2, paras. 226, 196.
[132] *Ibid.*, paras. 186, 195.
[133] *Ibid.*, para. 151; see also Kennett, *Dialogue*, pp. 30–8.
[134] Locke, *Two Treatises*, 2, paras. 17, 199.

rule claimed by Charles II's apologists which he and then James were believed to exercise was condemned because unrestrained: it abrogated obligations and oaths.

The issue of contract has been discussed earlier insofar as it reinforced a particular reading of the coronation oath; as I have suggested, arguments from breach of oath and contract could be simply variant formulations of office-abuse. Like the author of the *Friendly Debate*, Locke uses a notion of contract to insist that government is consensual and limited. Even in cases of invasion and usurpation, the point at which consent replaces war marks the beginning of a polity. The ground thus variously prepared, the resounding final chapter conflates notions of forfeiture of governing right, dissolution of government, resistance as self-defence, always only in the extremity of a state of war (created by the real rebels) and an appeal to heaven presupposing providential answer. Sir Robert Sawyer had suggested that the distinct terms used to describe James II's exit might be 'all one'; Locke went a long way to show just how much this could be so.

A contract motif is important in adding force to this popular affirmation of the enormity of office-abuse, but it was enough for Locke to be able to argue that specific political arrangements informed by prior understandings were reasonably taken to be contingent on mutual trust. Locke's use of contract is a polished repair of the mirror for magistrates that Hobbes had tried to shatter. And, as Hobbes's warlike natural condition was given verisimilitude by the Civil Wars, Locke's inconvenient but more social state of nature was a rough and reasonable match for the turbulent London in which the Convention met. The Lockian state of war had ended with James's departure.

Locke had a continuing close interest in the Americas, revising the constitutions of the Carolinas at about the same time as the *Two Treatises* were being written. David Armitage has persuasively argued that the work was probably only finished in 1682, with the late insertion of the chapter on property.[135] If so, its presence and character may be explained by casuistic opportunism. Locke had one eye on the natural condition of the Indians and what might be done about it. But one eye remained on London. The result was split vision. The need for 'property' to do double duty required a shift to an encompassing generality that drew on but erased the established distinction between *real* and *personal* property, or the one drawn by Ascham between subsistence and surplus property. Locke put much emphasis on rights of possession being contingent upon

---

[135] Armitage, 'John Locke, Carolina and the *Two Treatises of Government*', pp. 1-26.

good use, a point most relevant to *real* and Ascham's surplus property for which possession was not absolute. In the Americas, this could be employed to justify dispossessing the Indians who might not husband land as profitably as the colonisers. Conversely, in England an appeal to the sanctity of ownership could be used in an opposing way. When labour was mixed with material goods, especially those needed for subsistence, it was plausible to claim that an absolute right of ownership was created. The argument was medieval. Expropriation of such *personal* property without consent stood, then, as the traditional mark of the tyrant, and so could justify self-defence. Such arguments were much in the London air while the work was being written.[136]

Despite a strong family resemblance to tracts like *A Friendly Debate*, the *Second Treatise* gives remarkably little attention to religion. Locke evokes Thomas Bilson on the alienation of magistracy to a foreign power, but does not discuss the principal possibility of alienation to Rome, or Rome via France. Again, he only alludes to arbitrary power being used to change the religion of society, arguably the predominant fear of Charles II's last years.[137] Picking up the familiar ship and state imagery exploited by Trimmer, Locke remarks that if a man is always being steered towards Algiers despite the prevailing conditions, he can assume that is where he is being taken. This may be a direct allusion to a sequence of allegorical pamphlets printed in support of Charles between 1679 and 1680 about a ship off the coast of Algiers (Rome) and the captain's problems with the crew (rebels).[138] Locke's general account of property can easily be taken to embrace religion, for it was conventional enough to treat religion as a property, and Locke's discussion has been seen as a defence against the possible re-distribution of real estate under a Catholic prince. Such scaremongering arguments were voiced by Locke's contemporaries but they are not in the *Second Treatise*.[139]

On these counts, oversight seems less likely than strategic displacement; and it is the absence of sectarian polemic as much as anything present in the *Second Treatise* that has helped in the effective removal of the work from its intellectual milieu.[140] The point of bypassing religion might have

---

[136] Scott, *Algernon Sidney and the Restoration Crisis*, pp. 185–6, 271–3.
[137] Locke, *Two Treatises*, 2, paras. 239, 210.
[138] Anon., *The Seamans Dream* (1679); Anon., *A Letter from Leghorn*; Anon., *An Answer to Another Letter from Leghorn* (1680); Anon., *An Answer to a Second Letter from Leghorn* (1680); Anon., *A Newsletter from Leghorn . . . to a Merchant in London* (1680).
[139] Andrew Marvell, *An Account of the Growth of Popery and Arbitrary Government* (1677), pp. 13–14; Wildman, *Some Remarks*.
[140] On the analogous absence of historical reference, see J. G. A. Pocock, *The Ancient Constitution and the Feudal Law* (Cambridge, 1987 edn.), pp. 236–8.

been to render irrelevant priestly claims about their authority to guide consciences. Locke's work, however, has been further secularised, sitting ill with his devout antipathy to Catholicism. It is possible to take this revisionism too far and argue that Locke is modern because of what he did not say. Nevertheless, what he did say followed the same patterns of argument and relied on the same interchangeable casuistic *topoi*, axioms and adages as works now largely forgotten. Yet he remains a writer of whom we constantly expect too much, or the wrong sort of thing, perhaps because of the philosophical significance of the *Essay* and so the *Two Treatises* persistently incites the energies of rescue, rehabilitation and re-writing; all conditional on the silence of the text.

Locke's synoptic collapse of the vocabulary of casuistic justification is a response to James VI&I, *Trew Law of Free Monarchy* and Hobbes's *De cive*. Locke quotes James VI&I as an authority on kingship.[141] To 'the old question', however, of who is to judge the difference between exercise and abuse of office, he replies the people, so cutting through or deflecting all distinctions. In hearing no discrete clerical voice, Locke sides with men like Ascham and Hobbes on the question of the limits of the office of the priest. His notion of the people is as general and accommodating as that of their consent and property. Modern commentators expecting clear commitments in such language have had room to move in differing directions. For some, Locke's people were an exclusive élite, for others a proof of democratic commitment so advanced as to explain Locke's marginal status in contemporary debates.[142]

Such a polarisation unnecessarily confuses our priorities with Locke's. A broad and inclusive notion of the people in situations of emergency was neither new nor (to allude to the incoherent hyperbole) the preserve of those too radically modern for their times. It was implicit in the rhetorics of patriotism; and if found in the screaming injunctions of Ponet, Goodman, Cardinal Allen and Edward Sexby, it is also there in the panic of James VI&I after the Gunpowder Plot. In emergency every man has an office to come to the aid of his country. To recall William Ames, *in extremis*, every man becomes a public officer. Or, as White Kennett remarked, in extraordinary cases there are no rules.[143] The preface of the *Second Treatise*, like the final chapter, is at one with just this inclusive tradition of patriotic casuistry. It was '*the people of* England

---

[141] Locke, *Two Treatises*, 2, para. 200, see also para. 133, on 'commonwealth'; cf. also Fullwood, *Agreement*, p. 34.

[142] On the reception, see Mark Goldie, 'Introduction', in *The Reception of Locke's Politics* (London, 1999), vol. I, esp. pp. xx–xxiii.

[143] Kennett, *Dialogue*, pp. 33–6. His account of the origin of society and function of executive rule is also like Locke's, pp. 10–12.

whose love of their Just and Natural Right, with their Resolution to preserve them, [that] *saved the Nation when it was on the very brink of Slavery and Ruine*.[144] From this, however, we can neither infer that he was similarly inclusive in times of normality, nor that he countenanced only the people as a landed élite. The issue was beside the point. Modern analyses, insisting that he stand here or there on a democratic principle have missed the evident casuistic markers, put where they matter, at the outset and reinforced at the end. The common ground Locke shared with others about office and its abuse, threatening '*Slavery and Ruine*' and a looming state of war, defined the fault-line of necessary casuistry, and suggests that he was at one with many of those around him. Locke might not have been cited much because he, in particular, was not much needed. Yet, by evading so many specifics he was more easily used as the turmoils of the 1680s faded into the past. When he wrote, around 1682, however, he was indeed embarked on a dangerous enterprise; the protean potential was the unintended consequence of circumspect generality. The *Two Treatises* were a threat of future action and an act of great polemical courage; in 1690 they could superficially be given focus on the past; James II tamed the revolutionary Locke, for the time being.

[144] Locke, *Two Treatises*, Preface, p. 155.

Epilogue

> I know what *Persona* means in the Dictionary, and therein lies all your Divinity. And therefore, I say . . . Farewell.
> (John Eachard, *A Second Dialogue*, 1673)

I

Like Burnet's depiction of the reign of James II, the web of office has been broken, though by no single act. Dealing with language is, remarked Wittgenstein, like trying to mend a cobweb with your fingers, and it would be fruitless to try such a repair now. Cobwebs, however, do stick and can at a pinch bind wounds. Office has had an arachnidean virtue of tenacity, even in the processes by which it has been over-stretched, torn and used to patch up the fissures in later notions of what counts as ethical conduct and political theory. So what has happened to the spider and what help might an enhanced understanding of office provide? It is a difficult question, not least because it has to be asked almost at the same time as it has been powerfully argued that the modern state arose as a consequence of official entanglements: institutionalised offices became more formalised, and their functions were extended, in which processes a controlling centre became more robust.[1] If true, is this a case of the offspring consuming the parent; if the state is the result, what has happened to notions of office?

I have looked at a world in which some tacit understanding and expectation of office shaped the moral argument of early modern England, argument that was neither driven exclusively by a universalist deontology, nor by consequentialism. Insofar as office informed the political, that category of experience was itself compromised, or subordinated to the point of becoming contingent for those who might be expected to rely upon it. Any treatment of politics during this period as *sui generis* or independent is artificial – a convention of academic convenience and

---

[1] Braddick, *State Formation*, at length.

syllabus management. All this may be difficult to accept; we no longer live in that world, its vocabulary and patterns of use are not ours. If, to put it synoptically, a social domain constructed of offices was presupposed, the reasons for its decline, fragmentation and transformation must be intrinsic. And implicit in much of my discussion are explanations for the changed environment in which we live. The following hypotheses are as tentative as they are rudimentary.

First, then, from antiquity Carneadean scepticism, or cynicism, provides one clue in its recognition that whatever might be described as a virtue could be designated a vice and with its alternative thesis that what really drives the world is self-interest. The rise of what is called interest theory, out of the writings of figures like Machiavelli, Guicciardini and Lipsius, with a garnish of authority from Tacitus, may be seen as a graph charting disappointed expectations of office. There was no straightforward vector of replacement, for in part interest theorists regarded what I have called the negative register of office as of the greatest value in understanding the world. In an analogy drawn from relationships of office, Henri duc de Rohan wrote that as princes rule subjects, so interest rules princes and he clearly regarded interest, like a reified office, as a fundamental principle of continuity to be preserved. A state's interest, then, was not unlike the end of an office, the neglect of which was irresponsible. Yet, in adding that interests should be augmented, he compromised the similarly constitutive notion of a limit.[2] After a fashion, this ambivalent relationship with and development from notions of office allowed office and interest to rub along almost in as complementary a fashion as *honestas* and *utilitas*.[3] But it also allowed for forms of explanation independent of any ethics of office. A succinct illustration is found in Henry Neville's short allegory of the Civil Wars.[4] A number of players sit around a card table. Each is a *persona* for an interest that can be encapsulated in some maxim, of the sort de Rohan had formulated. And it is the interplay of these that explains the rules of the game; a partial control over events can be achieved only by manipulating the drives of other players. The problem for Neville was that no one understood this better than the Jesuits; they might, he concluded, still win in the end. In Neville's vision there may be doctrines of office, and behaviour that

---

[2] Henri duc de Rohan, *De l'interest des princes et estates de la Chrestiente* (Paris, 1639), pp. 104–6; cf. Bacon, *Advancement*, on the duties of augmentation and preservation.
[3] Godwyn, *The Negroe's and Indians Advocate*, A3.
[4] Henry Neville, *A Game of Piquet* (1660); see also John Locke, *The Correspondence of John Locke*, ed. Esmond de Beer, 8 vols. (Oxford: Clarendon Press, 1989), letter 81 (October 1659), on custom and interest as the only 'Luminarys of the world'.

conforms to them, but explanation and control require something else. The metaphors of risk and game-play he helped set upon their way would have a significant future in shaping a coherent conception of the political. While Neville was warning about the dangers of the republic and Reformation being trumped by Jesuitic cunning, William Cavendish's very different advice to Charles II exhibited a similar emphasis on control. An ethics of office is persistently shuffled to one side in order to concentrate on defeating or playing interests by tying them to the crown. Only in this way, Cavendish argued, would Charles survive.[5]

Overall, and analogous to the ways in which metaphors can become sufficiently established to allow conceptual use distinct from their origins, interest, fashioned from a vocabulary of office, became an idiom of critical analysis. John Selden indicates how much further matters could be taken, extrapolating from his anti-clerical and Carneadean vision of the priesthood. In contrast to a more elevated view of the clerical office in which ordination was radically transformative, consequent upon the grace that flowed through the ordaining hands, Selden took a starkly proclamatory and Lutheran line.[6] The imposition of hands is 'nothing but a designation of a Person to this or that Office'. There is no 'indelible Character'; a priest is like any man but for his title. Thus far this is an emphatic expression of a separation variant of nominal identity, but from this he generalised: 'Men that would get Power over others, make themselves as unlike them as they can.'[7] This is close to seeing interest not as an abuse but a function of office. A sub-theme of this study has concerned the specific and highly contested office of the priest; with Selden's reflection in mind, it can be suggested that anti-clericalism provided the arguments and exempla of contention that corroded notions of office as a whole. We do not have to extrapolate very far from Selden to conclude that all relationships of office are expressions of power, a term Selden uses not to mean the proper moral authority of office but a desire for domination.

Secondly, the rhetorics of office were themselves increasingly indiscriminate. One reason why I did not wish to shape my argument through a concept of ideology, so narrating a story of a core ideological concept, was to emphasise this persistently accommodating capacity in the language. As I have noted, there is an irony in that the protean, of which there was so much fear with respect to human conduct, was a feature of the

---

[5] Cavendish, 'Advice', at length.
[6] Compare Richard Vines, *The Authours, Nature and Danger of Haeresie* (1647), pp. 15–17.
[7] Selden, *Table Talk*, pp. 65–6.

language through which that conduct was depicted. The very adaptability of the vocabulary encouraged over-extension, especially as presuppositions of office cohabited with semiotic understandings of the world. Again, this problem was endemic, but after the Reformation there were additional pressures towards a protean pragmatics of office-talk. In a beleaguered Protestant country, in particular, there was the casuistic imperative to an ad hoc vertical extension of office. Beyond the higher reaches of theology, extending a notion of office to everyone, if only opportunistically, ran the risk of dissipating official identity while simultaneously entrapping everyone in the intricacies of multiple *personae*. To this was added incitement to stretch the vocabulary of office both to assimilate modal transformations in the intellectual world and to sanction anyone exercising the office of rule. Partly through sovereignty theory this latter form of horizontal extension began to reify government as an object of study. This, clearly realised during the Engagement controversy, threatened to make redundant any critical vocabulary for those actually in office – some seeds, perhaps, for the vision of an objective political science to be pursued from the nineteenth century.[8]

Selden's understanding of power was not unreasonable, although, as we have seen, more conventional Lockean uses of the word survived along with it. By the beginning of the eighteenth century, with the issues of the Civil Wars still fresh, the almost routine inflation of the vocabulary of office to justify anything was easily parodied, a point brilliantly demonstrated by 'Mrs Bull's Vindication of the Rights of Cuckoldom'. In this, Arbuthnot exploited a lack of discrimination in, and elision of, the political vocabulary. The merging of distinct conceptual terms seems to have been particularly evident in the debates around the Revolution of 1688–9. By the early eighteenth century, office-talk suffered, then, from conjoined problems of explanatory saliency, promiscuous adaptability and moral credibility.

It is in this context that alternative ethical theories arose, a little like newly formed states, from the armoury of office itself. Utilitarianism and Kantian deontology may, as I have indicated (above, chapter 8), be seen as responses to the difficulties of an ethics of office, and each involved turning aspects of arguments from office into global alternatives to it. Kant's hostility to casuistry needs little rehearsing. He condemned it as failing to provide any over-arching principle of conduct, and for mistaking an undifferentiated heap of arbitrary cases for morality itself. Casuistry could justify anything, but only retrospectively; it was

---

[8] Stefan Collini, Donald Winch and John Burrow, *That Noble Science of Politics* (Cambridge, 1983).

dangerous, self-serving and capricious – accusations that were all familiar from the conventional if selective abuse of casuistry in the name of official integrity. Instead, he destroyed the ethics of office by universalising a singular sense of it. *Persona* became person because it had to be a coherent moral singularity. The duty at the philological root of deontology became unitary. In this way, all putatively moral conduct defining the *noumenal* realm was subject to a uniform metaphysical principle. This single moral law would obviate the need for casuistry and render unethical consideration of the offices people actually held in their conduct in the *phenomenal* realm.[9]

Changes of emphasis in natural law theory provide a closely related dimension of the process of ethical attenuation. During the seventeenth and eighteenth centuries, until roughly the last re-issue of Pufendorf's works in 1759, natural law arose from and was a projection of relationships of office, but *ius*, as right or law, gradually became eased away from office, just as it was increasingly severed from divine law; the agent in the ambit of natural law became the rights-bearing individual. Additionally, it may be that the environment of laws in which agency operated became physical and, as with Mandeville, psychological, so embedding interest in a world view increasingly to one side of any notion of spheres of moral responsibility.

From the end of the nineteenth century Kantian deontology and utilitarianism have proved convenient abstractions, each of which, on its own, accounts poorly for the complexity of the world, but enables us to get along in it. So there has remained a more circumscribed, and perhaps more defensible arena in which a sense of office is vital, just as there remains a place for casuistry to mitigate the failings of aprioristic ethics. In theory, Max Weber provided a seminal example of the way in which a distinct sphere for an ethics of office could be maintained in an increasingly alien environment, through his theorisation of bureaucracy as *officium* and politics as a vocation. In practice, the professions of law and medicine, along with the priesthood, have remained paradigmatic of the official *persona*. But these provide locations for office *in*, rather than grounding *for*, an altered situation that makes an older world at once foreign but still intelligible. Yet here, in an ocean of commonsense deontology and consequentialism, the situation has become decidedly confused, the reliance on office and *persona* arbitrary. On the one hand, social groups aspiring to the lucrative status of the professions of law and medicine need at least the accoutrements of an official communal identity,

---

[9] Hunter, *Rival Enlightenments*, pp. 274–363.

with its distinctive ethics, ends and arcane knowledge. Sometimes this amounts to not much more than aping an ugly argot and the promulgation of reassuring codes of conduct. On the other, the reliance upon the fusion of duty and *persona* as constituting ethical conduct has suffered from misuse by oppressive bureaucracies and war machines called to account. In a different way, the relentless satire of the *persona* of the bureaucrat played a part in Britain, and countries like it, in establishing an environment in which civil service could be reformed on a model of business efficiency, and its traditionally proclaimed office as independent, institutionalised counsel of government compromised. Nevertheless, the patent shortcomings of post-Kantian moral certainties, and their unworldy metaphysics of social explanation, have led to some partial readjustment back to a reliance on conceptions of office as a moral category. This should remind us that all theories of ethics can be misused and that none does full justice to what we recognise as moral conduct.[10]

The general picture is one in which the ethics of office has at once contracted and its filaments been taken to repair its successors. Sometimes there is an inadvertence, or historical ignorance in this. The ethics of care, which in the western world has become something of a rationalisation of the ubiquitous social worker, is largely a massaged casuistry; practical ethics, at its best well cognisant of an ethics of office, a reaffirmation of casuistry's centrality to any philosophy that wishes to have serious engagement with the life beyond the seminar. More recently, what has been called 'virtue' ethics has been presented as a third way between utilitarianism and deontology, and an old way revived.[11] The emphasis has been upon relational identity and the moral qualities necessary for proper conduct. Character and communal value are made central to ethical judgement. This, too, it hardly needs labouring, rediscovers an aspect of the ethics of office highly sensitive to the characteristics, skills and qualities necessary for a given *persona*, defined only in reciprocal relationships. The abstracted point of continuity, however, has aided the retrojection of virtue ethics back into antiquity, so roping a classical tradition into an appropriate lineage; but to do this, the modality of an ethics of office has to be overlooked and the *personae* replaced by a post-Kantian person. The resultant vision of the past, as David Burchell has aptly remarked, is 'heroically primitive'.[12] It has played no small part

---

[10] Charles Taylor, *Sources of the Self: The Making of Modern Identity* (Cambridge, Mass., 1989), pp. 495–521.
[11] Alistair MacIntyre, *After Virtue: A Study in Moral Theory* (Notre Dame, 1981).
[12] David Burchell, 'Civic Personae: MacIntyre, Cicero and Moral Personality', *History of Political Thought*, 19 (1998), p. 103.

in continuing to keep an ethics of office obscure. It has created an inadequacy of perspective only reinforced by myth-making histories of ethics preoccupied with moral autonomy, regardless of whether they are celebrations, or lamentations for its being a dreadful mistake.[13] Rule utilitarianism, again, offers some reconstitution of an ethics of office by positing not utility per se as a criterion of ethical conduct, but the value of fixed patterns of rules. To judge rule-following by the ends served is close to a casuistry of office, as even a casual reading of Locke should make clear.[14]

II

Coinciding with the decline of a presupposition of office has been the rise of political theory as a discrete field of study with its own projected lineage, developing in the mid-nineteenth century and firming into its present shape only at the beginning of the twentieth.[15] It is possible, as I have indicated (above, chapter 10), that a decline in the ubiquity of office was one condition for the development of political theory, especially as it is now studied with its dogged attention to ideological conflict and the definition of our own political concepts; if so, the fashioning of a suitable pedigree into a decisively political shape, to give a depth and credibility to a juvenile discipline, has necessitated reconfiguring arguments about office and casuistic exception in which the political was often fleeting, unstable and subordinate. Many of the lineal figures of early modern political theory have had their casuistries of office re-tailored to our needs. Broad movements of political argument, relevant to major and minor figures alike, have been largely structured by concepts of ideology, intellectually cohesive and exclusive bodies of doctrinal commitment. On the basis of such patterns of alterity there has been no shortage of grandish narratives of the victory of one ideology at the expense of others. The propensity is not without merit, for there were divisive patterns of belief in the early modern world, and firm rationalisations for organised violence. Moreover, writing history on the model of ideological conflict has the attraction of making the past tidy, exciting, leading somewhere; the shock therapy of recognition pays dividends.

---

[13] Schneewind, *The Invention of Autonomy*, and Taylor, *Sources of the Self*, are two sides of the same coin.
[14] Brad Hooker, *Ideal, Code, Real World* (Oxford, 2000), pp. 3–30; and Robert Goodin, 'Utilitarianism as Public Philosophy', in A. Vincent, ed., *Polictical Theory: Tradition and Interpretation* (Cambridge, 1997), pp. 67–88.
[15] Robert Blakey, *A History of Political Literature from the Earliest Times*, 2 vols. (London, 1855); W. Dunning, *A History of Political Theories* (New York, 1902).

Nevertheless, any fascination we might have with pin-pointing the interplay of ideologies needs to be read against rather alien features of early modern text use. Consistency of argument was not always cherished and the fashion for the *cento*, for philosophical eclecticism and commonplace books all put it at a discount, allowing almost any respectable authority to sit down to tea with another. Additionally, the criteria of intellectual coherence have been stable neither over time nor intellectual space, and there was a pronounced tendency in seventeenth-century England to create oppositional groupings from projected patterns of inferential, or practical consequence. These are not straightforward evidence of social division, or stable intellectual allegiance.

Qualifications aside, the problem of identifying political ideologies is often less with previous text uses than with recent 'discoveries' of traditions, doctrines and languages. It is easy to forget that when we are the organising agents, discovery can be a matter of modelling and, in a subtle way, invention. In recent years we have been treated to mixed monarchy theory as a new dominant ideology;[16] to the replacement of Ciceronianism with Tacitism; the emergence of a theory of reason of state;[17] the rise of absolutism, Arminianism, republicanism and the synthesis of this last ideology with its imagined antithesis, liberalism. These replace, or refine the older surges of capitalism and puritanism, perhaps constitutionalism, and democracy. At all events, isms have proved indispensable in imposing a clarifying shape on the movements of time. John Locke's life has been presented as an apotheosis of enlightened development from conservatism to radicalism.[18] Some of these stories are more fanciful than others, but tidy history is apt to be fanciful history. The more a commonly shared register in the use of a vocabulary is mistaken for an exclusive ideolect, and the more the surviving evidence of language use is elided with modern categories of analysis, the more tidiness shifts into falsity and falsity trips to the brink of fantasy. There is something to be said for a rise of absolutism; reference to Tacitus can mark a weary disappointment with conduct in office; but there is less to say for a new ideology of civility (above, chapter 5), and rebellion as an emergent ideology is a step beyond the brink.[19]

I have, then, been canvassing something less than the discovery of yet another rising ideology in this yeasty world, namely the relative stability

---

[16] Weston and Greenberg, *Subjects and Sovereigns*.
[17] Tuck, *Philosophy and Government*.
[18] Richard Ashcraft, *Revolutionary Politics and Locke's Two Treatises of Government* (Princeton, 1986).
[19] Greenberg, *The Radical Face*, pp. 203–4, 244.

of the principal use patterns of a vocabulary that cut across what we see as ideological divisions. If the resources of office could undoubtedly be used divisively, they were also the means by which talismanic names we take as ideological markers could be brought together: expectation of office and its vocabulary were lubricants of textual assimilation. A linguistic consensus expressed in shared usage was the means of and condition for dispute, and we cannot hope to understand seventeenth-century political reflection without paying it attention independently of our own political vocabulary.

It has yet to be shown, one way or the other, whether ideology is a necessary agent in the study of the history of the pre-modern world, and addressing this issue has not been my direct concern. But historians have been rather too free with the label, usually without saying what they mean by it, yet treating it as a sort of natural kind, an adjunct to treating politics in a similar fashion.[20] It should also be apparent by now that we can get a long way in early modern political theory without automatic recourse to ideological modelling. I have shown how easily adjustable patterns of *sententiae* from the cultural capital of office-talk might, depending on circumstances, be accentuated, diminished or displaced from one writer to another. So, for example, we have a family resemblance between the maxims of 'absolutism' and 'de facto theory': those extolling allegiance to authority and those suspending it in extraordinary cases. The propensity to create reified political identities has obscured the resourcefulness and fluidity of argument. The effect has been as creatively parochialising as it has become familiar. This is not to eschew all explanatory models as such. In one way, the hypothesis of a presupposition of office, presented as an analytic abridgement (Introduction, chapter 1) is a rudimentary model intended to explain much of the character of early modern argument; but it is a descriptive synopsis, not the application of a neoteric vision of politics dependent upon much later conceptual relationships.

The projection of immediate enthusiasms, firmed up sometimes to create conceptual models of genuine insight, does serve to keep academic discourse buoyant, in part because it helps date it.[21] But for theoretical constructs with the virtues of abstraction, elegance and explanatory

---

[20] Condren, *Status and Appraisal*, a work much exercised by the anachronisms of political theory analysis, did not even question the universality of a concept of ideology. As far as I am aware, the work was never criticised for such myopia.

[21] It is salutary to recall that barely a generation ago, in literature now largely forgotten, it was fairly automatic to pull the history of political theory along with conceptual cold-war horses; which political theorists were totalitarians and who was really on the side of freedom?

suggestiveness, a little detail goes a long way. To return to a point made at the outset: the elegance of any model screens out material, thereby accentuating a pattern; but once the model is treated as the evidence, or embedded beneath it, differing forms of difficulty become apparent. Models as underlying truths become shibboleths and metaphysical principles to be defended and rescued by so much tinkering to accommodate deviant evidence that their virtues are lost in defensive tautology and anachronism. This has been the fate of Marxism. But nescient modelling may also generate historiographical blindness. Most western academics live in a fairly secular world, and so secularisation is likely to be seen as a salient feature of modernity, one requiring the development of explanatory models in the idioms of Feuerbach or Weber. Overlooking the oath, or not recognising it as problematic, above all because it was a religious act, has been a remarkably economical way of creating a premature secularisation of political debate in which issues of office then need to be pared down to suitably secular politics, of promises and agreements and of contractual rights, in order to conform to expectations.

The lineage of political theory, which it had taken barely a hundred years to fabricate into a near two-millennia achievement of (western) civilisation, began to unravel within a generation of the fall of the first atomic bombs. It survives as a teaching device and, although convenient, it should not be convenient to consider it true.[22] Yet the pressures to sell more books to students with partial and distracted interests has itself been enough to keep simple anachronistic outlines and old myths alive and well. Meanwhile it has been increasingly documented that the variety, depth and errant complexity of political thinking defies the simple linear shape that began with Plato and has proceeded ever since in self-conscious selection until it reached NATO. This study has been a part of this self-critical enterprise, raising the question of how far what is presented as early modern political theory is a mythic misconstrual of something else we have come near to forgetting. However that is answered, we are led to a more fundamental if ahistorical question. Is it feasible to construct an explanatory model of how political vocabularies are established and transformed: wherever it began, by what mechanisms have humans spun out that web of words in which to entrap the world as political in the first place? It is this interrupted speculation on bodies political that constitutes the work ahead.

---

[22] John G. Gunnell, *The Descent of Political Theory: The Genealogy of an American Vocation* (Chicago, 1993), for a thorough account of the invention of a discipline, its lineage and more recent fragmentation.

Bibliography

Some printed titles have been slightly abbreviated. Where modern printings have been used, the first date in brackets gives earlier or initial publication year, or period of composition. For pre-modern books the place of publication is London unless otherwise indicated. The place and publisher is given only for modern works. Where authors are known only by initials, I have kept to the order of printing.

UNPUBLISHED MATERIALS

A. A. (Anthony Ascham) (1647), 'Of Marriage', Cambridge University Library, MS Gg I.4 Tracts.

Anon. (1688), 'The Female Casuist', Huntington MS EL, 8770 (35/B/43).

(1688), 'An Epitaph for Passive Obedience', Huntington MS EL, 8770 (35/B/43).

Booth, Emily (2002), 'A Subtle and Mysterious Machine: Walter Charleton's Medical World', Ph.D. thesis, University of La Trobe, Melbourne.

Cavendish, William, 'Horae subsecivae', Chatsworth MS, D3.

Cavendish, William, Duke of Newcastle, 'Advice', Bodleian Library, Oxford, Clarendon MS 109.

Cornwallis, Sir William, Folger MS V.a.132.

Curtis, C. M. (1996), 'Richard Pace on Pedagogy, Counsel and Satire', Ph.D. thesis, Cambridge University.

'The Duchess of York's Ghost', Huntington MS EL 8770 (35/B/43).

Erle, Thomas, 'Paper of Instructions', Erle, Papers, Churchill College, Cambridge, Archives, 4/4 fol. 3.

Fitzmaurice, Andrew (1995), 'Classical Rhetoric and the Literature of Discovery, 1570–1630', Ph.D. thesis, Cambridge University.

Hilton, Philip (1999), 'Bitter Honey: The Disillusioned Philosophy of Mandeville's Treatise', Ph.D. thesis, University of New South Wales, Sydney.

Hobbes, Thomas, 'Questions' (Sovereignty Fragment), Chatsworth, Hobbes MSS, D5.

Johnson, Richard (2002), 'Early Modern Natural Law and the Problem of the Sacred State', Ph.D. thesis, Griffith University, Brisbane.

Kelly, M. R. L. L. (1996), 'King and Crown', 2 vols., Ph.D. thesis, Macquarie University, Sydney.

Lawson, George, 'Amica dissertatio', Baxter Treatises, 1, fols. 99–130b, item 9, Dr Williams's Library, London.

Mainstone Parish Records, Shropshire County Records Office, 3277/1/2.

More, Richard (c. 1681), 'The Defence of Richard More against the Rev. Mr. Billingsley's Charges', in private hands.

(c. 1695), 'A List of my Books', More papers relating to sixteenth and seventeenth centuries, Shropshire County Records Office.

Nelson, Eric (2001), 'The Greek Tradition in Early Modern Republican Thought', Ph.D. thesis, Cambridge University.

Palmer, Roger, Lord Castelmain, *The Englishman's Allegiance*, bound in with Samuel Butler, *Hudibras*, 1674, Caltech Archives, California, to be accessioned.

Sampson, Margaret (no date), '"Giving Obedience for Peace and Quietnesse": The Political Thought of Anthony Ascham and the Engagement Controversy, 1648–50', BA Hons. thesis, Australian National University, Canberra.

Saunders, David (2004), 'Our Artificial Conscience: Lord Nottingham, Judicial Impartiality, and the "conscientia politica et civilis"', unpublished paper.

Schuster, John A. and Taylor, Alan B. H. (2003), 'Organising the Experimental Life at the Early Royal Society: The Production and Communication of Experimentally Based Knowledge', Princeton University, History and Philosophy of Science Seminar.

Semler, Liam (2002), 'Designs on the Self: Inigo Jones, Marginal Writing and Renaissance Self-Assembly', 'The Theory and Practice of Early Modern Autobiography' seminar, Humanities Research Centre, Australian National University, December.

'Tarquin and Tullia' (1689), Huntington MS EL 8770 (35/B/43).

RE-PRINTED COLLECTIONS OF TRACTS AND DOCUMENTS

Anon. (1683), *Certain Sermons Reprinted from the Reign of Queen Elizabeth*.

Anon. (1705), *State Tracts*, vol. I.

Beddard, Robert (1988), *A Kingdom without a King: The Journal of the Provisional Government in the Revolution of 1688* (Oxford: Phaidon Press).

Emerton, Ephraim (1964), *Humanism and Tyranny* (Gloucester, Mass.: Smith).

Gardiner, Samuel Rawson, ed. (1979), *The Constitutional Documents of the Puritan Revolution, 1625–1660* (Oxford: Clarendon Press).

Jones, Edmund, ed. (1956), *English Critical Essays (Sixteenth, Seventeenth and Eighteenth Centuries)* (London: Oxford University Press).

Jones, David Lewis, ed. (1988), 'Grey's Debates', in *A Parliamentary History of the Glorious Revolution* (London: HMSO).

Legg, L. G. W. (1901), *English Coronation Records* (London: Constable).

Malcolm, Joyce Lee (1999), *The Struggle for Sovereignty: Seventeenth Century English Political Tracts*, 2 vols. (Indianapolis: Liberty Fund).

Sandoz, Ellis, ed. (1991), *The Political Sermons of the American Founding Era, 1730–1805* (Indianapolis: Liberty Fund).

A Selection from the Gentleman's Magazine (1811), 4 vols.

Somers Tracts (1688–9), 10 vols.

Stephenson, Carl and Marcham, Frederick (1937), *Sources of English Constitutional History* (New York: Harper).
Stubbs, William (1870, 1957), *Select Charters and Other Illustrations of English Constitutional History* (Oxford: Oxford University Press).
Tanner, J. R. (1930, 1961), *Constitutional Documents of the Reign of James I, 1603–1625* (Cambridge: Cambridge University Press).
Thornton, James (1934), *Table Talk from Ben Jonson to Leigh Hunt* (London: Dent).
Wolfe, Don, ed. (1967), *The Leveller Manifestoes* (London: Frank Cass).
Woodhouse, A. S. P. (1938), *Puritanism and Liberty: Being the Army Debates (1647–9) from the Clarke Manuscripts with Supplementary Documents* (London: Dent).

ANONYMOUS WORKS

(1584, 2000), 'Bond of Association for the Defense of Queen Elizabeth', in *Elizabeth I, Collected Works*, ed. Leah S. Marcus, Janel Mueller and Mary Beth Rose (Chicago: Chicago University Press), pp. 183–5.
(1604), *The Catholike's Supplication for Toleration.*
(1616), *Sir Thomas Overbury's Vision.*
(1616), *The Office of Christian Parents.*
(1639), *Laws and Ordinances.*
(1640, 1679), *The Letter of Sir John Suckling.*
(1642), *The Contra-Replicant, His Complaint to his Majestie.*
(1642), *Some Few Observations Upon his Majesties Late Answers to the Declaration or Remonstrance of the Lords.*
(1642), *A Discourse upon the Questions in Debate between the King and Parliament.*
(1642), *The Moderator Expecting Sudden Peace or Certaine Ruine.*
(1642), *The Observator Defended.*
(1643), *An Answer to a Seditious Pamphlett intituled Plain English.*
(1643), *A Letter of Spiritual Advice.*
(1643), *Certain Observations upon the New League or Covenant* (Bristol).
(1643), *Certaine Observations upon the Two Contrary Covenants* (Oxford).
(1643), *New Quaeres of Conscience Touching the Late Oath: Desiring Resolution.*
(1643), *The Anti-Covenant, or A Sad Complaint.*
(1643), *The Iniquity of the Late Solemn League or Covenant Discovered.*
(1643), *Plain English: Or a Discourse Concerning the Accommodation, The Armie, The Association.*
(1643), *A Looking Glass for Rebels.*
(1647), *A Mirror of Allegiance.*
(1649), *A Brief Answer to the Late Resolves of the Commons.*
(1649), *A Second Part of the Religious Demurrer.*
(1649, 1967), *No Papist nor Presbyterian*, in Don Wolfe, ed., *The Leveller Manifestoes.*
(1649), *Some considerations about the nature of an oath.*
(1649), *The Westminsterian Iunto's Self-Condemnation.*

(1649, 1999), *The Declaration of the Parliament of England*, in Malcolm, ed., *The Struggle for Sovereignty*, vol. I, pp. 369–90.
(1649, 1999), *The Grand Case for Conscience Stated*, in Malcolm, ed., *The Struggle for Sovereignty*, vol. I, pp. 405–34.
(1649), *The Booke of Oathes*.
(1649), *An enquiry after further satisfaction concerning obeying a change of government beleeved to be unlawful*.
(1650), *A briefe resolution of that grand case of conscience*.
(1650), *A Copie of a Letter*.
(1650), *A Pack of Old Puritans*.
(1650), *Conscience Puzzel'd About Subscribing to the New Engagement*, in Malcolm, ed., *The Struggle for Sovereignty*, vol. I, pp. 435–44.
(1650), *Memorandums of the Conferences held between The Brethren Scrupled at the Engagement and others who were satisfied with it*.
(1650), *The exercitation answered*.
(1650), *The Time Serving Proteus . . . Uncas'd to the World*.
(1650), *Trayters Deciphered*.
(1650?), *Arguments and Reasons to prove the inconvenience . . . of taking the New Engagement*.
(1651), *A word of councel to the disaffected*.
(1658?, 1680), *A Worthy Panegyrick upon Monarchy*.
(1659), *The Whole Duty of Man*.
(1659, 1673), *The Gentleman's Calling*.
(1660), *The Sage Senator*.
(c. 1666), *Urbis Londiniensis*.
(1670), *The Office of the Holy Week According to the Missall and Roman Breviary* (Paris).
(1673), *The Ladies Calling*.
(1675), *Reflections on a Catholick Ballad*.
(c. 1675), *A Satyr against Coffee*.
(1675, 1682), *A Letter from a Person of Quality to his Friend in the Country*.
(1678), *A Poem to His Sacred Majesty on the Plot, by a Gentleman*.
(1678), *The Trials of Edward Coleman and William Stacey*.
(1679), *A Letter from Leghorn from Aboard the Van Herring*.
(1679), *A Discourse on the Peerage and Jurisdiction of the Lords Spiritual*.
(1679), *A Letter from Leghorn*.
(1679), *The Character of a Quaker*.
(1679), *The Jesuit's Gospel*.
(1679), *The Seamans Dream*.
(1680), *A Newsletter from Leghorn . . . to a Merchant in London*.
(1680), *An Answer to the Second Letter from Leghorn*.
(1680), *That Bishops in England May and Ought to Vote in Cases of Blood*.
(1680), *The True Protestant's Appeal*.
(1680), *Magna veritas, or John Gadbury not a Papist*.
(1680), *The Sheriffs Case*.
(1680), *A Letter from the King of Morocco to Charles I*.
(1680), *An Answer to Another Letter from Leghorn*.
(1681), *Scandalum magnatum, Or the Great Tryal at Chelmsford Assizes*.

(1681), *The Certain way to Serve England.*
(1681), *Obsequium et veritas.*
(1681), *The Character of a Disbanded Courtier.*
(1681), *The Late Famous Tryal of Mr Hickeringill.*
(1681), *The Two Associations.*
(1681), *The Whole Duty of Nations.*
(1681), *Scandalum magnatum: or, The Great Tryal of Chelmsford Assizes.*
(1682), *A Pindarick Poem to his Grace Christopher Duke of Albermarle.*
(1682), *Remarques Upon the New Project of Association.*
(1682), *The Parallel: or a New Specious Association an Old Rebellious Covenant.*
(1682), *A Plea for the Succession.*
(1682), *The Addresses Imputing an Abhorrence of an Association Pretended to have been seized in the Earl of Shaftsbury's Closet.*
(1682), *The True Character of an Upstart Courtier.*
(1562, 1683), 'Of Excess in Apparel', in Anon., *Certain Sermons Reprinted from the Reign of Queen Elizabeth*, pp. 193–200.
(1562, 1683), 'The State of Matrimony', in *Certain Sermons*, pp. 319–27.
(1562, 1683), 'An Homily against Disobedience and Wilful Rebellion', in *Certain Sermons*, pp. 351–88.
(1683), *The Character of a Trimmer.*
(1684), *The Character of London Village.*
(1685), *Rebellious Antidotes: Or a Dialogue Between Tea and Coffee.*
(1688), *Vox cleri pro rege.*
(1689), *A Defence of Their Majesties.*
(1689), *A Discourse Concerning the Signification of Allegiance.*
(1689), *A Letter to a Member of the Convention*, in *Somers Tracts*, vol. VII.
(1689), *A Remonstrance and Protestation of all Good Protestants of This Kingdom . . . together with Reflections Upon it.*
(1689), *An Enquiry into the Present State of Affairs.*
(1689), *Reflections on our Late and Present Proceedings in England*, in *Somers Tracts*, vol. X.
(1689), *The Anatomy of a Jacobite Tory.*
(1689), *The Book of Oaths.*
(1689), *The Doctrine of Passive Obedience and Jure Divino Disproved by a Layman of the Church of England.*
[Jeremy Collier ?] (1689), *Vindiciae juris regii.*
(1689), *A Friendly Debate Between Dr. Kingsman, a Dissatisfied Clergy-Man and Gratianus Trimmer, a Neighbour Minister.*
(1689), *Proposals to this Present Convention*, in *Somers Tracts*, vol. VIII.
(1689), *The Anatomy of an Arbitrary Prince.*
(1689, 1705), *Some Short Considerations Relating to the Settling of the Government Humbly Offer'd*, in *State Tracts*, vol. I.
(1689, 1705), *A Discourse Concerning the Nature, Power and Proper Effects of the Present Convention*, in *State Tracts*, vol. I.
(1689), *A Justification of the Whole Proceedings.*
(1689?), *A Caution Against Inconsistency, Or The Connexion between Praying and Swearing in Relation to Civil Powers.*

(1688/9, 1988), 'A Jornall of the Convention', in Jones, ed., *A Parliamentary History of the Glorious Revolution*, pp. 231–48.
(1690), *The Case of Allegiance to a King in Possession*.
(1691), *A Confutation of Sundry Errors*.
(1691), *Animadversions on a Discourse*.
(1691), *Counsel to the True English: Or a Word of Advice to the Jacobites*.
(1698), *The Immorality of the Pulpit*.
(1700), *The Julian and Gregorian Year*.
(1705), *An Examination of the Scruples of those who refuse to take the oaths of allegiance*, in *State Tracts*, vol. I.
(1705), *Some Considerations Touching Succession and Allegiance*, in *State Tracts*, vol. I.
(1705), *The Case of oaths stated*, in *State Tracts*, vol. I.
(1705), *Important Questions of State, Law, Justice and Prudence both Civil and Religious*, in *State Tracts*, vol. I.
(1755), *The Whole Duty of an Apprentice*.
(1790), *Gentleman's Magazine* (London).

NAMED OR INITIALLED BOOKS AND TRACTS

Allen, William (1584), *A True Sincere and Modest Defence of English Catholics*.
 (1588), *An Admonition to the Nobility and People of England and Ireland*.
Allix, Peter (?) (1689), *An Examination of the Scruples of Those who Refuse to Take the Oath of Allegiance*.
Ames, William (1639), *Cases of Conscience and the Resolution thereof*.
Anderton, W. (1693), *Remarks on the Present Confederacy*.
Andrewes, Lancelot (1609), *Tortura Torti*.
Anton, Robert (1616), *The Philosophers Satyrs*.
Arbuthnot, John (1712, 1892), *The History of John Bull*, in George Aitken, ed., *The Life and Works of John Arbuthnot* (Oxford: Clarendon Press), pp. 191–290.
 (1712), *Pseudologia Politike, Or The Art of Political Lying*.
Argall, Charles (?) (1683), *The King of Poland's Ghost*.
Aristotle (c. 330 BC, 1954), *The Rhetoric*, trans. W. Rhys Roberts (New York: Random House).
 (1915, 1966) *Ethica Nicomachea*, trans. Sir David Ross, in *The Works of Aristotle* (Oxford: Clarendon Press), vol. IX.
Arnisaeus, Henning (1610), *De iure maiestatis libri tres* (Frankfurt).
 (1612) *De auctoritate principum in populum semper inviolabili* (Frankfurt).
Ascham, Anthony (1648), *A Discourse Wherein it is Examined, What is Particularly Lawful during the Confusions and Revolutions of Government*.
 (?) (1649), *The Bounds and Bonds of Publique Obedience*.
 (?) (1649), *A Combate Between Two Seconds*.
 (1649), *The Confusions and Revolutions of Governments*.
 (?) (1650), 'E. P.', *An Answer to the Vindication of Dr. Hammond*.
 (1650), *A Reply to a Paper*.
Atwood, William (1690), *The Fundamental Constitution of the English Government*.
 (1696), *Reflections upon a Treasonable Opinion ... Against Signing the National Association*.

Aubrey, John (c. 1660–97, 1949), *Brief Lives*, ed. Oliver Lawson Dick (Harmondsworth: Penguin).
B&Y (1683), *The Arraignment of Co-ordinate Power*.
B. R. (1689), *Satisfaction Tendered*.
Bacon, Sir Francis (1597, 1625, 1825), *Essays*, in *Works*, Basil Montague, ed. (London: Pickering), vol. I.
  (1605, 1825), *The Advancement of Learning*, in *Works*, vol. II.
  (c. 1605, 1826), 'An Explanation of What Manner of Persons Those Should be, That are to Execute the Power or Ordinance of the King's Prerogative', in *Works*, vol. VI, pp. 102–7.
  (1614, 1826), 'The Charge of Francis Bacon . . . Touching Duels', in *Works*, vol. VI, pp. 108–24.
  (1826), 'A Speech to the Speaker's Excuse', in *Works*, vol. VI, pp. 65–74.
Bagshawe, Edward (1660), *The Rights of the Crown*.
Baker, Sir Richard (1670), *Theatrum Triumphans*.
Baldwin, William (1557, 1610), *A Treatise of Morall Philosophie*, continuation by Thomas Palfreyman.
  (1559, 1938), *The Mirror for Magistrates*, ed. Lily B. Campbell (Cambridge: Cambridge University Press).
Ball, William (1642), *A Caveat to Subjects*.
Barbon, Nicholas (1678), *A Discourse Shewing the Great Advantages New-Buildings, And the Enlarging of Towns and Cities Do Bring to a Nation*.
Barclay, William (1611), *Of The Authoritie of the Pope*.
Barnes, John (1625), *Dissertatio contra aequivocationes* (Paris).
Barnes, Joshua (1703), *The Good Old Way*.
Bartolus of Sassoferrato (c. 1356, 1964), *Tractatus de tyrannia*, ed. and trans. Ephraim Emerton, in *Humanism and Tyranny*, pp. 126–54.
Baxter, Richard (1673), *The Christian Directory*.
  (1691), *Against the Revolt to a Foreign Jurisdiction*.
Beacon, Richard (1594), *Solon His Follie* (Oxford).
Becanus, Martin (1612), *Controversia anglicana de potestate regis et pontificis* (Mainz).
  (1612), *Dissidium anglicanum de primatu regis* (Mainz).
Bell, Thomas (1606), *The Regiment of the Church*.
Bellarmine, Robert (1607), *Admonitum . . . Georgio Blacuello* in George Blackwell, *A large Examination Taken at Lambeth*.
  (1608), *Matthaei Torti . . . responsio* (St Omer).
  (1609), *Apologia* (Rome).
  Of Passive Obedience (1712, 1953) in *Works*, Vol. VI, pp. 15–46.
Berkeley, George (1750, 1953), *Maxims Concerning Patriotism* (Dublin), in *The Works of George Berkeley*, ed. A. A. Luce and T. E. Jessop (London: Nelson), vol. VI, pp. 253–5.
Beza, Theodore (?) (1573, 1971), *Du droit des magistrats*, ed. R. M. Kingdon (Geneva: Droz).
Bilson, Thomas (1585), *The True Difference Between Christian Subjection and Unchristian Rebellion* (Oxford).
Blackwell, George (1607), *A Large Examination Taken at Lambeth . . . together with the Cardinal's Letter and M. Blacwell's said Answer to it. Also Blacwell's Letter to the Romish Catholickes in England*.

Blount, Charles (?) (1689), *The Proceedings of the Present Parliament Justified*.
Blow, John (?) (1664), *An Opera Performed Before the King*.
Bodin, Jean (1576, 1962), *Six livres de la République*, trans. Richard Knolles, in *The Six Bookes of a Commonweale*, ed. K. D. McRae (Cambridge, Mass.: Harvard University Press).
Bohun, Edmund de (1684), *The Justice of the Peace, His Calling: A Moral Essay*.
Boswell, James (1951), *London Journal, 1762–63*, ed. Frederick A. Pottle (London and Melbourne: Heinemann).
Boyle, Sir Robert (1646, 1991), 'The Dayly Reflection', 'The Aretology' and 'Of Piety', in John T. Harwood, ed., *The Early Essays and Ethics of Robert Boyle* (Carbondale and Edwardsville: Southern Illinois University Press), pp. 203–35.
  (*c*. 1647, 1695, 1772), *A Free Discourse Against Customary Swearing*, in *The Works of Sir Robert Boyle*, ed. Thomas Birch, vol. VI, pp. 1–26.
  (1661), *The Skeptical Chymist*.
  (1772), *The Christian Virtuoso*, in *Works*, vol. V, pp. 508–40; vol. VI, pp. 673–716, 717–96.
Bracton, Henry de (1968–77), *De legibus et consuetudinibus Angliae*, ed. G. E. Woodbine and S. E. Thorne (Cambridge, Mass.: Harvard University Press).
Bramhall, John (1655, 1999), *A Defence of True Liberty*, in Vere Chappell, ed., *Hobbes and Bramhall on Liberty and Necessity* (Cambridge: Cambridge University Press), pp. 43–68.
Brathwaite, Richard (1630), *The English Gentleman*.
Browne, Sir Thomas (1643, 1716, 1845), *Religio Medici, and True Christian Morals*, ed. Henry Gardiner (London: Pickering).
Buchanan, George (1579, 1642), *Baptistes, sive calumnia Tragoedia* (Frankfurt, 1579), trans. as *Tyrannical Government Anatomized*.
  (1579, 1725), *De jure regni apud Scotos* (Edinburgh), in *Opera omnia*, ed. Thomas Rudiman, 2 vols. (Lugdini Batavorum), vol. I.
Burnet, Gilbert (1823), *A History of his own Time*, 6 vols. (Oxford: Clarendon Press).
Burton, Robert (1621, 1989), *The Anatomy of Melancholy*, ed. T. C. Faulfer, N. K. Kiessling and R. L. Blair, 3 vols. (Oxford: Clarendon Press).
Butler, Samuel (1667–9, 1970), *Characters*, ed. Charles W. Daves (Cleveland: Case Western Reserve University Press).
Campion, Thomas (1602, 1956), *Observations on the Art of English Poesy*, in Jones, ed., *English Critical Essays*, pp. 55–60.
Canne, John (1649), *The Golden Rule*.
Cardano, Girolamo (1562, 2004), *De libris propriis*, ed. Ian Maclean (Milan: Franco Angeli).
Cary, Lucius, Lord Falkland and Culpepper, Nicholas (1643, 1999), *The King's Answer to the Nineteen Propositions*, in Malcolm, ed., *The Struggle for Sovereignty*, vol. I, pp. 145–78.
Caryl, Joseph (1650), *A Logical Demonstration of the Lawfulness of Subscribing to the New Engagement*.
Case, Stephen (?) (1783, 1991), *Defensive Arms Vindicated*, in Ellis Sandoz, ed., *The Political Sermons of the American Revolution, 1730–1805*, pp. 711–70.

Castiglione, Baldesar (1528, 1987), *Il Cortigiano, The Courtier*, trans. George Bull (Harmondsworth: Penguin).
Cavendish, Margaret, Duchess of Newcastle (1667, 1896), *The Life of the Thrice Noble, High and Puissant Prince, William Cavendish, Duke, Marquess and Earl of Newcastle*, ed. C. H. Firth (London).
Charles I (?) (1649), *Eikon Basilike*.
Charleton, Walter (1652), *The Darknes of Atheism Dispelled by Light*.
 (1659), *The Natural History of Nutrition*.
 (1680), *Enquiries into Human Nature*.
Charron, Pierre (1601), *De la Sargesse*, trans. S. Lennard, in *Of Wisdome Three Bookes*.
Cicero (c. 45 BC, 1913), *De officiis*, trans. Walter Miller (Cambridge, Mass.: Harvard University Press).
Claridge, Richard (1689), *A Defence of the Present Government*.
 (1689), *A Second Defence of the Present Government*.
Clarkson, David (1675), *The Practical Divinity of the Papists Discovered to be Destructive of Christianity and Men's Souls*.
Collier, Jeremy (1688), *The Office of the Chaplain*.
 (1691), *Dr. Sherlock's Case of Allegiance Considered*.
Collins, Anthony (1708), *An Answer to Mr Clarke's Third Defence*.
Comber, Thomas (1681/2), *The Nature and Usefulness of Judicial Swearing*.
 (1689), *A Discourse of Duels*.
 (1689), *A Letter to a Bishop Concerning the Present Settlement and the New Oaths*.
 (1692/3), *The Protestant Mask*.
Condren, Charles de (1643, 1847–8), *Traité des équivoques*, in *Oeuvres complètes*, ed. Abbé Pin (Paris).
Constant, Benjamin (1838, 1988), *Ancient and Modern Liberty*, in *The Political Writings of Benjamin Constant*, ed. Biancamaria Fontana (Cambridge: Cambridge University Press).
Cook, John (1649), *King Charls His Case: or, An Appeal to All Rational Men, Concerning His Tryal at the High Court of Justice*.
Cooper, Anthony Ashley, 1st Earl of Shaftesbury (1680), *A Speech made Lately by a Noble Peer of the Realm*.
Cooper, Anthony, 3rd Earl of Shaftesbury (1711, 1999), *The Characteristicks of Men, Manners, Opinions and Times*, ed. Philip J. Ayres, 2 vols. (Oxford: Clarendon Press).
Coply, Anthony (1601), *An Answer to a Letter of a Jesuitical Gentleman*.
Cornwallis, Sir William (1616), *Essays of Certain Paradoxes*.
Cotta, John (1612), *A Short Discovery of the Unobserved Dangers of . . . Physicke in England*.
 (1624), *The Assured Witch*.
Coverdale, Miles (?) (1548, 1574), *A Christe exhortacion*.
Crosse, Henry (1603), *Virtues common-wealth*.
Cumberland, Richard (1672), *De legibus naturae*.
 (1672, 1727), *De legibus naturae*, trans. John Maxwell as *A Treatise of the Laws of Nature*.
D. J. (1650), *Just Re-Proposals to Humble Proposals*.

Dalton, Michael (1635), *Country Justice*.
Daniel, Gabriel (1694, 1704), *The Discourses of Cleander and Eudoxus on the Provincial Letters*.
Daniel, Samuel (?) (1603, 1956), *A Defence of Rhyme*, in E. Jones, ed., *English Critical Essays* (London: Oxford University Press), pp. 61–87.
Dante Alighieri (1321, 1921), *De monarchia*, ed. E. Rostagno (Florence: Società Dantesca Italiana).
  (1970–5), *The Divine Comedy*, ed. and trans. Charles S. Singleton, 6 Vols. (Princeton: Princeton University Press).
Day, Angel (1586, 1592, 1967), *The English Secretary*, ed. Robert O. Evans (Gainesville, Fl.: Scholars' Facsimiles).
Defoe, Daniel (?) (1689), *The Advantages of the Present Settlement*.
  (1701, 1975), *The True Born Englishman*, in *Selected Writings*, ed. John Boulton (Cambridge: Cambridge University Press).
  (1706), *Jure Divino*.
Dekker, Thomas (1953–61), *Dramatic Works*, ed. F. Bowers (Cambridge: Cambridge University Press), vol. III.
Digges, Dudley (1642), *An Answer to a Printed Book*.
Dingley, Robert (1658), *Vox coeli, or Philosophical, Historicall and Theological Observations of Thunder*.
Dominis, Marco Antonio de (1617–22), *De respublica ecclesiastica*, 3 vols.
Donne, John (1610), *The Pseudo-Martyr*.
  (1624, 1700), *Biathanatos*.
  (1640), *Sermons*, ed. John Donne the younger.
  (1660), *Sermons*, ed. John Donne the younger.
Downes, Theophilus (1690), *A Discourse Concerning The Signification of Allegiance as it is to be Understood in the New Oath of Allegiance*.
  (1691), *An Examination of the Arguments Drawn from Scripture and Reason in Dr. Sherlock's Case of Allegiance and his Vindication of it*.
Downhame, George (1609), *Two Sermons*.
  (1611), *A Defence of the Sermon*.
Dryden, John (1668, 1956), *An Essay of Dramatic Poesy*, in Jones, ed., *English Critical Essays*, pp. 104–74.
  (1681), *Absalom and Achitophel*.
Dury, John (1649), *A Case of Conscience Resolved*.
  (1650), *A Disengaged Survey*.
  (1650), *Objections Against the taking of the Engagement answered*.
  (1650), *Just Re-Proposals to Humble Proposals*.
  (1651), *Conscience eased: or the main scruple against the taking of the Engagement removed*.
E. W., (1681), *The Bishops Courts Dissolved*.
Eachard, John (1671), *Mr Hobbs State of Nature Considered in a Dialogue Between Timothy and Philautus*, in *Works* (1773), vol. II.
Earle, John (1633), *Micro-cosmography, or a Piece of the World Discovered*.
Eaton, Samuel (1650), *A Resolution of Conscience*.
  (1650), *The Oath of Allegiance and the National Covenant Proved to be Non-Obligatory*.

Elizabeth I (1564, 2000), 'Oration at the University of Cambridge', August 1564, in *Collected Works*, ed. Leah S. Marcus, Janel Mueller and Mary Beth Rose (Chicago: Chicago University Press), pp. 87–9.
  (1567, 2000), 'Speech[es] Dissolving Parliament', January 1567, in *Collected Works*, pp. 105–8.
  (1576, 2000), 'Speech at the Close of Parliament', March 1576, in *Collected Works*, pp. 167–71.
  (1585, 2000), 'Speech at the Close of Parliament', March 1585, in *Collected Works*, pp. 181–3.
  (1586, 2000), 'The Queen's Speech to the Committee of Both Houses', November 1586, in *Collected Works*, pp. 186–90.
  (1593, 2000), 'Speech at the Closing of Parliament', April 1593, in *Collected Works*, pp. 328–30.
  (1601, 2000), 'Golden Speech', November 1601, in *Collected Works*, pp. 335–40.
  (1601, 2000), 'The Queen's Last Speech', December 1601, in *Collected Works*, pp. 346–51.
Elyot, Sir Thomas (1531, 1962), *The Book Named the Governor*, ed. S. E. Lehmberg (London: Dent).
Epictetus (*c.* 130 AD, 1925, 1928), *Discourses*, trans. W. A. Oldfather (Cambridge, Mass.: Harvard University Press).
Evelyn, John (1664), *Sylva, or a Discourse of Forest-Trees*.
  (1818, 1955), *The Diary of John Evelyn*, ed. E. S. de Beer, 6 vols. (Oxford: Clarendon Press).
Fanshawe, Sir Richard (1997), *Poems and Translations*, ed. Peter Dudson (Oxford: Oxford University Press).
Ferne, Henry (1642), *The Resolving of Conscience*.
Ficino, Marsilio (1489, 1989), *Libra da vita in tres libros divisos*, ed. Carol V. Kaske and John R. Clark (New York: Renaissance Society of America). Also *De vita libri tres*, ed. M. Plessner and F. Klein-Franke (Hildersheim, 1978).
Field, Richard (1606), *Of the Church, five books*.
Filmer, Robert (1652), *Observations Upon Aristotles Politiques*.
  (1680, 1949), *Patriarcha*, ed. Peter Laslett (Cambridge: Cambridge University Press).
Finch, Heneage (1965), 'A Treatise of Chancellery Learning', in D. E. C. Yale, ed., *Lord Nottingham's 'Manuel of Chancery Practice' and 'Prolegomena of Chancery and Equity'* (Cambridge: Cambridge University Press).
Fisher, Samuel (1660), *Rusticus ad Academicus, or . . . The Rustick's Alarm to the Rabbies*.
Fitzherbert, Thomas (1616), *An sic utilitas in scelere* (Rome).
Fortescue, Sir John (1949), *De laudibus legum Angliae*, ed. S. B. Chrimes (Cambridge: Cambridge University Press).
Fuller, Thomas (1642), *The Holy State and the Profane State*.
Fullwood, Francis (1689), *The Agreement Betwixt the Present and the Former Government*.
G. B., Dr (1689), *A Word to the Wavering*.

Garnet, Henry (1598, 1851), *A Treatise of Equivocation*, ed. David Jardine (London: Longmans).
Gee, Edward (1650), *An exercitation*.
  (1650), *A Plea for Non-Subscribers to the Engagement*.
  (1650), *A vindication of the oath of allegiance in answer to a paper disperst by Mr Sam: Eaton*.
  (1658), *The Divine Right and Original of Civill Magistracy*.
Gilby, Anthony (1581), *A Pleasaunt Dialogue Between A Soldier of Berwicke and an English Chaplaine*.
Gillespie, George (1637), *A Dispute Against the English Popish Ceremonies Obtruded onto the Church of Scotland*.
Glanvill, Joseph (1671), *Philosophia pia*.
Godwyn, Morgan (1680), *The Negroe's and Indians Advocate*.
Goodman, Christopher (1558), *How Superior Powers oght to be Obeyd of their Subjects*.
Goodwin, John (1649), *Right and Might Well Mett*, in Malcolm, ed., *The Struggle for Sovereignty: Seventeenth Century English Political Tracts*, vol. I, pp. 307–58.
Goslicius [Laurentius Grimalius] (1593), *De optimo senatore*, trans. Anon. (1598) as *The Counsellor, exactly portrayed in two bookes*.
Gosson, Stephen (1582), *Playes Confuted in Five Actions*.
  (1586), *The Ephemerides of Philo Divided into Three Bookes*.
Gouge, William (1622), *Domesticall Duties*.
Grand Remonstrance, The (1641, 1979), in S. R. Gardiner, ed., *The Constitutional Documents of the Puritan Revolution*, pp. 202–31.
Greville, Fulke (1633, 1990), 'An Inquisition upon Fame and Honour', in *Certaine Learned and Elegant Workes*, ed. A. D. Cousins (New York: Delmar) pp. 33–49.
Grimalde Nicholas (1556, 1583), *Marcus Tullius Ciceroes Three Bokes of Duties*.
Grotius, Hugo (1625), *De jure belli ac pacis* (Paris).
Guazzo, Stephano (1586), *The ciuile conuersation*, trans. George Pettie.
Hale, Sir Matthew (c. 1645, 1976), *The Prerogatives of the King* (London: Selden Society).
  (1677), *The Primitive Origination of Mankind*.
Hall, Edward (c. 1540, 1809), *Chronicles*.
Hall, John (1654), *Of Government and Obedience*.
Hall, Joseph (1643), *The Lawfulness and Unlawfulness of an Oath or Covenant* (Oxford).
Hammond, Henry (1650), *A Vindication*.
Harington, Sir John (1604, 1991), *The Sixth Book of Virgil's Aeneid*, ed. Simon Cauchi (Oxford: Clarendon Press).
Harrington, James (1656, 1977), *Oceana*, in *The Political Works of James Harrington*, ed. J. G. A. Pocock (Cambridge: Cambridge University Press).
Harvey, Christopher (1663), *Faction Supplanted*.
Hawke, Michael (1658), *Killing is Murder*.
Haworth, Samuel (1680), *Anthropologia: or a Philosophic Discourse Concerning Man*.
Head, Richard (1684), *Proteus Redivivus, or the art of Wheedling*.

Herbert, George (1652), *A Priest to the Temple*.
Herle, Charles (1642, 1999), *A Fuller Answer to a Treatise*, in Malcolm, *The Struggle for Sovereignty*, vol. I, pp. 223–60.
Hesiod (*c*. 700 BC, 1936), *Works and Days* and *Homerica*, trans. H. G. Evelyn-White (Cambridge, Mass.: Harvard University Press).
Heylyn, Peter (1643), *The Rebells Catechism*.
Heywood, Thomas (1633), *Londini euphoria*.
Hickeringill, Edmund (1680), *The Naked Truth, The First Part*.
  (1681), *The Naked Truth, The Second Part*.
  (1682), *The Horrid Sin of Man-Catching Explained in a Sermon*.
Hickeringill, Philip (1681), *A Vindication of The Naked Truth, The Second Part*.
Hickes, George (1689), *A Word to the Wavering*.
  (1691), *An Apology for the New Separation*.
  (1692), *A Vindication of Some Among Ourselves*.
Higgons, Theophilus (1611), *A Sermon Preached at St. Paul's Cross* (3 March 1610).
Hitchcock John (1617), *A Sanctuary for Honest Men: or an Abstract of Humane Wisdom*.
Hobbes, Thomas (1640, 1969), *The Elements of Law*, ed. Ferdinand Tönnies (London: Frank Cass).
  (1642, 1646), *De cive* (Amsterdam).
  (1643, 1973), *Critique du De mundo de Thomas White*, ed. J. Jacquot and H. W. Jones (Paris: Vrin-CNRS).
  (1651, 1845), *The Answer to the Preface Before Gondibert*, in *The English Works of Thomas Hobbes*, ed. Sir William Molesworth, vol. IV, pp. 441–60.
  (1651, 1991), *Leviathan*, ed. Richard Tuck (Cambridge: Cambridge University Press).
  (1651), *Philosophicall Rudiments Concerning Government and Society*, *De cive*, trans. Charles Cotton.
  (1655, 1839), *De corpore*, in *English Works*, vol. I.
  (1655, 1845), *De corpore*, in *Opera latine*, ed. Sir William Molesworth, vol. I.
  (*c*. 1668, 1843), *An Historical Narration Concerning Heresy and the Punishment thereof*, in *English Works*, vol. IV, pp. 385–408.
  (1679, 1680), *Thomae Hobbesii Malmesburiensis Vita, The Life of Mr. Thomas Hobbes of Malmesbury*.
  (1679, 1840), *Considerations upon the Reputation, Loyalty, Manners and Religion of Thomas Hobbes*, in *English Works*, vol. IV, pp. 409–40.
  (1994), *The Correspondence of Thomas Hobbes*, ed. Noel Malcolm, 2 vols. (Oxford: Clarendon Press).
Hoby, Sir Edward (1615), *A Curry-Combe for a Cox-Combe*.
Hodges, Thomas (1647), *The Growth and Spreading of Haeresie*.
Horn, Andrew (?) (*c*. 1300, 1642, 1968), *Speculum justiciorum*, trans. *The Mirror of Justices* (New York: Kelly).
Hotman, François (1573, 1972), *Francogallia*, ed. Ralph Giesey and J. H. M. Salmon (Cambridge: Cambridge University Press).
Hume, David (1772, 1994), *Political Essays*, ed. Knud Haakonssen (Cambridge: Cambridge University Press).
  (1745, 1978), *A Treatise of Human Nature*, ed. L. A. Selby-Bigge (1894), second edn. ed. P. H. Niddich (Oxford: Clarendon Press).

Humfrey, John (1662), *A Second Discourse*.
  (?) (1688), *Good Advice Before it is Too Late*.
  (1702), *The Free State of the People Maintained*.
Hunton, Philip (1643), *A Treatise of Monarchie*.
Hutchinson, Lucy (*c.* 1670, 1968), *Memoirs of the Life of Colonel Hutchinson* (London: Dent).
Hyde, Edward, Lord Clarendon (1662), *The Lord Chancellor's Speech to the Two Houses at their Prorogation*.
  (1670, 1815), *Essays Moral and Entertaining*.
  (1888, 1958), *The History of the Great Rebellion*, ed. W. D. Macray, 6 vols. (Oxford: Clarendon Press).
J. K. (1598), *The Courtiers Academie*, translation of Annibale Romei, *Discorsi divisi in sette giornate*, 1586.
James II (1685), *His Majesties Most Gracious Speech to Both Houses of Parliament*, 9 November.
James VI&I (1588, 1616), *A Fruitful Meditation*, in *The Workes of the Most High and Mighty Prince Iames . . .*, ed. James Montague, pp. 73–80.
  (1597, 1616), *Daemonologie*, in *Workes*, pp. 94–136.
  (1598, 1616), *The Trew Law of Free Monarchies*, in *Workes*, pp. 191–210.
  (1599, 1603), *Basilicon Doron*, in *Workes*, pp. 137–89.
  (1603, 1616), Speech of 19 March, in *Workes*, pp. 485–97.
  (1605, 1616), *A Discourse of the Manner of the Discovery of the Late Intended Treason*, in *Workes*, pp. 223–46.
  (1605, 1616), *His Maiesties Speech in This Last Session of Parliament*, in *Workes*, pp. 499–508.
  (1609), *An Apologie for the Oath of Allegiance*, in *Workes*, pp. 247–86.
  (1609), *The Kings Majesties Speech to the Lords and Commons*, 21 March in *Workes*, pp. 527–8.
  (1609, 1616), *A Praemonition of His Maiesties to all the most Mightie Monarches, Kings, Free Princes and States of Christendome*, in *Workes*, pp. 287–338.
  (1616), *A Catalogue of the Lyes of Tortus, Together with a Briefe Confutation of them*, in *Workes*, pp. 339–46.
  (1615), *God and the King*.
  (1918), *Political Works*, ed. C. H. McIlwain (Cambridge, Mass.: Harvard University Press).
John of Salisbury (*c.* 1180, 1990), *Policraticus*, trans. Cary J. Nederman (Cambridge: Cambridge University Press).
Johnson, Robert (1601), *Essais, or Rather Imperfect Offers*.
Johnson, Samuel, (1774, 1968), *The Patriot*, in *The Political Works of Samuel Johnson*, ed. J. P. Hardy (London: Routledge), pp. 91–9.
Jonson, Ben (1641, 1875), *Timber, or Discoveries made upon Men and Matter*, in *Works of Ben Jonson*, ed. W. Gifford (London: Bickers and Sotheran), vol. IX, pp. 129–228.
Kennett, White (1689), *A Dialogue Between Friends*.
King, John (1608), *A Sermon Preached at Whitehall* (Oxford).
Lacey, John (1604), *A Petition Apologeticall*.
Latimer, Hugh (1537–48, 1635), *Fruitful Sermons*.

Lawson, George (1657), *An Examination of Mr Hobbs, His Leviathan*.
  (1660, 1689, 1992), *Politica sacra et civilis*, ed. Conal Condren (Cambridge: Cambridge University Press).
  (1665), *Magna charta ecclesiae universalis*.
Lawson, Jeremy (1681), *Lawson Of Oaths and Witnesses*.
L'Estrange, Roger (1681), *The Casuist Uncas'd in a Dialogue with Richard Baxter*.
  (1682), *A Memento*.
  (1685), *A Vindication of the Observator*.
Lilbourne, John (1646, 1967), *A Remonstrance of Many Thousand Citizens and other Free-born People of England*, in D. Wolfe, ed., *The Leveller Manifestoes*, pp. 109–30.
  (1650), *The Engagement Vindicated and Explained*.
Locke, John (1660, 1967), *Two Tracts on Government*, ed. Philip Abrams (Cambridge: Cambridge University Press).
  (1690, 1694), *An Essay Concerning Human Understanding*.
  (1690, 1963), *Two Treatises of Government*, ed. Peter Laslett (Cambridge: Cambridge University Press).
  (c. 1700, 1830), 'Thus I think', in Peter King, *The Life of John Locke*, vol. II.
  (1989), *The Correspondence of John Locke*, ed. Esmond de Beer, 8 vols. (Oxford: Clarendon Press).
Long, Thomas (?) (1689, 1705), *A Resolution of Certain queries concerning submission to the Present Government*.
  (1689), *Reflections upon a Later Book*.
Lowman, R. (1685), *An Exact Narrative and Description of the Wonderful and Stupendous Fire-Works in Honour of Their Majesties Coronations*.
Lucian (1960), *Bion Prasis, Philosophies for Sale*, in *Works*, vol. II, trans. A. M. Harmon (Cambridge Mass.: Harvard University Press).
Ludlow, Edmund (1698–9), *Memoirs*, 3 vols. (Vivay).
M. S. (1695), *A Philosophical Discourse on the Nature of Immaterial Souls*.
Machiavelli, Niccolò (1513, 1973), *Il Principe*, ed. Sergio Bertelli (Milan: Feltrinelli).
  (1513, 1988), *The Prince*, trans. Russell Price, introduction by Quentin Skinner (Cambridge: Cambridge University Press).
Malcolm, James (1811), *Anecdotes of the Manners and Customs of London*, 3 vols.
Mandeville, Bernard de (1711, 1730), *A Treatise of the Hypochondriack and Hysterick Passions*.
Marlowe, Christopher (c. 1590, 1604, 1985), *Doctor Faustus*, ed. David Ormerod and Christopher Wortham (Perth: University of Western Australia Press).
Marshall, Stephen (1641), *Meroz Curs'd*.
Marsilius of Padua (1324, 1958), *Defensor pacis*, ed. H. Kusch (Berlin: Rütten and Loening).
Marvell, Andrew (1650, 1681, 1978), 'An Horatian Ode of Cromwell's Return From Ireland', in Elizabeth Donno, ed., *The Complete Poems of Andrew Marvell* (Harmondsworth: Penguin).
  (1667, 1689, 1978), '*The Last Instructions to a Painter*', in Donno, *Complete Poems*.
  (1677), *An Account of the Growth of Popery and Arbitrary Government* (Amsterdam).

Mason, Henry (1624), *The New Art of Lying Covered by Jesuits under a Vaile of Equivocation*.
  (1627), *The Tribunal of Conscience*.
Maxwell, John (1644), *Sacro-sancta regnum majestas* (Oxford).
Merbury, Charles (1581), *A briefe discourse of royall monarchie, as of the best commonweal*.
Meriton, George (1607), *A Sermon of nobilitie*.
Milton, John (1644, 1959), *Areopagitica*, in *The Complete Prose Works*, vol. II, ed. Ernest Sirluck (New Haven: Yale University Press), pp. 486–570.
  (1650, 1962), *Eikonoklastes*, in *The Complete Prose Works*, vol. III, ed. Merritt Y. Hughes (New Haven: Yale University Press), pp. 337–601.
  (1650, 1962), *The Tenure of Kings and Magistrates*, in *Complete Prose Works*, vol. III, pp. 190–258.
  (1654), *Pro populo Anglicano Defensio, The Second Defence of the English People* in *The Complete Prose Works*, vol. IV, ed. Don M. Wolfe (New Haven: Yale University Press), pp. 547–686.
  (1667, 1960), *Paradise Lost*, in *The Poems of John Milton*, ed. Helen Darbishire (London: Oxford University Press) pp. 1–281.
Montaigne, Michel de (1575–6, 1578–80, 1992), *Essais*, trans. Donald M. Frame, in *The Complete Essays* (Stanford: Stanford University Press).
More, Thomas (1515, 1995), *Utopia*, ed. and trans. George Logan, Robert Adams and Clarence Miller (Cambridge: Cambridge University Press).
Morice, James (?) (1590), *A Briefe Treatise of Oathes*.
Morton, Thomas (1606), *A Full Satisfaction concerning a Double Romish Iniquitie*.
  (1608), *A Preamble unto an Incounter*.
Moulin, Lewis de (1650), *The Power of the Magistrate*.
Mulcaster, Richard (1581), *Positions wherein those primitive circumstances be examined*.
Mun, Thomas (1664, 1949), *England's Treasure By Forraign Trade* (Oxford: Blackwell).
Musculus, Wolfgang (1578), *Loci communes*, trans. John Man, as *The Commonplaces of Christian Religion*.
  (1600), *In Epistolam D. Apostoli Pauli ad Romanos commentarii* (Basel).
N. H. (1694), *The Ladies Dictionary*.
N. W. (1650), *A Discourse Concerning the Engagement, or The Northern Subscribers Plea*.
Nashe, Thomas (1594, 1972), *The Terrors of the Night*, in *The Unfortunate Traveller and other Works*, ed. J. B. Steane (Harmondsworth: Penguin), pp. 208–50.
Nedham, Marchamont (1650, 1969), *The Case of the Commonwealth Truly Stated*, ed. Philip Knachel (Virginia: Folger Library and University of Virginia Press).
Nelson, Abraham (?) (1644, 1660), *A Perfect Description of Antichrist*.
Neville, Henry (1660), *A Game of Piquet*.
  (1675), trans. *The Works of the Famous Niccolo Machiavell*.
Nicholes, Alexander (1615), *A Discourse of Marriage and Wiving*.
Nineteen Propositions made by Both Houses of Parliament (1642) in S. R. Gardiner, *Constitutional Documents*, pp. 249–53.
North, Francis, Chief Justice (1682), *The Lord Keeper's Speech*.

Orrery, Earl of (1672), *The Black Prince*.
Overbury, Sir Thomas (?) (1616, 1622), *Sir Thomas Overbury his Wife, with Additions of New Characters*.
Overton, Richard (1647, 1967), *An Appeale from the Degenerate Representative Body*, in D. Wolfe, ed., *The Leveller Manifestoes*, pp. 154–95.
Owen, David (1610), *Herode and Pilate Reconciled*.
Pace, Richard (1517, 1967), *De fructu qui ex doctrina percipitur*, ed. and trans. Frank Manley and Richard S. Sylvester (New York: Renaissance Society of America).
Parker, Henry (1642), *Some Few Observations upon His Majesties Late Answer to the Declaration . . . of May 1642*.
  (1642), *Observations upon Some of his Majesties Late Answers and Expresses*.
  (1643), *The Oath of Pacification*.
Parker, Samuel (1670), *The Rehearsal Transpos'd: A Discourse of Ecclesiastical Polities*.
Parsons, Robert (1594/5), *A Conference about the Next Succession* (Antwerp).
  (1607), *A Treatise Tending to Mitigation*.
  (1608), *The Judgement of a Catholicke English-man*.
Peacham, Henry (1622), *The Compleat Gentleman*.
Peele, George (1591, 1888), *Descenus Astraeae*, in *The Works of George Peele*, ed. A. H. Bullen, vol. I, pp. 361–8.
Pepys, Samuel (1660–9, 1977), *Diary*, ed. Robert Latham and William Matthews (London: Bell).
Percivall, M. (?) (1696), *The Tragedy Called the Popish Plot Reviv'd*.
Perkins, William (1608), *A Whole Treatise of the Cases of Conscience*.
  (1609), *A Treatise of the Vocations, or Callings of Men, with the sorts and kinds of them and the right use thereof*, in *Workes* (Cambridge), vol. I, pp. 728–55.
Phillips, Edward (1658, 1685), *The Mysteries of Love and Eloquence*.
'Philodemius' (1649), *The Original and End of Civil Power*.
Plato (*c*. 410 BC, 1969), *The Republic*, trans. Paul Shorey (Cambridge, Mass.: Harvard University Press).
  (*c*. 355 BC, 1965), *Timaeus*, trans. H. D. P. Lee (Harmondsworth: Penguin).
Pole, Reginald (1536), *Pro ecclesiasticae unitatis defensione* (Rome).
Ponet, John (1556), *A Shorte Treatise of Politicke Power* (Strasbourg).
Pope, Alexander (1727, 1952), *Peri Bathous, Or The Art of Sinking in Poetry*, ed. E. L. Steeves (New York: Columbia University, Crown Press).
Potocki, Jan (1815, 1995), *The Manuscript Found at Saragossa*, trans. Ian Maclean (Harmondsworth: Penguin).
Powell, Gabriel (?) (1604, 1606), *The Catholicke's Supplication*.
Price, Richard (1790, 1991), *A Discourse on the Love of our Country*, in Ellis Sandoz, ed., *Political Sermons of the American Revolution*, pp. 1005–28.
Protestation (1641, 1979), in S. R. Gardiner, ed., *Constitutional Documents*, p. 155.
Prynne, William (1633), *Histrio-mastix*.
  (1643), *The Treachery and Disloyalty of Papists to their Soveraignes: The Soveraigne Power of Parliaments and Kingdoms*.
  (1650), *A Briefe Apologie for all Non-Subscribers*.

(1659), *Concordia discors*.
(1661), *A Short, Sober pacific examination of some exhorbitances in Ceremonial Appurtinances to the Common Prayer*.
(1664), *Quakers Unmasked*.
Pufendorf, Samuel (1672, 1943), *De iure naturae et gentium, libri octo*, trans. C. H. and W. A. Oldfather (Oxford: Clarendon Press).
Puttenham, George (1589), *The Art of English Poesy*, introduction by Baxter Hatherway (Kent, Ohio: Kent State University Press).
Pym, John (1641), *The Speech or Declaration of John Pym*, in J. L. Malcolm, ed., *The Struggle for Sovereignty*, vol. I, pp. 127–44.
Quintilian (*c*. AD 90, 1920–2), *Institutio oratoria*, trans. H. E. Butler (Cambridge, Mass.: Harvard University Press).
R. A. (1661), *A Letter to a Friend*.
R. F. (1651), *Mercurius heliconicus. Or the result of a safe conscience*.
R. O. (1643), *Man's Mortalitie*.
Rainolds, John (1599), *Th'Overthrow of Stage-Playes*.
Raleigh, Sir Walter (1658), *The Cabinet Council*.
Reeves, William (1712), *The Nature of Truth and Falsity*.
Reynalds, J. (?) (1650), *The Humble Proposals of Several Learned Divines within the Kingdom Concerning the Engagement*.
Rich, Barnaby (1578), *Allarme to England*.
Rocket, John (1650), *The Christian Subject*.
Rogers, Thomas (1576), *A Philosophicall Discourse Entitled The Anatomy of the Mind*.
Rohan, Henri duc de (1639), *De l'interest des princes et estates de la Chrestiente* (Paris).
Rous, Francis (1649, 1999), *The Lawfulnes of Obeying the Present Government*, in J. L. Malcolm, ed., *The Struggle for Sovereignty*, vol. I, pp. 393–404.
Rutherford, Samuel (1644), *Lex, Rex, Or the Law and the Prince* (Edinburgh).
S. R. (1693), *The Life of M. Descartes*.
S. W. (1650), *The Constant man's character*.
Sacheverell, Henry (1709), *The Perils of False Brethren*.
Sadler, Sir Ralph (1809), *State Papers*, 2 vols. (Edinburgh).
Salutati, Coluccio (1400, 1964), *De tyranno*, in E. Emerton, ed., *Humanism and Tyranny*, pp. 70–116.
Sanderson, Robert (1621, 1854), *Sermons ad Populum* in *Works*, ed. W. Jacobson (Oxford: Oxford University Press), vol. III, pp. 91–144.
(1626, 1854), *Sermons ad Magistratum*, in *Works*, vol. I, pp. 171–362.
(1647, 1854), *The Reasons for the Present Judgement of the University of Oxford*, in *Works*, vol. IV, pp. 367–447 [erratic pagination].
(1649), *A Resolution of Conscience in Answer to a Letter Sent with Mr. Ascham's Book*.
(1650, 1854), 'The Case of the Engagement', in *Works*, vol. V, pp. 17–33.
(1854), 'The Case of the Validity of a Matrimonial Contract', [n.d.], in *Works*, vol. V, pp. 122–36.
(1854), 'The Case of the Rash Vow', in *Works*, vol. V, pp. 60–74.
(1655), *De juramento*, translation of *De juramenti promissorii* (1647), also in *Works*, vol. IV, pp. 231–361.

(1661, 1854), *Episcopacy not Prejudicial to Regal Power*, in *Works*, vol. V, pp. 137–192.

Saunders, Richard (1651), *Plenary Possession*.

Saville, George, Marquis of Halifax (c. 1684, 1912), *The Character of a Trimmer*, in Walter Raleigh, ed., *The Complete Works* (Oxford: Clarendon Press) pp. 47–103.

Scheibler, Christoph (1617, 1665), *Metaphysica duobus libris, universum hujus scientiae systema* (Giessen and Oxford).

Scott, William (1635), *An Essay on Drapery*.

Selden, John (1686, 1934), *Table Talk*, in James Thornton, ed., *Table Talk from Ben Jonson to Leigh Hunt*, pp. 18–108.

Sellar, A. (1689), *The History of Passive Obedience*.

Settle, E. (1685), *A Poem Upon the Coronation of His Most Sacred Majesty King James II*.

Sewell, George (1712), *The Patriot, A Poem*.

Sexby, Edward (1657, 1689), *Killing No Murder*.

Shakespeare, William (1959), *Complete Works*, ed. Peter Alexander, (London: Collins).

(1591), *Henry VI*.
(c. 1592–3), *The Comedy of Errors*.
(c. 1593), *Richard III*.
(c. 1594–5), *Two Gentlemen of Verona*.
(c. 1594–5), *Love's Labour's Lost*.
(c. 1595–6), *Richard II*.
(c. 1596), *A Midsummer Night's Dream*.
(c. 1596–7), *The Merchant of Venice*.
(c. 1596–7), *King John*.
(c. 1597–8), *2Henry IV*.
(c. 1598–1600), *Much Ado about Nothing*.
(c. 1598–1600), *As You Like It*.
(c. 1598–1600), *Twelfth Night*.
(1600), *Henry V*.
(c. 1600), *Hamlet*.
(1601), *The Phoenix and the Turtle*.
(c. 1601–2), *Troilus and Cressida*.
(c. 1600–1), *Julius Caesar*.
(c. 1601), *The Merry Wives of Windsor*.
(c. 1604), *Measure for Measure*.
(c. 1604–5), *Othello*.
(c. 1605–6), *Macbeth*.
(c. 1605–6), *King Lear*.
(c. 1609–10), *The Winter's Tale*.
(c. 1611–12), *The Tempest*.

Sharp, John (1688, 1754), 'On Heresy', in *Works*, vol. IV, pp. 1–24.

(c. 1690, 1754), 'All Oaths not Unlawful and Against Perjury', in *Works*, vol. IV, pp. 272–86.

(c. 1690, 1754), 'Arguments Against Common Swearing', in *Works*, vol. IV, pp. 287–302.

Bibliography

(1690, 1754), 'Rules of Conduct for Ourselves', in *Works*, vol. I , pp. 175–97.

(1691, 1754), 'General Directions for a Holy Life', in *Works*, vol. I, pp. 226–49.

(1699/1700, 1754), 'The Duty of Subjection to Higher Powers', in *Works*, vol. II, pp. 34–51.

(*c*. 1700, 1754), 'A Discourse of Conscience', in *Works*, vol. II, pp. 171–228.

(1754), 'A Discourse on the Various Callings in Life', in *Works*, vol. V, pp. 80–108.

Sheldon, Richard (1611), *Certain General Reasons Proving the Lawfulnesse of the Oath of Allegiance*.

Sherlock, William (1684), *The Case of Resistance to Supreme Powers*.

(1685), *A Sermon Preached at Westminster*.

(1691), *The Case of Allegiance due to Sovereign Powers*.

Sidney, Algernon (1681–3, 1698, 1996), *Discourses Concerning Government*, ed. Thomas G. West (Indianapolis: Liberty Fund).

Sidney, Sir Philip (1595, 1956), *An Apology for Poetry*, in E. Jones, *English Critical Essays*, pp. 1–54.

Smith, Adam (1790, 1984), *A Theory of Moral Sentiments*, ed. D. D. Raphael and A. L. Macfie (Indianapolis: Liberty Fund).

Smith, Sir Thomas (1583, 1906), *De republica Anglorum*, ed. L. Alston (Cambridge: Cambridge University Press).

Solemn League and Covenant (1643, 1979), in S. R. Gardiner, *Constitutional Documents*, pp. 267–70.

Southwell, Robert (1595, 1967), *St. Peter's Complaint*, in *The Poems of Robert Southwell, S.J*, ed. James H. McDonald and Nancy Pollard Brown (Oxford: Clarendon Press).

St German, Christopher (1530, 1638), *A Dyaloge in Englysshe bytwyxt a Doctoure of Dyvynyte and a Student in the Lawes of England: of the groundes of the sayd lawes and of Conscyence*.

St John, Henry, Lord Bolingbroke (1749, 1965), *The Idea of a Patriot King*, ed. Stanley W. Jackman (New York: Bobbs-Merrill).

Starkey, Thomas (?) (1532, 1989), *A Dialogue Between Cardinal Pole and Thomas Lupset*, ed. Thomas F. Mayer (London: Royal Historical Society).

Ste B. (1608), *Counsel to the Husband, to the Wife Instruction*.

Steele, Richard (1714), *The Englishman, being the Close of the Paper So-Called*.

Stephens, Edward (?) (1696, 1705), *Four Questions Debated*, in *State Tracts*, vol. I.

Stow, John (1598, 1603), *A Survay of London*.

Stuart, Richard (1656), *Three Sermons Preached by the Reverend and Learned Dr. Richard Stuart, to which is added a Fourth by Samuel Harsnett*.

Studeley, Peter (1635), *The Looking-Glasse of Schism*.

Suarez, Francisco de (1613), *Defensio fidei Catholicae et apostolicae adversus anglicanae sectae errores* (Coimbra).

T. B. (1649), *Logoi apologetikoi*.

Taylor, Jeremy (1651), *Rules for Holy Dying*.

(1660), *Ductor dubitantium*.

Taylor, John (1630), *Christian Admonitions against Cursing and Swearing*.

Thompson, Flora (1948, 1975), *Lark Rise to Candleford* (London: Oxford University Press).

Tillotson, John (1685, 1702), 'Of Diligence', in *Fifteen Sermons*, pp. 225–59.
Tooke, Andrew (1691, 2003), *The Whole Duty of Man According to the Law of Nature*, translation of Samuel Pufendorf, *De officio hominis* (1673), ed. Ian Hunter and David Saunders (Indianapolis: Liberty Fund).
Trenchard, John and Gordon, Thomas (1720–3, 1995), *Cato's Letters: or Essays on Liberty, Civil and Religious, and Other Important Subjects*, ed. Ronald Hamowy, 2 vols. (Indianapolis: Liberty Fund).
Tuvill, Daniel (1608), *Essayes Politicke and Morall.*
 (1609), *Essayes Morall and Theological.*
 (1614), *The Doue and the Serpent.*
Tynley, Robert (1609), *Two Learned Sermons.*
Valla, Lorenzo (1962), *Opera omnia*, 2 vols. (Turin: Bottega d'Erasmo).
Vermigli, Peter Martyr (1564–83, 1980), *The Political Thought of Peter Martyr Vermigli: Selected Works and Commentary*, ed. Robert Kingdon (Geneva: Droz).
Vienne, Philibert de (1575), *The Court Philosopher*, trans., G. North.
Vines, Richard (1647), *The Authors, Nature and Danger of Haeresie.*
Violet, Thomas (?) (1661), *A Petition Against the Jewes.*
Vitoria, Francisco (1528), *On Civil Power*, in *Political Writings*, ed. and trans. Anthony Pagden and Jeremy Lawrence (Cambridge: Cambridge University Press), pp. 1–44.
 (1532) *On The Power of the Church*, in *Political Writings*, pp. 45–151.
W. C. (1660), *A Discourse for King and Parliament.*
W. S. (1650), *The Constant Man's Character.*
Walter, Thomas (1679), *The Excommunicated Prince.*
Walwyn, William (1649, 1967), *A Manifestation*, in Don Wolfe, ed., *The Leveller Manifestoes*, pp. 384–96.
Ward, Nathaniel (?) (1649), *A Religious Demurrer.*
 (?) (1650), *A Discolliminium, Or Reply to a Late Book called Bounds and Bonds.*
Ward, Seth (1652), *A Philosophical Essay.*
 (1661, 1710), *Against Resistance to Lawful Powers.*
Warr, John (1649, 1992), *The Corruption and Deficiency of the Laws of England*, in *A Spark in the Ashes: The Pamphlets of John Warr*, ed. Stephen Sedley and Lawrence Kaplan (London: Verso).
Warren, Albertus (1650), *The Royalist Reform'd.*
White, Christopher (1627), *Of Oathes.*
Wildman, John (?) (1688/9, 1705), *Some Remarks Upon Government*, in *State Tracts*, vol. I.
Willett, Andrew (1607), *An Harmonie on the First Booke of Samuel.*
 (1614), *An Harmonie on the Second Booke of Samuel.*
William, K. (1689), *Wherein it is Set Forth.*
Williams, J. (1678), *The History of the Gunpowder Treason.*
Willis, Thomas (1683), *Two Discourses Concerning the Soul of Brutes*, trans. S. Pordage.
Willymat, William (1604), *A Loyal Subjects Looking-glasse.*
Wilson, John (1662), *The Cheats.*
Wilson, Thomas (1533, 1560, 1909), *The Art of Rhetoric*, ed. G. H. Mair (Oxford: Clarendon Press).

Wing, John (1620), *The Crown Conjugal*.
Winstanley, Gerrard (1652, 1973), *The Law of Freedom in a Platform: or True Magistracy Restored*, ed. Robert W. Kenny (New York: Schocken Books).
Wright, Leonard (1589, 1616), *A Display of Duty*.
Young, Edward (1759, 1956), *Conjectures on Original Composition*, in E. Jones, *English Critical Essays*, pp. 270–311.

SECONDARY SOURCES: BOOKS

Ackroyd, Peter (2000), *London, the Biography* (London: Chatto and Windus).
Adams, Robert M. (1977), *Bad Mouth: Fugitive Papers on the Dark Side* (Berkeley: University of California Press).
Alford, Stephen (1998), *The Early Elizabethan Polity: William Cecil and the British Succession Crisis, 1558–1569* (Cambridge: Cambridge University Press).
Anstey, Peter (2000), *The Philosophy of Robert Boyle* (London: Routledge).
Archer, Ian (1991), *The Pursuit of Stability: Social Relations in Elizabethan London* (Cambridge: Cambridge University Press).
Arrington, Robert L. (1998), *Western Ethics: An Historical Introduction* (Oxford: Blackwell).
Ashcraft, Richard (1986), *Revolutionary Politics and Locke's Two Treatises of Government* (Princeton: Princeton University Press).
Austin, John (1955), *How to Do Things with Words*, ed. J. O. Urmson (London: Oxford University Press).
Baker, J. H. (1979), *An Introduction to English Legal History* (London: Butterworth).
Barber, Sarah (1998), *Regicide and Republicanism: Politics and Ethics in the English Revolution, 1646–59* (Edinburgh: Edinburgh University Press).
Bartlett, John (1979), *A Complete Concordance to Shakespeare* (London: Macmillan).
Baxter, Stephen (1966), *William III* (London: Longmans).
Beattie, J. M. (2002), *Policing and Punishment in London, 1660–1750* (Oxford: Oxford University Press).
Bendall, Sarah, Brook, Christopher and Collinson, Patrick (1999), *A History of Emmanuel College Cambridge* (Woodbridge: Boydell).
Bennet, Joan (1989), *Reviving Liberty: Radical Christian Humanism in Milton's Poems* (Cambridge, Mass.: Harvard University Press).
Bergeron, David M. (1971), *English Civic Pageantry, 1558–1642* (London: Edward Arnold).
Berlin, Isaiah (1969), *Four Essays on Liberty* (Oxford: Oxford University Press).
Blakey, Robert (1855), *A History of Political Literature from the Earliest Times*, 2 vols. (London).
Bloom, Harold (1999), *Shakespeare: The Invention of the Human* (London: Fourth Estate).
Bourdieu, Pierre (1972), *Esquisse d'une théorie de la pratique* (Geneva: Droz), trans. Richard Nice, *An Outline of a Theory of Practice* (New York: Cambridge University Press, 1977).

Bowsma, William (1984), *Venice and the Defence of Republican Liberty* (Los Angeles: University of California Press).
Braddick, Michael, J. (2000), *State Formation in Early Modern England, c.1550–1700* (Cambridge: Cambridge University Press).
Brett, Annabel (1997), *Liberty, Right and Nature: Individual Rights in Later Scholastic Thought* (Cambridge: Cambridge University Press).
Brown, Meg Lota (1995), *Donne and the Politics of Conscience in Early Modern England* (Leiden: Brill).
Buc, Philippe (2001), *The Dangers of Ritual: Between Early Medieval Texts and Social Scientific Theory* (Princeton: Princeton University Press).
Burgess, Glenn (1992), *The Politics of the Ancient Constitution* (London: Macmillan).
— (1996), *Absolute Monarchy and the Stuart Constitution* (New Haven: Yale University Press).
Burke, Peter (1978), *Popular Culture in Early Modern Europe* (London: Temple Smith).
— (1986), *The Italian Renaissance: Culture and Society in Italy* (Princeton: Princeton University Press).
Caputo, John (2000), *On Religion* (London: Routledge).
Champion, Justin (1992), *The Pillars of Priestcraft Shaken: The Church of England and its Enemies, 1660–1730* (Cambridge: Cambridge University Press).
Collingwood, R. G. (1939), *An Autobiography* (Oxford: Oxford University Press).
Collini, Stefan, Winch, Donald and Burrow, John (1983), *That Noble Science of Politics: A Study in Nineteenth-Century Intellectual History* (Cambridge: Cambridge University Press).
Coltman, Irene (1962), *Private Men and Public Causes* (London: Faber).
Condren, Conal (1985), *The Status and Appraisal of Classic Texts* (Princeton: Princeton University Press).
— (1989), *George Lawson's 'Politica' and the English Revolution* (Cambridge: Cambridge University Press).
— (1994), *The Language of Politics in Seventeenth-Century England* (London: Macmillan).
— (1996), *Satire, Lies and Politics: The Case of Dr Arbuthnot* (London: Macmillan).
— (2000), *Thomas Hobbes* (New York: Twayne).
Cooper, Tim (2001), *Fear and Polemic in Seventeenth-Century England: Richard Baxter and Antinomianism* (Aldershot: Ashgate).
Cragg, Gerald R. (1975), *Freedom and Authority: A Study of English Thought in the Early Seventeenth Century* (Philadelphia: Westminster Press).
Craven, W. G. (1981), *Giovanni Pico della Mirandola, Symbol of his Age* (Geneva: Droz).
Cressy, David (1979), *Bonfires and Bells: National Memory and the Protestant Calendar in Elizabethan and Stuart England* (London: Weidenfeld and Nicolson).
— (1997), *Birth, Marriage and Death: Ritual, Religion and the Life-Cycle in Tudor and Stuart England* (Oxford: Oxford University Press).
Croce, Benedetto (1929, 1973), *Etica e politica* (Rome: Laterza).

Cromartie, Alan (forthcoming 2006), *The Constitutionalist Revolution in Early Modern England* (Cambridge: Cambridge University Press).
Davis, J. C. (1981), *Utopia and the Ideal Society: A Study of English Utopian Writings, 1516–1700* (Cambridge: Cambridge University Press).
 (1986), *Fear, Myth and History: The Ranters and the Historians* (Cambridge: Cambridge University Press).
Donaldson, Peter S. (1988), *Machiavelli and the Mystery of State* (Cambridge: Cambridge University Press).
Dunning, W. (1902), *A History of Political Theories* (New York: Macmillan).
Ferrante, Joan (1984), *The Political Vision of the Divine Comedy* (Princeton: Princeton University Press).
Fish, Stanley (1972), *Self-Consuming Artifacts* (Berkeley: University of California Press).
Fitzmaurice, Andrew (2003), *Humanism and America: An Intellectual History of English Colonialism, 1500–1625* (Cambridge: Cambridge University Press).
Forbes, Duncan (1975), *Hume's Philosophical Politics* (Cambridge: Cambridge University Press).
Fox, Christopher (1988), *Locke and the Scriblerians* (Los Angeles: University of California Press).
Franklin, Julian (1975), *John Locke and the Theory of Sovereignty* (Cambridge: Cambridge University Press).
Friedeburg, Robert von (2002), *Self-Defence and Religious Strife in Early Modern Europe: England and Germany, 1530–1680* (Aldershot: Ashgate).
Gallie, W. B. (1964), *Philosophy and the Historical Understanding* (London: Chatto and Windus).
Gaukroger, Stephen (2000), *Francis Bacon and the Transformation of Early-Modern Philosophy* (Cambridge: Cambridge Univervsity Press).
Geertz, Clifford (1980), *Negara: The Theatre State in Nineteenth-Century Bali* (Princeton: Princeton University Press).
Gennep, Arnold van (1908, 1960), *The Rites of Passage*, trans. M. B. Vizidom and G. L. Caffee (Chicago: Chicago University Press).
Gillies, John (1996), *Shakespeare and the Geography of Difference* (Cambridge: Cambridge University Press).
Goffman, Erving (1959), *The Presentation of the Self in Everyday Life* (New York: Doubleday).
 (1983), *Frame Analysis: An Essay on the Organisation of Experience* (New York: Harper).
Greenberg, Janelle (2001), *The Radical Face of the Ancient Constitution: St Edward's Laws in Early Modern Political Thought* (Cambridge: Cambridge University Press).
Greenblatt, Stephen (1980), *Renaissance Self-Fashioning, from More to Shakespeare* (Chicago: Chicago University Press).
 (1988), *Shakespearean Negotiations: The Circulation of Social Energy* (Berkeley: University of California Press).
 (2002), *Hamlet in Purgatory* (Princeton: Princeton University Press).
Gunnell, John G. (1993), *The Descent of Political Theory: The Genealogy of an American Vocation* (Chicago: Chicago University Press).

Haakonssen, Knud (1996), *Natural Law and Moral Philosophy: From Grotius to the Scottish Enlightenment* (Cambridge: Cambridge University Press).
Habermas, Jürgen (1992), *The Structural Transformation of the Public Sphere: An Enquiry into a Category of Bourgeois Society*, trans. T. Burger and F. Lawrence (Cambridge: Polity Press).
Hadot, Pierre (1995), *Philosophy as a Way of Life: Spiritual Exercises from Socrates to Foucault*, ed. Arnold Davidson, trans. Michael Chase, from *Exercices spirituels et philosophie antique*.
Haigh, Christopher (1998), *Elizabeth I* (New York: Longmans).
Harris, Tim (1987), *London Crowds in the Reign of Charles II: Propaganda and Politics from the Restoration to the Exclusion Crisis* (Cambridge: Cambridge University Press).
Hexter, J. H. (1973), *The Vision of Politics on the Eve of the Reformation* (London: Allen Lane).
Hindle, Steve (2000), *The State and Social Change in Early Modern England, c.1550–1640* (New York: Palgrave).
Hole, Christina (1943–4), *English Custom and Usage* (London: Batsford).
Hooker, Brad (2000), *Ideal, Code, Real World* (Oxford: Clarendon Press).
Höpfl, Harro (1982), *The Christian Polity of John Calvin* (Cambridge: Cambridge University Press).
Hunter, Ian (2001), *Rival Enlightenments: Civil and Metaphysical Philosophy in Early Modern Germany* (Cambridge: Cambridge University Press).
Hunter, Michael (2000), *Robert Boyle (1627–91): Scrupulosity and Science* (Woodbridge: Boydell Press).
Hunter, M., Mandelbrote, G., Ovendon, R. and Smith, N., eds. (1999), *A Radical's Books: The Library Catalogue of Samuel Jeakes of Rye, 1623–90* (Woodbridge: Brewer).
Ihalainen, Pasi (1999), *The Discourse on Political Pluralism in Early Eighteenth-Century England* (Helsinki: Suomaen Historiallinen Seura).
Jolliffe, J. E. A. (1970), *Angevin Kingship* (London: Adam Black).
Jones, David Martin (1999), *Conscience and Allegiance in Seventeenth-Century England* (New York: University of Rochester Press).
Kantorowicz, Ernst (1958), *The King's Two Bodies: A Study in Medieval Political Theology* (Princeton: Princeton University Press).
Kent, J. R. (1986), *The Village Constable, 1580–1642* (Oxford: Clarendon Press).
Kenyon, J. P. (1977), *Revolutionary Principles: The Politics of Party, 1689–1720* (Cambridge: Cambridge University Press).
Kernan, Alvin B. (1979), *The Playwright as Magician: Shakespeare's Image of the Poet in the English Public Theater* (New Haven: Yale University Press).
Killcullen, John (1988), *Sincerity and Truth* (Oxford: Blackwell).
Lacey, Douglas R. (1969), *Dissent and Parliamentary Politics in England, 1661–1689* (New Brunswick, N. J.: Rutgers University Press).
Lamont, William (1979), *Richard Baxter and the Millennium* (London: Croom Helm).
Lewis, C. S. (1976), *Studies in Words* (Cambridge: Cambridge University Press).
McGrath, Patrick (1967), *Papists and Puritans Under Elizabeth I* (London: Blandford Press).

McIlwain, C. H. (1932, 1964), *The Growth of Political Thought in the West* (New York: Macmillan).
McInnes, Angus (1980), *English Towns* (London: Historical Association).
MacIntyre, Alistair (1967), *A Short History of Ethics* (London: Routledge).
  (1981), *After Virtue: A Study in Moral Theory* (Notre Dame, Ind.: Notre Dame University Press).
Mack, Peter (2002), *Elizabethan Rhetoric in Theory and Practice* (Cambridge: Cambridge University Press).
McKeon, Michael (1975), *Politics and Poetry in Restoration England: The Case of Dryden's Annus Mirabilis* (Cambridge, Mass.: Harvard University Press).
Maclean, Ian (1992), *Interpretation and Meaning in the Renaissance: The Case of Law* (Cambridge: Cambridge University Press).
  (2002), *Logic, Signs and Nature in the Renaissance* (Cambridge: Cambridge University Press).
Malcolm, Noel (1984), *De Dominis (1560–1624): Venetian, Anglican, Ecumenicist and Relapsed Heretic* (London: Strickland).
  (1997), *The Origins of English Nonsense* (London: Fontana).
  (2002), *Aspects of Hobbes* (Oxford: Clarendon Press).
Malcolmson, Christina (1999), *Heart Work: George Herbert and the Protestant Ethic* (Stanford: Stanford University Press).
Martin, Julian (1992), *Francis Bacon, the State and the Reform of Natural Philosophy* (Cambridge: Cambridge University Press).
Mayer, Thomas F. (1989), *Thomas Starkey and the Commonweal: Humanist Politics in the Reign of Henry VIII* (Cambridge: Cambridge University Press).
Mendle, Michael (1995), *Dangerous Positions: Mixed Government, the Estates of the Realm and the Making of the xix Propositions* (Tuscaloosa, Ala.: Alabama University Press).
  (1995), *Henry Parker and the English Civil War: The Political Thought of the Public's 'Privado'* (Cambridge: Cambridge University Press).
Milton, Anthony (1995), *Catholic and Reformed: The Roman and the Protestant Churches in English Protestant Thought, 1600–1640* (Cambridge: Cambridge University Press).
Monod, Paul Kléber (1993), *Jacobitism and the English People, 1688–1788* (Cambridge: Cambridge University Press).
Morrill, J. B. (1976), *The Revolt of the Provinces: Conservatives and Radicals in the English Civil War, 1630–1650* (London: Allen and Unwin).
  (1996), *The Nature of the English Revolution* (Harlow: Longmans).
Morris, Wesley (1972), *Towards a New Historicism* (Chicago: Chicago University Press).
Mous, Katherine Eisaman (1980), *Inwardness and Theater in the English Renaissance* (Chicago: Chicago University Press).
Muir, Edwin (1997), *Ritual in Early Modern Europe* (Cambridge: Cambridge University Press).
Muldrew, Craig (1998), *The Economy of Obligation: The Culture of Credit and Social Relations in Early Modern England* (New York: St Martins Press).
Myers, J. L. (1927, 1968), *The Political Ideas of the Greeks* (New York: Greenwood).

Norbrook, David (2000), *Writing the English Republic: Poetry, Rhetoric and Politics, 1627–1660* (Cambridge: Cambridge University Press).
Nussbaum, Martha (1994), *The Therapy of Desire: Theory and Practice in Hellenistic Ethics* (Princeton: Princeton University Press).
Oakeshott, Michael (1933, 1966), *Experience and its Modes* (Cambridge: Cambridge University Press).
Onians, R. B. (1951, 1973), *The Origins of European Thought* (New York: Arno).
Orgel, Stephen (1965), *The Jonsonian Masque* (Cambridge, Mass.: Harvard University Press).
Parnham, David (1997), *Sir Henry Vane, Theologian: A Study in Seventeenth-Century Religious Political Discourse* (London: Associated University Press).
Parrow, Kathleen (1993), *From Defense to Resistance: Justification of Violence during the French Wars of Religion* (Philadelphia: APS).
Patterson, Annabelle (1976), *Marvell and the Civic Crown* (Princeton: Princeton University Press).
  (1994), *Reading Hollingshed's Chronicles* (Chicago: Chicago University Press).
Patterson, W. Brown (2000), *James VI&I and the Reunion of Christendom* (Cambridge: Cambridge University Press).
Peltonen, Markku (1995), *Classical Humanism and Republicanism in English Political Thought, 1570–1640* (Cambridge: Cambridge University Press).
  (2003), *The Duel in Early Modern England: Civility, Politeness and Honour* (Cambridge: Cambridge University Press).
Perelman, Chaim (1979), *The New Rhetoric and the Humanities: Essays on Rhetoric and its Applications* (Dordrecht: Reidel).
Petchey, W. J. (1985), *The Intentions of Thomas Plume* (Maldon: Trustees of the Plume Library).
Peters, F. E. (1967), *Greek Philosophical Terms: A Historical Lexicon* (New York: New York University Press).
Pettit, Philip (1997), *Republicanism: A Theory of Freedom and Government* (Oxford: Oxford University Press).
Phillipson, Nicholas and Skinner, Quentin, eds. (1993), *Political Discourse in Early Modern Britain* (Cambridge: Cambridge University Press).
Piaia, Gregorio (1977), *Marsilio da Padova nella Riforma e nella Controriforma* (Padua: Antenore).
Pilhens, Hugh (1983), *The Story of Hungerford* (Newbury: Local Heritage).
Pocock, J. G. A. (1973), *Obligation and Authority in Two English Revolutions* (Wellington: Victoria University Press).
  (1975), *The Machiavellian Moment* (Princeton: Princeton University Press).
  (1987), *The Ancient Constitution and the Feudal Law: A Reissue with a Retrospect* (Cambridge: Cambridge University Press).
Porter, Roy (2000), *Enlightenment Britain and the Creation of the Modern World* (Harmondsworth: Allen Lane).
Post, Gaines (1964), *Studies in Medieval Legal Thought. Public Law and the State, 1100–1322* (Princeton: Princeton University Press).
Powell, Sumner Chilton (1963), *Puritan Village: The Formation of a New England Town* (Middletown, Conn.: Wesleyan University Press).
Pritchard, Arnold (1979), *Catholic Loyalism in Elizabethan England* (London: Scolar Press).

Prokhovnik, Raia (1991), *Rhetoric and Philosophy in Hobbes's Leviathan* (New York: Garland).
  (1999), *Rational Woman* (London: Routledge).
  (2004), *Spinoza and Republicanism* (London: Palgrave).
Racken, Phyllis (1990), *Stages of History: Shakespeare's English Chronicles* (New York: Cornell University Press).
Rawls, John (1971), *A Theory of Justice* (Cambridge, Mass.: Harvard University Press).
  (2000), *Lectures on the History of Moral Philosophy* (Cambridge, Mass.: Harvard University Press).
Reeve, L. J. (1989), *Charles I and the Road to Personal Rule* (Cambridge: Cambridge University Press).
Ricoeur, Paul (1992), *Oneself as Another*, trans. Kathleen Blamey (Chicago: Chicago University Press).
Romilly, Jacqueline de (1975), *Magic and Rhetoric in Ancient Greece* (Cambridge, Mass.: Harvard University Press).
Rorty, Richard (1979), *Philosophy and the Mirror of Nature* (Princeton: Princeton University Press).
Rose, Margaret (1979), *Parody: Meta-Fiction* (London: Croom Helm).
Russell, Conrad (1988), *The Crisis of Parliaments* (Oxford: Oxford University Press).
  (1990), *The Causes of the English Civil War* (Oxford: Clarendon Press).
Russell, F. W. (1859), *Kett's Rebellion in Norfolk* (London).
Ryle, Gilbert (1949), *The Concept of Mind* (London: Hutchinson).
Sandel, Michael, ed. (1984), *Liberalism and its Critics* (Oxford: Blackwell).
Sasso, Gennaro (1958), *Niccolò Machiavelli. Storia del suo pensiero politico* (Naples: Morano).
Schneewind, J. B. (1998), *The Invention of Autonomy: A history of Modern Moral Philosophy* (Cambridge: Cambridge University Press).
Scott, Jonathan (1988), *Algernon Sidney and the English Republic, 1623–1677* (Cambridge: Cambridge University Press).
  (1991), *Algernon Sidney and the Restoration Crisis, 1677–83* (Cambridge: Cambridge University Press).
  (2000), *England's Troubles: Seventeenth-Century English Political Instability in European Context* (Cambridge: Cambridge University Press).
Shapin, Stephen (1994), *A Social History of Truth: Civility and Science in Seventeenth-Century England* (Chicago: Chicago University Press).
Shapiro, Barbara (1969), *John Wilkins, 1614–1672: An Intellectual Biography* (Los Angeles: University of California Press).
Sharpe, Kevin (1987), *Criticism and Compliment* (Cambridge: Cambridge University Press).
  (2000), *Re-Mapping Early-Modern England: The Culture of Seventeenth-Century Politics* (Cambridge: Cambridge University Press).
Shennon, J. H. (1969), *Government and Society in France, 1461–1661* (London: Allen and Unwin).
Shirley, Frances (1979), *Swearing and Perjury in Shakespeare's Plays* (London: Allen and Unwin).

Shuger, Deborah (1990), *Habits of Thought in the English Renaissance: Religion, Politics and the Dominant Culture* (Berkeley: University of California Press).
Skinner, Quentin (1998), *Liberty Before Liberalism* (Cambridge: Cambridge University Press).
— (1996), *Reason and Rhetoric in Philosophy of Hobbes* (Cambridge: Cambridge University Press).
Smith, David L. (1994), *Constitutional Royalism and the Search for a Settlement, c.1640–1649* (Cambridge: Cambridge University Press).
Sommerville, J. P. (1986), *Politics and Ideology in England, 1603–1640* (London: Longmans).
Stater, V. L. (1994), *Noble Government: The Stuart Lord Lieutenancy and the Transformation of English Politics* (Athens, Ga.: University of Georgia Press).
Strawson, P. F. (1959, 1971), *Individuals: An Essay in Descriptive Metaphysics* (London: Methuen).
Sullivan, Vickie B. (2004), *Machiavelli, Hobbes and the Formation of a Liberal Republicanism in England* (Cambridge: Cambridge University Press).
Sutton, Anne F. and Hammond, P. W., eds. (1983), *The Coronation of Richard III* (Gloucester: Alan Sutton).
Targoff, Rami (2001), *Common Prayer: The Language of Devotion in Early Modern England* (Chicago: Chicago University Press).
Taylor, Charles (1989), *Sources of the Self: The Making of Modern Identity* (Cambridge, Mass.: Harvard University Press).
Tierney, Brian (1997), *The Idea of Natural Rights: Studies on Natural Rights, Natural Law and Church Law, 1150–1625* (Atlanta: Scholars Press).
Toulmin, Stephen and Jonsen, A. R. (1988), *The Abuse of Casuistry: A History of Moral Reasoning* (Los Angeles: University of California Press).
Trinkhaus, Charles (1970), *In our Image and Likeness: Humanity and Divinity in Italian Humanist Thought*, 2 vols. (Chicago: Chicago University Press).
Tuck, Richard (1993), *Philosophy and Government, 1572–1651* (Cambridge: Cambridge University Press).
Tully, James (1982), *A Discourse on Property: John Locke and his Adversaries* (Cambridge: Cambridge University Press).
Tuve, Rosemund (1972), *Elizabethan Metaphysical Imagery* (Chicago: Chicago University Press).
Ullmann, Walter (1975), *Law and Politics in the Middle Ages* (Cambridge: The Sources of History).
Underdown, David (1973), *Somerset and the Civil War and Interregnum* (Newton Abbot: David and Charles).
— (2000), *Start of Play: Cricket and Culture in Eighteenth-Century England* (London: Allen Lane).
Vickers, Brian (1993), *Appropriating Shakespeare: Contemporary Critical Quarrels* (New Haven: Yale University Press).
Viroli, Maurizio (1992), *From Politics to Reason of State: The Acquisition and Transformation of the Language of Politics, 1250–1600* (Cambridge: Cambridge University Press).

Weston, Corrine Comstock and Greenberg, Janelle (1981), *Subjects and Sovereigns: The Grand Controversy over Legal Sovereignty in Stuart England* (Cambridge: Cambridge University Press).
Whitfield, J. H. (1947), *Machiavelli* (Oxford: Oxford University Press).
  (1969), *Discourses on Machiavelli* (Cambridge: Heffer).
Wiggins, David (1988), *Identity and Spatio-Temporal Continuity* (Oxford: Blackwell).
Wilcox, David (1969), *The Development of Florentine Humanist Historiography in the Fifteenth Century* (Cambridge, Mass.: Harvard University Press).
Wilkinson, Bertie (1951), *The Coronation in History* (London: History Association).
Wilks, Michael (1963), *The Problem of Sovereignty in the Later Middle Ages* (Cambridge: Cambridge University Press).
Wilson, John Dover (1970), *The Fortunes of Falstaff* (Cambridge: Cambridge University Press).
Worden, Blair (1974), *The Rump Parliament* (Cambridge: Cambridge University Press).
Wrightson, Keith (1993), *English Society* (London: Routledge).
Yates, Frances (1993), *Astraea: The Imperial Theme in the Sixteenth Century* (London: Pimlico).
Zagorin, Perez (1954, 1977), *A History of Political Thought in the English Revolution* (New York: Thoemmes Press).
  (1990), *Ways of Lying: Dissimulation, Persecution and Conformity in Early Modern Europe* (Cambridge, Mass.: Harvard University Press).

SECONDARY SOURCES: ARTICLES

Alford, Stephen (forthcoming), 'The Politics of Emergency in the Reign of Elizabeth I', in Glenn Burgess and Matthew Feinstein, eds., *English Radicalism, 1550–1850* (Cambridge: Cambridge University Press).
Anselment, R. (1993), '*Stone Walls* and *Iron Bars*: Richard Lovelace and the Conventions of Seventeenth-Century Literature', *Renaissance and Reformation*, 29, pp. 15–34.
Armitage, David (2004), 'John Locke, Carolina and the *Two Treatises of Government*', *Political Theory*, 32, 5, pp. 1–26.
Armstrong, C. and Squires, J. (2002), 'Beyond the Public/Private Dichotomy: Relational Space and Sexual Inequalities', *Contemporary Political Theory*, 1, pp. 261–83.
Baldwin, Geoff (2001), 'Individual and Self in the Late Renaissance', *Historical Journal*, 44, 2, pp. 341–64.
Berlin, Sir Isaiah (1969), 'Negative and Positive Liberty', in *Four Essays on Liberty* (Oxford: Oxford University Press).
Borny, Geoffrey (2002), 'Direct Address and the Fourth Wall: The Then and Now of Shakespearean Performance', in Philippa Kelly, ed., *The Touch of the Real: Essays in Early Modern Culture* (Perth: University of Western Australia Press), pp. 221–38.
Boschiero, L. (2002), 'Natural Philosophizing inside the Late Seventeenth-Century Tuscan Court', *British Journal for the History of Science*, 35, 4, pp. 383–410.

Burchell, David (1988), 'Civic Personae: MacIntyre, Cicero and Moral Personality', *History of Political Thought*, 19, pp. 101–18.

Burgess, Glenn (1986), 'Usurpation, Obligation and Obedience in the Thought of the Engagement Controversy', *Historical Journal*, 29, pp. 515–36.

(1988), 'Contexts for the Writing and Publication of Hobbes's *Leviathan*', *History of Political Thought*, 11, pp. 675–702.

(1996), 'Review', *History of Political Thought*, 16, 4, pp. 632–9.

(2001), 'Religious War and Constitutional Defence: Justifications for Resistance in English Puritan Thought, 1590–1643', in Robert von Friedeburg, ed., *Widerstandsrecht in der frühen Neuzeit* (Berlin: Duncker und Humblot), pp. 185–206.

(2004), 'The Execution of Charles I and English Political Thought', in Robert von Friedeburg, ed., *Murder and Monarchy: Regicide in European History, 1300–1800* (Basingstoke: Palgrave), pp. 212–36.

Burke, Peter (1985), 'Popular Culture in Seventeenth-Century London', in Barry Reay, ed., *Popular Culture in Seventeenth-Century England* (London: Croom Helm), pp. 31–58.

Canning, J. P. (1998), 'Law, Sovereignty and Corporation Theory, 1300–1450', in J. H. Burns, ed., *The Cambridge History of Political Thought, c.350–1450* (Cambridge: Cambridge University Press), pp. 454–76.

Clark, Carol (1982), 'Talking about Souls: Montaigne and Human Psychology', in I. D. MacFarlane and Ian Maclean, eds., *Montaigne, Essays in Memory of Richard Sayce* (Oxford: Clarendon Press), pp. 57–76.

Clark, J. C. D. (2002), 'Religion and Political Identity: Samuel Johnson as Nonjuror', in J. C. D. Clark and Howard Erskine-Hill, eds., *Samuel Johnson in Historical Context* (Aldershot: Palgrave), pp. 79–145.

Claydon, Tony (2000), 'The Sermon, the "Public Sphere" and the Political Culture of Late Seventeenth-Century England', in Lori Ann Ferrell and Peter McCullough, eds., *The English Sermon Revised: Literature and History, 1600–1750* (Manchester: Manchester University Press), pp. 208–34.

Collinson, Patrick (1994), 'De republica Anglorum: Or History with the Politics Put Back', in *Elizabethan Essays* (London: Hambledon Press), pp. 1–30.

(1994), 'The Monarchical Republic of Elizabeth I', in *Elizabethan Essays*, pp. 31–58.

Condren, Conal (1987), 'More Parish Library, Salop' (Appendix with F. Carleton), *Library History*, 7, 5, pp. 141–61.

(1988), 'Confronting the Monster: George Lawson's Reactions to Hobbes's Leviathan', *Political Science*, 40, pp. 67–83.

(1993), 'Casuistry to Newcastle: *The Prince* in the World of the Book', in Nicholas Phillipson and Quentin Skinner, eds., *Political Discourse in Early Modern Britain*, pp. 164–86.

(1997), 'Liberty of Office and its Defence in Seventeenth-Century Political Argument', *History of Political Thought*, 18, pp. 460–82.

(2001), 'Between Social Constraint and the Public Sphere: Methodological Problems in Reading Early-Modern Political Satire', *Contemporary Political Theory*, 1, 1, pp. 79–101.

(2004), 'The Office of Rule and the Rhetorics of Tyrannicide in Medieval and Early-Modern Europe: An Overview', in R. von Friedeburg, ed., *Murder and*

Monarchy: Regicide in European History, 1300–1800 (Basingstoke: Palgrave), pp. 48–72.

(forthcoming), 'Radicalism Revised', in G. Burgess and M. Feinstein, eds., *British Radicalism 1500–1800*.

Coole, Diana (2000), 'Cartographic Convulsions: Public and Private Reconsidered', *Political Theory*, 28, 3, pp. 337–54.

Coulton, Barbara (2003), 'Rivalry and Religion: The Borough of Shrewsbury in the Early Stuart Period', *Midland History*, 28, pp. 28–50.

Cousins, A. D. (1990), 'Marvell's "Upon Appleton House, to My Lord Fairfax" and the Regaining of Paradise', in Conal Condren and A. D. Cousins, eds., *The Political Identity of Andrew Marvell* (Aldershot: Scolar Press), pp. 53–84.

(2003), 'Role-Play and Self-Portrayal in More's *A Dialogue of Comfort Against Tribulation*', *Christianity and Literature*, 52, 4, pp. 457–70.

Crawford, Patricia (2001), '"The Poorest She": Women and Citizenship in Early Modern England', in Michael Mendle, ed., *The Putney Debates, 1647* (Cambridge: Cambridge University Press), pp. 197–218.

Cressy, David (2002), 'The Protestation Protested, 1641 and 1642', *Historical Journal*, 52, 2, pp. 251–79.

Davis, J. C. (1992), 'Religion and the Struggle for Freedom in the English Revolution', *Historical Journal*, 35, pp. 507–30.

De Luna, D. N. (1996), '*Jure Divino*: Defoe's "volume in a Folio by Way of Answer to, and Confutation of *Clarendon's* History of the Rebellion"', *Philological Quarterly*, 75, pp. 43–66.

Dietz, Mary (1989), 'Patriotism', in Terence Ball, James Farr and Russell Hanson, eds., *Political Innovation and Conceptual Change* (Cambridge: Cambridge University Press), pp. 177–93.

Donagan, Barbara (2001), 'The Web of Honour: Soldiers, Christians and Gentlemen in the English Civil War', *Historical Journal*, 44, 2, pp. 365–89.

Edwards, Philip (1970), 'Person and Office in Shakespeare's Plays', *Proceedings of the British Academy*, 56, pp. 93–109.

Ewbank, Inga-Stina (1967), '"Those Pretty Devices": A Study of Masques in Plays', in *A Book of Masques, in Honour of Allardyce Nicoll* (Cambridge: Cambridge University Press), pp. 412–33.

Fatovic, C. (2004), 'Constitutionalism and Contingency: Locke's Theory of Prerogative', *History of Political Thought*, 25, 2, pp. 276–97.

Fitzmaurice, Andrew, (2000), '"Every Man, that Prints, Adventures": The Rhetoric of the Virginia Company Sermons', in L. A. Ferrell and P. McCullough, eds., *The English Sermon Revised: Religion, Literature and History, 1600–1750* (Manchester: Manchester University Press), pp. 24–42.

Franklin, James (1984), 'Natural Sciences as Textual Interpretation: The Hermeneutics of the Natural Sign', *Philosophy and Phenomenological Research*, 44, 4, pp. 509–20.

Friedeburg, Robert von (2002), 'Self Defence and Sovereignty. The Reception and Application of German Political Thought in England and Scotland, 1628–1669', *History of Political Thought*, 23, pp. 238–65.

(2004), 'Introduction', in R. von Friedeburg, ed., *Murder and Monarchy: Regicide in European History, 1300–1800* (Basingstoke: Macmillan), pp. 3–47.

Glazov-Corrigan, Elena (1991), 'The New Function of Language in Shakespeare's Pericles: Oath versus "Holy Word"', in Stanley Wells, ed., *Shakespeare Survey*, vol. XLIII (Cambridge: Cambridge University Press), pp. 131–40.
Goldie, Mark (1980), 'The Revolution of 1689 and the Structure of Political Argument', *Bulletin of Research in the Humanities*, 83, pp. 473–564.
  (1980), 'The Roots of True Whiggism', *History of Political Thought*, 1, pp. 195–236.
  (1991), 'The Political Thought of the Anglican Revolution' in Robert Beddard, ed., *The Revolution of 1688* (Oxford: Oxford University Press), pp. 102–36.
  (1993), 'James II and the Dissenters' Revenge: The Commission of Enquiry of 1688', *Historical Research*, 66, 159, pp. 53–88.
  (1999), 'Introduction', in *The Reception of Locke's Politics* (London: Pickering and Chatto), pp. xvii–lxxxiv.
  (2001), 'The Unacknowledged Republic: Office-Holding in Early Modern England', in Tim Harris, ed., *The Politics of the Excluded, c.1500–1850* (London: Palgrave), pp. 153–94.
Goodin, Robert, E. (1997), 'Utilitarianism as Public Philosophy', in Andrew Vincent, ed., *Political Theory: Tradition and Diversity* (Cambridge: Cambridge University Press), pp. 67–88.
Grace, Damian (1988), 'Subjects or Citizens? Populi and Cives in More's *Epigrammata*', *Moreana*, 97, pp. 133–6.
Grantly, Darryll (1988),'Masques and Murderers: Dramatic Method and Ideology in Revenge Tragedy and the Court Masque', in Clive Bloom, ed., *Jacobean Poetry and Prose: Rhetoric, Representation and the Popular Imagination* (London: Macmillan), pp. 194–212.
Greengrass, Mark (2004), 'Regicide, Martyrs and Monarchical Authority in France in the Wars of Religion', in R. von Friedeburg, ed., *Murder and Monarchy: Regicide in European History, 1300–1800* (Basingstoke: Macmillan), pp. 176–92.
Grunnart, Frank (2002), 'Sovereignty and Resistance: The Development of a Right of Resistance in German Natural Law', in Ian Hunter and David Saunders, eds., *Natural Law and Civil Sovereignty: Moral Right and State Authority in Early Modern Political Thought* (London: Palgrave), pp. 123–38.
Guervich, Aaron (1997), 'Bakhtin and his Theory of Carnival', in Jan Bremmer and Herman Roodenburg, eds., *A Cultural History of Humour From Antiquity to the Present Day* (Cambridge and Oxford: Polity Press and Blackwell), pp. 54–60.
Guy, John (1995), 'The Rhetoric of Counsel in Early Modern England', in Dale Hoak, ed., *Tudor Political Culture* (Cambridge: Cambridge University Press), pp. 291–310.
Harris, Tim (1995), 'Problematising Popular Culture', in Tim Harris, ed., *Popular Culture in England, c.1500–1850* (Basingstoke: Macmillan), pp. 1–27.
  (2001), 'The Leveller Legacy: From Restoration to Exclusion Crisis', in M. Mendle, ed., *The Putney Debates* (Cambridge: Cambridge University Press), pp. 219–40.
Haskins, George (1965), 'Representative Government in Early New England: The Corporate and Parliamentary Traditions', in *Liber Memorialis: Maurice*

Powicke, The International Commission for the History of Representative and Parliamentary Institutions, XXVII (Louvain: Editions Nauwelaerts), pp. 85–98.

Höpfl, Harro and Thompson, Martyn P. (1979), 'The History of Contract as a Motif in Political Thought', *American Historical Review*, 4, 84, pp. 919–44.

(2002), 'Orthodoxy and Reason of State', *History of Political Thought*, 23, pp. 211–37.

Horton, Craig (2003), '"... *the* Country *must diminish*": Jacobean London and the Production of Pastoral Space in *The Winter's Tale*', *Parergon*, new series, 20, pp. 85–108.

Huizinga, Johann (1940, 1965), 'Patriotism and Nationalism in European History', in *Men and Ideas*, trans. James S. Holmes and Hans van Marle (New York: Meridian), pp. 97–155.

Israel, Jonathan (1991), 'The Dutch Role in the Glorious Revolution', in J. Israel, ed., *The Anglo-Dutch Moment: Essays on the Glorious Revolution and its World Impact* (Cambridge: Cambridge University Press), pp. 105–62.

Jack, Sybil M. (2001), 'National Identities within Britain and the Proposed Union in 1603–1607', *Parergon*, new series, 18, 2, pp. 75–102.

Kelley, Donald R. (1996), 'On the Margins of Begriffsgeschichte', in Hartmut Lehmann and Melvin Richter, eds., *The Meaning of Historical Terms and Concepts: New Studies in Begriffsgeschichte* (Washington, D. C.: German Historical Institute), pp. 35–40.

Kendall, Wilmore (1966), 'How to Read Milton's *Areopagitica*', *Journal of Politics*, 22, pp. 439–73.

Kessler, Eckhard (1988), 'The Intellective Soul', in Charles B. Schmitt and Quentin Skinner, eds., *The Cambridge History of Renaissance Philosophy* (Cambridge: Cambridge University Press), pp. 485–534.

Kittsteiner, H. D. (1998), 'Kant and Casuistry', in Edmund Lietes, ed., *Conscience and Casuistry in Early Modern Europe* (Cambridge: Cambridge University Press), pp. 185–213.

Koselleck, Reinhart (1996), 'Response' in H. Lehmann and M. Richter, eds., *The Meaning of Historical Terms and Concepts: New Studies in Begriffsgeschichte* (Washington, D. C.: German Historical Institute), pp. 59–70.

Koster, Patricia (1969), 'Arbuthnot's Use of Quotation and Parody', *Philological Quarterly*, 48, pp. 201–11.

Lake, Peter (1981), 'Anti-Popery: The Structure of Prejudice', in R. Cust and A. Hughes, eds., *Conflict in Early Stuart England* (London: Longmans), pp. 72–106.

(1994), 'Deeds Against Nature: Cheap Print, Protestantism and Murder in Early Seventeenth Century England', in Kevin Sharpe and Peter Lake, eds., *Culture and Politics in Early Stuart England* (Basingstoke: Macmillan), pp. 257–84.

Lamont, William (1966), 'The Rise and Fall of Bishop Bilson', *Journal of British Studies*, 5, 2, pp. 22–32.

(2002), 'Richard Baxter, Popery and the Origins of the English Civil War', *History*, 87, pp. 336–52.

Lohr, Charles H. (1988), 'Metaphysics', in Charles B. Schmitt and Quentin Skinner, eds., *The Cambridge History of Renaissance Philosophy* (Cambridge: Cambridge University Press), pp. 537–638.
Love, Harold (2003), 'Early Modern Print Culture: Assessing the Models', *Parergon*, new series, 20, 1, pp. 45–64.
Lund, William (2003), 'Neither *Behemoth* nor *Leviathan*: Explaining Hobbes's Illiberal Politics', *Filozofski vestnik*, 24, 2, pp. 59–83.
McCulloch, Diarmaid (2002), 'Richard Hooker's Reputation', *English Historical Review*, 117, pp. 773–88.
MacCullum, Gerald, C. (1967), 'Positive and Negative Freedom', *Philosophical Review*, 76, pp. 314–19.
McKeon, Michael (1987), 'Politics of Discourses and the Rise of the Aesthetic in Seventeenth-Century England', in Kevin Sharpe and Steven Zwicker, eds., *Politics of Discourse: The Literature and History of Seventeenth-Century England* (Los Angeles: University of California Press), pp. 35–51.
MacLachlan, Alistair (1996), 'Patriotic Scripture: The Making and Unmaking of English National Identity', *Parergon*, new series, 14, 1, pp. 1–30.
Maclean, Ian (forthcoming), 'La doctrine de la preuve dans les procès intentés contre les sorciers en Lorraine et en Franche-Comté autour de 1600', in J.-P. Pittion, ed., *Droit et justice à la Renaissance* (Tours: CESR).
Malcolm, Noel (2000), 'Charles Cotton, Translator of Hobbes's *De cive*', *Huntington Library Quarterly*, 61, 2, pp. 259–87.
—— (2002), 'Hobbes's Theory of International Relations' in N. Malcolm, *Aspects of Hobbes* (Oxford: Clarendon Press), pp. 242–56.
—— (2003), '*Behemoth Latinus*: Adam Ebert, Tacitism and Hobbes', *Filozofski vestnik*, 24, 2, pp. 85–120.
Mason, Roger (2001), 'George Buchanan on Resistance and the Common Man', in R. von Friedeburg, ed., *Widerstandsrecht in der frühen Neuzeit* (Berlin: Duncker and Humblot), pp. 163–81.
Mazzeo, A. J. (1962), 'Cromwell as Davidic King', in A. J. Mazzeo, ed., *Reason and the Imagination* (New York: Columbia University Press), pp. 29–56.
Mears, Natalie (2001), 'Counsel, Public Debate and Queenship: John Stubb's The Discoverie of a Gaping Gulf, 1579', *Historical Journal*, 44, 3, pp. 629–50.
Miller, John (1982), 'The Glorious Revolution: Contract and Abdication Reconsidered', *Historical Journal*, 25, 3, pp. 541–56.
Moos, Peter von (2003), 'Literary Aesthetics in the Latin Middle Ages: The Rhetorical Theology of Peter Abelard', in Constant J. Mews, Cary J. Nederman and Rodney Thompson, eds., *Rhetoric and Renewal in the Latin West, 1100–1540* (Turnhout: Brepols), pp. 81–97.
Muldrew, Craig (1993), 'Interpreting the Market: The Ethics of Credit and Community Relations in Early Modern England', *Social History*, 18, 2, pp. 163–83.
Nederman, Cary J. (1988), 'The Royal Will and the Baronial Bridle: The Place of the *addicio de cartis* in Bractonian Political Thought', *History of Political Thought*, 9, pp. 419–29.
Oakley, Francis (1973), 'Celestial Hierarchies Revisited: Walter Ullmann's Vision of Medieval Politics', *Past and Present*, 60, pp. 1–48.

Park, Katherine (1988), 'The Organic Soul', in Charles B. Schmitt and Quentin Skinner, eds., *The Cambridge History of Renaissance Philosophy* (Cambridge: Cambridge University Press), pp. 464–484.

Park, Katherine and Kessler, Eckhard (1988), 'The Concept of Psychology', in Charles B. Schmitt and Quentin Skinner, eds., *The Cambridge History of Renaissance Philosophy* (Cambridge: Cambridge University Press), pp. 455–63.

Peck, Linda Levy (1996), 'Kingship, Council and Law in Early Stuart Britain', in J. G. A. Pocock, et. al., *The Varieties of British Political Thought* (Cambridge: Cambridge University Press), pp. 80–115.

Peltonen, Markku (2001), 'Francis Bacon, the Earl of Northampton and the Jacobean Anti-Duelling Campaign', *Historical Journal*, 44, 1, pp. 1–28.

Pocock, J. G. A. (1973), 'Political Thought in the Cromwellian Interregnum', in P. S. O'Connor and G. A. Woods, eds., *W. P. Morrell, A Tribute: Essays in Early Modern History* (Dunedin: University of Otago Press), pp. 21–36.

Poppi, Antonino (1988), 'Fate, Fortune, Providence and Human Freedom', in Charles B. Schmitt and Quentin Skinner, *The Cambridge History of Renaissance Philosophy* (Cambridge: Cambridge University Press), pp. 641–67.

Prest, Wilfred (1991), 'Judicial Corruption in Early Modern England', *Past and Present*, 133, pp. 67–95.

Price, Russell (1973), 'The Senses of *Virtù* in Machiavelli', *European Studies Review*, 3, pp. 315–45.

Rahe, P. A. (2004), 'The Classical Republicanism of John Milton', *History of Political Thought*, 25, 2, pp. 243–75.

Reichardt, Dosia (2003), '"At my grates no Althea": Prison Poetry and the Consolations of Sack in the Interregnum', *Parergon*, new series, 20, 1, pp. 139–61.

Richards, Judith (2001), 'English Allegiance in a British Context', *Parergon*, new series, 18, 2, pp. 103–21.

Salmon, J. H. M. (1991), 'Catholic Resistance Theory, Ultramontanism and the Royalist Response, 1580–1620', in J. H. Burns, ed., assisted by Mark Goldie, *The Cambridge History of Political Thought, 1450–1700* (Cambridge: Cambridge University Press), pp. 219–53.

Sampson, Margaret, (1990), 'Property in Seventeenth-Century English Political Thought', in Gordon Schochet, ed., *Religion, Resistance and Civil War* (Washington, D. C.: Folger Library), pp. 259–76.

(1990), ' "Will you Hear what a Casuist he is?" Thomas Hobbes as Director of Conscience', *History of Political Thought*, 11, 4, pp. 721–36.

(1998), 'Liberty and Laxity in Seventeenth-Century English Political Thought', in Edmund Lietes, ed., *Conscience and Casuistry in Early Modern Europe* (Cambridge: Cambridge University Press), pp. 72–119.

Schmitt, Charles B. (1988), 'The Rise of the Philosophical Textbook', in C. B. Schmitt and Q. Skinner, eds., *The Cambridge History of Renaissance Philosophy* (Cambridge: Cambridge University Press), pp. 792–804.

Schmitz, Leonhard (1882), 'Persona', in William Smith, ed., *A Dictionary of Greek and Roman Antiquities* (London: Murray), pp. 889–93.

Schochet, Gordon J. (1993), 'Between Lambeth and *Leviathan*: Samuel Parker on the Church of England and Political Order', in Nicholas Phillipson and Quentin Skinner, eds., *Political Discourse in Early Modern Britain* (Cambridge: Cambridge University Press), pp. 189–208.

Schuster, John A. and Taylor, Alan H. B. (1997), 'Blind Trust: The Gentlemanly Origins of Experimental Science', *Social Studies of Science*, 27, pp. 503–36.

Seidler, Michael J. (2001), 'Qualification and Standing in Pufendorf's Two English Revolutions', in R. von Friedeburg, ed., *Widerstandsrecht in der frühen Neuzeit, Zeitschrift für Historische Forschung*, Beiheft 26 (Berlin: Duncker and Humblot), pp. 329–52.

Shami, Jeanne (2000), 'Anti Catholicism in the Sermons of John Donne', in L. A. Ferrell and P. McCullough, eds., *The English Sermon Revised: Literature and History, 1600–1750* (Manchester: Manchester University Press), pp. 136–66.

Slaughter, Thomas P. (1981), '"Abdicate" and "Contract" in the Glorious Revolution', *Historical Journal*, 24, 2, pp. 323–37.

Skinner, Quentin (1972), 'Conquest and Consent: Thomas Hobbes and the Engagement Controversy', in G. E. Aylmer, ed., *The Interregnum: The Quest for Settlement* (London: Macmillan), pp. 79–98.

(2002), 'Ambrogio Lorenzetti and the Portrayal of Virtuous Government', in *Visions of Politics*, vol. II: *Renaissance Virtues* (Cambridge: Cambridge University Press), pp. 9–92.

(2002), 'Classical Liberty, Renaissance Translation and the English Civil War', in *Visions of Politics*, vol. II, pp. 308–43.

(2002), 'Thomas More's *Utopia* and the Virtue of True Nobility', in *Visions of Politics*, vol. II, pp. 213–44.

(2002), 'The Context of Hobbes's Theory of Political Obligation', in *Visions of Politics*, vol. III: *Hobbes and Civil Science* (Cambridge: Cambridge University Press), pp. 264–86.

(2002), 'Hobbes on Rhetoric and the Construction of Morality', in *Visions of Politics*, vol. III, pp. 116–20.

Somers, Margaret R. (1995), 'The "Misteries" of Property. Relationality Rural-Industrialization and Community in Chartist Narratives of Political Rights', in John Brewer and Susan Staves, eds., *Early Modern Conceptions of Property* (London: Routledge), pp. 62–94.

Sommerville, Johann (1988), 'The New Art of Lying', in Edmund Lietes, ed., *Conscience and Casuistry in Early Modern Europe* (Cambridge: Cambridge University Press), pp. 159–84.

(1991), 'Absolutism and Revolution in the Seventeenth Century', in J. H. Burns, ed., assisted by M. Goldie, *The Cambridge History of Political Thought, 1450–1700* (Cambridge: Cambridge University Press), pp. 347–73.

Spurr, John (1993), 'Perjury, Profanity and Politics', *Seventeenth Century*, 8, 1, pp. 29–50.

Swanson, S. G. (1997), 'The Medieval Foundations of Locke's Theory of Natural Rights: The Rights of Subsistence and the Principle of Extreme Necessity', *History of Political Thought*, 18, 3, pp. 399–459.

Taylor, Charles (1985), 'What's Wrong with Negative Liberty', in *Philosophy and the Human Sciences* (Cambridge: Cambridge University Press), pp. 221–9.

Thiel, Udo (1998), 'Individuation', in Daniel Garber and Michael Ayers, eds., *The Cambridge History of Seventeenth-Century Philosophy* (Cambridge: Cambridge University Press), pp. 212–62.
—— (1998), 'Personal Identity', in Garber and Ayers, eds., *The Cambridge History of Seventeenth-Century Philosophy*, pp. 868–911.
Tierney, Brian (1983), 'The Origins of Natural Rights Language: Texts and Contexts 1150–1250', *History of Political Thought*, 4, pp. 429–41.
Tuck, Richard (1998), 'Optics and Sceptics', in E. Lietes, ed., *Conscience and Casuistry in Early Modern Europe* (Cambridge: Cambridge University Press), pp. 235–63.
Vallance, Edward (2001), 'Oaths, Casuistry and Equivocation: Anglican Responses to the Engagement Controversy', *Historical Journal*, 44, 1, pp. 59–77.
Walker, William (2001), '*Paradise Lost* and the Forms of Government', *History of Political Thought*, 22, 2, pp. 270–300.
Wallace, John M. (1964), 'The Engagement Controversy, 1649–52: An Annotated Check List of Pamphlets', *Bulletin of the New York Public Library*, 68, 6, pp. 384–405.
West, Francis (1999), 'The Colonial History of the Norman Conquest', *History*, 84, pp. 219–36.
Wood, Neal (1967), 'Machiavelli's Concept of Virtue Reconsidered', *Political Studies*, 15, pp. 159–72.
—— (2001), 'Introduction', in *Niccolo Machiavelli, The Art of War*, trans. Ellis Farneworth (Cambridge, Mass.: Da Capo), pp. iii–lxxxvii.
Wootton, David (1983), 'The Fear of God in Early Modern Political Theory', in *Historical Papers* (Vancouver: Canadian Historical Association), pp. 56–80.
Wortham, Christopher, J. (1990) 'Marvell's Cromwell Poems: An Accidental Triptych', in C. Condren and A. D. Cousins, eds., *The Political Identity of Andrew Marvell* (Aldershot: Scolar Press), pp. 16–29.
—— (1996), 'Shakespeare, James I and the Matter of Britain', *English*, 97, 45, pp. 97–122.
Zwicker, Steven (1990), 'Virgins and Whores: The Politics of Sexual Misconduct in the 1660s', in C. Condren and A. D. Cousins, eds., *The Political Identity of Andrew Marvell* (Aldershot: Scolar Press), pp. 85–110.

Index

Note

The index is comprehensive but not exhaustive. We have not indexed footnotes, passing references or passages which allude to, or foreshadow, extensive argument elsewhere. Titled persons appear under the style in which they are referred to in the text and (m) indicates a modern author.

Abjuration Oath, see allegiance, oath of
absolutism, *see* sovereignty theory
Accursius, 28
active/contemplative life, 17, 18, 74–76, 117–18, 123
actor, *see* player, office of
adiaphora, 39, 241, 303
allegiance, oath of (1606), 270–6, 281–5, 295; oath of allegiance and supremacy (1689), 294, 331–3; Oath of Abjuration (1702), 237, 249, 333; *see also* oaths
Allegiance controversy (1688–90), 320–42; *Friendly Debate* (Anon.), 334–7; *see also* Locke, John; oaths; spiritual/temporal authority
Allen, Cardinal William, 155, 190, 276
Althusius, Johannes, 192
Americas, 154–5, 197, 264, 389
Ames, William, 73, 156, 176
Ammirato, Scipione, 223–5
Anderton, W., 323
Andrewes, Bishop Lancelot, 282
Antichrist, 151, 190, 202, 283–4
Apology (1604), 101, 169, 170
Aquinas, St Thomas, 117, 130, 178
arbitrary rule, *see* prerogative
Arbuthnot, Dr John, 150, 206–8, 226–7
Archer, Ian (m), 58, 62
Argyll, Archibald Campbell, ninth Earl of, 242, 255
aristocrat, office of, 28, 56, 65–71, 170; as courtier, 86, 106–9; revenge and duelling, 68, 120; virtues of, 47, 67–69, 120, 194–5; *see also* counsel, office of

Aristotle, 16, 97, 117, 172, 174, 178; *De Anima*, 125, 132; *Poetics*, 111–12, 116; *Rhetoric*, 16, 212
Armitage, David (m), 339
Arnisaeus, Henning, 156, 311
Ascham, Anthony, 192, 265, 292, 304–8, 328, 339
Association, Bonds of (Elizabethan), 61, 151, 152, 242–3; (of 1681), 152, 243–4; (of 1696), 244; *see also* oaths, associative
Aubrey, John, 22, 71, 118
Augustine, of Hippo, St, 24, 151, 181, 198, 304, 307
Austin, John (m), 285
Azpilcueta, Martin, 286

Bacon, Sir Francis, 70, 83, 119–20; *Advancement of Learning*, 75–76, 87, 113, 117–118, 151; *Essays*, 164
Bacon, Nathaniel, 158
Baker, Sir Richard, 110–11
Bakhtin, Mikhail (m), 49, 52
Baldus de Ubaldus, 28, 101, 102
Baldwin, William, 20
baptism, *see* ceremonies of office
Barbon, Nicholas, 63
Barclay, William, 189, 199
Baxter, Richard, 65, 152, 182, 199, 249
Beacon, Richard, 74, 176, 225
Bellarmine, Cardinal Robert, 272, 274–5, 276, 281, 282–3, 313
Bentham, Jeremy, 184
Bergeron, David (m), 47

391

Index

Berkeley, Bishop George, 154, 204
Berlin, Isaiah (m), 91
Bethel, Slingsby, 248
Beza, Theodore, 192
Bilson, Thomas, 190, 198–9
Blackwell, George, 271, 275
Bodin, Jean, 278, 310
Bohun, Edward de, 54, 74, 86
Bolingbroke, Henry St John, Viscount, 154
Boniface VIII, Pope, 273
Book(e) of Oath(e)s, 40, 233, 238, 243, 258, 260, 261
Boswell, James, 23
Bourdieu, Pierre (m), 4
Boyle, Sir Robert, 117, 119, 120–1, 173, 235, 251
Bracton, Henry de, 167, 191
Braddick, Michael (m), 213–14, 218
Bradley, F. H. (m), 24
Brathwaite, Richard, 65
Brown, Meg Lota (m), 182
Browne, Sir Thomas, 9, 85, 101, 129, 132, 144, 181, 224, 248
Buchanan, George, 202, 205, 265, 276
Burckardt, Jacob, 122, 146, 220
bureaucrat, office of, 347
Burgess, Glenn (m), 278, 310
Burghley, William Cecil, Lord, 225
Burnet, Bishop Gilbert, 96, 156, 175, 177, 196, 237, 241, 314–15, 316, 317, 322–3
Burton, Robert, 87
Butler, Samuel, 62, 67, 74, 83, 107–8, 108–9, 110, 118, 244

Calvin, John, 191
Caputo, John (m), 34, 94
Cardano, Girolamo, 140
Carneades, 16, 17, 29, 85, 117, 179
carnivals, *see* office, inversion of
Caryl, Joseph, 296, 298
Case, Stephen, 197, 199
Castiglione, Baldesar, 69, 106–7
casuistry, 28, 172–85, 186–90, 206–8, 220, 222, 278, 306, 346–7, 348; exceptional/extensive, 176–8; modal, 30, 178–85, 191, 224–7, 273, 289; presumptive, 31, 178–85, 190–1, 302; *see also* ethics of office
Catholicism/anti-Catholicism, 50, 112, 152, 174, 189, 192, 243–4, 269–72, 275–6, 281–4, 315–17; 'popery', 38, 41, 42, 271, 274, 275, 318, 322–3; *see also* Jesuits
Cavendish, Margaret, Duchess of Newcastle, 67, 223

Cavendish, William, Duke of Newcastle, 36, 55, 61, 64–65, 66, 67, 161, 223–4, 344
ceremonies of office, 25, 36, 53, affirmative/transformative, 40, 43–46, 47–48; rites of passage (birth, marriage, death), 39–43, 215, 216, 256; witnesses to, 43–44; *see also* coronations
Chambers, Ephraim, 88
Champion, Justin (m), 159
Charles I, 102–4, 132–3, 158, 166–71, 202–3, 258, 260–3, *Eikon Basilike*, 160, 166
Charles II, 43–44, 108, 162, 171, 211, 223, 241, 243, 258, 291
Charleton, Walter, 80, 82, 87, 213
Charron, Pierre, 128–9
childbirth, *see* ceremonies of office
Chiver, Robert, 76
Christ, *see* God
Christendom, 162–3, 190, 273–4, 282, 283–4; conciliarism in, 283
church and state relations, *see* spiritual/temporal authority
Church of England, 189, 206–8, 241–2, 269, 276, 281–5, 316–18, 319
Cicero, Marcus Tullius, 15–20, 74, 82, 106, 114, 128, 151, 180
circles, symbolism of, 41–42, 44–45
citizen, office of, 17, 63–65, 104, 155
Civil Wars, 35, 67, 92, 102, 150, 166–71, 187–8, 195, 202–3
Clapmarius, Arnoldus, 223, 224–5
Clarendon, Edward Hyde, Earl of, 76
Clubmen, 150, 243
coffee-houses, 77–78
Coke, Sir Edward, 63, 240
Collier, Jeremy, 89
Collingwood, R. G. (m), 4
Collinson, Patrick (m), 60
Colyngbourne, William ('The Cat, the Rat...'), 112–13
Coltman, Irene (m), 306
Comber, Thomas, 70, 251
Commonwealth, *see* republic, English
Condren, Charles de, 289
conscience, 130–4, 172, 307; as duty of office, 132–3, 279; as judge, 131–2; mind as synonym for, 131; *see also* soul
consent/contract, 52, 146, 206, 242, 264–7, 304–5, 309, 324–6, 328–31, 333–4; *see also* coronation oath
constable, parish office of, 56–57, 59, 62, 245
Constant, Benjamin, 93
Convention parliament of 1689, 319–20, 328–31; debates in, 329–31

Cornwallis, Sir William, 99–100
coronations, 43, 52, 255–6, 315; coronation oath, 254–67, 315, as contract, 255, 257, 326; and laws of Edward the Confessor, 102, 255, 257, 259, 263; and laws of God, 259, 260; and oath text of Edwards II and III, 260, 263
Cotta, John, 5, 6, 98, 127, 129
counsel, office of, 27, 123, 149, 149, 162–71, 183–4, 191, 199, 213, 262, 316; evil counsel, 163, 166–71, 188; and Privy Council, 164, 167; *see also* aristocrat
courtier, office of, *see* aristocrat, office of
Cousins, A. D. (m), 128
Coverdale, Miles, 239, 240
Cranmer, Archbishop Thomas, 255
Craven, W. (m), 122
Cressy, David (m), 39, 41
Croce, Benedetto (m), 219
Cromwell, Oliver, 161, 177, 203, 258, 300; *see also* Protector, office of
Crosse, Henry, 20
cuckoldom, rights of, 206–8, 345
Curtis, Catherine (m), 123
Cusacke, John, 76

Dalton, Michael, 73
Daniel, Gabriel, 179
Daniel, Samuel, 89, 111, 119
Dante Alighieri, 163, 236, 273
Darlington, Robert, 176
David, king of Israel, 108, 112, 187, 198, 266
de facto theory, 295–8, 327–8; *see also* Engagement controversy
death, *see* ceremonies of office; soul, office of
Decker, Thomas, 46, 47
Declarations: (1649), 300; (1689), 331
defence of office, *see* casuistry
definition, nominal, 26–28, 198, 256–7; real, 26
Defoe, Daniel, 98, 191, 326
democracy, 60, 67, 193; *see also* extension of office
Derrida, Jacques (m), 287
Descartes, René, 141, 144
Devonshire, William Cavendish, third Earl of, 204, 205
Digby, Sir Kenelm, 275
Dingley, Robert, 9, 10
dissolution, 196–7, 205–6, 330, 334; *see also* rebellion; Revolution, 'Glorious'
Dominis, Antonio de, 271, 283
domino effect, 197, 234

Donne, John, 8, 129, 275; *Biathanatos*, 172, 173, 174, 179, 182; 'The Sunne Rising', 8, 182–3
dress/costume, symbolism of, 23, 107–8, 108–9, 110
Dryden, John, 108
Dury, John, 299–300
Dutch republic, *see* republic, Dutch

Eachard, John, 111
Earle, John, 110
economy, 211
Edward I, 256
Edward II, 260, 297
Edward III, 257–8
Edward IV, 64
Edward VI, 262
Edward the Confessor, laws of, *see* coronations
Eliot, Sir John, 156
Elizabeth I, 50, 64, 151, 155, 158, 190, 242–3, 269, 271, 276; progresses of, 45–46
Ellesmere, Thomas Egerton, Lord, 135, 206
Elyot, Sir Thomas, 65
Engagement, 1, 324, 330; Engagement controversy, 290, 331
entia moralia, *see* identity
Epictetus, 128
Epicurus, 125
equivocation/lying, *see* Jesuits
Essex, Robert Devereux, second Earl of, 66, 71
Essex, Robert Devereux, third Earl of, 193
ethics, 6, 12, 28; consequentialist, 184–5, 343, 346; deontological, 16, 85–86, 184, 185, 346; of office, 17–18, 23–24, 26, 30–31, 85–104, 216–25, 250, 280, 286, 346–7; prudence in, 173, 181, 179, 221, 224; and virtue ethics, 347; *see also* casuistry
Evan, Enock ap, 42–43
Evelyn, John, 215–16
executions, *see* ceremonies of office
extension of office, 18–19, 345; horizontal, 296–7, 302, 304, 310; vertical 26, 155–6, 157, 163, 244; lesser magistracy as, 191–3; *see also* military office; rule, office of

Ferne, Henry, 187, 202
Ficino, Marsilio, 114
Field, Richard, 283
Finch, Heneage, 133
Fisher, Samuel, 131, 251

Index

FitzHerbert, Thomas, 176
FitzJames, Sir John, 68
flattery, *see* counsel
Forbes, Duncan (m), 186
Fortescue, Sir John, 259
Foscarini, Antonio, Venetian ambassador, 281
Foucault, Michel (m), 139
Foxe, John, 155, 282
France, 254–5
freedom, *see* liberty
Friendly Debate, *see* Allegiance controversy
Fullwood, Francis, 331

Galileo Galilei, 111
Gallicans of the Sorbonne, 272
Garnet, Henry, 269, 285, 286
Gawen, Katharine, 269
Gaynsford, Elizabeth (midwife), 40
Gee, Edward, 217, 294, 300, 308
gift-giving, *see* aristocrat
Gilby, Anthony, 192
Gillespie, George, 41
God, 76; and appeal to Heaven, 195–6, 279, 318; concept of, 101, 98–99, 114, 126–7, 200, 280; as counsellor, 163; fear of, 9, 307; and Heaven, 161–2; love of, 151; office as duty to, 89, 190, 191, 266, 296–8, 328; office of, 10, 19, 101, 115, 117, 127–8, 129–30, 212, 279–80; and Christ, office of, 100, 130–4, 181, 275; and revenge, 194; as source of all authority, 18, 83, 196, 274, 276, 277, 301–3, 324; and truth-telling, 285, 289; *see also* presuppositions; soul, office of
Goffman, Erving (m), 6, 137
Goldie, Mark (m), 58, 59, 60, 317, 333
Goodman, Christopher, 190, 198
Goodwin, John, 192, 204
Goslicius (Laurentius Grimalius), 59, 76, 89, 164, 165, 180
Gosson, Stephen, 106, 108, 110, 111
Gouge, William, 61, 74–75
Grand Case for Conscience, The (Anon.), 302–3
Greenberg, Janelle (m), 263
Greenblatt, Stephen (m), 136, 139
Greville, Fulke, 85
Griffith, Matthew, 45
Grimalde, Nicholas, 20, 74, 215
Grotius, Hugo, 33, 134–5, 195, 308
Guicciardini, Francesco, 222
Gunpowder Plot, 156, 191, 269–70, 278, 285

Haakonssen, Knud (m), 23, 134
Habermas, Jürgen (m), 22, 34, 77
Hakluyt, Richard, 155
Hale, Sir Matthew, 21, 22, 68, 129, 261
Halifax, George Savile, Marquess of, 108, 153
Hall, John, 96
Hammond, Henry, 297
Harcourt, Sir Simon, 175
Harington, Sir John, 19
Harrington, James, 74, 133, 159
Harvey, Christopher, 188
Harvey, William, 118
Hawke, Michael, 203
Haworth, Samuel, 127
Henry II, 256
Henry IV, 256
Henry VIII, 164, 241, 258, 318
Herbert, Rev. George, 86, 129, 139
Herle, Charles, 202
Herod, king of Judea, 245
Hesiod, 21
Heylyn, Peter, 72, 188, 192, 311
Heywood, Thomas, 20, 22, 46
Hickeringill, Edmund, 42, 246
Hickeringill, Philip, 318
Hickes, George, 154, 324, 333–4
Hindle, Steve (m), 56
historiography, *see* intellectual history
Hitchcock, John, 180
Hoadley, Benjamin, 196
Hobbes, Thomas, 88, 97, 99, 121, 140, 196, 294; contract theory of, 266–7; reputation and persona of, 118–19, 145, 324; Works: *Answer to ... Gondibert*, 96, 119; *De cive*, 65, 98, 134, 205, 341; *Elements*, 68, 98, 134; *Letters*, 70, 127; *Leviathan*, 49, 66, 72, 76, 84, 93, 130, 165, 205; and Engagement, 304, 308–13, natural condition, 146, 288, priests in, 95, 212, 312–13, 322, sovereign in, 84, 205
honestas/utilitas, 26, 88, 124, 184–5, 200, 295, 301–3, 312, 344; *see also* rhetoric
Hooker, Richard, 282, 282–3
Höpfl, Harro (m), 222
house of office, 22
Hugh of St Victor, 217
Hume, David, 57, 92, 142, 197
Humfrey, John, 59, 199, 237, 241
humours, theory of, 87–88, 211
Hungerford, 44, 58
Hunter, Michael (m), 173
Hunton, Philip, 188, 189, 196–7, 201, 236, 279, 280

Index 395

husbandry, office of, 21, 76, 215–16
Hutchinson, Colonel John, 73

identity, corporeal/nominal, 100–2, 128–9, 138, 140–2, 201, 279; and autonomy, 105, 140, 142–4, 144–5; and role-play, 6–7, 26, 38, 111, 136–8, 227; and self, 18, 23–24, 69, 120–1, 122–4, 220; and 'self-fashioning', 33, 137–40, 222; *see also* soul
ideology, 149, 157–8, 185, 228–9, 277, 278–9, 281, 345, 348–9
Ihalainen, Pasi (m), 153, 154
individual, *see* identity
intellectual history, 1, 3, 5, 7, 159; and conceptualisation, 2, 4–5
interest theory, 344 *see also* identity
Ireton, Henry, 262

James II, 10, 152, 208, 252, 258–9, 260, 314, 319, 325–6, 333–4
James VI&I, 157, 169, 191, 258, 269–72, 275–6, 305, 313, 332; and conscience, 132; *Basilicon Doron*, 66, 100–1; *Daemonologie*, 98; *Discourse ... of the Powder Treason*, 156; *Praemonition*, 189, 284–5; *Speeches*, 216, 280–1; *Trew Law of Free Monarchy*, 151–2, 186, 266, 276–7, 279–281, 311, 341; *see also* prerogative; sovereignty theory
Jeakes, Samuel, 214
jesters, 51, 164; *see also* office, inversion of
Jesuits, 105, 172, 174, 175, 251–2, 270, 344; English, 189, 248, 271, 283, 285–NaN; and equivocation/lying, 181, 248–50, 253, 270–1, 285–9, 292, 293, 299, 332–3; and poetry, 112; and probabilism, 174;
  see also Catholicism; oaths
John of Salisbury 101, 199–200, 322
John XXII, Pope, 102
John, king of England, 256
Johnson, Richard (m), 135
Johnson, Dr Samuel, 154–5
Jolliffe, J. E. A. (m), 60
Jones, David Martin (m), 260
Jones, Inigo, 209–10
Jonson, Ben, 113–14, 116
justice, 15, 42–43

Kant, Immanuel, 18, 22, 24, 28, 33, 143, 184
Kantorowicz, Ernst (m), 1, 100
Kelly, M. R. L. (m), 261–2
Kennett, White, 233, 248
King's Answer to the Nineteen Propositions, *see* Nineteen Propositions

king's two bodies, 80, 100–4, 168; *see also* rule, office of
Knox, John, 198
Koselleck, Reinhart (m), 5, 6

Latimer, Bishop Hugh, 64, 81, 244, 274, 299
Laud, Archbishop William, 261, 322
law, 30, 280, 279; divine, 134–5; natural, 16, 23; and casuistry, 175, 177; and ethics of office, 89, 346; and rule, 309, 335; and priesthood, 274, 307–8; and rights, 33–34, 173, 176–7, 225
Lawes and Ordinances of Warre (1639), 250
Lawson, George, 97, 99, 103, 130, 157, 187, 188, 196, 224, 261, 264, 335
lawyer, office of, 23, 30, 118, 172, 178, 179, 299, 346
Lee, Sir Henry, 46
legislation, *see* sovereignty
Leibniz, Gottfried Wilhelm, 23, 141
Lessius, Leonhard, 70
L'Estrange, Roger, 90, 98, 152–3
Letter from a Person of Quality, 246–7
Levellers, 84, 152, 158
Lewis of Bavaria, 102
Lewis, C. S. (m), 29
liberalism, 33–34, 90, 94, 228
liberty, of office, 59, 73, 77, 80, 89–94, 113, 164–5, 279–80, 305; and licence, 92–94, 167; positive/negative, 90–91, 227; and slavery, 93, 99; as service to God, 129
Lilbourne, John, 293
Locke, John, 349; *Essay*, 121–2, 134, 141–2; *Two Treatises*, 57, 83, 157, 205–6, 280, 304, and Allegiance controversy, 337–42
London, 63–65, 78, 150, 314, 315, 318, 319; offices in, 20, 46–47, 50, 56, 58, 59, 192, 238; pageantry of, 20, 45, 46–47
Longinus, 114
Louis VI of France, 151, 158
Louis XIV of France, 316
Lovejoy, A. O. (m), 5
Lucian, 17, 118, 123
Lucifer, *see* Satan
Lucretius, 125

McCallum, Gerald (m), 90
Machiavelli, Niccolò, 86, 124, 151, 164, 166; *Prince*, 176, 177, 218, 219–22, 224
McKeon, Michael (m), 214
Mandeville, Bernard de, 23, 88, 140

396 Index

Marian question, *see* rebellion
marital office, 206–8, 215, 216, 217, 302–3;
 and flitching, 48; *see also* ceremonies of office
Marlowe, Christopher, 88, 143;
 Dr Faustus, 145
Marshall, William, 274
Marsilio, Giovanni, 275
Marsilius of Padua, 127, 273–4
Marvell, Andrew, 38, 171, 294
Mary I, 151, 198
Mason, Henry, 86, 131, 288
masques, 48, 49, 108; *see also* ceremonies of office
mathematics, 111–12, 120
May, Tom (Lucan's *Pharsalia*), 96
mayor, *see* London
Medici, Lorenzo de', 165
Medina, Bartolomeo, 174
Melanchthon, Philipp, 126, 194
Mendle, M. (m), 170, 173
Merbury, Charles, 158
merchant, office of, 61–62, 82
Meriton, George, 66, 71
metaphor, 2, 31–32, 37, 52, 110, 209–18;
 autochthonous and analytic, 210–11
Meyer, Thomas (m), 63
Middleton, Thomas, 47
midwife, office of, 40–41, 61
military office, 88, 144, 184, 220–2; as lesser magistracy, 192–3, 203; *see also* extension of office
Milton, John, 74, 87, 93, 98, 159, 168;
 Eikonoklastes, 161, 160; *Paradise Lost*, 115, 161–2, 202–3
mob, *see* London
models/explanatory modelling, 2–3, 10, 54, 77, 213–16, 228–9, 281, 349–50; *see also* ideology
Monod, Paul (m), 333
Montaigne, Michel de, 29, 128–9
moral discourse, *see* ethics
More, Richard, the Younger, 161, 214, 218
More, Sir Thomas, 63, 128, 335; *Utopia*, 65, 123–4, 163–4
Morice, James, 240
Morrill, John (m), 202
Morton, Thomas, 272, 288
motivation, 32, 87, 187; *see also* humours, theory of
Mous, Katherine Eisaman (m), 138
Muggletonians, 141
Muir, Edwin (m), 38
Mulcaster, Richard, 72, 111
Muldrew, Craig (m), 62

Mun, Thomas, 61–62, 72
Musculus, Wolfgang, 200

Nashe, Thomas, 9
nationalism, *see* patriot, office of
natural condition/state of war, *see* consent; Hobbes, Thomas
Nedham, Marchamont, 299, 308, 310
Nelson, Eric (m), 123
Neville, Henry, 219, 344
Newton, Sir Isaac, 119,
Nineteen Propositions, 168–71
non-jurors, 323–4, 326, 327–8
Norbrook, David (m), 96
North, Justice Francis, 224
Northampton, Henry Howard, Earl of, 69, 70
Noy, William, 89

oaths, 9, 12, 233–53, 301–2, 303, 306, 309–10; abuse of, 240, 244–6, 247; breaking, 265; and God, 235–7, 271; and hostility to swearing, 250–2; and perjury, 248; and subscription, 247, 293, 294–5; as symbolic, 270; synonyms for, 233–4; typology: of allegiance, 263–4, 318; assertory/promissory, 233–4, 237, 247, 255–6, 270, 285, 291; associative, 242–4; circumstantial, 241–2; diurnal, 239–40; of explication, 239; of passage, 25, 238–9, 252, 255, 256, 263–4; proclamatory/transformative, 238–9, 255–6, 258; state, 237, 241, 242, 256; *see also* Allegiance controversy; casuistry; consent; coronations; Engagement controversy; Jesuits; vocabulary of office
oath-text (Edward II), *see* coronations
obedience, 188, 189, 190–1, 199, 204–5, 206–8, 259, 316–17
office, 1–2, 25, 29, 343–5; abuse of, 6, 10, 17, 48, 57, 74, 99–100, 162, 223, *see also* tyranny; defence of, 194, *see also* self-defence; institutionalised, 54, 56–62, 150, 213–14; intellectual, 122, 145; inversion of, 37, 49–51; neglect or alienation of, 198–9; rationale and limit of, 26–27, 28–29, 83, 176, 263–4, 297–8; *see also* ceremonies of; ethics of; extension of; liberty of; presuppositions of; vocabulary of; *see also* specific offices under name of office
originality, 143–4
Otway, Thomas, 245
Overbury, Sir Thomas, 107

Index

Overton, Richard, 103
Owen, David, 63, 189, 191

Pace, Richard, 114
pageants, *see* London; ceremonies of office
Palmer, Roger, Lord Castlemaine, 153, 233
parental office, 31–32, 41, 61, 75, 210, 216; *see also* ceremonies of office
Parker, Henry, 165, 166, 173, 195, 202, 262
Parker, Samuel, 72
parliament, office of, 89, 101, 103, 166–7, 169–71, 195, 202, 260–3; *see also* sovereignty; counsel
parody and satire, 26–52, 142, 208, 226, 347; *see also* cuckoldom
Parsons, Robert, 252, 255, 263, 265, 272, 285, 287, 288
party/faction, 153–4, 207, 208
patriot, office of, 28, 149–58, 193, 244–6
Patterson, W. Brown (m), 270
Paul V, Pope, 272, 274, 275
Pearl, Valerie (m), 58
Peel, George, 46
Peltonen, Markku (m), 1, 61, 67–68, 106, 107
Pepys, Samuel, 22
Perkins, William, 81, 129
persona, 6–7, 89–90, 101–4, 179, 183–4, 237, 286, 299, 300–3; Ciceronian typology of, 17; natural philosopher, 120–1; and private conduct, 73–74, 91; as ruling council, 163; as role play, 23–24; social and temporal continuity of, 25–26, 28–29; as subject, 191; 204–5; *see also* identity; soul; for specific *personae* see under name of office
Petrarch, 111, 116
Pettie, George, 113
Pettit, Philip (m), 91
Philodemius (pseud.), 192
philosophy/philosopher, office of, 3, 16–17, 17–18, 75–76, 116–24; natural philosophy, 119–21; as relationship to God, 128–9, 131; see also active/contemplative life
physician, office of, 23, 131, 346
Pico della Mirandola, Giovanni, 122–3, 211
Plato, 3, 66, 113, 114, 116; *Republic*, 15–20, 27, 120, imagery in, 19–20, 31, 66, 132, philosopher in, 17–18, 114; and Gyges, 199, 201; and Socrates, 15, 22, 118; *Timaeus*, 125, 140
player, office of, 86, 109–11, 181
Plume, Thomas (Plume Library), 56

Pocock, J. G. A. (m), 159
poet, office of, 110, 111–16; decorum of 115–16
Pole, Cardinal Reginald, 274
political autonomy, 35, 219–27; domain, 37, 52–53, 95–97, 218, 343; *see also* ethics; casuistry
political theory, 3, 10, 22, 34, 146, 216–19, 348; lineage of, 349, 350; and science, 345
Pomponazzi, Pietro, 181
Ponet, John, 151, 157, 198, 217, 283
pope, *see* priest, office of; spiritual/temporal authority
Pope, Alexander, 150
Porter, Roy (m), 23, 24, 42, 94, 142, 144
Powell, Sumner Chilton (m), 59
power, 83; *see also* office, synonyms for
prerogative/arbitrary rule, 89, 160, 173, 257–8, 261–2, 278–81; *see also* tyranny
Prest, Wilf (m), 68
presuppositions, 3–4, 211–14; of God, 9, 211; of office, 2, 3, 6–10, 12, 24–25, 30, 215–18, 329; semiotic, 8–9, 37, 211–12
Price, Dr Richard, 157
priest, office of, 21–22, 37–38, 129, 178–9, 246, 318, 321; assumption of, 39–40, 241–2, 344–5; scope of, 89, 133, 134, 226, 272, 280, 286–7, 298–300, 318, 321–4, 345; and papal and episcopal office, 273–4, 282, 321, 332; as shape shifter, 105; *see also* soul
print culture, 155, 334
probability, *see* Jesuit
property, 177, 305, 339–40; *see also* Locke, John
Protector, office of, 258, 260; *see also* Cromwell, Oliver
Protestation, The, 156, 235, 293
providence, 298, 321; *see also* God and appeal to Heaven
Prynne, William, 41, 110, 167, 236, 237, 260–2, 298
public/private, 26, 34, 71–77, 123, 132–3, 201, 203–4, 225–6, 227–8; and oaths, 246
public sphere, 34, 54, 77–79, 91, 94, 227
Pufendorf, Samuel, 8, 23, 27–28, 173, 225
Puttenham, George, 115, 116
Pym, John, 164–5, 178
Pythagoras, 19

Quakers, 109, 251–2
Quintilian, 16, 109, 124

Racken, Phyllis (m), 139
Raleigh, Sir Walter, 88, 158, 165–6, 180
reason of state, *see* state
rebellion/resistance, 9, 31, 150, 167, 187–208, 333–4; *see also* self-defence; office, defence of; tyranny
redescription, 95–100, 154–5, 155–6, 170–1, 187, 191, 256, 320, 327–31, 344; and *amphibologia* 285–6; antonymity in, 96; decorum of, 97; metaphor/allegory in, 96; moral/ethical, 198, 201; radical, 97–98; as repredication, 95, 150; softening of, 95, 96; *see also* equivocation; vocabulary of office
Reeves, Dr William, 181
Reformation, 37–38, 39, 114–16, 151, 247, 345; and citizenship, 155; ecumenicalism in, 58–59
representation, 83–84, 330, 331
republic/republicanism, 35, 54, 60–61, 91; Dutch, 318; English, 35, 152, 162, 259, 260, 290–1, 310; *see also* Engagement controversy
resistance theory, 187, 188; *see also* rebellion
Revolution, French, 35, 135, 157
Revolution, 'Glorious' (1688/9), 191, 207, 333
rhetoric, 16–17, 72, 109, 113, 114–20, 124, 209; as protean, 97, 98, 145; and *skiagraphia*, 254–5, 286; *see also honestas/utilitas*; poet, office of
Richard II, 256
Richard III, 99, 112, 256, 262
rights, 23, 33–34, 89, 135; *see also* law
rites of passage, *see* ceremonies of office
rituals, *see* ceremonies of office
Rocket, John, 83, 296, 300
Rohan, Henri, duc du, 344
Rome (Ancient), 64, 192, 282, 303
Rous, Francis, 293, 300–3, 313
Royal Society, 97, 119–20, 251
rule, office of, 18, 27, 32, 52–53, 89–90, 101–2, 179, 180, 182–3, 191, 275–6, 279, 295–8; abuse of, 192; and coronation, 256–9; and counsel, 165–71; purpose of, 266–7; *see also* counsel; king's two bodies; sovereignty; monarchs under individual names
Rutherford, Samuel, 132–3, 175, 201, 216, 265
Ryle, Gilbert (m), 139

Sacheverell, Dr Henry, 153, 175, 196, 206, 207

Sacred Vow and Covenant, The (1643), 249
Sadler, Sir Ralph, 73, 151, 164
Sanderson, Robert, 76, 81, 234, 235, 244, 290, 292–3, 309, 334
Sarpi, Paolo, 283, 284
Satan, 98, 101, 110, 115; as evil counsellor, 163; in *Paradise Lost*, 161–2; as rebel, 87, 187, 202–3; as tyrant, 9, 10, 200
Scheibler, Christoph, 127
Schmitt, Carl (m), 278
Schmitt, Charles (m), 119
Scott, Jonathan (m), 159
Scroggs, Lord Chief Justice, 82
secularisation, 307–8, 350
Selden, John, 28, 36, 85, 248, 252, 344–5
self, *see* identity
self-defence, 89, 177, 194, 204, 205–6, 302; *see also* office, defence of
Settle, Elkanah, 50
Sexby, Edward, 203
Shaftesbury, Anthony Ashley Cooper, first Earl of, 108, 152, 171, 317
Shakespeare, William, works cited: *Hamlet*, 107, 109–10, 142, 245; *Henriad (Henry IV and V)*, 92, 136–8, 175, 183–4; *Julius Caesar*, 9, 10; *Love's Labour's Lost*, 245; *Macbeth*, 253; *Measure for Measure*, 199; *Merchant of Venice*, 245; *Othello*, 144–5, 181, 208; *Richard II*, 82, 137; *Tempest*, 102; *Troilus and Cressida*, 55; *Twelfth Night*, 80, 233, *Wars of the Roses (Henry VI and Richard III)*, 144
Shapin, Steven (m), 120
Sharp, Bishop John, 84, 93, 133, 134, 244, 245, 322, 324
Sharpe, Kevin (m), 215
Sheldon, Richard, 272, 275, 299
shepherd, office of, and wolf, 15, 18, 19–20, 22, 46, 47, 279; *see also* tyranny
Shepherd's Calendar, The (Anon.), 21
sheriff, office of, 59; *see also* London
Sherlock, William, 197, 317, 317–28
Sidney, Algernon, 74, 90, 159, 263, 264
Sidney, Sir Philip, 111, 113–14, 115–16, 116
Skinner, Quentin (m), 91, 288, 310
slavery, *see* liberty
Smith, Adam, 157
Smith, David (m), 168
Smith, Henry, 211
Smith, Sir Thomas, 163
soldier, *see* military office
Solemn League and Covenant, 235, 243, 292–3, 299, 300, 302, 303

Index

soul, office of, 19, 38, 42, 81, 86, 127–35, 146; equivocation and, 286; as everyman in office 193; as general principle of life, 125–30, 140–2; and *persona*, 134, 140–2; secularisation of, 34, 135, 138–9, 211, 306; study of (*psychologia*), 126; *see also* conscience; identity
Southwell, Robert, 112, 285
sovereignty theory, 167, 168–71, 188, 217, 261–3, 267, 275–81, 310; *see also* rule, office of
spiritual/temporal authority, 55–59, 183–4, 270–89, 295, 298–300, 307–8, 313, 315–18, 321–4, 332–3; and two swords theory, 273–6, 310, 322
spiritual realm, 6, 98–99, 127; and witchcraft, 5, 51, 98
St German, Christopher, 130
Starkey, John, 214, 218, 219
Starkey, Thomas, 20
state, concept of, 218, 219–27; formation, In.1, In.2–3, 54–58, 213–14, 343; reason of, 222–7, 307; *see also* oaths; political autonomy
Steel, Richard, 153
Stillingfleet, Edward, 237
Stow, John, 45, 46, 48, 64, 150
Strafford, William Wentworth, Earl of, 164, 168, 177
Strawson, P. F. (m), 7, 8
Stuart, Richard, 37
Suarez, Francisco de, 174, 201, 272, 281, 283
swearing, *see* oaths
Swift, Jonathan, 94

Tacitus, 107
Taylor, Jeremy, 70, 131, 174, 188, 201, 249
Thomas, Keith (m), 44
Tillotson, Archbishop John, 81, 236
Toland, John, 133
Tönnies, Ferdinand, 57
Tooke, Andrew, 173, 225, 311
Toulmin, S. and Jonsen, A. R., 180
trade, *see* merchant
tradition, 30, 38–39
Tuck, Richard (m), 308
Tuve, Rosamund (m), 115
Tuvill, Daniel, 69, 72, 87, 105, 176, 178, 225–6
Tyndale, Mathew, 72
tyranny, 31, 87, 112–13, 199–208, 216, 280–281, 305–6, 325–6; of acquisition and exercise, 197–8, 294–8, 301, 302, 317; as affront to God, 190–1; legal, 160, 199; obedience owed to, 190–1, 196, 198; as redundant classifier, 205, 312; and tyrannicide, 199–205, 276, 325–6; *see also* office, abuse of; rule, office of; rebellion

Ullmann, Walter (m), 277
Underdown, David (m), 49
universities, 46, 109, 111–12, 210, 252

Van Gennep, Arnold (m), 39–40
Vane, Sir Harry, the Younger, 130
Venice, 158, 262, 271, 274–275, 277, 283, 284
Vermigli, Peter Martyr, 192, 194–5, 196, 198
Vico, Gianbatista, 210–11
Vienne, Philibert de, 107
Virgil, 19
Viroli, Maurizio (m) 217, 223
Vitoria, Francisco, 274
vocabulary of office, 2, 10, 12, 22, 24–25, 80–104, 161–2, 281, 321–4, 345; registers of, 84, 149, 150, 159–63, 167–8; negative, 29, 32, 87–88, 92–94, 94–95, 143, 160, 161, 187–8, 344; positive, 84–87, 88–92, 143, 160; synonyms for, 25, 80, 83; *see also* equivocation; redescription

Wallace, John (m), 293
Walpole, Sir Robert, 154
Warner, Walter, 127
Warren, Albertus, 66, 299
Washbourne, Thomas, 290–1
Weber, Max (m), 24, 213, 346
Wentworth, Peter, 73
White, Thomas, 275
Willett, Andrew, 90, 108, 164, 166, 190, 198, 201
William I, 64, 254
William III, 259, 260, 314–15, 318–20; and Mary II, 326–7
William of Malmesbury, 63
Willis, Thomas, 88, 140–1
Willymat, William, 72, 311
Wilson, Thomas, 114, 116
Wing, John, 216
Winstanley, Gerard, 61, 82
Wolsey, Cardinal Thomas, 87
Wood, Neal (m), 220–1
Worden, Blair (m), 291
Wright, Leonard, 181, 190

Zagorin, Perez (m), 286, 295